# CRIMINOLOGICAL THEORY

## Readings and Retrospectives

### Heith Copes

*University of Alabama at Birmingham*

### Volkan Topalli

*Georgia State University*

Mc Graw Hill

Connect
Learn
Succeed™

Published by McGraw-Hill, an imprint of The McGraw-Hill Companies, Inc., 1221 Avenue of the Americas, New York, NY 10020. Copyright © 2010. All rights reserved. No part of this publication may be reproduced or distributed in any form or by any means, or stored in a database or retrieval system, without the prior written consent of The McGraw-Hill Companies, Inc., including, but not limited to, in any network or other electronic storage or transmission, or broadcast for distance learning.

This book is printed on acid-free paper.

1 2 3 4 5 6 7 8 9 0 DOC/DOC 0 9

ISBN: 978-0-07-338001-8
MHID: 0-07-338001-6

Editor in Chief: *Michael Ryan*
Editorial Director: *Beth Mejia*
Publisher: *Frank Mortimer*
Executive Editor: *Katie Stevens*
Editorial Coordinator: *Teresa Treacy*
Executive Marketing Manager: *Leslie Oberhuber*
Media Project Manager: *Vivek Iyer*
Production Editor: *Alison Meier*
Design Coordinator: *Margarite Reynolds*
Cover Design: *Kay Lieberherr*
Production Supervisor: *Louis Swaim*
Composition: *10/12 Times by Laserwords*
Printer: *45# New Era Matte Plus, R. R. Donnelley & Sons*

Credits: A credits section for this book begins on page 483 and is considered an extension of the copyright page.

**Library of Congress Cataloging-in-Publication Data**

Criminological theory: readings and retrospectives / edited by Heith Copes and Volkan Topalli.—1st ed.
    p. cm.
  Includes bibliographical references and index.
  ISBN-13: 978-0-07-338001-8 (alk. paper)
  ISBN-10: 0-07-338001-6 (alk. paper)
1.  Criminology.   I. Copes, Heith. II. Topalli, Volkan.
HV6018.C734 2009
364.01—dc22

                                                                          2009019990

The Internet addresses listed in the text were accurate at the time of publication. The inclusion of a Web site does not indicate an endorsement by the authors or McGraw-Hill, and McGraw-Hill does not guarantee the accuracy of the information presented at these sites.

www.mhhe.com

# ABOUT THE EDITORS

**HEITH COPES** is an associate professor in the Department of Justice Sciences at the University of Alabama at Birmingham. His primary research combines symbolic interactionism and rational choice theory to better understand the criminal decision-making process. His recent publications appear in *The British Journal of Criminology, Crime and Justice: A Review of Research, Criminology and Public Policy,* and *Social Problems,* and he has received funding from the National Institute of Justice.

**VOLKAN TOPALLI** is an associate professor at Georgia State University (GSU) in the Department of Criminal Justice and is a Research Fellow with the GSU Partnership for Urban Health Research and the International Centre for Research on Forensic Psychology (Portsmouth University, UK). His research focuses on the general areas of offender decision making and retaliatory criminal behavior of urban street offenders. His work employs mixed method (i.e., quantitative and ethnographic) approaches, relying on theoretical principles found in traditional criminology as well as social and ecological psychology. He has numerous publications in journals such as *Criminology, Justice Quarterly, The British Journal of Criminology,* and *Aggressive Behavior* and has received funding from the National Institute of Justice and the National Science Foundation.

# ACKNOWLEDGMENTS

We appreciate very much the support of our associates at McGraw-Hill in providing us the opportunity to present this book to you. To call them visionary would probably come off as self-serving, so we will merely offer our gratitude that they believed enough in the concept of this book and the two of us as editors to green light the project and put up with the plodding process that is academic work. In particular, we thank Katie Stevens, our managing editor, for her patience and enthusiasm. We get the feeling that said patience and enthusiasm derived not only from her good nature but also from our ability to amuse her.

We also thank our research assistants (Jessica Stein and Jacquie Rion at Georgia State University, and Joel Kiser at the University of Alabama at Birmingham) for putting up with a number of incredibly annoying, cryptic, and unreasonable requests. They have been patient, good-natured, and diligent in their aid to us and we dare say that this book would have a publication date far in the future were it not for their efforts. Hopefully, karma will provide them the opportunity to persecute their own graduate students in similar fashion in the not-too-distant future.

We would be remiss not to thank our lovely wives, Buffy and Çigdem, for their support, encouragement, patience, and good senses of humor. This book frequently took our attention away from them, and they have (for the most part) put up with us in the way that only wives married to academics can.

# DEDICATION

*We dedicate this book to our mentors and friends, Neal Shover and Richard Wright, not only because they have provided us with terrific guidance, counsel, and support throughout our careers, but also because they would most certainly hate being mentioned in the dedication of any book. Thank you, gentlemen!*

# PREFACE

In the past decade the number and size of criminology and criminal justice departments have increased substantially and nearly all of these departments require a class in criminological theory. Those who teach these theory classes have three options when choosing texts: they can assign a theory textbook that summarizes the theories and the major research on them; they can assign a reader that includes one or two original articles explaining each theory; or they can put together their own packet of readings. We believe that each of these options has major limitations. In an effort to address these limitations and provide researchers, instructors, and students with a comprehensive treatment of criminological theory, we put together the book you now hold in your hands. This book is unique among edited theoretical volumes in that it provides a comprehensive collection of the most impactful classical theoretical pieces in criminology, combined with original retrospective pieces on each theory written exclusively for this book by some of the best-established and up-and-coming criminologists today. This combination of classical articles and contemporary retrospectives provides the reader with a solid foundation for understanding the original theories and with a contemporary understanding of how the theories have evolved through testing and developments.

This book contains the most important and influential theories used to understand crime and criminality. As a course text, this book is designed for upper-division courses in criminology, criminal justice, and sociology. As a research resource, it should be of interest to researchers and professionals because it provides a compendium of the most important theories combined with keen contemporary analysis that presents the latest research and theoretical modifications regarding each of them. This book's greatest strength, and indeed its future impact, derives from the retrospective pieces found at the end of each chapter. Great care and deliberation were taken to identify and recruit contemporary criminologists whose current and past work marks them as experts in the theoretical perspectives at hand. In each chapter, these individuals have provided retrospective analyses of the theories so users can "see" how each theory has progressed and been implemented since its development. We strove to ensure a consistency in the retrospectives. Thus, in soliciting these unique pieces from our authors we asked them to consider five aspects of each theory. First, authors provide the theoretical foundation of the theory they wrote about. This includes a brief overview and summary of the theory, with some detail on how the theory came about and what its preceding philosophical foundations may have been. Second, authors reviewed the various critiques of the theory. Here they provide a critical assessment of the theory, delineating its shortcomings and identifying areas that require further attention from researchers and theorists. Third, for theories to be valid they must be subject to empirical evaluation. In reviewing evaluations authors address the major research evaluating the theory, as well as how the theory has held up to empirical tests and how scholars have measured core concepts. Fourth, each retrospective discusses the various theoretical refinements that have been made. This includes a description of the advances and reformulations of the original theory and a description of how the theory has grown since its inception. Finally, authors address the potential policy applications of the theory. This includes addressing how the theory can be used to inform and guide policies relevant to crime and justice.

In our opinion, these critical analyses have the capacity to enlighten our understanding of criminological theory as a whole, and it is likely that a number of them will at some point in the future be considered classical pieces in their own right. To our knowledge there is not another criminology theory textbook like this on the market, and we are grateful beyond words to the authors who submitted their work to us for this book. A perusal of the author biographies will surely impress the reader, and we are humbled (if not outright shocked) that these exceptional scholars were willing to pause their busy and productive careers to contribute to this effort. What is evident from their writings, research, and careers is that they feel as passionately about the place and importance of criminology in contemporary society as we do. Crime is an unfortunately enduring characteristic of life, and our ability to respond to it would be severely hampered were it not for the existence and advancement of criminological theory. The contributing authors continue to advance theory and research in this critical area. This book would simply not be possible without them.

# CONTRIBUTORS' BIOGRAPHICAL INFORMATION

**BRUCE A. ARRIGO** is a professor of crime, law, and society within the Department of Criminal Justice at the University of North Carolina–Charlotte. He is an internationally acclaimed researcher and award-winning author, having published some 25 books and edited volumes as well as more than 150 articles, chapters, and essays.

**J. C. BARNES** is a doctoral student in the College of Criminology and Criminal Justice at Florida State University. His research interests include the etiology of delinquency, especially the biosocial correlates to delinquency, and evolutionary psychology. His work has appeared in *Crime and Delinquency, Criminal Justice and Behavior, Youth Violence and Juvenile Justice, Criminal Justice Policy Review, American Journal of Criminal Justice*, and the *Journal of Criminal Justice Education*.

**KEVIN M. BEAVER** earned his PhD from the University of Cincinnati in 2006 and was awarded the Graduate Research Fellowship from the National Institute of Justice. He is currently an assistant professor in the College of Criminology and Criminal Justice at Florida State University. His research examines the ways in which the environment intersects with biological and genetic factors to produce delinquent and criminal behaviors. Dr. Beaver is author of *Biosocial Criminology: A Primer* and coeditor (with Anthony Walsh) of *Biosocial Criminology: New Directions in Theory and Research*.

**MARK T. BERG** is an assistant professor in the school of Public and Environmental Affairs at Indiana-Purdue University. His current research focuses on the structural-cultural context of social behavior, criminological theory, and longitudinal patterns of violent offending. His dissertation research is supported by a fellowship from the H. F. Guggenheim Foundation.

**JÓN GUNNAR BERNBURG** is an associate professor of sociology at the University of Iceland. His current research focuses on two areas of crime and deviance research: labeling theory and neighborhood effects. His work has appeared in several scholarly journals, most recently in *Criminology, Social Forces*, and *Social Science & Medicine*.

**JEFFREY A. BOUFFARD** is an associate professor in the College of Criminal Justice at Sam Houston State University, in Huntsville, Texas. He received his PhD (criminology and criminal justice) in 2000 from the University of Maryland–College Park. He also holds a master's degree in clinical psychology from St. Michael's College in Vermont, where he spent several years working as a psychologist with adult and juvenile inmates. In addition to studying rational choice and self-control theories, he has conducted several evaluations of the operation and effectiveness of drug courts and drug treatment programs, adult and juvenile offender reentry programs, restorative justice and community service programs, as well as juvenile mentoring and after-school prevention programs. He has published numerous peer-reviewed articles in scholarly journals such as *Justice Quarterly, Journal of Criminal Justice, Prison Journal, Journal of Offender Rehabilitation*, and *Journal of Drug Issues*.

**AMANDA BURGESS-PROCTOR** received her PhD in criminal justice from Michigan State University. She is an assistant professor in the Department of Sociology at Oakland University. Her primary research interests include feminist criminology, criminological theory, intimate partner violence, and intersections of race, class, and gender. She has published articles in *Feminist Criminology, Violence Against Women, Violence & Victims*, and *Women & Criminal Justice*.

**MATT DELISI** is coordinator of Criminal Justice Studies, associate professor in the Department of Sociology, and faculty affiliate with the Center for the Study of Violence at Iowa State University. He has produced approximately 100 scholarly publications, including articles in *Addictive Behaviors, American Journal of Public Health, Behavioral and Brain Functions, Behavioral Sciences and the Law, Crime & Delinquency, Criminal Behaviour and Mental Health, Criminal Justice and Behavior, Criminal Justice Policy Review, Criminology, Forensic Science International, Homicide Studies, International Journal of Law and Psychiatry, International Journal of Offender Therapy and Comparative Criminology, Journal of Adolescent Research, Journal of Criminal Justice, Journal of Criminal Justice Education, Journal of Forensic Sciences, Journal of Genetic Psychology, Justice Quarterly, Psychological Reports, Social Science Journal, Social Science Research, Women & Criminal Justice*, and *Youth Violence and Juvenile Justice*.

**JACINTA M. GAU** is an assistant professor in the Department of Criminal Justice at California State University–San Bernardino. Her primary research interests relate to broken windows theory and include police–community relationships and the measurement of disorder. Her recent work has appeared in *Justice Quarterly, Criminology & Public Policy*, and *Policing: An International Journal of Police Strategies and Management*.

**ANDY HOCHSTETLER** is associate professor of sociology at Iowa State University. He writes on self-conception and the choice to offend with emphasis on identity and decision making. With Neal Shover, he wrote *Choosing White-Collar Crime* for Cambridge University Press.

**JOHN P. HOFFMANN** is a professor in the Department of Sociology at Brigham Young University. His research interests include theories of delinquency and the influences of religious beliefs and practices on attitudes and behaviors.

**SCOTT JACQUES** is a PhD candidate in the Department of Criminology and Criminal Justice at the University of Missouri–St. Louis. He is primarily concerned with conceptualizing, documenting, and explaining the behavior of drug dealers.

**SANDRA LEGGE** is a research assistant at Bielefeld University, Germany. Her research interest focuses on anomie theory, deviant behavior, and prejudices and discrimination. She is co–guest editor of the special issue *Youth, Violence, and Social Disintegration* for the journal *New Directions for Youth Development*, and coauthor of *Social Structural Effects on the Level and Development of the Individual Experience of Anomie in the German Population*.

**CATHERINE D. MARCUM** is assistant professor of justice studies in the Political Science Department at Georgia Southern University. She graduated in December 2008 from Indiana University of Pennsylvania with a doctorate of philosophy in criminology. Her main research interests are applications of criminological theory, cybercrime, sexual offenders and victims, and corrections.

**STEVEN F. MESSNER** is Distinguished Teaching Professor of Sociology, University at Albany, State University of New York. His research focuses on social institutions and crime, understanding trends in crime, and crime and social control in China. In addition to his publications in professional journals, he is coauthor of *Crime and the American Dream* and *Perspectives on Crime and Deviance;* and coeditor of *Theoretical Integration in the Study of Deviance and Crime* and *Crime and Social Control in a Changing China*.

**J. MITCHELL MILLER** is a professor in the Department of Criminal Justice at the University of Texas–San Antonio. His research is oriented around criminological theory testing in applied programmatic context, including a current evaluation of a cognitive restructuring initiative for serial inebriates incarcerated in the Texas Department of Criminal Justice East Texas Treatment Facility. His recent published works include *Criminological Theory: A Brief Introduction* (second edition, with Chris Schreck and Rick Tewksbury) and *Criminology* (second edition, with Leonard Glick).

**ALEX R. PIQUERO** is a professor of criminology and criminal justice and affiliate with the Maryland Population Research Center at the University of Maryland–College Park. He is also executive counselor of the American Society of Criminology and coeditor of the *Journal of Quantitative Criminology*. His research interests include criminological theory, criminal careers, and quantitative research methods.

**NICOLE LEEPER PIQUERO** is an assistant professor of criminal justice in the Wilder School of Government and Public Affairs at Virginia Commonwealth University. She is also secretary of the Academy of Criminal Justice Sciences. Her current research focuses on the etiology of white-collar crime, personality dimensions and traits associated with white-collar and corporate crime decision making, and white-collar crime victimization.

**TRAVIS PRATT** is an associate professor in the School of Criminology and Criminal Justice at Arizona State University. He earned his PhD from the University of Cincinnati and is the author of more than 45 refereed articles that have appeared in journals such as *Criminology, Justice Quarterly, Crime and Delinquency*, the *Journal of Research in Crime and Delinquency, Advances in Criminological Theory*, and *Crime and Justice: An Annual Review*. He is also the author of *Addicted to Incarceration: Corrections Policy and the Politics of Misinformation in the United States*. He is the recipient of the Ruth Shonle Cavan Award for the Outstanding Young Scholar of the American Society of Criminology.

**CHRISTOPHER J. SCHRECK** is an associate professor in the Department of Criminal Justice at the Rochester Institute of Technology. His research focuses on using criminological theory to better understand the antecedents of victimization and the linkages between victimization and offending. His more recent work explores the origins of differential patterns in violent and nonviolent crime at the microlevels and macrolevels.

**J. EAGLE SHUTT** is an assistant professor at the University of Louisville's Department of Justice Administration. A former prosecutor and public defender, his research interests include evolutionary psychology, biosocial criminology, subcultures, and law.

**ERIC A. STEWART** is an associate professor in the College of Criminology and Criminal Justice at Florida State University. He is also a member of the Racial Democracy, Crime and Justice Network. His research interests include racial inequality and criminal outcomes and crime over the life course, as well as contextual processes and microprocesses on adolescent development.

**JEFFERY T. ULMER** is currently an associate professor of sociology and crime, law, and justice at Pennsylvania State University. He has published journal articles on topics such as courts and sentencing, criminological theory, symbolic interactionism, recidivism, fear of crime, criminal enterprise, and the integration of ethnographic and quantitative methods. In addition, he is the author or coauthor of three books: *Social Worlds of Sentencing: Court Communities Under Sentencing Guidelines, Confessions of a Dying Thief: Understanding Criminal Careers and Illegal Enterprise* (with Darrell Steffensmeier), and *Sentencing Guidelines: Lessons From Pennsylvania* (with John Kramer). *Confessions of a Dying Thief* won the 2006 Hindelang Award from the American Society of Criminology.

**MICHAEL G. VAUGHN** is currently an assistant professor in the School of Social Work and holds appointments in public policy and the Department of Community Health, Division of Epidemiology, Saint Louis University School of Public Health. He has written over 60 publications and his interdisciplinary research has appeared in such journals as *Addictive Behaviors, American Journal of Public Health, American Journal of Psychiatry, Behavioral and Brain Functions, Drug and Alcohol Dependence, Criminal Justice and Behavior, Behavioral Sciences and the Law, Youth Violence and Juvenile Justice, Journal of Emotional and Behavioral Disorders, Criminology, Journal of Criminal Justice, Social*

*Service Review*, and *Children and Youth Services Review*. In addition to several projects examining psychopathy, adolescent health, adolescent substance abuse, self-regulation, and violence, he is developing and testing a general biosocial public health model for research and intervention applications.

**CHRISTOPHER R. WILLIAMS** is an associate professor of criminology within the Department of Sociology and Criminology at the University of West Georgia. His books include *Law, Psychology, and Justice: Chaos Theory and the New (Dis)Order; Theory, Justice, and Social Change: Theoretical Integrations and Critical Applications*; the edited volume *Philosophy, Crime, and Criminology*; and *Ethics, Crime, and Criminal Justice*. He has also published numerous scholarly articles and book chapters, most confronting issues and controversies in social and criminological theory; the sociology of deviance; the philosophical foundations of crime, law, and justice; and the sociological and legal dimensions of mental health and illness.

**JOHN PAUL WRIGHT** is an associate professor of criminal justice at the University of Cincinnati, Division of Criminal Justice. His research interests focus on the nexus of biological, genetic, and social sources of variance in criminal propensity. He has published over 80 scientific articles in a variety of journals, as well as four books.

# CONTENTS

## PART I    Classical and Neoclassical Theories

# PART VII   Control Theories

# PART VIII   Interactionist Theories

# PART IX   Critical Theories

# PART I

# CLASSICAL AND NEOCLASSICAL THEORIES

# RATIONAL CHOICE THEORIES

## AN ESSAY ON CRIMES AND PUNISHMENTS

*Cesare Beccaria*

### Chap. I

#### Of the origin of punishments

Laws are the conditions, under which men, naturally independent, united themselves in society. Weary of living in a continual state of war, and of enjoying a liberty, which became of little value, from the uncertainty of its duration, they sacrificed one part of it, to enjoy the rest in peace and security. The sum of all these portions of the liberty of each individual constituted the sovereignty of a nation; and was deposited in the hands of the sovereign, as the lawful administrator. But it was not sufficient only to establish this deposite; it was also necessary to defend it from the usurpation of each individual, who will always endeavour to take away from the mass, not only his own portion, but to encroach on that of others. Some motives, therefore, that strike the senses, were necessary, to prevent the despotism of each individual from plunging society into its former chaos. Such motives are the punishments established against the infractors of the laws. I say, that motives of this kind are necessary; because, experience shows, that the multitude adopt no established principle of conduct; and because, society is prevented from approaching to that dissolution, (to which, as well as all other parts of the physical, and moral world, it naturally tends) only by motives, that are the immediate objects of sense, and which being continually presented to the mind, are sufficient to counterbalance the effects of the passions of the individual, which oppose the general good. Neither the power of eloquence, nor the sublimest truths, are sufficient to restrain, for any length of time, those passions, which are excited by the lively impressions of present objects.

### Chap. II

#### Of the right to punish

Every punishment, which does not arise from absolute necessity, says the great *Montesquieu,* is tyrannical. A proposition which may be made more general, thus. Every act of authority of one man over another, for which there is not an absolute necessity, is tyrannical. It is upon this then, that the sovereign's right to punish crimes is founded; that is, upon the necessity of defending the public liberty, entrusted to his care, from the usurpation of individuals; and punishments are just in proportion, as the liberty, preserved by the sovereign, is sacred and valuable.

Let us consult the human heart, and there we shall find the foundation of the sovereign's right to punish; for no advantage in moral policy can be lasting, which is not founded on the indelible sentiments of the heart of man. Whatever law deviates from this principle will always meet with a resistance, which will destroy it in the end; for the smallest force, continually applied, will overcome the most violent motion communicated to bodies.

No man ever gave up his liberty, merely for the good of the public. Such a chimera exists only in romances. Every individual wishes, if possible, to be exempt from the compacts, that bind the rest of mankind.

The multiplication of mankind, though slow, being too great for the means, which the earth, in its natural state, offered to satisfy necessities, which every day became more numerous, obliged men to separate again, and form new societies. These naturally opposed the first, and a state of war was transferred from individuals to nations.

Thus it was necessity, that forced men to give up a part of their liberty; it is certain then, that every individual would chuse to put into the public stock the smallest portion possible; as much only as was sufficient to engage others to defend it. The aggregate of these, the smallest portions possible, forms the right of punishing: all that extends beyond this is abuse, not justice.

Observe that by *justice* I understand nothing more, than that bond, which is necessary to keep the interest of individuals united; without which, men would return to their original state of barbarity. All punishments, which exceed the necessity of preserving this bond, are in their nature unjust. We should be cautious how we associate with the word *justice,* an idea of any thing real, such as a physical power, or a being that actually exists. I do not, by any means, speak of the justice of God, which is of another kind, and refers immediately to rewards and punishments in a life to come.

## Chap. III

### Consequences of the foregoing principles

The laws only can determine the punishment of crimes; and the authority of making penal laws can only reside with the legislator, who represents the whole society, united by the social compact. No magistrate then, (as he is one of the society) can, with justice, inflict on any other member of the same society, punishment, that is not ordained by the laws. But as a punishment, increased beyond the degree fixed by the law, is the just punishment, with the addition of another; it follows, that no magistrate, even under a pretence of zeal, or the public good, should increase the punishment already determined by the laws.

If every individual be bound to society, society is equally bound to him, by a contract, which from its nature, equally binds both parties. This obligation, which descends from the throne to the cottage, and equally binds the highest, and lowest of mankind, signifies nothing more, than that it is the interest of all, that conventions, which are useful to the greatest number, should be punctually observed. The violation of this compact by any individual, is an introduction to anarchy.

The sovereign, who represents the society itself, can only make general laws, to bind the members; but it belongs not to him to judge whether any individual has violated the social compact, or incurred the punishment in consequence. For in this case, there are two parties, one represented by the sovereign, who insists upon the violation of the contract, and the other is the person accused, who denies it. It is necessary then that there should be a third person to decide this contest; that is to say, a judge, or magistrate, from whose determination there should be no appeal; and this determination should consist of a simple affirmation, or negation of fact.

If it can only be proved, that the severity of punishments, though not immediately contrary to the public good, or to the end for which they were intended, viz. to prevent crimes, be useless; then such severity would be contrary to those beneficent virtues, which are the consequence of enlightened reason, which instructs the sovereign to wish rather to govern men in a state of freedom and happiness, than of slavery. It would also be contrary to justice, and the social compact.

## Chap. IV

### Of the interpretation of laws

Judges, in criminal cases, have no right to interpret the penal laws, because they are not legislators. They have not received the laws from our ancestors as a domestic tradition, or as the will of a testator, which his heirs, and executors, are to obey; but they receive them from a society actually existing, or from the sovereign, its representative. Even the authority of the laws is not founded on any pretended obligation, or ancient convention; which must be null, as it cannot bind those who did not exist at the time of its institution; and unjust, as it would reduce men, in the ages following, to a herd of brutes, without any power of judging, or acting. The laws receive their force, and authority from an oath of fidelity, either tacit, or expressed, which living subjects have sworn to their sovereign, in order to restrain the intestine fermentation of the private interest of individuals. From hence springs their true and natural authority. Who then is their lawful interpreter? The sovereign, that is, the representative of society, and not the judge, whose office is only to examine, if a man have, or have not committed an action contrary to the laws.

In every criminal cause the judge should reason syllogistically. The *major* should be the general law; the *minor,* the conformity of the action, or its opposition to the laws; the *conclusion,* liberty, or punishment. If the judge be obliged by the imperfection of the laws, or chuses, to make any other, or more syllogisms than this, it will be an introduction to uncertainty.

There is nothing more dangerous than the common axiom: *the spirit of the laws is to be considered.* To adopt it is to give way to the torrent of opinions. This may seem a paradox to vulgar minds, which are more strongly affected by the smallest disorder before their eyes, than by the most pernicious, though remote, consequences produced by one false principle adopted by a nation.

Our knowledge is in proportion to the number of our ideas. The more complex these are, the greater is the variety of positions, in which they may be considered. Every man hath his own particular point of view, and at different times, sees the same objects in very different lights. The spirit of the laws will then be the result of the good, or bad logic of the judge; and this will depend on his good or bad digestion; on the violence of his passions; on the rank, and condition of the accused, or on his connections with the judge; and on all those little circumstances, which change the appearance of objects in the fluctuating mind of man. Hence we see the fate of a delinquent changed many times in passing through the different courts of judicature, and his life and liberty, victims to the false ideas, or ill humour of the judge; who mistakes the vague result of his own confused reasoning, for the just interpretation of the laws. We see the same crimes punished in a different manner at different times in the same tribunals; the consequence of not having consulted the constant, and invariable voice of the laws, but the erring instability of arbitrary interpretation.

The disorders, that may arise from a rigorous observance of the letter of penal laws, are not to be compared with those produced by the interpretation of them. The first are temporary inconveniences which will oblige the legislature to correct the letter of the law, the want of preciseness, and uncertainty of which has occasioned these disorders; and this will put a stop to the fatal liberty of explaining; the source of arbitrary and venal declamations. When the code of laws is once fixed, it should be observed in the literal sense, and nothing more is left to the judge, than to determine, whether an action be, or be not conformable to the written law. When the rule of right which ought to direct the actions of the philosopher, as well as the ignorant, is a matter of controversy, not of fact, the people are slaves to the magistrates. The despotism of this multitude of tyrants is more insupportable, the less the distance is between the oppressor and the oppressed; more fatal than that of one, for the tyranny of many is not to be shaken off, but by having recourse to that of one alone. It is more cruel, as it meets with more opposition, and the cruelty of a tyrant is not in proportion to his strength, but to the obstacles that oppose him.

These are the means, by which security of person and property is best obtained; which is just, as it is the purpose of uniting in society; and it is useful, as each person may calculate exactly the inconveniences attending every crime. By these means, subjects will acquire a spirit of independence and liberty; however it may appear to those, who dare to call the weakness of submitting blindly to their capricious and interested opinions, by the sacred name of virtue.

These principles will displease those, who have made it a rule with themselves, to transmit to their inferiors the tyranny they suffer from their superiors. I should have every thing to fear, if tyrants were to read my book; but tyrants never read.

## Chap. V

### Of the obscurity of laws

If the power of interpreting laws be an evil, obscurity in them must be another, as the former is the consequence of the latter. This evil will be still greater, if the laws be written in a language unknown to the people; who, being ignorant of the consequences of their own actions, become necessarily dependent on a few, who are interpreters of the laws, which, instead of being public, and general, are thus rendered private, and particular. What must we think of mankind, when we reflect, that such is the established custom of the greatest part of our polished, and enlighten'd Europe? Crimes will be less frequent, in proportion as the code of laws is more universally read, and understood; for there is no doubt, but that the eloquence of the passions is greatly assisted by the ignorance, and uncertainty of punishments.

Hence it follows, that without written laws, no society will ever acquire a fixed form of government, in which the power is vested in the whole, and not in any part of the society; and in which, the laws are not to be altered, but by the will of the whole, nor corrupted by the force of private interest. Experience and reason show us, that the probability of human traditions diminishes in proportion as they are distant from their sources. How then can laws resist the inevitable force of time, if there be not a lasting monument of the social compact?

Hence we see the use of printing, which alone makes the public, and not a few individuals, the guardians and defenders of the laws. It is this art, which, by diffusing literature, has gradually dissipated the gloomy spirit of cabal and intrigue. To this art it is owing, that the atrocious crimes of our ancestors, who were alternately slaves, and tyrants, are become less frequent. Those who are acquainted with the history of the two or three last centuries, may observe, how from the lap of luxury and effeminacy, have sprung the most tender virtues, humanity, benevolence, and toleration of human errors. They may contemplate the effects of, what was so improperly called, ancient simplicity, and good faith; humanity groaning under implacable superstition; the avarice and ambition of a few, staining, with human blood, the thrones and palaces of kings; secret treasons, and public massacres; every noble a tyrant over the people; and the ministers of the gospel of Christ, bathing their hands in blood, in the name of the God of all mercy. We may talk as we please of the corruption and degeneracy of the present age, but happily we see no such horrid examples of cruelty and oppression.

## Chap. VI

### Of the proportion between crimes and punishments

It is not only the common interest of mankind, that crimes should not be committed, but that crimes of every kind should be less frequent, in proportion to the evil they produce to society. Therefore, the means made use of by the legislature to prevent crimes, should be more powerful, in proportion as they are destructive of the public safety and happiness, and as the inducements to commit them are stronger. Therefore there ought to be a fixed proportion between crimes and punishments.

It is impossible to prevent entirely all the disorders which the passions of mankind cause in society. These disorders increase in proportion to the number of people, and the opposition of private interests. If we consult history, we shall find them increasing, in every state, with the extent of dominion. In political arithmetic, it is necessary to substitute a calculation of probabilities, to mathematical exactness. That force, which continually impels us to our own private interest, like gravity, acts incessantly, unless it meets with an obstacle to oppose it. The effects of this force are the confused series of human actions. Punishments, which I would call political obstacles, prevent the fatal effects of private interest, without destroying the impelling cause, which is that sensibility inseparable from man. The legislator acts, in this case, like a skilful architect, who endeavours to counteract the force of gravity by combining the circumstances which may contribute to the strength of his edifice.

The necessity of uniting in society being granted, together with the conventions, which the opposite interests of individuals must necessarily require, a scale of crimes may be formed, of which the first degree should consist of those, which immediately tend to the dissolution of society, and the last, of the smallest possible injustice done to a private member of that society. Between these extremes will be comprehended, all actions contrary to the public good, which are called criminal, and which descend by insensible degrees, decreasing from the highest to the lowest. If mathematical calculation could be applied to the obscure and infinite combinations of human actions, there might be a corresponding scale of punishments, descending from the greatest to the least: but it will be sufficient that the wise legislator mark the principal divisions, without disturbing the order, left to crimes of the *first* degree, be assigned punishments of the *last*. If there were an exact and universal scale of crimes and punishments, we should there have a common measure of the degree of liberty and slavery, humanity and cruelty of different nations.

Any action, which is not comprehended in the above-mentioned scale, will not be called a crime, or punished as such, except by those who have an interest in the denomination. The uncertainty of the extreme points of this scale, hath produced a system of morality which contradicts the laws; a multitude of laws that contradict each other; and many, which expose the best men to the severest punishments, rendering the ideas of *vice* and *virtue* vague, and fluctuating, and even their existence doubtful. Hence that fatal lethargy of political bodies, which terminates in their destruction.

Whoever reads, with a philosophic eye, the history of nations, and their laws, will generally find, that the ideas of virtue and vice, of a good or a bad citizen, change with the revolution of ages; not in proportion to the alteration of circumstances, and consequently conformable to the common good; but in proportion to the passions and errors by which the different law-givers were successively influenced. He will frequently observe, that the passions and vices of one age, are the foundation of the morality of the following; that violent passion, the offspring of fanaticism and enthusiasm, being weakened by time, which reduces all the phenomena of the natural and moral world to an equality, become, by degrees, the prudence of the age, and an useful instrument in the hands of the powerful, or artful politician. Hence the uncertainty of our notions of honour and virtue; an uncertainty which will ever remain, because they change with the revolutions of time, and names survive the things they originally signified; they change with the boundaries of states, which are often the same both in physical and moral geography.

Pleasure and pain are the only springs of action in beings endowed with sensibility. Even amongst the motives which incite men to acts of religion, the invisible legislator has ordained rewards and punishments. From a partial distribution of these, will arise that contradiction, so little observed, because so common; I mean, that of punishing by the laws, the crimes which the laws have occasioned. If an equal punishment be ordained for two crimes that injure society in different degrees, there is nothing to deter men from committing the greater, as often as it is attended with greater advantage.


## Chap. VII

### Of estimating the degree of crimes

The foregoing reflections authorise me to assert, that crimes are only to be measured by the injury done to society.

They err, therefore, who imagine that a crime is greater, or less, according to the intention of the person by whom it is committed; for this will depend on the actual impression of objects on the senses, and on the previous disposition of the mind; both which will vary in different persons, and even in the same person at different times, according to the succession of ideas, passions, and circumstances. Upon that system, it would be necessary to form, not only a particular code for every individual, but a new penal law for every crime.

Men, often with the best intention, do the greatest injury to society, and with the worst, do it the most essential services.

Others have estimated crimes rather by the dignity of the person offended, than by their consequences to society. If this were the true standard, the smallest irreverence to the divine Being ought to be punished with infinitely more severity, than the assassination of a monarch.

In short, others have imagined, that the greatness of the sin should aggravate the crime. But the fallacy of this opinion will appear on the slightest consideration of the relations between man and man, and between God and man. The relations between man and man, are relations of equality. Necessity alone hath produced, from the opposition of private passions and interests, the idea of public utility, which is the foundation of human justice. The other are relations of dependence, between an imperfect creature and his creator, the most perfect of beings, who has reserved to himself the sole right of being both lawgiver, and judge; for he alone can, without injustice, be, at the same time, both one and the other. If he hath decreed eternal punishments for those who disobey his will, shall an insect dare to put himself in the place of divine justice, or pretend to punish for the Almighty, who is himself all-sufficient; who cannot receive impressions of pleasure, or pain, and who alone, of all other beings, acts without being acted upon? The degree of sin depends on the malignity of the heart, which is impenetrable to finite beings. How then can the degree of sin serve as a standard to determine the degree of crimes? If that were admitted, men may punish when God pardons, and pardon when God condemns; and thus act in opposition to the supreme Being.

## Chap. VIII

### Of the division of crimes

We have proved, then, that crimes are to be estimated by *the injury done to society*. This is one of those palpable truths, which, though evident to the meanest capacity, yet, by a combination of circumstances, are only known to a few thinking men in every nation, and in every age. But opinions, worthy only of the despotism of Asia, and passions, armed with power and authority, have, generally by insensible and sometimes by violent impressions on the timid credulity of men, effaced those simple ideas, which perhaps constituted the first philosophy of infant society. Happily the philosophy of the present enlightened age seems again to conduct us to the same principles, and with that degree of certainty, which is obtained by a rational examination, and repeated experience.

A scrupulous adherence to order would require, that we should now examine, and distinguish the different species of crimes, and the modes of punishment; but they are so variable in their nature, from the different circumstances of ages, and countries, that the detail would be tiresome, and endless. It will be sufficient for my purpose, to point out the most general principles, and the most common and dangerous errors, in order to undeceive, as well those, who, from a mistaken zeal for liberty, would introduce anarchy and confusion, as those, who pretend to reduce society in general to the regularity of a convent.

Some crimes are immediately destructive of society, or its representative; others attack the private security of the life, property, or honour of individuals; and a third class consists of such actions as are contrary to the laws which relate to the general good of the community.

The first, which are of the highest degree, as they are most destructive to society, are called crimes of *Leze-majesty*. Tyranny, and ignorance, which have confounded the clearest terms and ideas, have given this appellation to crimes of a different nature, and consequently have established the same punishment for each; and on this occasion, as on a thousand others, men have been sacrificed, victims to a word. Every crime, even of the most private nature, injures society; but every crime does not threaten its immediate destruction. Moral, as well as physical actions, have their sphere of activity differently circumscribed, like all the movements of nature, by time and space; it is therefore a sophistical interpretation, the common philosophy of slaves, that would confound the limits of things, established by eternal truth.

To these succeed crimes which are destructive of the security of individuals. This security being the principal end of all society, and to which every citizen hath an undoubted right, it becomes indispensably necessary, that to these crimes the greatest of punishments should be assigned.

The opinion, that every member of society has a right to do any thing, that is not contrary to the laws, without fearing any other inconveniences, than those which are the natural consequences of the action itself, is a political dogma, which should be defended by the laws, inculcated by the magistrates, and believed by the people; a sacred dogma, without which there can be no lawful society; a just recompence for our sacrifice of that universal liberty of action, common to all sensible beings, and only limited by our natural powers. By this principle, our minds become free, active, and vigorous; by this alone we are inspired with that virtue which knows no fear, so different from that pliant prudence, worthy of those only who can bear a precarious existence.

Attempts, therefore, against the life, and liberty of a citizen, are crimes of the highest nature. Under this head we comprehend not only assassinations, and robberies, committed by the populace, but by grandees, and magistrates; whose example acts with more force, and at a greater distance, destroying the ideas of justice and duty among the subjects, and substituting that of the right of the strongest, equally dangerous to those who exercise it, and to those who suffer. . . .

## Chap. XII

### Of the intent of punishments

From the foregoing considerations it is evident, that the intent of punishments, is not to torment a sensible being, nor to undo a crime already committed. Is it possible that torments, and useless cruelty, the instrument of furious fanaticism, or of impotency of tyrants, can be authorized by a political body? which, so far from being influenced by passion, should be the cool moderator of the passions of individuals. Can the groans of a tortured wretch recall the time past, or reverse the crime he has committed?

The end of punishment, therefore, is no other, than to prevent the criminal from doing further injury to society, and to prevent others from committing the like offence. Such punishments, therefore, and such a mode of inflicting them, ought to be chosen, as will make the strongest and most lasting impressions on the minds of others, with the least torment to the body of the criminal.

# MODELING OFFENDERS' DECISIONS:
# A FRAMEWORK FOR RESEARCH AND POLICY

*Ronald V. Clarke and Derek B. Cornish*

Most theories about criminal behavior have tended to ignore the offender's decision making—the conscious thought processes that give purpose to and justify conduct, and the underlying cognitive mechanisms by which information about the world is selected, attended to, and processed. The source of this neglect is the apparent conflict between decision-making concepts and the prevailing determinism of most criminological theories. Whether framed in terms of social or psychological factors, these theories have traditionally been concerned to explain the criminal dispositions of particular individuals or groups. More recently, faced with the need to explain not just the genesis of people's involvement in crime but also the occurrence of particular criminal acts, greater attention has been paid by theory to the immediate environmental context of offending. But the resulting accounts of criminal behavior have still tended to suggest deterministic models in which the criminal appears as a relatively passive figure; thus he or she is seen either as prey to internal or external forces outside personal control, or as the battlefield upon which these forces resolve their struggle for the control of behavioral outcomes. . . .

## Models of Criminal Decision Making

Even allowing for some selective perception on our part, we believe that during the past decade there has been a notable confluence of interest in the rational choice, nondeterministic view of crime. This is a natural perspective for law and economics, but it has also achieved wide currency in criminology's other parent disciplines—sociology and psychology—as well as within the different schools of criminology itself. That the shift is part of a broader intellectual movement is suggested by the increasing popularity of economic and rational choice analyses of behaviors other than crime. Why there should be this movement at the present time and what social forces and events might be implicated is difficult to say, but cross-fertilization of ideas between different groups of people working on similar problems always occurs, and certain individuals have deliberately applied the same theoretical perspective to a variety of different problems. For instance, Gary Becker pioneered his economic analyses of crime when dealing with the economics of discrimination and has since extended his method to choice of marriage partner. . . .

The models of crime presented below also offer a way of synthesizing a diverse range of concepts and findings for the purpose of guiding policy and research, but they are developed within the context of much more explicit decision making. They are not models in which relationships are expressed either in mathematical terms (as in, e.g., economic models) or in the form of testable propositions. Nor are they even "decision trees" that attempt to model the successive steps in a complex decision process. Rather, they are schematic representations of the key decision points in criminal behavior and of the various social, psychological, and environmental factors bearing on the decisions reached. Our models resemble most closely the kind of flow diagrams frequently employed to represent complex social processes—for example, the explanatory models for fear of crime developed by Skogan and Maxfield and for victimization proneness by Hindelang, Gottfredson, and Garofalo.

The models, which need to be separately developed for each specific form of crime, are not theories in themselves but rather the blueprints for theory. They owe much to early attempts to model aspects of criminal decision making by Brantingham and Brantingham, Brown and Altman, and Walsh. But these earlier models were largely confined to just one of the criminal decision processes—target selection—and they also depended upon a commonsense explication of the likely decision steps taken by the "rational" criminal. Our models are concerned not just with the decision to commit a particular crime, but also with decisions relating to criminal "readiness" or involvement in crime; and they also take some account of the recent psychological research on cognitive processing.

This research is still at a relatively early stage, and as yet there is only a comparatively small body of criminological data relevant to decision making upon which to draw. Any attempt to develop decision models of crime must at this stage be tentative. Thus our aim is only to provide models that are at present "good enough" to accommodate existing knowledge and to guide research and policy initiatives. Even such "good enough" models, however, have to meet the criticism that they assume too much rationality on the part of the offender. But rationality must be conceived of in broad terms. For instance, even if the choices made or the decision processes themselves are not optimal ones, they may make sense to the offender and represent his best efforts at optimizing outcomes. Moreover, expressive as well as economic goals can, of course, be characterized as rational. And lastly, even where the motivation appears to have a pathological component, many of the subsequent planning and decision-making activities (such as choice of victims or targets) may be rational.

### A. Modeling criminal involvement and criminal events

There is a fundamental distinction to be made between explaining the involvement of particular individuals in crime and explaining the occurrence of criminal events. Most criminological theorists have been preoccupied with the former problem and have neglected the latter. They have sought to elucidate the social and psychological variables underlying criminal dispositions, on the apparent assumption that this is all that is needed to explain the commission of crime itself. But the existence of a suitably motivated individual goes only part of the way to explaining the occurrence of a criminal event—a host of immediately precipitating, situational factors must also be taken into account. And a further distinction that must be recognized by theorists concerns the various stages of criminal involvement—initial involvement, continuance, and desistance. That these separate stages of involvement may require different explanatory theories, employing a range of different variables, has been made clear by the findings of recent research into criminal careers.

The distinctions between event and involvement have to be maintained when translating traditional perspectives into decision terms. It may be that the concepts of choice or decision are more readily translatable and more fruitful in relation to continuance and desistance than to initial involvement, but to some extent this may depend on the particular offense under consideration. For some offenses, such as shoplifting or certain acts of vandalism, it might be easier to regard the first offense as determined by the multiplicity of factors identified in existing criminological theory and as committed more or less unthinkingly, that is, without a close knowledge or consideration of the implications. But however much people may be propelled by predisposing factors to the point where crime becomes a realistic course of action, it may still be legitimate (or, at least, useful) to see them as having a choice about whether to become involved. Once the offense is committed, however, the individual acquires direct knowledge about the consequences and implications of that behavior; and this knowledge becomes much more salient to future decisions about continuance or desistance. It may also provide the background of experience to render initial involvement in another crime a considered choice.

### B. The need for models to be crime specific

The discussion above has anticipated another important requirement of decision models of crime: whether of involvement or of event, these must be specific to particular kinds of crime. Recent preoccupation with offender pathology and the desire to construct general statements about crime, deviancy, and rule breaking have consistently diverted attention from the important differences between types of crime—the people committing them, the nature of the motivations involved, and the behaviors required. Whatever the purposes and merits of academic generalization, it is essential for policy goals that these important distinctions be maintained. And, moreover, it will usually be necessary to make even finer distinctions between crimes than those provided by legal categories. For instance, it will not usually be sufficient to develop models for a broad legal category such as burglary. Rather it will be necessary to differentiate at least between commercial and residential burglary (as has already been done in a number of studies) and perhaps even between different kinds of residential and commercial burglaries. For example, burglary in public housing projects will be a quite different problem from burglary in affluent commuter areas, or from burglary in multioccupancy inner-city dwellings. And the same is obviously true of many other crimes, such as vandalism, robbery, rape, and fraud. The degree of specificity required will usually demand close attention to situational factors, especially in event models.

The emphasis on specificity, however, should not be taken as contradicting the fact, established in research on criminal careers, that particular individuals may be involved in a variety of criminal activities. But their involvement in separate activities does not necessarily derive from the same sources, though *in practice* the separate processes of involvement in different crimes may be interrelated. This means that in explaining a particular individual's pattern of criminal activity it may be necessary to draw upon a variety of specific models and perhaps to describe the links between them. However, this is a matter for those interested in the etiology of individual criminality and in related policies—such as rehabilitation and incapacitation—focused upon the individual offender. Whether they be specialists or generalists, our own interest in offenders is primarily restricted to occasions when they are involved in the offense under consideration. This is because each form of crime is likely to require specific remedies and, by shifting the focus from offender to offense, a range of neglected options is likely to be brought into the policy arena. All our models reflect this focus of interest and our purpose below is to lay out their formal requirements.

### C. The example of residential burglary

We have chosen below to illustrate the construction of decision models of crime through the example of residential burglary in a middle-class suburb. Although it might have made more interesting reading to have selected a less obviously instrumental offense, our choice in the end was made for reasons of convenience: knowledge about this offense is relatively well advanced and we have been involved in some of the recently completed research. This work suggests that the offenders involved are generally rather older and more experienced than those operating in public housing estates, but less sophisticated than those preying on much wealthier residences. Since decision models are for us primarily intended to make criminological theorizing of greater relevance to crime control policies, we believe that practical considerations should play a large part in determining the specificity of the model: the offense modeled should be as specific as current knowledge allows, while at the same time sufficiently common or serious to justify the development of special preventive policies.

In the following pages we will present four models—one concerned with the criminal event and the others with the three stages of criminal involvement—since the decision processes for each model are quite different. It may not always be necessary for policy purposes to model all four processes; indeed, as said above, decisions about which models to develop, and at what level of detail, ought to be governed by policy goals. Our present aim is primarily didactic: first, to set out the models in order to identify the links between them; second, to locate and to give some hint of the ways in which existing criminological data might be interpreted within a decision framework; and third, to illustrate how, through development and examination of the models, the most fruitful points of intervention in the criminal decision process might be identified. As our purpose is not to develop fully elaborated decision models of residential burglary, but only to demonstrate their feasibility, we shall not usually indicate where they draw upon empirical findings (which in any case have been mentioned above) and where they rely upon our own armchair theorizing.

One obvious implication of the need for specificity is that the configuration of the models may vary significantly among different kinds of crime. For instance, models involving offenses which appear to depend primarily upon "presented" opportunities (e.g., shoplifting) will probably be simpler than those (such as residential burglary) involving opportunities that must be "sought." And these in turn will be simpler than those involving offenses where the opportunities are created or planned (e.g., bank robberies).

### D. Initial involvement

Figure 1 represents the process of initial involvement in residential burglary in a middle-class suburb. There are two important decision points: the first (box 7) is the individual's recognition of his "readiness" to commit this particular offense in order to satisfy certain of his needs for money, goods, or excitement. Readiness involves rather more than receptiveness: it implies that the individual has actually contemplated this form of crime as a solution to his needs and has decided that under the right circumstances he would commit the offense. In reaching this decision he will have evaluated other ways of satisfying his needs and this evaluation will naturally be heavily influenced by his previous learning and experience—his moral code, his view of the kind of person he is, his personal and vicarious experiences of crime, and the degree to which he can plan and exercise foresight. These variables in turn are related to various historical and contemporaneous background factors—psychological, familial, and sociodemographic (box 1). It is with the influence of these background factors that traditional criminology has been preoccupied; they have been seen to determine the values, attitudes, and personality traits that dispose the individual to crime. In a decision-making context, however, these background influences are less directly criminogenic; instead they have an orienting function—exposing

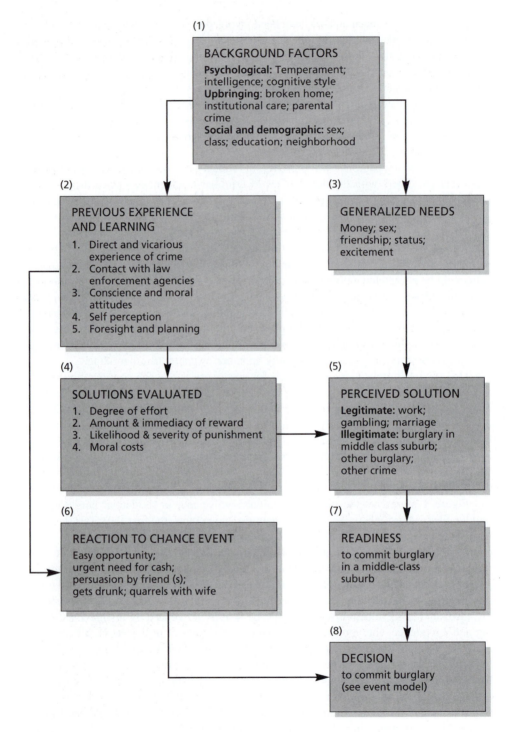

**FIGURE 1**
Initial involvement model (example: burglary in a middle-class suburb).

people to particular problems and particular opportunities and leading them to perceive and evaluate these in particular (criminal) ways. Moreover, the contribution of background factors to the final decision to commit crime would be much moderated by situational and transitory influences; and for certain sorts of crime (e.g., computer fraud) the individual's background might be of much less relevance than his immediate situation.

The second decision (box 8), actually to commit a burglary, is precipitated by some chance event. The individual may suddenly need money, he may have been drinking with associates who suggest committing a burglary (for many offenses, especially those committed by juveniles, immediate pressure from the peer group is important), or he may perceive an easy opportunity for the offense during the course of his routine activities. In real life, of course, the two decision points may occur almost simultaneously and the chance event may not only precipitate the decision to burgle, but may also play a part in the perception and evaluation of solutions to generalized needs.

### E. The criminal event

Figure 2 depicts the further sequence of decision making that leads to the burglar selecting a particular house. As mentioned above, for some other crimes the sequence will be much lengthier; and the less specific the offense being modeled, the more numerous the alternative choices. For example, should a more general model of burglary be required,

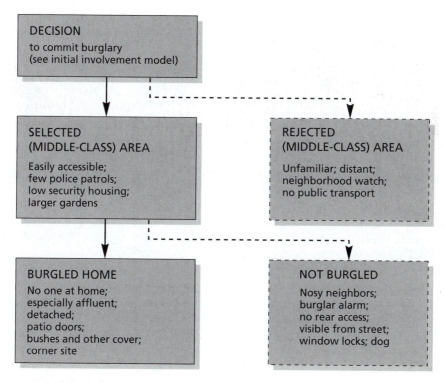

**FIGURE 2**
Event model (example: burglary in a middle-class suburb).

a wider range of areas and housing types would have to be included. In the present case, however, there may be little choice of area in which to work, and in time this decision (and perhaps elements of later decisions) may become routine.

This is, of course, an idealized picture of the burglar's decision making. Where the formal complexity of the decision task is laid out in detail, as in Walsh's work, there may be a temptation to assume that it entails equally complex decision making. In real life, however, only patchy and inaccurate information will be available. Under these uncertain circumstances the offender's perceptions, his previous experience, his fund of criminal lore, and the characteristic features of his information processing become crucial to the decision reached. Moreover, the external situation itself may alter during the time span of the decision sequence. The result is that the decision process may be telescoped, planning may be rudimentary, and there may be last-minute (and perhaps ill-judged) changes of mind. Even this account may overemphasize the deliberative element, since alcohol may cloud judgment. Only research into these aspects of criminal decision making will provide event models sufficiently detailed and accurate to assist policy-making.

### F. Continuance

Interviews with burglars have shown that in many cases they may commit hundreds of offenses; the process of continuing involvement in burglary is represented in Figure 3. It is assumed here that, as a result of generally positive reinforcement, the frequency of

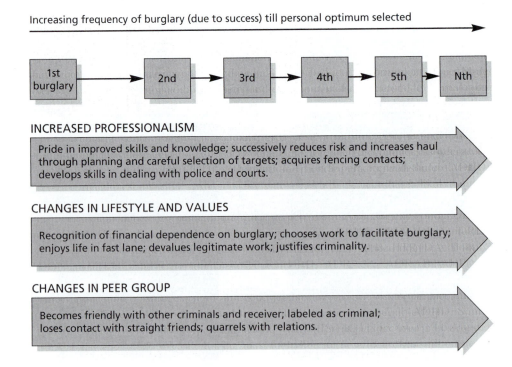

**FIGURE 3**
Continuing involvement model (example: burglary in a middle-class suburb).

offending increases until it reaches (or subsequently reduces to) some optimum level. But it is possible to conceive of more or less intermittent patterns of involvement for some individuals; and intermittent patterns may be more common for other types of offenses (e.g., those for which ready opportunities occur less frequently). It is unlikely that each time the offender sets out to commit an offense he will actively consider the alternatives, though this will sometimes be necessary as a result of a change in his circumstances or in the conditions under which his burglaries have to be committed. (These possibilities are discussed in more detail in regard to the "desistance" model of Figure 4.)

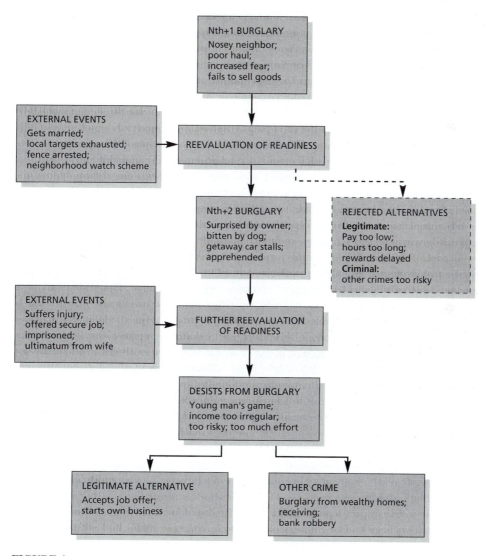

**FIGURE 4**
Desistance model (example: burglary in a middle-class suburb).

More important to represent in the continuing involvement model are the gradually changing conditions and personal circumstances that confirm the offender in his readiness to commit burglary. The diagram summarizes three categories of relevant variables. The first concerns an increase in professionalism: pride in improved skills and knowledge; successive reductions of risk and an improvement in haul through planning and careful selection of targets; and the acquisition of reliable fencing contacts. The second reflects some concomitant changes in lifestyle: a recognition of increased financial dependence on burglary; a choice of legitimate work to facilitate burglary; enjoyment of "life in the fast lane"; the devaluation of ordinary work; and the development of excuses and justifications for criminal behavior. Third, there will be changes in the offender's network of peers and associates and his relationship to the "straight" world. These trends may be accelerated by criminal convictions as opportunities to obtain legitimate work decrease and as ties to family and relations are weakened.

This picture is premised upon a more open criminal self-identification. There will be, however, many other offenses (e.g., certain sexual crimes) that are more encapsulated and hidden by the offender from everyone he knows.

### G. Desistance

It is in respect of the subject of Figure 4 in particular—desistance from burglary—that paucity of relevant criminological information is especially evident. While the work of, for example, Parker, Greenberg, Trasler, and West provides some understanding of the process of desistance, empirical data, whether relating to groups or individuals and in respect of particular sorts of crime, are very scanty. Nevertheless, there is sufficient information to provide in Figure 4 an illustration of the offender's decision processes as he begins a renewed evaluation of alternatives to burglary. This follows aversive experiences during the course of offending and changes in his personal circumstances (age, marital status, financial requirements) and the neighborhood and community context in which he operates (changes of policing, depletion of potential targets). These result in his abandoning burglary in favor of some alternative solution either legitimate or criminal. While desistance may imply the cessation of all criminal activity, in other cases it may simply represent displacement to some other target (commercial premises rather than houses) or to another form of crime. Desistance is, in any case, not necessarily permanent and may simply be part of a continuing process of lulls in the offending of persistent criminals or even, perhaps, of a more casual drifting in and out of particular crimes. . . .

### Conclusions

During the course of this discussion a number of deficiencies in current criminological theorizing have been identified. Many of these flow from two underlying assumptions: that offenders are different from other people and that crime is a unitary phenomenon. Hence, the preoccupation with the issue of initial involvement in crime and the failure to develop explanations for specific kinds of offending. Moreover, explanatory theories have characteristically been confined to a limited selection of variables derived from one or another of criminology's contributory disciplines; and none of the dominant theories has taken adequate account of situational variables. A decision-making approach, however, stresses the rational elements in criminal behavior and requires explanations to be specific to particular forms of crime. It also demands that attention be paid to the crucial distinction between criminal involvement (at its various stages) and criminal events. By doing so it provides a framework that can accommodate the full range of potentially relevant variables (including situational ones) and the various competing but partial theories.

# CONTEMPORARY RETROSPECTIVE ON RATIONAL CHOICE THEORIES

## CLASSICAL AND RATIONAL CHOICE PERSPECTIVES

*Andy Hochstetler, Iowa State University; and*
*Jeffrey A. Bouffard, Sam Houston State University*

Classical theorists, those who support rational choice and deterrence theories in criminology, apply a philosophically "economic" logic and tradition to the study of crime. That is, these authors suppose that individuals decide to engage in crime because at some level they determine that the potential benefits of the behavior outweigh the potential costs. Unlike some of the other theoretical areas covered in this book, there is no clear boundary around the works in classical and rational choice criminology. In fact, it is probably better to refer to this "classical" approach, with its central focus on choice, rather than some form of "determinism" as a broad perspective, rather than as a singular theory of crime. In essence, the classical perspective on crime is akin to other "control" approaches to crime, in that it does not assume that special motives or personality underlie criminal behavior, but rather focuses on the question of why some people behave (because the costs outweigh the rewards) than on why some misbehave.

Papers that draw on the tradition usually do not include easily spotted key words in their titles. The influence of the camps crosses many particular areas of inquiry and is sometimes identifiable only in the spirit of the piece or in respectful citations to key studies. Some proponents of this view, for instance, espouse a literal translation of "economic" notions, seeing crime as the result of calculations of monetary costs and rewards (see Becker, 1968, for instance). Others (see Cornish & Clarke, 1986) propose a less financial calculation, suggesting merely that would-be offenders consider—even if only in a rudimentary way—a range of costs and benefits of crime (social and emotional consequences, for instance), only some of which may be material or financial in nature. Given this wide array of specific theories and studies it is difficult to say with authority how many classical criminology or rational choice studies exist. The tradition began hundreds of years ago and has drawn interest of scholars and students from inside and outside sociology and criminology for centuries. Its subtle influence is everywhere in criminology and in the operation of the criminal justice system with its focus on deterrence through the imposition of formal penalties (i.e., imprisonment).

The degree to which adherents view crime as an outcome of a choice that is subject to general economic principles and that results from maximizing behavior on the part of decision makers distinguishes the camps from other areas of criminology. From this perspective, offending rates result from optimizing individuals' reactions to incentives (referred to as perceptual deterrence—the role of individuals' perceptions of costs as these deter crime) and are aggregate results of individuals' assessments of costs and benefits. The offender is traditionally portrayed as a normal person (with no peculiar motives or individual defects that are thought to predispose crime) who responds predictably so that "when the probable costs exceed the probable benefits, an individual will not commit crime" (Banfield, 1970, p. 160). Reflecting a tradition of methodological individualism, individuals' combined decisions to commit or abstain from crime based on judgments of its net payoff are thought to explain variation in crime rates across space and time. This view of aggregate crime rates is characterized by the body of research on objective deterrence—the study of the relationship between imprisonment rates and crime rates, for instance.

There are many variants to the formula. Some theorists lean toward integration, incorporating a wide range of psychological and social variables as controls or potential moderators of base economic considerations (see Wilson & Herrnstein, 1985, for a thorough accounting of one such perspective). One relatively inclusive version notes that benefits of crime that figure heavily in the choice are tangible satisfactions from the criminal act while costs include expected out-of-pocket expenses, opportunity costs of the criminal's time, and criminal punishment (Posner, 1992). Others err on the side of parsimony by focusing strictly on economic variables.

The distinction between the objective deterrence and perceptual deterrence–rational choice perspectives rests on the former's focus on aggregate variation and tendency to use macrolevel variables that reflect variation in opportunity for crime and spatial and temporal differences in payoff and punishment. Perceptual deterrence–rational choice theorists are more likely to focus on individual variation in crime and varying individual criminal propensity. They also are more likely to incorporate a wider array of variables into explanations, often drawing insight from traditional domains of psychology and sociology.

Gary Becker's work represents the classic economic camp. He is a Nobel Prize, Medal of Science, and Presidential Medal of Freedom winning economist and Distinguished Professor of Economics, Business and Sociology at the University of Chicago. Becker proposed what is now known as the subjective expected utility (SEU) model of crime, which has proven to be surprisingly controversial. It notes that crime will be more likely if the individual's perceived expected utility (expressed in monetary terms) for criminal behavior is greater than the expected utility of some legal alternative. This model is often represented mathematically with the following formula: $EU = pU(Y - f) + (1 - p)U(Y)$, where EU = the expected utility from the behavior; p = the probability of punishment, and U = the "utility" (the severity) of costs or benefits. Becker contends also that those who might consider crime calculate (1) practical opportunities of earning legitimate income, (2) amounts of income offered by these opportunities, (3) amounts of income offered by various illegal methods, (4) probabilities of being arrested for illegal acts, and (5) probabilities of punishment if caught. The act or occupation with the highest discounted return is likely to be chosen (Sullivan, 1973). As an economic purist, he asserts provocatively that there is little reason for theorizing that treats offenders as if they have a special character that leads them to crime. Becker extends his logic to conclude that the most prominent theories of motivation in criminology are not needed; basic economics addresses their problem sufficiently. Criminal offenders are normal, reasoning economic actors responding to market forces. Understandably, this dogma leaves him out of favor with many sociologists of crime who specialize in these criminological theories.

If classical criminology is accurate, we should expect that rates of crime will be stable if the costs and benefits of it remain so. Modified versions used by those who claim *rational choice* as their perspective often allow for the possibility that the prevalence of criminal thinking might also vary between individuals and populations. Like classical theorists, rational choice theorists tend to emphasize self-interested actors that behave according to predictable logics that are, in the main, normal. Basic "economic" principles—that is, maximizing gain while minimizing loss—underlie crime's occurrence and distribution, but attention is devoted to understanding group and individual differences in interpretation of crime's costs and benefits. These *thick* versions of classical–rational choice thinking depart from the assumption that preferences are stable in individuals (or groups), and that offenders have no peculiar tastes that lead them to crime. Recognizing that not all preferences and objectives that lead to crime are stable, such models also are likely to adopt what economists call the present aim standard.

*Rational* behaviors become those that reflect cost and benefit for the objective at the moment a decision is made (McCarthy, 2002), and "rationality" occurs where people attempt to "choose the best means to the chooser's ends" (Posner, 1998). Note that *rational* in this instance is not used to necessarily refer to a lengthy, deliberative process in which all available behavioral options and their consequences are logically assessed and weighed against one another (the idea of "pure rationality"), but rather that the decision maker does at least attempt to make a decision that attempts to maximize gains relative to losses. Thus crime results from a choice or the exercise of free will, even if that decision process itself is not "optimal" in a purely objective sense. This notion of limited or "bounded" rationality is central to most modern versions of rational choice theory.

Thick (sometimes called "wide") models may incorporate common cognitive quirks, particular preferences that shape assessment of costs and benefits, and recurring departures from pure rationality as well. Typically, thicker models of choice are found in those papers that focus on microeconomics or other influences on *how* individuals reach criminal decisions rather than aggregate rates of them. The specific subject of how decision makers look at and perceive opportunities and situations and allocate finite cognitive resources to make choices is at center stage in these thicker models.

The intellectual seeds for classical and rational choice criminology were sown in the eighteenth-century Enlightenment. Many of the central questions and biases in the approaches were formed then. When the theories are recapped in textbooks, one is as likely to see reference to Beccaria and Bentham as well as to lesser thinkers of the last half century. Although the mathematics in contemporary applications sometimes are overwhelming to those of us not accustomed to reading formulas, the thinking in older and newer versions of classical criminology at least is familiar. Much in our system of justice rests on the same foundations and we live with the cultural and intellectual legacy spawned by those who inspired classical criminology. The scholarly influence of classical criminology is most clear, however, among contemporary scholars who look to economics and its assumptions for guidance on how to proceed in understanding crime and evaluating policy.

Perhaps due in part to its conventionality, classical criminology sometimes is associated with contemporary conservative political thought. By no means is it a necessarily conservative approach, and there is scant reason for assuming that practitioners are more conservative than those in most other areas of criminology. Part of the confusion may be because laissez-faire approaches to government were part of the early tradition and still may receive credence among more proponents than in some overtly political, left-of-center areas of criminology. Those who accept only targeted and efficient government interventions and crime-fighting strategies may find a more comfortable theoretical home in the classical tradition because these ideals are associated with its founders.

Certainly, the punitive could find some rationale for their sentiments in classical criminology as well. Descendants of the classical camp in criminology generally agree that individuals have "free will," and they tend to portray individuals as hedonistic optimizers and their decisions as pragmatic responses to economic forces and other situational factors. It follows that crime can be dissuaded, in certain circumstances, by raising the perceived costs of it (the focus of the "get tough" movement over the last 30 years in America). And, traditional acceptance that properly applied pain might in some cases reduce crime by specific or general deterrence doubtless turns some away from the tradition for political reasons, but there are few who do not share considerable ground with classical criminology in making a case that economic conditions contribute to crime or that understanding the role of choice can improve our ability to understand, prevent, and control crime. Both deterrence and other rational choice perspectives tend to emphasize potential sanctions, but they also draw attention to costs and benefits within offending decisions relative to alternative options, including those offered by the legitimate labor market (Ehrlich, 1996).

Major figures of the Enlightenment, some of whom commented extensively on crime, believed that citizenry should enjoy freedoms to select their own path. To treat them otherwise was to demean the meaning and potential of citizenry. (For these reasons, many were influential and early abolitionists.) They asserted reason as policy and as the truest source of legitimacy for the state and adhered to a faith in democratically selected representatives to make reasonable policy based on accord from the populace. They also leaned toward small government believing that wherever possible the state should in the interest of liberty leave persons to their own affairs and free from government intrusion. Planning and government intervention on some matters always was part of their shared vision of government, however; citizens would follow a rational course leading to national progress and improved industry only if the state could modify the environment so that the most individually beneficial path for citizens led to societal benefit. The state must not offer interference where matters already were so arranged but could make efficient improvements where the interest of society and individuals was far out of its natural balance. Influential Enlightenment figures were not blinded to the fact that personal interest conflicted with public interest in inevitable ways.

If the state's authority should be limited, it extended at least as far as protection from crime and hostile nations which is why these subjects received due attention from great thinkers of the time. Adam Smith (1763/1896) contended that humankind has ultimate rights "to the preservation of the body and reputation from injury" as well as the right to have "liberty free from infringement unless there is a proper cause." The sovereignty of a nation is grounded in the deposit of individuals with the sovereign and this trust must be protected "from the usurpation of each individual who will always endeavor to take away from the mass, not only his own portion, but to encroach on that of others" (Beccaria, 1764/1986).

Early classical theorists knew that crime required management; they intended to calibrate the law and justice system for the task and agreed generally that the state should do no more than required or than was pragmatic and effective. Precise visions of the philosophical underpinnings of rights, the law, and justice varied widely, but there was near universal agreement among classical and enlightened thinkers that the deterrent value of the law should be used at the least possible harm to society and to the individual, that is, without undue or unneeded cruelty to offenders. From this perspective costs should only slightly outweigh potential benefits, in order to tip the decisional scales toward compliance with the law; however, any punishment beyond that needed to accomplish this task was seen as cruel and unnecessary. Classical visions eventually came to reflect the utilitarian ideas that balancing private and individual interests against public interest required optimizing liberty, minimizing harm and, wherever possible, close correspondence between the two objectives. From inception, theorists contended that implementing rational law and legal measures required dispassionate judgment of what would be most effective and scientific evaluation of attempted improvements. Crime control should be measured and its effectiveness evaluated objectively to ensure the proper balance of costs and benefits.

As previously described, perspectives that imagine crime to be the outcome of a deliberative calculation have limitations. They may contain a "rather uncomplicated view of the rational man" as homoeconomicus (Sykes, 1978). Clearly, the strengths of classical criminology, and rational choice, are not found in their sophisticated depiction of the intricacies and diverse workings of human cognition and psychology. The mind and meaning are not where the core of tradition suggests that its investigators look for answers about the occurrence and distribution of crime. Moreover, the fact that crime is often a stupid mistake leads many to incorrectly and intuitively believe that rational choice perspectives miss the mark based on the colloquial use of the word *rational* as synonym for prudent, careful, or cautious. No reasonable rational choice or classical camp scholar ever contended that deliberating criminals choose carefully. All recognize that decisions and options can be constrained, and that most daily and significant decisions are not made with ledgers in hand. In fact, recent research from neuropsychology and the decision-making sciences suggest that human decision making is aided, for instance, by the individual being in an optimal state of emotional arousal—that is, not too "hot" so as to make rash decisions, but not so "cold" as to be unmoved by potential consequences (see Damasio, 1994). Similarly, emotional processing of information has been demonstrated to aid decision making by allowing heuristic "shortcuts" in the decision process. Moreover, no "perfect knowledge, lightning-fast calculation, or any of the other caricatures of economic theory" are required to make efficient sense of crime with economic logic and methods (Becker, 1968).

An analogy may be useful. The way in which many of the legitimately employed find their way to chosen occupations may not be all that different analytically from an offender's choice of a sustained criminal course. A shortage of physical therapists can be corrected by raising wages, getting the word out about high wages, and keeping required investment for entry into the career relatively low. Wait for a generation of the college bound to adjust their career paths, and odds are that you will have a bounty of therapists, all else being equal. With sufficient reward the quality of therapist might improve by drawing away some who otherwise would be medical doctors. Doubtless many of the careerists drawn to the therapy profession will later claim that they chose the field mainly for altruistic reasons, due to the intervention of significant mentors, or because unanticipated life events and location made the job accessible. Some will not know that economics figured in their professional choice and many will not recall making any such calculation. Similarly, evidence mounts that different perceptions of the rewards of crime draw and repel offenders at various points in their careers (Pezzin, 1995). Economic forces also have immediate effect. When perceived costs rise relative to payoff of crime and rewards of avoiding crime, more offenders turn away from it.

## Critiques

The most difficult issues for classical criminologists to address surround methodological challenges of measuring and incorporating potentially important variables. For example, some of the functions of a crime control apparatus and some costs and benefits of penalties are difficult to measure or monetize. Similar difficulties confront those who would measure offenders' nonfinancial perceived costs and benefits of crime, which may include considerations foreign to those used in other economic analyses. Classical criminologists can counter that imaginative economists can measure more than the critics assume, but it is true that the approach is weak when it comes to understanding cultural and symbolic elements of crime and its control. In addition, there is a certain moral/political detachment in many equations used by classical criminologists. In classical perspectives, crime is often portrayed as a simple interaction between state and potential offender; almost nothing is said of the social/collateral costs of controlling it or other influences on offender thinking. Due credit is not generally given to offender psychology and its origins, although it is well known that many offenders have mental and thinking problems. Socialization largely is set aside, although we know it to be critically important in criminal careers and other relevant aspects of the lifecourse. Moreover, the fact that crime results from long-term cumulative and recent learning on the part of the offender and that this learning alters opportunity assessments often is slighted by treating rational choice as static rather than as a dynamic process. These shortcomings are reflected in the often static, cross-sectional analyses that characterize many rational choice studies and mischaracterize the process of real decision making. Fortunately, the trend is to incorporate these types of variables and complexities into integrated models and to account for changing perceptions (Matsueda, Kreager, & Huizinga, 2006; Pogarsky, Kim, & Paternoster, 2005).

Unifying themes within this perspective are so abstract and general that they are difficult for critics to dismantle with a point-by-point attack. Classical criminology and its rational choice derivatives are too close to the core of any discipline that studies patterns in human behavior to generate weaknesses that do not apply widely; the architecture is similar outside the rational choice and classical glass houses. Specific papers in the classical tradition contain many firm and formal hypotheses and findings that can and are put to the test, but some critics maintain that rational choice perspectives provide few falsifiable statements and can incorporate so many diverse findings as to be meaningless. In response, classical criminologists could respond that more of their fundamental statements have been tested in experiments (usually by experimental economists) than those made in other areas. Moreover, in the sciences, it generally is particular hypotheses generated within schools of thought and in particular papers that can be falsified. Entire camps of scholarship in time may topple as a result, but they seldom stand on a few testable hypotheses. Critics of classical perspectives have yet to develop a model that explains as much of the variation in a wide range of phenomena consistently and that offer a more sensible starting point than the classical camp. A handful of classically inspired variables (economic and otherwise) often can make fairly good sense of a problem.

Rational choice theory is best seen as a "framework, a rubric or a family of theories" that serves to "organize findings, link theoretical statements and logically guide theory construction" (Hechter & Kanazawa, 1997, p. 194). In criminology, attempts to dismantle or criticize the general perspective rather than specific hypotheses derived from it might be particularly futile because "most rational choice theorists appreciate that at best they are supporting an approach that is a sensitizing principle, that . . . suggests things that you probably ought to look at if you are trying to understand such matters" (Geis, 2007, p. 170). Those who adhere to even purist, or thin, versions of rational choice and classical depictions of crime are not blinded to the way things really are or the complexities of crime and cognition, so much as they have clear notions about where to begin, with a focus on the content and process of individuals' decisions to engage in criminal behavior. Other factors may well be incorporated into such a model, with particular emphasis on how these other theories and correlates of crime help shape the content and process of the choice that is made. Despite this potential for the fruitful integration of choice and other perspectives in the explanation of crime, because classical and rational choice perspectives are as much toolboxes as they are theories of criminal behavior, few will be persuaded to abandon their allegiances by followers of competing perspectives.

Dismissive statements about classical and rational choice perspectives are common in textbooks where authors sometimes are motivated by fear that use of words like *rational*, *decision making*, and *choice* lend themselves to confirming what students who are unsympathetic to offenders already believe about causes of crime and how to best deal with it. Words such as those listed might lead to unsettling and unfortunate political conclusions, endorsement of harsh penalties, or undue attention to personal responsibility—all outcomes of the recent "get tough on crime" stance predominant in American society. One important text frets that even social scientists' eyes might be turned in the wrong political direction when "emphasis on rationality becomes an ideological commitment rather than a theoretical one. And . . . such ideology leads to advocacy of certain policy interventions—criminal justice sanctions, situational crime prevention, and so on—and to a disinterest in, if not skepticism about, other policy interventions that would attack the conditions that place individuals in situations where crime is, among all their choices, the most rational one available" (Lilly, Cullen, & Ball, 2007, p. 279). Although one might think otherwise from the preceding passage, there is little danger about rational choice approaches or their supposed convenient liaison with correctional practice.

Every theoretical approach tends to focus attention and classical perspectives often make short work of correlations between poverty and crime; it results from varying aggregate estimates of prospects from legitimate pursuits versus illegal ones under changing market conditions (Fender, 1999). There is nothing mean-spirited or that should be particularly displeasing to the charitable in that hypothesis. Moreover, an overriding theme of many writers in the area has been that costly policies without beneficial effects that outweigh costs should be abandoned, and many of these policies are sure to be punitive. The increased use of prisons for incapacitation in recent years with little evidence of cost-effectiveness or accompanying, substantial reductions in crime rates are a prominent example. If mischaracterizations of rational choice can be used or threaten to turn attention from material causes of crime, there is not much more that informed students of the classical perspective can do but correct laypersons' portrayals where possible and move on with their work. If anything, a more thorough understanding of when, how, and for whom large-scale attempts at deterrence (increased sentence lengths, for instance) are effective can help policy makers determine the most effective ways to utilize punishments for the greatest social benefit, as the Enlightenment thinkers proposed with the least unnecessary cost to society and the individual.

Because conversion of simple exchanges into mathematical or economic statements makes them seem complex and artificial, it can appear that classical models cannot possibly capture considerations in real-world street-offenders' minds and contexts. However, many who center their work firmly in the classical tradition could care less about individual offenders' conscious thought processes while committing discrete offenses and all know that at that level of analysis decision-making processes are sure to be *bounded* by accessible information, context, and abilities to estimate. Still, as scholars of cognition are keen to point out, students of human behavior and thought should be amazed at the capacity of individuals to intuitively and rapidly calculate remote and uncertain outcomes, to select behaviors using salient criteria, to improvise, take mental shortcuts, and modify desired ends to suit emerging outcomes. Often people somehow manage to approximate rationality and generally maximize gains in their daily decisions, as if it comes naturally. Humans possess minds that make profound and rapid sense of their environment and contingencies, as well as likely and remote possibilities even if no sophisticated economic calculator is required for economics to work.

## Empirical Evaluations

Underlying much writing in the classical tradition is the objective of determining what a reasonable system of justice would look like. This includes evaluation of what the optimum level of enforcement and sanctions should be, and whether or not deterrent measures have worthwhile prospects. Following the belief that "criminal law should minimize the social cost of crime, which equals the sum of the harm it causes and the cost of punishing it," one offshoot of classical criminology, the deterrence literature, analyzes penalties and their effects (Cooter & Ulen, 1997, p. 396).

A small but increasing share of the voluminous literature on deterrence reflects emerging interest in modeling formally and testing game theoretic and other exchanges occurring between those who would deter crime and those who would commit it (see Basinger, 2001; Fender, 1999). One notion is that aggregate offender (and state) choices reflect the ongoing mouse and mousetrap relationship as crime fighters and those who might consider illegal acts learn and react to changing environments. There also is increasing theoretical attention to the possibility that lawmakers can use deterrent penalties to shift moral and cultural qualms about crime and change the public's cost–benefit analyses as a result (Dau-Schmidt, 1990). The integration of game theory and other dynamic views on feedback between penalties and assessments of crime into classical criminology is in infancy, however.

The thrust of most deterrence research is to investigate how changes in policies affect the subsequent behavior of population aggregates, such as by examining what stringent enforcement of laws prohibiting drunk driving and accompanying public information campaigns did to rates of drunk driving (they worked), or the number of crimes prevented by executions (a highly contested series of findings). In discussing effects of punishment operating by way of deterrence, it will suffice to share a few general observations.

Methodological difficulties surrounding attempts to distinguish incapacitation effects from deterrence effects in aggregate models complicate the issue, but evidence for deterrent effects remains strong, and is also found in studies that assess perceived costs of crime (see Mocan & Rees, 2005, for an interesting test of perceptual deterrence). Certainty of punishment seems to decrease crime more than severity. There are contingencies, however. The most apparent is that the point of diminishing return for investing in deterrent efforts varies by crime, probably according to the size and characteristics of the population that remains presently undeterred when a new policy is imposed. Crimes committed by many, by the nondesperate or lightly motivated, by the legally informed, and with currently lenient penalties must be easier to reduce with new measures than are crimes committed by a few desperate persons who are presently capable of ignoring penalties that already are stiff. In the former case, the easy work is yet to be done. Partially because natural consequences and shame are powerful deterrents (Pratt, Cullen, Blevins, Daigle, & Madensen, 2006), relatively rare crimes that have tremendously devastating natural or informal consequences are difficult to deter further by formal means. For this reason, Beccaria observed that laws forbidding suicide are ineffective. Crimes with already stiff penalties are also unlikely to yield significant additional deterrence by adjusting formal penalties upward; some people don't scare easily and even those who may be scared had they considered a consequence may not be deterred if, at the moment of decision, that consequence is not recalled or attended to. Herein is a trap for proponents of deterrence as the central crime control policy—evidence supports the notion that deterrence works; however, it cannot work if the cost is not relevant to the individual at the time of the decision. Any number of factors work to make costs seem unimportant or irrelevant to would-be offenders, including but not limited to substance abuse, low intelligence, incomplete information, heightened emotional state, and so on.

By contrast to the classical tradition's concern with aggregate rates of crime, contemporary rational choice investigators typically zoom in to examine the elements of thinking and rationality that figure in discrete criminal decisions. These may examine real decision making or experimental data, but more often data come from vignettes in surveys. Examining perceptual variation is a key component and one that can potentially prove very fruitful for understanding when and why deterrent effects fail to materialize. For example, one might give surveys to or interview some subgroup of the population that might consider theft to see how they think and what they think about when considering the crime and how it differs from a comparison group. This is similar to marketing research where the choice to commit crime compares to the decision to go through with some purchase or investment. Such an approach adds detailed information to analyses of markets, providing specifics on who chooses, when they choose, and what considerations affect the decision outcome. There are numerous studies where subjects of varying background put pen to paper to explain how they would evaluate costs and benefits presented in vignettes and also answer background questions about their own decisions and experiences to see if they predict (Tibbetts & Gibson, 2002). Only a few in criminology use experimental methods to assess whether rewards and punishment affect cheating or risk-taking on assigned tasks (Ward, Stafford, & Gray, 2006). When presented vignettes that contain calculable and finite costs and benefits, respondents usually answer accordingly, leading to the conclusion that the decision to commit crime generally is rational and strongly affected by estimated costs and gains. On the whole, and with many caveats, there can be no doubt based on the results of this research that deterrence works where other relevant factors can be controlled (Pratt et al., 2006). Pen-and-paper studies also reveal some contingencies that interact with or mediate the effects of cost–benefit estimates.

Similar techniques for examining criminal decisions include exercises where known offenders describe in detail what they consider when deciding to commit or selecting real crimes by responding to vignettes. There also have been interviews about rationality in the target selection process and on how offenders sequentially proceed through decisions leading to crime. Here, we have confirmed what those who study target selection and routine activities approaches already showed by survey and geographic methods; where crime is eased and the odds of getting away with something are made high by environmental arrangements and circumstance, offending is likely.

Rational choice and classical perspective also have a long history of being used as a device in framing qualitative interviews of persistent offenders concerning their criminal decision making. Qualitative interviews of known criminals allow offenders to speak freely or with few constraints and to provide more complex narratives of their lives and decisions. These studies allow better understanding of how offenders choose sustained criminal careers as well as how they select particular targets, although there is general agreement that each aspect of crime merits some separate attention. Cornish and Clarke (1986) explained that offenders decide whether to commit crime according to immediate needs and their assessments of immediate threats, but also take into account what they have learned in sequences of decisions.

Once their eyes are turned to crime, targets are selected as reasonably as offenders can manage with the aim of achieving their humble goals conveniently and with limited information. Most who go through with crime invest little in acquiring information, planning particular offenses, or considering carefully cost and benefits. Generally, qualitative studies add some caveats to portrayals of offenders as rational calculating individuals and complicate the picture by revealing the significance of psychology, subculturally derived imperatives, interpersonal dynamics, and emergent foreground contingencies on decisions to offend (Shover, 1996; Wright & Decker, 1994).

It is difficult to say whether the recurring finding that offenders already known to be persistent do not consider getting caught is confirmation or disconfirmation of rational choice (Shover & Honaker, 1992). There is no comparison group of people who did not commit crime in most studies. It is often noted that some mental effort, criminal experience that makes crime routine, and a good bit of drug and alcohol abuse help in ignoring consequences, which is only to say that most thieves do not weigh heavily financial payoff against careful estimates of risk and cost. Offenders can make efforts and use techniques such as getting drunk or having convenient rationalizations prepared that aid in putting consequence out of mind. Qualitative studies also remind of the chaos in many offenders' lives; a significant number of offenders, it seems, do not set out to reap benefits of crime so much as they stumble into criminal opportunities and decisions. Typical contexts that lead to repeat street crime impede careful decision making or proper attention to fear. Young, drunk, and addicted persons do not choose wisely and they are especially unlikely to do so when in like-minded company. These occasional reminders from qualitative researchers are needed and can add meaning to analyses of choice, but in no way imperil the rational choice perspective. Despite their unnecessary use of a *rational choice* straw man as adversary to format presentation, we learn that criminal lifestyles and situations conduce to form criminal events by making criminal opportunities stand out and seem more reasonable than they might in deliberative contexts.

It should not be surprising that research on aggregate, economic deterrence and bottom-up interview research sometimes lead to different conclusions. Analyses of aggregate variation smooth out some of the complexities and detail found in decisions and generally attempt to model the effects of only a few variables that might influence the rate of occurrence of crime generally. The tradeoff is that these necessarily obscure important details and peculiar thinking that affect decisions in many offenses. This empirical–theoretical divide is not unique to criminology. Economists might examine how purchasers respond to price changes. The microconsiderations of real buyers and their idiosyncrasies are more likely to be found in interviews, captured in surveys, or seen in laboratories by watching them closely than they are to be discovered in big national-level studies of price and buying. The analogy reveals that aggregate and bottom-up decision making approaches the same phenomena from different angles and levels of analysis.

Differences in approach and errant assumptions of both groups about the other can make communicating across disciplines and methodologies difficult. The approaches are commensurable and in some cases each type of analysis might incorporate variables discovered in models done in the other. Often with large numbers many idiosyncratic influences on decisions cancel, but both normal and exceptional psychological patterns can be discovered and modeled in aggregate data. In fact, almost all contemporary economists recognize that there is a complex psychology of markets that incorporates external variables and logics but that affects the aggregate outcome significantly. It is widely accepted that learning, ignorance, convenience, and the tendency to satisfy (as opposed to maximize) affect choice.

Some of those who attempt to model relevant and recurring behavioral components into macrolevel models are at the forefront of the discipline. For example, Daniel Kahenman was awarded a Nobel Prize for his examinations of decision making under uncertainty and for his version of prospect theory modeling heuristic shortcuts that depart systematically from principles of probability affecting choice (see also the works of Amos Tversky and Vernon Smith). There have also been advances in theorizing behavioral/economic approaches to law, which attempt to improve models of rational choice by relaxing assumptions that people purely are rational optimizers of self-interest and by incorporating complexities of learned strategies for decision making under uncertainty (Ellickson, 1989; Jolls, Sunstein, & Thaler, 1998). Criminology has far to go in understanding even the simplest intersections of psychology, decision-making considerations, and changing markets for crime and further still before it can incorporate cultural shifts and changing preferences into traditional aggregate economic models.

## Theoretical Refinements

Despite the advantages of parsimonious economic models, the trend in social sciences is toward analytic and theoretical models that are more complex than those used in the past. They often recognize that individual ways of looking to environments are nested within economic and geographic localities as well as in groups. They are likely to incorporate many variables and more likely to analyze hierarchical, multilevel effects. Attempts to explain consumer purchasing decisions based on a consideration of the perceived utility of a product parallels and might have contributed to increased emphasis on perception and *perceptual deterrence* in understanding crime choice. There is an emerging consensus within the classical camp, especially among legal scholars with an interest in moral shifts, that crime rates probably reflect fluctuation in the size and tastes of a likely customer base as well as in changing estimates of incentives and sanctions by the general population (Cooter, 2000a, 2000b). Crimes with payoff that objectively is stable over time, for example, might ebb and flow in their perceptual attractiveness in part due to the public's multifaceted response to law. This view acknowledges that if there is a market for crime, there may be limited numbers of participants under normal historical conditions; many citizens will ignore completely variation in the things intended to raise or lower net criminal benefits, for one reason or another. There is almost no reason to think that the size of the likely offender population is stable or contingent only on economic variables, and models of crime that want to increase explained variation probably should take account [of this]. There is less for assuming that individual offenders thinking is intractable rather than developed over time and contingent on varying ways of thinking, events, and previous outcomes.

### Preferences, commitments, and impediments

There is a commonly held suspicion and a good deal of evidence that peculiar characteristics of offenders' thinking lead to crime. Many of the complications of examining rational choice come down to preferences, commitments, and mental impediments that make crime more likely. All may be characteristic disproportionately of identifiable groups of persons that are prone to offending.

Individuals or categories of people may desire things that are not apparently objective costs or rewards of a given decision for all observers. Advertisers, for example, know that they can play on our irrational preferences by cleverly and expensively packaging goods even when it is thrown away immediately on purchase; marketers know that some are more enticed than others and how to play to the tastes of particular groups. Preferences affect what is chosen when confronting criminal opportunity much as they determine what persons choose when deciding whether to purchase or walk away from a product in a store. For example, problem gamblers not only have increased desire for arousal that comes from the activity but also have increased expectations that gambling will result in positive and arousing experiences, as has been shown in a sample of criminal offenders (Walters & Contri, 1998). Despite the admonition that explanations of crime that focus on abnormality are superfluous by advocates of pure economics, it is likely that offenders are drawn to elements of criminal activity in a way that others are not.

Individuals or groups also may have ways of thinking that skew their analysis of costs and benefits, apart from utilities. It is now widely accepted that there are thinking mistakes associated with addiction, for example. They include willingness to act without full information, mistaken retention of practiced behaviors in simple tasks, and discounting of future consequences. If we look to gamblers, and experiments that emulate gambling, we can see that a great many people are overoptimistic about their ability to calculate outcomes, consider sunk costs errantly, are too loss averse to play rationally, see only the most available options, and misinterpret near misses as near wins rather than losses. Indeed, the earliest statements of classical criminology recognized that the severity of punishment generally is discounted according to the amount of time (celerity) until it will be imposed and it was implied that the discount is greater for some than others. There is a long and continuing history of examining whether offenders discount future costs more than nonoffenders, and of extrapolating the implications for law (Listokin, 2002, 2007). Discounting at greater rates than others may be one manifestation of impulsivity, a construct increasingly integrated into individual-level analyses of crime inspired by rational choice.

A currently prominent theory that claims descent from classical criminology asserts that offenders are likely to have low levels of self-control. Those who engage in crime and analogous behavior are hyperphysical, self-centered, impulsive, hot-tempered, risk-takers, and enjoy simple unchallenging tasks (Gottfredson & Hirschi, 1990). For these persons, crime is a particularly attractive prospect. There is considerable evidence in psychology and criminology that there are persons predisposed by such tastes to offending. The source of the thinking problems may lie in inattentive parenting (Gottfredson & Hirschi, 1990). In the language of rational choice perspectives, those without self-control, which is conceptualized as a stable characteristic, prefer crime and similar present-oriented activities more so than do others. Given equivalent costs and benefits, we should expect those who have exhibited the condition to be more likely to choose crime than those who have not. Such impediments, in combination with the fact that many active criminals are intoxicated much of the time and the significant percentage of whom are not the sharpest tacks in the box, might indicate that offenders occupy the high tail of the curve for impediments to reason. In fact, in a recent restatement on the measurement of self-control, Hirschi (2004) suggested that self-control is best measured as the number of costs considered during an offending decision, coupled with the perceived importance of these costs. Clearly Hirschi is (intentionally or otherwise) suggesting a correspondence between self-control and rational choice as explanations of crime.

Preferences that lead to crime need not be those tastes that lead to stupid decisions and need not be especially peculiar. Some are widely shared and can lead to other healthy outcomes. For example, base desires for money and material trappings underlie a great deal of offending, but also can lead to hard work. McCarthy and Hagan (2001) showed that a disposition for risk-taking and competence interact to raise the rewards of crime much as the characteristics lead to successful entrepreneurship. This suggests that there are some people suited to crime and gaining its returns, just as there those suited to becoming entrepreneurs. It is small inference to assume that they might find crime more attractive than criminals destined to low returns. In a study of predictors of white-collar crime, Piquero, Exum, and Simpson (2005) showed that a desire for control is correlated with the crimes. It is well known also that some rewards of crime are interpreted differently by known offenders and others; for example, subcultural dictates lead some offenders to interpret interpersonal confrontations using a particular set of costs and benefits that likely will elude those outside their cultures. Those who stand up for themselves might also be rewarded by deference from those who would harass them otherwise.

It might be said that some have a strong preference for law abidance and some do not. Where one falls on the spectrum of preference for and against illegality can determine attentiveness to rational choice considerations. Likewise, there is considerable reason to think that criminally prone individuals are influenced differently by sanctions (Wright, Caspi, Moffitt, & Paternoster, 2004). Greg Pogarsky's (2002) survey of 412 university students about drinking and driving is illustrative of the point. After reading a vignette about deciding to drive from a bar or find another means home after drinking too much, students estimated the chances of being caught and the severity of the punishment if they were. They were then provided with the same vignette and asked if they would drive if they knew there was no chance of being caught. Students were classified into those who would not consider drinking and driving at all (acute conformists), those whose chances increased when they had knowledge that they would get away with it (deterrables), and those who reported that they were more than likely to offend in the first instance and with no risk of being caught (incorrigibles). Acute conformists were influenced heavily by self and social disapproval. Predictors were analyzed further by comparing incorrigible and deterrable offender categories. Importantly, incorrigibles' offending likelihood was not subject to certainty or severity estimates of the varied consequences. The effects of severity operated strongly on deterrable students. Certainty of being caught and self-disapproval had significant effects in the expected directions. This serves as one of the many sources of evidence for the interaction of rational choice variables with other variables and what should by now be an obvious point: There are patterns of influence for rational choice variables in subcomponents of the population that affect the general population differently.

Commitments are externally created considerations that are imported into a discrete decision; they would have little bearing on its outcome and would not shape immediate costs and benefits except for the fact that those who harbor them assign them importance. They often make behavior seem irrational to those not aware of outside obligations affecting decisions. Imagine a rational choice theorist attempting to understand when a loan shark shoots the indebted by looking only at a particular transaction with a deadbeat. Our investigator might assume that the loan shark will do what maximizes his chances of financial return. But, it is necessary to understand that the usurer has an image to uphold that allows the work to be done. Apart from the job and best strategy for sustaining a career, if the shark has promised that delinquent borrowers will be hurt the general value of credibility for interpersonal exchange might lead to an unfortunate result. A promise is a promise.

Of course, commitments also can work to impede crime. Travis Hirschi asserts that his control theories of crime are extensions of classical theory and highly compatible with rational choice theories. In calculating the costs of crime, individuals consider their investments in conformity and institutions. Sally Simpson has findings from multiple works that bear upon rational choice and prospects for deterrence among people with differing opinions. In one such study, Simpson (2002) administered surveys to business students and corporate executives containing vignettes of white-collar decision-making contexts and possible criminal responses. Estimates of personal benefit predicted intentions to offend as did risk perceptions. Those who saw opportunity for career advancement and thrills also were more likely to choose crime than others. An ethical reasoning scale, shame, and the possibility of informal sanctions from family, friends, and business associates affected criminal intention. The threat of being fired or corrected by superiors decreased it and being ordered to commit crime increased intent. Most relevant for understanding the place of commitment is that for highly moral "good citizens" neither sanction threats nor other variables made much difference. Respondents who scored low on personal morality (low commitment to a moral code) were another matter; they were deterred by threat. Evidence for similar interaction between morality (self-disapproval, capacity for shame) and perceived opportunity is reported by many others (Grasmick & Bursik, 1990; Grasmick,

Bursik, & Kinsey, 1991; Makkai & Braithwaite, 1994; Nagin & Pogarsky, 2003; Pogarsky, 2002). The good guys probably do not abide by the law because they concluded that they should in amoral calculations of costs and benefits, but because they abide by a practiced code of behavior.

Bouffard (2002, 2007) improves upon the typical approaches for using surveys to study criminal decision making by allowing respondents to generate and assign relevance to their own consequences. This reduces the chances that researchers will continue to misconstrue what is measured by would-be offenders as they select crime or law abidance. Bouffard finds that subject-generated consequences predict crime, include many crime-specific practical considerations of each offense, and do not include some of the rational choice considerations appearing prominently as consequences in lists provided by researchers. In a recent article, Bouffard (2007) presented students with scenarios about drunk driving, shoplifting, and fighting. Participants were asked to provide up to seven cost items and seven benefits of each act. They then rated the certainty and severity of each consequence. Although legal costs were the most frequently considered and were listed most often in two of the three scenarios, a number of costs and benefits appear that are not included in most deductive constructions of costs and benefits of crime. Characteristics of individuals determined which costs and benefits they see as most relevant. For example, males were much more likely to see relationship benefits of fighting a rival, but saw much less emotional benefit for themselves from fighting than did females. (Perhaps chivalry is not dead.) Those with low self-control were the most likely to list emotional benefit for self as a main benefit of fighting. These findings and others suggest that criminal decisions are best construed as highly situational and personal, but also indicate that there are patterns in criminal calculus. Even artificial situations are open to a wide range of interpretations; of course, real-world situations are much richer tapestries.

## Policy Applications

As a general approach, rational choice could be used as grounding to endorse most any policy that aims at making crime less attractive relative to other options. Any program that reduces the payoff of crime by increasing the certainty, severity, and celerity of punishment fits nicely in the tradition as would any program that raises the relative payoff of law abidance with incentives or attempts to make offenders better aware of penalties. Efforts to formally define predictable punishments and advertise them to the public—such as found in campaigns to advertise enhanced penalties for gun crime—certainly fit.

The variety of potential criminal justice topics related to classical and choice perspectives is almost unlimited, which makes elaborating the place of the tradition in policy difficult. Nevertheless, there are two general policies that have transformed how crime fighting is done in recent decades where the theoretical fit is sufficient. These are cognitive restructuring and situational crime prevention programs.

Situational crime prevention shares assumptions about how offenders gravitate toward opportunities to maximize gain, convenience, and ease in common with classical criminological thinking. It borrows from the classical tradition the idea that offenders assess the situational costs and benefits of crime, assess the risks of sanctions in the immediate context, and often wander into potentially criminal situations following paths of least resistance. No commitment to criminal cultures or aberrant personality is emphasized. It follows that changes in movements of persons, routines, and activities that ease crime will result in more of it. In response, Marcus Felson (1994) advocates what he calls natural crime prevention or "the chunking and channeling of human activities, in imitation of nature, to reduce crime temptations and increase controls" (p. 133). This can be accomplished through environmental designs that make the prospects of crime unappealing by either changing its risks, reminding of them, or increasing the effort and investment required. This approach stands in contrast to large-scale changes in the severity of punishment accomplished by increasing the sentence length for a given crime or set of crimes, the net result on the would-be offender's perception of costs of which may be negligible. By making crime seem inconvenient and clearly and immediately more risky, the rate of it is reduced; and many criminal impulses will pass if the situation does not allow them to be easily and conveniently carried out. Target hardening efforts and anticrime environmental design have inspired redesign of large housing projects, entertainment districts, dressing rooms in shops, and particular targets (such as when manufacturers make packaging bulky to discourage shoplifting). Such efforts, if sufficiently large and aimed where crimes concentrate, are almost inevitably successful, and often improve the quality of life in a place at minimal cost to consumers and citizens. This lends real-world evidence to conceptions of the offender as a rational actor inspired by situations and who reacts predictably to altered costs, benefits, and obstacles. The number of offenses and harm is reduced because many crimes result from passing thoughts or undeniable local opportunities. Of course, there are some criminally minded or highly motivated offenders whose crimes may be displaced rather than prevented, but the best available evidence on displacement shows that it is generally less than 100%. Thankfully, minds can be changed and criminal calculus altered so that some of those crimes that might otherwise only be displaced are rejected by the offenders that consider them.

Cognitive restructuring programs do not stem from the purist or thin classification models but from thick models of choice that acknowledge that offenders have peculiar ways of thinking about and weighing costs and benefits that potentially can be made normal. They place emphasis on choice, but do not share the belief that crime results from ordinary thought processes. Rather, they are based on models of decision making that incorporate peculiar commitments, impediments, and preferences of offenders. The focus is on choice and changing what offenders assess and how they will think about the prospects of crime the next time enticements present. Cognitive restructuring looks to change attitudes, beliefs, and interpretations that are thought to adversely affect inmate prospects, especially when it comes to how they assess attractions and disadvantages of the criminal lifestyle, particular stimuli that might contribute to criminal scenes, or events that turn thoughts to crime. Offenders are trained through various "cog-based" curriculums to recognize thinking errors, such as rationalization, failure to recognize the cost of crime to others including family members and victims, failure to calculate accumulated costs of crime, and failure to recognize that discreet criminal events often are part of a series of acts that will lead to the same unfortunate outcomes already experienced. The hope is that the next time criminal opportunities emerge they will appear differently in the mind's eye. Also, offenders will readjust their thinking so that they cannot easily put the likely course and potential negative outcomes out of mind when they start down a potentially criminal path.

For example, the next time a few criminal acquaintances ask to "go for a ride," the potential costs of the seemingly innocuous decision to ride along will enter the calculus before the point of unlikely return is reached. As simple as they sound, cog-based programs are effective at reducing recidivism among convicted felons, revealing that to a significant extent crime is subject to will and choice (Wilson, Bouffard, & Mackenzie, 2005). Many states are reaching the evidence-based conclusion that in combination with substance abuse treatment, they are the most worthwhile investment for treating large numbers of incarcerated offenders.

# ROUTINE ACTIVITY THEORY

## SOCIAL CHANGE AND CRIME RATE TRENDS:
## A ROUTINE ACTIVITY APPROACH

*Lawrence E. Cohen and Marcus Felson*

In its summary report [for 1969] the National Commission on the Causes and Prevention of Violence presents an important sociological paradox:

> Why, we must ask, have urban violent crime rates increased substantially during the past decade when the conditions that are supposed to cause violent crime have not worsened —have, indeed, generally improved?
>
> The Bureau of the Census, in its latest report on trends in social and economic conditions in metropolitan areas, states that most "indicators of well-being point toward progress in the cities since 1960." Thus, for example, the proportion of blacks in cities who completed high school rose from 43 percent in 1960 to 61 percent in 1968; unemployment rates dropped significantly between 1959 and 1967 and the median family income of blacks in cities increased from 61 percent to 68 percent of the median white family income during the same period. Also during the same period the number of persons living below the legally-defined poverty level in cities declined from 11.3 million to 8.3 million.

Despite the general continuation of these trends in social and economic conditions in the United States, the *Uniform Crime Report* indicates that between 1960 and 1975 reported rates of robbery, aggravated assault, forcible rape and homicide increased by 263%, 164%, 174%, and 188%, respectively. Similar property crime rate increases reported during this same period (e.g., 200% for burglary rate) suggest that the paradox noted by the Violence Commission applies to nonviolent offenses as well.

In the present paper we consider these paradoxical trends in crime rates in terms of changes in the "routine activities" of everyday life. We believe the structure of such activities influences criminal opportunity and therefore affects trends in a class of crimes we refer to as *direct-contact predatory violations*. Predatory violations are defined here as illegal acts in which "someone definitely and intentionally takes or damages the person or property of another." Further, this analysis is confined to those predatory violations involving direct physical contact between at least one offender and at least one person or object which that offender attempts to take or damage.

We argue that structural changes in routine activity patterns can influence crime rates by affecting the convergence in space and time of the three minimal elements of direct-contact predatory violations: (1) motivated offenders, (2) suitable targets, and (3) the absence of capable guardians against a violation. We further argue that the lack of any one of these elements is sufficient to prevent the successful completion of a direct-contact predatory crime, and that the convergence in time and space of suitable targets and the absence of capable guardians may even lead to large increases in crime rates without necessarily requiring any increase in the structural conditions that motivate individuals to engage in crime. That is, if the proportion of motivated offenders or even suitable targets were to remain stable in a community, changes in routine activities could nonetheless alter the likelihood of their convergence in space and time, thereby creating more opportunities for crimes to occur. Control therefore becomes critical. If controls through routine activities were to decrease, illegal predatory activities could then be likely to increase. In the process of developing this explanation and evaluating its consistency with existing data, we relate our approach to classical human ecological concepts and to several earlier studies.

## The Structure of Criminal Activity

Sociological knowledge of how community structure generates illegal acts has made little progress since Shaw and McKay and their colleagues published their pathbreaking work, *Delinquency Areas*. Variations in crime rates over space long have been recognized and current evidence indicates that the pattern of these relationships within metropolitan communities has persisted. Although most spatial research is quite useful for describing crime rate patterns and providing post hoc explanations, these works seldom consider—conceptually or empirically—the fundamental human ecological character of illegal acts as *events* which occur at specific locations in *space* and *time*, involving specific persons and/or objects. These and related concepts can help us to develop an extension of the human ecological analysis to the problem of explaining changes in crime rates over time. Unlike many criminological inquiries, we do not examine why individuals or groups are inclined criminally, but rather we take criminal inclination as given and examine the manner in which the spatio-temporal organization of social activities helps people to translate their criminal inclinations into action. Criminal violations are treated here as routine activities which share many attributes of, and are interdependent with, other routine activities. This interdependence between the structure of illegal activities and the organization of everyday sustenance activities leads us to consider certain concepts from human ecological literature.

## Selected Concepts from Hawley's Human Ecological Theory

While criminologists traditionally have concentrated on the *spatial* analysis of crime rates within metropolitan communities, they seldom have considered the *temporal* interdependence of these acts. In his classic theory of human ecology, Amos Hawley treats the community not simply as a unit of territory but rather as an organization of symbiotic and commensalistic relationships as human activities are performed over both space and time.

Hawley identified three important temporal components of community structure: (1) *rhythm*, the regular periodicity with which events occur, as with the rhythm of travel activity; (2) *tempo*, the number of events per unit of time, such as the number of criminal violations per day on a given street; and (3) *timing*, the coordination among different activities which are more or less interdependent, such as the coordination of an offender's rhythms with those of a victim; the examples are ours. These components of temporal organization, often neglected in criminological research, prove useful in analyzing how illegal tasks are performed—a utility which becomes more apparent after noting the spatio-temporal requirements of illegal activities.

## The Minimal Elements of Direct-Contact Predatory Violations

As we previously stated, despite their great diversity, direct-contact predatory violations share some important requirements which facilitate analysis of their structure. Each successfully completed violation minimally requires an *offender* with both criminal inclinations and the ability to carry out those inclinations, a person or object providing a *suitable target* for the offender, and *absence of guardians* capable of preventing violations. We emphasize that the lack of any one of these elements normally is sufficient to prevent such violations from occurring. Though guardianship is implicit in everyday life, it usually is marked by the absence of violations; hence it is easy to overlook. While police action is analyzed widely, guardianship by ordinary citizens of one another and of property as they go about routine activities may be one of the most neglected elements in sociological research on crime, especially since it links seemingly unrelated social roles and relationships to the occurrence or absence of illegal acts.

The conjunction of these minimal elements can be used to assess how social structure may affect the tempo of each type of violation. That is, the probability that a violation will occur at any specific time and place might be taken as a function of the convergence of likely offenders and suitable targets in the absence of capable guardians. Through consideration of how trends and fluctuations in social conditions affect the frequency of this convergence of criminogenic circumstances, an explanation of temporal trends in crime rates can be constructed.

## The Ecological Nature of Illegal Acts

This ecological analysis of direct-contact predatory violations is intended to be more than metaphorical. In the context of such violations, people, gaining and losing sustenance, struggle among themselves for property, safety, territorial hegemony, sexual outlet, physical control, and sometimes for survival itself. The interdependence between offenders and victims can be viewed as a predatory relationship between functionally dissimilar individuals or groups. Since predatory violations fail to yield any net gain in sustenance for the larger community, they can only be sustained by feeding upon other activities. As offenders cooperate to increase their efficiency at predatory violations and as potential victims organize their resistance to these violations, both groups apply the symbiotic principle to improve their sustenance position. On the other hand, potential victims of predatory crime may take evasive actions which encourage offenders to pursue targets other than their own. Since illegal activities must feed upon other activities, the spatial and temporal structure of routine legal activities should play an important role in determining the location, type and quantity of illegal acts occurring in a given community or society. Moreover, one can analyze how the structure of community organization as well as the level of technology in a society provide the circumstances under which crime can thrive. For example, technology and organization affect the capacity of persons with criminal inclinations to overcome their targets, as well as affecting the ability of guardians to contend with potential offenders by using whatever protective tools, weapons and skills they have at their disposal. Many technological advances designed for legitimate purposes—including the automobile, small power tools, hunting weapons, highways, telephones, etc.—may enable offenders to carry out their own work more effectively or may assist people in protecting their own or someone else's person or property.

Not only do routine legitimate activities often provide the wherewithal to commit offenses or to guard against others who do so, but they also provide offenders with suitable targets. Target suitability is likely to reflect such things as value (i.e., the material or symbolic desirability of a personal or property target for offenders), physical visibility, access, and the inertia of a target against illegal treatment by offenders (including the weight, size, and attached or locked features of property inhibiting its illegal removal and the physical capacity of personal victims to resist attackers with or without weapons). Routine production activities probably affect the suitability of consumer goods for illegal removal by determining their value and weight. Daily activities may affect the location of property and personal targets in visible and accessible places at particular times. These activities also may cause people to have on hand objects that can be used as weapons for criminal acts or self-protection or to be preoccupied with tasks which reduce their capacity to discourage or resist offenders.

While little is known about conditions that affect the convergence of potential offenders, targets and guardians, this is a potentially rich source of propositions about crime rates. For example, daily work activities separate many people from those they trust and the property they value. Routine activities also bring together at various times of day or night persons of different background, sometimes in the presence of facilities, tools or weapons which influence the commission or avoidance of illegal acts. Hence, the timing of work, schooling and leisure may be of central importance for explaining crime rates.

The ideas presented so far are not new, but they frequently are overlooked in the theoretical literature on crime. Although an investigation of the literature uncovers significant examples of descriptive and practical data related to the routine activities upon which illegal behavior feeds, these data seldom are treated within an analytical framework. The next section reviews some of this literature.

### Relation of the routine activity approach to extant studies

A major advantage of the routine activity approach presented here is that it helps assemble some diverse and previously unconnected criminological analyses into a single substantive framework. This framework also serves to link illegal and legal activities, as illustrated by a few examples of descriptive accounts of criminal activity.

### Descriptive Analyses

There are several descriptive analyses of criminal acts in criminological literature. For example, Thomas Reppetto's study, *Residential Crime*, considers how residents supervise their neighborhoods and streets and limit access of possible offenders. He also considers how distance of households from the central city reduces risks of criminal victimization. Reppetto's evidence—consisting of criminal justice records, observations of comparative features of geographic areas, victimization survey data and offender interviews—indicates that offenders are very likely to use burglary tools and to have at least minimal technical skills, that physical characteristics of dwellings affect their victimization rates, that the rhythms of residential crime rate patterns are marked (often related to travel and work patterns of residents), and that visibility of potential sites of crime affects the risk that crimes will occur there. Similar findings are reported by Pope's study of burglary in California and by Scarr's study of burglary in and around the District of Columbia. In addition, many studies report that architectural and environmental design as well as community crime programs serve to decrease target suitability and increase capable guardianship, while many biographical or autobiographical descriptions of illegal activities note that lawbreakers take into account the nature of property and/or the structure of human activities as they go about their illegal work.

Evidence that the spatio-temporal organization of society affects patterns of crime can be found in several sources. Strong variations in specific predatory crime rates from hour to hour, day to day, and month to month are reported often, and these variations appear to correspond to the various tempos of the related legitimate activities upon which they feed. Also at a microsociological level, Short and Strodtbeck describe opportunities for violent confrontations of gang boys and other community residents which arise in the context of community leisure patterns, such as "quarter parties" in black communities, and the importance, in the calculus of decision making employed by participants in such episodes, of low probabilities of legal intervention. In addition, a wealth of empirical evidence indicates strong spatial variations over community areas in crime and delinquency rates (for an excellent discussion and review of the literature on ecological studies of crimes, see Wilks). Recently, Albert Reiss has argued convincingly that these spatial variations (despite some claims to the contrary) have been supported consistently by both official and unofficial sources of data. Reiss further cites victimization studies which indicate that offenders are very likely to select targets not far from their own residence.

## Macrolevel Analyses of Crime Trends and Cycles

Although details about how crime occurs are intrinsically interesting, the important analytical task is to learn from these details how illegal activities carve their niche within the larger system of activities. This task is not an easy one. For example, attempts by Bonger, Durkheim, Henry and Short, and Fleisher to link the rate of illegal activities to the economic condition of a society have not been completely successful. Empirical tests of the relationships postulated in the above studies have produced inconsistent results which some observers view as an indication that the level of crime is not related systematically to the economic conditions of a society.

It is possible that the wrong economic and social factors have been employed in these macro studies of crime. Other researchers have provided stimulating alternative descriptions of how social change affects the criminal opportunity structure, thereby influencing crime rates in particular societies. For example, at the beginning of the nineteenth century, Patrick Colquhoun presented a detailed, lucid description and analysis of crime in the London metropolitan area and suggestions for its control. He assembled substantial evidence that London was experiencing a massive crime wave attributable to a great increment in the assemblage and movement of valuable goods through its ports and terminals.

A similar examination of crime in the period of the English industrial expansion was carried out by a modern historian, J. J. Tobias, whose work on the history of crime in nineteenth century England is perhaps the most comprehensive effort to isolate those elements of social change affecting crime in an expanding industrial nation. Tobias details how farreaching changes in transportation, currency, technology, commerce, merchandising, poverty, housing, and the like, had tremendous repercussions on the amount and type of illegal activities committed in the nineteenth century. His thesis is that structural transformations either facilitated or impeded the opportunities to engage in illegal activities. In one of the few empirical studies of how recent social change affects the opportunity structure for crime in the United States, Leroy Gould demonstrated that the increase in the circulation of money and the availability of automobiles between 1921 and 1965 apparently led to an increase in the rate of bank robberies and auto thefts, respectively. Gould's data suggest that these relationships are due more to the abundance of opportunities to perpetrate the crimes than to short-term fluctuations in economic activities.

Although the sociological and historical studies cited in this section have provided some useful *empirical* generalizations and important insights into the incidence of crime, it is fair to say that they have not articulated systematically the *theoretical* linkages between routine legal activities and illegal endeavors. Thus, these studies cannot explain how changes in the larger social structure generate changes in the opportunity to engage in predatory crime and hence account for crime rate trends. To do so requires a conceptual framework such as that sketched in the preceding section. Before attempting to demonstrate the feasibility of this approach with macrolevel data, we examine available microlevel data for its consistency with the major assumptions of this approach.

## Microlevel Assumptions of the Routine Activity Approach

The theoretical approach taken here specifies that crime rate trends in the post-World War II United States are related to patterns of what we have called routine activities. We define these as any recurrent and prevalent activities which provide for basic population and individual needs, whatever their biological or cultural origins. Thus routine activities would include formalized work, as well as the provision of standard food, shelter, sexual outlet, leisure, social interaction, learning and childrearing. These activities may go well beyond the minimal levels needed to prevent a population's extinction, so long as their prevalence and recurrence makes them a part of everyday life.

Routine activities may occur (1) at home, (2) in jobs away from home, and (3) in other activities away from home. The latter may involve primarily household members or others. We shall argue that, since World War II, the United States has experienced a major shift of routine activities away from the first category into the remaining ones, especially those nonhousehold activities involving nonhousehold members. In particular, we shall argue that this shift in the structure of routine activities increases the probability that motivated offenders will converge in space and time with suitable targets in the absence of capable guardians, hence contributing to significant increases in the direct-contact predatory crime rates over these years.

If the routine activity approach is valid, then we should expect to find evidence for a number of empirical relationships regarding the nature and distribution of predatory violations. For example, we would expect routine activities performed within or near the home and among family or other primary groups to entail lower risk of criminal victimization because they enhance guardianship capabilities. We should also expect that routine daily activities affect the location of property and personal targets in visible and accessible places at particular times, thereby influencing their risk of victimization. Furthermore, by determining their size and weight and in some cases their value, routine production activities should affect the suitability of consumer goods for illegal removal. Finally, if the routine activity approach is useful for explaining the paradox presented earlier, we should find that the circulation of people and property, the size and weight of consumer items etc., will parallel changes in crime rate trends for the post-World War II United States.

The veracity of the routine activity approach can be assessed by analyses of both microlevel and macrolevel interdependencies of human activities. While consistency at the former level may appear noncontroversial, or even obvious, one nonetheless needs to show that the approach does not contradict existing data before proceeding to investigate the latter level. . . .

### Discussion

In our judgment many conventional theories of crime (the adequacy of which usually is evaluated by cross-sectional data, or no data at all) have difficulty accounting for the annual changes in crime rate trends in the post-World War II United States. These theories may prove useful in explaining crime trends during other periods, within specific communities, or in particular subgroups of the population. Longitudinal aggregate data for the United States, however, indicate that the trends for many of the presumed causal variables in these theoretical structures are in a direction opposite to those hypothesized to be the causes of crime. For example, during the decade 1960–1970, the percent of the population below the low-income level declined 44% and the unemployment rate declined 186%. Central city population as a share of the whole population declined slightly, while the percent of foreign stock declined 0.1%, etc.

On the other hand, the convergence in time and space of three elements (motivated offenders, suitable targets, and the absence of capable guardians) appears useful for understanding crime rate trends. The lack of any of these elements is sufficient to prevent the occurrence of a successful direct-contact predatory crime. The convergence in time and space of suitable targets and the absence of capable guardians can lead to large increases in crime rates without any increase or change in the structural conditions that motivate individuals to engage in crime. Presumably, had the social indicators of the variables hypothesized to be the causes of crime in conventional theories changed in the direction of favoring increased crime in the post-World War II United States, the increases in crime rates likely would have been even more staggering than those which were observed. In any event, it is our belief that criminologists have underemphasized the importance of the convergence of suitable targets and the absence of capable guardians in explaining recent increases in the crime rate. Furthermore, the effects of the convergence in time and space of these elements may be multiplicative rather than additive. That is, their convergence by a fixed percentage may produce increases in crime rates far greater than that fixed percentage, demonstrating how some relatively modest social trends can contribute to some relatively large changes in crime rate trends. . . .

Without denying the importance of factors motivating offenders to engage in crime, we have focused specific attention upon violations themselves and the prerequisites for their occurrence. However, the routine activity approach might in the future be applied to the analysis of offenders and their inclinations as well. For example, the structure of primary group activity may affect the likelihood that cultural transmission or social control of criminal inclinations will occur, while the structure of the community may affect the tempo of criminogenic peer group activity. We also may expect that circumstances favorable for carrying out violations contribute to criminal inclinations in the long run by rewarding these inclinations.

We further suggest that the routine activity framework may prove useful in explaining why the criminal justice system, the community and the family have appeared so ineffective in exerting social control since 1960. Substantial increases in the opportunity to carry out predatory violations may have undermined society's mechanisms for social control. For example, it may be difficult for institutions seeking to increase the certainty, celerity and severity of punishment to compete with structural changes resulting in vast increases in the certainty, celerity and value of rewards to be gained from illegal predatory acts.

It is ironic that the very factors which increase the opportunity to enjoy the benefits of life also may increase the opportunity for predatory violations. For example, automobiles provide freedom of movement to offenders as well as average citizens and offer vulnerable targets for theft. College enrollment, female labor force participation, urbanization, suburbanization, vacations and new electronic durables provide various opportunities to escape the confines of the household while they increase the risk of predatory victimization. Indeed, the opportunity for predatory crime appears to be enmeshed in the opportunity structure for legitimate activities to such an extent that it might be very difficult to root out substantial amounts of crime without modifying much of our way of life. Rather than assuming that predatory crime is simply an indicator of social breakdown, one might take it as a byproduct of freedom and prosperity as they manifest themselves in the routine activities of everyday life.

# CONTEMPORARY RETROSPECTIVE ON ROUTINE ACTIVITY THEORY

## ROUTINE ACTIVITY THEORY: AN ASSESSMENT OF A CLASSICAL THEORY

*Catherine D. Marcum, Georgia Southern University*

Routine activity theory has proven itself to be useful in explaining different types of criminal victimization. It has been tested and supported by several studies that have examined victimization on the macrolevel, but a more voluminous amount of supporting literature is based on microlevel research, which has examined individual offending behaviors. According to routine activity theory, three elements must be present in order for a crime to occur: a suitable target, lack of capable guardianship, and exposure to motivated offenders (Cohen & Felson, 1979).

Meier and Miethe (1993) asserted that target suitability is based on a person's availability as a victim, as well as his or her attractiveness to the offender. Persons who are available for victimization are those who have not taken certain precautions to protect themselves. For example, leaving a car in the driveway with the keys in the ignition increases victimization risk, because the owner of the car did not take precautions to prevent theft. Attractiveness refers to the appeal of the target based on the value of what the victim has to offer, such as property or sexual favors. With these two aspects present, a person becomes a more likely and suitable candidate for criminal victimization.

The second component necessary for a crime to occur, according to Cohen and Felson (1979), is a lack of capable guardianship. Guardianship is the ability of persons and objects to prevent a crime from occurring (Garofalo & Clark, 1992; Miethe & Meier, 1990; Tseloni, Wittebrood, Farrell, & Pease, 2004) and can take two forms: social and physical. Social guardianship can exist through such factors as household composition, lifestyle, marital status, and employment type. For example, working full-time may ensure that a person will be away from the home roughly 8 hours a day, therefore leaving the home unattended. In contrast, physical guardianship refers to self-protective measures taken by a person, such as burglar alarms and outside lighting. These types of measures have been supported as a method of decreasing burglary rates in neighborhoods (Miethe & McDowall, 1993; Miethe & Meier, 1990; Tseloni et al., 2004).

A motivated offender is a person who is willing to commit a crime when opportunities are presented through the presence and absence of the other two components (Cohen & Felson, 1979; Mustaine & Tewksbury, 2002). In other words, the theory asserts that if a motivated offender is presented with a suitable target that is not properly guarded against victimization, a crime is likely to occur. Schwartz and Pitts (1995) also suggested that offenders are motivated to commit crime because of the support of society to continue the behavior. For example, a person who burglarized an automobile for a compact disc player may be likely to continue this behavior because of a lack of punishment received and the encouragement provided by friends to participate in this lucrative behavior. In summary, situations conducive to crime are those that provide the opportunity to inspired people to take advantage of persons or property left unguarded.

An examination of these three components demonstrates that in general, individuals who enter unsafe environments and participate in risky activities are more likely to become victims of crime. For example, a younger woman who walks home through a dangerous neighborhood every evening at 10:00 p.m. after she gets off work has drastically increased her likelihood of victimization (e.g., rape, assault, murder) based on her routine activities. However, an absence of one or more of the three components of routine activity theory will significantly reduce the potential for victimization. In the previous example, taking public transportation or changing the work shift to daytime could reduce the likelihood of victimization.

Routine activity theory also challenges the "pestilence fallacy" (Felson, 1994), which is the assumption that crime is a result of the occurrence of other negative events. The theory insists that crime is actually a result of the sociostructural occurrences of people's everyday activities. For example, Cohen and Felson (1979) originally stated that the rate of direct-contact predatory crime is dependent on the amount of opportunities available to commit crime in everyday situations. More recently, factors such as social structure and demographic characteristics have been found to influence daily routines, which in turn influence exposure to motivated offenders (Gaetz, 2004; Miethe, Stafford, & Long, 1987; Sampson & Wooldredge, 1987). Overall, "the convergence in time and space of suitable targets and the absence of capable guardians can lead to large increases in crime rates" (Cohen & Felson, 1979, p. 604).

## Critiques

The first criticism of routine activity theory is in regard to its usefulness in explaining actual criminal behavior. Routine activity theory is primarily a theory of victimization (Akers & Sellers, 2009); therefore, it only indirectly provides an explanation of why people are motivated to commit a specific type of crime. Rather than attempting to explain the reason for criminal activity, it assumes that people exist who want to commit crimes based on the opportunities and victims presented to them. Osgood and Anderson (2004) suggested that measuring routine activities through individual-level data would better link offending and victimization.

A larger criticism of the theory involved the type of data utilized. Overall, studies examining crime with the theory were found to have strong predictive capabilities, whether utilizing macro- or microlevel research. However, criminologists have presented arguments criticizing the use of each type of data. For example, according to Bennett (1991), macrolevel research usually does not measure routine activities directly. Instead, it relies on aggregate measures, which often can lead to overlooking important factors identified through individual-level analysis. With this in mind, in the mid-1990s Osgood, Wilson, O'Malley, Bachman, and Johnston (1996) argued there was a lack of use of individual data to explain victimization, with too many studies relying on the use of aggregate data.

On the other hand, support for the theory found through microlevel data has been criticized by some scholars who assert that it does not demonstrate as strong of support as found through macrolevel studies (Miethe et al., 1987; Sampson & Wooldredge, 1987). Furthermore, Sherman, Gartin, and Buerger (1989), as well as Tita and Griffiths (2005), have argued there has been an abundance of use of individual-level data, but little utilization of spatial data. Nevertheless, the volume of support found in microlevel studies, in conjunction with the macrolevel studies also examined, presents a collaborative and undeniable verification of the value of the theory and its usefulness in explaining various types of victimization. This can be seen in the following section which provides a thorough examination of these studies.

## Empirical Studies

A key aspect of routine activity theory is that crime is not a random occurrence, but rather is a result of regular activity patterns converging in time and space (Mustaine & Tewksbury, 2002). Certain lifestyles and activities enhance victimization risk, based on increased involvement with dangerous persons and places. Routine activity theory has been tested and supported by several studies that have explained victimization on the macro- and microlevel. This section will discuss the findings from these various studies, as well as provide an assessment of the criticisms of routine activity theory revealed through its empirical tests.

### Macrolevel studies

As stated, the theory has been used to explain victimization on a macrolevel. In general, macrolevel research seeks to explain variation in crime rates, such as differences in crime rates between counties, areas within a county, or neighborhoods (Cohen & Felson, 1979). Sherman et al. (1989), as well as Tita and Griffiths (2005), have argued that there has been an abundance of use of individual-level data, but not enough utilization of spatial data. The supporting macrolevel studies that are available compare crime data for neighborhoods (LaGrange, 1999; Roncek & Bell, 1981; Roncek & Maier, 1991), census tracks (Copes, 1999), cities (Cao & Maume, 1993; Cook, 1987; Sampson, 1987a), and even countries (Tseloni et al., 2004), to better understand the effect of routine activities in these particular areas.

*Neighborhoods.* A benefit of conducting macrolevel research is the ability to compare crime rates in areas that share a common link, whether it is location or organizational structure. Roncek and Maier (1991), building off the previous work of Roncek and Bell (1981), examined the effect of taverns and cocktail lounges on the crime rate in Cleveland's residential city blocks between 1979 and 1981. The researchers stated there were several reasons that areas with such businesses should experience higher crime rates, consistent with routine activity theory. First, cash would be present on the patrons, as well as in the businesses, making them suitable targets for crime. Second, routine activities in a tavern (e.g., drinking) takes persons away from their intimate handlers and weakens social controls (Hirschi, 1969), in turn influencing them to participate in, or be victims of, deviant activities. Finally, Roncek and Maier (1991) found persons inhabiting these types of businesses may not be residents of the area. Results of their study showed that in all of the residential blocks, the number of taverns and lounges had a significant effect on the crime rate. Further analyses revealed that the number of taverns and lounges were associated with a higher probability of crime in an area deemed safe, as well as on blocks that already had more crime (Roncek & Maier, 1991).

LaGrange (1999) also examined the effect of certain factors in residential areas and neighborhoods. She examined the distribution of minor property crimes in a Canadian city during a one-year period in relation to three predictors: neighborhood demographics, proximity of shopping malls, and proximity of public and Catholic junior and senior high schools. The study hypothesized that physical features of an environment with malls and schools were expected to produce an increased rate of minor crimes. Shopping malls and schools hinder effective guardianship because of the difficulty in determining legitimate and illegitimate patrons and the large amount of traffic, along with the considerable amount of young people loitering in the area (LaGrange, 1999). Results determined that the presence of high schools and shopping malls within an area were significant predictors of an increase in mischievous events. According to LaGrange, her contribution to the literature provided support for routine activity theory by demonstrating how a lack of guardianship in an area causes significant increases in criminal activity.

*Cities.* Macrolevel studies can be used to compare structural aspects of different areas, such as cities or towns. Cao and Maume (1993) performed one of the more noted macrolevel studies by examining structural factors that cause robbery occurrences to vary depending on the urban environment. They argued that robbery is a unique violent crime because it disproportionately occurs in cities and is generally a crime between strangers (Cook, 1987). Cao and Maume (1993) selected 296 standard metropolitan statistical areas (SMSAs), which provided continuity with previous related research (Messner & Blau, 1987). Analyses indicated that urbanization had a direct positive effect on robbery. Large, urbanized areas have residents who are less likely to own a car or home, and people's daily routines are dependent on public transportation. Based on this, people are more likely to cross paths with strangers and motivated offenders, without guardianship, thereby leading to robbery victimization. In summary, urbanism is a strong determinant of a risky routine lifestyle.

*Countries.* The recent research of Tseloni et al. (2004) examined factors related to burglary occurrences in three countries, based on three victimization surveys taken at approximately the same time: the 1994 British Crime Survey, the 1994 National Crime Victimization Survey, and the 1993 Netherlands Police Monitor. Although there were differences in the frequencies across datasets, several similar lifestyle characteristics were shown to be significant indicators of victimization. Negative binomial regression models revealed that proximity to potential offenders (motivated offenders), a city size of 250,000 persons or more (availability of suitable targets), and lone parenthood (lack of guardianship) provided the strongest impact on potential victimization in all three areas. The results of this study provided additional support for routine activity theory (Tseloni et al., 2004).

## Microlevel studies

Osgood et al. (1996) further asserted that routine activity theory would be useful in explaining individual offending through microlevel research. They suggested a person's increased exposure to easy opportunities for deviant behavior would increase the likelihood of a crime. Furthermore, they argued microlevel research allows for a better explanation of this phenomenon, while holding constant alternative causal factors. Several previous studies had, in fact, examined the routine activities of individuals and provided support for the hypothesis that crime is more likely to occur when these activities increase the likelihood of the union of the three key theoretical components: a suitable target, a lack of guardianship, and a motivated offender (Forde & Kennedy, 1997; Hawdon, 1996; Lasley, 1989; Meier & Miethe, 1993; Miethe et al., 1987; Osgood et al., 1996; Schreck & Fisher, 2004).

The following microlevel research examines individual offending and victimization in different forms. These studies focus on offending behavior, personal and property crime victimization, and domain-specific models. Also, an examination of routine activity theory from the feminist perspective will be presented, as well as miscellaneous studies that examined the general risk of victimization. The review of this literature will demonstrate the value of using routine activity theory to explain victimization, based on the continued support found in these studies.

*Offending behavior.* The majority of the research on this theory examines the behaviors and experiences of the victim. However, some research has examined the behaviors of offenders and how the components of routine activity theory affect their choice to commit crime. One cross-sectional study focused on the third component of routine activity theory, lack of guardianship, by examining survey data from Icelandic adolescents (Bernburg & Thorlindsson, 2001). All students in the compulsory ninth and tenth grades of Icelandic secondary schools were administered anonymous questionnaires. Unstructured peer interaction was found to have a significant positive effect on property offending. Moreover, the data also indicated that unstructured peer interaction had a weaker effect on deviant behavior when the level of social bonding increased; therefore, this study provided only moderate support for routine activity theory regarding the tenet of lack of guardianship.

An offending behavior receiving much scrutiny is sexual assault. One study on this particular type of behavior came from Sasse (2005), who examined the motivating variables of sex offenders. He asserted that motivation to commit these types of offenses is acted upon not only because the motivation is available, but also because it originates from histories of past abuse, low self-esteem, and other psychological variables. This study hypothesized that according to routine activity theory, these variables should influence behavior based on the proximity of the offender to the victim, which influences the level of motivation.

Data were collected from 163 men and women in three counties in a midwestern community-based sex offender program. At intake, the respondents were subjected to a variety of assessments that included questions on personal demographics, offense characteristics, victim relationship, and abuse histories (Sasse, 2005). Results found general support for the theory. Home offenders were more likely to be abused and have younger victims compared to their community correspondents. These types of offenders have an advantage, as they have more time to groom their victims and influence them to conceal the behavior. Community offenders were younger, with older victims, and were more likely to have used alcohol before the offense. Again, support was found for the theory, as the targets for these offenders were at the age that roaming the community unsupervised is allowed.

Another examination of sexually deviant behavior more recently came from Jackson, Gililand, and Veneziano (2006). Their purpose was twofold: (1) to examine the prior and current deviance of male college students in relationship with athletic participation, fraternity participation, and opportunity, specifically in the prediction of sexual aggression; and (2) to assess the relationship between prior delinquency and sexual aggression. A sample of 304 college men involved in various contact and noncontact sports, as well as fraternity and nonfraternity members, was surveyed on previous and current behaviors. Analyses indicated that prior deviance had a positive and significant effect on levels of sexually aggressive behavior. College-level deviance was also a significant indicator of sexually aggressive behavior. There is a higher likelihood an offender will be sexually aggressive if the opportunity to potentially commit the offense is present (Jackson et al., 2006).

***Personal and property crime victimization.*** Routine activity theory has been used frequently in the past to explore personal and property crime victimization (Arnold, Keane, & Baron, 2005; Cohen & Cantor, 1980; Collins, Cox, & Langan, 1987; Gaetz, 2004; Lasley, 1989; Moriarty & Williams, 1996; Mustaine & Tewksbury, 1999; Schreck & Fisher, 2004; Spano & Nagy, 2005; Tewksbury & Mustaine, 2000). For example, early research by Cohen and Cantor (1980) and Cohen, Cantor, and Kluegel (1981) analyzed data from the National Crime Survey to consider the relationships between lifestyle and demographic characteristics and larceny victimization. The findings from both studies supported the theory. Risk of victimization was found to be higher for younger persons who lived alone and were unemployed (Cohen & Cantor, 1980; Cohen et al., 1981).

The theory suggests that the social context of criminal victimization is a central factor in the risk of victimization (Cohen & Felson, 1979; Lynch, 1987; Wooldredge, Cullen, & Latessa, 1992). In other words, even though a person may be motivated to commit an offense, the lack of a suitable target and the presence of proper guardianship will make a crime unlikely to occur. To illustrate, college students are often victims of property crime, especially vandalism (Sloan, 1994). Tewksbury and Mustaine (2000) tested the hypothesis that a target increases its chances of becoming a victim of vandalism based on the movement of property in public domains. Data for this study were taken from surveys given to 1,513 university students enrolled in introductory-level criminal justice and sociology courses at nine universities and colleges in eight different states.

Analyses indicated that a person's drug and alcohol use, as well as his or her leisure activities, were not significant predictors of vandalism victimization. Home security measures also had no effect on the victimization of these college students. However, employment status and neighborhood characteristics were found to be significant predictors. Tewksbury and Mustaine (2000) reasoned that this is because those who are unemployed leave their property unsupervised for long periods of time, possibly because they are in class or looking for work, and therefore expose it to potential offenders. In regard to neighborhood characteristics, persons who lived near a park were more likely to be victimized, seemingly because parks contain a large number of unsupervised persons (i.e., potential offenders) who are exposed to suitable targets to victimize.

Situational factors, such as personal activities and the places frequented, are a central feature of routine activity theory. In Gaetz's (2004) study, the theory was extended by applying the concept of social exclusion, which explores the restriction of a person's access to institutions and practices based on their economic, social, and political conditions. Homeless youth are restricted in the most obvious resource for enhancing safety: constant shelter. According to Gaetz (2004), data from this study support the theory, as it was shown that homeless youth experience twice the amount of victimization as youth who have constant shelter. They are therefore unable to avoid dangerous persons and situations because of their inability to obtain shelter, and in turn are restricted in the manner in which they can protect themselves.

In general, family and peer connections are life mechanisms that allow for exposure to motivated offenders, as well as the presentation of suitable targets, for young people. The level of social bonds a person develops has been shown to contribute to routine activities that affect the risk of victimization (Felson, 1986; Horney, Osgood, & Marshall, 1995). A recent study by Schreck and Fisher (2004) examined the hypothesis that strong attachment to family encourages a better quality of guardianship by parents, in turn making children less attractive targets by limiting their contact with motivated offenders because they are spending more time at home (Felson, 1986; Shreck, Wright, & Miller, 2002). Data were obtained from the first wave of the National Longitudinal Study of Adolescent Health. The results of the study identified several variables that influenced violent victimization in adolescents. First, minorities were more likely to experience victimization than white youth. Second, family climate and parental feelings toward children were the strongest family-related predictors of victimization. Adolescents living in homes with a loving environment appear to be at less risk for victimization, because they spend more time in the home rather than unsafe environments that make them suitable targets. Finally, peer delinquency and activities with friends were the strongest peer-context variables that influenced victimization, and teenagers who participated in higher levels of delinquency were more likely to be victimized because they were exposed to other motivated offenders. Overall, these results were supportive of the main hypothesis of the study (Schreck & Fisher, 2004).

Although there is a voluminous amount of research investigating adolescent violence, Spano and Nagy (2005) argued that little research has been conducted examining determinants of rural violence using targeted samples of rural youth. Using data from the

Alabama Adolescent Survey, administered in 2001, routine activity theory was utilized to explain assault and robbery victimization among rural adolescents, and social isolation was assessed as a risk or protective factor. The statistical analysis indicated that deviant lifestyle indicators and teasing increased the probability of assault victimization. Gender, level of teasing, and social isolation had a significant effect on robbery victimization.

Surprisingly, in this same study, black adolescents were less likely than white adolescents to become victims of assault and robbery, which deviated from the national trend. Spano and Nagy (2005) accredited this difference to the possibility that black residents of rural areas may be more watchful and have stronger friendship connections, and that more blacks go to the public school system in the rural portion of Alabama that was surveyed. Based on these findings, the authors suggested that routine activity theory may need to be altered to accommodate community influences in rural areas that affect victimization.

A more recent study by Arnold et al. (2005) examined how causal factors affect the risk of personal and property victimization for the general population. Rather than concentrating on offender motivation, which Cohen and Felson (1979) asserted was always present, the researchers focused on suitable targets and lack of guardianship in the equation. Data were collected in the Canadian General Social Survey of 1988, through the random digit dialing technique. The participants were questioned on their experiences with various lifestyle aspects and criminal victimization falling into four categories: violence, theft of personal property, household crime, and vehicle theft (Arnold et al., 2005).

The analysis indicated a few significant predictors of victimization. First, respondents under the age of 24 were more likely to be victimized. Second, the main activities of the respondent (such as drinking and leisure activities) drastically increased a person's likelihood of being a victim of violence or a household crime. Finally, it was discovered that respondents with a high risk of one form of victimization were more likely to have a high risk of another form, due to their lifestyle choices. In other words, people who participate in activities that make them vulnerable as targets, with little guardianship, are likely to be victimized in many forms (Arnold et al., 2005).

In sum, much of the past research testing routine activity theory has provided support for it by exploring several types of property crime, such as vandalism and motor vehicle theft (Bennett, 1991; Cohen & Cantor, 1980; Cohen et al., 1981; Copes, 1999; Gaetz, 2004; Massey, Krohn, & Bonati, 1989; Tewksbury & Mustaine, 2000). Support for the effect of routine activities on personal crime, such as assault and robbery victimization, has also been revealed in past studies (Arnold et al., 2005; Gaetz, 2004; Spano & Nagy, 2005). In the next section, the idea of situational factors being related to victimization will be considered in more detail.

***Domain-specific models.*** Many researchers have used domain-specified models to better explain routine activities inside and outside the home environment (Ehrhardt-Mustaine & Tewksbury, 1997; Garofalo, Siegel, & Laub, 1987; Lynch, 1987; Madriz, 1996; Wooldredge et al., 1992). This approach allows for a closer examination of a specific area of criminal activity, allowing for a more focused look at a particular type of environment. By examining victimization in a certain area rather than in generalities, a better explanation of victimization potentially can be provided (Wooldredge, 1998). Although infrequently used, domain-specific models have been well supported when studying routine activities (Lynch, 1987; Madriz, 1996).

Wooldredge et al. (1992) analyzed victimization in the workplace by testing routine activity theory in a specific environment. These researchers stated that the majority of studies testing this theory were not domain-specific when questioning a person on victimization; therefore, it is difficult to conclude a direct relationship exists between routine activities and the likelihood of victimization (Lynch, 1987). Full-time faculty members at the University of Cincinnati were polled through a self-report questionnaire on their personal and property crime victimization experiences on campus.

One hundred sixteen faculty members reported being victims of property crimes, and 21 were victims of personal crimes. Demographic characteristics were not found to be significant predictors of victimization. However, variables representing extent of exposure to motivated offenders were significant predictors of property crime victimization. Level of guardianship variables, such as the amount of time faculty spent on campus after hours and faculty whose offices were not located within shouting distance of other faculty, were also significantly related to property crime victimization (Wooldredge et al., 1992). However, none of these guardianship variables were predictors of personal crime victimization, and target attractiveness, which was measured by the location of faculty offices on campus and possessions available in the office, was found to be an insignificant predictor of both types of crimes. The authors noted that these findings were not surprising, as faculty members generally have control over who enters their offices, as well as their possessions (Wooldredge et al., 1992).

Another study initiated by Wang (2002) examined criminal activity in the specific domain of banks. He asserted that bank robberies are not a random event, but instead are based on determinative social circumstances that allow banks to be suitable targets. The focus of this study was on the causal factors associated with bank robberies by Asian offenders. Wang considered all three components of routine activity theory when collecting the data, and he found support for his hypothesis that these components were important during the criminal event. First, he stated motivation was clearly present based on the careful planning and different approaches used by the gang members to rob the bank. Second, each bank was an apparent suitable target, having excessive amounts of cash and being located close to a major highway for easy escape. Finally, each bank lacked in guardianship, based on inadequate security measures at the time of the robbery. Either the banks were robbed early in the morning, when there was little to no security, or the security guards were unarmed.

Overall, domain-specific models of victimization allow for a closer examination of the specific area of the criminal activity, allowing for a narrow scope of inquiry. They have been used to examine victimization in the home, workplace, and other specific places containing a person's routine activities (Ehrhardt-Mustaine & Tewksbury, 1997; Garofalo et al., 1987; Lynch, 1987; Madriz, 1996; Wooldredge, 1998; Wooldredge et al., 1992). Scholars in this area have argued that although the activities of offenders and victims often are discussed, the location of the incident is often not considered. By examining the location of crime, it is felt that crime can be better understood and explained. However, this type of model is fairly new, and in order to accurately test routine activity theory, appropriate measures must be used, or the explanatory power of the model will be lower and the ability to generalize the findings to a larger population will be lessened (Wooldredge, 1998).

***Feminist interpretation of routine activities.*** One of the more interesting adaptations of routine activity theory is the feminist interpretation, made popular by Schwartz and Pitts

(1995). They attempted to better explain motivation by describing the reasons males sexually assault women (the suitable targets). They asserted that two factors increase female suitability: (1) women who go out drinking are more likely to be sexually assaulted; and (2) these women are more likely to report they know men that get women drunk in order to sexually assault them. In addition, the presence or absence of capable guardians influences the likelihood of the event (Schwartz & Pitts, 1995). This adaptation of the theory has been tested through data collected from undergraduate males and females, as described in the following text.

Schwartz, DeKeseredy, Tait, and Alvi (2001) investigated the likelihood of sexual assault on a college campus by applying the feminist model of routine activity theory. In this particular study, the data were derived from a Canadian sample of community college and university students. Two questionnaires, one for women and one for men, were administered in 95 undergraduate classrooms at 27 universities and 21 colleges. There was a drastic difference in victimization rates found for women who used drugs and those who did not. With regard to alcohol use and victimization, less than half of light drinkers were sexually assaulted, compared to slightly more than half of heavy drinkers. Analysis further revealed a significant relationship between sexual assault and level of alcohol and drug use for both men and women. The analysis indicated the following factors significantly increased the odds that a male will commit an act of sexual aggression: drinking two or more times a week; male peer support for emotional violence; and male peer support for physical and sexual violence. Furthermore, a male with all three of these characteristics was almost ten times as likely to commit an act of sexual aggression than a male with none of the characteristics (Schwartz et al., 2001).

This study provided support for feminist routine activity theory in several ways. First, the data showed that men who drink heavily are more likely to be motivated offenders, and women who consume large amounts of alcohol are more likely to be suitable targets. Second, male peer support for committing acts of sexual victimization against women can be viewed as a motivator, as well as a component of guardianship. Overall, the data from the study demonstrated that sexual victimization could be attributed to participation in routine activities.

A second study utilizing feminist routine activity theory assessed two items: (1) how women's lifestyles affect their suitability as potential victims of sexual assault and (2) whether the factors that influence sexual assault vary depending on the degree of sexual assault (Mustaine & Tewksbury, 2002). The data were collected from self-report surveys collected during the 1998 fall academic terms from undergraduates at twelve southern institutions. Guardianship behavior did not influence the likelihood of sexual assault. Also, lifestyle choices relating to alcohol did not have a significant effect in this sample, although they have been found to be significant predictors in other studies (Schwartz & Pitts, 1995; Vogel & Himelein, 1995). However, several significant influences on sexual assault were found in the data. Women who participated in leisure time with friends "doing nothing" had higher odds of being victimized than women who did not participate in that type of activity. Also, females who were members of a higher number of clubs and organizations had higher odds of being victimized compared to others in only a few clubs. Finally, and most significantly, women who bought drugs and women who spent more time in public while using drugs had higher odds of being victimized (Mustaine & Tewksbury, 2002).

The utilization of the feminist perspective of the theory is beneficial for theorists when trying to investigate female victimization. More specifically, routine activity theory has been supported through the examination of female sexual assault (Mustaine & Tewksbury, 2002; Schwartz & Pitts, 1995; Schwartz et al., 2001). However, an obvious limitation to this adaptation is that it disregards the importance of male victimization and experiences. Although useful for particular types of crimes, this limits the utilization of this particular adaptation of the theory.

Based on an examination of the relevant literature, routine activity theory has received support on both the macro- and microlevel. Although not as plentiful as microlevel research, macrolevel investigations of the theory have revealed empirical support for the components of the theory. In particular, lack of guardianship in areas with large amounts of traffic from nonresidents having no ties to the area was shown to produce a significant effect on crime rates in neighborhoods (LaGrange, 1999; Roncek & Bell, 1981; Roncek & Maier, 1991). Moreover, the lack of guardianship and risky lifestyles of city residents have a significant relationship with victimization (Cao & Maume, 1993; Cook, 1987; Forde & Kennedy, 1997; Sampson, 1987a). An examination of countries in different continents also revealed support for the theory, by demonstrating how not only a lack of guardianship, but also crossing paths with a motivated offender as a suitable target, increases the likelihood of victimization (Tseloni et al., 2004).

Microlevel studies utilize individual-level data, allowing for analysis of factors that specifically apply to individuals, rather than across large groups. Literature on offending behavior indicates unstructured peer interaction and lack of parental supervision and connection reflected a lack of guardianship that was a significant predictor of criminal offending (Bernburg & Thorlindsson, 2001; Felson, 1986; Horney et al., 1995; Schreck & Fisher, 2004; Sasse, 2005). Personal and property crime victimization studies suggest a person's routine activities, such as participating in leisure activities away from the home and other lifestyle choices, significantly increase the likelihood of victimization (Arnold et al., 2005; Cohen & Cantor, 1980; Cohen & Felson, 1981; Collins et al., 1987; Gaetz, 2004; LaGrange, 1999; Lasley, 1989; Lynch, 1987; Moriarty & Williams, 1996; Mustaine & Tewksbury, 1999; Spano & Nagy, 2005; Tewksbury & Mustaine, 2000; Wooldredge et al., 1992). Domain-specific models were noted to better explain routine activities in a specific environment (Ehrhardt-Mustaine & Tewksbury, 1997; Garofalo et al., 1987; Lynch, 1987; Madriz, 1996; Wang, 2002; Wooldredge et al., 1992). Finally, current studies reveal that drug and alcohol consumption is a significant predictor of sexual victimization of females (Mustaine & Tewksbury, 2002; Schwartz et al., 2001).

## Theoretical Refinements

The work of Cohen and Felson (1979) was preceded by the work of Hindelang et al. (1978), as well as Amos Hawley (1950). Hindelang et al. (1978) developed what is commonly termed "lifestyle/exposure theory," which was based on correlation between lifestyle choices and victimization. They asserted that the variance in victimization risk is related to differences in lifestyle choices. Lifestyle choices encompass the daily activities of a person's life, such as work, school, and extracurricular activities. Choices made by individuals influence their exposure to different persons and places, as well as deviant behaviors, which increases their own risk of victimization (Hindelang et al., 1978).

Routine activity theory is similar to lifestyle/exposure theory (Messner & Tardiff, 1985). According to Brantingham and Brantingham (1981), Cohen and Felson sought to expand and improve upon the work of Hindelang et al. (1978) by incorporating ecological concepts, specifically Hawley's (1950) components of temporal organization: rhythm, tempo, and timing. Rhythm is the regularity with which events occur. Tempo is the number of events that occur per unit of time. Finally, timing is the duration and recurrence of the events. According to Cohen and Felson (1979), the inclusion of these three components improves the explanation of how and why criminal activity is performed.

From the initial assertions of Cohen and Felson, and in conjunction with the works of various other scholars, the currently recognized routine activity theory has been formed. This theory states that there are three components necessary in a situation in order for a crime to occur: a suitable target, a lack of a capable guardian, and a motivated offender (Cohen & Cantor, 1980; Cohen & Felson, 1979, 1981; Felson, 1986, 1987; Hawdon, 1996; Lasley, 1989; Sampson & Wooldredge, 1987). Moreover, crime is not a random occurrence, but rather, follows regular patterns that require these three components.

## Policy Applications

As demonstrated previously in the text, there is extensive support in the literature for routine activity theory when it comes to explaining crime victimization. This indicates that implementing policies that reduce exposure to motivated offenders, decrease target suitability, and increase capable guardianship should in turn decrease the likelihood a person will become a victim of crime. Two particular types of policies that perform these functions are situational crime prevention strategies and target hardening.

Situational, or place-based, crime prevention strategies are successful with the same means as hot-spot police patrols: they are used when and where they are most needed. Rather than attempting to alter the behavior of the offender, the purpose of situational crime prevention strategies is to block the opportunity of commit criminal behavior in a specific place. In other words, the presence of motivated offenders and target suitability of victims are decreased and the guardianship in a specific place is increased. These types of prevention strategies do not specifically focus on decreasing victimization as a whole, but victimization in a particular location.

According to Eck (2002), place-based tactics could be more influential than offender-based plans because they pay closer attention to immediate situations rather than preparing a person for an uncertain period of time in the future. Referred to as place improvement processes (Brantingham & Brantingham, 1995), these types of plans are known for reducing crime by reducing the attractiveness of committing a crime in certain areas (Barclay, Buckley, Brantingham, Brantingham, & Whin-Yates, 1996; Brantingham & Brantingham, 1981). For example, New York City managers could reduce the occurrence of mugging in Central Park by adding additional lights and security guards throughout the park.

A particular type of situational crime prevention strategy that has been shown to be effective is target hardening, which is providing locks and improved security to access points. In regard to a crime in a physical location, burglary rates have reduced because of target hardening strategies (Bowers, Johnson, & Hirschfield, 2004). This type of strategy could be considered a secondary and tertiary prevention strategy (Pease, 2002) because of its aim to block those at high risk of committing an offense, as well as those who have a criminal history of burglary offenses.

Target hardening strategies increase the amount of guardianship in a specific location. Several empirical studies have demonstrated that lack of guardianship measures increase the occurrence of victimization (Bernburg & Thorlindsson, 2001; Cao & Maume, 1993; LaGrange, 1999; Tewksbury & Mustaine, 2000). By implementing different guardianship measures that focus specifically on reducing entry into certain locations, the amount of victimization that occurs in the area will hypothetically be reduced. For example, the utilization of "zoning" practices, as suggested by the Internet Community Ports Act (Preston, 2007), would allow for parents to limit or eliminate their children's access to areas on the Internet that could increase the likelihood of victimization. The guardianship of the parents is increased, as they hold the "key" to eliminating access to websites with inappropriate content.

# PART II

# BIOSOCIAL THEORIES

# CRIMINAL MAN

*Gina Lombroso-Ferrero*

. . . The Classical School based its doctrines on the assumption that all criminals, except in a few extreme cases, are endowed with intelligence and feelings like normal individuals, and that they commit misdeeds consciously, being prompted thereto by their unrestrained desire for evil. The offence alone was considered, and on it the whole existing penal system has been founded, the severity of the sentence meted out to the offender being regulated by the gravity of his misdeed.

The Modern, or Positive, School of Penal Jurisprudence, on the contrary, maintains that the antisocial tendencies of criminals are the result of their physical and psychic organisation, which differs essentially from that of normal individuals; and it aims at studying the morphology and various functional phenomena of the criminal with the object of curing, instead of punishing him. The Modern School is therefore founded on a new science, Criminal Anthropology, which may be defined as the Natural History of the Criminal, because it embraces his organic and psychic constitution and social life, just as anthropology does in the case of normal human beings and the different races.

If we examine a number of criminals, we shall find that they exhibit numerous anomalies in the face, skeleton, and various psychic and sensitive functions, so that they strongly resemble primitive races. It was these anomalies that first drew my father's attention to the close relationship between the criminal and the savage and made him suspect that criminal tendencies are of atavistic origin.

When a young doctor at the Asylum in Pavia, he was requested to make a postmortem examination on a criminal named Vilella, an Italian Jack the Ripper, who by atrocious crimes had spread terror in the Province of Lombardy. Scarcely had he laid open the skull, when he perceived at the base, on the spot where the internal occipital crest or ridge is found in normal individuals, a small hollow, which he called *median occipital fossa.* This abnormal character was correlated to a still greater anomaly in the cerebellum, the hypertrophy of the vermis, *i.e.,* the spinal cord which separates the cerebellar lobes lying underneath the cerebral hemispheres. This vermis was so enlarged in the case of Vilella, that it almost formed a small, intermediate cerebellum like that found in the lower types of apes, rodents, and birds. This anomaly is very rare among inferior races. . . . It is seldom met with in the insane or other degenerates, but later investigations have shown it to be prevalent in criminals.

This discovery was like a flash of light. "At the sight of that skull," says my father, "I seemed to see all at once, standing out clearly illumined as in a vast plain under a flaming sky, the problem of the nature of the criminal, who reproduces in civilised times characteristics, not only of primitive savages, but of still lower types as far back as the carnivora."

Thus was explained the origin of the enormous jaws, strong canines, prominent zygomæ, and strongly developed orbital arches which he had so frequently remarked in criminals, for these peculiarities are common to carnivores and savages, who tear and devour raw flesh. Thus also it was easy to understand why the span of the arms in criminals so often exceeds the height, for this is a characteristic of apes, whose fore-limbs are used in walking and climbing. The other anomalies exhibited by criminals—the scanty beard as opposed to the general hairiness of the body, prehensile foot, diminished number of lines in the palm of the hand, cheek-pouches, enormous development of the middle incisors and frequent absence of the lateral ones, flattened nose and angular or sugar-loaf form of the skull, common to criminals and apes; the excessive size of the orbits, which, combined with the hooked nose, so often imparts to criminals the aspect of birds of prey, the projection of the lower part of the face and jaws (prognathism) found in negroes and animals, and supernumerary teeth (amounting in some cases to a double row as in snakes) and cranial bones (epactal bone as in the Peruvian Indians): all these characteristics pointed to one conclusion, the atavistic origin of the criminal, who reproduces physical, psychic, and functional qualities of remote ancestors.

Subsequent research on the part of my father and his disciples showed that other factors besides atavism come into play in determining the criminal type. These are: disease and environment. Later on, the study of innumerable offenders led them to the conclusion that all law-breakers cannot be classed in a single species, for their ranks include very diversified types, who differ not only in their bent towards a particular form of crime, but also in the degree of tenacity and intensity displayed by them in their perverse propensities, so that, in reality, they form a graduated scale leading from the born criminal to the normal individual.

Born criminals form about one third of the mass of offenders, but, though inferior in numbers, they constitute the most important part of the whole criminal army, partly because they are constantly appearing before the public and also because the crimes committed by them are of a peculiarly monstrous character; the other two thirds are composed of criminaloids (minor offenders), occasional and habitual criminals, etc., who do not show such a marked degree of diversity from normal persons.

Let us commence with the born criminal, who as the principal nucleus of the wretched army of law-breakers, naturally manifests the most numerous and salient anomalies.

The median occipital fossa and other abnormal features just enumerated are not the only peculiarities exhibited by this aggravated type of offender. By careful research, my father and others of his School have brought to light many anomalies in bodily organs, and functions both physical and mental, all of which serve to indicate the atavistic and pathological origin of the instinctive criminal. . . .

The present volume will only touch briefly on the principal characteristics of criminals, with the object of presenting a general outline of the studies of criminologists.


## Physical Anomalies of the Born Criminal

### The head

As the seat of all the greatest disturbances, this part naturally manifests the greatest number of anomalies, which extend from the external conformation of the brain-case to the composition of its contents.

The criminal skull does not exhibit any marked characteristics of size and shape. Generally speaking, it tends to be larger or smaller than the average skull common to the region or country from which the criminal hails. It varies between 1200 and 1600 c.c.; i.e., between 73 and 100 cubic inches, the normal average being 92. This applies also to the cephalic index; that is, the ratio of the maximum width to the maximum length of the skull multiplied by 100, which serves to give a concrete idea of the form of the skull, because the higher the index, the nearer the skull approaches a spherical form, and the lower the index, the more elongated it becomes. The skulls of criminals have no characteristic cephalic index, but tend to an exaggeration of the ethnical type prevalent in their native countries. In regions where dolichocephaly (index less than 80) abounds, the skulls of criminals show a very low index; if, on the contrary, they are natives of districts where brachycephaly (index 80 or more) prevails, they exhibit a very high index.

In 15.5% we find trochocephalous or abnormally round heads (index 91). A very high percentage (nearly double that of normal individuals) have submicrocephalous or small skulls. In other cases the skull is excessively large (macrocephaly) or abnormally small and ill-shaped with a narrow, receding forehead (microcephaly, 0.2%). More rarely the skull is of normal size, but shaped like the keel of a boat (scaphocephaly, 0.1% and sub-scaphocephaly 6%). (See Figure 1.) Sometimes the anomalies are still more serious and we find wholly asymmetrical skulls with protuberances on either side (plagiocephaly 10.9%, see Figure 2), or terminating in a peak on the bregma or anterior fontanel (acrocephaly), or depressed in the middle (cymbocephaly, sphenocephaly). At times, there are crests or grooves along the sutures (11.9%) or the cranial bones are abnormally thick, a characteristic of savage peoples (36.6%) or abnormally thin (8.10%). Other anomalies of importance are the presence of Wormian bones in the sutures of the skull (21.22%), the bone of the Incas already alluded to (4%), and above all, the median occipital fossa. Of great importance also are the prominent frontal sinuses found in 25% (double that of normal individuals), the semicircular line of the temples, which is sometimes so exaggerated that it forms a ridge and is correlated to an excessive development of the temporal muscles, a common characteristic of primates and carnivores. Sometimes the forehead is receding, as in apes (19%), or low and narrow (10%).

### The face

In striking contrast to the narrow forehead and low vault of the skull, the face of the criminal, like those of most animals, is of disproportionate size, a phenomenon intimately

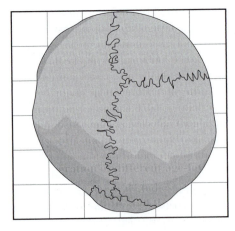

**FIGURE 1**
Skull formation.

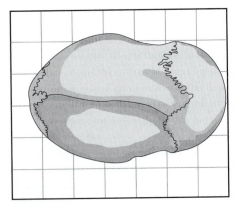

**FIGURE 2**
Skull formation.

connected with the greater development of the senses as compared with that of the nervous centres. Prognathism, the projection of the lower portion of the face beyond the forehead, is found in 45.7% of criminals. Progeneismus, the projection of the lower teeth and jaw beyond the upper, is found in 38%, whereas among normal persons the proportion is barely 28%. As a natural consequence of this predominance of the lower portion of the face, the orbital arches and zygomæ show a corresponding development (35%) and the size of the jaws is naturally increased, the mean diameter being 103.9 mm. (4.09 inches) as against 93 mm. (3.66 inches) in normal persons. Among criminals 29% have voluminous jaws.

The excessive dimensions of the jaws and cheekbones admit of other explanations besides the atavistic one of a greater development of the masticatory system. They may have been influenced by the habit of certain gestures, the setting of the teeth or tension of the muscles of the mouth, which accompany violent muscular efforts and are natural to men who form energetic or violent resolves and meditate plans of revenge.

Asymmetry is a common characteristic of the criminal physiognomy. The eyes and ears are frequently situated at different levels and are of unequal size, the nose slants towards one side, etc. This asymmetry, as we shall see later, is connected with marked irregularities in the senses and functions. . . .

### The cerebrum and the cerebellum

The chief and most common anomaly is the prevalence of macroscopic anomalies in the left hemisphere, which are correlated to the sensory and functional left-handedness common to criminals and acquired through illness. The most notable anomaly of the cerebellum is the hypertrophy of the vermis, which represents the middle lobe found in the lower mammals. Anomalies in the cerebral convolutions consist principally of anastomotic folds, the doubling of the fissure of Rolando, the frequent existence of a fourth frontal convolution, the imperfect development of the precuneus (as in many types of apes), etc. Anomalies of a purely pathological character are still more common. These are: adhesions of the meninges, thickening of the pia mater, congestion of the meninges, partial atrophy, centres of softening, seaming of the optic thalami, atrophy of the corpus callosum, etc. . . .

These anomalies in the limbs, trunk, skull and, above all, in the face, when numerous and marked, constitute what is known to criminal anthropologists as the criminal type, in exactly the same way as the sum of the characters peculiar to cretins form what is called the cretinous type. In neither case have the anomalies an intrinsic importance, since they are neither the cause of the anti-social tendencies of the criminal nor of the mental deficiencies of the cretin. They are the outward and visible signs of a mysterious and complicated process of degeneration, which in the case of the criminal evokes evil impulses that are largely of atavistic origin.

### Sensory and Functional Peculiarities of the Born Criminal

The above-mentioned physiognomical and skeletal anomalies are further supplemented by functional peculiarities, and all these abnormal characteristics converge, as mountain streams to the hollow in the plain, towards a central idea—the atavistic nature of the born criminal.

An examination of the senses and sensibility of criminals gives the following results:

### General sensibility

Tested simply by touching with the finger, a certain degree of obtuseness is noted. By using an apparatus invented by Du Bois–Reymond and adopted by my father, the degree of sensibility obtained was 49.6 mm. in criminals as against 64.2 mm. in normal individuals. Criminals are more sensitive on the left side, contrary to normal persons, in whom greater sensibility prevails on the right.

### Sensibility to pain

Compared with ordinary individuals, the criminal shows greater insensibility to pain as well as to touch. This obtuseness sometimes reaches complete analgesia or total absence of feeling (16%), a phenomenon never encountered in normal persons. The mean degree of dolorific sensibility in criminals is 34.1 mm. whereas it is rarely lower than 40 mm. in normal individuals. Here again the left-handedness of criminals becomes apparent, 39% showing greater sensibility on the left.

### Tactile sensibility

The distance at which two points applied to the finger-tips are felt separately is more than 4 mm. in 30% of criminals, a degree of obtuseness only found in 4% of normal individuals. Criminals exhibit greater tactile sensibility on the left. Tactile obtuseness varies with the class of crime practised by the individual. While in burglars, swindlers, and assaulters, it is double that of normal persons, in murderers, violators, and incendiaries it is often four or five times as great. . . .

### Meteoric sensibility

This is far more apparent in criminals and the insane than in normal individuals. With variations of temperature and atmospheric pressure, both criminals and lunatics become agitated and manifest changes of disposition and sensations of various kinds, which are rarely experienced by normal persons.

### Sight

[Sight] is generally acute, perhaps more so than in ordinary individuals, and in this the criminal resembles the savage. Chromatic sensibility, on the contrary, is decidedly defective, the percentage of colour-blindness being twice that of normal persons. The field of vision is frequently limited by the white and exhibits much stranger anomalies, a special irregularity of outline with deep peripheral scotoma, which we shall see is a special characteristic of the epileptic.

### Hearing, smell, taste

[Hearing, Smell, Taste] are generally of less than average acuteness in criminals. Cases of complete anosmia and qualitative obtuseness are not uncommon.

### Agility

Criminals are generally agile and preserve this quality even at an advanced age. When over seventy, Vilella sprang like a goat up the steep rocks of his native Calabria, and the celebrated thief "La Vecchia," when quite an old man, escaped from his captors by leaping from a high rampart at Pavia.

### Strength

Contrary to what might be expected, tests by means of the dynamometer show that criminals do not usually possess an extraordinary degree of strength. There is frequently a slight difference between the strength of the right and left limbs, but more often ambidexterity, as in children, and a greater degree of strength in the left limbs.

## Psychology of the Born Criminal

The physical type of the criminal is completed and intensified by his moral and intellectual physiognomy, which furnishes a further proof of his relationship to the savage and epileptic.

### Natural affections

These play an important part in the life of a normally constituted individual and are in fact the *raison d'être* of his existence, but the criminal rarely, if ever, experiences emotions of this kind and least of all regarding his own kin. On the other hand, he shows exaggerated and abnormal fondness for animals and strangers. La Sola, a female criminal, manifested about as much affection for her children as if they had been kittens and induced her accomplice to murder a former paramour, who was deeply attached to her; yet she tended the sick and dying with the utmost devotion.

In the place of domestic and social affections, the criminal is dominated by a few absorbing passions: vanity, impulsiveness, desire for revenge, licentiousness.

## Moral Sense

The ability to discriminate between right and wrong, which is the highest attribute of civilised humanity, is notably lacking in physically and psychically stunted organisms. Many criminals do not realise the immorality of their actions. In French criminal jargon conscience is called "la muette," the thief "l'ami," and "travailler" and "servir" signify to steal. A Milanese thief once remarked to my father: "I don't steal. I only relieve the rich of their superfluous wealth." Lacenaire, speaking of his accomplice Avril, remarked, "I realised at once that we should be able to work together." A thief asked by Ferri what he did when he found the purse stolen by him contained no money, replied, "I call them rogues." The notions of right and wrong appear to be completely inverted in such minds. They seem to think they have a right to rob and murder and that those who hinder them are acting unfairly. Murderers, especially when actuated by motives of revenge, consider their actions righteous in the extreme.

### Repentance and remorse

We hear a great deal about the remorse of criminals, but those who come into contact with these degenerates realise that they are rarely, if ever, tormented by such feelings. Very few confess their crimes: the greater number deny all guilt in a most strenuous manner and are fond of protesting that they are victims of injustice, calumny, and jealousy. As Despine once remarked with much insight, nothing resembles the sleep of the just more closely than the slumbers of an assassin.

Many criminals, indeed, allege repentance, but generally from hypocritical motives; either because they hope to gain some advantage by working on the feelings of philanthropists, or with a view to escaping, or, at any rate, improving their condition while in prison. . . .

## The Criminal Type

All the physical and psychic peculiarities of which we have spoken are found singly in many normal individuals. Moreover, crime is not always the result of degeneration and atavism; and, on the other hand, many persons who are considered perfectly normal are not so in reality. However, in normal individuals, we never find that accumulation of physical, psychic, functional, and skeletal anomalies in one and the same person, that we do in the case of criminals, among whom also entire freedom from abnormal characteristics is more rare than among ordinary individuals.

Just as a musical theme is the result of a sum of notes, and not of any single note, the criminal type results from the aggregate of these anomalies, which render him strange and terrible, not only to the scientific observer, but to ordinary persons who are capable of an impartial judgment.

Painters and poets, unhampered by false doctrines, divined this type long before it became the subject of a special branch of study. The assassins, executioners, and devils painted by Mantegna, Titian, and Ribera the Spagnoletto embody with marvellous exactitude the characteristics of the born criminal; and the descriptions of great writers, Dante, Shakespeare, Dostoyevsky, and Ibsen, are equally faithful representations, physically and psychically, of this morbid type. . . .

## Criminality in Children

The criminal instincts common to primitive savages would be found proportionally in nearly all children, if they were not influenced by moral training and example. This does not mean that without educative restraints, all children would develop into criminals. According to the observations made by Prof. Mario Carrara at Cagliari, the bands of neglected children who run wild in the streets of the Sardinian capital and are addicted to thievish practices and more serious vices, spontaneously correct themselves of these habits as soon as they have arrived at puberty.

This fact, that the germs of moral insanity and criminality are found normally in mankind in the first stages of his existence, in the same way as forms considered monstrous when exhibited by adults, frequently exist in the fœtus, is such a simple and common phenomenon that it eluded notice until it was demonstrated clearly by observers like Moreau, Perez, and Bain. The child, like certain adults, whose abnormality consists in a lack of moral sense, represents what is known to alienists as a morally insane being and to criminologists as a born criminal, and it certainly resembles these types in its impetuous violence.

Perez remarks on the frequency and precocity of anger in children:

During the first two months, it manifests by movements of the eyebrows and hands undoubted fits of temper when undergoing any distasteful process, such as washing or when deprived of any object it takes a fancy to. At the age of one, it goes to the length of striking those who incur its displeasure, of breaking plates or throwing them at persons it dislikes, exactly like savages.

Moreau cites numerous cases of children who fly into a passion if their wishes are not complied with immediately. In one instance observed by him a very intelligent child of eight, when reproved, even in the mildest manner by his parents or strangers, would give way to violent anger, snatching up the nearest weapon, or if he found himself unable to take revenge, would break anything he could lay his hands on.

A baby girl showed an extremely violent temper, but became of gentle disposition after she had reached the age of two (Perez). Another, observed by the same author, when only eleven months old, flew into a towering rage, because she was unable to pull off her grandfather's nose. Yet another, at the age of two, tried to bite another child who had a doll like her own, and she was so much affected by her anger that she was ill for three days afterwards.

Nino Bixio, when a boy of seven on seeing his teacher laugh because he had written his exercise on office letter-paper, threw the inkstand at the man's face. This boy was literally the terror of the school, on account of the violence he displayed at the slightest offence.

Infants of seven or eight months have been known to scratch at any attempt to withdraw the breast from them, and to retaliate when slapped.

A backward and slightly hydrocephalous boy whom my father had under observation, began at the age of six to show violent irritation at the slightest reproof or correction. If he was able to strike the person who had annoyed him, his rage cooled immediately; if not, he would scream incessantly and bite his hands with gestures similar to those often witnessed in caged bears who have been teased and cannot retaliate.

The above cases show that the desire for revenge is extremely common and precocious in children. Anger is an elementary instinct innate in human beings. It should be guided and restrained, but can never be extirpated.

Children are quite devoid of moral sense during the first months or first years of their existence. Good and evil in their estimation are what is allowed and what is forbidden by their elders, but they are incapable of judging independently of the moral value of an action.

"Lying and disobedience are very wrong," said a boy to Perez, "because they displease mother." Everything he was accustomed to was right and necessary.

A child does not grasp abstract ideas of justice, or the rights of property, until he has been deprived of some possession. He is prone to detest injustice, especially when he is the victim. Injustice, in his estimation, is the discord between a habitual mode of treatment and an accidental one. When subjected to altered conditions, he shows complete uncertainty. A child placed under Perez's care modified his ways according to each new arrival. He began ordering his companions about and refused to obey any one but Perez.

Affection is very slightly developed in children. Their fancy is easily caught by a pleasing exterior or by anything that contributes to their amusement; like domestic animals that they enjoy teasing and pulling about, and they exhibit great antipathy to unfamiliar objects that inspire them with fear. Up to the age of seven or even after, they show very little real attachment to anybody. Even their mothers, whom they appear to love, are speedily forgotten after a short separation.

In conclusion, children manifest a great many of the impulses we have observed in criminals; anger, a spirit of revenge, idleness, volubility and lack of affection.

We have also pointed out that many actions considered criminal in civilised communities, are normal and legitimate practices among primitive races. It is evident, therefore, that such actions are natural to the early stages, both of social evolution and individual psychic development.

In view of these facts, it is not strange that civilised communities should produce a certain percentage of adults who commit actions reputed injurious to society and punishable by law. It is only an atavistic phenomenon, the return to a former state. In the criminal, moreover, the phenomenon is accompanied by others also natural to a primitive stage of evolution. These have already been referred to in the first chapter, which contains a description of many strange practices common to delinquents, and evidently of primitive origin—tattooing, cruel games, love of orgies, a peculiar slang resembling in certain features the languages of primitive peoples, and the use of hieroglyphics and pictography.

The artistic manifestations of the criminal show the same characteristics. In spite of the thousands of years which separate him from prehistoric savages, his art is a faithful reproduction of the first, crude artistic attempts of primitive races. The museum of criminal anthropology created by my father contains numerous specimens of criminal art, stones shaped to resemble human figures, like those found in Australia, rude pottery covered with designs that recall Egyptian decorations or scenes fashioned in terra-cotta that resemble the grotesque creations of children or savages.

The criminal is an atavistic being, a relic of a vanished race. This is by no means an uncommon occurrence in nature. Atavism, the reversion to a former state, is the first feeble indication of the reaction opposed by nature to the perturbing causes which seek to alter her delicate mechanism. Under certain unfavourable conditions, cold or poor soil, the common oak will develop characteristics of the oak of the Quaternary period. The dog left to run wild in the forest will in a few generations revert to the type of his original wolf-like progenitor, and the cultivated garden roses when neglected show a tendency to reassume the form of the original dog-rose. Under special conditions produced by alcohol, chloroform, heat, or injuries, ants, dogs, and pigeons become irritable and savage like their wild ancestors.

This tendency to alter under special conditions is common to human beings, in whom hunger, syphilis, trauma, and, still more frequently, morbid conditions inherited from insane, criminal, or diseased progenitors, or the abuse of nerve poisons, such as alcohol, tobacco, or morphine, cause various alterations, of which criminality—that is, a return to the characteristics peculiar to primitive savages—is in reality the least serious, because it represents a less advanced stage than other forms of cerebral alteration.

The ætiology of crime, therefore, mingles with that of all kinds of degeneration: rickets, deafness, monstrosity, hairiness, and cretinism, of which crime is only a variation. It has, however, always been regarded as a thing apart, owing to a general instinctive repugnance to admit that a phenomenon, whose extrinsications are so extensive and penetrate every fibre of social life, derives, in fact, from the same causes as socially insignificant forms like rickets, sterility, etc. But this repugnance is really only a sensory illusion, like many others of widely diverse nature.

### Pathological origin of crime

The atavistic origin of crime is certainly one of the most important discoveries of criminal anthropology, but it is important only theoretically, since it merely explains the phenomenon. Anthropologists soon realised how necessary it was to supplement this discovery by that of the origin, or causes which call forth in certain individuals these atavistic or criminal instincts, for it is the immediate causes that constitute the practical nucleus of the problem and it is their removal that renders possible the cure of the disease.

These causes are divided into organic and external factors of crime: the former remote and deeply rooted, the latter momentary but frequently determining the criminal act, and both closely related and fused together.

Heredity is the principal organic cause of criminal tendencies. It may be divided into two classes: indirect heredity from a generically degenerate family with frequent cases of insanity, deafness, syphilis, epilepsy, and alcoholism among its members; direct heredity from criminal parentage.

### Indirect heredity

Almost all forms of chronic, constitutional diseases, especially those of a nervous character: chorea, sciatica, hysteria, insanity, and above all, epilepsy, may give rise to criminality in the descendants.

Of 559 soldiers convicted of offences, examined by Brancaleone Ribaudo, 10% had epileptic parents. According to Dejerine, this figure reaches 74.6% among criminal epileptics. Arthritis and gout have been known to generate criminality in the descendants. But the most serious, and at the same time most common, form of indirect heredity is alcoholism, which, contrary to general belief, wreaks destruction in all classes of society, amongst the rich and poor without distinction of sex, for alcohol may insinuate itself everywhere under the most refined and pleasant disguises, in liqueurs, sweets, and coffee.

According to calculations made by my father, 20% of Italian criminals descend from inebriate families; according to Penta the percentage is 27 and in dangerous criminals, 33%. The Jukes family, of whom we shall speak later, descended from a drunkard.

The first salient characteristic in hereditary alcoholism is the precocious taste for intoxicants; secondly, the susceptibility to alcohol, which is infinitely more injurious to the offspring of inebriates than to normal individuals; and thirdly, the growth of the craving for strong drinks, which inevitably undermine the constitution.

### Direct heredity

The effects of direct heredity are still more serious, for they are aggravated by environment and education. Official statistics show that 20% of juvenile offenders belong to families of doubtful reputation and 26% to those whose reputation is thoroughly bad. The criminal Galletto, a native of Marseilles, was the nephew of the equally ferocious anthropophagous violator of women, Orsolano. Dumollar was the son of a murderer; Patetot's grandfather and great-grandfather were in prison, as were the grandfathers and fathers of Papa, Crocco, Serravalle and Cavallante, Comptois and Lempave; the parents of the celebrated female thief Sans Refus, were both thieves.

The genealogical study of certain families has shown that there are whole generations, almost all the members of which belong to the ranks of crime, insanity, and prostitution (this last being amongst women the equivalent of criminality amongst men). A striking example is furnished by the notorious Jukes family, with 77 criminal descendants.

Ancestor, Max Jukes: 77 criminals; 142 vagabonds; 120 prostitutes; 18 keepers of houses of ill-fame; 91 illegitimates; 141 idiots or afflicted with impotency or syphilis; 46 sterile females.

A like criminal contingent may be found in the pedigrees of Chrêtien, the Lemaires, the Fieschi family, etc.

### Race

This is of great importance in view of the atavistic origin of crime. There exist whole tribes and races more or less given to crime, such as the tribe Zakka Khel in India. In all regions of Italy, whole villages constitute hot-beds of crime, owing, no doubt, to ethnical causes: Artena in the province of Rome, Carde and San Giorgio Canavese in Piedmont, Pergola in Tuscany, San Severo in Apulia, San Mauro and Nicosia in Sicily. The frequency of homicide in Calabria, Sicily, and Sardinia is fundamentally due to African and Oriental elements.

In the gipsies we have an entire race of criminals with all the passions and vices common to delinquent types: idleness, ignorance, impetuous fury, vanity, love of orgies, and ferocity. Murder is often committed for some trifling gain. The women are skilled thieves and train their children in dishonest practices. On the contrary, the percentage of crimes among Jews is always lower than that of the surrounding population; although there is a prevalence of certain specific forms of offences, often hereditary, such as fraud, forgery, libel, and chief of all, traffic in prostitution; murder is extremely rare. . . .

## Social Causes of Crime

### Education

We now come to the second series of criminal factors, those which depend, not on the organism, but on external conditions. We have already stated that the best and most careful education, moral and intellectual, is powerless to effect an improvement in the morally insane, but that in other cases, education, environment, and example are extremely important, for which reason neglected and destitute children are easily initiated into evil practices. . . .

### Meteoric causes

[Meteoric causes] are frequently the determining factor of the ultimate impulsive act, which converts the latent criminal into an effective one. Excessively high temperature and rapid barometric changes, while predisposing epileptics to convulsive seizures and the insane to uneasiness, restlessness, and noisy outbreaks, encourage quarrels, brawls, and stabbing affrays. To the same reason may be ascribed the prevalence during the hot months, of rape, homicide, insurrections, and revolts. In comparing statistics of criminality in France with those of the variations in temperature, Ferri noted an increase in crimes of violence during the warmer years. An examination of European and American statistics shows that the number of homicides decreases as we pass from hot to cooler climates. Holzendorf calculates that the number of murders committed in the Southern States of North America is fifteen times greater than those committed in the Northern States. A low temperature, on the contrary, has the effect of increasing the number of crimes against property, due to increased need, and both in Italy and America the proportion of thefts increases the farther north we go.

### Density of population

The agglomeration of persons in a large town is a certain incentive to crimes against property. Robbery, frauds, and criminal associations increase, while there is a decrease in crimes against the person, due to the restraints imposed by mutual supervision. . . .
In all large cities, low lodging-houses form the favourite haunts of crime.

### Imitation

The detailed accounts of crimes circulated in large towns by newspapers, have an extremely pernicious influence, because example is a powerful agent for evil as well as for good. . . .

### Immigration

The agglomeration of population produced by immigration is a strong incentive to crime, especially that of an associated nature,—due to increased want, lessened supervision and the consequent ease with which offenders avoid detection. In New York the largest contingent of criminality is furnished by the immigrant population.
The fact of agglomeration explains the greater frequency of homicide in France in thickly populated districts.
The criminality of immigrant populations increases in direct ratio to its instability. This applies to the migratory population in the interior of a country, specially that which has no fixed destination, as peddlers, etc. Even those immigrants whom we should naturally assume to be of good disposition—religious pilgrims—commit a remarkable number of associated crimes. The Italian word *mariuolo* which signifies "rogue" owes its origin to the behaviour of certain pilgrims to the shrines of Loreto and Assisi, who, while crying *Viva Maria!* ("Hail to the Virgin Mary!") committed the most atrocious crimes, confident that the pilgrimage itself would serve as a means of expiation. In his *Reminiscences* Massimo d' Azeglio notes that places boasting of celebrated shrines always enjoy a bad reputation.

### Prison life

The density of population in the most criminal of cities has not such a bad influence as has detention in prisons, which may well be called "Criminal Universities."
Nearly all the leaders of malefactors: Maino, Lombardo, La Gala, Lacenaire, Soufflard, and Hardouin were escaped convicts, who chose their accomplices among those of their fellow-prisoners who had shown audacity and ferocity. In fact, in prison, criminals have an opportunity of becoming acquainted with each other, of instructing those less skilled in infamy, and of banding together for evil purposes. Even the expensive cellular system, from which so many advantages were expected, has not attained its object and does not prevent communication between prisoners. Moreover, in prison, mere children of seven or eight, imprisoned for stealing a bunch of grapes or a fowl, come into close contact with

adults and become initiated into evil practices, of which these poor little victims of stupid laws were previously quite ignorant.

### Education

Contrary to general belief, the influence of education on crime is very slight.

The number of illiterates arrested in Europe is less, proportionally, than that of educated individuals. Nevertheless, although a certain degree of instruction is often an aid to crime, its extension acts as a corrective, or at least tends to mitigate the nature of crimes committed, rendering them less ferocious, and to decrease crimes of violence, while increasing fraudulent and sexual offences.

### Professions

The trades and professions which encourage inebriety in those who follow them (cooks, confectioners, and inn-keepers), those which bring the poor (servants of all kinds, especially footmen, coachmen, and chauffeurs) into contact with wealth, or which provide means for committing crimes (bricklayers, blacksmiths, etc.) furnish a remarkable share of criminality. Still more so is this the case with the professions of notary, usher of the courts, attorneys, and military men.

It should be observed, however, that the characteristic idleness of criminals makes them disinclined to adopt any profession, and when they do, their extreme fickleness prompts them to change continually.

### Economic conditions

Poverty is often a direct incentive to theft, when the miserable victims of economic conditions find themselves and their families face to face with starvation, and it acts further indirectly through certain diseases: pellagra, alcoholism, scrofula, and scurvy, which are the outcome of misery and produce criminal degeneration; its influence has nevertheless often been exaggerated. If thieves are generally penniless, it is because of their extreme idleness and astonishing extravagance, which makes them run through huge sums with the greatest ease, not because poverty has driven them to theft. On the other hand the possession of wealth is frequently an incentive to crime, because it creates an ever-increasing appetite for riches, besides furnishing those occupying high public offices or important positions in the banking and commercial world with numerous opportunities for dishonesty and persuading them that money will cover any evil deed.

### Sex

Statistics of every country show that women contribute a very small share of criminality compared with that furnished by the opposite sex. This share becomes still smaller when we eliminate infanticide, in view of the fact that the guilty parties in nearly all such cases should be classed as criminals from passion. . . .

However, this applies only to serious crimes. For those of lesser gravity, statistics are at variance with the results obtained by the Modern School, which classes prostitutes as criminals. According to this mode of calculation, the difference between the criminality of the two sexes shows a considerable diminution, resulting perhaps in a slight prevalence of crime in women. In any case, female criminality tends to increase proportionally with the increase of civilisation and to equal that of men.

**Age**

The greater number of crimes are committed between the ages of 15 and 30, whereas, outbreaks of insanity between these ages are extremely rare, the maximum number occurring between 40 and 50. On the whole, criminality is far more precocious than mental alienation, and its precocity, which is greater among thieves than among murderers, swindlers, and those guilty of violence and assault is another proof of the congenital nature of crime and its atavistic origin, since precocity is a characteristic of savage races.

Seldom do we find among born criminals any indication of that so-called criminal scale, leading by degrees from petty offences to crimes of the most serious nature. As a general rule, they commence their career with just those crimes which distinguish it throughout, even when these are of the gravest kind, like robbery and murder. Rather may it be said that every age has its specific criminality, and this is the case especially with criminaloids. On the borderland between childhood and adolescence, there seems to be a kind of instinctive tendency to law-breaking, which by immature minds is often held to be a sign of virility. The Italian novelist and poet Manzoni describes this idea very well in his *Promessi Sposi,* when speaking of the half-witted lad Gervaso, who "because he had taken part in a plot savouring of crime, felt that he had suddenly become a man."

This idea lurks in the slang word *omerta* used by Italian criminals, which signifies not only to be a man but a man daring enough to break the law.


# CRIME AND HUMAN NATURE

*James Q. Wilson and Richard J. Herrnstein*

## Crime as Choice: The Theory in Brief

Our theory rests on the assumption that people, when faced with a choice, choose the preferred course of action. This assumption is quite weak; it says nothing more than that whatever people choose to do, they choose it because they prefer it. In fact, it is more than weak; without further clarification, it is a tautology. When we say people "choose," we do not necessarily mean that they consciously deliberate about what to do. All we mean is that their behavior is determined by its consequences. A person will do that thing the consequences of which are perceived by him or her to be preferable to the consequences of doing something else. What can save such a statement from being a tautology is how plausibly we describe the gains and losses associated with alternative courses of action and the standards by which a person evaluates those gains and losses.

These assumptions are commonplace in philosophy and social science. Philosophers speak of hedonism or utilitarianism, economists of value or utility, and psychologists of reinforcement or reward. We will use the language of psychology, but it should not be hard to translate our terminology into that of other disciplines. Though social scientists differ as to how much behavior can reasonably be described as the result of a choice, all agree that at least some behavior is guided, or even precisely controlled, by things variously termed pleasure, pain, happiness, sorrow, desirability, or the like. Our object is to show how this simple and widely used idea can be used to explain behavior.

At any given moment, a person can choose between committing a crime and not committing it (all these alternatives to crime we lump together as "noncrime"). The consequences of committing the crime consist of rewards (what psychologists call "reinforcers") and punishments; the consequences of not committing the crime (i.e., engaging in noncrime) also entail gains and losses. The larger the ratio of the net rewards of crime to the net rewards of noncrime, the greater the tendency to commit the crime. The net rewards of crime include, obviously, the likely material gains from the crime, but they also include intangible benefits, such as obtaining emotional or sexual gratification, receiving the approval of peers, satisfying an old score against an enemy, or enhancing one's sense of justice. One must deduct from these rewards of crime any losses that accrue immediately—that are, so to speak, contemporaneous with the crime. They include the pangs of conscience, the disapproval of onlookers, and the retaliation of the victim.

The value of noncrime lies all in the future. It includes the benefits to the individual of avoiding the risk of being caught and punished and, in addition, the benefits of avoiding penalties not controlled by the criminal justice system, such as the loss of reputation or the sense of shame afflicting a person later discovered to have broken the law and the possibility that, being known as a criminal, one cannot get or keep a job.

The value of any reward or punishment associated with either crime or noncrime is, to some degree, uncertain. A would-be burglar can rarely know exactly how much loot he will take away or what its cash value will prove to be. The assaulter or rapist may exaggerate the satisfaction he thinks will follow the assault or the rape. Many people do not know how sharp the bite of conscience will be until they have done something that makes them feel the bite. The anticipated approval of one's buddies may or may not be forthcoming. Similarly, the benefits of noncrime are uncertain. One cannot know with confidence whether one will be caught, convicted, and punished, or whether one's friends will learn about the crime and as a result withhold valued esteem, or whether one will be able to find or hold a job.

Compounding these uncertainties is time. The opportunity to commit a crime may be ready at hand (an open, unattended cash register in a store) or well in the future (a bank that, with planning and preparation, can be robbed). And the rewards associated with noncrime are almost invariably more distant than those connected with crime, perhaps many weeks or months distant. The strength of reinforcers tends to decay over time at rates that differ among individuals. As a result, the extent to which people take into account distant possibilities—a crime that can be committed only tomorrow, or punishment that will be inflicted only in a year—will affect whether they choose crime or noncrime. All of these factors—the strength of rewards, the problems of uncertainty and delay, and the way in which our sense of justice affects how we value the rewards—will be examined in the remainder of this chapter. . . .

## The Theory as a Whole

We assert that the chief value of a comprehensive theory of crime is that it will bring to our attention all the factors that explain individual differences in criminality and thus prevent us from offering partial explanations or making incomplete interpretations of research findings. The larger the ratio of the rewards (material and nonmaterial) of noncrime to the rewards (material and nonmaterial) of crime, the weaker the tendency to commit crimes. The bite of conscience, the approval of peers, and any sense of inequity will increase or decrease the total value of crime; the opinions of family, friends, and employers are important benefits of noncrime, as is the desire to avoid the penalties that can be imposed by the criminal justice system. The strength of any reward declines with time, but people differ in the rate at which they discount the future. The strength of a given reward is also affected by the total supply of reinforcers.

Some implications of the theory are obvious: Other things being equal, a reduction in the delay and uncertainty attached to the rewards of noncrime will reduce the probability of crime. But other implications are not so obvious. For instance, increasing the value of the rewards of noncrime (by increasing the severity of punishment) may not reduce a given individual's tendency to commit crime if he believes that these rewards are not commensurate with what he deserves. In this case, punishing him for preferring crime to noncrime may trigger hostility toward society in retaliation for the shortfall. The increased rewards for noncrime may be offset by an increased sense of inequity and hence an increased incentive for committing a crime. Or again: It may be easier to reduce crime by making penalties swifter or more certain, rather than more severe, if the persons committing crime are highly present-oriented (so that they discount even large rewards very sharply) or if they are likely to have their sense of inequity heightened by increases in the severity of punishment. Or yet again: An individual with an extroverted personality is more likely than one with an introverted one to externalize his feelings of inequity and act directly to correct them.

In laboratory settings involving both human and animal subjects, each element of the theory has received at least some confirmation and the major elements have been confirmed extensively. Extrapolating these findings outside the laboratory, into real-world settings, is a matter on which opinions differ. We propose to bring together evidence from a variety of disciplines bearing on the connection between elements of the theory and the observed characteristics of crime and criminals.

The connection between crime and impulsiveness has been demonstrated as has the link between (low) intelligence and crime. Those features of family life that produce stronger or weaker internalized inhibitions will be seen to have a connection to the presence or absence of aggressiveness and criminality. Certain subcultures, such as street-corner gangs, appear to affect the value members attach to both crime and noncrime. The mass media, and in particular television, may affect both aggressiveness directly and a viewer's sense of inequity that can affect crime indirectly. Schooling may affect crime rates by bringing certain persons together into groups that reinforce either crime or noncrime and by determining the extent to which children believe that their skills will give them access to legitimate rewards. The condition of the economy will have a complex effect on crime depending on whether the (possibly) restraint-weakening impact of affluence dominates the restraint-strengthening influence of employment opportunities.

Though we will be using, for the most part, examples of rather common criminality to illustrate our argument, the theory is quite consistent with the more bizarre and unusual forms of crime. Psychopathic personalities lack to an unusual degree internalized inhibitions on crime. Persons possessed by some obsessive interest—for example, pyromania— attach an inordinately high value to the rewards of certain crimes. If everyone loved fire too much, society would try hard to teach the moral evil of fire, as well as its practical danger. As it is, what society does teach is sufficient to overcome whatever slight tendency toward pyromania every average person may have, but it is insufficient to inhibit the rare pyromaniac. One reason society punishes arsonists is not only to make it more costly for persons to use fire for material gain but also to provide extra moral education to the occasional person who loves fire for its own sake.

In addition to pathological drives, there are ordinary ones that can, under certain conditions, become so strong as to lead to crime. History and literature abound with normal men and women in the grip of a too powerful reinforcement. Many people have broken the law for love, honor, family, and country, as well as for money, sex, vengeance, or delusion. Such criminals may be psychologically unremarkable; they transgressed because as they perceived the situation the reward for crime exceeded that for noncrime, and an opportunity presented itself. The legal system often tries to minimize the punishment inflicted on such people.

# CONTEMPORARY RETROSPECTIVE ON BIOSOCIAL THEORIES

## CONTEMPORARY PERSPECTIVES ON BIOLOGICAL AND BIOSOCIAL THEORIES OF CRIME

*Matt DeLisi, Iowa State University; Kevin M. Beaver, Florida State University; Michael G. Vaughn, Saint Louis University; and John Paul Wright, University of Cincinnati*

The search for the environmental plasticity of behavior will undoubtedly continue, but the situationalist is well-advised not to ignore the data from allied fields. Like gravity, genotypes seem to exert a pervasive effect on behavioral phenotypes that unless we look at their effect on the trajectories of people's lives, will pass unnoticed because they are an invisible part of everyone. (David Rowe, 1987, p. 226)

No area of criminological thought has more baggage than biological theory. It is the most caricaturized, most vilified, and least understood body of theory and research in criminology. Most professional criminologists will be the first to admit that they have little to no training, knowledge, or understanding of biological processes and correlates of antisocial behavior. Much of this antagonistic relationship between criminological theory and biological theory stems from disciplinary viewpoints and training. Most professional criminologists were trained as sociologists and the preponderance of criminological theory is sociological in orientation (see Wright & Miller, 1998). According to this view, the environment and phenomena *external* to people are viewed as causal agents, not characteristics internal to the individual. Thus, if Edwin Sutherland and Donald Cressey decreed that delinquent behavior is learned and not inherited, that tended to be sufficient proof for many criminologists. Consequently, some have simply pretended that biology had nothing to say about the study of crime. For instance, in his presidential address to the American Sociological Association, Douglas Massey (2002) admonished, "Somehow we have allowed the fact that we are social beings to obscure the biological foundation upon which our behavior ultimately rests. Most sociologists are woefully ignorant of even the most elementary precepts of biological science. If we think about biology at all, it is usually in terms of discredited eugenic arguments and crude evolutionary theorizing long since discarded in the natural sciences" (p. 1).

There are other reasons why biological theory has baggage, namely the dark history of repressive policies that were based in biological theory. Francis Galton, a cousin of Charles Darwin, coined the term *eugenics* to describe the science of improving the human race through better breeding. According to eugenicists, an inherited substance in the blood called "germ plasma" that is present at conception determines *all* of an individual's mental, moral, and physical characteristics. The moment someone commits a crime, that fact is encoded in his or her blood and is transmitted to any off-spring. In 1877, Richard Dugdale used this idea to study intelligence and deviancy. In *The Jukes,* he located more than 1,000 descendants of Ada Jukes and found they included 140 criminals, 280 paupers, 40 people with venereal disease, and assorted other deviant types. Dugdale concluded that the Jukes suffered from "degeneracy and innate depravity." In *The Kallikak Family,* Henry Goddard (1912) traced the descendants of Martin Kallikak, who "had two lines of progeny, one from a 'feeble-minded' barmaid and the other from a 'respectable' girl of a good family." The illegitimate union produced many paupers, criminals, alcoholics, and people with mentally deficiencies, while there were few of these types found among descendants of the legitimate union.

Eugenics was popular in the early twentieth century. It had become so much a part of the American landscape that laws were passed making it illegal for African Americans and whites and for Asian Americans and whites to marry. In 1922 and 1924 federal laws were passed to restrict the immigration of southern and eastern Europeans into the United States. The "inferior" people who already lived in the United States were institutionalized and sterilized in record numbers. In 1907, Indiana passed the first sterilization law, with Connecticut following soon after. In total, 33 states passed laws prescribing the compulsory sterilization of citizens who were feebleminded, mentally ill, and chronic criminal offenders. In spite of these statutes, sterilization did not gain widespread acceptance in the United States until the 1920s. In 1927, the U.S. Supreme Court ruled in *Buck v. Bell* that sterilization laws were constitutional. Borrowing from the Court's reasoning in *Buck,* the German Nazi government passed legislation that provided the legal basis for sterilizing at least 350,000 people. The second Supreme Court case to examine the legality of sterilization was based on a 1935 Oklahoma law that prescribed the involuntary sexual sterilization of chronic criminal offenders. In *Skinner v. Oklahoma* (1942), the Court ruled that involuntary sexual sterilization of criminals was illegal.

With such a dark history, it is easy to understand why biological approaches to criminology have been viewed as controversial. Early scholars, such as Cesare Lombroso, Henry Goodard, Charles Goring, and Enrico Ferri, focused on biological traits purported to contribute to criminal behavior. In many cases, these early approaches were crude, such as Lombroso's idea that criminals were evolutionary savages with distinct flaws or *stigmata* or the general fixation on intelligence as the determinant of a person's total capacity, character, and worth. In other cases, biological criminology was campy and difficult to take seriously (e.g., "Hunchbacks are extremely rare among murderers but are more common among rapists, forgers, and arsonists" [Lombroso, 1876/2006, p. 56]).

But that is history. The crude and insensitive inquiry that typified biological theory no longer exists and the status of biological theory can be effectively summarized with four points. First, biological theory is no longer called biological theory because it is evident that human behavior is the product of an interaction between individual-level factors and environmental factors. Criminological research that incorporates biological constructs is today called *biosocial criminology*. Second, there is no unified biosocial theory of crime in the same way that self-control, anomie, or general strain theories are coherent bodies of thought. Instead, biosocial theory is comprised of dozens of areas of research spanning the fields of psychology, psychiatry, pediatrics, behavioral genetics, molecular genetics, and related fields. Third, biosocial theory does not cite physical appearances as causes or correlates of criminality. Instead biosocial theory asserts that variations in individual-level traits, behaviors, personality and cognitive features, hormones, physiological factors, genetic factors, and brain functioning contribute to criminality. Fourth, and perhaps most importantly, biosocial theory seeks to explain the ways that *nature and nurture interact to produce human behavior.* In this way, biosocial theory not only affirms the importance of environmental (read, social) causes of behavior, but also is dependent on social causes of behavior.

Three articles exemplify the latter point and are reviewed here. These articles were chosen because they represent the four aspects of contemporary biosocial research. David Rowe's (1987) work is a primer on behavioral genetics and shows how variation in behavioral outcomes can be decomposed into genetic factors (heritability), family factors (shared or common-family environment), and selection factors (nonshared environment). Using personality as an illustration, Rowe's (1987, 1994, 2002) work shows that the stability across situations in terms of personality expression has significantly less to do with situational exigencies and more to do with heredity or genetics. Rowe's article builds on developmental psychology research, especially the seminal work of Sandra Scarr (see Scarr, 1992; Scarr & Carter-Saltzman, 1979; Scarr & McCartney, 1983; Scarr & Weinberg, 1978). The reason that Rowe's essay is reviewed here is that he was principally a criminologist and indeed was arguably the most influential biosocial criminologist in recent decades.

Terrie Moffitt's (1993) developmental taxonomy is among the most cited and influential recent developments in criminology. In it, Moffitt suggests two archetypal categories of offenders: a normative group called adolescence-limited offenders that represent about 90% of the offender population, and a pathological group called life-course-persistent offenders that represent about 10% or less of the offender population. Generally, adolescence-limited offenders engage in benign, rebellious forms of delinquency and have nonexistent or sparse criminal careers. Conversely, life-course-persistent offenders engage in many types of delinquency, including serious and violent forms, and are likely to become habitual criminals.

Moffitt was very clear that different factors work to produce life-course-persistent offenders and adolescence-limited offenders. The origin of life-course-persistent offending is due to the interaction between two different factors, neuropsychological deficits and an adverse home environment. Moffitt's identification of neuropsychological problems as a causal agent in the etiology of life-course-persistent offenders was an important contribution to the criminological literature. Children with neuropsychological problems are frequently hard to manage, manifest difficult temperaments, and engage in serious troublesome behavior from a very early age (Moffitt, 1990). The constellation of problems caused by neurological deficits thus places these children at high risk for becoming a life-course-persistent offender. Moffitt also identified the child's home environment as a second factor implicated in the development of life-course-persistent offending. What happens is that a transactional process unfolds where children with neurological impairments elicit responses from their rearing environment. Most of the time parents are equipped with the necessary skills to respond to and deal with difficult children in an appropriate manner. When this occurs, the environment is able to blunt the problems associated with neuropsychological problems. However, in some situations a child who is neuropsychologically impaired is raised by abusive or otherwise criminogenic parents. The reactions by these types of parents exacerbate the antisocial propensities of their child and the end result is the formation of a life-course-persistent offender. In short, life-course-persistent offenders are created by complex interactions between neuropsychological deficiencies and an adverse home environment.

Heavily rooted in the behavioral genetics literature, Judith Rich Harris (1995) answers the question "Do parents have any important long-term effects on the development of their child's personality?" with a resounding "No!" Harris argues that the peer relationships that children form with other children are primarily responsible for inculcating culture and modifying innate personality features. It is within these friendship groups that the psychological traits that a child is born with become permanently modified by the environment. Harris (1995, p. 482) argues that two processes occur. Assimilation transmits cultural norms, smoothes off rough edges of the personality, and makes children more like their peers. Differentiation exaggerates individual differences and increases variability. Whether assimilation or differentiation occurs at a given point depends on the context of the interaction (e.g., participating in a sporting event, sitting in the classroom, playing at recess, etc.). In behavioral genetic parlance, this means that the effects of the nonshared environment are significantly more powerful than shared environmental effects. Harris's work has had the greatest public impact and is most controversial mainly because *it destroys the notion that parents are most responsible for people's personalities and behaviors because of the ways that they socialize their children.* Instead, parents are important because they pass on their genetic information to their children. Otherwise, personality and behaviors are molded by peer relationships occurring outside the home.

## Critiques

On the surface, the three works just reviewed seem to be very different and not part of a coherent area of criminological theory. Taken together, the works make two main contributions. First, they make explicit the reality that nature and nurture, biology and sociology, and genetics and environment work in tandem to explain behavioral outcomes. In this way, they challenge the orthodoxy of major schools of thought, especially Harris's and Rowe's work that shows the power of nonshared over shared or familial effects on behavior. Second, by showing the extreme variation that exists across individual-level traits and behaviors, they provide compelling evidence that there are different "types" of people who can be scientifically classified according to personality characteristics and traits (Rowe) or criminality (Moffitt). For example, although both adolescence-limited and life-course-persistent offenders engage in delinquency, it would be a mistake to conclude that they are similar (i.e., that they are differently named delinquent groups). Instead, they are quantitatively and qualitatively different forms of antisocial behavior. Particularly in the case of life-course-persistent offenders, Moffitt's theory shows that various behavioral manifestations are differently influenced by the nature–nurture duality. The etiology of adolescence-limited offending is primarily social; the etiology of life-course-persistent offending is biosocial. That is a critically important distinction.

If there is a legitimate critique of these articles and the areas of scholarship they represent, it is that they provide too little guidance to criminologists as a way to test the theories as they relate to criminal behavior. These works are the foundation upon which more recent research can build. For example, Rowe's work provides a clear primer on behavioral genetics and the ways to decompose variation into its three constitutive parts (heredity, shared environment, and nonshared environment). What is missing is guidance on conducting molecular genetic research where measured genes are used as predictors of behavior (see Rowe, 2002). In other words, it is one thing to specify that a certain percentage of variance is attributable to heredity, but it is more specific to show that specific genes (e.g., MAOA, DRD2, DAT1, 5HTT, etc.) are associated with specific behaviors (e.g., psychopathy, conduct disorder, ADHD, violent crime, etc.). (This limitation is discussed later in this chapter.) Fortunately, these works served as the impetus for subsequent researchers to use new datasets, including datasets with measured genes, to specify the ways that biosocial factors result in crime.

## Empirical Evaluations

In the past few decades, there has been extensive research supporting the link between biological phenomena such as low resting heart rate; autonomic functioning; genetic basis of ADHD and related behavioral syndromes; links between cortisol, testosterone, and violence, and so on (see Raine, 1993; Walsh, 2002; Walsh & Beaver, 2008) and crime. In terms of the articles showcased in this chapter, there has also been a flurry of empirical research that resoundingly supports the claims of the authors.

In terms of Rowe's and Harris's research, it is now simply understood that genetic factors account for between 40 and 60% of the variance in antisocial behaviors as shown by several recent meta-analyses (Mason & Frick, 1994; Miles & Carey, 1997; Moffitt, 2005; Rhee & Waldman, 2002). More than criminology thought possible and would perhaps like to admit, the etiology of delinquent behavior is deeply rooted in our genes. On this, the evidence is incontrovertible. Another empirical trend suggests that heredity or genetic factors are implicated more strongly in more pathological forms of antisocial behavior (DeLisi, 2008). For instance, callous-unemotional traits including guiltlessness, lack of consideration of other people's feelings, meanness, disinterest in school and behavioral performance, social isolation, and rare display of feelings or emotion are prodromes of psychopathy (see Rutter, 2005). Importantly, the early warning signs of severe antisocial behavior are strongly heritable. To illustrate, a recent study of callous-unemotional traits and antisocial behavior among 3,687 twin pairs indicated that 67% of variation in extreme callous-unemotional traits among 7-year-old children was attributable to genetics. When examining extreme antisocial behavior in 7-year-olds with psychopathic tendencies, genes accounted for 81% of the variation (Viding, Blair, Moffitt, & Plomin, 2005). A subsequent study found that 71% of conduct problems in boys and 77% in girls were attributable to genetic influences (Viding, Frick, & Plomin, 2007).

Of course, genetics do not account for all the variance in criminological outcomes; environmental influences are also crucial, but all environmental influences are not equal. Research clearly shows that 40 to 50% of variance in crime is attributable to nonshared environment factors and that between 0 and 10% is the result of shared (family) environment (see Beaver, 2008; Plomin, DeFries, Craig, & McGuffin, 2003; Rowe & Plomin, 1981). According to Robert Plomin and Denise Daniels (1987), "behavioral genetic studies consistently point to nonshared environment as the most important source of environmental variance for personality, psychology, and IQ after childhood . . . children in the same family experience practically no shared environmental influence that makes them similar for behavior traits" (pp. 15–16). That the nonshared environment is so important and the shared environment so comparatively unimportant is precisely the thesis of Harris's (1995) work. In fact, Harris (1998, 2007) has since produced two national bestsellers that build on the empirical foundations of behavioral genetic and biosocial research to show the primacy of heredity and nonshared environment as determinants of human behavior. In this way, the biosocial approach has entered the Zeitgeist.

While Harris's ideas diffused into American culture, Terrie Moffitt's developmental taxonomy has been nothing short of a juggernaut in the research community. To date, her 1993 article has been cited nearly 1,900 times and her delineation of a normative, delayed criminal onset group and a pathological, early criminal onset group has been influential, appearing in the American Psychiatric Association's fourth edition of the *Diagnostic and Statistical Manual of Mental Disorders (DSM–IV)*; numerous theories of delinquency in the social sciences; and summary reports or fact sheets produced by the National Institute of Mental Health, United States Surgeon General, World Health Organization, National Institutes of Health, and others (Cullen, Wright, & Blevins, 2006). Empirically, the pathology of the life-course-persistent offender has been differentially predicted by individual-level, biosocial factors, including neurological abnormalities, autonomic hypoactivity (e.g., low resting heart rate), low cognitive ability, low birth weight, maternal cigarette use, perinatal complications, and neuropsychological deficits (Gibson & Tibbetts, 2000; Moffitt & Caspi, 2001; Raine, Brennan, & Mednick, 1997; Tibbetts & Piquero, 1999). The essential conclusion to distill from this area of research is the combinatory importance of biological, sociological, and biosocial variables that *interact and mutually reinforce* to produce antisocial behavior (Caspi, Henry, McGee, Moffitt, & Silva, 1995).

## Theoretical Refinements

The current state and the foreseeable future of theory and research in the biosocial area can cogently be summarized by two words: molecular genetics. The work of Rowe, Moffitt, and Harris provided the conceptual foundation on which molecular genetic research is based, which can use measured genes as variables in multivariate models to show precisely the ways that some of the approximately 30,000 genes work to influence antisocial behavior. Basically, molecular genetics research adds specificity and refinement to the story of how biological and environmental constructs interact. Interestingly, much of the research that informs biosocial criminology is conducted by noncriminologists, many of whom study other behavioral outcomes relating to psychopathology (but see Beaver et al., 2007a, 2007b). There are many examples of this research. For instance, drawing on data from the

E-Risk Study, a nationally representative cohort of 1,116 5-year-old British twin pairs and their families, Louise Arseneault and her colleagues (2003) found that 82% of the etiology of childhood antisocial behavior was explained by genetic factors. Moreover, genetic vulnerabilities interact with abusive environments to produce antisocial behavior. To illustrate, children who were victims of maltreatment were significantly likely to present conduct problems. The effect of maltreatment on conduct problems was *12 times* stronger among youths with genetic risk factors than those without genetic risks (Jaffee et al., 2005).

Based on data from the Minnesota Twin Family Study, Blonigen, Hicks, Krueger, Patrick, and Iacono (2005) found that adolescent psychopathic traits are also differentially predicted by genetic factors. Specifically, fearless dominance, which is marked by social potency, stress immunity, and fearlessness, was associated with reduced genetic risk for internalizing psychopathology. Impulsive antisociality, which is marked by negative emotionality (aggression and alienation) and low behavioral constraint (impulsivity and sensation seeking), was associated with increased genetic risk for externalizing psychopathology. For both males and females, the heritability estimates for fearless dominance (45%), impulsive antisociality (49%), internalizing of psychopathology (36%), and externalizing of psychopathology (73%) were moderate to high.

In a landmark study, Avshalom Caspi and his colleagues (2002) studied the polymorphism in the gene that encodes the neurotransmitter-metabolizing enzyme monoamine oxidase A (MAOA), which metabolizes neurotransmitters such as norepinephrine, serotonin, and dopamine. They examined the interaction between MAOA levels and childhood maltreatment for four antisocial outcomes: conduct disorder, disposition toward violence, antisocial personality disorder, and conviction for a violent offense. For all four outcomes, the association between maltreatment and antisocial behavior was conditional on the MAOA genotype. Although just 12% of the sample had genetic risk (low MAOA levels) and maltreatment, they accounted for an alarming 44% of the total cohort convictions for violent crime. Moreover, 85% of youths who had both genetic and environmental risk factors developed some form of antisocial behavior. In the absence of maltreatment, the genotypic risk factor did not manifest because genetic expression is contingent on environmental conditions.

Molecular genetics research has yielded great insight into the genetic underpinnings of childhood and adolescent forms of antisocial behavior, such as conduct disorder (CD), oppositional defiant disorder (ODD), and attention deficit hyperactivity disorder (ADHD). If co-occurring, these psychiatric diagnoses create a cascading effect that is likely to result in serious delinquency and even habitual criminal conduct (DeLisi, 2005). David Comings and his colleagues (2000a) explored the predictive value of 20 genes on CD, ODD, and ADHD. The analyses included 6 dopaminergic genes (DRD1, DRD2, DRD3, DRD4, DRD5, and DAT1), 7 serotonergic genes (5HTT, HTR1A, HTR1B, HTR1DA, HTR2A, TDO2, and TRH), and 7 noradrenergic genes (DBH, ADRA2A, ADRAB, ADRA2C, PNMT, NET, and COMT). The 3 strongest dopamine genes contributed to just over 2% of the variance, the 3 strongest serotonin genes contributed to 3% of the variance, and the 6 strongest adrenergic genes accounted for about 7% of the variance in ADHD. Similar predictive effects were found for CD and ODD.

A follow-up study included 42 genes including 6 new neurotransmitter genes: CHNRA4, ADOA2A, NOS3, NMDAR1, GRIN2B, and GABRB3. Comings and his colleagues (2000b) again found that noradrenergic genes were the strongest predictors of ADHD and ODD. On the other hand, the genes that were most helpful in predicting CD were hormone and neuropeptide genes, such as CCK, CYP19, ESRI, and INS. While this listing of genes may appear confusing to the casual reader, it is important to note that the use of measured genes is a natural extension of the behavioral genetic approach described in the Rowe and Harris articles. Behavioral genetics estimates the explanatory power of heredity; molecular genetics dives into that explanatory power to show the proportional predictive value of individual genes or groups of similar genes.

Jonathan Mill and his colleagues (2006) explored the links between two dopamine genes (DRD4 and DAT1) on ADHD and intellectual functioning. Their longitudinal epidemiologic investigation examined two birth cohorts: the E-Risk Study of 2,232 children in England and the Dunedin New Zealand birth cohort including 1,037 children. The findings were alarming. Both DRD4 and DAT1 predicted intellectual functioning and ADHD. Respondents in the Dunedin study were followed up to age 26 and evaluated for 10 adult outcomes, including violent conviction, nonviolent conviction, substance abuse diagnosis, psychiatric diagnoses, aggression against partner, aggression against minors, no high school qualification, out-of-wedlock parenthood, government welfare benefits, and long-term unemployment of more than six months. Children who had been diagnosed with ADHD were significantly likely to experience multiple negative adult outcomes and the effects were largely accounted for by DRD4 and DAT1. In other words, the influence of just two genes on 10 forms of psychopathology was shown nearly three decades into life.

Just as the dopaminergic system relates to antisocial behavior, the serotonergic system is important because it is the system that modulates behavior, specifically the 5HTT gene which has consistently been associated with ADHD (Bobb, Castellanos, Addington, & Rapoport, 2006). The 5HTT gene is also associated with criminal and violent behavior in adulthood as well as personality disorders that co-occur with crime. In this sense, 5HTT is one of likely many genes that contribute to antisocial behavior across the life course. For example, Wolfgang Retz, Retz-Junginger, Supprian, Thome, and Rosler (2004) explored the effects of 5HTT among 153 male forensic psychiatric patients, 72 of which were violent offenders. Nearly 1 in 4 violent patients had two risk alleles for 5HTT, a prevalence estimate that was nearly three times greater than the prevalence among nonviolent psychiatric patients. Nearly 81% of violent patients had at least one risk allele and there was a significant overrepresentation of the risk 5HTT genotype among subgroups with personality disorders. Recent research also reported that 5HTT plays a part in the functioning of the amygdala, bilateral parts of the limbic system of the brain that play a primary role in the processing and memory of emotions in particular the modulation of fear (also see Meyer-Lindenberg et al., 2006). The significance of this is that the emotional impairments produced by amygdala dysfunction are at the heart of recent causal explanations for psychopathy (Blair, Mitchell, & Blair, 2005).

## Policy Applications

The beginning of this chapter noted that biological theories of crime carry considerable baggage and the bulk of this negative connotation pertains to historical policies rooted in a biological-based understanding of behavior. Even today, when we present our own behavioral genetic or molecular genetic research at conferences, there is always concern, sometimes vociferously voiced concern, about the potentially repressive policies that will result from an informed scientific understanding of the biological basis of crime. This concern originates from ignorance of biosocial criminology and the misguided prejudice that some hold against biosocial criminology. Actually, the public policies that logically stem from a biological and biosocial view of crime have been in place for decades and will continue to be used indefinitely.

Having a biological risk for antisocial behavior—such as a low resting heart rate, elevated levels of testosterone or cortisol, male gender, or risk alleles of a specific gene—is simply one facet of the multifaceted network of characteristics, traits, and behaviors found in the background of serious offenders. In fact, there are dozens of powerful risk factors for antisocial behavior. Difficult temperament, impulsivity, hyperactivity, disruptive behavior, aggression, substance use, withdrawn behaviors, low verbal intelligence, exposure to environmental toxins such as lead and the like are child factors that contribute to crime. For family factors, parental psychopathology, parental crime, parental criminal justice system involvement, abuse, neglect, poor child-rearing practices, poor supervision and monitoring, teenage motherhood, prenatal exposure to cigarettes and other pathogens, large family size, family poverty, unemployed father, and many other variables contribute to delinquency. Associating with delinquent siblings and peers, being rejected by one's peers, being poorly bonded to school, having poor school performance, residing in a disorganized neighborhood with exposure to drugs, guns, and violence are additional risk factors for antisocial behavior (Loeber & Farrington, 2001). Prevention and treatment programs are well aware of these risk factors; indeed, they are designed to develop and bolster prosocial characteristics that serve to protect people from crime while reducing risk factors. The prevention and treatment of crime is the identification and management of risk. There is nothing extraordinary about a biological risk factor for crime; it is one of many elemental determinants of behavior (see Farrington & Welsh, 2007).

A landmark prevention study that demonstrated the long-term effects of early life interventions based on assessments of risk is the Nurse-Family Partnership program supervised by David Olds and his colleagues (1998a). Based on a sample of 400 women and 315 infants born in upstate New York between April 1978 and September 1980, the women in the sample posed a variety of risk factors for their children becoming antisocial. All were unmarried, 48% were less than 15 years of age, and 59% of the mothers lived in poverty. Via random assignment to four groups receiving various social services, the comprehensive experimental group received 9 home visits during pregnancy and 23 home visits from nurses from birth until the child's second birthday. Control subjects received standard, but less comprehensive prenatal care. All groups were followed up 15 years later.

The results were impressive in the reduction of a variety of problem behaviors associated with chronic delinquency. Compared to controls, boys who were in the treatment groups had a lower incidence of running away; accumulated significantly fewer arrests and convictions; accrued fewer probationary sentences and subsequent violations; had fewer lifetime sexual partners; and had a lower prevalence of smoking, alcoholism, and casual alcohol use. In short, the experiment offered compelling evidence that early-life interventions that teach parents the skills they need to raise healthy children were achievable (Olds et al., 1998a).

The Nurse-Family Partnership program is one of the model prevention programs in the country and is part of the Blueprints for Violence Prevention Program at the Center for the Study and Prevention of Violence at the University of Colorado at Boulder. The Blueprints for Violence Prevention Program is a national violence prevention initiative that identifies programs that meet the most scientifically rigorous standards of program effectiveness. They have found that the nurse visits in the Olds study resulted in 79% fewer verified reports of child abuse and neglect; 31% fewer subsequent births and increased interval between births; 30-month reduction in the receipt of Aid to Families with Dependent Children, a social welfare subsidy; 44% fewer maternal behavioral problems due to substance abuse; 69% fewer maternal arrests; and 56% fewer children arrests. Most impressively from a policy perspective, the costs of the program, approximately $3,200 per family annually, were recouped by the child's fourth birthday (Olds, Hill, Mihalic, & O'Brien, 1998b). The approach has since been replicated on other study populations (e.g., African American and Hispanic), continued over longer follow-up periods, and shown to be an effective intervention for a host of antisocial outcomes (Olds, 2002).

That research findings emanating from biosocial criminology are so amenable to prevention, treatment, and public policy is good news and hopefully will mark an era in criminology where biological constructs are rightfully seen as integral to the study of crime. We are proud to announce that this shifting paradigm is already underway. For example, Mary Gibson and Nicole Hahn Rafter recently translated all five editions of Lombroso's *Criminal Man* into English. Their description of that project is illuminating (1876/2006):

> We began this project with a disdain for what we understood as the simplemindedness of Lombroso's theory of atavism and with a fear that his biological determinism was prejudicial to women, blacks, and other social groups that he deemed inferior. Many of his conclusions seemed silly, and his project a particularly frightful example of bad science. But our views have changed, based on our careful reading of his criminological oeuvre . . . Lombroso now appears to have been a curious, engaged and energetic polymath with a tremendous appetite for literature, art, folklore, as well as natural science, medicine, psychiatry, and law. That he was careless and often wrong about the conclusions that he drew from the disparate data provided by these fields does not detract from the significance of his enterprise. (pp. 1–2)

In the genomic era, cataclysmic scientific discoveries are made on an almost weekly basis. Neuroscience is shining light on the mechanisms of nature and nurture that underscore human existence and human behavior. This scientific advance has already infiltrated criminology. If not now then very soon, biosocial theory, an area once completely marginalized and ridiculed within criminology, will become the definite statement of crime.

# PART III

# SOCIAL DISORGANIZATION THEORY

# JUVENILE DELINQUENCY AND URBAN AREAS

*Clifford R. Shaw and Henry D. McKay*

## Differential Systems of Values

In general, the more subtle differences between types of communities in Chicago may be encompassed within the general proposition that in the areas of low rates of delinquents there is more or less uniformity, consistency, and universality of conventional values and attitudes with respect to child care, conformity to law, and related matters; whereas in the high-rate areas systems of competing and conflicting moral values have developed. Even though in the latter situation conventional traditions and institutions are dominant, delinquency has developed as a powerful competing way of life. It derives its impelling force in the boy's life from the fact that it provides a means of securing economic gain, prestige, and other human satisfactions and is embodied in delinquent groups and criminal organizations, many of which have great influence, power, and prestige.

In the areas of high economic status where the rates of delinquents are low there is, in general, a similarity in the attitudes of the residents with reference to conventional values, as has been said, especially those related to the welfare of children. This is illustrated by the practical unanimity of opinion as to the desirability of education and constructive leisure-time activities and of the need for a general health program. It is shown, too, in the subtle, yet easily recognizable, pressure exerted upon children to keep them engaged in conventional activities, and in the resistance offered by the community to behavior which threatens the conventional values. It does not follow that all the activities participated in by members of the community are lawful; but, since any unlawful pursuits are likely to be carried out in other parts of the city, children living in the low-rate communities are, on the whole, insulated from direct contact with these deviant forms of adult behavior.

In the middle-class areas and the areas of high economic status, moreover, the similarity of attitudes and values as to social control is expressed in institutions and voluntary associations designed to perpetuate and protect these values. Among these may be included such organizations as the parent-teachers associations, women's clubs, service clubs, churches, neighborhood centers, and the like. Where these institutions represent dominant values, the child is exposed to, and participates in a significant way in one mode of life only. While he may have knowledge of alternatives, they are not integral parts of the system in which he participates.

In contrast, the areas of low economic status, where the rates of delinquents are high, are characterized by wide diversity in norms and standards of behavior. The moral values range from those that are strictly conventional to those in direct opposition to conventionality as symbolized by the family, the church, and other institutions common to our general society. The deviant values are symbolized by groups and institutions ranging from adult criminal gangs engaged in theft and the marketing of stolen goods, on the one hand, to quasi-legitimate businesses and the rackets through which partial or complete control of legitimate business is sometimes exercised, on the other. Thus, within the same community, theft may be defined as right and proper in some groups and as immoral, improper, and undesirable in others. In some groups wealth and prestige are secured through acts of skill and courage in the delinquent or criminal world, while in neighboring groups any attempt to achieve distinction in this manner would result in extreme disapprobation. Two conflicting systems of economic activity here present roughly equivalent opportunities for employment and for promotion. Evidence of success in the criminal world is indicated by the presence of adult criminals whose clothes and automobiles indicate unmistakably that they have prospered in their chosen fields. The values missed and the greater risks incurred are not so clearly apparent to the young.

Children living in such communities are exposed to a variety of contradictory standards and forms of behavior rather than to a relatively consistent and conventional pattern. More than one type of moral institution and education are available to them. A boy may be familiar with, or exposed to, either the system of conventional activities or the system of criminal activities, or both. Similarly, he may participate in the activities of groups which engage mainly in delinquent activities, those concerned with conventional pursuits, or those which alternate between the two worlds. His attitudes and habits will be formed largely in accordance with the extent to which he participates in and becomes identified with one or the other of these several types of groups.

Conflicts of values necessarily arise when boys are brought in contact with so many forms of conduct not reconcilable with conventional morality as expressed in church and school. A boy may be found guilty of delinquency in the court, which represents the values of the larger society, for an act which has had at least tacit approval in the community in which he lives. It is perhaps common knowledge in the neighborhood that public funds are embezzled and that favors and special consideration can be received from some public officials through the payment of stipulated sums; the boys assume that all officials can be influenced in this way. They are familiar with the location of illegal institutions in the community and with the procedures through which such institutions are opened and kept in operation; they know where stolen goods can be sold and the kinds of merchandise for which there is a ready market; they know what the rackets are; and they see in fine clothes, expensive cars, and other lavish expenditures the evidences of wealth among those who openly engage in illegal activities. All boys in the city have some knowledge of these activities; but in the inner-city areas they are known intimately, in terms of personal relationships, while in other sections they enter the child's experience through more impersonal forms of communication, such as motion pictures, the newspapers, and the radio.

Other types of evidence tending to support the existence of diverse systems of values in various areas are to be found in the data on delinquency and crime. When translated into its significance for children, the presence of a large number of adult criminals in certain areas means that children there are in contact with crime as a career and with the criminal way of life, symbolized by organized crime. In this type of organization can be seen the delegation of authority, the division of labor, the specialization of function, and all the other characteristics common to well-organized business institutions wherever found.

Similarly, the delinquency data presented graphically on spot maps and rate maps give plausibility to the existence of a coherent system of values supporting delinquent acts. In making these interpretations it should be remembered that delinquency is essentially group behavior. A study of boys brought into the Juvenile Court of Cook County during the year 1928 revealed that 81.8 per cent of these boys committed the offenses for which they were brought to court as members of groups. And when the offenses were limited to stealing, it was found that 89 per cent of all offenders were taken to court as group or gang members. In many additional cases where the boy actually committed his offense alone, the influence of companions was, nevertheless, apparent. This point is illustrated in certain cases of boys charged with stealing from members of their own families, where the theft clearly reflects the influence and instigation of companions, and in instances where the problems of the boy charged with incorrigibility reveal conflicting values, those of the family competing with those of the delinquent group for his allegiance.

The heavy concentration of delinquency in certain areas means, therefore, that boys living in these areas are in contact not only with individuals who engage in proscribed activity but also with groups which sanction such behavior and exert pressure upon their members to conform to group standards. Examination of the distribution map reveals that, in contrast with the areas of concentration of delinquents, there are many other communities where the cases are so widely dispersed that the chances of a boy's having intimate contact with other delinquents or with delinquent groups are comparatively slight.

The importance of the concentration of delinquents is seen most clearly when the effect is viewed in a temporal perspective. The maps representing distribution of delinquents at successive periods indicate that, year after year, decade after decade, the same areas have been characterized by these concentrations. This means that delinquent boys in these areas have contact not only with other delinquents who are their contemporaries but also with older offenders, who in turn had contact with delinquents preceding them, and so on back to the earliest history of the neighborhood. This contact means that the traditions of delinquency can be and are transmitted down through successive generations of boys, in much the same way that language and other social forms are transmitted.

The cumulative effect of this transmission of tradition is seen in two kinds of data, which will be presented here only very briefly. The first is a study of offenses, which reveals that certain types of delinquency have tended to characterize certain city areas. The execution of each type involves techniques which must be learned from others who have participated in the same activity. Each involves specialization of function, and each has its own terminology and standards of behavior. Jack-rolling, shoplifting, stealing from junkmen, and stealing automobiles are examples of offenses with well-developed techniques, passed on by one generation to the next.

The second body of evidence on the effects of the continuity of tradition within delinquent groups comprises the results of a study of the contacts between delinquents, made through the use of official records. The names of boys who appeared together in court were taken, and the range of their association with other boys whose names appeared in the same records was then analyzed and charted. It was found that some members of each delinquent group had participated in offenses in the company of other older boys, and so on, backward in time in an unbroken continuity as far as the records were available. The continuity thus traced is roughly comparable to that which might be established among baseball players through their appearance in official line-ups or regularly scheduled games. In baseball it is known that the techniques are transmitted through practice in back yards, playgrounds, sand lots, and in other places where boys congregate. Similarly in the case of delinquency traditions, if an unbroken continuity can be traced through formal institutions such as the Juvenile Court, the actual contacts among delinquents in the community must be numerous, continuous, and vital.

The way in which boys are inducted into unconventional behavior has been revealed by large numbers of case studies of youths living in areas where the rates of delinquents are high. Through the boy's own life-story the wide range of contacts with other boys has been revealed. These stories indicate how at early ages the boys took part with older boys in delinquent activities, and how, as they themselves acquired experience, they initiated others into the same pursuits. These cases reveal also the steps through which members are incorporated into the delinquent group organization. Often at early ages boys engage in malicious mischief and simple acts of stealing. As their careers develop, they become involved in more serious offenses, and finally become skilled workmen or specialists in some particular field of criminal activity. In each of these phases the boy is supported by the sanction and the approbation of the delinquent group to which he belongs. . . .

## Differential Social Organization

Other subtle differences among communities are to be found in the character of their local institutions, especially those specifically related to the problem of social control. The family, in areas of high rates of delinquents, is affected by the conflicting systems of values and the problems of survival and conformity with which it is confronted. Family organization in high-rate areas is affected in several different ways by the divergent systems of values encountered. In the first place, it may be made practically impotent by the existing interrelationships between the two systems. Ordinarily, the family is thought of as representing conventional values and opposed to deviant forms of behavior. Opposition from families within the area to illegal practices and institutions is lessened, however, by the fact that each system may be contributing in certain ways to the economic well-being of many large family groups. Thus, even if a family represents conventional values, some member, relative, or friend may be gaining a livelihood through illegal or quasi-legal institutions— a fact tending to neutralize the family's opposition to the criminal system.

Another reason for the frequent ineffectiveness of the family in directing boys' activities along conventional lines is doubtless the allegiance which the boys may feel they owe to delinquent groups. A boy is often so fully incorporated into the group that it exercises more control than does the family. This is especially true in those neighborhoods where most of the parents are European-born. There the parents' attitudes and interests reflect an Old World background, while their children are more fully Americanized and more sophisticated, assuming in many cases the role of interpreter. In this situation the parental control is weakened, and the family may be ineffective in competing with play groups and organized gangs in which life, though it may be insecure, is undeniably colorful, stimulating, and enticing.

A third possible reason for ineffectiveness of the family is that many problems with which it is confronted in delinquency areas are new problems, for which there is no traditional solution. An example is the use of leisure time by children. This is not a problem in the Old World or in rural American communities, where children start to work at an early age and have a recognized part in the system of production. Hence, there are no time-honored solutions for difficulties which arise out of the fact that children in the city go to work at a later age and have much more leisure at their disposal. In the absence of any accepted solution for this problem, harsh punishment may be administered; but this is often ineffective, serving only to alienate the children still more from family and home.

Other differences between high-rate and low-rate areas in Chicago are to be seen in the nature of the existing community organization. Thomas and Znaniecki have analyzed the effectively organized community in terms of the presence of social opinion with regard to problems of common interest, identical or at least consistent attitudes with reference to these problems, the ability to reach approximate unanimity on the question of how a problem should be dealt with, and the ability to carry this solution into action through harmonious co-operation.

Such practical unanimity of opinion and action does exist, on many questions, in areas where the rates of delinquents are low. But, in the high-rate areas, the very presence of conflicting systems of values operates against such unanimity. Other factors hindering the development of consistently effective attitudes with reference to these problems of public welfare are the poverty of these high-rate areas, the wide diversity of cultural backgrounds represented there, and the fact that the outward movement of population in a city like Chicago has resulted in the organization of life in terms of ultimate residence. Even though frustrated in his attempts to achieve economic security and to move into other areas, the immigrant, living in areas of first settlement, often has defined his goals in terms of the better residential community into which he hopes some day to move. Accordingly, the immediate problems of his present neighborhood may not be of great concern to him.

Another characteristic of the areas with high rates of delinquents is the presence of large numbers of nonindigenous philanthropic agencies and institutions—social settlements, boys' clubs, and similar agencies—established to deal with local problems. These are, of course, financed largely from outside the area. They are also controlled and staffed, in most cases, by persons other than local residents and should be distinguished from indigenous organizations and institutions growing out of the felt needs of the local citizens. The latter organizations, which include American institutions, Old World institutions, or a synthesis of the two, are rooted in each case in the sentiments and traditions of the people. The nonindigenous agencies, while they may furnish many services and be widely used, seldom become the people's institutions, because they are not outgrowths of the local collective life. The very fact that these nonindigenous private agencies long have been concentrated in delinquency areas without modifying appreciably the marked disproportion of delinquents concentrated there suggests a limited effectiveness in deterring boys from careers in delinquency and crime.

Tax-supported public institutions such as parks, schools, and playgrounds are also found in high-rate, as well as in low-rate, areas. These, too, are usually controlled and administered from without the local area; and, together with other institutions, they represent to the neighborhood the standards of the larger community. However, they may be actually quite different institutions in different parts of the city, depending on their meaning and the attitudes of the people toward them. If the school or playground adapts its program in any way to local needs and interests, with the support of local sentiment, it becomes a functioning part of the community; but, instead, it is often relatively isolated from the people of the area, if not in conflict with them. High rates of truants in the inner-city areas may be regarded as an indication of this separation.

These more subtle differences between contrasting types of areas are not assumed to be wholly distinct from the differences presented in quantitative form in earlier chapters. They are, no doubt, products or by-products of the same processes of growth which physically differentiate city areas and segregate the population on an economic basis. This economic segregation in itself, as has been said, does not furnish an explanation for delinquency. Negative cases are too numerous to permit such a conclusion. But in the areas of lowest economic status and least vocational opportunity a special setting is created in which the development of a system of values embodied in a social, economic, and prestige system in conflict with conventional values is not only a probability but an actuality.

The general theoretical framework within which all community data are interpreted will be fully stated in the concluding chapter. Briefly summarized, it is assumed that the differentiation of areas and the segregation of population within the city have resulted in wide variation of opportunities in the struggle for position within our social order. The groups in the areas of lowest economic status find themselves at a disadvantage in the struggle to achieve the goals idealized in our civilization. These differences are translated into conduct through the general struggle for those economic symbols which signify a desirable position in the larger social order. Those persons who occupy a disadvantageous position are involved in a conflict between the goals assumed to be attainable in a free society and those actually attainable for a large proportion of the population. It is understandable, then, that the economic position of persons living in the areas of least opportunity should be translated at times into unconventional conduct, in an effort to reconcile the idealized status and their practical prospects of attaining this status. Since, in our culture, status is determined largely in economic terms, the differences between contrasted areas in terms of economic status become the most important differences. Similarly, as might be expected, crimes against property are most numerous.

The physical, economic, and social conditions associated with high rates of delinquents in local communities occupied by [the] white population exist in exaggerated form in most of the Negro areas. Of all the population groups in the city, the Negro people occupy the most disadvantageous position in relation to the distribution of economic and social values. Their efforts to achieve a more satisfactory and advantageous position in the economic and social life of the city are seriously thwarted by many restrictions with respect to residence, employment, education, and social and cultural pursuits. These restrictions have contributed to the development of conditions within the local community conducive to an unusually large volume of delinquency. . . .

The development of divergent systems of values requires a type of situation in which traditional conventional control is either weak or nonexistent. It is a well-known fact that the growth of cities and the increase in devices for transportation and communication have so accelerated the rate of change in our society that the traditional means of social control, effective in primitive society and in isolated rural communities, have been weakened everywhere and rendered especially ineffective in large cities. Moreover, the city, with its anonymity, its emphasis on economic rather than personal values, and its freedom and tolerance, furnishes a favorable situation for the development of devices to improve one's status, outside of the conventionally accepted and approved methods. This tendency is stimulated by the fact that the wide range of secondary social contacts in modern life operates to multiply the wishes of individuals. The automobile, motion pictures, magazine and newspaper advertising, the radio, and other means of communication flaunt luxury standards before all, creating or helping to create desires which often cannot be satisfied with the meager facilities available to families in areas of low economic status. The urge to satisfy the wishes and desires so created has helped to bring into existence and to perpetuate the existing system of criminal activities.

It is recognized that in a free society the struggle to improve one's status in terms of accepted values is common to all persons in all social strata. And it is a well-known fact that attempts are made by some persons in all economic classes to improve their positions by violating the rules and laws designed to regulate economic activity. However, it is assumed that these violations with reference to property are most frequent where the prospect of thus enhancing one's social status outweighs the chances for loss of position and prestige in the competitive struggle. It is in this connection that the existence of a system of values supporting criminal behavior becomes important as a factor in shaping individual life-patterns, since it is only where such a system exists that the person through criminal activity may acquire the material goods so essential to status in our society and at the same time increase, rather than lose, his prestige in the smaller group system of which he has become an integral part.

## Summary and Interpretation

It is clear from the data included in this volume that there is a direct relationship between conditions existing in local communities of American cities and differential rates of delinquents and criminals. Communities with high rates have social and economic characteristics which differentiate them from communities with low rates. Delinquency—particularly group delinquency, which constitutes a preponderance of all officially recorded offenses committed by boys and young men—has its roots in the dynamic life of the community.

It is recognized that the data included in this volume may be interpreted from many different points of view. However, the high degree of consistency in the association between delinquency and other characteristics of the community not only sustains the conclusion that delinquent behavior is related dynamically to the community but also appears to establish that all community characteristics, including delinquency, are products of the operation of general processes more or less common to American cities. Moreover, the fact that in Chicago the rates of delinquents for many years have remained relatively constant in the areas adjacent to centers of commerce and heavy industry, despite successive changes in the nativity and nationality composition of the population, supports emphatically the conclusion that the delinquency-producing factors are inherent in the community.

From the data available it appears that local variations in the conduct of children, as revealed in differential rates of delinquents, reflect the differences in social values, norms, and attitudes to which the children are exposed. In some parts of the city attitudes which support and sanction delinquency are, it seems, sufficiently extensive and dynamic to become the controlling forces in the development of delinquent careers among a relatively large number of boys and young men. These are the low-income areas, where delinquency has developed in the form of a social tradition, inseparable from the life of the local community.

This tradition is manifested in many different ways. It becomes meaningful to the child through the conduct, speech, gestures, and attitudes of persons with whom he has contact. Of particular importance is the child's intimate association with predatory gangs or other forms of delinquent and criminal organization. Through his contacts with these groups and by virtue of his participation in their activities he learns the techniques of stealing, becomes involved in binding relationships with his companions in delinquency, and acquires the attitudes appropriate to his position as a member of such groups. To use the words of Frank Tannenbaum: "It is the group that sets the pattern, provides the stimulus, gives the rewards in glory and companionship, offers the protection and loyalty, and, most of all, gives the criminal life its ethical content without which it cannot persist."

In these communities many children encounter competing systems of values. Their community, which provides most of the social forms in terms of which their life will be organized, presents conflicting possibilities. A career in delinquency and crime is one alternative, which often becomes real and enticing to the boy because it offers the promise of economic gain, prestige, and companionship and because he becomes acquainted with it through relationships with persons whose esteem and approbation are vital to his security and to the achievement of satisfactory status. In this situation the delinquent group may become both the incentive and the mechanism for initiating the boy into a career of delinquency and crime and for sustaining him in such a career, once he has embarked upon it.

In cases of group delinquency it may be said, therefore, that from the point of view of the delinquent's immediate social world, he is not necessarily disorganized, maladjusted, or antisocial. Within the limits of his social world and in terms of its norms and expectations, he may be a highly organized and well-adjusted person.

The residential communities of higher economic status, where the proportion of persons dealt with as delinquents and criminals is relatively low, stand in sharp contrast to the situation described above. Here the norms and values of the child's social world are more or less uniformly and consistently conventional. Generally speaking, the boy who grows up in this situation is not faced with the problem of making a choice between conflicting systems of moral values. Throughout the range of his contacts in the community he encounters similar attitudes of approval or disapproval. Cases of delinquency are relatively few and sporadic. The system of conventional values in the community is sufficiently pervasive and powerful to control and organize effectively, with few exceptions, the lives of most children and young people.

In both these types of communities the dominant system of values is conventional. In the first, however, a powerful competing system of delinquency values exists; whereas in the second, such a system, if it exists at all, is not sufficiently extensive and powerful to exercise a strong influence in the lives of many children. Most of the communities of the city fall between these two extremes and represent gradations in the extent to which delinquency has become an established way of life.

It is important to ask what the forces are which give rise to these significant differences in the organized values in different communities. Under what conditions do the conventional forces in the community become so weakened as to tolerate the development of a conflicting system of criminal values? Under what conditions is the conventional community capable of maintaining its integrity and exercising such control over the lives of its members as to check the development of the competing system? Obviously, any discussion of this question at present must be tentative. The data presented in this volume, however, afford a basis for consideration of certain points which may be significant.

It may be observed, in the first instance, that the variations in rates of officially recorded delinquents in communities of the city correspond very closely with variations in economic status. The communities with the highest rates of delinquents are occupied by those segments of the population whose position is most disadvantageous in relation to the distribution of economic, social, and cultural values. Of all the communities in the city, these have the fewest facilities for acquiring the economic goods indicative of status and success in our conventional culture. Residence in the community is in itself an indication of inferior status, from the standpoint of persons residing in the more prosperous areas. It is a handicap in securing employment and in making satisfactory advancement in industry and the professions. Fewer opportunities are provided for securing the training, education, and contacts which facilitate advancement in the fields of business, industry, and the professions.

The communities with the lowest rates of delinquents, on the other hand, occupy a relatively high position in relation to the economic and social hierarchy of the city. Here the residents are relatively much more secure; and adequate provision is offered to young people for securing the material possessions symbolic of success and the education, training, and personal contacts which facilitate their advancement in the conventional careers they may pursue.

Despite these marked differences in the relative position of people in different communities, children and young people in all areas, both rich and poor, are exposed to the luxury values and success patterns of our culture. In school and elsewhere they are also exposed to ideas of equality, freedom, and individual enterprise. Among children and young people residing in low-income areas, interests in acquiring material goods and enhancing personal status are developed which are often difficult to realize by legitimate means because of limited access to the necessary facilities and opportunities.

This disparity in the facilities available to people in different communities for achieving a satisfactory position of social security and prestige is particularly important in relation to delinquency and crime in the urban world. In the city, relationships are largely impersonal. Because of the anonymity in urban life, the individual is freed from much of the scrutiny and control which characterize life in primary-group situations in small towns and rural communities. Personal status and the status of one's community are, to a very great extent, determined by economic achievement. Superior status depends not so much on character as on the possession of those goods and values which symbolize success. Hence, the kind of clothes one wears, the automobile one drives, the type of building in which one lives, and the physical character of one's community become of great importance to the person. To a large degree these are the symbols of his position—the external evidences of the extent to which he has succeeded in the struggle for a living. The urban world, with its anonymity, its greater freedom, the more impersonal character of its relationships, and the varied assortment of economic, social, and cultural backgrounds in its communities, provides a general setting particularly conducive to the development of deviations in moral norms and behavior practices.

In the low-income areas, where there is the greatest deprivation and frustration, where, in the history of the city, immigrant and migrant groups have brought together the widest variety of divergent cultural traditions and institutions, and where there exists the greatest disparity between the social values to which the people aspire and the availability of facilities for acquiring these values in conventional ways, the development of crime as an organized way of life is most marked. Crime, in this situation, may be regarded as one of the means employed by people to acquire, or to attempt to acquire, the economic and social values generally idealized in our culture, which persons in other circumstances acquire by conventional means. While the origin of this tradition of crime is obscure, it can be said that its development in the history of the community has been facilitated by the fact that many persons have, as a result of their criminal activities, greatly improved their economic and social status. Their clothes, cars, and other possessions are unmistakable evidence of this fact. That many of these persons also acquire influence and power in politics and elsewhere is so well known that it does not need elaboration at this point. The power and affluence achieved, at least temporarily, by many persons involved in crime and illegal rackets are well known to the children and youth of the community and are important in determining the character of their ideals.

It may be said, therefore, that the existence of a powerful system of criminal values and relationships in low-income urban areas is the product of a cumulative process extending back into the history of the community and of the city. It is related both to the general character of the urban world and to the fact that the population in these communities has long occupied a disadvantageous position. It has developed in somewhat the same way as have all social traditions, that is, as a means of satisfying certain felt needs within the limits of a particular social and economic framework.

It should be observed that, while the tradition of delinquency and crime is thus a powerful force in certain communities, it is only a part of the community's system of values. As was pointed out previously, the dominant tradition in every community is conventional, even in those having the highest rates of delinquents. The traditionally conventional values are embodied in the family, the church, the school, and many other such institutions and organizations. Since the dominant tradition in the community is conventional, more persons pursue law-abiding careers than careers of delinquency and crime, as might be expected.

In communities occupied by Orientals, even those communities located in the most deteriorated sections of our large cities, the solidarity of Old World cultures and institutions has been preserved to such a marked extent that control of the child is still sufficiently effective to keep at a minimum delinquency and other forms of deviant behavior. As Professor Hayner has pointed out in his chapter on five cities of the Pacific Northwest, the close integration of the Oriental family, the feeling of group responsibility for the behavior of the child, and the desire of these groups to maintain a good reputation in American communities have all been important elements in preserving this cultural solidarity.

It is the assumption of this volume that many factors are important in determining whether a particular child will become involved in delinquency, even in those communities in which a system of delinquent and criminal values exists. Individual and personality differences, as well as differences in family relationships and in contacts with other institutions and groups, no doubt influence greatly his acceptance or rejection of opportunities to engage in delinquent activities. It may be said, however, that if the delinquency tradition were not present and the boys were not thus exposed to it, a preponderance of those who become delinquent in low-income areas would find their satisfactions in activities other than delinquency.

In conclusion, it is not assumed that this theoretical proposition applies to all cases of officially proscribed behavior. It applies primarily to those delinquent activities which become embodied in groups and social organizations. For the most part, these are offenses against property, which comprise a very large proportion of all the cases of boys coming to the attention of the courts.

# NEIGHBORHOODS AND VIOLENT CRIME: A MULTILEVEL STUDY OF COLLECTIVE EFFICACY

*Robert J. Sampson, Stephen W. Raudenbush, and Felton Earls*

For most of this century, social scientists have observed marked variations in rates of criminal violence across neighborhoods of U.S. cities. Violence has been associated with the low socioeconomic status (SES) and residential instability of neighborhoods. Although the geographical concentration of violence and its connection with neighborhood composition are well established, the question remains: why? What is it, for example, about the concentration of poverty that accounts for its association with rates of violence? What are the social processes that might explain or mediate this relation? In this article, we report results from a study designed to address these questions about crime and communities.

Our basic premise is that social and organizational characteristics of neighborhoods explain variations in crime rates that are not solely attributable to the aggregated demographic characteristics of individuals. We propose that the differential ability of neighborhoods to realize the common values of residents and maintain effective social controls is a major source of neighborhood variation in violence. Although social control is often a response to deviant behavior, it should not be equated with formal regulation or forced conformity by institutions such as the police and courts. Rather, social control refers generally to the capacity of a group to regulate its members according to desired principles—to realize collective, as opposed to forced, goals. One central goal is the desire of community residents to live in safe and orderly environments that are free of predatory crime, especially interpersonal violence.

In contrast to formally or externally induced actions (for example, a police crackdown), we focus on the effectiveness of informal mechanisms by which residents themselves achieve public order. Examples of informal social control include the monitoring of spontaneous play groups among children, a willingness to intervene to prevent acts such as truancy and street-corner "hanging" by teenage peer groups, and the confrontation of persons who are exploiting or disturbing public space. Even among adults, violence regularly arises in public disputes, in the context of illegal markets (for example, prostitution and drugs), and in the company of peers. The capacity of residents to control group-level processes and visible signs of social disorder is thus a key mechanism influencing opportunities for interpersonal crime in a neighborhood.

Informal social control also generalizes to broader issues of import to the well-being of neighborhoods. In particular, the differential ability of communities to extract resources and respond to cuts in public services (such as police patrols, fire stations, garbage collection, and housing code enforcement) looms large when we consider the known link between public signs of disorder (such as vacant housing, burned-out buildings, vandalism, and litter) and more serious crime.

Thus conceived, neighborhoods differentially activate informal social control. It is for this reason that we see an analogy between individual efficacy and neighborhood efficacy: both are activated processes that seek to achieve an intended effect. At the neighborhood level, however, the willingness of local residents to intervene for the common good depends in large part on conditions of mutual trust and solidarity among neighbors. Indeed, one is unlikely to intervene in a neighborhood context in which the rules are unclear and people mistrust or fear one another. It follows that socially cohesive neighborhoods will prove the most fertile contexts for the realization of informal social control. In sum, it is the linkage of mutual trust and the willingness to intervene for the common good that defines the neighborhood context of collective efficacy. Just as individuals vary in their capacity for efficacious action, so too do neighborhoods vary in their capacity to achieve common goals. And just as individual self-efficacy is situated rather than global (one has self-efficacy relative to a particular task or type of task), in this paper we view neighborhood efficacy as existing relative to the tasks of supervising children and maintaining public order. It follows that the collective efficacy of residents is a critical means by which urban neighborhoods inhibit the occurrence of personal violence, without regard to the demographic composition of the population.

## What Influences Collective Efficacy?

As with individual efficacy, collective efficacy does not exist in a vacuum. It is embedded in structural contexts and a wider political economy that stratifies places of residence by key social characteristics. Consider the destabilizing potential of rapid population change on neighborhood social organization. A high rate of residential mobility, especially in areas of decreasing population, fosters institutional disruption and weakened social controls over collective life. A major reason is that the formation of social ties takes time. Financial investment also provides homeowners with a vested interest in supporting the commonweal of neighborhood life. We thus hypothesize that residential tenure and homeownership promote collective efforts to maintain social control.

Consider next patterns of resource distribution and racial segregation in the United States. Recent decades have witnessed an increasing geographical concentration of lower income residents, especially minority groups and female-headed families. This neighborhood concentration stems in part from macroeconomic changes related to the deindustrialization of central cities, along with the out-migration of middle-class residents. In addition, the greater the race and class segregation in a metropolitan area, the smaller the number of neighborhoods absorbing economic shocks and the more severe the resulting concentration of poverty will be. Economic stratification by race and place thus fuels the neighborhood concentration of cumulative forms of disadvantage, intensifying the social isolation of lower income, minority, and single-parent residents from key resources supporting collective social control.

Perhaps more salient is the influence of racial and economic exclusion on perceived powerlessness. Social science research has demonstrated, at the individual level, the direct role of SES in promoting a sense of control, efficacy, and even biological health itself. An analogous process may work at the community level. The alienation, exploitation, and dependency wrought by resource deprivation act as a centrifugal force that stymies collective efficacy. Even if personal ties are strong in areas of concentrated disadvantage, they may be weakly tethered to collective actions.

We therefore test the hypothesis that concentrated disadvantage decreases and residential stability increases collective efficacy. In turn, we assess whether collective efficacy explains the association of neighborhood disadvantages and residential instability with rates of interpersonal violence. It is our hypothesis that collective efficacy mediates a substantial portion of the effects of neighborhood stratification.

## Research Design

This article examines data from the Project on Human Development in Chicago Neighborhoods (PHDCN). Applying a spatial definition of neighborhood—a collection of people and institutions occupying a subsection of a larger community—we combined 847 census tracts in the city of Chicago to create 343 "neighborhood clusters" (NCs). The overriding consideration in formation of NCs was that they should be as ecologically meaningful as possible, composed of geographically contiguous census tracts, and internally homogeneous on key census indicators. We settled on an ecological unit of about 8000 people, which is smaller than the 77 established community areas in Chicago (the average size is almost 40,000 people) but large enough to approximate local neighborhoods. Geographic boundaries (for example, railroad tracks, parks, and freeways) and knowledge of Chicago's neighborhoods guided this process.

The extensive racial, ethnic, and social-class diversity of Chicago's population was a major criterion in its selection as a research site. At present, whites, blacks, and Latinos each represent about a third of the city's population. Table 1 classifies the 343 NCs according to race or ethnicity and a trichotomized measure of SES from the 1990 census. Although there are no low-SES white neighborhoods and no high-SES Latino neighborhoods, there are black neighborhoods in all three cells of SES, and many heterogeneous neighborhoods vary in SES. Table 1 at once thus confirms the racial and ethnic segregation and yet rejects the common stereotype that minority neighborhoods in the United States are homogeneous.

To gain a complete picture of the city's neighborhoods, 8782 Chicago residents representing all 343 NCs were interviewed in their homes as part of the community survey (CS). The CS was designed to yield a representative sample of households within each NC, with sample sizes large enough to create reliable NC measures. Henceforth, we refer to NCs as "neighborhoods," keeping in mind that other operational definitions might have been used.

## Measures

"Informal social control" was represented by a five-item Likert-type scale. Residents were asked about the likelihood ("Would you say it is very likely, likely, neither likely nor

**TABLE 1**
**Racial and ethnic composition by SES strata:**
**Distribution of 343 Chicago NCs in the PHDCN design**

| Race or ethnicity | SES | | |
|---|---|---|---|
| | Low | Medium | High |
| ≥75% black | 77 | 37 | 11 |
| ≥75% white | 0 | 5 | 69 |
| ≥75% Latino | 12 | 9 | 0 |
| ≥20% Latino and ≥20% white | 6 | 40 | 12 |
| ≥20% Latino and ≥20% black | 9 | 4 | 0 |
| ≥20% black and ≥20% white | 2 | 4 | 11 |
| NCs not classified above | 8 | 15 | 12 |
| Total | 114 | 114 | 115 |

unlikely, unlikely, or very unlikely?") that their neighbors could be counted on to inter-vene in various ways if (i) children were skipping school and hanging out on a street corner, (ii) children were spray-painting graffiti on a local building, (iii) children were showing disrespect to an adult, (iv) a fight broke out in front of their house, and (v) the fire station closest to their home was threatened with budget cuts. "Social cohesion and trust" were also represented by five conceptually related items. Respondents were asked how strongly they agreed (on a five-point scale) that "people around here are willing to help their neighbors," "this is a close-knit neighborhood," "people in this neighborhood can be trusted," "people in this neighborhood generally don't get along with each other," and "people in this neighborhood do not share the same values" (the last two statements were reverse coded).

Responses to the five-point Likert scales were aggregated to the neighborhood level as initial measures. Social cohesion and informal social control were closely associated across neighborhoods, which suggests that the two measures were tapping aspects of the same latent construct. Because we also expected that the willingness and intention to intervene on behalf of the neighborhood would be enhanced under conditions of mutual trust and cohesion, we combined the two scales into a summary measure labeled collec-tive efficacy.

The measurement of violence was achieved in three ways. First, respondents were asked how often each of the following had occurred in the neighborhood during the past 6 months: (i) a fight in which a weapon was used, (ii) a violent argument between neigh-bors, (iii) a gang fight, (iv) a sexual assault or rape, and (v) a robbery or mugging. The scale construction for perceived neighborhood violence mirrored that for social control and cohesion. Second, to assess personal victimization, each respondent was asked "While you have lived in this neighborhood, has anyone ever used violence, such as in a mugging, fight, or sexual assault, against you or any member of your household anywhere in your neighborhood?" Third, we tested both survey measures against independently recorded incidents of homicide aggregated to the NC level. Homicide is one of the most reliably measured crimes by the police and does not suffer the reporting limitations associated with other violent crimes, such as assault and rape.

Ten variables were constructed from the 1990 decennial census of the population to reflect neighborhood differences in poverty, race and ethnicity, immigration, the labor market, age composition, family structure, homeownership, and residential stability (see Table 2). . . .

Consistent with theories and research on U.S. cities, the poverty-related variables given in Table 2 are highly associated and load on the same factor. . . . Hence, the pre-dominant interpretation revolves around concentrated disadvantage—African Americans, children, and single-parent families are differentially found in neighborhoods with high concentrations of poverty. . . .

The second dimension captures areas of the city undergoing immigration, especially from Mexico. The two variables that define this dimension are the percentage of Latinos (approximately 70% of Latinos in Chicago are of Mexican descent) and the percentage of foreign-born persons. . . .

The third factor score is the percentage of persons living in the same house as 5 years earlier and the percentage of owner-occupied homes. The clear emergence of a residential stability factor is consistent with much past research. . . .

TABLE 2

**Oblique rotated factor pattern (Loadings ≥0.60) in 343
Chicago neighborhoods (Data are from the 1990 census)**

| Variable | Factor loading |
|---|---|
| **Concentrated disadvantage** | |
| Below poverty line | 0.93 |
| On public assistance | 0.94 |
| Female-headed families | 0.93 |
| Unemployed | 0.86 |
| Less than age 18 | 0.94 |
| Black | 0.60 |
| **Immigrant concentration** | |
| Latino | 0.88 |
| Foreign-born | 0.70 |
| **Residential stability** | |
| Same house as in 1985 | 0.77 |
| Owner-occupied house | 0.86 |

## Association between Neighborhood Social Composition and Collective Efficacy

The theory described above led us to expect that neighborhood concentrated disadvantage and immigrant concentration would be negatively linked to neighborhood collective efficacy and residential stability would be positively related to collective efficacy. . . .

We found some effects of personal background (Table 3): High SES, homeownership, and age were associated with elevated levels of collective efficacy, whereas high mobility was negatively associated with collective efficacy. Gender, ethnicity, and years in neighborhood were not associated with collective efficacy.

At the neighborhood level, when these personal background effects were controlled, concentrated disadvantage and immigrant concentration were significantly negatively associated with collective efficacy, whereas residential stability was significantly positively associated with collective efficacy (for metric co-efficients and $t$ ratios, see Table 3). . . .

## Collective Efficacy as a Mediator of Social Composition

Past research has consistently reported links between neighborhood social composition and crime. We assessed the relation of social composition to neighborhood levels of violence, violent victimization, and homicide rates, and asked whether collective efficacy partially mediated these relations.

### Perceived violence

Using a model that paralleled that for collective efficacy, we found that reports of neighborhood violence depended to some degree on personal background. Higher levels of violence were reported by those who were separated or divorced (as compared with those who were single or married), by whites and blacks (as opposed to Latinos), by younger

**TABLE 3**
**Correlates of collective efficacy**

| Variable | Coefficient | SE | t ratio |
|---|---|---|---|
| Intercept | 3.523 | 0.013 | 263.20 |
| Person-level predictors | | | |
| Female | −0.012 | 0.015 | −0.76 |
| Married | −0.005 | 0.021 | −0.25 |
| Separated or divorced | −0.045 | 0.026 | −1.72 |
| Single | −0.026 | 0.024 | −1.05 |
| Homeowner | 0.122 | 0.020 | 6.04 |
| Latino | 0.042 | 0.028 | 1.52 |
| Black | −0.029 | 0.030 | −0.98 |
| Mobility | −0.025 | 0.007 | −3.71 |
| Age | $2.09 \times 10^{-3}$ | $0.60 \times 10^{-3}$ | 3.47 |
| Years in neighborhood | $0.64 \times 10^{-3}$ | $0.82 \times 10^{-3}$ | 0.78 |
| SES | $3.53 \times 10^{-2}$ | $0.76 \times 10^{-2}$ | 4.64 |
| Neighborhood-level predictors | | | |
| Concentrated disadvantage | −0.172 | 0.016 | −10.74 |
| Immigrant concentration | −0.037 | 0.014 | −2.66 |
| Residential stability | 0.074 | 0.130 | 5.61 |
| Variance components | | | |
| Within neighborhoods | 0.320 | | |
| Between neighborhoods | 0.026 | | |
| Percent of variance explained | | | |
| Within neighborhoods | 3.2 | | |
| Between neighborhoods | 70.3 | | |

respondents, and by those with longer tenure in their current neighborhood. Gender, home-ownership, mobility, and SES were not significantly associated with responses within neighborhoods. When these personal background characteristics were controlled, the concentrations of disadvantage and immigrants were positively associated with the level of violence (see Table 4, model 1). Also, as hypothesized, residential stability was negatively associated with the level of violence. . . .

Next, collective efficacy was added as a predictor in the level 3 model (Table 4, model 2). . . . Hence, after social composition was controlled, collective efficacy was strongly negatively associated with violence. Moreover, the coefficients for social composition were substantially smaller than they had been without a control for collective efficacy. . . . As hypothesized, then, collective efficacy appeared to partially mediate widely cited relations between neighborhood social composition and violence.

### Violent victimization

Violent victimization was assessed by a single binary item. . . . Social composition, as hypothesized, predicted criminal victimization, with positive coefficients for concentrated disadvantage and immigrant concentration and a negative coefficient for residential stability (Table 4, model 1). . . . These estimates controlled for background characteristics associated with the risk of victimization. When added to the model, collective efficacy was negatively associated with victimization (Table 4, model 2). . . .

**TABLE 4**

**Neighborhood correlates of perceived neighborhood violence, violent victimization, and 1995 homicide events**

| Variable | Model 1: social composition | | | Model 2: social composition and collective efficacy | | |
|---|---|---|---|---|---|---|
| | Coefficient | SE | t | Coefficient | SE | t |
| **Perceived neighborhood violence**[*] | | | | | | |
| Concentrated disadvantage | 0.277 | 0.021 | 13.30 | 0.171 | 0.024 | 7.24 |
| Immigrant concentration | 0.041 | 0.017 | 2.44 | 0.018 | 0.016 | 1.12 |
| Residential stability | −0.102 | 0.015 | −6.95 | −0.056 | 0.016 | −3.49 |
| Collective efficacy | | | | −0.618 | 0.104 | −5.95 |
| **Violent victimization**[†] | | | | | | |
| Concentrated disadvantage | 0.258 | 0.045 | 5.71 | 0.085 | 0.054 | 1.58 |
| Immigrant concentration | 0.141 | 0.046 | 3.06 | 0.098 | 0.044 | 2.20 |
| Residential stability | −0.143 | 0.050 | −2.84 | −0.031 | 0.051 | −0.60 |
| Collective efficacy | | | | −1.190 | 0.240 | −4.96 |
| **1995 homicide events**[‡] | | | | | | |
| Concentrated disadvantage | 0.727 | 0.049 | 14.91 | 0.491 | 0.064 | 7.65 |
| Immigrant concentration | −0.022 | 0.051 | −0.43 | −0.073 | 0.050 | −1.45 |
| Residential stability | 0.093 | 0.042 | 2.18 | 0.208 | 0.046 | 4.52 |
| Collective efficacy | | | | −1.471 | 0.261 | −5.64 |

[*]Estimates of neighborhood-level coefficients control for gender, marital status, homeownership, ethnicity, mobility, age, years in neighborhood, and SES of those interviewed. Model 1 accounts for 70.5% of the variation between neighborhoods in perceived violence, whereas model 2 accounts for 77.8% of the variation.

[†]Neighborhood-level coefficients are adjusted for the same person-level covariates listed in the first footnote. Model 1 accounts for 12.3% of the variation between neighborhoods in violent victimization, whereas model 2 accounts for 44.4%.

[‡]Model 1 accounts for 56.1% of the variation between neighborhoods in homicide rates, whereas model 2 accounts for 61.7% of the variation.

## Homicide

To assess the sensitivity of the findings when the measure of crime was completely independent of the survey, we examined 1995 homicide counts. . . .

Although concentrated disadvantage was strongly positively related to homicide, immigrant concentration was unrelated to homicide, and residential stability was weakly positively related to homicide (Table 4, model 1). However, when social composition was controlled, collective efficacy was negatively related to homicide (Table 4, model 2). Moreover, when collective efficacy was controlled, the coefficient for concentrated disadvantage was substantially diminished, which indicates that collective efficacy can be viewed as partially mediating the association between concentrated disadvantage and homicide.

## Control for prior homicide

Results so far were mainly cross-sectional, which raised the question of the possible confounding effect of prior crime. For example, residents in neighborhoods with high levels of violence might be afraid to engage in acts of social control. We therefore reestimated all models controlling for prior homicide: the 3-year average homicide rate in 1988, 1989, and 1990. Prior homicide was negatively related to collective efficacy in 1995 and positively related to all three measures of violence in 1995, including a direct association with homicide (Table 5). However, even after prior homicide was controlled, the coefficient for collective efficacy remained statistically significant and substantially negative in all three models. . . .

TABLE 5

**Predictors of neighborhood level violence, victimization, and homicide in 1995, with prior homicide controlled. For violence and victimization as outcomes, the coefficients reported in this table were adjusted for 11 person-level covariates (see Table 3), but the latter coefficients are omitted for simplicity of presentation**

| Variable | Violence as outcome | | | Victimization as outcome | | | Homicide in 1995 as outcome | | |
|---|---|---|---|---|---|---|---|---|---|
| | Coefficient | SE | t | Coefficient | SE | t | Coefficient | SE | t |
| Intercept | 3.772 | 0.379 | 9.95 | −2.015 | 0.042 | −49.24 | 3.071 | 0.050 | 62.01 |
| Concentrated disadvantage | 0.157 | 0.025 | 6.38 | 0.073 | 0.060 | 1.22 | 0.175 | 0.072 | 2.42 |
| Immigrant concentration | 0.020 | 0.016 | 1.25 | 0.098 | 0.045 | 2.20 | −0.034 | 0.044 | −0.77 |
| Residential stability | −0.054 | 0.016 | −3.39 | −0.029 | 0.052 | −0.56 | 0.229 | 0.043 | 5.38 |
| Collective efficacy | −0.594 | 0.108 | −5.53 | −1.176 | 0.251 | −4.69 | −1.107 | 0.272 | −4.07 |
| Prior homicide | 0.018 | 0.014 | 1.27 | 0.017 | 0.049 | 0.34 | 0.397 | 0.070 | 5.64 |
| Variance | | | | | | | | | |
| Between-neighborhood variance | 0.030 | | | 0.091 | | | 0.207 | | |
| Percent of variance explained between neighborhoods | 78.0 | | | 43.8 | | | 73.0 | | |

## Discussion and Implications

The results imply that collective efficacy is an important construct that can be measured reliably at the neighborhood level by means of survey research strategies. In the past, sample surveys have primarily considered individual-level relations. However, surveys that merge a cluster sample design with questions tapping collective properties lend themselves to the additional consideration of neighborhood phenomena.

Together, three dimensions of neighborhood stratification—concentrated disadvantage, immigration concentration, and residential stability—explained 70% of the neighborhood variation in collective efficacy. Collective efficacy in turn mediated a substantial portion of the association of residential stability and disadvantage with multiple measures of violence, which is consistent with a major theme in neighborhood theories of social organization. After adjustment for measurement error, individual differences in neighborhood composition, prior violence, and other potentially confounding social processes, the combined measure of informal social control and cohesion and trust remained a robust predictor of lower rates of violence.

There are, however, several limitations of the present study. Despite the use of decennial census data and prior crime as lagged predictors, the basic analysis was cross-sectional in design; causal effects were not proven. Indicators of informal control and social cohesion were not observed directly but rather inferred from informant reports. Beyond the scope of the present study, other dimensions of neighborhood efficacy (such as political ties) may be important, too. Our analysis was limited also to one city and did not go beyond its official boundaries into a wider region.

Finally, the image of local residents working collectively to solve their own problems is not the whole picture. As shown, what happens within neighborhoods is in part shaped by socioeconomic and housing factors linked to the wider political economy. In addition to encouraging communities to mobilize against violence through "self-help" strategies of informal social control, perhaps reinforced by partnerships with agencies of formal social control (community policing), strategies to address the social and ecological changes that beset many inner-city communities need to be considered. Recognizing that collective efficacy matters does not imply that inequalities at the neighborhood level can be neglected.

# CONTEMPORARY RETROSPECTIVE ON SOCIAL DISORGANIZATION THEORY

## SOCIAL DISORGANIZATION THEORY

*Travis Pratt, Arizona State University; and*
*Jacinta M. Gau, California State University, San Bernardino*

Early perspectives on criminological theory and research were guided by the assumption that the explanation for crime can be found within the individual (see Part II, "Biosocial Theories"). These theories differed, however, in terms of their propositions regarding what it is about individuals that *should* cause crime. For example, some criminological theorists maintained that crime could be a function of biological determinism (Dugdale, 1877), of substandard intelligence or "feeble-mindedness" (Goddard, 1914), or of dissocial manifestations of psychic forces (Aichorn, 1925/1979). Others were even so bold as to assert that individuals' criminal propensity can be indicated by the existence of "criminal bumps" on their heads (Lombroso-Ferrero, 1911; see also Gould, 1996). Regardless of their differences, each of these early perspectives shared the underlying premise that individual variations, not social conditions, were responsible for criminal behavior (see the discussion by Pratt, Maahs, & Stehr, 1998).

Social and economic changes beginning in the early 1900s, which were largely fueled by mass industrialization, resulted in new social problems and new ways of thinking about the sources of criminal behavior. Rapid increases in urbanization, residential mobility, and the rise of racially heterogeneous neighborhoods in American cities seemed to occur in concert with increases in crime rates. In particular, crime became visibly concentrated among the urban poor. In the midst of the Progressive movement, a liberal reform movement that occurred in the early twentieth century America, criminologists began to reject the notion that the poor were somehow biologically inferior and that they therefore deserved their meager lot in life as the natural outcome of their collective pathology (Cullen & Gilbert, 1982; Rothman, 1980). Instead, the Progressives "preferred a more optimistic interpretation: The poor were pushed by their environment, not born, into a life of crime" (Lilly, Cullen, & Ball, 1995, p. 39). As a consequence, a number of new formulations of criminological thought began to emerge that sought to shift the assumed "causes" of crime "from the personal to the social plane" (Matza, 1969, p. 47).

Among these new traditions was the theory of social disorganization articulated by Chicago school of criminology researchers Shaw and McKay (1942). Following their research on juvenile delinquency in Chicago, they developed a neighborhood-level theory of crime that placed little to no blame on the individuals residing in high-crime neighborhoods. Rather, "Shaw and McKay believed that juvenile delinquency could be understood only by considering the social context in which youths lived" (Lilly et al., 1995, p. 44). With this concept in mind, in this article we lay out the theoretical foundation of social disorganization theory, discuss the major critiques that have been leveled against it, outline the empirical assessments of and refinements made to the theory, and highlight its policy applications.

## Theoretical Foundation

The social disorganization tradition grew out of the research conducted in the early 1900s in Chicago by Shaw and McKay (1942). Upon studying Chicago's juvenile court records over a period of several decades, Shaw and McKay noted that rates of crime were not evenly dispersed across time and space in the city. Rather, crime tended to be concentrated in particular areas of the city—namely, slum neighborhoods. Further, crime rates were highest in these neighborhoods regardless of which racial or ethnic group happened to reside there at any particular time; and, as the previously crime-prone groups moved to other lower-crime areas of the city, their rate of criminal activity decreased accordingly. These observations led Shaw and McKay to the conclusion that crime was likely a function of neighborhood dynamics and not necessarily a function of the individuals within such neighborhoods. The question that remained was: What are the characteristics of the "slum neighborhoods" that set them apart from low-crime neighborhoods, and therefore seemed to foster criminal activity?

In answering this question, Shaw and McKay focused on the urban areas experiencing rapid changes in their social and economic structure—or, in the "zone of transition."[1] In particular, they looked to neighborhoods that were low in socioeconomic status (SES), with high rates of residential mobility, and had higher degrees of racial heterogeneity. These neighborhoods were viewed as "socially disorganized," meaning that conventional institutions of social control (e.g., schools, churches, voluntary community organizations) were weak and unable to regulate the behavior of the neighborhood's youth. Shaw and McKay (1942) also noted that, aside from the lack of behavioral regulation, socially disorganized neighborhoods tended to produce "criminal traditions" that could be passed across successive generations of youths. This system of pro-delinquency attitudes could be easily learned by youths through their daily contact with older juveniles (see also Kornhauser, 1978). Thus, a neighborhood characterized by social disorganization would provide fertile soil for crime and delinquency in two ways: through a lack of behavioral control mechanisms, and through the cultural transmission of delinquent values.[2]

---

[1]This focus was based on Burgess's (1967) theory of urban development. The "zone in transition" was defined as the true "inner city," where residents were often displaced to live in slumlike conditions because of their inability to afford to live elsewhere.

[2]As another testament to the influence of the work of Shaw and McKay, these two "prongs" of social disorganization theory provided the basis for individual-level theories such as social control/social bond theory and Sutherland's differential association theory (see Lilly et al., 1995).

It is important to note that Shaw and McKay did not specify a *direct* relationship between social disorganization and crime (see the discussion by Bursik, 1988). Rather, the socially disorganized neighborhoods observed by Shaw and McKay could indirectly influence neighborhood rates of crime in two ways. First, areas characterized by social disorganization tended to experience high levels of population turnover, which meant that they were abandoned by most as soon as it was economically possible (see also Wilson, 1987). In addition, such neighborhoods often experienced rapid changes in racial composition (i.e., racial heterogeneity) that made it difficult to resist the influx of new racial or ethnic groups. Taken together, these characteristics hindered the ability of socially disorganized neighborhoods to effectively engage in "self-regulation" (Bursik, 1986). In short, Bursik (1988) states that "the dynamics of social disorganization lead to variations across neighborhoods in the strength of the commitment of the residents to groups standards" (p. 521) and, as a result, variations in community crime rates.

## Critiques of Social Disorganization Theory

The social disorganization perspective remained both popular and influential throughout the 1950s and 1960s. Nevertheless, thinking about crime in social disorganization terms became increasingly unfashionable among criminologists by the late 1960s. To be sure, around this time there was a risk that social disorganization theory would be altogether abandoned by criminologists for a number of reasons.

First, as Bursik and Grasmick (1993b) noted:

> [W]ith the refinement of survey approaches to data collection and the increased interest in social-psychological theories of control, deterrence, learning, and labeling, the focus of the discipline significantly began to shift from group dynamics to individual processes during the 1960s and 1970s. (p. ix)

This trend away from macrolevel criminological theory and research saw the social disorganization tradition fall into relative disfavor among criminologists, many of whom viewed it as irrelevant or, at best, marginal to modern criminology (see e.g., Arnold & Brungardt, 1983; Davidson, 1981; see also Byrne & Sampson, 1986).

Second, critics argued that social disorganization theory's emphasis on human ecology made the assumption that community dynamics—including the social processes highlighted by social disorganization theorists—are fairly stable. The problem, of course, is that communities are in a constant state of flux. This means that crime rates can be a cause of a breakdown in community control, yet such increases in crime rates can also cause the kinds of ecological changes (e.g., residential mobility, decreases in informal social control) that concern social disorganization theorists (Bursik, 1988). Critics of social disorganization theory noted that cross-sectional research, which was the staple of criminological research at this time, therefore failed to fully capture the nature of community dynamics.

Third, scholars noted that empirical tests of social disorganization theory had failed to include direct measures of social disorganization. Instead, it was more convenient for researchers to measure the structural antecedents of disorganization (e.g., low SES, racial heterogeneity, residential mobility) because of the availability of census data and to merely assume that the unmeasured intervening processes associated with social disorganization existed. Obtaining direct measures of social disorganization was, by comparison, far more difficult given the exigencies of social science research at the time.

Finally, and perhaps most importantly, in an ironic twist social disorganization theory was criticized by liberal criminologists as being—at least implicitly—a racist theory of criminal behavior. In particular, since members of racial minority groups tend to disproportionately occupy the kinds of neighborhoods specified by social disorganization theory as problematic, calling such neighborhoods "disorganized" (a term that scholars felt was value-loaded) amounted to a violation of political correctness (see the discussion by Bursik, 1988). Thus, scholars even sought to replace the language of the theory to that of "differential social organization theory" to soften the perceived racial slight associated with the prefix "dis" (see, e.g., the discussion by Matsueda & Heimer, 1987). Overall, factors ranging from the shifts in the social context to the absence of direct measures of social disorganization—coupled with new ways of thinking about individual deviance that could be easily studied with survey data—kicked social disorganization theory off the criminological radar screen for nearly three decades.

## Empirical Evaluations

Despite these criticisms, a large body of literature testing the validity of social disorganization theory exists. Empirical tests of social disorganization theory fall into two camps: those that fail to include intervening mechanisms in their statistical model, and those that do include such variables. In either case, most tests of the theory begin by specifying and measuring variables associated with the original social disorganization formulation of Shaw and McKay. This section discusses the variables specified by traditional social disorganization theory and the recently articulated intervening mechanisms, and how they are typically measured in empirical studies. A discussion of the different types of dependent variables used by researchers is also provided.

### Traditional social disorganization variables

Virtually all published tests of social disorganization theory include measures of neighborhood socioeconomic status, residential mobility, and racial heterogeneity. Accordingly, the "neighborhood" is typically the unit of analysis (or level of aggregation) across these studies. The *socioeconomic status,* or *SES,* of a neighborhood, especially in those studies where individual-level data are "aggregated up," is usually measured by either a factor or summed scale of economic variables (Sampson & Groves, 1989; Sampson et al., 1997). Other studies have used a combination of income inequality measures and unemployment rates[3] to proxy the relative economic health of a neighborhood (e.g., see Bursik, 1986; Heitgerd & Bursik, 1987; Sampson, 1986). *Residential mobility* has typically been measured as the proportion of residents in a neighborhood living in the same dwelling for the

---

[3]The income inequality measure used by Sampson (1986) was the Gini Index of Income Concentration. Unemployment rates, on the other hand, are measured less consistently. Sampson (1986) used the percentage of unemployed aged 16 or older; Bursik (1986) used the percentage of males who were unemployed in conjunction with the percentage of males who were employed in particular fields (e.g., the percentage employed in "professional" occupations) and the median neighborhood education levels.

last five years (Heitgerd & Bursik, 1987; Sampson, 1986; Sampson et al., 1997).[4] Finally, *racial heterogeneity* has typically been measured as the percentage of blacks (Sampson, 1986) or percentage of nonwhites (Bursik, 1986)[5] in a neighborhood.

In addition to the variables specified by Shaw and McKay, Sampson (1986) noted that much of the empirical work on social disorganization theory has failed to consider the impact of other social disorganization variables, such as *family structures and stability*. He suggested that traditional social disorganization variables may influence community crime rates when taking into account the effects of levels of family disruption. This may occur by (1) removing an important set of control structures over youths' behavior, and (2) creating greater opportunities for criminal victimization (i.e., through the lack of capable guardianship). Essentially, Sampson (1986) recognized the importance of how social disorganization theory relates to control theory and routine activity/lifestyle theory.

Sampson used three measures of family structure. First, he included a measure of the percentage of residents in a neighborhood who were ever married that were either divorced or separated. The second measure of family structure was the percentage of female-headed families. Finally, he included a measure of the percentage of primary (or single)-headed households. His analyses revealed that independent of the traditional social disorganization variables, the family structure variables each had a direct significant effect on community crime rates. Thus, Sampson's work identified an important and additional source of social disorganization (implicit in the work of Shaw & McKay) that had been previously overlooked in empirical studies.

It is also important to note that Shaw and McKay viewed social disorganization variables as having an "indirect" effect on community crime rates. As such, a body of literature has emerged that attempts to specify the intervening mechanisms between social disorganization variables and crime rates. While this pool of studies is still relatively small, the findings are substantively important and thus warrant special consideration.

**Intervening mechanisms**

The trend toward specifying the indirect effects of social disorganization variables on crime was begun by Sampson and Groves (1989). Their study used aggregated data from the British Crime Survey. The intervening mechanisms between social disorganization variables[6] and crime rates specified in their study include informal control mechanisms such as youths' local friendship networks, the prevalence of unsupervised peer groups, and the level of organizational participation in the neighborhood.[7]

The most recent direction of the specification of intervening mechanisms for social disorganization theory can be seen in the work of Sampson et al. (1997). Their study

---

[4]This measure differed from that used by Sampson and Groves (1989), who used data from the British Crime Survey. Their measure of residential mobility was the percentage of residents in a neighborhood who grew up within a 15-minute walk from their current home.

[5]Bursik (1986) also included a measure of the percentage of foreign-born whites as a measure of racial heterogeneity. Bursik and Webb (1982) and Heitgerd and Bursik (1987) used residual change scores for the same variables in their study.

[6]The measure of "family disruption" used by Sampson and Groves (1989), unlike in the study conducted by Sampson (1986), was treated as one of the traditional social disorganization variables, and not as an intervening mechanism.

[7]Each of these variables was created by aggregating up individuals' responses to a number of scaled items.

argued that socially disorganized neighborhoods are likely to be low on *collective efficacy*, which is defined as "the willingness of local residents to intervene for the common good" (p. 919). The authors go on to state that community residents are "unlikely to intervene in a neighborhood context in which the rules are unclear and people mistrust or fear one another. It follows that socially cohesive neighborhoods will prove the most fertile contexts for the realization of social control" (p. 919). Using aggregated data from the Project on Human Development in Chicago Neighborhoods, they found that the traditional social disorganization variables explained 70% of the variation in their collective efficacy measures which, in turn, effectively mediated much of the direct effects of the social disorganization variables (see also Lowenkakamp, Cullen, & Pratt, 2003; Sampson, 2006).

### Dependent variables

Social disorganization variables have been used to predict rates of multiple types of crimes. For example, the theory has been tested to predict rates of general juvenile delinquency (Bursik, 1986), rates of personal violent victimization (Sampson, 1986; Sampson & Groves, 1989; Sampson et al., 1997), and rates of property victimization (Sampson, 1986; Sampson & Groves, 1989). Social disorganization variables have also been found to be significantly related to communities' levels of fear of crime (Pratt & Cullen, 2005). Accordingly, a recent meta-analysis of over 200 published criminological studies found that the variables specified by social disorganization are among the most consistently robust predictors of crime rates (Pratt & Cullen, 2000).

### Theoretical Refinements

Social disorganization theory was "rediscovered" in the 1980s. Research by scholars such as Bursik (1986, 1988), Sampson and Groves (1989), and Wilson (1987, 1996) helped revitalize, and partially reformulate and extend, the social disorganization tradition. In doing so, a number of problems leveled against the theory have been addressed effectively (see the discussion by Bursik, 1988). For example, research has been conducted to test for the "reciprocal effects"[8] of social disorganization (Bursik, 1986), and to test for the potential impact the levels of social disorganization of "surrounding communities" may have on neighboring communities (Heitgerd & Bursik, 1987).[9]

In addition, the scope of the theory was adjusted and expanded to include constructs beyond the macrolevel components originally specified by Shaw and McKay (e.g., low socioeconomic status, residential mobility, racial heterogeneity). New concepts have been

---

[8]The "reciprocal effects" mentioned by Bursik (1986) have to do with the assumption that "within the context of ongoing urban dynamics, the level of delinquency in an area may also directly or indirectly cause changes in the composition of an area [due to] out-migration" (p. 64). Thus Bursik estimated the simultaneous effects of social disorganization on crime, and crime on social disorganization. Similar approaches can be found in the work of Bursik and Webb (1982) and Morenoff and Sampson (1997), where changes in population characteristics were being predicted by changes in crime/delinquency rates.

[9]Heitgerd and Bursik (1987) showed that a relatively socially organized community may experience high rates of delinquency simply by virtue of being located geographically adjacent to a socially disorganized community.

added that have enhanced its theoretical clarity. In particular, as stated previously, recent research has explicitly tested for "intervening mechanisms" between the traditional social disorganization variables and crime rates. The intervening mechanisms noted by research-ers include the effect of social disorganization on rates of family disruption and "collective efficacy" (see Sampson & Groves, 1989; Sampson et al., 1997), which, in turn, directly influence crime rates.

Most recently, scholars have begun integrating concepts drawn from social disorganization theory into other individual-level theories of criminal behavior. Most notably, criminologists have linked social disorganization variables to the kinds of family processes that are related to the development of self-control in children (Pratt, Turner, & Piquero, 2004). This link is critical given the consistent empirical support for the relation-ship between self-control and criminal behavior (Pratt & Cullen, 2000). In particular, this research indicates that elements of parental efficacy (e.g., monitoring and supervi-sion of children) are determined to a large extent by neighborhood context (i.e., effective parenting is made more difficult in socially disorganized communities). Such parenting problems, in turn, result in a lower levels of self-control in children—an effect that also explains the apparent "race gap" in offending (see Pratt et al., 2004). In short, not only does social disorganization theory provide an explanation for community variations in crime rates, but it also provides the context for certain well-supported individual theories of criminal behavior.

## Policy Implications

The demise of macrolevel explanations for crime was a blow to social disorganization theory, but it did not mean the end of it in either the research (as discussed earlier) or pol-icy realms. In the late 1970s, changes began to happen in policing (see Kelling & Moore, 1988) that would soon bring this field to an intersection with social disorganization. Until this time, policing had been dominated by an emphasis on the apprehension of serious criminal offenders. Various methods were employed to enable police to react quickly when crimes were reported and to identify and arrest the culprits (Kelling & Moore, 1988). This so-called professional model of policing gradually came to be replaced by a more community-based or order maintenance model, which stressed the role of police as agents of *social* control, not just *crime* control (see Kelling & Moore, 1988; Walker, 1984).

A theory was proposed by Wilson and Kelling in 1982 that solidified the shift from the professional model to the order maintenance model (but see Walker, 1984). Dubbed "broken windows theory" for its creative use of window-related metaphor, this theory was premised on the contention that serious crime results when low-level offenses are allowed to flourish in a neighborhood or community. The theory's founders asserted that the failure to detect and quash disorderly public behaviors sends the message that the neighborhood is either unable or unwilling to exercise social control and prevent deviance. The area begins to decay physically as vandals, thieves, litterers, and graffiti taggers systematically destroy the infrastructure. At the same time, the area declines socially as prostitutes and small-time drug pushers peddle their trades with increasing boldness, panhandlers become aggressive in their solicitations for money, and gangs of teenagers loiter on street corners and harass or threaten passersby. Law-abiding residents of the area retreat into their homes out of the fear and discomfort inspired by these miscreants and the streets become devoid of "decent" people. Soon, it is not just vandals and vagabonds who feel at home in the slummy atmosphere—serious criminals, too, note the prime opportunity that the lack of social control affords and they descend upon the community (Wilson & Kelling, 1982).

The parallels between broken windows theory and its predecessor, social disorganization theory, are obvious. Like social disorganization theory, broken windows theory has at its core the criminogenic force inherent in the breakdown of the physical structure of a neighborhood or community. As with the newer conceptualizations of social disorganization theory (e.g., Sampson & Groves, 1989; Sampson et al., 1997), broken windows posits as an intervening mechanism the social stability of a neighborhood or community. Both theories revolve around the destabilizing effects that deficient levels of informal social control have upon neighborhoods. Both emphasize the damage done by physical decrepitation and the disappearance of law-abiding community residents whose watchful eyes discourage deviant behavior. In these ways, the two theories evince several commonalities.

There are, however, some key differences that set apart broken windows theory from social disorganization theory both on theoretical and policy levels. Foremost is that broken windows theory is more explicitly focused on the individual level of analysis. Indeed, social disorganization theory's ostensible focus is on the deterioration of a community at the macrolevel, as it is entire neighborhoods—not just individual people—that gradually succumb to social and structural failings. Broken windows, though, is not just about neighborhood- or community-level disorder—it is about disorderly *people*. It is, ultimately, *the* panhandler, *the* prostitute, and *the* loiterer who are responsible for the criminogenic conditions that appear on the macrolevel. The individuals classified as "disorderly" under the broken windows framework can be thought of as the molecules that make up a larger object: Individually, they are tiny and fairly insignificant, but when interlocked, they form something much larger than themselves. Social disorganization theory's traditional focus has been on the larger object; broken windows' focus is on the molecules.

The individualistic focus of broken windows theory had significant implications for police. The police, obviously, possess limited capacity to affect large-scale, systemic problems such as socioeconomic disadvantage. Broken windows offered the police a new angle. The original architects of broken windows contended that "the police are plainly key to order maintenance" (Wilson & Kelling, 1982, p. 36). Broken windows theory thus vests police with the responsibility for clearing the streets of offensive people in order to prevent (or reverse) the downward spiral of decay in neighborhoods and communities. By targeting the micro, police can—so the argument goes—change the macro.

Broken windows theory resounded with law enforcement officials nationwide. The first massive implementation began in New York City in 1994 when then-mayor Rudolph Giuliani appointed William Bratton as the head of the New York City Police Department. Bratton initiated a number of changes in the NYPD and one of these alterations entailed a shift to broken windows-style policing on the streets of the city. Crime—particularly violent crime—in New York City plummeted over the following years and Bratton, Guiliani, and others were quick to credit broken windows theory for this fortuitous development (Bratton & Knobler, 1998; Kelling & Coles, 1996; Kelling & Sousa, 2001). It was later established by social scientists that broken windows policing had had little, if any, effect on crime in New York City (Harcourt & Ludwig, 2006), but the empirical results failed to dampen the public and political popularity of this new-found crime "cure."

After the New York City experience, broken windows policing (or order maintenance policing, as it is often called) found its way into police departments across the country. Today, its influence can be seen in several facets of police tactics. Sometimes, it functions as a strategy in and of itself, wherein police departments announce crackdowns on certain types of disorder (see Braga et al., 1999; Novak, Harman, Holsinger, & Turner, 1999, for examples). Other times, it appears in the form of code enforcement programs, where police officers work with other city employees to enforce local civil ordinances that prohibit citizens from allowing their homes and surrounding properties to fall into disarray (see Mazerolle, Roehl, & Kadleck, 1998).

In still other police departments, broken windows tactics are embedded within a larger effort, such as community oriented policing (see Brunson, 2007). Broken windows theory was also the impetus behind the recent surge in antiloitering ordinances that were enacted by municipalities seeking to suppress gang activity (Meares & Kahan, 1998; Roberts, 1999). Despite having been functionally discredited by criminological studies (Gau & Pratt, 2008; Harcourt, 2001; Piquero, 1999; Sampson & Raudenbush, 1999, 2004; Spelman, 2004; Worrall, 2006), the theory's assumption that low-level disorder ultimately causes serious crime (an assumption perhaps drawn from a misreading of social disorganization theory) continues to garner widespread support from police officials and is now a staple of many law enforcement agencies' missions.

In sum, broken windows theory can be viewed as an offshoot of social disorganization theory and the impact of broken windows on various policies, likewise, offers a visible sign of the lingering influence of social disorganization theory on public policy. In the crime control realm, broken windows-style policing is the strategy of choice for many police leaders. The influences that social disorganization theory has had via its impact on the creation and implementation of broken windows theory shows that Shaw and McKay's (1942) ideas have endured, albeit in a form that has been modified in some significant ways.

## Summary of Social Disorganization Theory

Since its first articulation by Shaw and McKay in the early 1900s social disorganization theory has fallen both in and out of favor with criminologists. Despite being somewhat marginalized during the 1960s and 1970s, recent research has revived the theory and it continues to make an important contribution to criminological thought. In its current iteration, researchers have specified the links through which traditional social disorganization theory variables (e.g., low socioeconomic status, residential mobility, racial heterogeneity) may influence community crime rates. In particular, levels of social disorganization may affect informal control and criminal opportunity mechanisms (e.g., unsupervised peer groups, collective efficacy), which, in turn, directly influence neighborhood crime rates. Thus, in its contemporary form, social disorganization theory continues to be a parsimonious, yet dynamic, explanation of crime at the macrolevel that has received considerable empirical support.

# PART IV

# ANOMIE AND STRAIN THEORIES

# ANOMIE THEORIES

## SOCIAL STRUCTURE AND ANOMIE

*Robert K. Merton*

There persists a notable tendency in sociological theory to attribute the malfunctioning of social structure primarily to those of man's imperious biological drives which are not adequately restrained by social control. In this view, the social order is solely a device for "impulse management" and the "social processing" of tensions. These impulses which break through social control, be it noted, are held to be biologically derived. Nonconformity is assumed to be rooted in original nature. Conformity is by implication the result of an utilitarian calculus or unreasoned conditioning. This point of view, whatever its other deficiences, clearly begs one question. It provides no basis for determining the nonbiological conditions which induce deviations from prescribed patterns of conduct. In this paper, it will be suggested that certain phases of social structure generate the circumstances in which infringement of social codes constitutes a "normal" response.

The conceptual scheme to be outlined is designed to provide a coherent, systematic approach to the study of socio-cultural sources of deviate behavior. Our primary aim lies in discovering how some social structures *exert a definite pressure* upon certain persons in the society to engage in nonconformist rather than conformist conduct. The many ramifications of the scheme cannot all be discussed; the problems mentioned outnumber those explicitly treated.

Among the elements of social and cultural structure, two are important for our purposes. These are analytically separable although they merge imperceptibly in concrete situations. The first consists of culturally defined goals, purposes, and interests. It comprises a frame of aspirational reference. These goals are more or less integrated and involve varying degrees of prestige and sentiment. They constitute a basic, but not the exclusive, component of what Linton aptly has called "designs for group living." Some of these cultural aspirations are related to the original drives of man, but they are not determined by them. The second phase of the social structure defines, regulates, and controls the acceptable modes of achieving these goals. Every social group invariably couples its scale of desired ends with moral or institutional regulation of permissible and required procedures for attaining these ends. These regulatory norms and moral imperatives do not necessarily coincide with technical or efficiency norms. Many procedures which from the standpoint of *particular individuals* would be most efficient in securing desired values, e.g., illicit oil-stock schemes, theft, fraud, are ruled out of the institutional area of permitted conduct. The choice of expedients is limited by the institutional norms.

To say that these two elements, culture goals and institutional norms, operate jointly is not to say that the ranges of alternative behaviors and aims bear some constant relation to one another. The emphasis upon certain goals may vary independently of the degree of emphasis upon institutional means. There may develop a disproportionate, at times, a virtually exclusive, stress upon the value of specific goals, involving relatively slight concern with the institutionally appropriate modes of attaining these goals. The limiting case in this direction is reached when the range of alternative procedures is limited only by technical rather than institutional considerations. Any and all devices which promise attainment of the all important goal would be permitted in this hypothetical polar case. This constitutes one type of cultural malintegration. A second polar type is found in groups where activities originally conceived as instrumental are transmuted into ends in themselves. The original purposes are forgotten and ritualistic adherence to institutionally prescribed conduct becomes virtually obsessive. Stability is largely ensured while change is flouted. The range of alternative behaviors is severely limited. There develops a tradition-bound, sacred society characterized by neophobia. The occupational psychosis of the bureaucrat may be cited as a case in point. Finally, there are the intermediate types of groups where a balance between culture goals and institutional means is maintained. These are the significantly integrated and relatively stable, though changing, groups.

An effective equilibrium between the two phases of the social structure is maintained as long as satisfactions accrue to individuals who conform to both constraints, viz., satisfactions from the achievement of the goals and satisfactions emerging directly from the institutionally canalized modes of striving to attain these ends. Success, in such equilibrated cases, is twofold. Success is reckoned in terms of the product and in terms of the process, in terms of the outcome and in terms of activities. Continuing satisfactions must derive from sheer *participation* in a competitive order as well as from eclipsing one's competitors if the order itself is to be sustained. The occasional sacrifices involved in institutionalized conduct must be compensated by socialized rewards. The distribution of statuses and roles through competition must be so organized that positive incentives for conformity to roles and adherence to status obligations are provided *for every position* within the distributive order. Aberrant conduct, therefore, may be viewed as a symptom of dissociation between culturally defined aspirations and socially structured means.

Of the types of groups which result from the independent variation of the two phases of the social structure, we shall be primarily concerned with the first, namely, that involving a disproportionate accent on goals. This statement must be recast in a proper perspective. In no group is there an absence of regulatory codes governing conduct, yet groups do vary in the degree to which these folkways, mores, and institutional controls are effectively integrated with the more diffuse goals which are part of the culture matrix. Emotional convictions may cluster about the complex of socially acclaimed ends, meanwhile shifting their support from the culturally defined implementation of these ends. As we shall see, certain aspects of the social structure may generate countermores and antisocial behavior precisely because of differential emphases on goals and regulations. In the extreme case, the latter may be so vitiated by the goal-emphasis that the range of behavior is limited only by considerations of technical expediency. The sole significant question then becomes, which available means is most efficient in netting the socially approved value. The technically most feasible procedure, whether legitimate or not, is preferred to the institutionally prescribed conduct. As this process continues, the integration of the society becomes tenuous and anomie ensues.

Thus, in competitive athletics, when the aim of victory is shorn of its institutional trappings and success in contests becomes construed as "winning the game" rather than "winning through circumscribed modes of activity," a premium is implicitly set upon the use of illegitimate but technically efficient means. The star of the opposing football team is surreptitiously slugged; the wrestler furtively incapacitates his opponent through ingenious but illicit techniques; university alumni covertly subsidize "students" whose talents are largely confined to the athletic field. The emphasis on the goal has so attenuated the satisfactions deriving from sheer participation in the competitive activity that these satisfactions are virtually confined to a successful outcome. Through the same process, tension generated by the desire to win in a poker game is relieved by successfully dealing oneself four aces, or, when the cult of success has become completely dominant, by sagaciously shuffling the cards in a game of solitaire. The faint twinge of uneasiness in the last instance and the surreptious nature of public delicts indicate clearly that the institutional rules of the game *are known* to those who evade them, but that the emotional supports of these rules are largely vitiated by cultural exaggeration of the success-goal. They are microcosmic images of the social macrocosm.

Of course, this process is not restricted to the realm of sport. The process whereby exaltation of the end generates a *literal demoralization,* i.e., a deinstitutionalization, of the means is one which characterizes many groups in which the two phases of the social structure are not highly integrated. The extreme emphasis upon the accumulation of wealth as a symbol of success in our own society militates against the completely effective control of institutionally regulated modes of acquiring a fortune. Fraud, corruption, vice, crime, in short, the entire catalogue of proscribed behavior, becomes increasingly common when the emphasis on the *culturally induced* success-goal becomes divorced from a coordinated institutional emphasis. This observation is of crucial theoretical importance in examining the doctrine that antisocial behavior most frequently derives from biological drives breaking through the restraints imposed by society. The difference is one between a strictly utilitarian interpretation which conceives man's ends as random and an analysis which finds these ends deriving from the basic values of the culture.

Our analysis can scarcely stop at this juncture. We must turn to other aspects of the social structure if we are to deal with the social genesis of the varying rates and types of deviate behavior characteristic of different societies. Thus far, we have sketched three ideal types of social orders constituted by distinctive patterns of relations between culture ends and means. Turning from these types of *culture patterning*, we find five logically possible, alternative modes of adjustment or adaptation *by individuals* within the culture-bearing society or group. These are schematically presented in the following table, where (+) signifies "acceptance," (−) signifies "elimination" and (±) signifies "rejection and substitution of new goals and standards."

|  | Culture goals | Institutionalized means |
|---|:---:|:---:|
| I. Conformity | + | + |
| II. Innovation | + | − |
| III. Ritualism | − | + |
| IV. Retreatism | − | − |
| V. Rebellion | ± | ± |

Our discussion of the relation between these alternative responses and other phases of the social structure must be prefaced by the observation that persons may shift from one alternative to another as they engage in different social activities. These categories refer to role adjustments in specific situations, not to personality *in toto*. To treat the development of this process in various spheres of conduct would introduce a complexity unmanageable within the confines of this paper. For this reason, we shall be concerned primarily with economic activity in the broad sense, "the production, exchange, distribution and consumption of goods and services" in our competitive society, wherein wealth has taken on a highly symbolic cast. Our task is to search out some of the factors which exert pressure upon individuals to engage in certain of these logically possible alternative responses. This choice, as we shall see, is far from random.

In every society, Adaptation I (conformity to both culture goals and means) is the most common and widely diffused. Were this not so, the stability and continuity of the society could not be maintained. The mesh of expectancies which constitutes every social order is sustained by the modal behavior of its members falling within the first category. Conventional role behavior oriented toward the basic values of the group is the rule rather than the exception. It is this fact alone which permits us to speak of a human aggregate as comprising a group or society.

Conversely, Adaptation IV (rejection of goals and means) is the least common. Persons who "adjust" (or maladjust) in this fashion are, strictly speaking, *in* the society but not *of* it. Sociologically, these constitute the true "aliens." Not sharing the common frame of orientation, they can be included within the societal population merely in a fictional sense. In this category are *some* of the activities of psychotics, psychoneurotics, chronic autists, pariahs, outcasts, vagrants, vagabonds, tramps, chronic drunkards and drug addicts. These have relinquished, in certain spheres of activity, the culturally defined goals, involving complete aim-inhibition in the polar case, and their adjustments are not in accord with institutional norms. This is not to say that in some cases the source of their behavioral adjustments is not in part the very social structure which they have in effect repudiated nor that their very existence within a social area does not constitute a problem for the socialized population.

This mode of "adjustment" occurs, as far as structural sources are concerned, when both the culture goals and institutionalized procedures have been assimilated thoroughly by the individual and imbued with affect and high positive value, but where those institutionalized procedures which promise a measure of successful attainment of the goals are not available to the individual. In such instances, there results a twofold mental conflict insofar as the moral obligation for adopting institutional means conflicts with the pressure to resort to illegitimate means (which may attain the goal) and inasmuch as the individual is shut off from means which are both legitimate *and* effective. The competitive order is maintained, but the frustrated and handicapped individual who cannot cope with this order drops out. Defeatism, quietism and resignation are manifested in escape mechanisms which ultimately lead the individual to "escape" from the requirements of the society. It is an expedient which arises from continued failure to attain the goal by legitimate measures and from an inability to adopt the illegitimate route because of internalized prohibitions and institutionalized compulsives, *during which process the supreme value of the success-goal has as yet not been renounced.* The conflict is resolved by eliminating *both* precipitating elements, the goals and means. The escape is complete, the conflict is eliminated and the individual is a socialized.

Be it noted that where frustration derives from the inaccessibility of effective institutional means for attaining economic or any other type of highly valued "success," that Adaptations II, III and V (innovation, ritualism and rebellion) are also possible. The result will be determined by the particular personality, and thus, the *particular* cultural background, involved. Inadequate socialization will result in the innovation response whereby the conflict and frustration are eliminated by relinquishing the institutional means and retaining the success-aspiration; an extreme assimilation of institutional demands will lead to ritualism wherein the goal is dropped as beyond one's reach but conformity to the mores persists; and rebellion occurs when emancipation from the reigning standards, due to frustration or to marginalist perspectives, leads to the attempt to introduce a "new social order."

Our major concern is with the illegitimacy adjustment. This involves the use of conventionally proscribed but frequently effective means of attaining at least the simulacrum of culturally defined success,—wealth, power, and the like. As we have seen, this adjustment occurs when the individual has assimilated the cultural emphasis on success without equally internalizing the morally prescribed norms governing means for its attainment. The question arises, Which phases of our social structure predispose toward this mode of adjustment? We may examine a concrete instance, effectively analyzed by Lohman, which provides a clue to the answer. Lohman has shown that specialized areas of vice in the near north side of Chicago constitute a "normal" response to a situation where the cultural emphasis upon pecuniary success has been absorbed, but where there is little access to conventional and legitimate means for attaining such success. The conventional occupational opportunities of persons in this area are almost completely limited to manual labor. Given our cultural stigmatization of manual labor, and its correlate, the prestige of white collar work, it is clear that the result is a strain toward innovational practices. The limitation of opportunity to unskilled labor and the resultant low income can not compete *in terms of conventional standards of achievement* with the high income from organized vice.

For our purposes, this situation involves two important features. First, such antisocial behavior is in a sense "called forth" by certain conventional values of the culture *and* by the class structure involving differential access to the approved opportunities for legitimate, prestige-bearing pursuit of the culture goals. The lack of high integration between the means-and-end elements of the cultural pattern and the particular class structure combine to favor a heightened frequency of antisocial conduct in such groups. The second consideration is of equal significance. Recourse to the first of the alternative responses, legitimate effort, is limited by the fact that actual advance toward desired success-symbols through conventional channels is, despite our persisting open-class ideology, relatively rare and difficult for those handicapped by little formal education and few economic resources. The dominant pressure of group standards of success is, therefore, on the gradual attenuation of legitimate, but by and large ineffective, strivings and the increasing use of illegitimate, but more or less effective, expedients of vice and crime. The cultural demands made on persons in this situation are incompatible. On the one hand, they are asked to orient their conduct toward the prospect of accumulating wealth and on the other, they are largely denied effective opportunities to do so institutionally. The consequences of such structural inconsistency are psychopathological personality, and/or antisocial conduct, and/or revolutionary activities. The equilibrium between culturally designated means and ends becomes highly unstable with the progressive emphasis on attaining the prestige-laden ends by any means whatsoever. Within this context, Capone represents the triumph of amoral intelligence over morally prescribed "failure," when the channels of vertical mobility are closed or narrowed *in a society which places a high premium on economic affluence and social ascent for* all *its members.*

This last qualification is of primary importance. It suggests that other phases of the social structure besides the extreme emphasis on pecuniary success, must be considered if we are to understand the social sources of antisocial behavior. A high frequency of deviate behavior is not generated simply by "lack of opportunity" or by this exaggerated pecuniary emphasis. A comparatively rigidified class structure, a feudalistic or caste order, may limit such opportunities far beyond the point which obtains in our society today. It is only when a system of cultural values extols, virtually above all else, certain *common* symbols of success *for the population at large* while its social structure rigorously restricts or completely eliminates access to approved modes of acquiring these symbols *for a considerable part of the same population*, that antisocial behavior ensues on a considerable scale. In other words, our egalitarian ideology denies by implication the existence of noncompeting groups and individuals in the pursuit of pecuniary success. The same body of success-symbols is held to be desirable for all. These goals are held to *transcend class lines*, not to be bounded by them, yet the actual social organization is such that there exist class differentials in the accessibility of these *common* success-symbols. Frustration and thwarted aspiration lead to the search for avenues of escape from a culturally induced intolerable situation; or unrelieved ambition may eventuate in illicit attempts to acquire the dominant values. The American stress on pecuniary success and ambitiousness for all thus invites exaggerated anxieties, hostilities, neuroses and antisocial behavior.

This theoretical analysis may go far toward explaining the varying correlations between crime and poverty. Poverty is not an isolated variable. It is one in a complex of interdependent social and cultural variables. When viewed in such a context, it represents quite different states of affairs. Poverty as such, and consequent limitation of opportunity, are not sufficient to induce a conspicuously high rate of criminal behavior. Even the often mentioned "poverty in the midst of plenty" will not necessarily lead to this result. Only insofar as poverty and associated disadvantages in competition for the culture values approved for *all* members of the society is linked with the assimilation of a cultural emphasis on monetary accumulation as a symbol of success is antisocial conduct a "normal" outcome. Thus, poverty is less highly correlated with crime in southeastern Europe than in the United States. The possibilities of vertical mobility in these European areas would seem to be fewer than in this country, so that neither poverty *per se* nor its association with limited opportunity is sufficient to account for the varying correlations. It is only when the full configuration is considered, poverty, limited opportunity and a commonly shared system of success symbols, that we can explain the higher association between poverty and crime in our society than in others where rigidified class structure is coupled with *differential class symbols of achievement.*

In societies such as our own, then, the pressure of prestige-bearing success tends to eliminate the effective social constraint over means employed to this end. "The-end-justifies-the-means" doctrine becomes a guiding tenet for action when the cultural structure unduly exalts the end and the social organization unduly limits possible recourse to approved means. Otherwise put, this notion and associated behavior reflect a lack of cultural coordination. In international relations, the effects of this lack of integration are notoriously apparent. An emphasis upon national power is not readily coordinated with an inept organization of legitimate, i.e., internationally defined and accepted, means for attaining this goal. The result is a tendency toward the abrogation of international law, treaties become scraps of paper, "undeclared warfare" serves as a technical evasion, the bombing of civilian populations is rationalized, just as the same societal situation induces the same sway of illegitimacy among individuals.

The social order we have described necessarily produces this "strain toward dissolution." The pressure of such an order is upon outdoing one's competitors. The choice of means within the ambit of institutional control will persist as long as the sentiments supporting a competitive system, i.e., deriving from the possibility of outranking competitors and hence enjoying the favorable response of others, are distributed throughout the entire system of activities and are not confined merely to the final result. A stable social structure demands a balanced distribution of affect among its various segments. When there occurs a shift of emphasis from the satisfactions deriving from competition itself to almost exclusive concern with successful competition, the resultant stress leads to the breakdown of the regulatory structure. With the resulting attenuation of the institutional imperatives, there occurs an approximation of the situation erroneously held by utilitarians to be typical of society generally wherein calculations of advantage and fear of punishment are the sole regulating agencies. In such situations, as Hobbes observed, force and fraud come to constitute the sole virtues in view of their relative efficiency in attaining goals,—which were for him, of course, not culturally derived.

# DELINQUENCY AND OPPORTUNITY: A THEORY
# OF DELINQUENT GANGS

*Richard Cloward and Lloyd Ohlin*

## The Availability of Illegitimate Means

Social norms are two-sided. A prescription implies the existence of a prohibition, and *vice versa*. To advocate honesty is to demarcate and condemn a set of actions which are dishonest. In other words, norms that define legitimate practices also implicitly define illegitimate practices. One purpose of norms, in fact, is to delineate the boundary between legitimate and illegitimate practices. In setting this boundary, in segregating and classifying various types of behavior, they make us aware not only of behavior that is regarded as right and proper but also of behavior that is said to be wrong and improper. Thus the criminal who engages in theft or fraud does not invent a new way of life; the possibility of employing alternative means is acknowledged, tacitly at least, by the norms of the culture.

This tendency for proscribed alternatives to be implicit in every prescription, and *vice versa*, although widely recognized, is nevertheless a reef upon which many a theory of delinquency has foundered. Much of the criminological literature assumes, for example, that one may explain a criminal act simply by accounting for the individual's readiness to employ illegal alternatives of which his culture, through its norms, has already made him generally aware. Such explanations are quite unsatisfactory, however, for they ignore a host of questions regarding the *relative availability* of illegal alternatives to various potential criminals. The aspiration to be a physician is hardly enough to explain the fact of becoming a physician; there is much that transpires between the aspiration and the achievement.

This is no less true of the person who wants to be a successful criminal. Having decided that he "can't make it legitimately," he cannot simply choose among an array of illegitimate means, all equally available to him. As we have noted earlier, it is assumed in the theory of anomie that access to conventional means is differentially distributed, that some individuals, because of their social class, enjoy certain advantages that are denied to those elsewhere in the class structure. For example, there are variations in the degree to which members of various classes are fully exposed to and thus acquire the values, knowledge, and skills that facilitate upward mobility. It should not be startling, therefore, to suggest that there are socially structured variations in the availability of illegitimate means as well. In connection with delinquent subcultures, we shall be concerned principally with differentials in access to illegitimate means within the lower class.

Many sociologists have alluded to differentials in access to illegitimate means without explicitly incorporating this variable into a theory of deviant behavior. This is particularly true of scholars in the "Chicago tradition" of criminology. Two closely related theoretical perspectives emerged from this school. The theory of "cultural transmission," advanced by Clifford R. Shaw and Henry D. McKay, focuses on the development in some urban neighborhoods of a criminal tradition that persists from one generation to another despite constant changes in population. In the theory of "differential association," Edwin H. Sutherland described the processes by which criminal values are taken over by the individual. He asserted that criminal behavior is learned, and that it is learned in interaction with others who have already incorporated criminal values. Thus the first theory stresses the value systems of different areas; the second, the systems of social relationships that facilitate or impede the acquisition of these values.

Scholars in the Chicago tradition, who emphasized the processes involved in learning to be criminal, were actually pointing to differentials in the availability of illegal means— although they did not explicitly recognize this variable in their analysis. This can perhaps best be seen by examining Sutherland's classic work, *The Professional Thief*. "An inclination to steal," according to Sutherland, "is not a sufficient explanation of the genesis of the professional thief." The "self-made" thief, lacking knowledge of the ways of securing immunity from prosecution and similar techniques of defense, "would quickly land in prison; . . . a person can be a professional thief only if he is recognized and received as such by other professional thieves." But recognition is not freely accorded: "Selection and tutelage are the two necessary elements in the process of acquiring recognition as a professional thief. . . . A person cannot acquire recognition as a professional thief until he has had tutelage in professional theft, *and tutelage is given only to a few persons selected from the total population*." For one thing, "the person must be appreciated by the professional thieves. He must be appraised as having an adequate equipment of wits, front, talking-ability, honesty, reliability, nerve and determination." Furthermore, the aspirant is judged by high standards of performance, for only "a very small percentage of those who start on this process ever reach the stage of professional thief. . . ." Thus motivation and pressures toward deviance do not fully account for deviant behavior any more than motivation and pressures toward conformity account for conforming behavior. The individual must have access to a learning environment and, once having been trained, must be allowed to perform his role. Roles, whether conforming or deviant in content, are not necessarily freely available; access to them depends upon a variety of factors, such as one's socioeconomic position, age, sex, ethnic affiliation, personality characteristics, and the like. The potential thief, like the potential physician, finds that access to his goal is governed by many criteria other than merit and motivation.

What we are asserting is that access to illegitimate roles is not freely available to all, as is commonly assumed. Only those neighborhoods in which crime flourishes as a stable, indigenous institution are fertile criminal learning environments for the young. Because these environments afford integration of different age-levels of offender, selected young people are exposed to "differential association" through which tutelage is provided and criminal values and skills are acquired. To be prepared for the role may not, however, ensure that the individual will ever discharge it. One important limitation is that more youngsters are recruited into these patterns of differential associations than the adult criminal structure can possibly absorb. Since there is a surplus of contenders for these elite positions, criteria and mechanisms of selection must be evolved. Hence a certain propor-tion of those who aspire may not be permitted to engage in the behavior for which they have prepared themselves.

Thus we conclude that access to illegitimate roles, no less than access to legitimate roles, is limited by both social and psychological factors. We shall here be concerned primarily with socially structured differentials in illegitimate opportunities. Such differentials, we contend, have much to do with the type of delinquent subculture that develops.

## Learning and Performance Structures

Our use of the term "opportunities," legitimate or illegitimate, implies access to both learn-ing and performance structures. That is, the individual must have access to appropriate environments for the acquisition of the values and skills associated with the performance of a particular role, and he must be supported in the performance of the role once he has learned it.

Tannenbaum, several decades ago, vividly expressed the point that criminal role performance, no less than conventional role performance, presupposes a patterned set of relationships through which the requisite values and skills are transmitted by established practitioners to aspiring youth:

> It takes a long time to make a good criminal, many years of specialized training and much prep-aration. But training is something that is given to people. People learn in a community where the materials and the knowledge are to be had. A craft needs an atmosphere saturated with purpose and promise. The community provides the attitudes, the point of view, the philosophy of life, the example, the motive, the contacts, the friendships, the incentives. No child brings those into the world. He finds them here and available for use and elaboration. The community gives the criminal his materials and habits, just as it gives the doctor, the lawyer, the teacher, and the candlestick-maker theirs.

Sutherland systematized this general point of view, asserting that opportunity consists, at least in part, of learning structures. Thus "criminal behavior is learned" and, furthermore, it is learned "in interaction with other persons in a process of communication." However, he conceded that the differential-association theory does not constitute a full explanation of criminal behavior. In a paper circulated in 1944, he noted that "criminal behavior is partially a function of opportunities to commit [*i.e.*, to perform] specific classes of crime, such as embezzlement, bank burglary, or illicit heterosexual intercourse." Therefore, "while opportunity may be partially a function of association with criminal patterns and of the specialized techniques thus acquired, it is not determined entirely in that manner, and consequently differential association is not the sufficient cause of criminal behavior."

To Sutherland, then, illegitimate opportunity included conditions favorable to the performance of a criminal role as well as conditions favorable to the learning of such a role (differential associations). These conditions, we suggest, depend upon certain features of the social structure of the community in which delinquency arises.

## Differential Opportunity: A Hypothesis

We believe that each individual occupies a position in both legitimate and illegitimate opportunity structures. This is a new way of defining the situation. The theory of anomie views the individual primarily in terms of the legitimate opportunity structure. It poses questions regarding differentials in access to legitimate routes to success-goals; at the same time it assumes either that illegitimate avenues to success-goals are freely available or that differentials in their availability are of little significance. This tendency may be seen in the following statement by Merton:

> Several researches have shown that specialized areas of vice and crime constitute a "normal" response to a situation where the cultural emphasis upon pecuniary success has been absorbed, but where there is little access to conventional and legitimate means for becoming successful. The occupational opportunities of people in these areas are largely confined to manual labor and the lesser white-collar jobs. Given the American stigmatization of manual labor *which has been found to hold rather uniformly for all social classes*, and the absence of realistic opportunities for advancement beyond this level, the result is a marked tendency toward deviant behavior. The status of unskilled labor and the consequent low income cannot readily compete *in terms of established standards of worth* with the promises of power and high income from organized vice, rackets and crime. . . . [Such a situation] leads toward the gradual attenuation of legitimate, but by and large ineffectual, strivings and the increasing use of illegitimate, but more or less effective, expedients.

The cultural-transmission and differential-association tradition, on the other hand, assumes that access to illegitimate means is variable, but it does not recognize the significance of comparable differentials in access to legitimate means. Sutherland's "ninth proposition" in the theory of differential association states:

> *Though criminal behavior is an expression of general needs and values, it is not explained by those general needs and values since non-criminal behavior is an expression of the same needs and values.* Thieves generally steal in order to secure money, but likewise honest laborers work in order to secure money. The attempts by many scholars to explain criminal behavior by general drives and values, such as the happiness principle, striving for social status, the money motive, or frustration, have been and must continue to be futile since they explain lawful behavior as completely as they explain criminal behavior.

In this statement, Sutherland appears to assume that people have equal and free access to legitimate means regardless of their social position. At the very least, he does not treat access to legitimate means as variable. It is, of course, perfectly true that "striving for social status," "the money motive," and other socially approved drives do not fully account for either deviant or conforming behavior. But if goal-oriented behavior occurs under conditions in which there are socially structured obstacles to the satisfaction of these drives by legitimate means, the resulting pressures, we contend, might lead to deviance.

The concept of differential opportunity structures permits us to unite the theory of anomie, which recognizes the concept of differentials in access to legitimate means, and the "Chicago tradition," in which the concept of differentials in access to illegitimate means is implicit. We can now look at the individual, not simply in relation to one or the other system of means, but in relation to both legitimate and illegitimate systems. This approach permits us to ask, for example, how the relative availability of illegitimate opportunities affects the resolution of adjustment problems leading to deviant behavior. We believe that the way in which these problems are resolved may depend upon the kind of support for one or another type of illegitimate activity that is given at different points in the social structure. If, in a given social location, illegal or criminal means are not readily available, then we should not expect a criminal subculture to develop among adolescents. By the same logic, we should expect the manipulation of violence to become a primary avenue to higher status only in areas where the means of violence are not denied to the young. To give a third example, drug addiction and participation in subcultures organized around the consumption of drugs presuppose that persons can secure access to drugs and knowledge about how to use them. In some parts of the social structure, this would be very difficult; in others, very easy. In short, there are marked differences from one part of the social structure to another in the types of illegitimate adaptation that are available to persons in search of solutions to problems of adjustment arising from the restricted availability of legitimate means. In this sense, then, we can think of individuals as being located in two opportunity structures—one legitimate, the other illegitimate. Given limited access to success-goals by legitimate means, the nature of the delinquent response that may result will vary according to the availability of various illegitimate means.

## Illegitimate Opportunities and the Social Structure of the Slum

When we say that the form of delinquency that is adopted is conditioned by the presence or absence of appropriate illegitimate means, we are actually referring to crucial differences in the social organization of various slum areas, for our hypothesis implies that the local milieu affects the delinquent's choice of a solution to his problems of adjustment. One of the principal ways in which slum areas vary is in the extent to which they provide the young with alternative (albeit illegitimate) routes to higher status. Many of the works in the cultural-transmission and differential-association tradition are focused directly on the relationship between deviant behavior and lower-class social structure. By reconceptualizing aspects of the tradition, we hope to make our central hypothesis more explicit.

### Integration of different age-levels of offender

In their ecological studies of the urban environment, Shaw and McKay found that delinquency tended to be confined to limited areas and to persist in these areas despite demographic changes. Hence they spoke of "criminal traditions" and of the "cultural transmission" of criminal values. As a result of their observations of slum life, they concluded that particular importance must be assigned to the relationships between immature and sophisticated offenders—which we call the integration of different age-levels of offender. They suggested that many youngsters are recruited into criminal activities as a direct result of intimate associations with older and more experienced offenders:

> Stealing in the neighborhood was a common practice among the children and approved of by the parents. Whenever the boys got together they talked about robbing and made more plans for stealing. I hardly knew any boys who did not go robbing. The little fellows went in for petty stealing, breaking into freight cars, and stealing junk. The older guys did big jobs like stick-ups, burglary, and stealing autos. The little fellows admired the "big shots" and longed for the day when they could get into the big racket. Fellows who had "done time" were the big shots and looked up to and gave the little fellows tips on how to get by and pull off big jobs.

Thus the "big shots"—conspicuous successes in the criminal world—become role-models for youth, much more important as such than successful figures in the conventional world, who are usually socially and geographically remote from the slum area. Through intimate and stable associations with these older criminals, the young acquire the values and skills required for participation in the criminal culture. Further, structural connections between delinquents, semimature criminals, and the adult criminal world, where they exist, provide opportunities for upward mobility; where such integrative arrangements do not exist, the young are cut off from this alternative pathway to higher status.

### Integration of conventional and deviant values

Shaw and McKay were describing deviant learning structures—that is, alternative routes by which people seek access to the goals that society holds to be worthwhile. Their point was that access to criminal roles and advancement in the criminal hierarchy depend upon stable associations with older criminals from whom the necessary values and skills may be learned. Yet Shaw and McKay failed to give explicit recognition to the concept of illegitimate means and the socially structured conditions of access to them—probably because they tended to view slum areas as "disorganized." Although they consistently referred to illegitimate *activities* as "organized," they nevertheless tended to label high-rate delinquency *areas* "disorganized" because the values transmitted were criminal rather than conventional. Hence they sometimes made statements which we now perceive to be internally inconsistent, such as the following:

> This community situation was not only disorganized and thus ineffective as a unit of control, but it was characterized by a high rate of juvenile delinquency and adult crime, not to mention the widespread political corruption which had long existed in the area. Various forms of stealing and many organized delinquent and criminal gangs were prevalent in the area. These groups exercised a powerful influence and tended to create a community spirit which not only tolerated but actually fostered delinquent and criminal practices.

Sutherland was among the first to perceive that the concept of social disorganization tends to obscure the stable patterns of interaction which exist among carriers of criminal values: "the organization of the delinquent group, which is often very complex, is social disorganization only from an ethical or some other particularistic point of view." Like Shaw and McKay, he had observed that criminal activities in lower-class areas were organized in terms of a criminal value system, but he also observed that *this alternative value system was supported by a patterned system of social relations*. That is, he recognized the fact that crime, far from being a random, unorganized activity, is often an intricate and stable system of arrangements and relationships. He therefore rejected the "social disorganization" perspective: "At the suggestion of Albert K. Cohen, this concept has been changed to differential group organization, with organization for criminal activities on one side and organization against criminal activities on the other."

William F. Whyte, in his classic study of an urban slum, carried the empirical description of the structure and organization of illegal means a step further. Like Sutherland, Whyte rejected the position of Shaw and McKay that the slum is *dis*organized simply because it is organized according to principles different from those in the conventional world:

> It is customary for the sociologist to study the slum district in terms of "social disorganization" and to neglect to see that an area such as Cornerville has a complex and well-established organization of its own. . . . I found that in every group there was a hierarchical structure of social relations binding the individuals to one another and that the groups were also related hierarchically to one another. Where the group was formally organized into a political club, this was immediately apparent, but for informal groups it was no less true.

But Whyte's view of the slum differed somewhat from Sutherland's in that Whyte's emphasis was not on "differential group organization"—the idea that the slum is composed of two discrete systems, conventional and deviant. He stressed, rather, the way in which the occupants of various roles in these two systems become integrated in a single, stable structure which organizes and patterns the life of the community. Thus Whyte showed that individuals who participate in stable illicit enterprises do not constitute a separate or isolated segment of the community but are closely integrated with the occupants of conventional roles. He noted, for example, that "the rackets and political organizations extend from the bottom to the top of Cornerville society, mesh with one another, and integrate a large part of the life of the district. They provide a general framework for the understanding of the actions of both 'little guys' and 'big shots.'"

In a recent article, Kobrin has clarified our understanding of slum areas by suggesting that they differ in the *degree* to which deviant and conventional value systems are integrated with each other. This difference, we argue, affects the relative accessibility of illegal means. Pointing the way to the development of a "typology of delinquent areas based on variations in the relationship between these two systems," Kobrin describes the "polar types" on such a continuum. The integrated area, he asserts, is characterized not only by structural integration between carriers of the two value systems but also by reciprocal participation by carriers of each in the value system of the other. Thus, he notes:

> Leaders of [illegal] enterprises frequently maintain membership in such conventional institutions of their local communities as churches, fraternal and mutual benefit societies and political parties. . . . Within this framework the influence of each of the two value systems is reciprocal, the leaders of illegal enterprise participating in the primary orientation of the conventional elements in the population, and the latter, through their participation in a local power structure sustained in large part by illicit activity, participating perforce in the alternate, criminal value system.

The second polar type consists of areas in which the relationships between carriers of deviant and conventional values break down because of disorganizing forces such as "drastic change in the class, ethnic, or racial characteristics of [the] population." Kobrin suggests that in such slums "the bearers of the conventional culture and its value system are without the customary institutional machinery and therefore in effect partially demo-bilized with reference to the diffusion of their value system." At the same time, areas of this type are "characterized principally by the absence of systematic and organized adult activity in violation of the law, despite the fact that many adults in these areas commit vio-lations." Thus both value systems remain implicit, but the fact that neither is "systematic and organized" precludes the possibility of effective integration.

How does the accessibility of illegal means vary with the relative integration of conventional and criminal values in a given area? Although Kobrin does not take up this problem explicitly, he does note that the integrated area apparently constitutes a "training ground" for the acquisition of criminal values and skills. Of his first polar type he says:

> The stable position of illicit enterprise in the adult society of the community is reflected in the character of delinquent conduct on the part of children. While delinquency in all high-rate areas is intrinsically disorderly in that it is unrelated to official programs for the education of the young, in the [integrated community] boys may more or less realistically recognize the potentialities for personal progress in local society through access to delinquency. In a general way, therefore, delinquent activity in these areas constitutes a training ground for the acquisi-tion of skill in the use of violence, concealment of offense, evasion of detection and arrest, and the purchase of immunity from punishment. Those who come to excel in these respects are frequently noted and valued by adult leaders in the rackets who are confronted, as are the leaders of all income-producing enterprises, with problems of the recruitment of competent personnel.

Kobrin makes no mention of the extent to which learning structures and opportunities for criminal careers are available in the unintegrated area. Yet the fact that neither conven-tional nor criminal values are articulated in this type of area as he describes it suggests that the appropriate learning structures—principally integration of different age-levels of offenders—are not available. Furthermore, Kobrin's description of adult violative activ-ity in such areas as "unorganized" suggests that illegal opportunities are severely limited. Even if youngsters were able to secure adequate preparation for criminal roles, the social structure of such neighborhoods would appear to provide few opportunities for stable criminal careers. Kobrin's analysis—as well as that of Whyte and others before him— supports our conclusion that *illegal opportunity structures tend to emerge only when there are stable patterns of accommodation between the adult carriers of conventional and of deviant values.* Where these two value systems are implicit, or where the carriers are in open conflict, opportunities for stable criminal-role performance are limited. Where stable accommodative relationships exist between the adult carriers of criminal and conventional values, institutionalized criminal careers are available. The alienated adolescent need not rely on the vagaries of private entrepreneurship in crime, with the attendant dangers of detection and prosecution, imprisonment, fluctuations in income, and the like. Instead, he may aspire to rise in the organized criminal structure and to occupy a permanent position in some flourishing racket. Secure in such a position, he will be relatively immune from prosecution and imprisonment, can expect a more or less stable income, and can look forward to acceptance by the local community—criminal and conventional.

Some urban neighborhoods, in short, provide relief from pressures arising from limitations on access to success-goals by legitimate means. Because alternative routes to higher status are made available to those who are ambitious, diligent, and meritorious, the frustrations of youth in these neighborhoods are drained off. Where such pathways do not exist, frustrations become all the greater.

## Slum Organization and Subcultural Differentiation

Before we turn to a discussion of the relationship between particular forms of slum organization and the differentiation of subcultural content, it might be useful to note a recent article by Cohen and Short pertaining to subcultural differentiation. These authors assert that delinquency is basically "non-utilitarian, malicious, negativistic, versatile, and characterized by short-run hedonism and group-autonomy"—a position consistent with Cohen's earlier point of view, as expressed in *Delinquent Boys*. But the recent work of Cohen and Short also notes the existence of different types of delinquent subculture—principally of the criminal, conflict, and drug-use varieties. How, then, do they reconcile this conclusion about subcultural differentiation with their assertion that delinquency is "basically" non-utilitarian, malicious, and the like?

The point they make is that subcultural content varies depending on the age-level of the participants. Among younger delinquents, they suggest, a universal or generic form of subculture emerges which is *independent* of its specific social milieu. This subcultural form is characterized by a diffuse agglomeration of cultural traits, including an orientation toward the "kick," a "conflict" orientation, and an orientation toward the illegal acquisition of money or goods. These traits or orientations, some of which are more or less incompatible with others, can nevertheless coexist because the subculture is loosely organized and thus capable of considerable cultural versatility. As the participants mature, however, additional (unspecified) forces intervene which intensify the latent conflict between these orientations. Cliques within the subculture may then break away and form a more specialized sub-subculture which tends to value one orientation more than others (*e.g.,* disciplined theft rather than indiscriminate violence and destruction). If a particular cultural orientation comes to be widely diffused through the group, the generic culture as a whole may tend to become specialized. In either case, Cohen and Short believe that the process of subcultural differentiation occurs at later stages in the age cycle.

We question the validity of this point of view, for it rests upon what we consider an unwarranted premise; namely, that the social milieu influences the content of subcultural solutions at some points in the age cycle but not at other points. We prefer to make a quite different assumption; namely, that *the social milieu affects the nature of the deviant response whatever the motivation and social position* (i.e., *age, sex, socioeconomic level*) *of the participants in the delinquent subculture.* We assume that the local cultural and social structure impinges upon and modifies deviant responses from the very outset. The delinquent subculture may or may not be fully specialized at first, but we should not expect it to manifest all three delinquent orientations to the same extent, even at an early stage of development. In other words, we should expect the content of delinquent subcultures to vary predictably with certain features of the milieu in which these cultures emerge. And we should further expect these predominant traits to become all the more articulated and specialized as the subcultures become stabilized and integrated with their respective environments.

# THE PRESENT AND FUTURE OF
# INSTITUTIONAL-ANOMIE THEORY

*Steven F. Messner and Richard Rosenfeld*

Over a decade ago, we published the first edition of *Crime and the American Dream.* Our principal objectives in writing the book were twofold. One, we set out to offer an explanation of the empirical evidence about crime in the United States. Our point of departure was the claim of "American exceptionalism"—the view that levels and patterns of serious crime in the U.S. are distinctive when viewed in comparison with other advanced nations. Two, we were committed to applying a macro-sociological perspective to crime in American society. While the general influence of sociology on the development of criminology has been amply documented elsewhere, we were convinced that the promise of the sociological perspective for understanding crime had yet to be fully realized. The end result of our labors was a set of arguments about the interconnections between the basic features of the social organization of American society—its core cultural commitments and major social institutions—and observed levels and patterns of crime.

The original explanation of crime in the U.S. advanced in *Crime and the American Dream* has subsequently been interpreted more broadly as a macro-sociological *theory* of crime. In their widely cited article published in *Criminology* in 1995, Chamlin and Cochran christened our analytic framework and causal propositions with the felicitous label: "institutional-anomie theory." They proceeded to derive propositions from the theory and assessed these propositions using conventional regression-based techniques. The results of their analyses lent sufficient support to the hypotheses to encourage others to draw upon institutional-anomie theory to guide macro-level research on crime. . . .

## Synopsis of IAT

IAT incorporates central elements of the anomie perspective in criminology as developed by Robert K. Merton. In his classic essay "Social Structure and Anomie," Merton establishes the foundation for a sociological explanation of crime and other forms of deviant behavior by providing what might be regarded as an analytic accounting scheme. To understand crime, or for that matter virtually any form of patterned behavior at the macro-level, the analyst needs to direct attention to social organization—the prevailing culture and social structure. Merton applies his basic analytic accounting scheme to the case of the U.S.

As has been fully explicated in the literature, Merton's substantive thesis centers on alleged "contradictions" and "disjunctions" within the culture, and between the culture and a central feature of the social structure, the stratification system. Within American culture, Merton detects a disproportionate emphasis on the importance of realizing cultural goals, especially the goal of monetary success relative to the emphasis placed on the importance of using the legitimate means for pursuing goals. This cultural imbalance fosters *anomie,* wherein the selection of the means for social action is governed purely on the basis of considerations of technical efficiency. Merton further observes a structural strain built into the social organization of American society that derives from the combination of universal success goals and unequal access to the legitimate means for realizing success. Persons for whom access to the legitimate means is blocked are exposed to structural pressures to adapt in various ways, including the selection of technically efficient, but illegal, means to realize goals. Through these insightful and provocative arguments, Merton skillfully illustrates the utility of explaining macro-level phenomena, such as crime rates, with explicit reference to the fundamental features of the social organization of a society.

Our explanation of the interconnections between crime and social organization in the U.S. takes as its point of departure Merton's characterization of the goals-means imbalance in the culture. The disproportionate emphasis on achieving the goal of material success relative to the emphasis on the importance of using legitimate means is a defining feature of the culture: It is encapsulated in the cultural ethos of the "American Dream." Similarly, following Merton, we conceptualize anomie as a condition wherein the means of social action have been literally *de*-moralized; considerations of the legitimacy of the means are rendered subservient to assessments of their technical efficiency.

We then extend Merton's characterization of the cultural component of social organization in the U.S. by making explicit the value-foundations of the ethos of the American Dream. As noted by Parsons in his classic treatment of the "pattern variables" of social systems, the value complex in the U.S. is an exemplar of a "universalistic achievement" pattern. People are evaluated on the basis of what they have accomplished, what they have done, rather than who they are. This evaluative standard of achievement is applied broadly: Everyone is encouraged to succeed. Moreover, American culture exhibits a distinctive type of materialism. "Money" becomes the principal sign of success. As Marco Orru observes, money is the *"currency* for measuring achievement."American culture also places a particularly strong emphasis on individualism. Individual rights and entitlements are awarded priority over collective duties and obligations. In this manner, we elaborate Merton by proposing that the anomic type of culture in the U.S. that he so aptly describes rests upon a distinctive value-complex, one heavily tilted toward achievement orientation, universalism, individualism, and a pecuniary materialism.

While our approach to the cultural component of social organization follows Merton's lead rather closely, we shift attention in our analysis of social structure from the stratification system to selected institutions that bear primary responsibility for meeting the survival requirements of a society. Our analysis is based on the premise that the integration of institutions in a society or social system requires the balancing of sometimes competing "claims" of institutional roles. In any given society, a particular "institutional balance of power" emerges that reflects the ways in which its members accomplish this balancing task. The distinctive feature of the institutional structure in the U.S., we propose, is that it is characterized by dominance of the economy. Non-economic roles tend to be devalued relative to economic roles; non-economic roles typically are accommodated to economic roles when conflicts emerge; and the logic and mentality of the marketplace penetrates into the non-economic realms of social life. We illustrate economic dominance in the institutional balance of power in the U.S. with reference to the interconnections among the economy, the family, the polity, and the educational system.

Finally, to apply our characterization of the form of social organization in the U.S. specifically to the explanation of crime, we incorporate strands of conventional criminological theory. A high degree of anomie in the culture implies weak internal controls. Social norms are relatively ineffective in governing behavior, thus increasing the likelihood that people will pursue their goals "by any means necessary," including criminal means.

At the same time, economic dominance gives rise to enfeebled non-economic institutions. This leads to weak institutional controls—with the exception of the permissive "controls" emanating from a free-market economy—and meager institutional support which can be linked with crime via classical social disorganization theory and social support theory. As depicted schematically in Figure 1, the basic analytical model of social organization and crime underlying IAT thus incorporates values and norms from the culture, along with institutional interrelationships and corresponding controls and support from the social structure, to serve as the conceptual foundation for a macro-social explanation of crime.

## Analytic Review of Empirical Applications of IAT

IAT represents an attempt to understand the social sources of crime by applying core sociological concepts that are applicable to societies in general. Although this high level of abstraction enhances the scope of IAT, it renders empirical assessments difficult. Deriving specific causal propositions and identifying operational measures of the key concepts pose daunting challenges. Nevertheless, efforts to apply IAT in empirical analyses of crime have begun to accumulate. In our review of this literature, we restrict attention to macro-level research that has appeared in published sources and include studies that integrate IAT

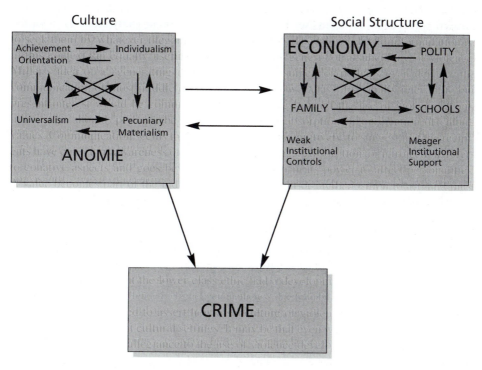

**FIGURE 1**
The analytical model of social organization and crime in IAT.

with other theoretical perspectives if the authors themselves regard the analyses as bearing directly on IAT. Our review is organized around two overarching themes: assessment of IAT's institutional dynamics and assessment of its cultural dynamics.

### Analyses of institutional dynamics

Researchers have confronted the challenge of applying the arguments about institutional structure and functioning advanced in IAT in several creative ways. Chamlin and Cochran, in their pioneering application of IAT cited above, draw on a policy recommendation presented in *Crime and the American Dream* to deduce specific propositions to guide their research. They note the claim in *Crime and the American Dream* that changes in economic conditions are unlikely to lead to significant reductions in crime in the absence of other changes in the culture and institutional structure of society and, more specifically, changes in the institutional balance of power. Building on the logic underlying this claim, they hypothesize that the effect of conventional indicators of adverse economic conditions that have been theoretically linked to crime will exhibit *interactive* rather than main effects on crime rates, reflecting a moderating role of the institutional balance of power.

Chamlin and Cochran thus elaborate the analytical model of IAT to incorporate the interrelationships between the institutional balance of power and "outputs" of the economy. They select poverty as the output of the economy to examine and conceptualize the institutional balance of power in terms of the vitality of three non-economic institutions: the family, religion, and the polity. This enables them to translate the highly abstract analytic model of IAT into a causal model that is amenable to empirical assessment via standard regression techniques (see Figure 2). Using data on property crime rates for the U.S. states in 1980 and indicators of the vitality of the non-economic institutions, they find evidence consistent with theoretical expectations. The regression coefficients for the product terms representing the hypothesized interactions are statistically significant in the predicted direction.

The Elaborated Analytical Model:

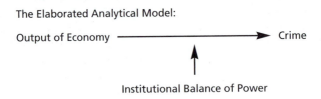

The Causal Model of Moderating Effects:

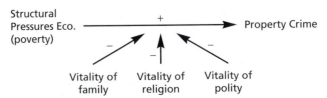

**FIGURE 2**
Chamlin and Cochran's translation of IAT into a casual model.

Several subsequent studies have followed the "moderating effects" framework to investigate the institutional dynamics depicted by IAT. Piquero and Piquero set out to replicate and extend Chamlin and Cochran's research. They conduct cross-sectional analyses of crime rates for the U.S. states with more recent data. In addition, they include violent crime rates as well as property crime rates in their analyses and assess the sensitivity of the results to alternative operationalizations of key concepts. The results of their analyses offer mixed support for IAT. The regression coefficients for the product terms are consistent with the theory in some instances, and this can be observed for both property and violence crimes but not in others. The authors accordingly caution that conclusions about IAT may be sensitive to decisions about operationalization.

Four other studies have extended the "moderating effects" framework to analyze additional institutional domains and different units of analysis. Hannon and DeFronzo draw on an integrated formulation of IAT and social support theory to hypothesize that levels of welfare assistance will moderate the effects of economic deprivation on crime rates. Using data on total, violent, and property crime rates for a sample of large metropolitan areas in the U.S. in 1990, they find that their composite index of "resource deprivation" exhibits the expected interaction effect with their welfare index: "higher levels of welfare assistance reduce the strength of the positive relationship between the size of the disadvantaged population and crime rates." They interpret these results as supportive of IAT.

Stucky also focuses on subnational units within the U.S., specifically cities. He combines insights from IAT and "systemic" social disorganization theory to predict that indicators of the responsiveness of local political structures will interact with indicators of deprivation (considering "family deprivation" as well as the more commonly studied "economic deprivation") in their effects on crime. He tests these hypotheses with data on violent crime rates for a sample of cities in 1990. His results are consistent with expectations. The effects of structural indicators of deprivation are mitigated in cities with local political structures that reflect greater responsiveness to citizens.

In addition to these studies based on data for population aggregates within the U.S., two analyses using cross-national data have adopted the "moderating effects" framework in the application of IAT. Savolainen employs a measure of "decommodification," or the generosity and extensiveness of social welfare policies, as an indicator of the vitality of non-economic institutions. He hypothesizes that the effects of income inequality and ascribed economic inequality on homicide rates should be less pronounced in nations that have "tamed the market" through policies of decommodification. His analyses of two cross-national samples offer support for the hypotheses. Subsequent research by Pratt and Godsey, using different operationalizations of key concepts, essentially reaffirms Savolainen's main conclusions. Pratt and Godsey observe that their indicator of social welfare policies (the percent of the nation's gross domestic product spent on health care) moderates the effect of an indicator of income inequality on homicide rates in the theoretically expected manner.

Although the bulk of the research on the institutional dynamics stipulated by IAT has followed the moderating effects strategy, two other approaches can also be discerned in the literature. In our study of "decommodification" that preceded Savolainen's work, we treat the measure of decommodification as an indicator of the balance between the polity and economy and hypothesize that it will exhibit a direct effect on homicide rates, net of controls. Our analyses of a cross-national sample offer evidence consistent with this "main effects" model. However, following the same logic but using data for a slightly different sample of nations, and employing a regression model with different control variables, Jensen does not replicate these findings about the effect of decommodification on homicide rates.

Batton and Jensen also examine the main effects of measures of decommodification in a time-series analysis of U.S. homicide rates for the period 1900 to 1997. Their analysis produces mixed support for IAT arguments. Although they find no significant effect of decommodification on homicide rates for the period as a whole, they do find an effect in the expected direction for the earlier subperiod 1900 to 1945. They interpret their results as suggesting that decommodification has a conditional effect on homicide that occurs under particular institutional circumstances.

Cullen et al. similarly apply IAT with a "main effects" approach but shift attention from the kinds of behaviors typically studied—violent and property crimes—to a very different dependent variable: managerial ethical reasoning. They examine the extent to which managers are willing to justify behavior that is ethically suspect. Drawing on IAT, they hypothesize that features of the institutional structure of a nation indicative of (or possibly casually related to) economic dominance will be positively associated with the tendency of managers to regard ethically suspect behavior as justified. The structural characteristics under consideration include indicators of welfare socialism, family breakdown, educational attainment and industrialization. Cullen et al. assess their hypotheses with data from a sample of 3,450 managers from 28 nations. Using the techniques of hierarchical linear modeling, they find support for three of the four hypotheses. The one unexpected finding emerges for the indicator of welfare socialism that is positively, rather than negatively, associated with managers' willingness to justify ethically suspect behaviors. The authors speculate that this finding may reflect the fact that members of the managerial classes are likely to be "net losers" under socialist policies.

A final approach to assessing the institutional dynamics of IAT in the literature assesses the possibility of "mediating" effects in the linkages among economic institutions, non-economic institutions, and crime. Maume and Lee argue that the language in *Crime and the American Dream* can be interpreted as consistent not only with the "moderating effects" model but also with a model wherein economic dominance undermines the vitality of non-economic institutions which, in turn, leads to high levels of crime in a manner suggested by classical social disorganization theory. They conceptualize family income inequality as an indictor of the dominance of the economy and estimate main and interaction effects of income inequality on homicides (disaggregated on the basis of "expressive" and "instrumental" motivation) with an array of indicators of the strength of non-economic institutions for a sample of U.S. counties circa 1990. They report that the evidence offers greater support for the mediation model than for the moderation model that has been assessed more frequently.

### Analyses of cultural dynamics

Research on the cultural dynamics of IAT is much more limited than that on institutional dynamics. To a large extent, this reflects the difficulties in obtaining valid and reliable measures of cultural orientations for quantitative analysis. Nevertheless, a few noteworthy efforts along these lines have appeared in the literature.

The research by Cullen et al. on managerial ethical reasoning discussed above includes an indirect assessment of claims about the interconnections among basic societal values, the normative orders, and attitudes that are presumably conducive to illegal behavior. Drawing on the arguments about the value foundations of the American Dream, the authors hypothesize that strong commitments to achievement, individualism, universalism, and pecuniary materialism should be related to high rates of crime because these kinds of value commitments give rise to relatively weak social norms. In the absence of measures of the weakness of norms or the degree of anomie, Cullen et al. assess their hypotheses by treating anomie as an unmeasured, intervening construct. The logic of this approach is depicted in the top panel of Figure 3.

Cullen et al. construct measures of the specified value orientations using cross-national survey responses from a variety of sources. As in the analyses of institutional dynamics, they employ hierarchical linear modeling to estimate the effect of the nation-level indicators of values on managers' willingness to justify ethically suspect behavior, net of selected individual-level variables. The results of their analyses offer mixed support for IAT. The measures of universalism and pecuniary materialism are related to managers' willingness to justify ethically suspect behavior in the expected positive direction. In contrast, the indicators of achievement orientation and individualism exhibit significant negative effects on the dependent variables. The authors once again speculate that the application of IAT to the specific population under investigation—managers—may not be straightforward because of the distinctive opportunity structures that confront this population.

Chamlin and Cochran adopt a different strategy. They apply IAT to the cultural component of social organization by directing attention to a hypothesized correlate of anomie: social altruism. They suggest that communities characterized by strong commitment to altruistic values are likely to be less anomic than those with a weaker commitment to altruism. IAT thus provides a rationale for anticipating a negative effect of measures of altruism on crime (see the bottom panel of Figure 3). Chamlin and Cochran operationalize altruism

Anomie as an Unmeasured Intervening Construct (Cullen et al.):

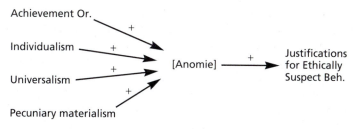

Altruism as an Unmeasured Correlate of Anomie (Chamlin & Cochran):

**FIGURE 3**
The logic of assessments of IAT cultural dynamics.

by means of the ratio of contributions to United Way campaigns, relative to aggregate income, and assess the effect of this measure on personal and property crime rates for a sample of U.S. cities. The results reveal significant, negative effects of altruism on both types of crime rates in multivariate analyses consistent with the logic of IAT.

Finally, studies by Jensen and Cao report evidence relevant to the empirical premise of American "cultural exceptionalism" underlying IAT. Jensen compares the U.S. with other nations on items from the World Values Survey (WVS) that might be regarded as indicators of the importance accorded economic roles relative to other activities, the embrace of pecuniary success goals, and the adoption of self-interested and utilitarian standards concerning law breaking. He concludes that respondents in the U.S. are not distinctive in displaying particularly utilitarian or materialistic orientations, nor do they stand out as having attitudes of expediency toward the law.

Cao similarly use items from the WVS to make cross-national comparisons of cultural orientations, focusing specifically on "anomie." Cao creates an anomie index by combining responses to six statements that refer to the justification of criminal or deviant scenarios: claiming government benefits the person is not entitled to, avoiding a fare on public transport, cheating on a tax if given the chance, buying stolen property, accepting a bribe, and failing to report damage the person has done to a parked vehicle. Cao reports that the mean level of anomie so measured in the U.S. "is not particularly high" raising questions about the claim that American society is exceptionally anomic. . . .

## Conclusion

Thirty years ago, in a collection of papers published in honor of Robert K. Merton, Stephen Cole traced the influence of the theory of social structure and anomie on deviance research during the period extending from the 1950s through the early 1970s. Cole examined all articles dealing with deviance that had appeared in four leading sociology journals: *American Sociological Review, American Journal of Sociology, Social Forces,* and *Social Problems*. On the basis of his analysis of the number and nature of citations to SS&A, Cole concluded that the era of great prominence for Mertonian anomie theory had passed. Cole further proposed that the declining influence of Merton's theory could not be attributed to any conclusive disconfirmation of its core claims. To the contrary, "there was certainly as much evidence in support of SS&A and derivative theories as in opposition." Instead, the fate of SS&A reflected a latent function of theory, namely, to provide "puzzles for research." The reason for the declining significance of Merton's theory, Cole speculated, was that the field had simply "exhausted most of the puzzles it had provided."

It certainly would be an exaggeration to claim that IAT has received overwhelming empirical support to date. Our review of the literature indicates that the results of efforts to evaluate hypotheses derived from the theory have been mixed and have been more supportive in some areas (institutional dynamics) than in others (cultural dynamics). In addition, the theory is clearly incomplete in important respects. We have noted, in particular, that Mertonian insights about the social structuring of criminal incentives and opportunities have yet to be incorporated systematically and formally into the framework of IAT. Nevertheless, an appreciable body of research informed by IAT has been steadily accumulating over recent years. This suggests to us the theory has served well the key latent function of replenishing the "puzzles" that stimulate criminological research.

# CONTEMPORARY RETROSPECTIVE ON ANOMIE THEORIES

## ANOMIE IN PERSPECTIVE

*Sandra Legge, University of Bielefeld; and*
*Steven F. Messner, University at Albany, State University of New York*

Robert K. Merton's "social structure and anomie" (hereafter referred to by the widely used acronym, SS&A) is the seminal work in the anomie research program in criminology. The original statement of SS&A was published in the *American Sociological Review* in 1938, but Merton continued to revise and elaborate the key arguments in subsequent publications, most notably in his book *Social Theory and Social Structure* (Merton, 1968). Merton was not the first to introduce the general concept of anomie to the scholarly community. The French sociologist Émile Durkheim (1897/1966b) had written about anomie as a problematic social condition that is likely to lead to high levels of suicide in his writings near the end of the nineteenth century. Merton deserves credit, however, for developing systematic accounts of how normal features of social organization can ironically promote crime and other forms of deviant behavior by fostering anomie, and how the pressures toward anomie are likely to be distributed unevenly across the class structure.

The starting point for SS&A is the demarcation of the scope conditions of the theory. Merton distances himself from popular, Freudian explanations of deviant behavior and makes clear that he is not interested in the social psychological processes that operate at the individual level. Rather, his interest lies in "macrolevel" phenomena. More specifically, he is concerned primarily with explaining why levels of crime and deviance vary across societies, and why levels of these phenomena vary systematically across the social structure within a given society. To address these sociological concerns, Merton concentrates his analysis on what he considers to be the two core properties of social organization— culture and social structure.

Merton further differentiates culture into two components: the "goals" and the "institutionalized means." The cultural goals are what people are encouraged to strive for, and the institutionalized means are the socially approved ways of pursuing these goals. In a well-integrated culture, these two components of the culture receive roughly comparable emphasis. Accepting the goals and abiding by the approved means are equally important. Merton suggests, however, that this is not the case for the culture of American society. To the contrary, American culture exhibits a peculiar imbalance. The goals are emphasized to a great extent, whereas the means receive much less emphasis. Merton highlights in particular the cultural goal of monetary success. The message to accumulate money and wealth comes across loud and clear. The rules about how to pursue these goals, in contrast, are not assigned nearly as much importance—what one gets is much more important than how one gets it. This imbalance or malintegration within the culture is the source of anomie or "normlessness." The rules that are supposed to govern behavior weaken and become relatively ineffective.

Alongside the imbalanced relationship between the core elements of the culture is another imbalanced relationship, that between the social structure and culture. Merton points out that the culturally determined goals in American society have a "universalistic" character. They are presumably valid for everyone. However, the access to the legitimate means to realize these goals is not universal. In particular, those located at the lower ends of the social class hierarchy confront barriers to the legitimate means for pursuing success. This combination of universalistic goals and inequality of opportunity undermines commitment to the social norms and is thus conducive to anomie in the culture. In Merton's (1968) words: "When the cultural and the social structure are malintegrated, the first calling for behavior and attitudes which the second precludes, there is a strain towards the breakdown of norms, toward normlessness" (p. 217).

But people encountering restricted access to the legitimate means for success do not necessarily react by committing crimes. In fact, the majority of people even in a malintegrated society tend to conform by embracing the cultural goals and following the institutionalized means. They do so largely because they blame their failure on themselves. The cultural system encourages individuals to make such attributions, and these attributions have the function of deflecting blame away from the system (Merton, 1968, pp. 191, 201–203, 222). Others, however, may adapt in a nonconformist or deviant manner.

The mode of adaptation that has been of greatest interest to criminologists is that of "innovation." The innovator accepts the cultural goals, especially the goal of monetary success, but substitutes technically expedient, sometimes illegal, means for the legitimate means. Instrumental property crimes can be interpreted as examples of the innovative adaptation. Others adapt by giving up on the cultural success goals but continuing to abide by the institutionalized means. Merton labels such an adaptation "ritualism" to indicate the ritualistic adherence to social rules. A further mode of adaptation is "retreatism." This entails the rejection of both the cultural goals and means, essentially dropping out of society. Criminal forms of retreatism include the consumption of illegal drugs. The final mode of adaptation is "rebellion." This involves rejecting both the goals and means and replacing them with alternative goals and means in an effort to transform the society.

In sum, SS&A proposes a sociological explanation for high rates of crime and other forms of deviant behavior that is cast in terms of the fundamental properties of social organization. An imbalance in the emphasis on goals and means in the culture, combined with a disjuncture between universalistic goals and unequal opportunities in the social structure, creates pressures to anomie and nonconformist behavior, including crime as a form of innovation. Moreover, these structural pressures are likely to be particularly acute for those on the lower rungs of the social class ladder. A distinctive feature of this explanation is the subtle interplay of cultural and social structural forces. Many criminological theorists focus exclusively on either culture or social structure (see Kornhauser, 1978). "By contrast, anomie theory incorporates both dimensions in an explanation, that whatever its empirical failings, has the great advantage of being conceptually complete. . . . Neither cultural conformity nor structural deprivation is, by itself, a sufficient cause of crime in Merton's formulation" (Messner & Rosenfeld, 2007, p. 57).

### Critiques

Merton's anomie theory certainly represents one of the most discussed sociological theories within the field of criminology, and its influence is impossible to deny (Abercombie, Hill, & Turner, 1988, p. 11). Nevertheless, the theory has also been heavily criticized over the decades (for overviews, see Bernard, 1984; Bohle, 1975; Clinard, 1964). These critiques refer especially to the adequacy of basic assumptions, the inexact/vague definitions of basic concepts, an inexact/insufficient formulation of the relationships among variables, and omissions and incompleteness in the theoretical arguments. One of the early critiques challenges the assumption that "monetary success" is a *unique and common goal* that is shared by all members of the society. Several studies have reported that lower- and upper-class people do not in fact aspire to the same values and goals (Agnew, 1983; Hyman, 1966; Mizruchi, 1960; Rushing, 1970). Developing this theme, Rodman (1963/1964) has theorized about a "value stretch," a means by which people try to adapt culturally determined values and goals to their social situation, thereby leading to cultural pluralism rather than uniformity.

Critics have also faulted Merton for not defining more clearly and explicitly his core concepts. In particular, despite its prominence in the very title of his essay, Merton does not devote much attention to developing a formal conceptualization of "anomie." This has provided ammunition to critics who have charged that Merton's unclear definition of this central concept has fostered "a pattern of steadily increasing semantic confusion" (Levine, 1985, p. 58).

A further, often criticized aspect of Merton's theoretical approach is the implication that the pressures toward anomie weigh mainly on members of the disadvantaged social classes. This might offer a plausible account for involvement in so-called street crimes, at least insofar as the official data on crime are accepted (see Tittle, Wayne, Villemez, & Smith, 1978). But how can these processes account for offending on the part of the well-to-do (i.e., for white-collar crimes)? Merton (1964) himself has responded to this criticism, pointing out that the upper classes are also vulnerable to anomic pressures. "It is not only that *their own* Faustian aspirations are ever escalating, becoming unlimited and insatiable. . . . It is also that, under still poorly understood conditions, more and more is expected of these men by others and this creates its own measure of stress. Less often than one might believe is there room for repose at the top" (p. 221). However, Merton never really integrates these observations about the intense expectations and concomitant stress among the upper classes with his general arguments about social organization and deviant behavior.

Finally, Merton's typology of modes of adaptation has been subjected to critical scrutiny as well (see especially Dubin, 1959; Harary, 1966). Merton has been commended for his "attempt to span both macrosocial and microsocial levels of analysis by tracing the individual-level consequences of cultural and social-structural phenomena" (Menard, 1995, p. 139). However, critics claim that the outcome of this commendable attempt does not reflect more than a descriptive scheme, without any formal criteria for differentiating the two categories referring to "acceptance" and "rejection" of goals and means, and with no unambiguous hypotheses about the factors which are responsible for the choice of the respective modes of adaptation (Baumer, 2007; Bohle, 1975; Dubin, 1959; Kitsuse & Cicourel, 1963). These criticisms certainly have merit, and an important task for further development of Merton's preliminary insights on modes of adaptations is to determine under which conditions passive or active forms of deviant behavior are selected. Merton offers some hints when he speculates that passive forms of deviant behavior (e.g., drug abuse) are more probable when an internal attribution is made, whereas active forms of deviant behavior are more probable if the affected individuals attribute their unfortunate situation to external circumstances. In their classic work on juvenile delinquency, Cloward and Ohlin (1960) in particular have made noteworthy strides in explicating how attributions of failure can facilitate the emergence of delinquent subcultures.

## Empirical Evaluations

A large body of research purporting to test hypotheses derived from Merton's anomie theory has accumulated over the years. The interpretations of these studies have been quite diverse. Some critics have confidently proclaimed that this theoretical approach has been "disconfirmed" (Kornhauser, 1978, p. 180), while others have suggested that the evidence in support of the theory has been at least on par with the evidence opposed to it (Cole, 1975, p. 212). In addition, when assessing the empirical literature, it is important to recall that Merton identified varying modes of individual adaption to structural pressures, and thus research focused solely on crime rather than deviant behavior more generally might not capture the full range of theoretical possibilities. In any event, the bulk of the empirical research has been directed primarily to two overarching issues: the commonly derived prediction of an inverse relationship between social class position and crime, and the role of perceived "strain" as the mechanism that links offending with structural barriers to achievement.

With respect to the issue of a class–crime relationship, an association between neighborhood levels of disadvantage and officially recorded rates of crime and delinquency was amply documented in the early decades of the twentieth century by researchers in the Chicago School.[1] The validity of this relationship, however, has been questioned as criminologists have increasingly moved away from the use of official crime data in favor of the self-report methodology. In self-report studies, samples of respondents, usually juveniles, are presented with questionnaire items asking about involvement in various forms of criminal and delinquent behavior. Analyses based on self-reported offending have typically detected little or no relationship with social class. This has led some to conclude that the widely held view that crime and delinquency are concentrated in the lower classes is a "myth" (Tittle et al., 1978).

Other researchers have urged caution in dismissing a class–crime relationship on conceptual and methodological grounds. One of the limitations of self-report studies is that they typically measure relatively minor forms of offending, especially self-report studies that are focused on juvenile delinquency. The "domain" of behavior in these studies thus differs from that represented in the official crime statistics, which record very serious offenses (along with some relatively minor offenses). Research that encompasses the more serious forms of illegal behavior in the measurement of self-reported offending has tended to find relationships between social class and crime that are more similar to those reported in studies based on official data (Bernard, 1984; Elliott, Huizinga, & Ageton, 1985).

---

[1]Our discussion of empirical assessments of the relationship between social class and crime is taken from Messner (in press), which relies on the review by Akers and Sellers (2004, pp. 170–172).

A second issue involves the nature of the relationship between social class and crime. Some researchers have proposed that high levels of offending are likely to be observed only among those at the very bottom of the social class hierarchy, and if so, standard socioeconomic status measures that cover the entire range of social classes might fail to detect much of an association because they do not focus on the strategic population. Studies using measures that differentiate the highly disadvantaged from others have revealed evidence consistent with the expected association between class and offending (Brownfield, 1986).

A second major body of empirical work informed by Merton's work is the literature on "strain" theory. As explained by Burton and Cullen (1992; see also Messner, 1988), "Merton's macro-level theory of *'social structure and anomie'* has evolved into an individual-level 'strain theory' that roots crime in the experience of blocked access to desired success goals" (p. 1). One variant of strain theory directs attention to a perceived gap between aspirations and expectations. The principal hypothesis here is that the probability of offending should be high for those who *aspire* to lofty goals but who do not *expect* to be able to realize them. The other variant of strain theory focuses on perceptions of blocked opportunities. The main hypothesis to be derived from this variant is that people who evaluate their chances for success unfavorably should exhibit relatively high involvement in criminal activity.

The research informed by strain theory has yielded mixed results. In their comprehensive review of the research extending from the early 1960s up through the early 1990s, Burton and Cullen (1992) conclude that studies operationalizing strain through indicators of perceptions of blocked opportunities have generally offered supportive evidence, whereas studies that operationalize strain with reference to a perceived gap between aspirations and expectations have been largely nonsupportive, although there are exceptions. The authors also observe, however, that the literature at the time of their writing is "woefully inadequate to the task of providing meaningful tests of strain theory" (p. 17).

Recently, Baumer and Gustafson (2007; see also Stults & Baumer, 2008) have developed a particularly innovative approach to testing hypotheses derived from "classic" anomie theory. They use data on individual value commitments taken from the General Social Survey (GSS) aggregated to counties and county clusters. By aggregating individual survey responses to the area level, they are able to characterize populations according to theoretically strategic cultural constructs—goals and means. Specifically, they are able to measure the strength of commitment to monetary success goals and the degree of respect for the legitimate means of attaining monetary success. Their analyses indicate that geographic areas characterized by the combination of a relatively high level of commitment to the goal of monetary success and a low level of commitment to the legitimate means tend to exhibit high rates of instrumental crime. These results are consistent with the logic of SS&A, although the authors note that some hypotheses are not supported, indicating the need for further theorizing in future research.

## Theoretical Refinements

The anomie perspective in criminology as originally set forth in SS&A has evolved continuously as criticisms have been raised and scholars sympathetic to the general approach have responded. Two developments have been particularly important: (1) extensions of the theory by the incorporation of subcultural dynamics, and (2) elaborations at both the macro- and microlevels by the introduction of new concepts.

The most noteworthy subcultural extensions are the influential works on juvenile delinquency by Albert Cohen (1955) and by Richard Cloward and Lloyd Ohlin (1960). Cohen directs attention to the problem of status deprivation shared by working-class boys. These youths tend to be judged according to the standards of the middle class—middle-class "measuring rods"—but their family upbringing makes them ill-suited to succeed according to these standards. One response to such a situation is to develop a delinquent subculture that embraces the exact opposite of middle-class values. Members of such a subculture are thus prone to behaviors that are distinctively "non-utilitarian, malicious, and negativistic" in character (i.e., behaviors that flagrantly flaunt the middle-class value system) (Cohen, 1955, p. 25).

Cloward and Ohlin (1960) similarly emphasize the importance of subcultural dynamics and class barriers to the pursuit of success when understanding juvenile delinquency, but they add an important original insight. They observe that opportunities to engage in various forms of illegitimate behaviors are differentially distributed, just as are the opportunities to engage in normatively approved forms of behavior. In other words, individuals are confronted with illegitimate as well as legitimate opportunity structures, and this "differential opportunity" influences the choice of any delinquent solution. They proceed to develop a typology of subcultural adaptations, differentiating "criminal," "conflict," and "retreatest" subcultures. The extensions of SS&A both by Cohen and by Cloward and Ohlin underscore the significance of social interactional processes and combine them with social structural analysis. Furthermore, Cloward and Ohlin's insights about access to illegitimate opportunities make an important contribution to the application of Merton' theory to the explanation of deviant behavior in the middle and upper class because of the different illegitimate opportunity structures. However, actual empirical tests of these theoretical extensions are very rare, and up to now, the main claims about distinctive types of subcultures have not been empirically supported (Hoffman & Ireland, 1995; Menard, 1997).

Some more recent extensions of anomie theory include the work of Cullen and Wright (1997) as well as Hagan and McCarthy (1997). Cullen and Wright propose that the concept of social support can be readily incorporated within the anomie theoretical framework. They argue that "social support theory is complementary and consistent with both individual-level and macrolevel strain theories" (Cullen & Wright, 1997, p. 189). In an effort to get a more detailed answer to how people respond to strain, the authors consider both the main effect of social support as well as its effect as an intervening variable (buffering effect) between strain and criminal outcomes. Furthermore, Cullen and Wright argue that this integrated model might contribute to a better understanding with respect to the following domains: the explanation of stability and changes in offending; the choice of adaptation; and the degree of resiliency in response to strain-inducing surroundings (Cullen & Wright, 1997, pp. 195–199). Similarly, Hagan and McCarthy (1997) suggest that the concept of "social capital" as developed by Coleman (1988, 1990) can enrich anomie theory by extending the focus beyond economic parameters. They explain that the concept of social capital captures "causal forces involving strains and opportunities that derive not just from the class position of families of origin but also from a variety of institutional sources—including work, family, school, neighborhood, and community" (Hagan & McCarthy, 1997, p. 136).

One of the more important new theoretical approaches that builds upon SS&A is institutional-anomie theory (IAT) formulated by Messner and Rosenfeld (2006, 2007). Consistent with Merton, the authors argue that a disproportionate emphasis on material success goals and a comparatively weak emphasis on the legitimate means are conducive to anomie. Under such cultural conditions, members of society are encouraged to pursue their goals "by any means necessary," including by criminal means. In contrast with Merton, however, the authors look beyond the social class system and direct attention to the role of the basic social institutions in regulating behavior. IAT also focuses on the ways in which culture and social structure operate in a complementary fashion in generating pressures toward anomie, in contrast with Merton's emphasis on the malintegration of these components of social organization (Messner, 2003).

Messner and Rosenfeld observe that each society has a unique balance of institutional forces, which they refer to as the "institutional balance of power." They further argue that in the United States the economy assumes a dominant position in the institutional structure. Such economic dominance is manifested in three interrelated ways: (1) by *devaluation* of noneconomic roles relative to economic roles (e.g., devaluation of work at home, minimal respect for purely academic achievement); (2) by *accommodation* of noneconomic roles to economic roles when conflicts occur (e.g., the adaptation of family life to the demands of the job); and (3) by *penetration* of the logic and mentality of the marketplace into noneconomic institutions (e.g., the tendency to adopt a calculative, utilitarian orientation in noneconomic relationships) (Messner & Rosenfeld, 2007, pp. 76–84). Messner and Rosenfeld further theorize that economic dominance tends to undermine the capacity of noneconomic institutions to exert effective social control and to provide meaningful social support. IAT thus offers an explanation of crime that, similar to Merton, explicitly joins cultural and social structural factors. High levels of crime can be expected when the culture exhibits a high degree of anomie, and when the social structure is characterized by the dominance of the economy over other social institutions. IAT is a relatively new perspective, and thus empirical assessments of it are limited. However, a growing body of research has offered some support for key claims of the theory (Messner & Rosenfeld, 1997b, 2006; Messner, Rosenfeld, & Baumer, 2004).

IAT represents an effort to develop and extend SS&A at the macrolevel of analysis. The most prominent and sophisticated version of the microtheoretical variant of Merton's anomie theory is general strain theory (GST) developed by Agnew (1992, 2001a, 2006a). The basic tenets of GST stipulate that various stressors increase the probability of deviant behavior by generating negative emotions. These stressors are defined as "relationships in which others are not treating the individual as he or she would like to be treated" (Agnew, 1992, p. 48). In later formulations of the theoretical argument, Froggio and Agnew (2007) additionally differentiate between objective kinds of strain (socioeconomic position, divorce, poverty), subjective kinds of strain (the personal evaluation of objective conditions), and vicarious experiences of strain.

SS&A calls attention to one important source of strain—restricted access to the legitimate means for success. However, Agnew postulates that other sources of strain (psychosocial stressors) affect the likelihood of deviant behavior as well. He refers specifically to three central sources of strain. The first type is the failure to achieve positive goals, which is the type recognized in Merton's theory. The second type is the loss of positively valued stimuli. This would include, for example, losing a job, money, boyfriends/girlfriends, and so on. Finally, the third type of strain is the presence of negative stimuli. This covers, for example, verbal or physical abuse, long-term unemployment, and so forth. According to Agnew, the presence of negative stimuli becomes particularly significant when it is associated with inevitability. Agnew further theorizes that the experience of strain and accompanying negative emotions do not automatically lead to criminal or delinquent conduct. Rather, responses to strain depend on coping capabilities, potential costs, and individual dispositions.

Agnew has continued to refine GST over the years in response to the findings of empirical assessments. For example, he has observed that some types of strain appear to be more important than others. Specifically, four conditions enhance the impact of strain on criminal behavior: first, when strain is seen as unjust; second, when strain is high in magnitude; third, when strain is accompanied by low social control; and finally, when the experience of strain is combined with pressure or incentives for criminal acts (Agnew, 2001a, p. 351). Overall, the empirical literature lends considerable support to the basic claim of GST that strain is related to crime and juvenile delinquency in particular. At the same time, efforts to document the hypothesized intervening mechanisms (negative emotions and conditioning variables) have yielded less supportive results (Tittle, Broidy, & Gertz, 2008). Resolving these theoretical anomalies is an important task for future work that continues to develop the microlevel branch of classic anomie theory.

## Policy Applications

The arguments advanced in SS&A have had an appreciable impact on social policy relevant to crime and criminal justice, especially in the United States. Merton's theory highlights in particular the potentially criminogenic consequences of the lack of opportunity. Accordingly, a logical policy response is to enhance opportunities for the disadvantaged. One major initiative along these lines was the Mobilization for Youth Program, which was implemented in the early 1960s and was organized to a large extent by Richard Cloward, a prominent scholar within the general anomie tradition (Liska & Messner, 1999, pp. 49–50). The program involved vocational training and educational enhancements for youths in low-income neighborhoods in New York City. In addition, the program encouraged the residents of disadvantaged communities to organize themselves to address their problems.

The Mobilization for Youth Program generated considerable controversy, and it was never fully implemented as planned. The community organization component did succeed in stimulating political activity and collective protests. There is little evidence the program was effective in reducing crime, and as might be expected, the accompanying political mobilization of a previously complacent citizenry was not received favorably by many local officials. Nevertheless, the implication of classical anomie theory that levels of crime will be reduced by expanding opportunity continues to inform the development of a wide range of social policies.

Institutional-anomie theory leads to a somewhat different perspective on how to deal with the crime problem. While not denying the potential benefits of providing greater equality of opportunity, IAT implies that social policies that focus exclusively on restricted access to the legitimate means are likely to be insufficient because they ignore the other key element of social organization—culture. Anomie arises not only because the stratification system "fails to deliver" but because the culture privileges monetary success goals over other goals and devalues social activities and relationships in the noneconomic institutional domain. From this perspective, fundamental reductions in crime will require not only policies that enhance educational and employment opportunities of the disadvantaged but also basic changes in the social organization of society—a rethinking of the dominant cultural goals and a restructuring of social institutions. This is indeed a tall order, but the historical record shows that societies can be (and have been) transformed in response to collective action and social movements.

Finally, the implications of general strain theory (GST) for crime reduction overlap to some extent with those of the macrolevel variants of anomie theory but supplement them as well. Insofar as policies that expand opportunities alleviate perceptions that individuals are unable to realize their goals, strain and negative emotions should be reduced, and levels of crime and delinquency should decrease. Alongside these macrolevel implications are opportunities to reduce the experience of strain and negative emotions at the microlevel. With respect to disadvantaged communities, it might be useful to promote different forms of participation in the community. The experience of self-efficacy might reduce strain in other domains. Furthermore, communities might provide special spaces and services for youth (e.g., youth clubs, sports clubs, crisis telephone lines for youth). The introduction of support systems for disadvantaged families to handle problems in a constructive way might also be highly beneficial.

At school it could be practical to identify and reduce potential sources of strain. Students who fail to achieve are especially likely to experience strain. Alongside the regular course schedule, schools might provide a broader array of activities to allow students to express their competencies in other, nonacademic fields (sports, social area, etc.). To be good in one subject (e.g., socially helpful behavior) might reduce the experience of strain. Furthermore, schools could implement different programs to handle conflicts among students (e.g., mediation). In so doing, students would learn to develop new coping strategies as alternatives to socially harmful behaviors. Alongside these desirable effects students would also receive the message that school means more than just excellent grades. Of course, it is unrealistic to reduce all potential sources of strain, and some negative experiences can also provide beneficial learning experiences. Nevertheless, general strain theory provides solid grounds for expecting that levels of crime and delinquency can be reduced by concerted efforts to minimize negative experiences and points toward practical policies to do so. These policies, along with the more macrolevel strategies that follow from the logic of anomie theory, offer promising possibilities for creating social environments that, if not "crime free," at least provide for a reasonable degree of public safety and security.

# GENERAL STRAIN THEORY

## FOUNDATION FOR A GENERAL STRAIN THEORY OF CRIME AND DELINQUENCY

*Robert Agnew*

This paper argues that strain theory has a central role to play in explanations of crime/delinquency, but that the theory has to be substantially revised to play this role. Most empirical studies of strain theory continue to rely on the strain models developed by Merton, A. Cohen, and Cloward and Ohlin. In recent years, however, a wealth of research in several fields has questioned certain of the assumptions underlying those theories and pointed to new directions for the development of strain theory. Most notable in this area is the research on stress in medical sociology and psychology, on equity/justice in social psychology, and on aggression in psychology—particularly recent versions of frustration-aggression and social learning theory. Also important is recent research in such areas as the legitimation of stratification, the sociology of emotions, and the urban underclass. Certain researchers have drawn on segments of the above research to suggest new directions for strain theory, but the revisions suggested have not taken full advantage of this research and, at best, provide only incomplete models of strain and delinquency. (Note that most of the theoretical and empirical work on strain theory has focused on delinquency.) This paper draws on the above literatures, as well as the recent revisions in strain theory, to present the outlines of a general strain theory of crime/delinquency.

The theory is written at the social-psychological level: It focuses on the individual and his or her immediate social environment—although the macroimplications of the theory are explored at various points. The theory is also written with the empirical researcher in mind, and guidelines for testing the theory in adolescent populations are provided. The focus is on adolescents because most currently available data sets capable of testing the theory involve surveys of adolescents. This general theory, it will be argued, is capable of overcoming the theoretical and empirical criticisms of previous strain theories and of complementing the crime/delinquency theories that currently dominate the field. . . .

### The Major Types of Strain

Negative relationships with others are, quite simply, relationships in which others are not treating the individual as he or she would like to be treated. The classic strain theories of Merton, A. Cohen, and Cloward and Ohlin focus on only one type of negative relationship: relationships in which others prevent the individual from achieving positively valued goals. In particular, they focus on the goal blockage experienced by lower-class individuals trying to achieve monetary success or middle-class status. More recent versions of strain theory have argued that adolescents are not only concerned about the future goals of monetary success/middle-class status, but are also concerned about the achievement of more immediate goals—such as good grades, popularity with the opposite sex, and doing well in athletics. The focus, however, is still on the achievement of positively valued goals. Most recently, Agnew has argued that strain may result not only from the failure to achieve positively valued goals, but also from the inability to escape legally from painful situations. If one draws on the above theories—as well as the stress, equity/justice, and aggression literatures—one can begin to develop a more complete classification of the types of strain.

Three major types of strain are described—each referring to a different type of negative relationship with others. Other individuals may (1) prevent one from achieving positively valued goals, (2) remove or threaten to remove positively valued stimuli that one possesses, or (3) present or threaten to present one with noxious or negatively valued stimuli. These categories of strain are presented as ideal types. There is no expectation, for example, that a factor analysis of strainful events will reproduce these categories. These categories, rather, are presented so as to ensure that the full range of strainful events are considered in empirical research.

## Strain as the failure to achieve positively valued goals

At least three types of strain fall under this category. The first type encompasses most of the major strain theories in criminology, including the classic strain theories of Merton, A. Cohen, and Cloward and Ohlin, as well as those modern strain theories focusing on the achievement of immediate goals. The other two types of strain in this category are derived from the justice/equity literature and have not been examined in criminology.

*Strain as the disjunction between aspirations and expectations/actual achievements.* The classic strain theories of Merton, A. Cohen, and Cloward and Ohlin argue that the cultural system encourages everyone to pursue the ideal goals of monetary success and/or middle-class status. Lower-class individuals, however, are often prevented from achieving such goals through legitimate channels. In line with such theories, adolescent strain is typically measured in terms of the disjunction between *aspirations* (or ideal goals) and *expectations* (or expected levels of goal achievement). These theories, however, have been criticized for several reasons. Among other things, it has been charged that these theories (1) are unable to explain the extensive nature of middle-class delinquency, (2) neglect goals other than monetary success/middle-class status, (3) neglect barriers to goal achievement other than social class, and (4) do not fully specify why only *some* strained individuals turn to delinquency. The most damaging criticism, however, stems from the limited empirical support provided by studies focusing on the disjunction between aspirations and expectations.

As a consequence of these criticisms, several researchers have revised the above theories. The most popular revision argues that there is a youth subculture that emphasizes a variety of immediate goals. The achievement of these goals is further said to depend on a variety of factors besides social class: factors such as intelligence, physical attractiveness, personality, and athletic ability. As a result, many middle-class individuals find that they lack the traits or skills necessary to achieve their goals through legitimate channels. This version of strain theory, however, continues to argue that strain stems from the inability to achieve certain ideal goals emphasized by the (sub)cultural system. As a consequence, strain continues to be measured in terms of the disjunction between *aspirations* and *actual achievements* (since we are dealing with immediate rather than future goals, actual achievements rather than expected achievements may be examined). . . .

***Strain as the disjunction between expectations and actual achievements.*** As indicated above, strain theories in criminology focus on the inability to achieve *ideal* goals derived from the cultural system. This approach stands in contrast to certain of the research on justice in social psychology. Here the focus is on the disjunction between *expectations* and *actual achievements* (rewards), and it is commonly argued that such expectations are existentially based. In particular, it has been argued that such expectations derive from the individual's past experience and/or from comparisons with referential (or generalized) others who are similar to the individual. Much of the research in this area has focused on income expectations, although the above theories apply to expectations regarding all manner of positive stimuli. The justice literature argues that the failure to achieve such expectations may lead to such emotions as anger, resentment, rage, dissatisfaction, disappointment, and unhappiness—that is, all the emotions customarily associated with strain in criminology. Further, it is argued that individuals will be strongly motivated to reduce the gap between expectations and achievements—with deviance being commonly mentioned as one possible option. This literature has not devoted much empirical research to deviance, although limited data suggest that the expectations-achievement gap is related to anger/hostility. . . .

***Strain as the disjunction between just/fair outcomes and actual outcomes.*** The above models of strain assume that individual goals focus on the achievement of specific outcomes. Individual goals, for example, focus on the achievement of a certain amount of money or a certain grade-point average. A third conception of strain, also derived from the justice/equity literature, makes a rather different argument. It claims that individuals do not necessarily enter interactions with specific outcomes in mind. Rather, they enter interactions expecting that certain distributive justice rules will be followed, rules specifying how resources should be allocated. The rule that has received the most attention in the literature is that of equity. An equitable relationship is one in which the outcome/input ratios of the actors involved in an exchange/allocation relationship are equivalent. Outcomes encompass a broad range of positive and negative consequences, while inputs encompass the individual's positive and negative contributions to the exchange. Individuals in a relationship will compare the ratio of their outcomes and inputs to the ratio(s) of specific others in the relationship. If the ratios are equal to one another, they feel that the outcomes are fair or just. This is true, according to equity theorists, even if the outcomes are low. If outcome/input ratios are not equal, actors will feel that the outcomes are unjust and they will experience distress as a result. Such distress is especially likely when individuals feel they have been underrewarded rather than overrewarded.

The equity literature has described the possible reactions to this distress, some of which involve deviance. In particular, inequity may lead to delinquency for several reasons—all having to do with the restoration of equity. Individuals in inequitable relationships may engage in delinquency in order to (1) increase their outcomes (e.g., by theft); (2) lower their inputs (e.g., truancy from school); (3) lower the outcomes of others (e.g., vandalism, theft, assault); and/or (4) increase the inputs of others (e.g., by being incorrigible or disorderly). In highly inequitable situations, individuals may leave the field (e.g., run away from home) or force others to leave the field. There has not been any empirical research on the relationship between equity and delinquency, although much data suggest that inequity leads to anger and frustration. A few studies also suggest that insulting and vengeful behaviors may result from inequity. . . .

**Summary: Strain as the failure to achieve positively valued goals.** Three types of strain in this category have been listed: strain as the disjunction between (1) aspirations and expectations/actual achievements, (2) expectations and actual achievements, and (3) just/fair outcomes and actual outcomes. Strain theory in criminology has focused on the first type of strain, arguing that it is most responsible for the delinquency in our society. Major research traditions in the justice/equity field, however, argue that anger and frustration derive primarily from the second two types of strain. To complicate matters further, one can list still additional types of strain in this category. Certain of the literature, for example, has talked of the disjunction between "satisfying outcomes" and reality, between "deserved" outcomes and reality, and between "tolerance levels" or minimally acceptable outcomes and reality. No study has examined all of these types of goals, but taken as a whole the data do suggest that there are often differences among aspirations (ideal outcomes), expectations (expected outcomes), "satisfying" outcomes, "deserved" outcomes, fair or just outcomes, and tolerance levels. This paper has focused on the three types of strain listed above largely because they dominate the current literature. . . .

### Strain as the removal of positively valued stimuli from the individual

The psychological literature on aggression and the stress literature suggest that strain may involve more than the pursuit of positively valued goals. Certain of the aggression literature, in fact, has come to de-emphasize the pursuit of positively valued goals, pointing out that the blockage of goal-seeking behavior is a relatively weak predictor of aggression, particularly when the goal has never been experienced before. The stress literature has largely neglected the pursuit of positively valued goals as a source of stress. Rather, if one looks at the stressful life events examined in this literature, one finds a focus on (1) events involving the loss of positively valued stimuli and (2) events involving the presentation of noxious or negative stimuli. So, for example, one recent study of adolescent stress employs a life-events list that focuses on such items as the loss of a boyfriend/girlfriend, the death or serious illness of a friend, moving to a new school district, the divorce/separation of one's parents, suspension from school, and the presence of a variety of adverse conditions at work.

Drawing on the stress literature, then, one may state that a second type of strain or negative relationship involves the actual or anticipated removal (loss) of positively valued stimuli from the individual. As indicated above, numerous examples of such loss can be found in the inventories of stressful life events. The actual or anticipated loss of positively valued stimuli may lead to delinquency as the individual tries to prevent the loss of the positive stimuli, retrieve the lost stimuli or obtain substitute stimuli, seek revenge against those responsible for the loss, or manage the negative affect caused by the loss by taking illicit drugs. While there are no data bearing directly on this type of strain, experimental data indicate that aggression often occurs when positive reinforcement previously administered to an individual is withheld or reduced. And as discussed below, inventories of stressful life events, which include the loss of positive stimuli, are related to delinquency.

### Strain as the presentation of negative stimuli

The literature on stress and the recent psychological literature on aggression also focus on the actual or anticipated presentation of negative or noxious stimuli. Except for the work of Agnew, however, this category of strain has been neglected in criminology.

And even Agnew does not focus on the presentation of noxious stimuli per se, but on the inability of adolescents to escape legally from noxious stimuli. Much data, however, suggest that the presentation of noxious stimuli may lead to aggression and other negative outcomes in certain conditions, even when legal escape from such stimuli is possible. Noxious stimuli may lead to delinquency as the adolescent tries to (1) escape from or avoid the negative stimuli; (2) terminate or alleviate the negative stimuli; (3) seek revenge against the source of the negative stimuli or related targets, although the evidence on displaced aggression is somewhat mixed; and/or (4) manage the resultant negative affect by taking illicit drugs.

A wide range of noxious stimuli have been examined in the literature, and experimental, survey, and participant observation studies have linked such stimuli to both general and specific measures of delinquency—with the experimental studies focusing on aggression. Delinquency/aggression, in particular, has been linked to such noxious stimuli as child abuse and neglect, criminal victimization, physical punishment, negative relations with parents, negative relations with peers, adverse or negative school experiences, a wide range of stressful life events, verbal threats and insults, physical pain, unpleasant odors, disgusting scenes, noise, heat, air pollution, personal space violations, and high density. In one of the few studies in criminology to focus specifically on the presentation of negative stimuli, Agnew found that delinquency was related to three scales measuring negative relations at home and school. The effect of the scales on delinquency was partially mediated through a measure of anger, and the effect held when measures of social control and deviant beliefs were controlled. And in a recent study employing longitudinal data, Agnew found evidence suggesting that the relationship between negative stimuli and delinquency was due to the *causal* effect of the negative stimuli on delinquency (rather than the effect of delinquency on the negative stimuli). Much evidence, then, suggests that the presentation of negative or noxious stimuli constitutes a third major source of strain.

Certain of the negative stimuli listed above, such as physical pain, heat, noise, and pollution, may be experienced as noxious largely for biological reasons (i.e., they may be unconditioned negative stimuli). Others may be conditioned negative stimuli, experienced as noxious largely because of their association with unconditioned negative stimuli. Whatever the case, it is assumed that such stimuli are experienced as noxious regardless of the goals that the individual is pursuing.

### The links between strain and delinquency

Three sources of strain have been presented: strain as the actual or anticipated failure to achieve positively valued goals, strain as the actual or anticipated removal of positively valued stimuli, and strain as the actual or anticipated presentation of negative stimuli. While these types are theoretically distinct from one another, they may sometimes overlap in practice. So, for example, the insults of a teacher may be experienced as adverse because they (1) interfere with the adolescent's aspirations for academic success, (2) result in the violation of a distributive justice rule such as equity, and (3) are conditioned negative stimuli and so are experienced as noxious in and of themselves. Other examples of overlap can be given, and it may sometimes be difficult to disentangle the different types of strain in practice. Once again, however, these categories are ideal types and are presented only to ensure that all events with the potential for creating strain are considered in empirical research.

Each type of strain increases the likelihood that individuals will experience one or more of a range of negative emotions. Those emotions include disappointment, depression, and fear. Anger, however, is the most critical emotional reaction for the purposes of the general strain theory. Anger results when individuals blame their adversity on others, and anger is a key emotion because it increases the individual's level of felt injury, creates a desire for retaliation/revenge, energizes the individual for action, and lowers inhibitions, in part because individuals believe that others will feel their aggression is justified. Anger, then, affects the individual in several ways that are conducive to delinquency. Anger is distinct from many of the other types of negative affect in this respect, and this is the reason that anger occupies a special place in the general strain theory. It is important to note, however, that delinquency may still occur in response to other types of negative affect—such as despair, although delinquency is less likely in such cases. The experience of negative affect, especially anger, typically creates a desire to take corrective steps, with delinquency being one possible response. Delinquency may be a method for alleviating strain, that is, for achieving positively valued goals, for protecting or retrieving positive stimuli, or for terminating or escaping from negative stimuli. Delinquency may be used to seek revenge; data suggest that vengeful behavior often occurs even when there is no possibility of eliminating the adversity that stimulated it. And delinquency may occur as adolescents try to manage their negative affect through illicit drug use. The general strain theory, then, has the potential to explain a broad range of delinquency, including theft, aggression, and drug use.

Each type of strain may create a *predisposition* for delinquency or function as a *situational event* that instigates a particular delinquent act. In the words of Hirschi and Gottfredson, then, the strain theory presented in this paper is a theory of both "criminality" and "crime" (or to use the words of Clarke and Cornish, it is a theory of both "criminal involvement" and "criminal events"). Strain creates a predisposition for delinquency in those cases in which it is chronic or repetitive. Examples include a continuing gap between expectations and achievements and a continuing pattern of ridicule and insults from teachers. Adolescents subject to such strain are predisposed to delinquency because (1) non-delinquent strategies for coping with strain are likely to be taxed; (2) the threshold for adversity may be lowered by chronic strains; (3) repeated or chronic strain may lead to a hostile attitude—a general dislike and suspicion of others and an associated tendency to respond in an aggressive manner; and (4) chronic strains increase the likelihood that individuals will be high in negative affect/arousal at any given time. A particular instance of strain may also function as the situational event that ignites a delinquent act, especially among adolescents predisposed to delinquency. Qualitative and survey data, in particular, suggest that particular instances of delinquency are often instigated by one of the three types of strain listed above. . . .

## Adaptations to (Coping Strategies for) Strain

The discussion thus far has focused on the types of strain that might promote delinquency. Virtually all strain theories, however, acknowledge that only *some* strained individuals turn to delinquency. Some effort has been made to identify those factors that determine whether one adapts to strain through delinquency. The most attention has been focused on the adolescent's commitment to legitimate means and association with other strained/delinquent individuals.

The following discussion builds on this effort and is in two parts. First, the major adaptations to strain are described. This discussion points to a number of cognitive, emotional, and behavioral coping strategies that have not been considered in the criminology literature. Second, those factors that influence whether one adapts to strain using delinquent or nondelinquent means are described. This discussion also expands on the criminology literature to include several additional factors that affect the choice of adaptation.

### Adaptations to strain

What follows is a typology of the major cognitive, emotional, and behavioral adaptations to strain, including delinquency.

*Cognitive coping strategies.* Several literatures suggest that individuals sometimes cognitively reinterpret objective stressors in ways that minimize their subjective adversity. Three general strategies of cognitive coping are described below; each strategy has several forms. These strategies for coping with adversity may be summarized in the following phrases: "It's not important," "It's not that bad," and "I deserve it." This typology represents a synthesis of the coping strategies described in the stress, equity, stratification, and victimization literatures. The stress literature, in particular, was especially useful. Stress has been found to have a consistent, although weak-to-moderate, main effect on outcome variables. Researchers have tried to explain this weak-to-moderate effect by arguing that the impact of stressors is conditioned by a number of variables, and much of the attention has been focused on coping strategies.

*Ignore/minimize the importance of adversity.* The subjective impact of objective strain depends on the extent to which the strain is related to the central goals, values, and/or identities of the individual. As Pearlin and Schooler state, individuals may avoid subjective strain "to the extent that they are able to keep the most strainful experiences within the least valued areas of their life." Individuals, therefore, may minimize the strain they experience by reducing the absolute and/or relative importance assigned to goals/values and identities.

In particular, individuals may claim that a particular goal/value or identity is unimportant in an absolute sense. They may, for example, state that money or work is unimportant to them. This strategy is similar to Merton's adaptations of ritualism and retreatism, and it was emphasized by Hyman. Individuals may also claim that a particular goal/value or identity is unimportant in a relative sense—relative to other goals/values or identities. They may, for example, state that money is less important than status or that work is less important than family and leisure activities.

The strategy of minimizing strain by reducing the absolute and/or relative emphasis placed on goals/values and identities has not been extensively examined in the strain literature. Certain evidence, however, suggests that it is commonly employed and may play a central role in accounting for the limited empirical support for strain theory. In particular, research on goals suggests that people pursue a wide variety of different goals and that they tend to place the greatest absolute and relative emphasis on those goals they are best able to achieve.

*Maximize positive outcomes/minimize negative outcomes.* In the above adaptation, individuals acknowledge the existence of adversity but relegate such adversity to an unimportant area of their life. In a second adaptation, individuals attempt to deny the existence of adversity by maximizing their positive outcomes and/or minimizing their negative outcomes. This may be done in two ways: lowering the standards used to evaluate outcomes or distorting one's estimate of current and/or expected outcomes.

Lowering one's standards basically involves lowering one's goals or raising one's threshold for negative stimuli. Such action, of course, makes one's current situation seem less adverse than it otherwise would be. Individuals may, for example, lower the amount of money they desire (which is distinct from lowering the importance attached to money). This strategy is also related to Merton's adaptations of ritualism and retreatism, and many of the critics of strain theory in criminology have focused on it. Hyman and others have argued that poor individuals in the United States are not strained because they have lowered their success goals—bringing their aspirations in line with reality. The data in this area are complex, but they suggest that this adaptation is employed by some—but not all—lower-class individuals.

In addition to lowering their standards, individuals may also cognitively distort their estimate of outcomes. As Agnew and Jones demonstrate, many individuals exaggerate their actual and expected levels of goal achievement. Individuals with poor grades, for example, often report that they are doing well in school. And individuals with little objective chance of attending college often report that they *expect* to attend college. In addition to exaggerating positive outcomes, individuals may also minimize negative outcomes—claiming that their losses are small and their noxious experiences are mild.

The self-concept literature discusses the many strategies individuals employ to accomplish such distortions. Two common strategies, identified across several literatures, are worth noting. In "downward comparisons," individuals claim that their situation is less worse or at least no worse than that of similar others (e.g., Brickman & Bulman, Gruder, Pearlin & Schooler, and Suls). This strategy is compatible with the equity literature, which suggests that one's evaluation of outcomes is conditioned by the outcomes of comparison others. Temporal comparisons may also be made, with individuals claiming that their situation is an improvement over the past. Recent research on the social comparison process suggests that individuals often deliberately make downward comparisons, especially when self-esteem is threatened. In a second strategy, "compensatory benefits," individuals cast "about for some positive attribute or circumstance within a troublesome situation . . . the person is aided in ignoring that which is noxious by anchoring his attention to what he considers the more worthwhile and rewarding aspects of experience." Crime victims, for example, often argue that their victimization benefited them in certain ways, such as causing them to grow as a person.

*Accept responsibility for adversity.* Third, individuals may *minimize* the subjective adversity of objective strain by convincing themselves that they *deserve* the adversity they have experienced. There are several possible reasons why *deserved* strain is less adverse than undeserved strain. Undeserved strain may violate the equity principle, challenge one's "belief in a just world", and—if attributed to the malicious behavior of another—lead one to fear that it will be repeated in the future. Such reasons may help explain why individuals who make internal attributions for adversity are less distressed than others.

Drawing on equity theory, one may argue that there are two basic strategies for convincing oneself that strain is deserved. First, individuals may cognitively minimize their positive inputs or maximize their negative inputs to a relationship. Inputs are conceived as contributions to the relationship and/or status characteristics believed to be relevant to the relationship. Second, individuals may maximize the positive inputs or minimize the negative inputs of others. Della Fave uses both of these strategies to explain the legitimation of inequality in the United States. Those at the bottom of the stratification system are said to minimize their own traits and exaggerate the positive traits and contributions of those above them. They therefore come to accept their limited outcomes as just.

**Behavioral coping strategies.** There are two major types of behavioral coping: those that seek to minimize or eliminate the source of strain and those that seek to satisfy the need for revenge.

*Maximizing positive outcomes/minimizing negative outcomes.* Behavioral coping may assume several forms, paralleling each of the major types of strain. Individuals, then, may seek to achieve positively valued goals, protect or retrieve positively valued stimuli, or terminate or escape from negative stimuli. Their actions in these areas may involve conventional or delinquent behavior. Individuals seeking to escape from an adverse school environment, for example, may try to transfer to another school or they may illegally skip school. This rather broad adaptation encompasses Merton's adaptations of innovation and rebellion, as well as those coping strategies described in the equity literature as "maximizing one's outcomes," "minimizing one's inputs," and "maximizing the other's inputs."

*Vengeful behavior.* Data indicate that when adversity is blamed on others it creates a desire for revenge that is distinct from the desire to end the adversity. A second method of behavioral coping, then, involves the taking of revenge. Vengeful behavior may also assume conventional or delinquent forms, although the potential for delinquency is obviously high. Such behavior may involve efforts to minimize the positive outcomes, increase the negative outcomes, and/or increase the inputs of others (as when adolescents cause teachers and parents to work harder through their incorrigible behavior).

**Emotional coping strategies.** Finally, individuals may cope by acting directly on the negative emotions that result from adversity. Rosenberg, Thoits, and others list several strategies of emotional coping. They include the use of drugs such as stimulants and depressants, physical exercise and deep-breathing techniques, meditation, biofeedback and progressive relaxation, and the behavioral manipulation of expressive gestures through playacting or "expression work." In all of these examples, the focus is on alleviating negative emotions rather than cognitively reinterpreting or behaviorally altering the situation that produced those emotions. Many of the strategies are beyond the reach of most adolescents, and data indicate that adolescents often employ illicit drugs to cope with life's strains. Emotional coping is especially likely when behavioral and cognitive coping are unavailable or unsuccessful.

It should be noted that individuals may employ more than one of the above coping strategies. Also, still other coping strategies, such as distraction, could have been listed. It is assumed, however, that the above strategies constitute the primary responses to strain. . . .

## Conclusion

Much of the recent theoretical work in criminology has focused on the integration of different delinquency theories. This paper has taken an alternative track and, following Hirschi's advice, has focused on the refinement of a single theory. The general strain theory builds upon traditional strain theory in criminology in several ways. First, the general strain theory points to several new sources of strain. In particular, it focuses on three categories of strain or negative relationships with others: (1) the actual or anticipated failure to achieve positively valued goals, (2) the actual or anticipated removal of positively valued stimuli, and (3) the actual or anticipated presentation of negative stimuli. Most current strain theories in criminology only focus on strain as the failure to achieve positively valued goals, and even then the focus is only on the disjunction between aspirations and expectations/actual achievements. The disjunctions between expectations and achievements and just/fair outcomes and achievements are ignored. The general strain theory, then, significantly expands the focus of strain theory to include all types of negative relations between the individual and others.

Second, the general strain theory more precisely specifies the relationship between strain and delinquency, pointing out that strain is likely to have a cumulative effect on delinquency after a certain threshold level is reached. The theory also points to certain relevant dimensions of strain that should be considered in empirical research, including the magnitude, recency, duration, and clustering of strainful events.

Third, the general strain theory provides a more comprehensive account of the cognitive, behavioral, and emotional adaptations to strain. This account sheds additional light on the reasons why many strained individuals do *not* turn to delinquency, and it may prove useful in devising strategies to prevent and control delinquency. Individuals, in particular, may be taught those nondelinquent coping strategies found to be most effective in preventing delinquency.

Fourth, the general strain theory more fully describes those factors affecting the choice of delinquent versus nondelinquent adaptations. The failure to consider such factors is a fundamental reason for the weak empirical support for strain theory.

Most of the above modifications in strain theory were suggested by research in several areas outside of traditional criminology, most notably the stress research in medical sociology and psychology, the equity/justice research in social psychology, and the aggression research in psychology. With certain exceptions, researchers in criminology have tended to cling to the early strain models of Merton, A. Cohen, and Cloward and Ohlin and to ignore the developments in related fields. And while these early strain models contain much of value and have had a major influence on the general strain theory in this paper, they do not fully exploit the potential of strain theory.

At the same time, it is important to note that the general strain theory is not presented here as a fully developed alternative to earlier theories. First, the macroimplications of the theory were only briefly discussed. It would not be difficult to extend the general strain theory to the macro level, however; researchers could focus on (1) the social determinants of adversity and (2) the social determinants of those factors that condition the effect of adversity on delinquency. Second, the theory did not concern itself with the nonsocial determinants of strain, such as illness. It seems doubtful that adversity caused by nonsocial sources is a major source of delinquency because, among other things, it is unlikely to generate anger. Nevertheless, nonsocial sources of adversity should be investigated. Third, the relationship between the general strain theory and other major theories of delinquency must be more fully explored. As hinted earlier, the relationship is rather complex. While the general strain theory is clearly distinct from control and differential association theory, strain may lead to low social control and association with delinquent others. Further, variables from the three theories may interact with one another in producing delinquency. Individuals with delinquent friends, for example, should be more likely to respond to strain with delinquency. The general strain theory then, is presented as a foundation on which to build.

# CONTEMPORARY RETROSPECTIVE ON GENERAL STRAIN THEORY

## THE STATUS OF GENERAL STRAIN THEORY

*John P. Hoffmann, Brigham Young University*

Strain theory has a relatively long history in criminology and sociology. However, its popularity has waxed and waned as researchers criticized and then extended it by broadening the scope of attention to a variety of strains that affect individuals. The recent resurgence is due to Robert Agnew's general strain theory. Agnew has taken earlier versions of strain theory, melded them with innovative concepts from contemporary criminological and psychological research, and created a new theoretical model of delinquent and criminal behavior. The goal of this article is to provide a general overview of the theory, offer some pointed critiques, discuss empirical evaluations, review some recent refinements, and conclude with how general strain theory might inform policies that are designed to diminish unlawful behaviors.

### Introduction to General Strain

Early versions of strain theory were based on French sociologist Émile Durkheim's musings about the effects of *anomie,* or the normlessness that occurs as societies undergo structural changes that upset the normal institutional and social balance that is of vital importance in functionalist thought. If, say, economic institutions are not functioning properly, perhaps due to a depression or recession, then other institutions, such as the family or the educational system, are affected and may become unstable. For instance, during an economic recession there may be more divorces as family finances are strained. Under conditions of anomie, social problems such as suicide and crime increase. Although Durkheim's functionalist ideas have been used as a source for social control theories (Hirschi, 1969), the American sociologist Robert Merton (1968) clearly emphasized the role that anomie plays in reducing an emphasis on institutional rules to gain valued cultural goals.

Merton proposed that, in some quarters of American society, an emphasis on the rules of society is weak compared to the drive to gain valuable resources such as money. Those who have few prospects for getting a good education or job realize that their path to economic success is blocked, so they look for alternative means to success. When the disjunction between the legitimate means and the prospects for success widens, people are placed under conditions of strain and are therefore more prone to use illegitimate means to obtain money and other culturally valuable resources.

Mertonian strain theory and its offspring such as Cloward and Ohlin's opportunity theory were pushed to the sidelines—mainly in the 1970s and 1980s—by criminologists who argued that delinquents and criminals did not experience more strain than others. Many observers claimed that there was little evidence that law violators sensed that their life opportunities were impeded by structural blockages. Therefore, strain and its consequent frustrations were not a sufficient explanation for people's involvement in illegal activities. Rather, as discussed by social control theorists, delinquents and criminals merely had low educational and occupational aspirations because they suffered from a lack of commitment to conventional society (see Part VII, "Control Theories," in this book). It was this lack of commitment—and other attenuated bonds—that led to their involvement in unlawful behaviors.

As twilight fell on what I will call traditional strain theory, a young criminologist revisited its basic propositions and pointed out that there might be a way to salvage strain theory. Instead of focusing simply on goals and expectations for success in school or at work, what was needed was much broader attention to the variety of strains that individuals may experience. As shown in the influential 1992 article, Robert Agnew proposed that there are several sources of strain that may affect delinquent and criminal behavior. Actually, though, his research on what is known as general strain theory predated the 1992 article, going back to Agnew's graduate school days. His 1980 PhD dissertation, titled *A Revised Strain Theory of Delinquency,* laid the groundwork for general strain theory. In this and subsequent publications that appeared during the 1980s, Agnew (1984, 1985b, 1989) argued that frustration among adolescents often mounts as they are unable to escape painful situations, such as a violent home life or a tough school environment. This may lead to escape attempts or to anger, which then result in delinquent activities such as running away from home or violent confrontations.

However, it was the 1992 article that brought these ideas together and elaborated the precise mechanisms by which various sources of strain lead to delinquent and criminal behavior. Agnew took earlier views of strain and generalized them to include all negative relations with others rather than just negative relations that are the result of striving for out-of-reach, yet culturally prescribed goals such as monetary success.[1] He also addressed the role that negative emotions, such as anger and frustration, play in the pathways that

---

[1]Albert Cohen (1997), a proponent of traditional strain theory, argued that what made the theory unique was "that it was couched in terms of the means-ends scheme and was concerned with the social origins and consequences of that disjunction between ends and means. If it did not deal with those things, it was not anomie [strain] theory. . . . The perspective of general strain theory is different. It looks at a variety of seemingly unrelated theories and research findings . . . and draws out what appears to be a commonality: the experience of noxious stimuli and consequent delinquent or otherwise deviant conduct" (p. 60).

lead from strain to crime and delinquency.[2] As discussed in the 1992 article, the particular sources of strain are categorized under three general headings: (1) blockage of positively valued goals, (2) loss of positively valued stimuli, and (3) the presence of negative stimuli. Although these are discussed in detail in Agnew's article reprinted in this volume, it is worthwhile to summarize them here.

### Blockage of positively valued goals

Agnew argued that traditional strain represents one aspect of a more general type of strain that he refers to as the "blockage of positively valued goals." This category includes strain in the form of disjunctions between "expectations and actual achievement" and disjunctions between "just/fair outcomes and actual outcomes." For example, adolescents value certain goals such as good grades, being treated well by others, and getting a good job or into a good school. When they perceive that their ability to achieve these goals is blocked due to unfair disadvantages or other barriers, they feel strained. For the same reasons that traditional strain theory saw a pathway to delinquency—frustration over blocked goals leading to delinquent adaptations as adolescents seek culturally valuable objects—Agnew thought that blockage of a variety of goals could affect crime and delinquency.

### Loss of positively valued stimuli

The second category of strain is "the removal or anticipated removal of positively valued stimuli." Agnew argued that stress research, especially in the field of social psychology, supports this position. He suggested that "numerous examples of such loss can be found in the inventories of stressful life-events," and events like the loss of a boyfriend/girlfriend, death or serious illness of a family member or friend, moving, and divorce or separation of parents all represent losses of positively valued stimuli. When families are disrupted through separation or divorce, for example, youths may feel the stress of the breakup and become frustrated as they feel they have little control over the situation. This stress and frustration causes an emotional overload that is channeled into some type of negative outcome such as delinquency, drug use, or emotional withdrawal.

### Negative stimuli

Agnew's third category of strain emphasized "relationships in which others present the individual with noxious or negative stimuli." Negative stimuli include aversive situations or environments (e.g., physically abusive parents, overly critical teachers) as well as negative life events (e.g., criminal victimization, family turmoil). Experiencing noxious stimuli increases the likelihood of delinquency or crime as individuals attempt to escape from the aversive situations, exact revenge on the source of the stimuli, or manage the resulting negative affect with drugs or alcohol. For example, if youths are physically or emotionally abused by parents or guardians, they may attempt to escape these noxious situations by running away from home, getting involved in gangs that provide alternative

---

[2]General strain theory draws considerably from the frustration-aggression hypothesis that was introduced to psychology in the late 1930s. This hypothesis proposed that aggression was a likely outcome of frustrating experiences (states that result when goals are blocked), especially when various social cues that are linked with violence, such as weapons, are present and the aggressive action alleviates the frustration in some way (Berkowitz, 1989).

family structures, or using drugs and alcohol to help them feel better or escape the emotional trauma of the abuse.

## Linking Strain to Crime and Delinquency

General strain theory thus posits that there are various sources of stress and strain that may affect individuals. However, the mere presence of strain—regardless of its source—is not sufficient for delinquent or criminal behavior to ensue. For example, not all strained individuals turn to deviance or delinquency; some may react to strain with conventional conduct. Agnew proposed that individuals respond to strain with a variety of cognitive, behavioral, or emotional adaptations. Within each of these adaptive strategies there exist both deviant and conventional options. Experienced or anticipated strain might, for instance, result in an emotional response in the form of "meditation, biofeedback, and progressive relaxation," or it might result in illicit drug use or violence.

A vital question for general strain theory is *why* some strained individuals get involved in delinquent or criminal behavior. The key condition that links strain to illegal behaviors is what Agnew referred to as *negative affect*. This is the crucial intervening condition between strain and illegal behavior. Negative affect includes a variety of negative emotions such as anger, frustration, guilt, depression, worthlessness, and anxiety (see Broidy & Agnew, 1997). Inclusion of negative affect, Agnew suggested, more clearly discriminates strain theory from other competing (or complementary) individual-level explanations of crime and delinquency. He also argued that while other affective states might lead to deviant adaptations, such as withdrawal or suicidal thoughts, anger is particularly influential in increasing the likelihood of delinquent and criminal behavior: "Anger results when individuals blame their adversity on others, and anger is the key emotion because it increases the individual's level of felt injury, creates a desire for retaliation/revenge, energizes the individual for action, and lowers inhibitions, in part because individuals believe that others will feel their aggression is justified" (pp. 59–60).

Strained individuals who locate the source of strain outside themselves are especially likely to become angry. The attribution of strain to external sources may be either actual or perceived, but when it occurs, anger increases and inhibitions diminish, thus allowing strained individuals to consider using deviant behaviors to remove or manage the strain. For example, adolescents whose parents divorce may become depressed or withdrawn. But, if they become aroused through anger, their reaction may be to lash out at others in an attempt to alleviate their frustration.

### Strain moderators

Agnew also identified conditions that diminish or increase the likelihood of an illicit response to strain. For example, individuals high in self-efficacy (which involves a sense of being able to control life situations to produce desired effects) might be strained, but they may not be inclined to direct adversity at external sources. Instead, a sense of control often leads to other coping strategies. This diminishes the probability that they will become angry when stressed, thus reducing their involvement in crime or delinquency. High self-esteem, a strong social support structure, or several personality factors may serve as similar strain "buffers." In addition, delinquent peers make it more likely that strained adolescents will turn to delinquency because they "reinforce the adolescent's delinquency, and instill delinquent values" (Agnew & White, 1992, p. 478). They may also remind youths of their stressful situations and encourage deviant methods to cope with the strain. However, conventional peers may reduce the effects of strain if they provide a supportive environment or can help minimize the negative stimuli that produce negative emotions such as anger and frustration.

Figure 1 provides a graphical illustration of Agnew's general strain theory. The illustration is quite general, providing only a rough overview of the theory.

## Critiques of General Strain Theory

General strain theory is rather unique as an individual-level explanation of crime and delinquency because it addresses specifically how particular social and psychological relationships and emotions may push people toward delinquency, crime, and drug use. Moreover, the theory is distinct in claiming that various goal blockages and noxious stimuli induce deviant behavior when other choices are not available or when the social environment is conducive to deviance (Agnew, 2006b; Cohen, 1997). Rather than claiming that learning must take place or that we should control adolescents lest their tendencies to

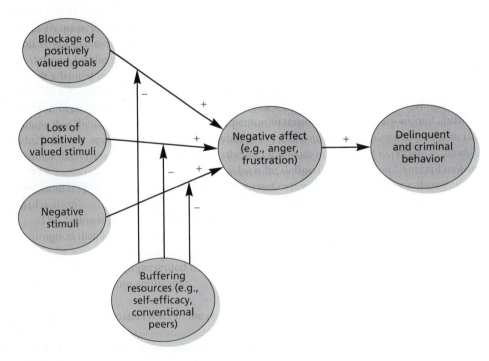

**FIGURE 1**
General strain theory.

become delinquent emerge as a natural consequence (see the articles on social learning and social control), strain theory exemplifies the way that life can push people down a road not of their own doing—a road that results in illegal behaviors. In particular, it offers an interesting model of adolescent behavior since the teenage years are a period of high risk of stresses and strains. Given the link between being treated poorly, such as when adolescents are abused physically or emotionally by adults, and delinquency—as well as the general finding that negative emotions such as anger and frustration are common correlates of delinquency—it is not surprising that general strain theory generates substantial interest as an explanation of delinquent and criminal behavior.

Nevertheless, there are limitations to the theory that should be considered. For example, the intervening steps that lead from strain to illegal behaviors may not be articulated well. It is not clear, for example, why some people get angry when presented with stressful situations, whereas others react by accepting the situation, overcoming it through willful action, or emotionally withdrawing. Aggression and anger, which are not the same trait but are closely related, often show up well before stressful situations. As discussed by psychologists, aggression is a relatively stable trait that begins early in life (Krahe, 2001). Yet, is strain a necessary condition for anger to turn into delinquency? Or, when we see strained youths becoming angry and then delinquent, is this merely a consequence of their anger? In general, then, the conditions thought to result from strain or that moderate the association between strain and crime or delinquency may themselves be the critical factors that produce these behaviors. Perhaps, as discussed in the articles on social learning, some people learn from an early age that the proper response to stress is aggression or violence, whereas others are taught to cope with stress in other ways. Thus, general strain theory may actually be a specific learning theory or at least reflective of what has been learned early in life. On the other hand, several empirical tests of strain theory suggest that stress is associated with illegal behavior regardless of anger, anxiety, or coping strategies. It is not clear why this should occur.

In addition, there are alternative explanations for the link between stressful life events or other strain mechanisms and aggression or violence. A social interactionist perspective, for instance, proposes that, rather than strain being the result of goal blockage which then leads to anger and violence, aggressive behavior is directly linked to seeking a particular goal. Richard B. Felson (1992), a proponent of this position, argued that aggressive and violent interactions usually begin when one person sees a "rule" violation, which presumably could include an informal rule of a particular peer group or neighborhood. The person then asks for an explanation. If it is not satisfactory, the accuser may attack the accused, and aggression and violence escalate. Retaliation by the accused is most likely when other people are present, perhaps as the accused tries to save face or uphold a reputation. In general, then, a social interactionist perspective emphasizes the perceptions and reactions of both parties in a dispute, as well as others who are present during an encounter. In a study that examined this perspective, Felson (1992) found that various feelings of frustration or strain did not predict violent or property delinquency, but that anger did. Moreover, being a target of another's aggression mediated the association between stressful life events and aggression. In other words, one form of strain led to what appeared to be retaliatory delinquent acts, rather than precipitating them directly. Although such a situational approach is not foreign to general strain theory, considering particular aggressive interactions offers a useful complement to the theory's original formulation.

A question regarding research on general strain theory is how negative or noxious stimuli or the removal of positively valued goals should be measured. These are broad terms that are difficult to objectify. They may vary tremendously among youths and adults; some may value personal relationships, whereas others may value their cars, iPods, or new shoes. This has implications for how strain is experienced in one's everyday life. For example, going through a family breakup is normally considered stressful for adolescents and parents, yet it may also reduce an abusive situation. It is also reasonable to consider that experiencing violent victimization is a stressful situation, but will likely be interpreted differently by adolescents in wealthy areas compared to those in violent, inner-city areas. In general, then, much more work is needed to fully determine the sources of strain and how they affect people's lives. It is conceivable that any criminal or delinquent act could be linked to some type of general strain, whether actual or perceived, if we look hard enough. Yet this runs the risk of broadening the sources of strain to an unmanageable set of factors.

## Empirical Evaluations of General Strain Theory

There have been numerous empirical studies of general strain theory since it was introduced. In fact, a recent review suggested that as of 2009, more than 50 articles in professional journals, as well as several theses and dissertations, have specifically examined various aspects of general strain theory and how it applies to delinquency, violence, young adult crime, traffic violations, workplace deviance, and even symptoms of depression. However, it can be a difficult theory to test since there are numerous sources of strain and several factors that presumably enhance or diminish the likelihood that strain results in delinquency. Moreover, Agnew (1992) proposed a comprehensive measurement strategy that takes into account the magnitude, duration, recency, and clustering of strain. He also maintained that using a composite strain score is needed to appropriately assess overall levels of strain among adolescents.

Although the results are not entirely consistent, there is general evidence that the introduction of strain in an adolescent's life is associated with a higher risk of delinquency (see, e.g., Agnew & White, 1992; Aseltine, Gore, & Gordon, 2000; Brezina, 1996; Broidy, 2001; Drapela, 2006; Hay & Evans, 2006; Hoffmann & Cerbone, 1999; Hoffmann & Miller, 1998; Hoffmann & Su, 1997; Mazerolle, Burton, Cullen, Evans, & Payne, 2000; Mazerolle & Piquero, 1998; Paternoster & Mazerolle, 1994; Spano, Rivera, & Bolland, 2006; Tittle et al., 2008). For example, researchers have counted the number of stressful life events (Agnew's loss of valued stimuli) or victimization experiences (Agnew's presence of noxious stimuli) and examined their statistical association with delinquency. Whether using cross-sectional data or longitudinal data, studies have found a consistent positive association with delinquent behavior (e.g., Broidy, 2001; Hoffmann & Miller, 1998; Mazerolle et al., 2000). However, there is also substantial variation in the degree to which various measures of strain are associated with delinquency. This may reflect the complexity of the theory and the difficulty in judging which particular aspects of general strain theory are most influential. Moreover, recall that Agnew proposed that several factors moderate and mediate the association between strain and delinquency.

Although only indirectly relevant to general strain theory, there is also a substantial body of literature indicating that child maltreatment is associated with later delinquency. In brief, numerous studies indicate that when children are physically or emotional abused, they are at a significantly higher risk of delinquency during adolescence (e.g., Ireland, Smith, & Thornberry, 2002; Ryan & Testa, 2005; Smith & Thornberry, 1995). However, similar to Agnew's proposals about general strain theory, this relationship is conditional. Maltreatment is especially likely to result in delinquency when (1) the child's family life is unstable (e.g., the child is placed in foster care or the parents trade off on custody), and (2) when maltreatment persists from childhood into adolescence rather than being limited to childhood only. This supports Agnew's idea that strain that is recent or persistent is most strongly linked to delinquency.

## General strain theory and moderating factors

Several studies have examined whether strain affects delinquency mainly in the presence of other factors such as low self-esteem, low self-efficacy, or delinquent peers. The evidence has been mixed. John P. Hoffmann and Alan S. Miller (1998), for example, determined that strain and delinquency were associated mainly for those high in self-esteem and self-efficacy, which is in the opposite direction to that proposed by Agnew. However, strain was also more strongly related to delinquency among those who had friends who were also delinquent, thus supporting one of Agnew's proposals.[3] Some studies have failed to find any moderating effect of self-esteem or self-efficacy (e.g., Hoffmann & Cerbone, 1999; Jang & Johnson, 2003; Paternoster & Mazerolle, 1994), whereas others have found supporting evidence (e.g., Baron, 2004; Mazerolle & Maahs, 2000). Therefore, it is not fully clear at present what role moderating variables play in the process that leads from strain to delinquency, although it is likely that associating with delinquent peers enhances the effects of strain on delinquency.

## General strain theory and negative affect

As mentioned earlier, an important proposition of general strain theory involves negative affect or emotions in general and anger in particular. Agnew argued that when those experiencing strain become angry or frustrated, they are more likely to respond to that strain with criminal or delinquent behavior. Generally, the research on negative affect as a mediator between strain and delinquency has received mixed support (e.g., Agnew, Brezina, Wright, & Cullen, 2002; Aseltine et al., 2000; Broidy, 2001; Jang & Johnson, 2003). For example, Robert H. Aseltine and colleagues (2000) found that stressful life events, family conflict, and peer conflict—all considered measures of strain—lead to anxiety and anger, and anger leads to aggression, but there is no mediating effect on delinquency. Rather, stressful life events alone are associated with increasing involvement in delinquency (see also Hoffmann & Cerbone, 1999; Mazerolle et al., 2000). Family conflict leads directly to marijuana use, but has no influence on delinquency. Peer conflict leads to anxiety, but not delinquency, aggression, or marijuana use. Figure 2 shows the model that Aseltine and colleagues examined.

---

[3]Hoffmann and Miller found this peer-enhanced effect only in a cross-sectional model. In a longitudinal model, there was inconsistent evidence that the link between strain and delinquency was affected by delinquent peers.

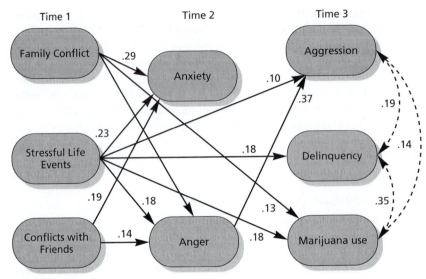

*Note:* Only significant path coefficients are shown. Dashed lines indicate correlations. The correlations among variables are omitted in Times 1 and 2.

**FIGURE 2**
A test of general strain theory. (*Source: Adapted from Aseltine et al., 2000, p. 267.*)

In a more complex and thorough analysis, Lisa Broidy (2001) collected self-report data from college students on the blockage of positively valued goals, unfair outcomes, negative stimuli/loss of positive stimuli (stress), anger, other negative affect, and both conventional and delinquent outcomes from a sample of college students. She showed that experiencing blocked goals decreases rather than increases anger—exactly the opposite of what general strain theory predicts. However, experiencing unfair outcomes as well as stress increases anger, which is consistent with general strain theory. In addition, Broidy found that anger increases the risk of illegitimate coping strategies, such as self-reported delinquency. Therefore, at least among this nonrandom sample of college students it appears that there is some relationship between strain and anger, and that anger increases the risk of illegitimate coping strategies.

**Theoretical Refinements of General Strain Theory**

There are several general issues that Agnew addressed to elaborate general strain theory. First, as suggested earlier, the duration, the frequency, and the recency of strain, as well as the actual number of strains or stressors converging upon the individual at any one time will, in part, determine the effects of these different dimensions of strain on delinquency. Thus, it is important to carefully consider each of these issues in order to fully assess general strain theory. Second, Agnew (2001a) claimed that researchers need to consider the difference between measuring strain subjectively and objectively. While subjective strain measures assess the degree to which individuals are not being treated as they would like to be treated, objective measures of strain assume that individuals experience an event or condition that is disliked, because it is usually disliked by members of his or her group (Agnew, 2001a; Froggio & Agnew, 2007). Sole reliance upon objective strain measures "may cause researchers to underestimate the support for strain theory because objective strains sometime create little subjective strain" (Agnew, 2001a, pp. 321–322). Thus, it is important to carefully delineate the various sources of strain in a person's life to get a full picture of how he or she may affect behavioral outcomes such as delinquency, crime, and other forms of misbehavior.

Third, Agnew argued that personality differences must be considered in research on general strain and crime/delinquency. Some individuals, perhaps because of distinct socialization experiences or genetic makeup, are much more likely to experience "negative emotionality," which involves attributing malicious behavior to others and becoming emotionally aroused. This is a more general term than "negative affect," the key mediator proposed by Agnew in the 1992 article. Although anger and frustration are significant negative emotions, there are also others such as stubbornness, irritability, and mood swings. Another trait involves constraint, or the ability of youths to reign in their impulses to act compulsively or without forethought. Those who lack constraint are reckless and risk-taking, with few feelings for the wants or needs of other people. They experience what Hirschi and Gottfredson have termed low "self-control." In a study of personality and strain, Agnew and colleagues (2002) found that strain, when combined with negative emotionality and low constraint, increase the risk of delinquency more so than if these personality traits are not present.

Finally, Agnew (1999, 2006b) has proposed that strain may be experienced at both the individual level and the macrolevel. He elaborated general strain theory in a manner consistent with much earlier work by Cloward and Ohlin by addressing how stressful social environments reinforce the effects of individual-level strain. Agnew made the obvious point that some communities are much more violent and disruptive than others, and it is these types of communities that are especially likely to highlight the effects of strain among residents. In other words, if we were to expose a group of, say, youths to the same degree of strain and place some in an impoverished, violent neighborhood and others in a safe middle-class neighborhood, we expect those experiencing strain at both the individual and the community level to be especially likely to react through delinquency.

Disorganized neighborhoods are conducive to both strain and crime or delinquency for a number of reasons. Residents of these neighborhoods are often unable to gain monetary or other valued resources, thus strain is higher than in better-off neighborhoods. In addition, various social problems, such as unemployment, family problems, and school problems, tend to be higher in these types of neighborhoods, so the chance of experiencing strain from multiple sources is high. Assuming that these various problems lead to strain, people in these neighborhoods will be exposed to a high proportion of residents who are strained and potentially angry, thus increasing their own propensity to have these experiences. When youths, for example, are provided with models of deviant or violent behavior, it is more likely that they will see deviance or violence as normal behavior. There are also fewer social support networks or other sources of coping in these areas. Finally, disorganized neighborhoods increase the chances of being a victim, which, as mentioned earlier, induces strain and creates an environment where retaliatory violence is expected (Agnew, 2006b).

There have been few tests of whether strain at the macrolevel affects delinquency or crime, although there are numerous studies of how disadvantaged neighborhood conditions affect crime and delinquency (see, e.g., Hoffmann, 2003; Taylor, 2001). John P. Hoffmann (2003) examined whether one measure of general strain—stressful life events—was associated with delinquency across different types of communities. He determined that, regardless of the poverty level or unemployment rates of the communities, stressful life events were significantly related to greater involvement in delinquency. Nevertheless, two studies using different datasets indicated that when schools—which is a type of community for adolescents—include many students who are aggressive and violent, or experience strain in their lives, other students are likely to be delinquent (Brezina, Piquero, & Mazerolle, 2001; Hoffmann & Ireland, 2004). In other words, there may be stressful schools that foster delinquent adaptations among a disproportionate number of students. However, John P. Hoffmann and Timothy O. Ireland (2004) also found that youths who experience many stressful events are more delinquent regardless of the level of stress or delinquency in their schools. Thus, there seems to be something about stress and strain that occurs among individual adolescents that leads to delinquency, but it is relatively independent of the broader environment within which they live or go to school.

## Policy and General Strain Theory

The ideas underlying traditional strain theory suggest that greater access to educational opportunities should be at the heart of any effort to reduce crime and delinquency. Since a good education is one of the best pathways toward legitimate success in American society, and lack of access to a good education is presumably a key blockage that increases the likelihood of deviant adaptations, it is important to make sure that all people have unimpeded access to a good education. General strain theory, because it addresses various frustrating and noxious experiences that may lead to deviant behaviors, recommends that not only access to a good education, but also the alleviation of a variety of strains should be a goal of delinquency prevention efforts. It is also important to find ways to limit the loss of positively valued stimuli or persistent exposure to negative stimuli among adults and adolescents (Agnew, 2006b). For example, as mentioned earlier, it is well established that child maltreatment, such as abuse and neglect, increases the risk of delinquency and later adult crime, as does exposure to violence in the home and in the community. Therefore, policies designed to limit exposure to violence should reduce strain, which in turn should reduce involvement in crime and delinquency.

### Alleviating negative emotions

Policies that are directed at anger specifically or negative affect/emotionality generally might offer effective strategies for reducing crime and delinquency. If strain increases the risk of anger and frustration, which in turn increases the risk of delinquency, then a strategy designed to reduce anger and frustration among adolescents might also reduce delinquency. This simple notion has spawned a litany of anger management programs around the country for adolescents and adults involved in the justice system (Hollenhorst, 1998). For example, Second Step is a school-based program designed to help children "recognize and understand feelings, make positive and effective choices, and keep anger from escalating into violence" (Amendola & Scozzle, 2004, p. 51). This and other programs may offer a useful palliative to the problems that lead up to involvement in delinquency and crime.

### Providing coping resources

Agnew argued that various cognitive and behavioral coping strategies are used by individuals when strain occurs. Some of these, such as social support from family members and close friends, could be used to alleviate the negative emotions that result from strain. Thus, in addition to teaching people to control their anger or frustrations in the face of adversities, programs that teach them cognitive coping strategies or that provide social support networks might reduce tendencies to resort to illegal behaviors when strains become overwhelming. For example, some of the most promising prevention and intervention programs involve *cognitive-behavior therapies (CBTs)*. The principal goals of CBTs are to teach individuals, usually adolescents, to learn to interpret social cues better, reduce their tendency to attribute hostile intentions to others, and gain interpersonal skills. They also attempt to teach people to monitor their behavior and increase their awareness of inappropriate conduct; to reinforce those behaviors that are socially appropriate; and to set clear and specific goals that foster interpersonal relations and lessen the likelihood of aggression. Many CBTs also teach adolescents social skills to avoid aggression and conflict situations, and develop prosocial and problem-solving skills (LeBlanc & Le, 1999).

There are a wide variety of CBTs, so it is difficult to assess their general success in reducing aggressive, criminal, and delinquent behavior. Nevertheless, David S. Bennett and Theresa A. Gibbons (2000) conducted a thorough review of 30 studies on CBTs and antisocial behavior. They concluded that they have a modest effect on reducing problem behaviors among children and adolescents. CBTs are especially effective among older children and adolescents and are moderately effective in reducing impulsivity (Hollon & Beck, 2003; McCart, Priester, Davies, & Azen, 2006), one aspect of low constraint that Agnew proposed as a mediating factor in general strain theory.

## Conclusions

Strain theory has a long history in criminology and delinquency research. Originally a sociological theory that addressed how cultural conditions and social structural arrangements lead some people to use criminal means to obtain valuable goods, it has evolved into a more sophisticated social-psychological theory that draws our attention to how stresses and strains lead some people toward crime, delinquency, and other deviant behaviors. The empirical support for Agnew's general strain theory is impressive, especially the consistent finding that negative life events and the removal of valuable things, whether they be emotional or tangible, are consistently associated with delinquency.

However, the results of studies that include anger or other negative emotions, or the role of social-psychological factors such as self-efficacy, are less impressive. It is still unclear if anger is a prerequisite for crime and delinquency, even the more violent forms (Felson, 1992). It is also not yet known whether the strain that leads to anger or negative affect uniformly produces delinquent or criminal responses. Thus far, the evidence suggests that these intermediate steps do not need to exist for illegal behaviors to occur. It is also clear, however, that more research using better and more thorough measures of strain and the mediating or moderating variables is necessary before we can draw any definitive conclusions.

Yet, it is also important to consider how strain at the macrolevel, such as across schools and neighborhoods, is implicated in crime and delinquency. Clearly, some schools and neighborhoods are more stressful than others. But it remains unclear how stresses and strains at the community level translate into strain at the individual level or motivate delinquency. However, this may be a key for general strain theory, for it may be how strain is experienced at both the macrolevel and individual levels that ultimately affects who gets involved in crime and delinquency and who does not.

# PART V

# SUBCULTURAL THEORIES

# DELINQUENT BOYS: THE CULTURE OF THE GANG

*Albert K. Cohen*

When we speak of a delinquent subculture, we speak of a way of life that has somehow become traditional among certain groups in American society. These groups are the boys' gangs that flourish most conspicuously in the "delinquency neighborhoods" of our larger American cities. The members of these gangs grow up, some to become law-abiding citizens and others to graduate to more professional and adult forms of criminality, but the delinquent tradition is kept alive by the age-groups that succeed them. This book is an attempt to answer some important questions about this delinquent subculture. The pages which follow will prepare the ground for the formulation of these questions. . . .

## Introduction

This is on subcultures in general, how they get started and what keeps them going. This seeming digression is really an integral part of our task. Any explanation of a particular event or phenomenon presupposes an underlying theory, a set of general rules or a model to which all events or phenomena of the same class are supposed to conform. Indeed, do we not mean by "explanation" a demonstration that the thing to be explained can be understood as a special case of the working out of such a set of general rules? For example, when we explain to a child why the rubber safety valve on a pressure cooker pops off when the interior of the cooker reaches a certain critical temperature, we first tell him that there are certain well-established relationships between pressure and temperature (which have been technically formulated in physics as Boyle's Law) and then we show him that the behavior of the valve is exactly what we should expect if the rules which describe those relationships are true. We do no more nor less when we explain the velocity of a falling body, the acquisition of a habit, an increase in the price of some commodity or the growth of a subculture. In every case, if the general theory which we invoke does not "fit" other phenomena of the same class, the explanation is not considered satisfactory. Thus, if *some* changes in the price level seem to be consistent with the "laws of supply and demand" but *other* changes in the price level are not, then the "laws" are considered unsatisfactory and *none* of the changes are explained by reference to these laws.

Therefore, it is appropriate that we set forth explicitly, if somewhat sketchily, the theory about subcultures in general that underlies our attempt to explain the delinquent subculture. If the explanation is sound; then the general theory should provide a key to the understanding of other subcultures as well. If the general theory does not fit other subcultures as well, then the explanation of this particular subculture is thrown into question.

## Action Is Problem-Solving

Our point of departure is the "psychogenic" assumption that all human action—not delinquency alone—is an ongoing series of efforts to solve problems. By "problems" we do not only mean the worries and dilemmas that bring people to the psychiatrist and the psychological clinic. Whether or not to accept a proffered drink, which of two ties to buy, what to do about the unexpected guest or the "F" in algebra are problems too. They all involve, until they are resolved, a certain tension, a disequilibrium and a challenge. We hover between doing and not doing, doing this or doing that, doing it one way or doing it another. Each choice is an act, each act is a choice. Not every act is a *successful* solution, for our choice may leave us with unresolved tensions or generate new and unanticipated consequences which pose new problems, but it is at least an attempt at a solution. On the other hand, not every problem need imply distress, anxiety, bedevilment. Most problems are familiar and recurrent and we have at hand for them ready solutions, habitual modes of action which we have found efficacious and acceptable both to ourselves and to our neighbors. Other problems, however, are not so readily resolved. They persist, they nag, and they press for novel solutions.

What people do depends upon the problems they contend with. If we want to explain what people do, then we want to be clear about the nature of human problems and what produces them. As a first step, it is important to recognize that all the multifarious factors and circumstances that conspire to produce a problem come from one or the other of two sources, the actor's "frame of reference" and the "situation" he confronts. All problems arise and all problems are solved through changes in one or both of these classes of determinants.

First, the situation. This is the world we live in and where we are located in that world. It includes the physical setting within which we must operate, a finite supply of time and energy with which to accomplish our ends, and above all the habits, the expectations, the demands and the social organization of the people around us. Always our problems are what they are because the situation limits the things we can do and have and the conditions under which they are possible. It will not permit us to satisfy equally potent aspirations, *e.g.,* to enjoy the blessings of marriage and bachelorhood at the same time. The resources it offers may not be enough to "go around," *e.g.,* to send the children to college, to pay off the mortgage and to satisfy a thousand other longings. To some of us it may categorically deny the possibility of success, as we define success. To others, it may extend the possibility of success, but the only means which it provides may be morally repugnant; *e.g.,* cheating, chicanery and bootlicking may be the only road open to the coveted promotion. . . .

Our really hard problems are those for which we have no ready-at-hand solutions which will not leave us without feelings of tension, frustration, resentment, guilt, bitterness, anxiety or hopelessness. These feelings and therefore the inadequacy of the solutions are largely the result of the frame of reference through which we contemplate these solutions. It follows that an effective, really satisfying solution *must entail some change in that frame of reference itself.* The actor may give up pursuit of some goal which seems unattainable, but it is not a "solution" unless he can first persuade himself that the goal is, after all, not worth pursuing; in short, his values must change. He may resolve a problem of conflicting loyalties by persuading himself that the greater obligation attaches to one rather than to the other, but this too involves a change in his frame of reference: a commitment to some standard for adjudicating the claims of different loyalties. "Failure" can be transformed into something less humiliating by imputing to others fraud, malevolence or corruption, but this means adopting new perspectives for looking at others and oneself. He may continue to strive for goals hitherto unattainable by adopting more efficacious but "illicit" means but, again, the solution is satisfying only to the degree that guilt is obviated by a change in moral standards. All these and other devices are familiar to us as the psychologist's and the psychoanalyst's "mechanisms of adjustment"—projection, rationalization, substitution, etc.—and they are all ways of coping with problems by a change within the actor's frame of reference.

A second factor we must recognize in building up a theory of subcultures is that human problems are not distributed in a random way among the roles that make up a social system. Each age, sex, racial and ethnic category, each occupation, economic stratum and social class consists of people who have been equipped by their society with frames of reference and confronted by their society with situations which are not equally characteristic of other roles. If the ingredients of which problems are compounded are likened to a deck of cards, your chances and mine of getting a certain hand are not the same but are strongly affected by where we happen to sit. The problems and preoccupations of men and women are different because they judge themselves and others judge them by different standards and because the means available to them for realizing their aspirations are different. It is obvious that opportunities for the achievement of power and prestige are not the same for people who start out at different positions in the class system; it is perhaps a bit less obvious that their levels of aspiration in these respects and therefore what it will take to satisfy them are likely also to differ. All of us must come to terms with the problems of growing old, but these problems are not the same for all of us. To consider but one facet, the decline of physical vigor may have very different meaning for a steel worker and a physician. There is a large and increasing scholarly literature, psychiatric and sociological, on the ways in which the structure of society generates, at each position within the system, characteristic combinations of personality and situation and therefore characteristic problems of adjustment. . . .

## How Subcultural Solutions Arise

Now we confront a dilemma and a paradox. We have seen how difficult it is for the individual to cut loose from the culture models in his milieu, how his dependence upon his fellows compels him to seek conformity and to avoid innovation. But these models and precedents which we call the surrounding culture are ways in which other people think and other people act, and these other people are likewise constrained by models in *their* milieux. *These models themselves, however, continually change.* How is it possible for cultural innovations to emerge while each of the participants in the culture is so powerfully motivated to conform to what is already established? This is the central theoretical problem of this book.

The crucial condition for the emergence of new cultural forms is the existence, *in effective interaction with one another, of a number of actors with similar problems of adjustment.* These may be the entire membership of a group or only certain members, similarly circumstanced, within the group. Among the conceivable solutions to their problems may be one which is not yet embodied in action and which does not therefore exist as a cultural model. This solution, except for the fact that is does not already carry the social criteria of validity and promise the social rewards of consensus, might well answer more neatly to the problems of this group and appeal to its members more effectively than any of the solutions already institutionalized. For each participant, this solution would be adjustive and adequately motivated provided that he could anticipate a simultaneous and corresponding transformation in the frames of reference of his fellows. Each would welcome a sign from the others that a new departure in this direction would receive approval and support. But how does one *know* whether a gesture toward innovation will strike a responsive and sympathetic chord in others or whether it will elicit hostility, ridicule and punishment? *Potential* concurrence is always problematical and innovation or the impulse to innovate a stimulus for anxiety.

The paradox is resolved when the innovation is broached in such a manner as to elicit from others reactions suggesting their receptivity; and when, at the same time, the innovation occurs by increments so small, tentative and ambiguous as to permit the actor to retreat, if the signs be unfavorable, without having become identified with an unpopular position. Perhaps all social actions have, in addition to their instrumental, communicative and expressive functions, this quality of being *exploratory gestures.* For the actor with problems of adjustment which cannot be resolved within the frame of reference of the established culture, each response of the other to what the actor says and does is a clue to the directions in which change may proceed further in a way congenial to the other and to the direction in which change will lack social support. And if the probing gesture is motivated by tensions common to other participants it is likely to initiate a process of *mutual* exploration and *joint* elaboration of a new solution. My exploratory gesture functions as a cue to you; your exploratory gesture as a cue to me. By a casual, semi-serious, non-committal or tangential remark I may stick my neck out just a little way, but I will quickly withdraw it unless you, by some sign of affirmation, stick *yours* out. I will permit myself to become progressively committed but only as others, by some visible sign, become likewise committed. The final product, to which we are jointly committed, is likely to be a compromise formation of all the participants to what we may call a cultural process, a formation perhaps unanticipated by any of them. Each actor may contribute something directly to the growing product, but he may also contribute indirectly by encouraging others to advance, inducing them to retreat, and suggesting new avenues to be explored. The product cannot be ascribed to any one of the participants; it is a real "emergent" on a group level.

We may think of this process as one of mutual conversion. The important thing to remember is that we do not first convert ourselves and then others. The acceptability of an idea to oneself depends upon its acceptability to others. Converting the other is part of the process of converting oneself.

A simple but dramatic illustration may help. We all know that soldiers sometimes develop physical complaints with no underlying organic pathology. We know that these complaints, which the soldier himself is convinced are real, are solutions to problems. They enable the soldier to escape from a hazardous situation without feeling guilty or to displace his anxiety, whose true cause he is reluctant to acknowledge even to himself, upon something which is generally acknowledged to be a legitimate occasion for anxiety. Edward A. Strecker describes an episode of mass psychoneurosis" in World War I. In a period of eight days, on a certain sector of the front, about 500 "gas casualties" reported for medical aid. There had been some desultory gas shelling but never of serious proportions.

Either following the explosion of a gas shell, or even without this preliminary, a soldier would give the alarm of "gas" to those in his vicinity. They would put on their masks, but in the course of a few hours a large percentage of this group would begin to drift into the dressing stations, complaining of indefinite symptoms. It was obvious upon examination that they were not really gassed.

Strecker tells us that these symptoms were utilized as "a route to escape from an undesirable situation." What he does not tell us, but what seems extremely probable, is that for many and probably most of the soldiers, this route to escape was available only because hundreds of other soldiers were "in the same boat" and in continual communicative interaction before, during and after the shelling. One soldier might be ripe for this delusion but if his buddies are not similarly ripe he will have a hard time persuading them that he has been gassed, and if they persist in not being gassed he will have a hard time persuading himself. If all are ripe, they may, in a relatively short time, collectively fabricate a false but unshakeable belief that all have been gassed. It is most unlikely that these 500 soldiers would have been able to "describe all the details with convincing earnestness and generally some dramatic quality of expression" if they had not been able to communicate with one another and develop a common vocabulary for interpreting whatever subjective states they did experience.

The literature on crowd behavior is another source of evidence of the ability of a propitious interaction situation to generate, in a short time, collective although necessarily ephemeral and unstable solutions to like problems. Students are agreed that the groundwork for violent and destructive mob behavior includes the prior existence of unresolved tensions and a period of "milling" during which a set of common sentiments is elaborated and reinforced. It is incorrect to assume, however, that a certain magic in numbers simply serves to lift the moral inhibitions to the expression of already established destructive urges. Kimball Young observes:

> Almost all commentators have noted that individuals engaged in mass action, be it attack or panic flight, show an amazing lack of what are, under calmer conditions, considered proper morals. There is a release of moral inhibitions, social taboos are off, and *the crowd enjoys a sense* of freedom and unrestraint.

He goes on to add, however:

> Certainly those engaged in a pogrom, a lynching or a race riot have a great upsurge of moral feelings, the sense of righting some wrong . . . Though the acts performed may be viewed in retrospect as immoral, and may later induce a sense of shame, remorse and guilt, at the time they seem completely justified.

It is true that ordinary moral restraints often cease to operate under mob conditions. These conditions do not, however, produce a suspension of all morality, a blind and amoral outburst of primitive passions. The action of each member of the mob is in accordance with a collective solution which has been worked out during the brief history of the mob itself. This solution includes not only something to do but a positive morality to justify conduct at such gross variance with the mob members' ordinary conceptions of decency and humanity. In short, what occurs under conditions of mob interaction is not the annihilation of morality but a rapid transformation of the moral frame of reference.

Here we have talked about bizarre and short-lived examples of group problem-solving. But the line between this sort of thing and large-scale social movements, with their elaborate and often respectable ideologies and programs, is tenuous. No fundamentally new principles have to be invoked to explain them.

We quote from one more writer on the efficacy of the interaction situation in facilitating transformations of the frame of reference. The late Kurt Lewin, on the basis of his experience in attempts at guided social change, remarks:

> . . . Experience in leadership training, in changing of food habits, work production, criminality, alcoholism, prejudices, all seem to indicate that it is usually easier to change individuals formed into a group than to change any one of them separately. As long as group values are unchanged the individual will resist changes more strongly the farther he is to depart from group standards. If the group standard itself is changed, the resistance which is due to the relationship between individual and group standard is eliminated.

The emergence of these "group standards" of this shared frame of reference, is the emergence of a new subculture. It is cultural because each actor's participation in this system of norms is influenced by his perception of the same norms in other actors. It is *sub*cultural because the norms are shared only among those actors who stand somehow to profit from them and who find in one another a sympathetic moral climate within which these norms may come to fruition and persist. In this fashion culture is continually being created, re-created and modified wherever individuals sense in one another like needs, generated by like circumstances, not shared generally in the larger social system. Once established, such a subcultural system may persist, but not by sheer inertia. It may achieve a life which outlasts that of the individuals who participated in its creation, but only so long as it continues to serve the needs of those who succeed its creators.

### Subcultural Solutions to Status Problems

One variant of this cultural process interests us especially because it provides the model for our explanation of the delinquent subculture. Status problems are problems of achieving respect in the eyes of one's fellows. Our ability to achieve status depends upon the criteria of status applied by our fellows, that is, the standards or norms they go by in evaluating people. These criteria are an aspect of their cultural frames of reference. If we lack the characteristics or capacities which give status in terms of these criteria, we are beset by one of the most typical and yet distressing of human problems of adjustment. One solution is for individuals who share such problems to gravitate toward one another and jointly to establish new norms, new criteria of status which define as meritorious the characteristics they *do* possess, the kinds of conduct of which they *are* capable. It is clearly necessary for each participant, if the innovation is to solve his status problem, that these new criteria be shared with others, that the solution be a group and not a private solution. If he "goes it alone" he succeeds only in further estranging himself from his fellows. Such new status criteria would represent new subcultural values different from or even antithetical to those of the larger social system.

In general conformity with this pattern, social scientists have accounted for religious cults and sects such as the Oxford Group and Father Divine's Kingdom as attempts on the part of people who feel their status and self-respect threatened to create little societies whose criteria of personal goodness are such that those who participate can find surcease from certain kinds of status anxiety. They have explained such social movements as the Nazi Party as coalitions of groups whose status is unsatisfactory or precarious within the framework of the existing order and who find, in the ideology of the movement, reassurance of their importance and worth or the promise of a new society in which their importance and worth will be recognized. They have explained messianic and revivalistic religious movements among some American Indian and other non-literate groups as collective reactions to status problems which arise during the process of assimilation into a culture and social system dominated by white people. In this new social system the natives find themselves relegated to the lowest social strata. They respond by drawing closer together to one another and elaborating ideologies which emphasize the glories of the tribal past, the merit of membership in the tribe and an early millennium in which the ancient glory and dignity of the tribe will be reestablished. All these movements may seem to have little in common with a gang of kids bent on theft and vandalism. It is true that they have little in common on the level of the concrete content of ideologies and value systems. In later chapters, however, we will try to show that the general principles of explanation which we have outlined here are applicable also to the culture of the delinquent gang. . . .

## What the Delinquent Subculture Has to Offer

The delinquent subculture, we suggest, is a way of dealing with the problems of adjustment we have described. These problems are chiefly status problems: certain children are denied status in the respectable society because they cannot meet the criteria of the respectable status system. The delinquent subculture deals with these problems by providing criteria of status which these children *can* meet.

This statement is highly elliptical and is based upon a number of assumptions whose truth is by no means self-evident. It is not, for example, self-evident that people whose status positions are low must necessarily feel deprived, injured or ego-involved in that low status. Whether they will or not depends upon several considerations.

We remarked earlier that our ego-involvement in a given comparison with others depends upon our "status universe." "Whom do we measure ourselves against?" is the crucial question. In some other societies virtue may consist in willing acceptance of the role of peasant, low-born commoner or member of an inferior caste and in conformity to the expectations of that role. If others are richer, more nobly-born or more able than oneself, it is by the will of an inscrutable Providence and not to be imputed to one's own moral defect. The sting of status inferiority is thereby removed or mitigated; one measures himself only against those of like social position. We have suggested, however, that an important feature of American "democracy," perhaps of the Western European tradition in general, is the tendency to measure oneself against "all comers." This means that, for children as for adults, one's sense of personal worth is at stake in status comparisons with all other persons, at least of one's own age and sex, whatever their family background or material circumstances. It means that, in the lower levels of our status hierarchies, whether adult or juvenile, there is a chronic fund of motivation, conscious or repressed, to elevate one's status position, either by striving to climb within the established status system or by redefining the criteria of status so that one's present attributes become status-giving assets. It has been suggested, for example, that such typically working-class forms of Protestantism as the Holiness sects owe their appeal to the fact that they reverse the respectable status system; it is the humble, the simple and the dispossessed who sit at the right hand of God, whereas worldly goods, power and knowledge are as nothing in His eyes. In like manner, we offer the view that the delinquent subculture is one solution to a kindred problem on the juvenile level.

Another consideration affecting the degree of privation experienced in a given status position is the "status source." A person's status, after all, is how he stands in somebody's eyes. Status, then, is not a fixed property of the person but varies with the point of view of whoever is doing the judging. I may be revered by some and despised by others. A crucial question then becomes: "Whose respect or admiration do I value?" That *you* think well or ill of me may or may not *matter* to me.

It may be argued that the working-class boy does not *care* what middle-class people think of him, that he is ego-involved only in the opinions of his family, his friends, his working-class neighbors. A definitive answer to this argument can come only from research designed to get at the facts. This research, in our opinion, is yet to be done. There is, however, reason to believe that most children are sensitive *to some degree* about the attitudes of *any persons* with whom they are thrown into more than the most superficial kind of contact. The contempt or indifference of others, particularly of those like school-mates and teachers, with whom we are constrained to associate for long hours every day, is difficult, we suggest, to shrug off. It poses a problem with which one may conceivably attempt to cope in a variety of ways. One may make an active effort to change himself in conformity with the expectations of others; one may attempt to justify or explain away his inferiority in terms which will exculpate him; one may tell oneself that he really doesn't care what these people think; one may react with anger and aggression. But the least prob-able response is simple, uncomplicated, honest indifference. If we grant the probable truth of the claim that most American working-class children are most sensitive to status sources on their own level, it does not follow that they take lightly rejection, disparagement and censure from other status sources.

Even on their "own" social level, the situation is far from simple. The "working class," we have repeatedly emphasized, is not culturally homogeneous. Not only is there much diversity in the cultural standards applied by one's own working-class neighbors and kin so that it is difficult to find a "working-class" milieu in which "middle-class" standards are not important. In addition, the "working-class" culture we have described is, after all, an ideal type; most working-class *people* are culturally ambivalent. Due to lack of capac-ity, of the requisite "character structure" or of "luck," they may be working-class in terms of job and income; they may have accepted this status with resignation and rationalized it to their satisfaction; and by example, by class-linked techniques of child training and by failure to support the middle-class agencies of socialization they may have produced children deficient in the attributes that make for status in middle-class terms. Neverthe-less, all their lives, through all the major media of mass indoctrination—the schools, the movies, the radio, the newspapers and the magazines—the middle-class powers-that-be that manipulate these media have been trying to "sell" them on middle-class values and the middle-class standard of living. Then there is the "propaganda of the deed," the fact that they have seen with their own eyes working-class contemporaries "get ahead" and "make the grade" in a middle-class world. In consequence of all this, we suspect that few working-class parents unequivocally repudiate as intrinsically worthless middle-class objectives. There is good reason to believe that the modesty of working-class aspirations is partly a matter of trimming one's sails to the available opportunities and resources and partly a matter of unwillingness to accept the discipline which upward striving entails.

However complete and successful one's accommodation to an humble status, the vitality of middle-class goals, of the "American dream," is nonetheless likely to manifest itself in his aspirations for his children. His expectations may not be grandiose, but he will want his children to be "better off" than he. Whatever his own work history and social reputation may be, he will want his children to be "steady" and "respectable." He may exert few positive pressures to "succeed" and the experiences he provides his children may even incapacitate them for success; he may be puzzled at the way they "turn out." But whatever the measure of his own responsibility in accounting for the product, he is not likely to judge that product by unadulterated "corner-boy" standards. Even "corner-boy" parents, although they may value in their children such corner-boy virtues as generosity to friends, personal loyalty and physical prowess, are likely also to be gratified by recognition by middle-class representatives and by the kinds of achievement for which the college-boy way of life is a prerequisite. Even in the working-class milieu from which he acquired his incapacity for middle-class achievement, the working-class corner-boy may find himself at a status disadvantage as against his more upwardly mobile peers.

Lastly, of course, is that most ubiquitous and inescapable of status sources, one-self. Technically, we do not call the person's attitudes towards himself "status" but rather "self-esteem, or, when the quality of the self-attitude is specifically moral, "conscience" or "superego." The important question for us is this: To what extent, if at all, do boys who are typically "working-class" and "corner-boy" in their overt behavior evaluate themselves by "middle-class," "college-boy" standards? For our overt behavior, however closely it conforms to one set of norms, need not argue against the existence or effectiveness of alternative and conflicting norms. The failure of our own behavior to conform to our own expectations is an elementary and commonplace fact which gives rise to the tremendously important consequences of guilt, self-recrimination, anxiety and self-hatred. The reasons for the failure of self-expectations and overt conduct to agree are complex. One reason is that we often internalize more than one set of norms, each of which would dictate a different course of action in a given life-situation; since we can only *do* one thing at a time, however, we are forced to choose between them or somehow to compromise. In either case, we fall short of the full realization of our own expectations and must somehow cope with the residual discrepancy between those expectations and our overt behavior. . . .

This interpretation of the delinquent subculture has important implications for the "sociology of social problems." People are prone to assume that those things which we define as evil and those which we define as good have their origins in separate and distinct features of our society. Evil flows from poisoned wells; good flows from pure and crystal fountains. The same source cannot feed both. Our view is different. It holds that those values which are at the core of "the American way of life," which help to motivate the behavior which we most esteem as "typically American," are among the major determinants of that which we stigmatize as "pathological." More specifically, it holds that the problems of adjustment to which the delinquent subculture is a response are determined, in part, by those very values which respectable society holds most sacred. The same value system, impinging upon children differently equipped to meet it, is instrumental in generating both delinquency and respectability.

# LOWER CLASS CULTURE AS A GENERATING MILIEU OF GANG DELINQUENCY

*Walter B. Miller*

The etiology of delinquency has long been a controversial issue, and is particularly so at present. As new frames of reference for explaining human behavior have been added to traditional theories, some authors have adopted the practice of citing the major postulates of each school of thought as they pertain to delinquency, and going on to state that causality must be conceived in terms of the dynamic interaction of a complex combination of variables on many levels. The major sets of etiological factors currently adduced to explain delinquency are, in simplified terms, the physiological (delinquency results from organic pathology), the psychodynamic (delinquency is a "behavioral disorder" resulting primarily from emotional disturbance generated by a defective mother-child relationship), and the environmental (delinquency is the product of disruptive forces, "disorganization," in the actor's physical or social environment).

This paper selects one particular kind of "delinquency"—law-violating acts committed by members of adolescent street corner groups in lower class communities—and attempts to show that the dominant component of motivation underlying these acts consists in a directed attempt by the actor to adhere to forms of behavior, and to achieve standards of value as they are defined within that community. It takes as a premise that the motivation of behavior in this situation can be approached most productively by attempting to understand the nature of cultural forces impinging on the acting individual as they are perceived *by the actor himself*—although by no means only that segment of these forces of which the actor is consciously aware—rather than as they are perceived and evaluated from the reference position of another cultural system. In the case of "gang" delinquency, the cultural system which exerts the most direct influence on behavior is that of the lower class community itself—a long-established, distinctively patterned tradition with an integrity of its own—rather than a so-called "delinquent subculture" which has arisen through conflict with middle class culture and is oriented to the deliberate violation of middle class norms.

The bulk of the substantive data on which the following material is based was collected in connection with a service-research project in the control of gang delinquency. During the service aspect of the project, which lasted for three years, seven trained social workers maintained contact with twenty-one corner group units in a "slum" district of a large eastern city for periods of time ranging from ten to thirty months. Groups were Negro and white, male and female, and in early, middle, and late adolescence. Over eight thousand pages of direct observational data on behavior patterns of group members and other community residents were collected; almost daily contact was maintained for a total time period of about thirteen worker years. Data include workers' contact reports, participant observation reports by the writer—a cultural anthropologist—and direct tape recordings of group activities and discussions.

## Focal Concerns of Lower Class Culture

There is a substantial segment of present-day American society whose way of life, values, and characteristic patterns of behavior are the product of a distinctive cultural system which may be termed "lower class." Evidence indicates that this cultural system is becoming increasingly distinctive, and that the size of the group which shares this tradition is increasing. The lower class way of life, in common with that of all distinctive cultural groups, is characterized by a set of focal concerns—areas or issues which command widespread and persistent attention and a high degree of emotional involvement. The specific concerns cited here, while by no means confined to the American lower classes, constitute a distinctive *patterning* of concerns which differs significantly, both in rank order and weighting from that of American middle class culture. [Table 1] presents a highly schematic and simplified listing of six of the major concerns of lower class culture. Each is conceived as a "dimension" within which a fairly wide and varied range of alternative behavior patterns may be followed by different individuals under different situations. They are listed roughly in order of the degree of *explicit* attention accorded each, and, in this sense represent a weighted ranking of concerns. The "perceived alternatives" represent polar positions which define certain parameters within each dimension. As will be explained in more detail, it is necessary in relating the influence of these "concerns" to the motivation of delinquent behavior to specify *which* of its aspects is oriented to, whether orientation is *overt* or *covert, positive* (conforming to or seeking the aspect), or *negative* (rejecting or seeking to avoid the aspect).

The concept "focal concern" is used here in preference to the concept "value" for several interrelated reasons: (1) It is more readily derivable from direct field observation. (2) It is descriptively neutral—permitting independent consideration of positive and negative valences as varying under different conditions, whereas "value" carries a built-in positive valence. (3) It makes possible more refined analysis of subcultural differences, since it

**TABLE 1**
**Focal concerns of lower class culture**

| Area | Perceived alternatives (state, quality, condition) | |
|---|---|---|
| 1. *Trouble:* | law-abiding behavior | law-violating behavior |
| 2. *Toughness:* | physical prowess, skill; "masculinity"; | weakness, ineptitude; effeminacy; |
| | fearlessness, bravery, daring | timidity, cowardice, caution |
| 3. *Smartness:* | ability to outsmart, dupe, "con"; | gullibility, "con-ability"; |
| | gaining money by "wits"; shrewdness, adroitness in repartee | gaining money by hard work; slowness, dull-wittedness, verbal maladroitness |
| 4. *Excitement:* | thrill; risk, danger; change, activity | boredom; "deadness," safeness; sameness, passivity |
| 5. *Fate:* | favored by fortune, being "lucky" | ill-omened, being "unlucky" |
| 6. *Autonomy:* | freedom from external constraint; freedom from superordinate authority; independence | presence of external constraint; presence of strong authority; dependency, being "cared for" |

reflects actual behavior, whereas "value" tends to wash out intracultural differences since it is colored by notions of the "official" ideal.

### Trouble

Concern over "trouble" is a dominant feature of lower class culture. The concept has various shades of meaning; "trouble" in one of its aspects represents a situation or a kind of behavior which results in unwelcome or complicating involvement with official authorities or agencies of middle class society. "Getting into trouble" and "staying out of trouble" represent major issues for male and female, adults and children. For men, "trouble" frequently involves fighting or sexual adventures while drinking; for women, sexual involvement with disadvantageous consequences. Expressed desire to avoid behavior which violates moral or legal norms is often based less on an explicit commitment to "official" moral or legal standards than on a desire to avoid "getting into trouble," e.g., the complicating consequences of the action.

The dominant concern over "trouble" involves a distinction of critical importance for the lower class community—that between "law-abiding" and "non-law-abiding" behavior. There is a high degree of sensitivity as to where each person stands in relation to these two classes of activity. Whereas in the middle class community a major dimension for evaluating a person's status is "achievement" and its external symbols, in the lower class, personal status is very frequently gauged along the law-abiding-non-law-abiding dimension. A mother will evaluate the suitability of her daughter's boyfriend less on the basis of his achievement potential than on the basis of his innate "trouble" potential. This sensitive awareness of the opposition of "trouble-producing" and "non-trouble-producing" behavior represents both a major basis for deriving status distinctions, and an internalized conflict potential for the individual.

As in the case of other focal concerns, which of two perceived alternatives—"law-abiding" or "non-law-abiding"—is valued varies according to the individual and the circumstances; in many instances there is an overt commitment to the "law-abiding" alternative, but a covert commitment to the "non-law-abiding." In certain situations, "getting into trouble" is overtly recognized as prestige-conferring; for example, membership in certain adult and adolescent primary groupings ("gangs") is contingent on having demonstrated an explicit commitment to the law-violating alternative. It is most important to note that the choice between "law-abiding" and "non-law-abiding" behavior is still a choice *within* lower class culture; the distinction between the policeman and the criminal, the outlaw and the sheriff, involves primarily this one dimension; in other respects they have a high community of interests. Not infrequently brothers raised in an identical cultural milieu will become police and criminals respectively.

For a substantial segment of the lower class population "getting into trouble" is not in itself overtly defined as prestige-conferring, but is implicitly recognized as a means to other valued ends, e.g., the covertly valued desire to be "cared for" and subject to external constraint, or the overtly valued state of excitement or risk. Very frequently "getting into trouble" is multi-functional, and achieves several sets of valued ends.

### Toughness

The concept of "toughness" in lower class culture represents a compound combination of qualities or states. Among its most important components are physical prowess, evidenced both by demonstrated possession of strength and endurance and athletic skill; "masculinity," symbolized by a distinctive complex of acts and avoidances (bodily tatooing; absence of sentimentality; non-concern with "art," "literature," conceptualization of women as conquest objects, etc.); and bravery in the face of physical threat. The model for the "tough guy"—hard, fearless, undemonstrative, skilled in physical combat—is represented by the movie gangster of the thirties, the "private eye," and the movie cowboy.

The genesis of the intense concern over "toughness" in lower class culture is probably related to the fact that a significant proportion of lower class males are reared in a predominantly female household, and lack a consistently present male figure with whom to identify and from whom to learn essential components of a "male" role. Since women serve as a primary object of identification during pre-adolescent years, the almost obsessive lower class concern with "masculinity" probably resembles a type of compulsive reaction-formation. A concern over homosexuality runs like a persistent thread through lower class culture. This is manifested by the institutionalized practice of baiting "queers," often accompanied by violent physical attacks, an expressed contempt for "softness" or frills, and the use of the local term for "homosexual" as a generalized pejorative epithet (e.g., higher class individuals or upwardly mobile peers are frequently characterized as "fags" or "queers"). The distinction between "overt" and "covert" orientation to aspects of an area of concern is especially important in regard to "toughness." A positive overt evaluation of behavior defined as "effeminate" would be out of the question for a lower class male; however, built into lower class culture is a range of devices which permit men to adopt behaviors and concerns which in other cultural milieux fall within the province of women, and at the same time to be defined as "tough" and manly. For example, lower class men can be professional short-order cooks in a diner and still be regarded as "tough." The highly intimate circumstances of the street corner gang involve the recurrent expression of strongly affectionate feelings towards other men. Such expressions, however, are disguised as their opposite, taking the form of ostensibly aggressive verbal and physical interaction (kidding, "ranking," roughhousing, etc.).

### Smartness

"Smartness," as conceptualized in lower class culture, involves the capacity to outsmart, outfox, outwit, dupe, "take," "con" another or others, and the concomitant capacity to avoid being outwitted, "taken," or duped oneself. In its essence, smartness involves the capacity to achieve a valued entity—material goods, personal status—through a maximum use of mental agility and a minimum use of physical effort. This capacity has an extremely long tradition in lower class culture, and is highly valued. Lower class culture can be characterized as "non-intellectual" only if intellectualism is defined specifically in terms of control over a particular body of formally learned knowledge involving "culture" (art, literature, "good" music, etc.), a generalized perspective on the past and present conditions of our own and other societies, and other areas of knowledge imparted by formal educational institutions. This particular type of mental attainment is, in general, overtly disvalued and frequently associated with effeminacy; "smartness" in the lower class sense, however, is highly valued.

The lower class child learns and practices the use of this skill in the street corner situation. Individuals continually practice duping and out-witting one another through recurrent card games and other forms of gambling, mutual exchanges of insults, and "testing" for mutual "conability." Those who demonstrate competence in this skill are accorded considerable prestige. Leadership roles in the corner group are frequently allocated according to demonstrated capacity in the two areas of "smartness" and "toughness"; the ideal leader combines both, but the "smart" leader is often accorded more prestige than the "tough" one—reflecting a general lower class respect for "brains" in the "smartness" sense.

The model of the "smart" person is represented in popular media by the card shark, the professional gambler, the "con" artist, the promoter. A conceptual distinction is made between two kinds of people: "suckers," easy marks, "lushes," dupes, who work for their money and are legitimate targets of exploitation; and sharp operators, the "brainy" ones, who live by their wits and "getting" from the suckers by mental adroitness.

Involved in the syndrome of capacities related to "smartness" is a dominant emphasis in lower class culture on ingenious aggressive repartee. This skill, learned and practiced in the context of the corner group, ranges in form from the widely prevalent semi-ritualized teasing, kidding, razzing, "ranking," so characteristic of male peer group interaction, to the highly ritualized type of mutual insult interchange known as "the dirty dozens," "the dozens," "playing house," and other terms. This highly patterned cultural form is practiced on its most advanced level in adult male Negro society, but less polished variants are found throughout lower class culture—practiced, for example, by white children, male and female, as young as four or five. In essence, "doin' the dozens" involves two antagonists who vie with each other in the exchange of increasingly inflammatory insults, with incestuous and perverted sexual relations with the mother a dominant theme. In this form of insult interchange, as well as on other less ritualized occasions for joking, semi-serious, and serious mutual invective, a very high premium is placed on ingenuity, hair-trigger responsiveness, inventiveness, and the acute exercise of mental faculties.

### Excitement

For many lower class individuals the rhythm of life fluctuates between periods of relatively routine or repetitive activity and sought situations of great emotional stimulation. Many of the most characteristic features of lower class life are related to the search for excitement or "thrill." Involved here are the highly prevalent use of alcohol by both sexes and the widespread use of gambling of all kinds—playing the numbers, betting on horse races, dice, cards. The quest for excitement finds what is perhaps its most vivid expression in the highly patterned practice of the recurrent "night on the town." This practice, designated by various terms in different areas ("honky-tonkin' "; "goin' out on the town"; "bar hoppin' "), involves a patterned set of activities in which alcohol, music, and sexual adventuring are major components. A group or individual sets out to "make the rounds" of various bars or night clubs. Drinking continues progressively throughout the evening. Men seek to "pick up" women, and women play the risky game of entertaining sexual advances. Fights between men involving women, gambling, and claims of physical prowess, in various combinations, are frequent consequences of a night of making the rounds. The explosive potential of this type of adventuring with sex and aggression, frequently leading to "trouble," is semi-explicitly sought by the individual. Since there is always a good likelihood that being out on the town will eventuate in fights, etc., the practice involves elements of sought risk and desired danger.

Counterbalancing the "flirting with danger" aspect of the "excitement" concern is the prevalence in lower class culture of other well established patterns of activity which involve long periods of relative inaction, or passivity. The term "hanging out" in lower class culture refers to extended periods of standing around, often with peer mates, doing what is defined as "nothing," "shooting the breeze," etc. A definite periodicity exists in the pattern of activity relating to the two aspects of the "excitement" dimension. For many lower class individuals the venture into the high risk world of alcohol, sex, and fighting occurs regularly once a week, with interim periods devoted to accommodating to possible consequences of these periods, along with recurrent resolves not to become so involved again.

### Fate

Related to the quest for excitement is the concern with fate, fortune, or luck. Here also a distinction is made between two states—being "lucky" or "in luck," and being unlucky or jinxed. Many lower class individuals feel that their lives are subject to a set of forces over which they have relatively little control. These are not directly equated with the supernatural forces of formally organized religion, but relate more to a concept of "destiny," or man as a pawn of magical powers. Not infrequently this often implicit world view is associated with a conception of the ultimate futility of directed effort towards a goal: if the cards are right, or the dice good to you, or if your lucky number comes up, things will go your way; if luck is against you, it's not worth trying. The concept of performing semi-magical rituals so that one's "luck will change" is prevalent; one hopes that as a result he will move from the state of being "unlucky" to that of being "lucky." The element of fantasy plays an important part in this area. Related to and complementing the notion that "only suckers work" (Smartness) is the idea that once things start going your way, relatively independent of your own effort, all good things will come to you. Achieving great material rewards (big cars, big houses, a roll of cash to flash in a fancy night club), valued in lower class as well as in other parts of American culture, is a recurrent theme in lower class fantasy and folk lore; the cocaine dreams of Willie the Weeper or Minnie the Moocher present the components of this fantasy in vivid detail.

The prevalence in the lower class community of many forms of gambling, mentioned in connection with the "excitement" dimension, is also relevant here. Through cards and pool which involve skill, and thus both "toughness" and "smartness"; or through race horse betting, involving "smartness"; or through playing the numbers, involving predominantly "luck," one may make a big killing with a minimum of directed and persistent effort within conventional occupational channels. Gambling in its many forms illustrates the fact that many of the persistent features of lower class culture are multi-functional—serving a range of desired ends at the same time. Describing some of the incentives behind gambling has involved mention of all of the focal concerns cited so far—Toughness, Smartness, and Excitement, in addition to Fate.

### Autonomy

The extent and nature of control over the behavior of the individual—an important concern in most cultures—has a special significance and is distinctively patterned in lower class culture. The discrepancy between what is overtly valued and what is covertly sought is particularly striking in this area. On the overt level there is a strong and frequently expressed resentment of the idea of external controls, restrictions on behavior, and unjust or coercive authority. "No one's gonna push *me* around," or "I'm gonna tell him he can

take the job and shove it. . . ." are commonly expressed sentiments. Similar explicit attitudes are maintained to systems of behavior-restricting rules, insofar as these are perceived
as representing the injunctions, and bearing the sanctions of superordinate authority. In
addition, in lower class culture a close conceptual connection is made between "authority"
and "nurturance." To be restrictively or firmly controlled is to be cared for. Thus the overtly
negative evaluation of superordinate authority frequently extends as well to nurturance,
care, or protection. The desire for personal independence is often expressed in such terms
as "I don't need *nobody* to take care of me. I can take care of myself!" Actual patterns of
behavior, however, reveal a marked discrepancy between expressed sentiment and what
is covertly valued. Many lower class people appear to seek out highly restrictive social
environments wherein stringent external controls are maintained over their behavior. Such
institutions as the armed forces, the mental hospital, the disciplinary school, the prison
or correctional institution, provide environments which incorporate a strict and detailed
set of rules defining and limiting behavior, and enforced by an authority system which
controls and applies coercive sanctions for deviance from these rules. While under the
jurisdiction of such systems, the lower class person generally expresses to his peers continual resentment of the coercive, unjust, and arbitrary exercise of authority. Having been
released, or having escaped from these milieux, however, he will often act in such a way
as to insure recommitment, or choose recommitment voluntarily after a temporary period
of "freedom."

Lower class patients in mental hospitals will exercise considerable ingenuity to insure
continued commitment while voicing the desire to get out; delinquent boys will frequently
"run" from a correctional institution to activate efforts to return them; to be caught and
returned means that one is cared for. Since "being controlled" is equated with "being
cared for," attempts are frequently made to "test" the severity or strictness of superordinate
authority to see if it remains firm. If intended or executed rebellion produces swift and
firm punitive sanctions, the individual is reassured, at the same time that he is complaining
bitterly at the injustice of being caught and punished. Some environmental milieux, having been tested in this fashion for the "firmness" of their coercive sanctions, are rejected,
ostensibly for being too strict, actually for not being strict enough. This is frequently so in
the case of "problematic" behavior by lower class youngsters in the public schools, which
generally cannot command the coercive controls implicitly sought by the individual.

A similar discrepancy between what is overtly and covertly desired is found in the area
of dependence-independence. The pose of tough rebellious independence often assumed
by the lower class person frequently conceals powerful dependency cravings. These are
manifested primarily by obliquely expressed resentment when "care" is not forthcoming
rather than by expressed satisfaction when it is. The concern over autonomy-dependency
is related both to "trouble" and "fate." Insofar as the lower class individual feels that his
behavior is controlled by forces which often propel him into "trouble" in the face of an
explicit determination to avoid it, there is an implied appeal to "save me from myself."
A solution appears to lie in arranging things so that his behavior will be coercively restricted
by an externally imposed set of controls strong enough to forcibly restrain his inexplicable
inclination to get in trouble. The periodicity observed in connection with the "excitement"
dimension is also relevant here; after involvement in trouble-producing behavior (assault,
sexual adventure, a "drunk"), the individual will actively seek a locus of imposed control (his wife, prison, a restrictive job); after a given period of subjection to this control,

resentment against it mounts, leading to a "break away" and a search for involvement in further "trouble."

## Focal Concerns of the Lower Class Adolescent Street Corner Group

The one-sex peer group is a highly prevalent and significant structural form in the lower class community. There is a strong probability that the prevalence and stability of this type of unit is directly related to the prevalence of a stabilized type of lower class child-rearing unit—the "female-based" household. This is a nuclear kin unit in which a male parent is either absent from the household, present only sporadically, or, when present, only minimally or inconsistently involved in the support and rearing of children. This unit usually consists of one or more females of child-bearing age and their offspring. The females are frequently related to one another by blood or marriage ties, and the unit often includes two or more generations of women, e.g., the mother and/or aunt of the principal child-bearing female.

The nature of social groupings in the lower class community may be clarified if we make the assumption that it is the *one-sex peer unit* rather than the two-parent family unit which represents the most significant relational unit for both sexes in lower class communities. Lower class society may be pictured as comprising a set of age-graded one-sex groups which constitute the major psychic focus and reference group for those over twelve or thirteen. Men and women of mating age leave these groups periodically to form temporary marital alliances, but these lack stability, and after varying periods of "trying out" the two-sex family arrangement, gravitate back to the more "comfortable" one-sex grouping, whose members exert strong pressure on the individual *not* to disrupt the group by adopting a two-sex household pattern of life. Membership in a stable and solidary peer unit is vital to the lower class individual precisely to the extent to which a range of essential functions—psychological, educational, and others, are not provided by the "family" unit.

The adolescent street corner group represents the adolescent variant of this lower class structural form. What has been called the "delinquent gang" is one subtype of this form, defined on the basis of frequency of participation in law-violating activity; this subtype should not be considered a legitimate unit of study per se, but rather as one particular variant of the adolescent street corner group. The "hanging" peer group is a unit of particular importance for the adolescent male. In many cases it is the most stable and solidary primary grroup he has ever belonged to; for boys reared in female-based households the corner group provides the first real opportunity to learn essential aspects of the male role in the context of peers facing similar problems of sex-role identification.

The form and functions of the adolescent corner group operate as a selective mechanism in recruiting members. The activity patterns of the group require a high level of intra-group solidarity; individual members must possess a good capacity for subordinating individual desires to general group interests as well as the capacity for intimate and persisting interaction. Thus highly "disturbed" individuals, or those who cannot tolerate consistently imposed sanctions on "deviant" behavior cannot remain accepted members; the group itself will extrude those whose behavior exceeds limits defined as "normal." This selective process produces a type of group whose members possess to an unusually high degree both the *capacity* and *motivation* to conform to perceived cultural norms, so that the nature of the system of norms and values oriented to is a particularly influential component of motivation.

Focal concerns of the male adolescent corner group are those of the general cultural milieu in which it functions. As would be expected, the relative weighting and importance of these concerns pattern somewhat differently for adolescents than for adults. The nature of this patterning centers around two additional "concerns" of particular importance to this group—concern with "belonging," and with "status." These may be conceptualized as being on a higher level of abstraction than concerns previously cited, since "status" and "belonging" are achieved *via* cited concern areas of Toughness, etc.

## Belonging

Since the corner group fulfills essential functions for the individual, being a member in good standing of the group is of vital importance for its members. A continuing concern over who is "in" and who is not involves the citation and detailed discussion of highly refined criteria for "in-group" membership. The phrase "he hangs with us" means "he is accepted as a member in good standing by current consensus"; conversely, "he don't hang with us" means he is not so accepted. One achieves "belonging" primarily by demonstrating knowledge of and a determination to adhere to the system of standards and valued qualities defined by the group. One maintains membership by acting in conformity with valued aspects of Toughness, Smartness, Autonomy, etc. In those instances where conforming to norms of this reference group at the same time violates norms of other reference groups (e.g., middle class adults, institutional "officials"), immediate reference group norms are much more compelling since violation risks invoking the group's most powerful sanction: exclusion.

## Status

In common with most adolescents in American society, the lower class corner group manifests a dominant concern with "status." What differentiates this type of group from others, however, is the particular set of criteria and weighting thereof by which "status" is defined. In general, status is achieved and maintained by demonstrated possession of the valued qualities of lower class culture—Toughness, Smartness, expressed resistance to authority, daring, etc. It is important to stress once more that the individual orients to these concerns *as they are defined within lower class society;* e.g., the status-conferring potential of "smartness" in the sense of scholastic achievement generally ranges from negligible to negative.

The concern with "status" is manifested in a variety of ways. Intra-group status is a continued concern, and is derived and tested constantly by means of a set of status-ranking activities; the intra-group "pecking order" is constantly at issue. One gains status within the group by demonstrated superiority in Toughness (physical prowess, bravery, skill in athletics and games such as pool and cards), Smartness (skill in repartee, capacity to "dupe" fellow group members), and the like. The term "ranking," used to refer to the pattern of intra-group aggressive repartee, indicates awareness of the fact that this is one device for establishing the intra-group status hierarchy.

The concern over status in the adolescent corner group involves in particular the component of "adultness," the intense desire to be seen as "grown up," and a corresponding aversion to "kid stuff." "Adult" status is defined less in terms of the assumption of "adult" responsibility than in terms of certain external symbols of adult status—a car, ready cash, and, in particular, a perceived "freedom" to drink, smoke, and gamble as one wishes and to come and go without external restrictions. The desire to be seen as "adult" is often a more significant component of much involvement in illegal drinking, gambling, and automobile driving than the explicit enjoyment of these acts as such.

The intensity of the corner group member's desire to be seen as "adult" is sufficiently great that he feels called upon to demonstrate qualities associated with adultness (Toughness, Smartness, Autonomy) to a much greater degree than a lower class adult. This means that he will seek out and utilize those avenues to these qualities which he perceives as available with greater intensity than an adult and [with] less regard for their "legitimacy." In this sense the adolescent variant of lower class culture represents a maximization or an intensified manifestation of many of its most characteristic features.

Concern over status is also manifested in reference to other street corner groups. The term "rep" used in this regard is especially significant, and has broad connotations. In its most frequent and explicit connotation, "rep" refers to the "toughness" of the corner group as a whole relative to that of other groups; a "pecking order" also exists among the several corner groups in a given interactional area, and there is a common perception that the safety or security of the group and all its members depends on maintaining a solid "rep" for toughness vis-a-vis other groups. This motive is most frequently advanced as a reason for involvement in gang fights: "We *can't* chicken out on this fight; our rep would be shot!"; this implies that the group would be relegated to the bottom of the status ladder and become a helpless and recurrent target of external attack.

On the other hand, there is implicit in the concept of "rep" the recognition that "rep" has or may have a dual basis—corresponding to the two aspects of the "trouble" dimension. It is recognized that group as well as individual status can be based on both "law-abiding" and "law-violating" behavior. The situational resolution of the persisting conflict between the "law-abiding" and "law-violating" bases of status comprises a vital set of dynamics in determining whether a "delinquent" mode of behavior will be adopted by a group, under what circumstances, and how persistently. The determinants of this choice are evidently highly complex and fluid, and rest on a range of factors including the presence and perceptual immediacy of different community reference-group loci (e.g., professional criminals, police, clergy, teachers, settlement house workers), the personality structures and "needs" of group members, the presence in the community of social work, recreation, or educational programs which can facilitate utilization of the "law-abiding" basis of status, and so on.

What remains constant is the critical importance of "status" both for the members of the group as individuals and for the group as a whole insofar as members perceive their individual destinies as linked to the destiny of the group, and the fact that action geared to attain status is much more acutely oriented to the fact of status itself than to the legality or illegality, morality or immorality of the means used to achieve it.

### Lower Class Culture and the Motivation of Delinquent Behavior

The customary set of activities of the adolescent street corner group includes activities which are in violation of laws and ordinances of the legal code. Most of these center around assault and theft of various types (the gang fight; auto theft; assault on an individual; petty pilfering and shoplifting; "mugging"; pocketbook theft). Members of street corner gangs are well aware of the law-violating nature of these acts; they are not psychopaths, nor physically or mentally "defective"; in fact, since the corner group supports and enforces a rigorous set of standards which demand a high degree of fitness and personal competence, it tends to recruit from the most "able" members of the community.

Why, then, is the commission of crimes a customary feature of gang activity? The most general answer is that the commission of crimes by members of adolescent street corner groups is motivated primarily by the attempt to achieve ends, states, or conditions which are valued, and to avoid those that are disvalued within their most meaningful cultural milieu, through those culturally available avenues which appear as the most feasible means of attaining those ends.

The operation of these influences is well illustrated by the gang fight—a prevalent and characteristic type of corner group delinquency. This type of activity comprises a highly stylized and culturally patterned set of sequences. Although details vary under different circumstances, the following events are generally included. A member or several members of group A "trespass" on the claimed territory of group B. While there they commit an act or acts which group B defines as a violation of its rightful privileges, an affront to their honor, or a challenge to their "rep." Frequently this act involves advances to a girl associated with group B; it may occur at a dance or party; sometimes the mere act of "trespass" is seen as deliberate provocation. Members of group B then assault members of group A, if they are caught while still in B's territory. Assaulted members of group A return to their "home" territory and recount to members of their group details of the incident, stressing the insufficient nature of the provocation ("I just *looked* at her! Hardly even said anything!"), and the unfair circumstances of the assault ("About *twenty* guys jumped just the *two* of us!"). The highly colored account is acutely inflammatory; group A, perceiving its honor violated and its "rep" threatened, feels obligated to retaliate in force. Sessions of detailed planning now occur; allies are recruited if the size of group A and its potential allies appears to necessitate larger numbers; strategy is plotted, and messengers dispatched. Since the prospect of a gang fight is frightening to even the "toughest" group members, a constant rehearsal of the provocative incident or incidents and the essentially evil nature of the opponents accompanies the planning process to bolster possibly weakening motivation to fight. The excursion into "enemy" territory sometimes results in a full scale fight; more often group B cannot be found, or the police appear and stop the fight, "tipped off" by an anonymous informant. When this occurs, group members express disgust and disappointment; secretly there is much relief; their honor has been avenged without incurring injury; often the anonymous tipster is a member of one of the involved groups.

The basic elements of this type of delinquency are sufficiently stabilized and recurrent as to constitute an essentially ritualized pattern, resembling both in structure and expressed motives for action classic forms such as the European "duel," the American Indian tribal war, and the Celtic clan feud. Although the arousing and "acting out" of individual aggressive emotions are inevitably involved in the gang fight, neither its form nor motivational dynamics can be adequately handled within a predominantly personality-focused frame of reference.

It would be possible to develop in considerable detail the processes by which the commission of a range of illegal acts is either explicitly supported by, implicitly demanded by, or not materially inhibited by factors relating to the focal concerns of lower class culture. In place of such a development, the following three statements condense in general terms the operation of these processes:

1. *Following cultural practices which comprise essential elements of the total life pattern of lower class culture automatically violates certain legal norms.*
2. *In instances where alternate avenues to similar objectives are available, the non-law-abiding avenue frequently provides a relatively greater and more immediate return for a relatively smaller investment of energy.*
3. *The "demanded" response to certain situations recurrently engendered within lower class culture involves the commission of illegal acts.*

The primary thesis of this paper is that the dominant component of the motivation of "delinquent" behavior engaged in by members of lower class corner groups involves a positive effort to achieve states, conditions, or qualities valued within the actor's most significant cultural milieu. If "conformity to immediate reference group values" is the major component of motivation of "delinquent" behavior by gang members, why is such behavior frequently referred to as negativistic, malicious, or rebellious? Albert Cohen, for example, in *Delinquent Boys* describes behavior which violates school rules as comprising elements of "active spite and malice, contempt and ridicule, challenge and defiance." He ascribes to the gang "keen delight in terrorizing 'good' children, and in general making themselves obnoxious to the virtuous." A recent national conference on social work with "hard-to-reach" groups characterized lower class corner groups as "youth groups in conflict with the culture of their *(sic)* communities." Such characterizations are obviously the result of taking the middle class community and its institutions as an implicit point of reference.

A large body of systematically interrelated attitudes, practices, behaviors, and values characteristic of lower class culture are designed to support and maintain the basic features of the lower class way of life. In areas where these differ from features of middle class culture, action oriented to the achievement and maintenance of the lower class system may violate norms of middle class culture and be perceived as deliberately non-conforming or malicious by an observer strongly cathected to middle class norms. This does not mean, however, that violation of the middle class norm is the dominant component of motivation; it is a by-product of action primarily oriented to the lower class system. The standards of lower class culture cannot be seen merely as a reverse function of middle class culture—as middle class standards "turned upside down"; lower class culture is a distinctive tradition many centuries old with an integrity of its own.

From the viewpoint of the acting individual, functioning within a field of well-structured cultural forces, the relative impact of "conforming" and "rejective" elements in the motivation of gang delinquency is weighted preponderantly on the conforming side. Rejective or rebellious elements are inevitably involved, but their influence during the actual commission of delinquent acts is relatively small compared to the influence of pressures to achieve what is valued by the actor's most immediate reference groups. Expressed awareness by the actor of the element of rebellion often represents only that aspect of motivation of which he is explicitly conscious; the deepest and most compelling components of motivation—adherence to highly meaningful group standards of Toughness, Smartness, Excitement, etc.—are often unconsciously patterned. No cultural pattern as well-established as the practice of illegal acts by members of lower class corner groups could persist if buttressed primarily by negative, hostile, or rejective motives; its principal motivational support, as in the case of any persisting cultural tradition, derives from a positive effort to achieve what is valued within that tradition, and to conform to its explicit and implicit norms.

# THE SUBCULTURE OF VIOLENCE: TOWARDS AN INTEGRATED THEORY IN CRIMINOLOGY

*Marvin E. Wolfgang and Franco Ferracuti*

## The Thesis of a Subculture of Violence

This section examines the proposition that there is a subculture of violence. Since results of the kinds of scaling analysis suggested in the last section are not available, it is necessary to build upon previous related research and theory in order to extend a theoretical formulation regarding the existence of subcultures in general if we are to hypothesize a particular subculture of violence. It would be difficult to support an argument that a subculture exists in relation to a single cultural interest, and the thesis of a subculture of violence does not suggest a monolithic character. It should be remembered that the term itself—subculture—presupposes an already existing complex of norms, values, attitudes, material traits, etc. What the subculture-of-violence formulation further suggests is simply that there is a potent theme of violence current in the cluster of values that make up the life-style, the socialization process, the interpersonal relationships of individuals living in similar conditions.

The analysis of violent aggressive behavior has been the focus of interest of many social and biological researches, and psychology has attempted to build several theories to explain its phenomenology, ranging from the death-aggression instinct of the psychoanalytic school to the frustration-aggression hypothesis. The present discussion is the result of joint explorations in theory and research in psychology and in sociology, using the concept of subculture as a learning environment. Our major area of study has been assaultive behavior, with special attention to criminal homicide. The following chapter will present a more detailed analysis of the pertinent literature, but some of the main trends in criminological thinking related to this topic must now be anticipated for the proper focus of the present discussion.

Isolated sectional studies of homicide behavior are extremely numerous, and it is not our intention to examine them in this chapter. There are basically two kinds of criminal homicide: (1) premeditated, felonious, intentional murder; (2) slaying in the heat of passion, or killing as a result of intent to do harm but without intent to kill. A slaying committed by one recognized as psychotic or legally insane, or by a psychiatrically designated abnormal subject involves clinical deviates who are generally not held responsible for their behavior, and who, therefore, are not considered culpable. We are eliminating these cases from our present discussion, although subcultural elements are not irrelevant to the analysis of their psychopathological phenomenology.

Probably fewer than five per cent of all known homicides are premeditated, planned intentional killings, and the individuals who commit them are most likely to be episodic offenders who have never had prior contact with the criminal law. Because they are rare crimes often planned by rationally functioning individuals, perhaps they are more likely to remain undetected. We believe that a type of analysis different from that presented here might be applicable to these cases.

Our major concern is with the bulk of homicides—the passion crimes, the violent slayings—that are not premeditated and are not psychotic manifestations. Like Cohen, who was concerned principally with most delinquency that arises from the "working-class" ethic, so we are focusing on the preponderant kind of homicide, although our analysis, particularly in the next chapter, will include much of the available data on homicide in general. . . .

We have said that overt use of force or violence, either in interpersonal relationships or in group interaction, is generally viewed as a reflection of basic values that stand apart from the dominant, the central, or the parent culture. Our hypothesis is that this overt (and often illicit) expression of violence (of which homicide is only the most extreme) is part of a subcultural normative system, and that this system is reflected in the psychological traits of the subculture participants. In the light of our discussion of the caution to be exercised in interpretative analysis, in order to tighten the logic of this analysis, and to support the thesis of a subculture of violence, we offer the following corollary propositions:

1. *No subculture can be totally different from or totally in conflict with the society of which it is a part.* A subculture of violence is not entirely an expression of violence, for there must be interlocking value elements shared with the dominant culture. It should not be necessary to contend that violent aggression is the predominant mode of expression in order to show that the value system is set apart as subcultural. When violence occurs in the dominant culture, it is usually legitimized, but most often is vicarious and a part of phantasy. Moreover, subcultural variations, we have earlier suggested, may be viewed as quantitative and relative. The extent of difference from the larger culture and the degree of intensity, which violence as a subcultural theme may possess, are variables that could and should be measured by known socio-psychological techniques. At present, we are required to rely almost entirely upon expressions of violence in conduct of various forms—parent–child relationships, parental discipline, domestic quarrels, street fights, delinquent conflict gangs, criminal records of assaultive behavior, criminal homicides, etc.—but the number of psychometrically oriented studies in criminology is steadily increasing in both quantity and sophistication, and from them a reliable differential psychology of homicides should emerge to match current sociological research.

2. *To establish the existence of a subculture of violence does not require that the actors sharing in these basic value elements should express violence in all situations.* The normative system designates that in some types of social interaction a violent and physically aggressive response is either expected or required of all members sharing in that system of values. That the actors' behavior expectations occur in more than one situation is obvious. There is a variety of circumstances in which homicide occurs, and the history of past aggressive crimes in high proportions, both in the victims and in the offenders, attests to the multisituational character of the use of violence and to its interpersonal characteristics. But, obviously, persons living in a subcultural milieu designated as a subculture of violence cannot and do not engage in violence continuously, otherwise normal social functioning would be virtually impossible We are merely suggesting, for example, that ready access to weapons in this milieu may become essential for

protection against others who respond in similarly violent ways in certain situations, and that the carrying of knives or other protective devices becomes a common symbol of willingness to participate in violence, to expect violence, and to be ready for its retaliation.

3. *The potential resort or willingness to resort to violence in a variety of situations empha-sizes the penetrating and diffusive character of this culture theme.* The number and kinds of situations in which an individual uses violence may be viewed as an index of the extent to which he has assimilated the values associated with violence. This index should also be reflected by quantitative differences in a variety of psychological dimensions, from differential perception of violent stimuli to different value expres-sions in questionnaire-type instruments. The range of violence from minor assault to fatal injury, or certainly the maximum of violence expected, is rarely made explicit for all situations to which an individual may be exposed. Overt violence may even occa-sionally be a chance result of events. But clearly this range and variability of behavioral expressions of aggression suggest the importance of psychological dimensions in mea-suring adherence to a subculture of violence.

4. *The subcultural ethos of violence may be shared by all ages in a subsociety, but this ethos is most prominent in a limited age group, ranging from late adolescence to middle age.* We are not suggesting that a particular ethnic, sex, or age group all share in com-mon the use of potential threats of violence. We are contending merely that the known empirical distribution of conduct, which expresses the sharing of this violence theme, shows greatest localization, incidence, and frequency in limited subgroups and reflects differences in learning about violence as a problem-solving mechanism.

5. *The counter-norm is nonviolence.* Violation of expected and required violence is most likely to result in ostracism from the group. Alienation of some kind, depending on the range of violence expectations that are unmet, seems to be a form of punitive action most feasible to this subculture. The juvenile who fails to live up to the conflict gang's requirements is pushed outside the group. The adult male who does not defend his honor or his female companion will be socially emasculated. The "coward" is forced to move out of the territory, to find new friends and make new alliances. Membership is lost in the subsociety sharing the cluster of attitudes positively associated with vio-lence. If forced withdrawal or voluntary retreat are not acceptable modes of response to engaging in the counter-norm, then execution, as is reputed to occur in organized crime, may be the extreme punitive measure.

6. *The development of favorable attitudes toward, and the use of, violence in a subculture usually involve learned behavior and a process of differential learning, association, or identification.* Not all persons exposed—even equally exposed—to the presence of a subculture of violence absorb and share in the values in equal portions. Differential per-sonality variables must be considered in an integrated social-psychological approach to an understanding of the subcultural aspects of violence. We have taken the posi-tion that aggression is a learned response, socially facilitated and integrated, as a habit, in more or less permanent form, among the personality characteristics of the aggres-sor. Aggression, from a psychological standpoint, has been defined by Buss as "the delivery of noxious stimuli in an interpersonal context." Aggression seems to possess two major classes of reinforcers: the pain and injury inflicted upon the victim and its extrinsic rewards. Both are present in a subculture of violence, and their mechanism

of action is facilitated by the social support that the aggressor receives in his group. The relationship between aggression, anger, and hostility is complicated by the habit characteristics of the first, the drive state of the second, and the attitudinal interpretative nature of the third. Obviously, the immediacy and the short temporal sequence of anger with its autonomic components make it difficult to study a criminal population that is some distance removed from the anger-provoked event. Hostility, although amenable to easier assessment, does not give a clear indication or measure of physical attack because of its predominantly verbal aspects. However, it may dispose to or prepare for aggression.

Aggression, in its physical manifest form, remains the most criminologically relevant aspect in a study of violent assaultive behavior. If violent aggression is a habit and possesses permanent or quasi-permanent personality trait characteristics, it should be amenable to psychological assessment through appropriate diagnostic techniques. Among the several alternative diagnostic methodologies, those based on a perceptual approach seem to be able, according to the existing literature, to elicit signs and symptoms of behavioral aggression, demonstrating the existence of this "habit" and/or trait in the personality of the subject being tested. Obviously, the same set of techniques being used to diagnose the trait of aggression can be used to assess the presence of major psychopathology, which might, in a restricted number of cases, have caused "aggressive behavior" outside, or in spite of, any cultural or subcultural allegiance.

7. *The use of violence in a subculture is not necessarily viewed as illicit conduct and the users therefore do not have to deal with feelings of guilt about their aggression.* Violence can become a part of the life style, the theme of solving difficult problems or problem situations. It should be stressed that the problems and situations to which we refer arise mostly within the subculture, for violence is used mostly between persons and groups who themselves rely upon the same supportive values and norms. A carrier and user of violence will not be burdened by conscious guilt, then, because generally he is not attacking the representatives of the nonviolent culture, and because the recipient of this violence may be described by similar class status, occupational, residential, age, and other attribute categories which characterize the subuniverse of the collectivity sharing in the subculture of violence. Even law-abiding members of the local subculture area may not view various illegal expressions of violence as menacing or immoral. Furthermore, when the attacked see their assaulters as agents of the same kind of aggression they themselves represent, violent retaliation is readily legitimized by a situationally specific rationale, as well as by the generally normative supports for violence.

Probably no single theory will ever explain the variety of observable violent behavior. However, the subculture-of-violence approach offers, we believe, the advantage of bringing together psychological and sociological constructs to aid in the explanation of the concentration of violence in specific socio-economic groups and ecological areas.

Some questions may arise about the genesis of an assumed subculture of violence. The theoretical formulation describes what is believed to be a condition that may exist in varying manifestations from organized crime, delinquent gangs, political subdivisions, and subsets of a lower-class culture. How these variations arise and from what base, are issues that have not been raised and that would require research to describe. Moreover, the literature on the sociology of conflict, derived principally from Simmel on the social psychology of conflict, and on the more specific topic of the sociology of violence would have to be carefully examined. That there may be some universal derivatives is neither asserted nor denied. One could argue (1) that there is a biological base for aggressive behavior which may, unless conditioned against it, manifest itself in physical violence; (2) that, in Hegelian terms, each culture thesis contains its contraculture antithesis, that to develop into a central culture, nonviolence within must be a dominant theme, and that therefore a subtheme of violence in some form is an invariable consequence. We do not find either of these propositions tenable, and there is considerable evidence to contradict both.

Even without returning philosophically to a discussion of man's pre-political or pre-societal state, a more temporally localized question of genesis may be raised. The descriptions current in subcultural theorizing in general sociology or sociological criminology are limited principally to a modern urban setting, although applications of these theories could conceivably be made to the criminal machinations in such culture periods as Renaissance Florence. At present, we create no new statement of the genesis of a subculture of violence, nor do we find it necessary to adopt a single position. The beginning could be a Cohen-like negative reaction that turned into regularized, institutionalized patterns of prescription. Sufficient communication of dominant culture values, norms, goals, and means is, of course, implicitly assumed if some subset of the population is to react negatively. The existence of violent (illegitimate) means also requires that some of the goals (or symbols of goals) of the dominant culture shall have been communicated to subcultural groups in sufficient strength for them to introject and to desire them and, if thwarted in their pursuit of them, to seek them by whatever illegal means are available. The Cloward–Ohlin formulation is, in this context, an equally useful hypothesis for the genesis of a subculture of violence. Miller's idea of a "generating milieu" does not assume—or perhaps even denies—the communication of most middle-class values to the lower class. Especially relevant to our present interest would be communication of attitudes toward the use of violence. Communication should, perhaps, be distinguished from absorption or introjection of culture values. Communication seems to imply transmission cognitively, to suggest that the recipients have conscious awareness of the existence of things. Absorption, or introjection, refers to conative aspects and goes beyond communication in its power to affect personalities. A value becomes part of the individual's attitudinal set or predisposition to act, and must be more than communicated to be an integral element in a prepotent tendency to respond to stimuli. It might be said that, both in Cohen's and in Cloward–Ohlin's conceptualizations, middle-class values are communicated but not absorbed as part of the personality or idioverse of those individuals who deviate. In Miller's schema, communication from middle to lower class is not required. A considerable degree of isolation of the latter class is even inferred, suggesting that the lower-class ethic had a developmental history and continuity of its own.

We are not prepared to assert how a subculture of violence arises. Perhaps there are several ways in different cultural settings. It may be that even within the same culture a collective conscience and allegiance to the use of violence develop into a subculture from the combination of more than one birth process, i.e. as a negative reaction to the communication of goals from the parent culture, as a positive reaction to this communication coupled with a willingness to use negative means, and as a positive absorption of an indigenous set of subcultural values that, as a system of interlocking values, are the antithesis of the main culture themes.

Whatever may be the circumstances creating any subculture at variance, the problems before us at present are those requiring more precision in defining a subculture, fuller descriptions and measurements of normative systems, and research designed to test hypotheses about subcultures through psychological, sociological, and other disciplinary methods. In the present chapter we have tried to provide an outline of how some of these problems might be resolved. We have used the conceptualization of a subculture of violence as a point of theoretical departure for an integrated sociological and psychological approach to definition, description, and measurement. It now seems appropriate to examine in more detail some of the relevant theory and data on homicide and other assaultive offenses in order to show how these formulations and empirical facts may lead into and be embraced or rejected by the thesis of a subculture of violence.

# THE CODE OF THE STREETS

*Elijah Anderson*

Of all the problems besetting the poor inner-city black community, none is more pressing than that of interpersonal violence and aggression. It wreaks havoc daily with the lives of community residents and increasingly spills over into downtown and residential middle-class areas. Muggings, burglaries, carjackings, and drug-related shootings, all of which may leave their victims or innocent bystanders dead, are now common enough to concern all urban and many suburban residents. The inclination to violence springs from the circumstances of life among the ghetto poor—the lack of jobs that pay a living wage, the stigma of race, the fallout from rampant drug use and drug trafficking, and the resulting alienation and lack of hope for the future.

Simply living in such an environment places young people at special risk of falling victim to aggressive behavior. Although there are often forces in the community which can counteract the negative influences, by far the most powerful being a strong, loving, "decent" (as inner-city residents put it) family committed to middle-class values, the despair is pervasive enough to have spawned an oppositional culture, that of "the streets," whose norms are often consciously opposed to those of mainstream society. These two orientations—decent and street—socially organize the community, and their coexistence has important consequences for residents, particularly children growing up in the inner city. Above all this environment means that even youngsters whose home lives reflect mainstream values—and the majority of homes in the community do—must be able to handle themselves in a street-oriented environment.

This is because the street culture has evolved what may be called a code of the streets, which amounts to a set of informal rules governing interpersonal public behavior, including violence. The rules prescribe both a proper comportment and a proper way to respond if challenged. They regulate the use of violence and so allow those who are inclined to aggression to precipitate violent encounters in an approved way. The rules have been established and are enforced mainly by the street-oriented, but on the streets the distinction between street and decent is often irrelevant; everybody knows that if the rules are violated, there are penalties. Knowledge of the code is thus largely defensive; it is literally neces-sary for operating in public. Therefore, even though families with a decency orientation are usually opposed to the values of the code, they often reluctantly encourage their children's familiarity with it to enable them to negotiate the inner-city environment.

At the heart of the code is the issue of respect—loosely defined as being treated "right," or granted the deference one deserves. However, in the troublesome public environment of the inner city, as people increasingly feel buffeted by forces beyond their control, what one deserves in the way of respect becomes more and more problematic and uncertain. This in turn further opens the issue of respect to sometimes intense interpersonal negotiation. In the street culture, especially among young people, respect is viewed as almost an exter-nal entity that is hard-won but easily lost, and so must constantly be guarded. The rules of the code in fact provide a framework for negotiating respect. The person whose very appearance—including his clothing, demeanor, and way of moving—deters transgressions feels that he possesses, and may be considered by others to possess, a measure of respect. With the right amount of respect, for instance, he can avoid "being bothered" in public. If he is bothered, not only may he be in physical danger but he has been disgraced or "dissed" (disrespected). Many of the forms that dissing can take might seem petty to middle-class people (maintaining eye contact for too long, for example), but to those invested in the street code, these actions become serious indications of the other person's intentions. Con-sequently, such people become very sensitive to advances and slights, which could well serve as warnings of imminent physical confrontation.

This hard reality can be traced to the profound sense of alienation from mainstream society and its institutions felt by many poor inner-city black people, particularly the young. The code of the streets is actually a cultural adaptation to a profound lack of faith in the police and the judicial system. The police are most often seen as representing the dominant white society and not caring to protect inner-city residents. When called, they may not respond, which is one reason many residents feel they must be prepared to take extraordinary measures to defend themselves and their loved ones against those who are inclined to aggression. Lack of police accountability has in fact been incorporated into the status system: the person who is believed capable of "taking care of himself" is accorded a certain deference, which translates into a sense of physical and psychological control. Thus the street code emerges where the influence of the police ends and personal respon-sibility for one's safety is felt to begin. Exacerbated by the proliferation of drugs and easy access to guns, this volatile situation results in the ability of the street-oriented minority (or those who effectively "go for bad") to dominate the public spaces.

## Decent and Street Families

Although almost everyone in poor inner-city neighborhoods is struggling financially and therefore feels a certain distance from the rest of America, the decent and the street family in a real sense represent two poles of value orientation, two contrasting conceptual cat-egories. The labels "decent" and "street," which the residents themselves use, amount to evaluative judgments that confer status on local residents. The labeling is often the result of a social contest among individuals and families of the neighborhood. Individuals of the two orientations often coexist in the same extended family. Decent residents judge themselves to be so while judging others to be of the street, and street individuals often present themselves as decent, drawing distinctions between themselves and other people. In addition, there is quite a bit of circumstantial behavior—that is, one person may at different times exhibit both decent and street orientations, depending on the circumstances. Although these designations result from so much social jockeying, there do exist concrete features that define each conceptual category.

Generally, so-called decent families tend to accept mainstream values more fully and attempt to instill them in their children. Whether married couples with children or single-parent (usually female) households, they are generally "working poor" and so tend to be better off financially than their street-oriented neighbors. They value hard work and self-reliance and are willing to sacrifice for their children. Because they have a certain amount of faith in mainstream society, they harbor hopes for a better future for their children, if not for themselves. Many of them go to church and take a strong interest in their children's schooling. Rather than dwelling on the real hardships and inequities facing them, many such decent people, particularly the increasing number of grandmothers raising grandchildren, see their difficult situation as a test from God and derive great support from their faith and from the church community.

Extremely aware of the problematic and often dangerous environment in which they reside, decent parents tend to be strict in their child-rearing practices, encouraging children to respect authority and walk a straight moral line. They have an almost obsessive concern about trouble of any kind and remind their children to be on the lookout for people and situations that might lead to it. At the same time, they are themselves polite and considerate of others, and teach their children to be the same way. At home, at work, and in church, they strive hard to maintain a positive mental attitude and a spirit of cooperation.

So-called street parents, in contrast, often show a lack of consideration for other people and have a rather superficial sense of family and community. Though they may love their children, many of them are unable to cope with the physical and emotional demands of parenthood, and find it difficult to reconcile their needs with those of their children. These families, who are more fully invested in the code of the streets than the decent people are, may aggressively socialize their children into it in a normative way. They believe in the code and judge themselves and others according to its values.

In fact the overwhelming majority of families in the inner-city community try to approximate the decent-family model, but there are many others who clearly represent the worst fears of the decent family. Not only are their financial resources extremely limited, but what little they have may easily be misused. The lives of the street-oriented are often marked by disorganization. In the most desperate circumstances people frequently have a limited understanding of priorities and consequences, and so frustrations mount over bills, food, and, at times, drink, cigarettes, and drugs. Some tend toward self-destructive behavior; many street-oriented women are crack-addicted ("on the pipe"), alcoholic, or involved in complicated relationships with men who abuse them. In addition, the seeming intractability of their situation, caused in large part by the lack of well-paying jobs and the persistence of racial discrimination, has engendered deep-seated bitterness and anger in many of the most desperate and poorest blacks, especially young people. The need both to exercise a measure of control and to lash out at somebody is often reflected in the adults' relations with their children. At the least, the frustrations of persistent poverty shorten the fuse in such people—contributing to a lack of patience with anyone, child or adult, who irritates them.

In these circumstances a woman—or a man, although men are less consistently present in children's lives—can be quite aggressive with children, yelling at and striking them for the least little infraction of the rules she has set down. Often little if any serious explanation follows the verbal and physical punishment. This response teaches children a particular lesson. They learn that to solve any kind of interpersonal problem one must quickly resort to hitting or other violent behavior. Actual peace and quiet, and also the appearance of calm, respectful children conveyed to her neighbors and friends, are often what the young mother most desires, but at times she will be very aggressive in trying to get them. Thus she may be quick to beat her children, especially if they defy her law, not because she hates them but because this is the way she knows to control them. In fact, many street-oriented women love their children dearly. Many mothers in the community subscribe to the notion that there is a "devil in the boy" that must be beaten out of him or that socially "fast girls need to be whupped." Thus much of what borders on child abuse in the view of social authorities is acceptable parental punishment in the view of these mothers.

Many street-oriented women are sporadic mothers whose children learn to fend for themselves when necessary, foraging for food and money any way they can get it. The children are sometimes employed by drug dealers or become addicted themselves. These children of the street, growing up with little supervision, are said to "come up hard." They often learn to fight at an early age, sometimes using short-tempered adults around them as role models. The street-oriented home may be fraught with anger, verbal disputes, physical aggression, and even mayhem. The children observe these goings-on, learning the lesson that might makes right. They quickly learn to hit those who cross them, and the dog-eat-dog mentality prevails. In order to survive, to protect oneself, it is necessary to marshal inner resources and be ready to deal with adversity in a hands-on way. In these circumstances physical prowess takes on great significance.

In some of the most desperate cases, a street-oriented mother may simply leave her young children alone and unattended while she goes out. The most irresponsible women can be found at local bars and crack houses, getting high and socializing with other adults. Sometimes a troubled woman will leave very young children alone for days at a time. Reports of crack addicts abandoning their children have become common in drug-infested inner-city communities. Neighbors or relatives discover the abandoned children, often hungry and distraught over the absence of their mother. After repeated absences, a friend or relative, particularly a grandmother, will often step in to care for the young children, sometimes petitioning the authorities to send her, as guardian of the children, the mother's welfare check, if the mother gets one. By this time, however, the children may well have learned the first lesson of the streets; survival itself, let alone respect, cannot be taken for granted; you have to fight for your place in the world.

## Campaigning for Respect

These realities of inner-city life are largely absorbed on the streets. At an early age, often even before they start school, children from street-oriented homes gravitate to the streets, where they "hang"—socialize with their peers. Children from these generally permissive homes have a great deal of latitude and are allowed to "rip and run" up and down the street. They often come home from school, put their books down, and go right back out the door. On school nights eight- and nine-year-olds remain out until nine or ten o'clock (and teenagers typically come in whenever they want to). On the streets they play in groups that often become the source of their primary social bonds. Children from decent homes tend to be more carefully supervised and are thus likely to have curfews and to be taught how to stay out of trouble.

When decent and street kids come together, a kind of social shuffle occurs in which children have a chance to go either way. Tension builds as a child comes to realize that he must choose an orientation. The kind of home he comes from influences but does not determine the way he will ultimately turn out—although it is unlikely that a child from a thoroughly street-oriented family will easily absorb decent values on the streets. Youths who emerge from street-oriented families but develop a decency orientation almost always learn those values in another setting—in school, in a youth group, in church. Often it is the result of their involvement with a caring "old head" (adult role model).

In the street, through their play, children pour their individual life experiences into a common knowledge pool, affirming, confirming, and elaborating on what they have observed in the home and matching their skills against those of others. And they learn to fight. Even small children test one another, pushing and shoving, and are ready to hit other children over circumstances not to their liking. In turn, they are readily hit by other children, and the child who is toughest prevails. Thus the violent resolution of disputes, the hitting and cursing, gains social reinforcement. The child in effect is initiated into a system that is really a way of campaigning for respect.

In addition, younger children witness the disputes of older children, which are often resolved through cursing and abusive talk, if not aggression or outright violence. They see that one child succumbs to the greater physical and mental abilities of the other. They are also alert and attentive witnesses to the verbal and physical fights of adults, after which they compare notes and share their interpretations of the event. In almost every case the victor is the person who physically won the altercation, and this person often enjoys the esteem and respect of onlookers. These experiences reinforce the lessons the children have learned at home: might makes right, and toughness is a virtue, while humility is not. In effect they learn the social meaning of fighting. When it is left virtually unchallenged, this understanding becomes an ever more important part of the child's working conception of the world. Over time the code of the streets becomes refined.

Those street-oriented adults with whom children come in contact—including mothers, fathers, brothers, sisters, boyfriends, cousins, neighbors, and friends—help them along in forming this understanding by verbalizing the messages they are getting through experience: "Watch your back." "Protect yourself." "Don't punk out." "If somebody messes with you, you got to pay them back." "If someone disses you, you got to straighten them out." Many parents actually impose sanctions if a child is not sufficiently aggressive. For example, if a child loses a fight and comes home upset, the parent might respond. "Don't you come in here crying that somebody beat you up: you better get back out there and whup his ass. I didn't raise no punks! Get back out there and whup his ass. If you don't whup his ass, I'll whup your ass when you come home." Thus the child obtains reinforcement for being tough and showing nerve.

While fighting, some children cry as though they are doing something they are ambivalent about. The fight may be against their wishes, yet they may feel constrained to fight or face the consequences—not just from peers but also from caretakers or parents, who may administer another beating if they back down. Some adults recall receiving such lessons from their own parents and justify repeating them to their children as a way to toughen them up. Looking capable of taking care of oneself as a form of self-defense is a dominant theme among both street-oriented and decent adults who worry about the safety of their children. There is thus at times a convergence in their child-rearing practices, although the rationales behind them may differ.

## Self-Image Based on "Juice"

By the time they are teenagers, most youths have either internalized the code of the streets or at least learned the need to comport themselves in accordance with its rules, which chiefly have to do with interpersonal communication. The code revolves around the presentation of self. Its basic requirement is the display of a certain predisposition to violence. Accordingly, one's bearing must send the unmistakable if sometimes subtle message to "the next person" in public that one is capable of violence and mayhem when the situation requires it, that one can take care of oneself. The nature of this communication is largely determined by the demands of the circumstances but can include facial expressions, gait, and verbal expressions—all of which are geared mainly to deterring aggression. Physical appearance, including clothes, jewelry, and grooming, also plays an important part in how a person is viewed; to be respected, it is important to have the right look.

Even so, there are no guarantees against challenges, because there are always people around looking for a fight to increase their share of respect—or "juice," as it is sometimes called on the street. Moreover, if a person is assaulted, it is important, not only in the eyes of his opponent but also in the eyes of his "running buddies," for him to avenge himself. Otherwise he risks being "tried" (challenged) or "moved on" by any number of others. To maintain his honor he must show he is not someone to be "messed with" or "dissed." In general, the person must "keep himself straight" by managing his position of respect among others; this involves in part his self-image, which is shaped by what he thinks others are thinking of him in relation to his peers.

Objects play an important and complicated role in establishing self-image, Jackets, sneakers, gold jewelry, reflect not just a person's taste, which tends to be tightly regulated among adolescents of all social classes, but also a willingness to possess things that may require defending. A boy wearing a fashionable, expensive jacket, for example, is vulnerable to attack by another who covets the jacket and either cannot afford to buy one or wants the added satisfaction of depriving someone else of his. However, if the boy forgoes the desirable jacket and wears one that isn't "hip," he runs the risk of being teased and possibly even assaulted as an unworthy person. To be allowed to hang with certain prestigious crowds, a boy must wear a different set of expensive clothes—sneakers and athletic suit— every day. Not to be able to do so might make him appear socially deficient. The youth comes to covet such items—especially when he sees easy prey wearing them.

In acquiring valued things, therefore, a person shores up his identity—but since it is an identity based on having things, it is highly precarious. This very precariousness gives a heightened sense of urgency to staying even with peers, with whom the person is actually competing. Young men and women who are able to command respect through their presentation of self—by allowing their possessions and their body language to speak for them—may not have to campaign for regard but may, rather, gain it by the force of their manner. Those who are unable to command respect in this way must actively campaign for it—and are thus particularly alive to slights.

One way of campaigning for status is by taking the possessions of others. In this context, seemingly ordinary objects can become trophies imbued with symbolic value that far exceeds their monetary worth. Possession of the trophy can symbolize the ability to violate somebody—to "get in his face," to take something of value from him, to "dis" him, and thus to enhance one's own worth by stealing someone else's. The trophy does not have to be something material. It can be another person's sense of honor, snatched away with a derogatory remark. It can be the outcome of a fight. It can be the imposition of a certain standard, such as a girl's getting herself recognized as the most beautiful. Material things, however, fit easily into the pattern. Sneakers, a pistol, even somebody else's girlfriend, can become a trophy. When a person can take something from another and then flaunt it, he gains a certain regard by being the owner, or the controller, of that thing. But this display of ownership can then provoke other people to challenge him. This game of who controls what is thus constantly being played out on inner-city streets, and the trophy—extrinsic or intrinsic, tangible or intangible—identifies the current winner.

An important aspect of this often violent give-and-take is its zero-sum quality. That is, the extent to which one person can raise himself up depends on his ability to put another person down. This underscores the alienation that permeates the inner-city ghetto community. There is a generalized sense that very little respect is to be had, and therefore everyone competes to get what affirmation he can of the little that is available. The craving for respect that results gives people thin skins. Shows of deference by others can be highly soothing, contributing to a sense of security, comfort, self-confidence, and self-respect. Transgressions by others which go unanswered diminish these feelings and are believed to encourage further transgressions. Hence one must be ever vigilant against the transgressions of others or even *appearing* as if transgressions will be tolerated. Among young people, whose sense of self-esteem is particularly vulnerable, there is an especially heightened concern with being disrespected. Many inner-city young men in particular crave respect to such a degree that they will risk their lives to attain and maintain it.

The issue of respect is thus closely tied to whether a person has an inclination to be violent, even as a victim. In the wider society people may not feel required to retaliate physically after an attack, even though they are aware that they have been degraded or taken advantage of. They may feel a great need to defend themselves *during* an attack, or to behave in such a way as to deter aggression (middle-class people certainly can and do become victims of street-oriented youths), but they are much more likely than street-oriented people to feel that they can walk away from a possible altercation with their self-esteem intact. Some people may even have the strength of character to flee, without any thought that their self-respect or esteem will be diminished.

In impoverished inner-city black communities, however, particularly among young males and perhaps increasingly among females, such flight would be extremely difficult. To run away would likely leave one's self-esteem in tatters. Hence people often feel constrained not only to stand up and at least attempt to resist during an assault but also to "pay back"—to seek revenge—after a successful assault on their person. This may include going to get a weapon or even getting relatives involved. Their very identity and self-respect, their honor, is often intricately tied up with the way they perform on the streets during and after such encounters. This outlook reflects the circumscribed opportunities of the inner-city poor. Generally people outside the ghetto have other ways of gaining status and regard, and thus do not feel so dependent on such physical displays.

## By Trial of Manhood

On the street, among males these concerns about things and identity have come to be expressed in the concept of "manhood." Manhood in the inner city means taking the prerogatives of men with respect to strangers, other men, and women—being distinguished as a man. It implies physicality and a certain ruthlessness. Regard and respect are associated with this concept in large part because of its practical application: if others have little or no regard for a person's manhood, his very life and those of his loved ones could be in jeopardy. But there is a chicken-and-egg aspect to this situation: one's physical safety is more likely to be jeopardized in public *because* manhood is associated with respect. In other words, an existential link has been created between the idea of manhood and one's self-esteem, so that it has become hard to say which is primary. For many inner-city youths, manhood and respect are flip sides of the same coin: physical and psychological well-being are inseparable, and both require a sense of control, of being in charge.

The operating assumption is that a man, especially a real man, knows what other men know—the code of the streets. And if one is not a real man, one is somehow diminished as a person, and there are certain valued things one simply does not deserve. There is thus believed to be a certain justice to the code, since it is considered that everyone has the opportunity to know it. Implicit in this is that everybody is held responsible for being familiar with the code. If the victim of a mugging, for example, does not know the code and so responds "wrong," the perpetrator may feel justified even in killing him and may feel no remorse. He may think, "Too bad, but it's his fault. He should have known better."

So when a person ventures outside, he must adopt the code—a kind of shield, really—to prevent others from "messing with" him. In these circumstances it is easy for people to think they are being tried or tested by others even when this is not the case. For it is sensed that something extremely valuable is at stake in every interaction, and people are encouraged to rise to the occasion, particularly with strangers. For people who are unfamiliar with the code—generally people who live outside the inner city—the concern with respect in the most ordinary interactions can be frightening and incomprehensible. But for those who are invested in the code, the clear object of their demeanor is to discourage strangers from even thinking about testing their manhood. And the sense of power that attends the ability to deter others can be alluring even to those who know the code without being heavily invested in it—the decent inner-city youths. Thus a boy who has been leading a basically decent life can, in trying circumstances, suddenly resort to deadly force.

Central to the issue of manhood is the widespread belief that one of the most effective ways of gaining respect is to manifest "nerve." Nerve is shown when one takes another person's possessions (the more valuable the better), "messes with" someone's woman, throws the first punch, "gets in someone's face," or pulls a trigger. Its proper display helps on the spot to check others who would violate one's person and also helps to build a reputation that works to prevent future challenges. But since such a show of nerve is a forceful expression of disrespect toward the person on the receiving end, the victim may be greatly offended and seek to retaliate with equal or greater force. A display of nerve, therefore, can easily provoke a life-threatening response, and the background knowledge of that possibility has often been incorporated into the concept of nerve.

True nerve exposes a lack of fear of dying. Many feel that it is acceptable to risk dying over the principle of respect. In fact, among the hard-core street-oriented, the clear risk of violent death may be preferable to being "dissed" by another. The youths who have internalized this attitude and convincingly display it in their public bearing are among the most threatening people of all, for it is commonly assumed that they fear no man. As the people of the community say, "They are the baddest dudes on the street." They often lead an existential life that may acquire meaning only when they are faced with the possibility of imminent death. Not to be afraid to die is by implication to have few compunctions about taking another's life. Not to be afraid to die is the quid pro quo of being able to take somebody else's life—for the right reasons, if the situation demands it. When others believe this is one's position, it gives one a real sense of power on the streets. Such credibility is what many inner-city youths strive to achieve, whether they are decent or street-oriented, both because of its practical defensive value and because of the positive way it makes them feel about themselves. The difference between the decent and the street-oriented youth is often that the decent youth makes a conscious decision to appear tough and manly; in another setting—with teachers, say, or at his part-time job—he can be polite and deferential. The street-oriented youth, on the other hand, has made the concept of manhood a part of his very identity; he has difficulty manipulating it—it often controls him. . . .

### "Going for Bad"

In the most fearsome youths such a cavalier attitude toward death grows out of a very limited view of life. Many are uncertain about how long they are going to live and believe they could die violently at any time. They accept this fate; they live on the edge. Their manner conveys the message that nothing intimidates them; whatever turn the encounter takes, they maintain their attack—rather like a pit bull, whose spirit many such boys admire. The demonstration of such tenacity "shows heart" and earns their respect.

This fearlessness has implications for law enforcement. Many street-oriented boys are much more concerned about the threat of "justice" at the hands of a peer than at the hands of the police. Moreover, many feel not only that they have little to lose by going to prison but that they have something to gain. The toughening-up one experiences in prison can actually enhance one's reputation on the streets. Hence the system loses influence over the hard core who are without jobs, with little perceptible stake in the system. If mainstream society has done nothing *for* them, they counter by making sure it can do nothing *to* them.

At the same time, however, a competing view maintains that true nerve consists in backing down, walking away from a fight, and going on with one's business. One fights only in self-defense. This view emerges from the decent philosophy that life is precious, and it is an important part of the socialization process common in decent homes. It discourages violence as the primary means of resolving disputes and encourages youngsters to accept nonviolence and talk as confrontational strategies. But "if the deal goes down," self-defense is greatly encouraged. When there is enough positive support for this orientation, either in the home or among one's peers, then nonviolence has a chance to prevail. But it prevails at the cost of relinquishing a claim to being bad and tough, and therefore sets a young person up as at the very least alienated from street-oriented peers and quite possibly a target of derision or even violence.

Although the nonviolent orientation rarely overcomes the impulse to strike back in an encounter, it does introduce a certain confusion and so can prompt a measure of soul-searching, or even profound ambivalence. Did the person back down with his respect intact or did he back down only to be judged a "punk"—a person lacking manhood? Should he or she have acted? Should he or she have hit the other person in the mouth? These questions beset many young men and women during public confrontations. What is the "right" thing to do? In the quest for honor, respect, and local status—which few young people are uninterested in—common sense most often prevails, which leads many to opt for the tough approach, enacting their own particular versions of the display of nerve. The presentation of oneself as rough and tough is very often quite acceptable until one is tested. And then that presentation may help the person pass the test, because it will cause fewer questions to be asked about what he did and why. It is hard for a person to explain why he lost the fight or why he backed down. Hence many will strive to appear to "go for bad," while hoping they will never be tested. But when they are tested, the outcome of the situation may quickly be out of their hands, as they become wrapped up in the circumstances of the moment.

## An Oppositional Culture

The attitudes of the wider society are deeply implicated in the code of the streets. Most people in inner-city communities are not totally invested in the code, but the significant minority of hard-core street youths who are have to maintain the code in order to establish reputations, because they have—or feel they have—few other ways to assert themselves. For these young people the standards of the street code are the only game in town. The extent to which some children—particularly those who through upbringing have become most alienated and those lacking in strong and conventional social support—experience, feel, and internalize racist rejection and contempt from mainstream society may strongly encourage them to express contempt for the more conventional society in turn. In dealing with this contempt and rejection, some youngsters will consciously invest themselves and their considerable mental resources in what amounts to an oppositional culture to preserve themselves and their self-respect. Once they do, any respect they might be able to garner in the wider system pales in comparison with the respect available in the local system: thus they often lose interest in even attempting to negotiate the mainstream system.

At the same time, many less alienated young blacks have assumed a street-oriented demeanor as a way of expressing their blackness while really embracing a much more moderate way of life; they, too, want a nonviolent setting in which to live and raise a family. These decent people are trying hard to be part of the mainstream culture, but the racism, real and perceived, that they encounter helps to legitimate the oppositional culture. And so on occasion they adopt street behavior. In fact, depending on the demands of the situation, many people in the community slip back and forth between decent and street behavior.

A vicious cycle has thus been formed. The hopelessness and alienation many young inner-city black men and women feel, largely as a result of endemic joblessness and persistent racism, fuels the violence they engage in. This violence serves to confirm the negative feelings many whites and some middle-class blacks harbor toward the ghetto poor, further legitimating the oppositional culture and the code of the streets in the eyes of many poor young blacks. Unless this cycle is broken, attitudes on both sides will become increasingly entrenched, and the violence, which claims victims black and white, poor and affluent, will only escalate.

# CONTEMPORARY RETROSPECTIVE ON SUBCULTURAL THEORIES

## EXAMINING THE LOGIC OF SUBCULTURAL MODELS

*Mark T. Berg, University of Missouri–St. Louis; and*
*Eric A. Stewart, Florida State University*

It stands as a social fact that criminal behavior is not uniformly distributed throughout society. Much empirical evidence shows that rates of crime are disproportionably concentrated across place and time and within segments of the population. Numerous criminological theories attempt to account for the source of such variation. Each is conceptually anchored in descriptive information, suggesting a link between the distribution of crime and social conditions. Causal propositions are devised that configure theoretical relationships among these empirical patterns (Taylor, Walton, & Young, 1973). Cultural factors figure prominently into the logical framework of theories formulated to explain the uneven representation of violence within society. The point of departure for these works is that neither violent crime rates nor culture are characterized by a homogeneous pattern. Cultural theories posit that variation in value systems predicts simultaneous variation in the scope and form of violent actions (e.g., Gastil, 1971; Pettigrew & Spier, 1962).

   The readings authored by Cohen, Miller, Wolfgang and Ferracuti, and Anderson represent a collection of theoretical models that rely on culture as their predominant organizing principle. They share in common the assertion that *subcultural* processes in particular play a prominent role in the production of crime, especially violence. As we illustrate in this chapter, this theoretical inventory does not fuse into a coherent perspective on subcultures and violence. Instead, the components of the multiple models form a conceptual web identifying the ways in which value orientations allegedly procure violent actions. A relatively modest amount of effort has been dedicated to disentangling the unique contribution of the various subcultural models. Perhaps this is because a flurry of contentiousness surrounds their basic premise. Such state of affairs is owed in part to the abstractness of culture and its attendant causal processes, but also to the notion that a nonconventional culture is analogous to a pathological condition. Critics who adhere to the latter view more or less reject cultural explanations, claiming that this brand of theorizing victimizes persons for being mired in circumstances beyond their power (Pfohl, 1985). In fact, since the early 1970s empirical efforts to identify social processes underlying violence have largely neglected the role of culture. Publications by Lewis (1969) and others documenting the experience of urban poverty set off a firestorm of criticisms both from within and outside of academia (see Valentine, 1968; Wilson, 1987). As a consequence, later research in this arena moved away from a discussion of culture and criminology followed suit for many years. Now the discipline appears to again be open to the potential for nonconventional culture as a variable.

Scientific discourse should avoid the pitfall of ideological biases with respect to subculture in order to make significant progress toward understanding the nature of crime. It is also imperative that the logical structure of subcultural theories be extracted and explicitly defined prior to assessing the proposed relationships. In this chapter, we outline the major subcultural theories, while articulating the distinctiveness and similarity of their arguments with respect to patterns of violence. More specifically, we (1) synthesize the ideas in each theory concerning the etiology and content of subcultural systems, (2) discuss their alignment vis-à-vis social structure, and (3) determine how subcultural values are transmitted across time and place. Along the way we highlight the empirical evidence and critiques for these positions, drawing on both qualitative and quantitative sources. We conclude with advice for future research on subcultural theory and the implications of this work for policy.

## Foundations of Subcultural Theories

### Social structure, culture, and subculture

Social structure and culture unite to comprise social organization, the conceptual platform of the sociological paradigm (Jaeger & Selznick, 1964). Each concept is an "analytical [device]" that calls attention to a unique aspect of society (Messner & Rosenfeld, 1997b). Each serves as a distinct lens through which to understand the nature of social life. On one hand, culture represents the symbolic dimension comprised of values and norms directing behavior. On the other, social structure embodies the roles and relational properties that place constraints upon behavior. If culture is the roadmap to our actions, then structure is the chain that restricts our impulses. Violent behavior is a product of both factors (Messner & Rosenfeld, 1997b). The nexus of culture and social structure is essentially the cornerstone of any scholarly venture into the effects of culture on patterns of violence. We proceed accordingly, by incorporating the role of structure throughout our discussion of subcultural models.

There is not a precise or uniform definition of subculture in the criminological literature. For this reason it is vulnerable to critique, and the theories organized around the term are prone to misinterpretation. Subculture is, of course, a deductive artifact of culture though it is substantively distinctive. An explicit classification of culture holds that it is the meaning humans generate and apply to their environment (Geertz, 1973). This perspective permits culture to take on a variant shape across society. And it permits social consensus on values implying that, while values may differ, they do converge and assemble among groups, providing the empirical possibility of subculture. Some values are more widespread; in contrast, those less conventional are said to be shared by a subculture. Theoretically, what signifies membership into subcultures is not simply commonality in behavior patterns, but a sense of mutual cognitions pertaining to objects and actions (e.g., behaviors). To be part of a subculture necessitates that persons hold a salient and intense degree of identification with others who also make a "strategic" decision to attribute similar meaning to "objects" in their social world (Fine & Kleinman, 1979). Social structural conditions *potentially* function as stimulus for group identification, serving as a salient force in collective organization and ultimately facilitating subculture formations. Matsueda, Gartner, Piliavin, and Polakowski (1992) in fact argue that "subcultures . . . are intimately tied to structural opportunities" (pp. 767–768). As with culture, the concept of subculture cannot be logically divorced from the social structure. At the same time it is critical not to confound the concept of subculture with that of structure to prevent the occasion where structural collectivities are artificially imputed a shared subculture (e.g., Kornhauser, 1978).

While this conceptualization of subculture does not conform verbatim to the varying definitions used by the authors reviewed in the text, it serves as a useful reference point in the discussion that follows.

### Backdrop to subcultural models

By the first half of the twentieth century the study of deviance was situated in a vibrant intellectual environment, setting the stage for the development of what are now regarded as core theories of criminology. Criminologists at the time began to assume the analytical posture of positivism, in that they sought to discover the "law-like" structure governing social actions (Taylor et al., 1973). Their objective was to develop a science of crime by way of theoretical construction. Scholars in the Chicago School of sociology applied this strategy while investigating the implications of normative shifts on behavioral patterns among rural populations negotiating the transition to urban life (Thomas & Znaniecki, 1918). Others contrasted the complex interdependence of urban growth dynamics and human behavior to the notion of symbiotic development found in the study of plant ecology. It is in this vein that the early subcultural theories of delinquency emerged from the Chicago School.

Subsequent empirical research conducted by Shaw and McKay (1942) in Chicago neighborhoods contributed importantly to conceptual efforts in the study of crime. Based on analyses of county juvenile court records they concluded that rates of delinquency decreased precipitously with gains in distance from the city center, and rates tended to remain relatively stable across neighborhoods, despite population turnover. Shaw and McKay (1942, 1969) believed that such marked stability in the spatial concentration of crime was sustained by ecologically situated value systems espousing criminal behavior. This idea converged with Thrasher's (1927) earlier research and it was ultimately incorporated as the "cultural transmission" dimension of Shaw and McKay's social disorganization theory (Bursik & Webb, 1982; Cullen, 1984). To Shaw and McKay, deviant subcultures not only acted as hosts for the system of nonconventional values (Shaw & McKay, 1942), but were also responsible for disseminating it across generations. Further, structural conditions eroded social control mechanisms thereby permitting the proliferation of subcultures within neighborhoods (Kornhauser, 1978).

During this time period Sutherland (1947) formulated his social interactive theory of criminal behavior. Somewhat consistent with Shaw and McKay's position on cultural transmission, his intellectual approach posited that the stimulus for delinquency was produced in interaction with others. Stated succinctly, Sutherland's model of differential association stipulates that greater exposure to persons holding values supportive of law violation amplifies the odds that one will engage in this behavior. His propositions involve both the content of what is learned as well as the process through which it is done so. Most relevant to subcultural theory is his notion that exposure to "definitions" favorable or unfavorable to law violation constitutes the content of acquired knowledge in interaction. Definitions are essentially ideas regarding appropriate behavior (Vold, Bernard, & Snipes, 2002). Sutherland's thinking can be traced throughout subsequent versions of subcultural theory. Many, including those emphasized here, take the position "that it is ideas themselves . . . that directly cause criminal behavior" (Vold et al., 2002, p. 165).

## Substance and Evaluation of Subcultural Models

### Albert Cohen

The confluence of Shaw and McKay's ecological research and Sutherland's interaction-based theory inspired Albert Cohen's (1955) theory of the delinquent subculture. Cohen sought to overcome what he perceived as the limitations of these models while also expanding on their unique strengths. Where Shaw and McKay emphasized structural sources of behavior and offered ideas about the transmission of cultural orientations, Sutherland largely overlooked structural factors opting instead to focus more exclusively on the symbolic dimension of crime causation. But Merton's (1938) theory of anomie is the primary point of departure for Cohen's (1955) model. According to Merton's (1938) perspective, motivation for criminal behavior can be explained by the disjuncture between the culture structure and social structure. Persons confronting the reality of blocked structural opportunities either conform to or seek alternative mechanisms to attain the culturally defined American success goal. Crime represents one route to this end. Cohen insists that Merton's anomie theory proves inadequate to explain crimes devoid of financial motive. Moreover, Cohen (1955) believes Merton's notion of individual adaptations is "too atomistic." It depicts individuals as isolated in their quest to resolve the strain of means–end disjuncture. Unlike Merton, Cohen argues that adaptations to strain are influenced by individuals' "associations" in their local environment and "dependent upon [their] reference group" (Pfohl, 1985, p. 269). Cohen applauded criminological theory for granting a causal role to subcultural systems. He faulted these works on the whole, however, for failing to account for the origins of the delinquent subculture, its particular content, and its disproportionate presence in working-class populations. While lamenting these omissions, Cohen (1955) comments that "any subculture calls for explanation in its own right. It is never a random growth" (p. 18).

Cohen (1955) grounds his critiques of prior theorizing and he also formulates his own theory based on the empirical nature of juvenile delinquency. First, citing Thrasher (1927) Cohen claims that much delinquent behavior is "negativistic" or expressive, versus utilitarian. He emphasizes its social structural patterning—unlike Sutherland—by demonstrating that juvenile delinquency is "generally a working class phenomenon." Then, drawing again from Thrasher (1927) and, this time Sutherland (1947), Cohen notes that the "hallmark" of juvenile delinquency is its group-based character. In the book *Delinquent Boys: The Culture of the Gang,* Cohen (1955) progresses forward from these "facts" to state his theory of delinquent subcultures. Not unlike Merton, Cohen implicates wider conventional culture as the primary force underlying delinquent behavior. Cohen argues that the group-based, negativistic, and working-class character of delinquency is the product of the middle-class

American cultural standard. Specifically, Cohen believes that the status configuration of the wider value complex dominates all aspects of American life. By virtue of their socialization into working-class families, youth are poorly equipped to abide by the criteria of a middle-class existence (e.g., self-reliance, worldly asceticism, exercise of forethought, manners, and sociability). The structural deficits of the working class also translate into cultural deficits, according to Cohen. Furthermore, he argues that middle-class cultural standards are used to evaluate one's worth; for instance, Cohen (1955) remarks that "success is itself a sign of the exercise of moral qualities" (p. 87).

The school represents the arena in which working-class children's status "handicap" is most evident. Youth of all class positions assemble together in classrooms openly "competing for status in terms of the same set of . . . criteria." As Cohen (1955) remarks, that school is "where working-class children are most likely to be found wanting" (p. 112). Failing to fit the criteria of the "middle-class measuring rod" incurs a loss of respect within society, inviting a "status frustration." According to Cohen (1955), working-class youths consequently confront a "problem of adjustment" and therefore youth are "in the market for a solution" (p. 118). Cohen maintains that similarly situated youths find common ground and ultimately band together to reject middle-class values. They collectively devise an alternative status system that turns the tenets of the middle-class existence "upside down" (p. 28). Cohen argues that respect is conferred by the subculture to those members who excel at fighting, who are physically aggressive, and who display an all-around disregard for middle-class standards. Due to their repudiation of the conventional culture and deep reliance on their own social milieu for status, members of the delinquent subculture develop a strong dependence on their system for identity. This trait helps uphold its distinct degree of permanence across contexts.

The extent to which Cohen expands prior theory to forge his own contribution is apparent. Relying on the group as the catalyst for behavior, Cohen effectively merges the interactive contribution of Sutherland's work into his model, addressing what he sees as the atomistic limitation of Merton's anomie theory. At the same time he pinpoints the etiology of the contemporary delinquent subculture as a collective "reaction formation" against conventional culture. Cohen seems to expand on Shaw and McKay (1942), positing that the reservoir of identity provided by the subculture incurs its "transmission."

Later on in *Social Theory and Structure,* Merton (1968) acknowledged the contribution of Cohen's model to the development of his own thinking about the nature of the deviant response (see also Merton, 1997). Merton (1997) admits that Cohen's model plausibly bridges the conceptual framework of anomie with the learning premises of Sutherland's perspective. Subsequent theorizing by Merton regarding patterns of criminal behavior incorporated the notion of reference group influences. This is possibly due to Cohen's model (Merton, 1968; Pfohl, 1985). Yet, despite Cohen's contribution Merton appeared to argue that his theoretical position and Cohen's made comparable statements with regard to the etiology of the subculture. Cohen and Merton both posit that criminal behavior originates from the gap between the goals of the wider culture and the structurally available means to attain them. Merton believed that the group-based explanation was sufficient to account for the malicious character of delinquency that Cohen emphasized, but Merton seemed to suggest that the group dimension was not logically necessary because the subculture would not exist (or be needed) absent the means–ends disjuncture.

## Walter Miller

Like Cohen, Walter Miller (1958) unmistakably consolidates social structure in the framework of his theoretical perspective. He focuses more broadly on explaining the cultural milieu in which lower-class youth find themselves. Yet Miller's specific intent is to delineate the unique cultural conditions motivating lower-class "adolescent street corner groups" to engage in delinquency. Miller develops his model based on what he sees as the limitations of Cohen's theory. He forcefully differentiates his views from Cohen's, claiming that the fundamental "premise" of his theory asserts that delinquency among the lower class is shaped by members' desire to adhere to the "distinctly patterned tradition" of lower-class culture. In contrast, Miller claims the so-called delinquent subculture envisioned by Cohen has less "integrity" since it is assembled as a reaction against the middle class. Miller perceives that the lower-class culture as a whole—versus Cohen's reaction-based rendition—exerts a powerful influence on individuals' involvement in delinquent behavior. A central component of both theories is the actor's structural position. However, they take widely different positions on this point. Miller believes that lower-class delinquents are not motivated to violate the law by a referent value complex, but their actions are "dominated" by the dictates of their *absolute* position—as members in the lower class. Cohen's model assumes that delinquency is motivated according to one's *relative* status ranking in the class stratum.

According to Miller (1958), the lower-class cultural system is distinctive in its symbolic content, or what he refers to as focal concerns. He is careful to point out that his usage of the term "focal concerns" permits him to remain neutral when discussing their implications for behavior. Miller recognizes that focal concerns are analogous to values in the sense that they represent components of a culture and each attracts deep "emotional involvement." The focal concerns or values he speaks of include trouble, toughness, smartness, excitement, fate, and autonomy.

A unique feature of social life among the lower class according to Miller (1958) is the "adolescent street corner group." This single-sex social conglomerate provides a certain degree of affective and material resources unmet in the widespread absence of the two-parent family unit. Participants are socialized to the normative demeanor of the male "sex-role," an opportunity not otherwise available in their surroundings. Two additional focal concerns—"belonging" and "status"—are critically important to the lower-class peer group. Miller suggests that each is a by-product of adherence to the general array of focal concerns held by the lower class. The concept of belonging implies a preoccupation with "in-group membership" and the concern with status refers to youths' desire to achieve a position of good standing among group members. Personal status or rank is earned by exhibiting skills in the behavioral hallmarks of toughness and smartness. Showing physical prowess in the face of a rival group incurs a reputation for toughness, a quality that engenders a high ranking in one's group.

Miller (1958) proposes that for lower-class youth to conform to the normative imperatives of their group is to act inconsistent with the conventional values of wider society. Therefore in direct contrast to Cohen's strain-based perspective, Miller asserts that lower-class youths' criminal involvement is not motivated by the desire to defy the lofty demands of the middle-class value system. He maintains that such a logical configuration is advocated by those (e.g., Cohen) who use the middle-class principles as an "implicit point of reference."

Miller (1958) does not describe the origins of the lower-class value system; instead he is content with stating that it is a custom "centuries old." With regard to its permanence, he suggests lower-class culture is transmitted over time to the extent that lower-class persons aspire for membership into street-corner groups. Membership, again, is granted to those who overtly commit to focal concerns. But here the causal role of the cultural and structural components of Miller's model is imprecise. As explicated earlier, Cohen more clearly defined the structural genesis of the alternative status system, and described how the system's continuity arises from members' increased reliance on its cultural precepts. Cohen's and Miller's ideas converge somewhat in their treatment of the process aspects of Sutherland's theorizing. Both suggest that the principles of unconventional status systems operate as acute behavioral imperatives. The definitions or ideas common to these systems fuel law-violating behavior. However, the group concept in Miller's model assumes a more autonomous form, or in other words—it exists independent of other class-based systems (Brownfield, 1996). In Cohen's depiction the group establishes an autonomous norm structure, yet it subsists—at least initially—by virtue of its polarization against middle-class standards.

Cloward and Ohlin (1960) criticize Miller for imputing an alternative culture to all lower-class peer groups independent of the breadth of their involvement in delinquent behavior. They remark that "there is a tendency to classify as delinquent any group in which delinquent acts occur" (p. 69). Such thinking indeed leads to a logical trap that constrains all behaviors as being subcultural in origin. Similarly, Tittle (1983) notes that Miller's "theory reduces to the tautological assertion that the lower class is criminal because it is criminal" (p. 340). Structural patterns of class unequivocally facilitate the configuration of subcultural formation, but as we remarked earlier, actors must identify with the group ideals and artifacts in order to merge with them. Shared behavior and shared structural position make subculture probable by proxy, but without shared cognitions these factors are insufficient for group formation. Relating to this point, Miller is also faulted by Cloward and Ohlin for making no claims regarding the existence of a distinctively middle-class subculture—despite the fact that middle-class persons are also responsible for a considerable proportion of crime. But to be fair, Miller focuses explicitly on the lower class due to their disproportionate involvement in criminal behavior. Perhaps if the middle class displayed a similar pattern of law violation he would have constructed a theory to explain their actions.

Cloward and Ohlin (1960) also object to the fact that Miller invokes cultural conflict as his theoretical platform. A criminological explanation anchored in the concept of between-person value dissimilarity assumes that actors are "unacculturated" to the predominant values of American culture. They find this idea unconvincing given that the success goals of modern society appear so pervasive across social groupings. To Cloward and Ohlin, Miller's (1958) model is equipped to explain the transmission of subcultural norms; however, they insist the culture conflict approach is particularly lacking at identifying the origin of normative discrepancies (Cloward & Ohlin, 1960; Kornhauser, 1978).

### Empirical research: Cohen and Miller

Empirical evidence is somewhat ambiguous with respect to the validity of the propositions put forth by Miller and Cohen. Short and Strodtbeck's (1965) multimethod study shows that middle- and lower-class nongang and gang members positively value conventional standards. However, they also discover that with a decline in one's social class level the salience of *proscriptive* norms grows increasingly untenable among the study sample. Lower-class participants' behavior is also less consistent with their values, suggesting that the degree to which they actually conformed to middle-class standards is weaker than among their higher-status counterparts. Furthermore, Short and Strodtbeck found that while there is consensus between groups on values, the middle-class respondents are more adamantly opposed to negotiating comprises with their own standards. In support of Miller's argument their analysis indicates that lower-class boys place greater value on displaying a tough-guy reputation and being skilled at fighting. Miller generated his theory based on observations of behavior, but Short and Strodtbeck capture values as measured by semantic differentials. Any inconsistencies in the results of the two projects are perhaps attributable to their different methodological approaches, a fact that Short and Strodtbeck admit.

Likewise, Hirschi's (1969) analysis of data from the Richmond Youth Project provided little evidence in support of subcultural theory, in particular Miller's model (see Brownfield, 1996). His analysis shows that social status was unrelated to statements regarding the legitimacy of the law and notions of smartness. Also, family status had no effect on respondents' valuation of autonomy. Consistent with Miller's theory, however, Hirschi's results indicate that lower-class persons are more apt to hold fatalistic views. Also, Kornhauser (1978) relies on a diverse body of empirical evidence to question the validity of cultural-based approaches. To her "the subculture of the lower class, as portrayed by Walter Miller, exists only in his imagination" (p. 208).

More recent empirical evidence offers a greater degree of support for the subcultural propositions articulated by Miller and Cohen. Both theorists' models, when stated in causal language, assume that oppositional values are endogenous to structural positions and the distribution of these values vary closely with patterns of violent behaviors. Heimer (1997) examines if such a theoretical configuration explains violent actions among respondents in the National Youth Survey. She hypothesizes that youth reared in lower-class homes are inculcated with definitions favoring violence as a result of differential parenting practices. As expected, her findings indicate that "lower SES youths are more likely . . . to engage in violent delinquency because they have learned definitions favorable to violence through interactions with parents and peers" (p. 820). Heimer's strategy does not conform exactly to the expectations of Cohen's and Miller's propositions. Yet, her findings are consistent with the authors' general logic. Markowitz and Felson (1998) modified the structure-culture-behavior formulation of subcultural models (e.g., Miller and Cohen) as an "attitude mediation hypothesis." Similar to Heimer, they speculated that attitudes in favor of violence account for the link between SES and violent behavior. Results of their study showed that "the lower the status of persons, the more likely they were to emphasize courage and retribution" (Markowitz & Felson, 1998, p. 132); moreover nonconventional attitudes mediated the pathway between actors' class position and violence. An investigation conducted by Cao, Adams, and Jensen (1997) also unearthed findings suggesting a negative relationship between SES and violent attitudes.

### Marvin Wolfgang and Franco Ferracuti

Social structural and cultural processes make up the foundation of Miller's and Cohen's models; in contrast, culture is seemingly the sole strand binding together Wolfgang and Ferracuti's (1967) subcultural theory of violence. It was constructed to explain patterns of violence; a primary source of information was Marvin Wolfgang's

(1958) comprehensive study of homicides in Philadelphia. He discovered (1) incidents of homicide were often preceded by relatively innocuous verbal and physical disagreements between the parties involved, and (2) "high rates" of murder among African Americans reflected a pattern widely disproportionate to the white population. Wolfgang (1958) proposed that the exceptional levels of violence could be "symptoms of unconscious, destructive impulses laid bare in a subculture where toleration—if not encouragement—of violence is part of the normative structure" (p. 329). Merging this idea with the empirical reality of the data, he further argued that "a subculture of violence exists among a certain portion of the lower socioeconomic group—especially comprised of males and Negroes" (p. 330). Wolfgang set the foundation for an integrated criminological theory invoking culture to explain the distribution of violent behavior within the population. Most notably, it bridged racially differentiated patterns of violence with oppositional value orientations, construing social structural factors with a relatively minimal degree of explanatory power.

Wolfgang and Ferracuti (1967) develop their ideas fully in their book the *Subculture of Violence*. The authors stress that a subculture cannot fully differ from the "parent culture." Societies in their view tend to have a common value pattern to the extent that even subcultures remain within the wider "cultural system" (pp. 99–100). Most importantly, Wolfgang and Ferracuti suggest that their theory, like Miller's, is a theory of culture conflict. They state that some of the "values of a subculture . . . may . . . be in conflict" (p. 100) with the larger culture. Schaefer (1968) reaffirms this interpretation in his discussion of Sellin's research. He remarks that the criminal in Wolfgang and Ferracuti's formulation is "in a culture conflict." Schaefer argues that in their model the "normative structure" of subcultures conflicted with the predominant cultural dictates driving such behavior.

Sellin (1938) proposed years earlier that actors abide by rules "based on the attitudes of groups" regarding appropriate behavior in certain situations. He termed this system of expectations "conduct norms" (see Cressey, 1968, pp. 43–46). Wolfgang and Ferracuti (1967) applied this line of thought to their framework arguing that social groups modulate conduct norms. For conduct norms or values to be salient they must be situationally invariant. If not—according to Wolfgang and Ferracuti—they reflect no "enduring allegiance" (p. 105). Moreover, normative systems develop around values in that values engender the "normative standards" relating to proper behavioral "responses." Wolfgang and Ferracuti, however, allow for values to affect behavior independent of propinquity to like-minded others. On this point the authors deviate theoretically from Cohen and Miller in stating that their subculture is not "restricted by spatial proximity" (p. 115).

After sorting through the litany of theories of aggression, Wolfgang and Ferracuti (1967) assert that "constructs of social learning are the most directly related to subculture theory" (p. 150). They suggest that persons acquire the precepts of the subculture through processes of "differential learning." Similar to Miller (1958), Wolfgang and Ferracuti (1967) infer values from behavior. They claim that the extent to which persons identified with subcultural values is made obvious to the observer in light of their actions. Their theory focuses largely on understanding the cultural foundation underlying "passionate," or nonpremeditated acts of homicide. To the perpetrators who commit this category of crimes they impute the subculture of violence. Persons occupy a subculture of violence by virtue of the fact that they are violent. They concede that this approach is tautological.

In fact, Wolfgang and Ferracuti seem to brush aside the utility of the anomie concept as an explanatory mechanism (e.g., advocated by Cohen, Cloward & Ohlin, and Merton), arguing instead that homicide occurs among homogeneous groups that develop a self-contained normative repertoire. Wolfgang and Ferracuti (1967) insist that among groups who display the highest rates of homicide "we should find in the most intense degree a subculture of violence" (p. 153). An actor's integration into the subculture (measured by behavior) reflects his or her degree of adherence to its "prescriptions" for behavior. Violence does not represent the constant mode of action among subcultural members. Wolfgang and Ferracuti argue that if this were the case the social system itself would become debilitated. In this regard, their perspective is relatively limited in scope since it illuminates only the value set translating situations into violence, rather than the entire array of values held by a class position (e.g., Miller).

With regard to the etiology of subcultural traditions, Wolfgang and Ferracuti (1967) intentionally remain silent. They suggest that structural factors may contribute to the genesis of subcultures through the process hypothesized by Cohen, and Cloward and Ohlin. However, they concede that subcultural norms favoring violence are perhaps causally related with socioeconomic factors. For instance, Wolfgang and Ferracuti (1967, pp. 263–264) indicate that the concentration of a subcultural orientation among African Americans, as reflected by their involvement in "homicide and assaultive crimes," *may* be a product of the "urban deterioration" and economic disparities affecting this population (p. 298). But they make no consistent and precise statement about the linkage between social structural factors and the subcultural traditional they delineate. Interestingly, however, Wolfgang and Ferracuti appear to contend that it is structural factors like poverty and deprivation that account for the generational *transmission* of the subculture. Persons beleaguered by impoverished conditions become "frustrated" and "aggressive." Parents pass on this experience to their children where it blossoms fully into a subculture of violence (see Heimer, 1997). To prevent the continual cycling of the subcultural tradition, Wolfgang and Ferracuti (1967) suggest that the persons who carry it should be forcefully dispersed and resocialized into the middle-class system (p. 307). For some analysts this programmatic implication of their theory makes it less palatable on the whole.

### Elijah Anderson

To reiterate, perhaps what most distinguishes Wolfgang and Ferracuti (1967) from their cohort is the fact that they relied heavily upon a cultural interpretation. They did not link this subcultural condition with the structural factors affecting those to whom they assigned the cultural inventory—African Americans. Early studies in the social sciences did in fact note the high rate of crime among African Americans, leading some scholars at the time to attribute this behavior to structural arrangements and other factors—"pauperism," "alcohol," and the acrimonious nature of race relations in society (see DuBois, 1899/1996, pp. 261–286; see also Clark, 1965; Moynihan, 1969; Rainwater, 1970). Wolfgang and Ferracuti (1967) made some reference to but largely circumnavigated the political and social structural dimensions of this work, and instead emphasize the existence of a counterproductive culture among those demonstrating extensive involvement in violence—namely African Americans as well as lower-class persons. Elijah Anderson's research expands on this tradition. Like Wolfgang and Ferracuti (1967), he focuses on the symbolic or normative aspects of violent actions among urban blacks. Anderson's approach, however, goes beyond this and examines the social structural, historical and political backdrop against which these values subsist.

The substance of Anderson's article "The Code of the Streets"—printed in the *Atlantic Monthly* (1994)—is expanded on in his subsequent book titled *Code of the Street: Decency, Violence, and the Moral Life of the Inner City* (Anderson, 1999). It is open for debate as to whether this body of work represents a theory of violence per se. By most standards it does not (see Blalock, 1969; Gibbs, 1985). The book conveys a rich description of the symbolic and behavioral patterns characterizing social life in urban areas. Evidence is presented in noncausal language. Analysts have deduced ideas from these observations and translate them into testable theorems. Anderson's study of the cultural origins of violence is perhaps better referred to as a scientific perspective, an ethnographic study affording important conceptual insight into the complex reality of urban life.

Anderson's work is similar to early ethnographic studies conducted by Liebow (1967) and Hannerz (1969), which also concentrated on the African American experience in urban places. Both works described the microcontext encapsulating the social life of urban blacks facing structural barriers. Hannerz (1969), for instance, suggests that black "street corner men" become affixed to a "ghetto-specific culture" primarily because it prescribes alternative means to demonstrate masculinity in their local environment.

Violent crime rates climbed in America's cities throughout the 1970s and 1980s. By the early 1990s rates of homicide involving black youth peaked to an unprecedented level. William Julius Wilson's (1987) research was crucial to understanding this phenomenon because it systematically unraveled the sheer magnitude of the structural component behind urban violence. His work reveals that urban communities are distinguished by a dispropor-tionate concentration "of the most disadvantaged segments of the black population—poor, black, female headed families with children" (quoted from Sampson & Lauritsen, 1994, p. 69). Wilson indicates that the coexistence of structural deprivations undermines the formation of dense person–institution networks, consequently the urban poor are socially isolated from mainstream roles (Wilson, 1987). Wilson proposes that alternative behav-ior protocols emerge that are similar in nature to the nonconventional cultural patterns described by Liebow (1967) and Rainwater (1970). These *socially structured cultural pro-cesses* are less apt to assign negative sanctions to deviant behaviors, and consequently the probability of violent actions is magnified (see also Sampson & Wilson, 1995).

It was in this intellectual context in which Anderson (1994, 1999) researched the cul-tural mechanisms driving violence in contemporary urban America. His perspective is not unlike Wilson's, as well as Massey and Denton's (1993) with regard to how structural organization affects the values toward behavioral protocols. And it shares themes found in earlier ethnographies demonstrating the diversity of conduct norms among residents of urban centers (Horowitz & Schwartz, 1974). But Anderson differs primarily from Wilson in that the cultural substrate he defines purportedly sanctions the use of violence, whereas Wilson's conceptualization holds that violent behavior is less condoned or tolerated. More critically, Anderson suggests that for black males (and females) in disadvantaged urban areas, their very identity is constructed early in life according to the standards of the oppo-sitional culture (see especially Anderson, 1999; Sampson & Bean, 2006).

Anderson (1994, 1999) proposes that the social "alienation" brought about by eco-nomic transformation has spawned an oppositional "street culture" or "street code" in inner-city settings. It supplies the "rules" regarding the proper to way to defend oneself; at the same time it assigns the normative rational for those seeking to provoke aggressive actions. The code serves as a shared relational script that both victims and offenders must abide by if they are to successfully navigate their precarious social world. Miller's (1958) and Anderson's ideas are similar in this respect, as both authors argue that the nonconventional culture they observed is useful in the ecological context in which it exists.

The content of the code is comprised foremost of the rules to achieve honor, Similar to Miller (1958), Anderson posits that deference is a valuable commodity in the subculture. Someone who is respected is better equipped to avoid potential threats of violence plus the unwanted situation of being "bothered" by others. But perhaps more importantly, respect is an end in itself that affords the luxury of self-worth. By displaying a confident demeanor and wearing the appropriate attire actors communicate a "predisposition" to violence. The street code requires actors to express their willingness to engage in physical aggression if the situation demands it. When an attack occurs, the code dictates that it should be met with a retaliatory response of like proportion. Otherwise, respect is undermined and the victim invites future attacks. With regard to victimization, how persons respond illuminates the broad cultural disparities between the conventional and the oppositional system. In the case of the former, persons who are victimized will either contact formal authorities, or move on without rectifying the situation despite the degradation they experienced. In contrast, persons whose existence is dominated by the imperatives of the street code actively pursue a strategy for revenge. The former group's status does not hinge on whether or not they avenge their aggressor; rather, rank is determined by their merit in conventional avenues. Wolfgang and Ferracuti (1967) constructed a similar argument with respect to the impact of oppositional values on the response to victimization.

Anderson notes that not everyone accepts the oppositional culture as a legitimate value system. Much like Horowitz and Schwartz (1974), the urban landscape he observes is occupied by two coexisting groups of people: those who hold a "decent" orientation, and those whose lives conform more closely to standards of the code—a group he refers to as "street." Decent people socialize their children according to mainstream values. They believe that success is earned, in part, by working hard and maintaining a law-abiding lifestyle. Anderson (1994) also notes that parents in decent families rely on strict methods of discipline in order to socialize their children according to mainstream values. Cognizant of the hazardous social environment they occupy, decent parents establish curfews and keep a watchful eye on their children's activities.

As opposed to decent families, street families are more devoted to the oppositional orientation embodied in the code. Both their interpretations of their reality as well as their interpersonal behaviors rigidly conform to its precepts. Their orientation approximates that held by youths in the subculture envisioned by Cohen (1955). The cluster of values street folks abide by are antithetical to the precepts of middle-class, conventional existence. Street families place less emphasis on work and education, which is underpinned by their deep distrust in the formal structure as a whole (Anderson, 1994). Most are financially disadvantaged; whatever income they earn is "misused," spent on other priorities like cigarettes and alcohol. Children of street families witness numerous incidents suggesting that violent aggression versus verbal negotiation is a means to achieve a desired end. For youths reared in a street family, their unfavorable early life experiences and the inept, aggressive socialization they receive culminate to shape their strong proclivity toward an orientation consistent with the street code (Anderson, 1994).

According to Anderson's portrayal, the cultural standards that decent and street families adhere to are diametric opposites. Since both groups are immersed in the same contextual environment, their orientations are prone to clash—although the aggressive posture of the street orientation generally prevails. Because of this circumstance, Anderson argues that decent folks have an incentive to become intimately familiar with the behavioral imperatives of the code; moreover they must be prepared to momentarily perform them. The code represents an ecologically situated property directing individuals' behavioral responses, independent of their own culturally defined inclinations. Matseuda, Drakulich, et al. (2006) stress that Anderson's depiction of the code as a spatially bounded "objective property" is perhaps his most "novel observation" (p. 340).

### Empirical research: Wolfgang and Ferracuti, Anderson

A body of findings generated from survey data are inconsistent with Wolfgang and Ferracuti's postulates, suggesting no evidence of between-group differences with regard to support for the dictates of an oppositional subculture (Austin, 1980; Ball-Rokeach, 1973; Poland, 1978). One author remarks that "the subculture of violence, is at best, incomplete and at worst invalid as an explanation of violent behavior" (Ball-Rokeach, 1973, p. 748). Some scholars explicitly examine Wolfgang and Ferracuti's proposition suggesting blacks are more apt to adhere to subcultural values. Erlanger (1974) examined value disparities by race and income using survey data. His results failed to support Wolfgang and Ferracuti's hypothesis suggesting racial differences. More recent results coincide with these findings. For instance, based on analyses of the General Social Survey (GSS) Cao et al. (1997) conclude that "blacks in the general U.S. population are no more likely than whites to embrace values favorable to violence" (p. 376; see also Heimer, 1997). Multilevel research shows that blacks hold more negative views toward the agents of government authority (e.g., police, courts), but after incorporating neighborhood measures the relationship diminishes, suggesting that blacks' attitudes are strongly influenced by their contextual circumstances (Sampson & Bartusch, 1998).

Quantitative studies also examine the purported association between people's adherence to the oppositional subculture and unlawful behavior. The combined result of this work is somewhat ambiguous. Some investigators have explicitly examined the linkage between race, oppositional values, and patterns of violence implied in subcultural theory. For instance, Harer and Steffensmeier (1996) surmise from Wolfgang and Ferracuti's logic that if blacks are more invested in the subculture of violence, then they should display higher rates of violent offending irrespective of their contextual surroundings. Applying this idea to prison data, they find that blacks are in fact more likely to commit violent prison infractions in comparison to their white counterparts. Macrolevel research uses census data to investigate the validity of the subculture of violence thesis as it relates to violence across population segments. Using this method, Messner (1983) uncovers a positive effect of racial composition on violence, net of economic factors, which lends some evidence to Wolfgang and Ferracuti's thesis.

Data derived from survey questionnaires are also employed by researchers to test subcultural ideas, enabling more precise estimation of the attitude–behavior relationship. Felson, Liska, McNulty, and South (1994) find that youths' delinquent behavior is affected by the strength of school-level values in favor of violence, apart from their own value orientation. Anderson's ideas are consistent with Felson et al.'s findings. To recapitulate his depiction stipulates that oppositional values act as blanket imperatives shaping the distribution of public behaviors, regardless of persons' own orientations.

More recent research generates a construct approximating the attitudinal components of the street code. Findings from this work show that youths who reside in disadvantaged neighborhoods and who feel discriminated against are likely to adopt the street code (Stewart & Simons, 2006). Results also show that the street code predicts violent delinquency. Similar studies report that the street code has a positive effect on individuals' odds of victimization (Stewart, Schreck, & Simons, 2006); furthermore, neighborhood disadvantage exacerbates this relationship (Stewart et al., 2006). Related to this work, Sampson, Morenoff, and Raudenbush (2005) find that a latent construct capturing moral and legal cynicism within neighborhoods predicts youth violence net of social structural conditions. Research has also shown that structural correlates (or proxies) of the street code affect the nature of violence and victimization within neighborhoods. For instance, respondents are less likely to fight back against aggressors in structurally disadvantaged locations (Baumer, Horney, Felson, & Lauritsen, 2003). Again, these results tend to support Anderson's work. Kubrin and Weitzer (2003b) apply regression techniques to St. Louis police homicide reports. They show that retaliatory homicides—those reflecting subcultural imperatives regarding honor—are more likely to occur in disadvantaged neighborhoods. This finding closely coincides with the subcultural theory in general. Also, it supports Anderson's view that oppositional culture thrives in places lacking social structural resources, where honor is an indispensable ideal.

Much qualitative research also uncovers evidence in support of Anderson's claims regarding the nature of individuals' identification with the subcultural system. For instance, in research interviews active offenders express their obligations to dictates requiring retributive actions against aggressors. Many provide examples of serious violence they have committed consistent with these values (Jacobs & Wright, 2006; Wilkinson, 2003). Echoing Anderson's observations, a prominent finding throughout the qualitative literature is offenders' desire for respect and status in their local context (see also Kubrin & Weitzer, 2003b). People report pursuing this joint ideal by way of showing "nerve"—a willingness to engage in aggressive actions, and through the acquisition of material items representative of economic success (Wilkinson, 2003).

The link between individuals' lack of faith in the justice system and adherence to the street code is also clearly illuminated in qualitative studies (see Anderson, 1999). For instance, offenders indicate that they rely on informal means of dispute resolution such as lethal attacks, due to their strong disdain for the formal law (Jacobs & Wright, 2006). Reinforcing this theme, informants in similar studies report that the cultural imperative opposing the criminal justice system is so salient within their neighborhoods that those who cooperate with the police risk their own lives (Rosenfeld, Jacobs, & Wright, 2003).

To summarize, empirical research gives very little support to the notion that, as a whole, blacks are more involved in violence because they are more strongly wedded to values promoting such behavior. This finding does not confirm with a core proposition stated in Wolfgang and Ferracuti's theory. However, consistent with Anderson's perspective, estimates tend to suggest that in disadvantaged urban areas, (1) behavior is shaped by an oppositional cultural orientation that assigns less credibility to conventional modes of conduct, and (2) such value systems are influenced by contextual factors. With respect to the question of whether values favoring violence predict violent behavior, a significant body of evidence indicates that oppositional values in fact vary closely with involvement in violence. Results also show that values measured in the aggregate affect individuals' behavior, independent of their own commitment to these values; Anderson's observations regarding decent and street orientations seem to anticipate this finding.

The weight of the empirical evidence fails to disconfirm the idea that nonconventional culture plays a powerful role in stimulating violent behavior. Again, what appears untenable is the notion that black violence is driven by an inherent subculture (e.g., Wolfgang & Ferracuti, 1967). Despite this, research focused on the high rates of violence among the black population has not abandoned cultural explanations entirely. A prominent example is a model developed by Sampson and Wilson (1995). They provide a theory of the social ecology of violence emphasizing both social structural and cultural mechanisms. A point of departure for their reasoning is the inability of Wolfgang and Ferracuti's subcultural theory to logically account for the uneven distribution of black violence. If Wolfgang and Ferracuti are correct in their insistence that blacks adhere to a culture of violence, then according to Sampson and Wilson rates of black violent crime should be equal across place. This is not the case. Blacks are differentially involved in violence across America's cities. But this does not render cultural explanations entirely flawed. Expanding on Shaw and McKay's (1942) insight, Sampson and Wilson propose that black violence is the outcome of social disorganization as well as cultural social isolation. Both ecological processes arise due to "the concentration of poverty, family disruption, and residential instability." Social disorganization erodes informal regulation, while cultural social isolation "[shapes] cognitive landscapes or ecologically structured norms, regarding appropriate standards . . . of conduct" (p. 72). In turn, these mechanisms are hypothesized to jointly impact rates of violence. Sampson and Wilson's (1995) logic assumes that since black communities disproportionately experience structural disadvantage they also disproportionately experience the processes that fuel violent crime. Under the same social structural conditions blacks and whites should exhibit similar rates of involvement in violent offending.

## The Current State of Subcultural Theory

Perhaps the most widely read, and most blistering critique of subculture theory, was leveled by Kornhauser (1978) in her monograph titled the *Social Sources of Delinquency*. She questions the very possibility of a coherent deviant subculture, and accuses Sutherland and his contemporaries for assuming a theoretical position of "boundless cultural relativism" (p. 13). The society envisioned by Sutherland, she argues, is one "without a center" (p. 192). She charges Cohen with holding "biases against control theory" (p. 154) while also criticizing him for blindly pursuing subcultural to the point that he "obviates the possibility of strain" (p. 153). As noted earlier, her ruminations about Miller's (1958) theory are equally uncomplimentary. As for Wolfgang and Ferracuti, Kornhauser concludes that they are "restricted to the empty search for a subculture to account for the roots of violence" (p. 188). More broadly, Kornhauser challenges the possibility of deviant subcultures. She argues that the proliferation of oppositional values among groups, particularly those sanctioning destructive behavior, would cause a society to more or less collapse. Based on her reasoning, exchange-based economies are particularly susceptible to violence because it threatens the ability of important information and resources to flow throughout networks.

The intensity of Kornhauser's (1978) antipathy toward subcultural models is matched by her degree of affinity for structural approaches. In her quest to resurrect the social structure, she reexamines the structural aspects of Thrasher's (1927) exposé on gangs, and scrutinizes Shaw and McKay's (1942) formulation of social disorganization, eventually reinterpreting the latter as a consensus-based model. To build her case, she produces additional evidence suggesting that "subculture lacks complete definition and manifests considerable inauthenticity" (p. 134). Her position is heavily informed by Suttles's (1968) and Liebow's (1967) descriptions of the "provincial" nature of cultural adaptations in poor communities, and by Matza's (1964) assessment of subcultural influences restating them as normative drift.

Kornhauser (1978) concludes that what other theorists conceived as subcultures are actually collective representations of weakened commitment to conventional culture, a condition produced by social structural patterns, namely social disorganization (Warner, 2003). Her interpretation indicates that were it not for social disorganization, nonconventional protocols would not exist within communities, nor would acts of law violation.

Subsequent research in criminology and sociology examined sources of violence mainly through the analytical lens of the social structure. For instance, many of the most prominent theoretical works published in the latter 1980s and early 1990s relied on social consensus as their substantive principle (e.g., Sampson & Laub, 1993). Empirical research followed suit (see Sampson, 1987a; see also Wilson, 1987). Bursik and Grasmick's (1993a) widely cited systemic model drew much of its content from Kornhauser's interpretation of Shaw and McKay's work. Rather than settle with a subcultural component in their theory, Bursik and Grasmick accounted for the crime-generating effects of nonconventional processes via the absence of public formal social controls—a social structural property (Bursik & Grasmick, 1993b; Rosenfeld, 1994). To be clear, this is not to say that investigations into culture were entirely lacking in criminology during this time period (e.g., Bernard, 1990; Luckenbill & Doyle, 1989). But control-based studies of crime causation certainly dominated scientific discourse.

The trend has since shown signs of a reversal. Once again the potential causal role of culture has been granted important consideration in theoretical explanations of crime. Kornhauser's (1978) assessment remains influential, but her argument regarding the uniformity of cultural precepts is also the object of criticism (Matsueda, 1988; Messner & Rosenfeld, 1997b). Ethnographic findings generated in the last 15 or so years provide a wealth of findings challenging her purist structural assumptions. Similar research conducted in other social science disciples serves to reaffirm these critiques (Baumer & South, 2001; Small & Newman, 2001). Additionally, informal social organization has proved meaningful with respect to explaining community effects on patterns of crime, but residual variation in outcome measures suggests that another social process is operating to affect behaviors (Fischer, 1995; Sampson & Bean, 2006; Warner & Rountree, 1997). All of this has forced scholars to reevaluate the conceptualization of nonconventional culture, its relationship to the reality of structural circumstances in urban America, and the precise nature of the link between normative cultural standards and the procurement of violent actions.

Within criminology, culture is now regularly treated as an adaptation to the social structure, and behavior is considered endogenous to both factors. But this explanation is problematic because "individual actions are part of creating violent neighborhoods" (Sampson & Bean, 2006, p. 29). Early subcultural models (e.g., Sutherland) were in fact criticized for assuming a deterministic order since they implied that the causal chain flows one way, from value systems to action (Pfhol, 1985). A culture-as-adaptation perspective fails to recognize the independent casual force of cultural symbols. In response to this limitation researchers have moved away from a subcultural strategy (i.e., values and ends) and focused on how culture is responded to, mobilized, and re-created through individual choice situated within spatial milieus.

Sampson and Bean (2006) stress that a "culture in action" conceptualization of cultural processes is useful since it posits a nonrecursive sequence between action and the value complex. According to this view culture is "simultaneously an emergent product and producer of social organization" (p. 29). More critically, this perspective endows actors with considerable agency in navigating their social milieu. Swidler's (1986) popular conceptualization is a prominent example of this approach. She describes culture metaphorically as a set of disposable symbolic devices or a "tool kit." Actors are said to construct "strategies of action" from this symbolic resource enabling them to navigate the terrain of their social landscape. According to Swidler, actions cannot be accomplished without the proper "cultural equipment" (p. 275) and conversely, certain actions are more probable if these symbolic means are available. Individual variation in the composition of tool kits represents diversity of culture, and hence diversity in behavior is equally possible. The gap between conventional ideals and actual behavior is produced by the absence of symbolic devices. Applied this way, violence is practical to implement as a means if one's tool kit contains the requisite resources, and violent events may be difficult to avoid if repertories are unavailable that direct one's strategy to do so. Empirical research is needed to validate the utility of this conceptualization to explain the cultural sources of violent behavior.

# PART VI

# DIFFERENTIAL ASSOCIATION, SOCIAL LEARNING, AND NEUTRALIZATION THEORIES

# DIFFERENTIAL ASSOCIATION

*Edwin H. Sutherland and Donald Cressey*

Scientific explanations of criminal behavior may be stated either in terms of the processes which are operating at the moment of the occurrence of crime or in terms of the processes operating in the earlier history of the criminal. In the first case, the explanation may be called "mechanistic," "situational," or "dynamic"; in the second, "historical" or "genetic." Both types of explanation are desirable. The mechanistic type of explanation has been favored by physical and biological scientists, and it probably could be the more efficient type of explanation of criminal behavior. However, criminological explanations of the mechanistic type have thus far been notably unsuccessful, perhaps largely because they have been formulated in connection with the attempt to isolate personal and social pathologies among criminals. Work from this point of view has, at least, resulted in the conclusion that the immediate determinants of criminal behavior lie in the person-situation complex.

The objective situation is important to criminality largely to the extent that it provides an opportunity for a criminal act. A thief may steal from a fruit stand when the owner is not in sight but refrain when the owner is in sight; a bank burglar may attack a bank which is poorly protected but refrain from attacking a bank protected by watchmen and burglar alarms. A corporation which manufacturers automobiles seldom violates the pure food and drug laws, but a meat-packing corporation might violate these laws with great frequency. But in another sense, a psychological or sociological sense, the situation is not exclusive of the person, for the situation which is important is the situation as defined by the person who is involved. That is, some persons define a situation in which a fruit-stand owner is out of sight as a "crime-committing" situation, while others do not so define it. Furthermore, the events in the person-situation complex at the time a crime occurs cannot be separated from the prior life experiences of the criminal. This means that the situation is defined by the person in terms of the inclinations and abilities which he has acquired. For example, while a person could define a situation in such a manner that criminal behavior would be the inevitable result, his past experiences would, for the most part, determine the way in which he defined the situation. An explanation of criminal behavior made in terms of these past experiences is an historical or genetic explanation.

The following paragraphs state such a genetic theory of criminal behavior on the assumption that a criminal act occurs when a situation appropriate for it, as defined by the person, is present. The theory should be regarded as tentative, and it should be tested by the factual information presented in the later chapters and by all other factual information and theories which are applicable.

The following statements refer to the process by which a particular person comes to engage in criminal behavior.

1. *Criminal behavior is learned.* Negatively, this means that criminal behavior is not inherited, as such; also, the person who is not already trained in crime does not invent

criminal behavior, just as a person does not make mechanical inventions unless he has had training in mechanics.

2. *Criminal behavior is learned in interaction with other persons in a process of communication.* This communication is verbal in many respects but includes also "the communication of gestures."

3. *The principal part of the learning of criminal behavior occurs within intimate personal groups.* Negatively, this means that the impersonal agencies of communication, such as movies and newspapers, play a relatively unimportant part in the genesis of criminal behavior.

4. *When criminal behavior is learned, the learning includes* (a) *techniques of committing the crime, which are sometimes very complicated, sometimes very simple;* (b) *the specific direction of motives, drives, rationalizations, and attitudes.*

5. *The specific direction of motives and drives is learned from definitions of the legal codes as favorable or unfavorable.* In some societies an individual is surrounded by persons who invariably define the legal codes as rules to be observed, while in others he is surrounded by persons whose definitions are favorable to the violation of the legal codes. In our American society these definitions are almost always mixed, with the consequence that we have culture conflict in relation to the legal codes.

6. *A person becomes delinquent because of an excess of definitions favorable to violation of law over definitions unfavorable to violation of law.* This is the principle of differential association. It refers to both criminal and anticriminal associations and has to do with counteracting forces. When persons become criminal, they do so because of contacts with criminal patterns and also because of isolation from anticriminal patterns. Any person inevitably assimilates the surrounding culture unless other patterns are in conflict; a southerner does not pronounce *r* because other southerners do not pronounce *r*. Negatively, this proposition of differential association means that associations which are neutral so far as crime is concerned have little or no effect on the genesis of criminal behavior. Much of the experience of a person is neutral in this sense, e.g., learning to brush one's teeth. This behavior has no negative or positive effect on criminal behavior except as it may be related to associations which are concerned with the legal codes. This neutral behavior is important especially as an occupier of the time of a child so that he is not in contact with criminal behavior during the time he is so engaged in the neutral behavior.

7. *Differential associations may vary in frequency, duration, priority, and intensity.* This means that associations with criminal behavior and also associations with anticriminal behavior vary in those respects. "Frequency" and "duration" as modalities of associations are obvious and need no explanation. "Priority" is assumed to be important in the sense that lawful behavior developed in early childhood may persist throughout life, and also that delinquent behavior developed in early childhood may persist throughout life. This tendency, however, has not been adequately demonstrated, and priority seems to be important principally through its selective influence. "Intensity" is not precisely defined, but it has to do with such things as the prestige of the source of a criminal or anticriminal pattern and with emotional reactions related to the associations. In a precise description of the criminal behavior of a person, these modalities would be rated in quantitative form and a mathematical ratio be reached. A formula in this sense has not been developed, and the development of such a formula would be extremely difficult.

8. *The process of learning criminal behavior by association with criminal and anticriminal patterns involves all of the mechanisms that are involved in any other learning.* Negatively, this means that the learning of criminal behavior is not restricted to the process of imitation. A person who is seduced, for instance, learns criminal behavior by association, but this process would not ordinarily be described as imitation.

9. *While criminal behavior is an expression of general needs and values, it is not explained by those general needs and values, since noncriminal behavior is an expression of the same needs and values.* Thieves generally steal in order to secure money, but likewise honest laborers work in order to secure money. The attempts by many scholars to explain criminal behavior by general drives and values, such as the happiness principle, striving for social status, the money motive, or frustration, have been, and must continue to be, futile, since they explain lawful behavior as completely as they explain criminal behavior. They are similar to respiration, which is necessary for any behavior, but which does not differentiate criminal from noncriminal behavior.

It is not necessary, at this level of explanation, to explain why a person has the associations he has; this certainly involves a complex of many things. In an area where the delinquency rate is high, a boy who is sociable, gregarious, active, and athletic is very likely to come in contact with the other boys in the neighborhood, learn delinquent behavior patterns from them, and become a criminal; in the same neighborhood the psychopathic boy who is isolated, introverted, and inert may remain at home, not become acquainted with the other boys in the neighborhood, and not become delinquent. In another situation, the sociable, athletic, aggressive boy may become a member of a scout troop and not become involved in delinquent behavior. The person's associations are determined in a general context of social organization. A child is ordinarily reared in a family; the place of residence of the family is determined largely by family income; and the delinquency rate is in many respects related to the rental value of the houses. Many other aspects of social organization affect the kinds of associations a person has.

The preceding explanation of criminal behavior purports to explain the criminal and noncriminal behavior of individual persons. As indicated earlier, it is possible to state sociological theories of criminal behavior which explain the criminality of a community, nation, or other group. The problem, when thus stated, is to account for variations in crime rates and involves a comparison of the crime rates of various groups or the crime rates of a particular group at different times. The explanation of a crime rate must be consistent with the explanation of the criminal behavior of the person, since the crime rate is a summary statement of the number of persons in the group who commit crimes and the frequency with which they commit crimes. One of the best explanations of crime rates from this point of view is that a high crime rate is due to social disorganization. The term *social disorganization* is not entirely satisfactory, and it seems preferable to substitute for it the term *differential social organization*. The postulate on which this theory is based, regardless of the name, is that crime is rooted in the social organization and is an expression of that social organization. A group may be organized for criminal behavior or organized against criminal behavior. Most communities are organized for both criminal and anticriminal behavior, and, in that sense the crime rate is an expression of the differential group organization. Differential group organization as an explanation of variations in crime rates is consistent with the differential association theory of the processes by which persons become criminals.

# A DIFFERENTIAL ASSOCIATION-REINFORCEMENT THEORY OF CRIMINAL BEHAVIOR

*Robert L. Burgess and Ronald L. Akers*

In spite of the body of literature that has accumulated around the differential association theory of criminal behavior, it has yet to receive crucial empirical test or thorough restatement beyond Sutherland's own revision in 1947. Recognizing that the theory is essentially a learning theory, Sutherland rephrased it to state explicitly that criminal behavior is learned as any behavior is learned. In Cressey's two revisions of the textbook, the theory has been deliberately left unchanged from Sutherland's revision. Thus, the theory as it stands now is postulated upon the knowledge of the learning process extant 20–25 years ago.

Sutherland, himself, never was able to test directly or find specific empirical support for his theory, but he was convinced that the two-edged theory—(1) genetic, differential association and (2) structural, differential social organization—accounted for the known data on the full range of crimes, including conventional violations and white-collar crimes. The theory has received some other empirical support, but negative cases have also been found. The attempts to subject the theory to empirical test are marked by inconsistent findings both within the same study and between studies, as well as by highly circumscribed and qualified findings and conclusions. Whether the particular researcher concludes that his findings do or do not seem to support the theory, nearly all have indicated difficulty in operationalizing the concepts and recommend that the theory be modified in such a way that it becomes more amenable to empirical testing.

Suggested theoretical modifications have not been lacking, but the difficulty with these restatements is that they are no more readily operationalized than Sutherland's. One recent paper, however, by DeFleur and Quinney, offers new promise that the theory can be adequately operationalized. They have presented a detailed strategy for making specific deductions for empirical testing. But while they have clarified the problems in the derivation and generation of testable hypotheses from differential association, they still see its empirical validation as a very difficult, though not impossible task.

Regardless of the particular criticisms, the exceptions taken, and the difficulties involved in testing and reformulating the theory that have been offered, few take exception to the central learning assumptions in differential association. If we accept the basic assumption that criminal behavior is learned by the same processes and involves the same mechanisms as conforming behavior, then we need to recognize and make use of the current knowledge about these processes and mechanisms. Neither the extant statement of the theory nor the reformulations of it make explicit the nature of the underlying learning process involved in differential association. In short, no major revisions have been made utilizing established learning principles.

That this type of revision of the theory is needed has been recognized and some criticism of differential association has revolved around the fact that it does not adequately portray the process by which criminal behavior is learned. But as Cressey explains:

> It is one thing to criticise the theory for failure to specify the learning process accurately and another to specify which aspects of the learning process should be included and in what way.

Sutherland, of course, was as interested in explaining the "epidemiology" of crime as in explaining how the individual comes to engage in behavior in violation of the law and insisted that the two explanations must be consistent. Differential social organization (normative conflict) has been successful in "making sense" of variations in crime rates. But differential association has been less successful in explicating the process by which this differential organization produces individual criminality. This seems to be due not to the lack of importance of associations for criminal behavior but:

> . . . rather to the fact that the theory out-ran the capacity of either psychology or social psychology to give adequate, scientific answers to the question of why there are such qualitative (selective) differences in human association.

It now appears, however, that there is a body of verified theory which is adequate to the task of accurately specifying this process. Modern learning theory seems capable of providing insights into the problem of uniting structural and genetic formulations. While sociologists know a great deal about the structure of the environment from which deviants come, we know very little about the determining variables operating within this environment. The burden of criminological theory today is to combine knowledge of structural pressures with explanations of "why only *some* of the persons on whom this pressure is exerted become non-conformists."

It is for this reason that the recent effort by C. R. Jeffery to re-examine differential association in light of modern learning theory marks a new departure in the abundance of thinking and writing that has characterized the intellectual history of this theory. In spite of their intricate axiomatization of the theory, DeFleur and Quinney, for example, recognize that even they have left the learning process in differential association unspecified. But, they note, "modern reinforcement learning theory would handle this problem. . . ." This is precisely what Jeffery proposed to do and to the extent that this objective is served by discussing learning theory and criminal behavior together, he is at least partially successful. However, Jeffery does not in fact make it clear just how Sutherland's differential association theory may be revised. His explanation incorporates differential reinforcement:

> . . . [A] criminal act occurs in an environment in which in the past the actor has been reinforced for behaving in this manner, and the aversive consequences attached to the behavior have been of such a nature that they do not control or prevent the response.

This statement, as it stands, bears no obvious or direct relation to Sutherland's differential association, and nowhere else does Jeffery make it clear how differential reinforcement is a reformulation of differential association. Jeffery does discuss modern learning principles, but he does not show how these principles may be incorporated within the framework of Sutherland's theory, nor how these principles may lead to explanations of past empirical findings.

Jeffery's theory and his discussion of criminal behavior and learning theory remains not so much incorrect as unconvincing. His presentation of learning principles is supported wholly by reference to experiments with lower organisms and his extension to criminal behavior is mainly through anecdotal and illustrative material. The potential value and impact of Jeffery's article is diminished by not calling attention to the already large and growing body of literature in experimental behavioral science, especially evidence using human subjects, that has direct implications for differential association theory. We are basically in agreement with Jeffery that learning theory has progressed to the point where it seems likely that differential association can be restated in a more sophisticated and testable form in the language of modern learning theory. But that restatement must be attempted in a thorough fashion before we can expect others to accept it. Jeffery begins to do this and his thoughts are significant, but they do not take into account the theory as a whole.

The amount of empirical research in the social psychology of learning clearly has shown that the concepts in learning theory are susceptible to operationalization. Therefore, applying an integrated set of learning principles to differential association theory should adequately provide the revision needed for empirical testing. These learning principles are based on literally thousands of experimental hours covering a wide range of the phylogenetic scale and more nearly constitute empirically derived *laws* of behavior than any other set of principles. They enable the handling of a great variety of observational as well as experimental evidence about human behavior.

It is the purpose of this paper to take the first step in the direction to which Jeffery points. A restatement of the theory, not an alternative theory, will be presented, although, of necessity, certain ideas not intrinsic to differential association will have to be introduced and additions will be made to the original propositions. It should be pointed out that DeFleur and Quinney have been able to demonstrate that Sutherland's propositions, when stated in the form of set theory, appear to be internally consistent. By arranging the propositions in axiomatic form, stating them in logical rather than verbal symbols, they have brought the theoretical grammar up to date. Such is not our intention in this paper, at all. We recognize and appreciate the importance of stating the propositions in a formal, deductive fashion. We do feel, however, that this task is, at the present time, subsidiary to the more urgent task of: (1) making explicit the learning process, as it is now understood by modern behavioral science, from which the propositions of differential association can be derived; (2) fully reformulating the theory, statement by statement, in light of the current knowledge of this learning process; and (3) helping criminologists become aware of the advances in learning theory and research that are directly relevant to an explanation of criminal behavior. No claim is made that this constitutes a final statement. If it has any seminal value at all, that is, if it provokes a serious new look at the theory and encourages further effort in this direction, our objective will have been served.

## Differential Association and Modern Behavior Theory

In this section the nine formal propositions in which Sutherland expressed his theory will be analyzed in terms of behavior theory and research and will be reformulated as seven new propositions. (See Table 1.)

I. "Criminal behavior is learned." VIII. "The process of learning criminal behavior by association with criminal and anti-criminal patterns involves all of the mechanisms that are involved in any other learning."

Since both the first and eighth sentences in the theory obviously form a unitary idea, it seems best to state them together. Sutherland was aware that these statements did not sufficiently describe the learning process but these two items leave no doubt that differential association theory was meant to fit into a general explanation of human behavior and, as much is unambiguously stated in the prefatory remarks of the theory: an "explanation of criminal behavior should be a specific part of a general theory of behavior." Modern behavior theory as a general theory provides us with a good idea of what the mechanisms are that are involved in the process of acquiring behavior.

According to this theory, there are two major categories of behavior. On the one hand, there is reflexive or *respondent* behavior which is behavior that is governed by the stimuli that elicit it. Such behaviors are largely associated with the autonomic system. The work of Pavlov is of special significance here. On the other hand, there is *operant* behavior: behavior which involves the central nervous system. Examples of operant behavior include verbal behavior, playing ball, driving a car, and buying a new suit. It has been found that this class of behavior is a function of its past and present environmental consequences. Thus, when a particular operant is followed by certain kinds of stimuli, that behavior's frequency of occurrence will increase in the future. These stimuli are called reinforcing stimuli or reinforcers and include food, money, clothes, objects of various sorts, social attention, approval, affection and social status. This entire process is called positive reinforcement. One distinguishing characteristic of operant behavior as opposed to respondent behavior, then, is that the latter is a function of its antecedent stimuli, whereas the former is a function of its antecedent environmental consequences.

Typically, operant and respondent behaviors occur together in an individual's everyday behavior, and they interact in extremely intricate ways. Consequently, to fully understand any set of patterned responses, the investigator should observe the effects of the operants on the respondents as well as the effects of the respondents on the operants. The connections between operant and respondent behaviors are especially crucial to an analysis of attitudes, emotional and conflict behaviors.

In everyday life, different consequences are usually contingent upon different classes of behavior. This relationship between behavior and its consequences functions to alter the rate and form of behavior as well as its relationship to many features of the environment. The process of operant reinforcement is the most important process by which behavior is generated and maintained. There are, in fact, six possible environmental consequences relative to the Law of Operant Behavior. (1) A behavior may produce certain stimulus events and thereby increase in frequency. As we have indicated above, such stimuli are called positive reinforcers and the process is called positive reinforcement. (2) A behavior may remove, avoid, or terminate certain stimulus events and thereby increase in frequency. Such stimuli are termed negative reinforcers and the process, negative reinforcement. (3) A behavior may produce certain stimulus events and thereby decrease in frequency. Such stimuli are called aversive stimuli or, more recently, punishers. The entire behavioral process is called positive punishment. (4) A behavior may remove or terminate certain stimulus events and thereby decrease in frequency. Such stimuli are positive reinforcers and the process is termed negative punishment. (5) A behavior may produce or remove certain stimulus events which do not change the behavior's frequency at all. Such stimuli are called neutral stimuli. (6) A behavior may no longer produce customary stimulus events and thereby decrease in frequency. The stimuli which are produced are neutral stimuli, and the process, extinction. When a reinforcing stimulus no longer functions to increase the future probability of the behavior which produced it, we say the individual is satiated. To restore the reinforcing property of the stimulus we need only deprive the individual of it for a time. . . .

Again, we cannot review all of the relevant literature, yet perhaps the three investigations cited will serve to emphasize that many forms of deviant behavior are shaped and maintained by various contingencies of reinforcement. Given this experimental evidence we would amend Sutherland's first and eighth propositions to read:

I. *Criminal behavior is learned according to the principles of operant conditioning.*

II. "Criminal behavior is learned in interaction with other persons in the process of communication."

As DeFleur and Quinney have noted, the major implication of this proposition is that symbolic interaction is a necessary condition for the learning of criminal behavior. Of direct relevance to this is an experiment designed to test the relative significance of verbal instructions and reinforcement contingencies in generating and maintaining a certain class of behaviors. In brief, the results indicated that behavior could not be maintained solely through verbal instructions. However, it was also discovered that it was an extremely arduous task to shape a set of complex behaviors without using verbal instructions as discriminative stimuli. Behavior was quickly and effectively developed and maintained by a combination of verbal instructions *and* reinforcement consequences. Symbolic interaction is, then, not enough, contingencies of reinforcement must also be present.

From the perspective of modern behavior theory, two aspects of socialization are usually considered to distinguish it from other processes of behavioral change: (1) Only those behavioral changes occurring through learning are considered relevant; (2) only the changes in behavior having their origins in interaction with other persons are considered products of socialization. Sutherland's theory may, then, be seen to be a theory of differential socialization since he, too, restricted himself to learning having its origin in interaction with other persons. While social learning is, indeed, important and even predominant, it certainly does not exhaust the learning process. In short, we may learn (and, thus, our behavior would be modified) without any direct contact with another person. As such, Sutherland's theory may be seen to suffer from a significant lacuna in that it neglected the possibility of deviant behavior being learned in nonsocial situations. Consequently, to be an adequate theory of deviant behavior, the theory must be amended further to include those forms of deviant behavior that are learned in the absence of social reinforcement. Other people are not the only source of reinforcement although they are the most important. As Jeffery has aptly noted, stealing is reinforcing in and by itself whether other people know about it and reinforce it socially or not. The same may be said to apply to many forms of aggressive behaviors. . . .

In addition to the reinforcing function of an individual or group, there is, as seen in the Cohen and the Bandura and Ross studies, the discriminative stimulus function of a group. For example, specific individuals as physical stimuli may acquire discriminative control over an individual's behavior. The child in our example above is reinforced for certain kinds of behaviors in the presence of his parent, thus the parent's presence may come to control this type of behavior. He is reinforced for different behaviors in the presence of his peers, who then come to set the occasion for this type of behavior. Consequently this proposition must be amended to read:

II. *Criminal behavior is learned both in nonsocial situations that are reinforcing or discriminative, and through that social interaction in which the behavior of other persons is reinforcing or discriminative for criminal behavior.*

III. "The principal part of the learning of criminal behavior occurs within intimate personal groups."

In terms of our analysis, the primary group would be seen to be the major source of an individual's social reinforcements. The bulk of behavioral training which the child receives occurs at a time when the trainers, usually the parents, possess a very powerful system of reinforcers. In fact, we might characterize a primary group as a generalized reinforcer (one associated with many reinforcers, conditioned as well as unconditioned). And, as we suggested above, as the child grows older, groups other than the family may come to control a majority of an individual's reinforcers, e.g., the adolescent peer group.

To say that the primary group is the principal molder of an individual's behavioral repertoire is not to ignore social learning which may occur in other contexts. As we noted above, learning from social models can be adequately explained in terms of these behavioral principles. The analysis we employed there can also be extended to learning from the mass media and from "reference" groups. In any case, we may alter this proposition to read: III. *The principal part of the learning of criminal behavior occurs in those groups which comprise the individual's major source of reinforcements.*

IV. "When criminal behavior is learned, the learning includes (a) techniques of committing the crime, which are sometimes very complicated, sometimes very simple; (b) the specific direction of motives, drives, rationalizations, and attitudes."

A study by Klaus and Glaser as well as many other studies indicate that reinforcement contingencies are of prime importance in learning various behavioral techniques. And, of course, many techniques, both simple and complicated, are specific to a particular deviant act such as jimmying, picking locks of buildings and cars, picking pockets, short- and big-con techniques, counterfeiting and safe-cracking. Other techniques in criminal behavior may be learned in conforming or neutral contexts, e.g., driving a car, signing checks, shooting a gun, etc. In any event, we need not alter the first part of this proposition.

The second part of this proposition does, however, deserve some additional comments. Sutherland's major focus here seems to be motivation. Much of what we have already discussed in this paper often goes under the general heading of motivation. The topic of motivation is as important as it is complex. This complexity is related to the fact that the same stimulus may have two functions: it may be both a reinforcing stimulus and a discriminative stimulus controlling the behavior which is followed by reinforcement. Thus, motivation may be seen to be a function of the processes by which stimuli acquire conditioned reinforcing value and become discriminative stimuli. Reinforcers and discriminative stimuli here would become the dependent variables; the independent variables would be the conditioning procedures previously mentioned and the level of deprivation. For example, when a prisoner is deprived of contact with members of the opposite sex, such sex reinforcers will become much more powerful. Thus, those sexual reinforcers that are available, such as homosexual contact, would come to exert a great deal of influence and would shape behaviors that would be unlikely to occur without such deprivation. And, without going any further into this topic, some stimuli may be more reinforcing, under similar conditions of deprivation, for certain individuals or groups than for others. Furthermore, the satiation of one or more of these reinforcers would allow for an increase in the relative strength of others.

Much, therefore, can be learned about the distinctive characteristics of a group by knowing what the available and effective reinforcers are and the behaviors upon which they are contingent. Basically, we are contending that the nature of the reinforcer system and the reinforcement contingencies are crucial determinants of individual and group behavior. Consequently, a description of an individual's or group's reinforcers, and an understanding of the principles by which reinforcers affect behavior, would be expected to yield a great deal of knowledge about individual and group deviant behavior.

Finally, the rationalizations which Cressey identifies with regard to trust violators and the peculiar extensions of "defenses to crimes" or "techniques of neutralization" by which deviant behavior is justified, as identified by Sykes and Matza, may be analyzed as operant behaviors of the escape or avoidance type which are maintained because they have the effect of avoiding or reducing the punishment that comes from social disapproval by oneself as well as by others. We may, therefore, rewrite this proposition to read: IV. *The learning of criminal behavior, including specific techniques, attitudes, and avoidance procedures, is a function of the effective and available reinforcers, and the existing reinforcement contingencies.*

V. "The specific direction of motives and drives is learned from definitions of the legal codes as favorable or unfavorable."

In this proposition, Sutherland appears to be referring, at least in part, to the concept "norm" which may be defined as a statement made by a number of the members of a group, not necessarily all of them, prescribing or proscribing certain behaviors at certain times. We often infer what the norms of a group are by observing reaction to behavior, i.e., the sanctions applied to, or reinforcement and punishment consequences of, such behavior. We may also learn what a group's norms are through verbal or written statements. The individual group member also learns what is and is not acceptable behavior on the basis of verbal statements made by others, as well as through the sanctions (i.e., the reinforcing or aversive stimuli) applied to his behavior (and other norm violators) by others.

Behavior theory specifies the place of normative statements and sanctions in the dynamics of acquiring "conforming" or "normative" behavior. Just as the behavior and even the physical characteristics of the individual may serve discriminative functions, verbal behavior, and this includes normative statements, can be analyzed as $S^D$'s. A normative statement can be analyzed as an $S^D$ indicating that the members of a group ought to behave in a certain way in certain circumstances. Such "normative" behavior would be developed and maintained by social reinforcement. As we observed in the Ayllon-Azrin study of instructions and reinforcement contingencies, such verbal behavior would not maintain any particular class of behaviors if it were not at least occasionally backed by reinforcement consequences. Extending their analysis, an individual would not "conform" to a norm if he did not have a past history of reinforcement for such conforming behavior. This is important, for earlier we stated that we can learn a great deal about a group by knowing what the effective reinforcers are and the behaviors upon which they are contingent. We may now say that we can learn a great deal about an individual's or a group's behavior when we are able to specify, not only what the effective reinforcers are, but also what the rules or norms are by which these reinforcers are applied. For these two types of knowledge will tell us much about the types of behavior that the individual will develop or the types of behaviors that are dominant in a group.

For example, it has often been noted that most official criminal acts are committed by members of minority groups who live in slums. One distinguishing characteristic of a slum is the high level of deprivation of many important social reinforcers. Exacerbating this situation is the fact that these people, in contrast to other groups, lack the behavioral repertoires necessary to produce reinforcement in the prescribed ways. They have not been and are not now adequately reinforced for lawful or normative behavior. And as we know from the Law of Operant Reinforcement, a reinforcer will increase the rate of occurrence of any operant which produces it. Furthermore, we would predict that given a large number of individuals under similar conditions, they are likely to behave in similar ways. Within such groups, many forms of social reinforcement may become contingent upon classes of behaviors which are outside the larger society's normative requirements. Norms and legal codes, as discriminative stimuli, will only control the behavior of those who have experienced the appropriate learning history. If an individual has been, and is, reinforced for such "normative" behavior, that behavior will be maintained in strength. If he has not been, and is not now reinforced for such behaviors they would be weak, if they existed in his repertoire at all. And, importantly, the reinforcement system may shape and maintain another class of behaviors which do result in reinforcement and such behaviors may be considered deviant or criminal by other members of the group. Thus we may formulate this proposition to read: V. *The specific class of behaviors which are learned and their frequency of occurrence are a function of the reinforcers which are effective and available, and the rules or norms by which these reinforcers are applied.*

VI.  "A person becomes delinquent because of an excess of definitions favorable to violation of law over definitions unfavorable to violation of law."

This proposition is generally considered the heart of Sutherland's theory; it is the principle of differential association. It follows directly from proposition V, and we must now refer back to that proposition. In proposition V, the use of the preposition "from" in the phrase, "learned from definitions of the legal codes as favorable or unfavorable," is somewhat misleading. The meaning here is not so much that learning results *from* these definitions as it is that they form part of the *content* of one's learning, determining which direction one's behavior will go in relation to the law, i.e., law-abiding or lawbreaking.

These definitions of the law make lawbreaking seem either appropriate or inappropriate. Those definitions which place lawbreaking in a favorable light in a sense can be seen as essentially norms of evasion and/or norms directly conflicting with conventional norms. They are, as Sykes and Matza and Cressey note, "techniques of neutralization," "rationalizations," or "verbalizations" which make criminal behavior seem "all right" or justified, or which provide defenses against self-reproach and disapproval from others. The principle of negative reinforcement would be of major significance in the acquisition and maintenance of such behaviors.

This analysis suggests that it may not be an "excess" of one kind of definition over another in the sense of a cumulative ratio, but rather in the sense of the relative amount of discriminative stimulus value of one set of verbalizations or normative statements over another. As we suggested in the last section, normative statements are, themselves, behaviors that are a function of reinforcement consequences. They, in turn, may serve as discriminative stimuli for other operant behaviors (verbal and nonverbal). But recall that reinforcement must be forthcoming, at least occasionally, before a verbal statement can continue as a discriminative stimulus. Bear in mind, also, that behavior may produce reinforcing consequences even in the absence of any accompanying verbal statements.

In other terms, a person will become delinquent if the official norms or laws do not perform a discriminative function and thereby control "normative" or conforming behavior. We know from the Law of Differential Reinforcement that that operant which produces the most reinforcement will become dominant if it results in reinforcement. Thus, if lawful behavior did not result in reinforcement, the strength of the behavior would be weakened, and a state of deprivation would result, which would, in turn, increase the probability that other behaviors would be emitted which are reinforced, and such behaviors would be strengthened. And, of course, these behaviors, though common to one or more groups, may be labelled deviant by the larger society. And such behavior patterns, themselves, may acquire conditioned reinforcing value and, subsequently, be enforced by the members of a group by making various forms of social reinforcement, such as social approval, esteem, and status contingent upon that behavior.

The concept "excess" in the statement, "excess of definitions favorable to violation of law," has been particularly resistant to operationalization. A translation of this concept in terms of modern behavior theory would involve the "balance" of reinforcement consequences, positive and negative. The Law of Differential Reinforcement is crucial here. That is, a person would engage in those behaviors for which he had been reinforced most highly in the past. . . . Criminal behavior would, then, occur under those conditions where an individual has been most highly reinforced for such behavior, and the aversive consequences contingent upon the behavior have been of such a nature that they do not perform a "punishment function." This leads us to a discussion of proposition VII. But, first, let us reformulate the sixth proposition to read: VI. *Criminal behavior is a function of norms which are discriminative for criminal behavior, the learning of which takes place when such behavior is more highly reinforced than noncriminal behavior.*

VII. "Differential associations may vary in frequency, duration, priority, and intensity."

In terms of our analysis, the concepts frequency, duration, and priority are straightforward enough. The concept *intensity* could be operationalized to designate the number of the individual's positive and negative reinforcers another individual or group controls, as well as the reinforcement value of that individual or group. As previously suggested the group which can mediate the most positive reinforcers and which has the most reinforcement value, as well as access to a larger range of aversive stimuli, will exert the most control over an individual's behavior.

There is a good reason to suspect, however, that Sutherland was not so much referring to differential associations with other persons, as differential associations with criminal *patterns*. If this supposition is correct, then this proposition can be clarified by relating it to differential contingencies of reinforcement rather than differential social associations. From this perspective, the experimental evidence with regard to the various schedules of reinforcement is of major importance. There are three aspects of the schedules of reinforcement which are of particular importance here: (1) the *amount* of reinforcement: the greater the amount of reinforcement, the higher the response rate; (2) the *frequency* of reinforcement which refers to the number of reinforcements per given time period: the shorter the time period between reinforcements, the higher the response rate; and (3) the *probability* of reinforcement which is the reciprocal of responses per reinforcement: the lower the ratio of responses per reinforcement, the higher the rate of response.

Priority, frequency, duration, and intensity of association with criminal persons and groups are important to the extent that they insure that deviant behavior will receive greater amounts of reinforcement at more frequent intervals or with a higher probability than conforming behavior. But the frequency, probability, and amount of reinforcement are the crucial elements. This means that it is the coming under the control of contingencies of reinforcement that selectively produces the criminal definitions and behavior. Consequently, let us rewrite this proposition to read: VII. *The strength of criminal behavior is a direct function of the amount, frequency, and probability of its reinforcement.*

IX. "While criminal behavior is an expression of general needs and values, it is not explained by those general needs and values since noncriminal behavior is an expression of the same needs and values."

In this proposition, Sutherland may have been reacting, at least in part, to the controversy regarding the concept "need." This controversy is now essentially resolved. For, we have finally come to the realization that "needs" are unobservable, hypothetical, fictional inner-causal agents which were usually invented on the spot to provide spurious explanations of some observable behavior. Futhermore, they were inferred from precisely the same behavior they were supposed to explain.

While we can ignore the reference to needs, we must discuss values. Values may be seen as reinforcers which have salience for a number of the members of a group or society. We agree with Sutherland to the extent that he means that the nature of these general reinforcers do not necessarily determine which behavior they will strengthen. Money, or something else of general value in society, will reinforce any behavior that produces it. This reinforcement may depend upon noncriminal behavior, but it also may become contingent upon a set of behaviors that are labelled as criminal. Thus, if Sutherland can be interpreted as meaning that criminal and noncriminal behavior cannot be maintained by the same set of reinforcers, we must disagree. However, it may be that there are certain reinforcing consequences which only criminal behavior will produce, for the behavior finally shaped will depend upon the reinforcer that is effective for the individual. Nevertheless, it is the reinforcement, not the specific nature of the reinforcer, which explains the rate and form of behavior. But since this issue revolves around contingencies of reinforcement which are handled elsewhere, we will eliminate this last proposition.

## Concluding Remarks

The purpose of this paper has been the application of the principles of modern behavior theory to Sutherland's differential association theory. While Sutherland's theory has had an enduring effect upon the thinking of students of criminal behavior, it has, till now, undergone no major theoretical revision despite the fact that there has been a steady and cumulative growth in the experimental findings of the processes of learning.

**TABLE 1**
**A differential association-reinforcement theory of criminal behavior**

| Sutherland's statements | Reformulated statements |
|---|---|
| 1. "Criminal behavior is learned."<br>8. "The process of learning criminal behavior by association with criminal and anti-criminal patterns involves all of the mechanisms that are involved in any other learning." | 1. Criminal behavior is learned according to the principles of operant conditioning. |
| 2. "Criminal behavior is learned in interaction with other persons in a process of communication." | 2. Criminal behavior is learned both in nonsocial situations that are reinforcing or discriminative and through that social interaction in which the behavior of other persons is reinforcing or discriminative for criminal behavior. |
| 3. "The principal part of the learning of criminal behavior occurs within intimate personal groups." | 3. The principal part of the learning of criminal behavior occurs in those groups which comprise the individual's major source of reinforcements. |
| 4. "When criminal behavior is learned, the learning includes (a) techniques of committing the crime, which are sometimes very complicated, sometimes very simple; (b) the specific direction of motives, drives, rationalizations, and attitudes." | 4. The learning of criminal behavior, including specific techniques, attitudes, and avoidance procedures, is a function of the effective and available reinforcers, and the existing reinforcement contingencies. |
| 5. "The specific direction of motives and drives is learned from definitions of the legal codes as favorable or unfavorable." | 5. The specific class of behaviors which are learned and their frequency of occurrence are a function of the reinforcers which are effective and available, and the rules or norms by which these reinforcers are applied. |
| 6. "A person becomes delinquent because of an excess of definitions favorable to violation of law over definitions unfavorable to violation of law." | 6. Criminal behavior is a function of norms which are discriminative for criminal behavior, the learning of which takes place when such behavior is more highly reinforced than noncriminal behavior. |
| 7. "Differential associations may vary in frequency, duration, priority, and intensity." | 7. The strength of criminal behavior is a direct function of the amount, frequency, and probability of its reinforcement. |
| 9. "While criminal behavior is an expression of general needs and values, it is not explained by those general needs and values since noncriminal behavior is an expression of the same needs and values." | 9. (Omit from theory.) |

There are three aspects of deviant behavior which we have attempted to deal with simultaneously, but which should be separated. First, how does an individual *become* delinquent, or how does he learn delinquent behavior? Second, what *sustains* this delinquent behavior? We have attempted to describe the ways in which the principles of modern behavior theory are relevant to the development and maintenance of criminal behavior. In the process, we have seen that the principle of differential reinforcement is of crucial importance. But we must also attend to a third question, namely, what sustains the pattern or *contingency* of reinforcement? We only have hinted at some of the possibly important variables. We have mentioned briefly, for example, structural factors such as the level of deprivation of a particular group with regard to important social reinforcers, and the lack of effective reinforcement of "lawful" behavior and the concomitant failure to develop the appropriate behavioral repertoires to produce reinforcement legally. We have also suggested that those behaviors which do result in reinforcement may, themselves, gain reinforcement value and be enforced by the members of the group through the manipulation of various forms of social reinforcement such as social approval and status, contingent upon such behaviors. In short, new norms may develop and these may be termed delinquent by the larger society.

There are many other topics that are of direct relevance to the problem of deviant behavior which we have not been able to discuss given the requirements of space. For instance, no mention has been made of some outstanding research in the area of punishment. This topic is, of course, of prime importance in the area of crime prevention. To illustrate some of this research and its relevance, it has been found experimentally that the amount of behavior suppression produced by response-contingent aversive stimuli is a direct function of the intensity of the aversive stimulus, but that a mild aversive stimulus may produce a dramatic behavior-suppression if it is paired with reinforcement for an alternative and incompatible behavior. Furthermore, it has been discovered that if an aversive stimulus is repeatedly paired with positive reinforcement, and reinforcement is not available otherwise, the aversive stimulus may become a discriminative stimulus ($S^D$) for reinforcement and, consequently, not decrease the behavior's frequency of occurrence.

There are, in conclusion, numerous criteria that have been used to evaluate theories. One such set is as follows:

1. The amount of empirical support for the theory's basic propositions.
2. The "power" of the theory, i.e., the amount of data that can be derived from the theory's higher-order propositions.
3. The controlling possibilities of the theory, including (a) whether the theory's propositions are, in fact, *causal* principles, and (b) whether the theory's propositions are stated in such a way that they suggest possible *practical* applications.

What dissatisfaction there has been with differential association can be attributed to its scoring low on these criteria, especially (1) and (3). We submit that the reformulated theory presented here answers some of these problems and better meets each of these criteria. It is our contention, moreover, that the reformulated theory not only specifies the conditions under which criminal behavior is learned, but also some of the conditions under which deviant behavior in general is acquired. Finally, while we have not stated our propositions in strictly axiomatic form, a close examination will reveal that each of the later propositions follow from, modify, or clarify earlier propositions.

# TECHNIQUES OF NEUTRALIZATION:
# A THEORY OF DELINQUENCY

*Gresham M. Sykes and David Matza*

In attempting to uncover the roots of juvenile delinquency, the social scientist has long since ceased to search for devils in the mind or stigma of the body. It is now largely agreed that delinquent behavior, like most social behavior, is learned and that it is learned in the process of social interaction.

The classic statement of this position is found in Sutherland's theory of differential association, which asserts that criminal or delinquent behavior involves the learning of (a) techniques of committing crimes and (b) motives, drives, rationalizations, and attitudes favorable to the violation of law. Unfortunately, the specific content of what is learned—as opposed to the process by which it is learned—has received relatively little attention in either theory or research. Perhaps the single strongest school of thought on the nature of this content has centered on the idea of a delinquent sub-culture. The basic characteristic of the delinquent sub-culture, it is argued, is a system of values that represents an inversion of the values held by respectable, law-abiding society. The world of the delinquent is the world of the law-abiding turned upside down and its norms constitute a countervailing force directed against the conforming social order. Cohen sees the process of developing a delinquent sub-culture as a matter of building, maintaining, and reinforcing a code for behavior which exists by opposition, which stands in point by point contradiction to dominant values, particularly those of the middle class. Cohen's portrayal of delinquency is executed with a good deal of sophistication, and he carefully avoids overly simple explanations such as those based on the principle of "follow the leader" or easy generalizations about "emotional disturbances." Furthermore, he does not accept the delinquent sub-culture as something given, but instead systematically examines the function of delinquent values as a viable solution to the lower-class, male child's problems in the area of social status. Yet in spite of its virtues, this image of juvenile delinquency as a form of behavior based on competing or countervailing values and norms appears to suffer from a number of serious defects. It is the nature of these defects and a possible alternative or modified explanation for a large portion of juvenile delinquency with which this paper is concerned.

The difficulties in viewing delinquent behavior as springing from a set of deviant values and norms—as arising, that is to say, from a situation in which the delinquent defines his delinquency as "right"—are both empirical and theoretical. In the first place, if there existed in fact a delinquent sub-culture such that the delinquent viewed his illegal behavior as morally correct, we could reasonably suppose that he would exhibit no feelings of guilt or shame at detection or confinement. Instead, the major reaction would tend in the direction of indignation or a sense of martyrdom. It is true that some delinquents do react in the latter fashion, although the sense of martyrdom often seems to be based on the fact that others "get away with it" and indignation appears to be directed against the chance events or lack of skill that led to apprehension. More important, however, is the fact that there is a good deal of evidence suggesting that many delinquents *do* experience a sense of guilt or shame, and its outward expression is not to be dismissed as a purely manipulative gesture to appease those in authority. Much of this evidence is, to be sure, of a clinical nature or in the form of impressionistic judgments of those who must deal first hand with the youthful offender. Assigning a weight to such evidence calls for caution, but it cannot be ignored if we are to avoid the gross stereotype of the juvenile delinquent as a hardened gangster in miniature.

In the second place, observers have noted that the juvenile delinquent frequently accords admiration and respect to law-abiding persons. The "really honest" person is often revered, and if the delinquent is sometimes overly keen to detect hypocrisy in those who conform, unquestioned probity is likely to win his approval. A fierce attachment to a humble, pious mother or a forgiving, upright priest (the former, according to many observers, is often encountered in both juvenile delinquents and adult criminals) might be dismissed as rank sentimentality, but at least it is clear that the delinquent does not necessarily regard those who abide by the legal rules as immoral. In a similar vein, it can be noted that the juvenile delinquent may exhibit great resentment if illegal behavior is imputed to "significant others" in his immediate social environment or to heroes in the world of sport and entertainment. In other words, if the delinquent does hold to a set of values and norms that stand in complete opposition to those of respectable society, his norm-holding is of a peculiar sort. While supposedly thoroughly committed to the deviant system of the delinquent sub-culture, he would appear to recognize the moral validity of the dominant normative system in many instances.

In the third place, there is much evidence that juvenile delinquents often draw a sharp line between those who can be victimized and those who cannot. Certain social groups are not to be viewed as "fair game" in the performance of supposedly approved delinquent acts while others warrant a variety of attacks. In general, the potentiality for victimization would seem to be a function of the social distance between the juvenile delinquent and others and thus we find implicit maxims in the world of the delinquent such as "don't steal from friends" or "don't commit vandalism against a church of your own faith." This is all rather obvious, but the implications have not received sufficient attention. The fact that supposedly valued behavior tends to be directed against disvalued social groups hints that the "wrongfulness" of such delinquent behavior is more widely recognized by delinquents than the literature has indicated. When the pool of victims is limited by considerations of kinship, friendship, ethnic group, social class, age, sex, etc., we have reason to suspect that the virtue of delinquency is far from unquestioned.

In the fourth place, it is doubtful if many juvenile delinquents are totally immune from the demands for conformity made by the dominant social order. There is a strong likelihood that the family of the delinquent will agree with respectable society that delinquency is wrong, even though the family may be engaged in a variety of illegal activities. That is, the parental posture conducive to delinquency is not apt to be a positive prodding. Whatever may be the influence of parental example, what might be called the "Fagin" pattern of socialization into delinquency is probably rare. Furthermore, as Redl has indicated, the idea that certain neighborhoods are completely delinquent, offering the child a model for delinquent behavior without reservations, is simply not supported by the data.

The fact that a child is punished by parents, school officials, and agencies of the legal system for his delinquency may, as a number of observers have cynically noted, suggest to the child that he should be more careful not to get caught. There is an equal or greater probability, however, that the child will internalize the demands for conformity. This is not to say that demands for conformity cannot be counteracted. In fact, as we shall see shortly, an understanding of how internal and external demands for conformity are neutralized may be crucial for understanding delinquent behavior. But it is to say that a complete denial of the validity of demands for conformity and the substitution of a new normative system is improbable, in light of the child's or adolescent's dependency on adults and encirclement by adults inherent in his status in the social structure. No matter how deeply enmeshed in patterns of delinquency he may be and no matter how much this involvement may outweigh his associations with the law-abiding, he cannot escape the condemnation of his deviance. Somehow the demands for conformity must be met and answered; they cannot be ignored as part of an alien system of values and norms.

In short, the theoretical viewpoint that sees juvenile delinquency as a form of behavior based on the values and norms of a deviant sub-culture in precisely the same way as law-abiding behavior is based on the values and norms of the larger society is open to serious doubt. The fact that the world of the delinquent is embedded in the larger world of those who conform cannot be overlooked nor can the delinquent be equated with an adult thoroughly socialized into an alternative way of life. Instead, the juvenile delinquent would appear to be at least partially committed to the dominant social order in that he frequently exhibits guilt or shame when he violates its proscriptions, accords approval to certain conforming figures, and distinguishes between appropriate and inappropriate targets for his deviance. It is to an explanation for the apparently paradoxical fact of his delinquency that we now turn.

As Morris Cohen once said, one of the most fascinating problems about human behavior is why men violate the laws in which they believe. This is the problem that confronts us when we attempt to explain why delinquency occurs despite a greater or lesser commitment to the usages of conformity. A basic clue is offered by the fact that social rules or norms calling for valued behavior seldom if ever take the form of categorical imperatives. Rather, values or norms appear as *qualified* guides for action, limited in their applicability in terms of time, place, persons, and social circumstances. The moral injunction against killing, for example, does not apply to the enemy during combat in time of war, although a captured enemy comes once again under the prohibition. Similarly, the taking and distributing of scarce goods in a time of acute social need is felt by many to be right, although under other circumstances private property is held inviolable. The normative system of a society, then, is marked by what Williams has termed *flexibility;* it does not consist of a body of rules held to be binding under all conditions.

This flexibility is, in fact, an integral part of the criminal law in that measures for "defenses to crimes" are provided in pleas such such as nonage, necessity, insanity, drunkenness, compulsion, self-defense, and so on. The individual can avoid moral culpability for his criminal action—and thus avoid the negative sanctions of society—if he can prove that criminal intent was lacking. *It is our argument that much delinquency is based on what is essentially an unrecognized extension of defenses to crimes, in the form of justifications for deviance that are seen as valid by the delinquent but not by the legal system or society at large.*

These justifications are commonly described as rationalizations. They are viewed as following deviant behavior and as protecting the individual from self-blame and the blame of others after the act. But there is also reason to believe that they precede deviant behavior and make deviant behavior possible. It is this possibility that Sutherland mentioned only in passing and that other other writers have failed to exploit from the viewpoint of sociological theory. Disapproval flowing from internalized norms and conforming others in the social environment is neutralized, turned back, or deflected in advance. Social controls that serve to check or inhibit deviant motivational patterns are rendered inoperative, and the individual is freed to engage in delinquency without serious damage to his self image. In this sense, the delinquent both has his cake and eats it too, for he remains committed to the dominant normative system and yet so qualifies its imperatives that violations are "acceptable" if not "right." Thus the delinquent represents not a radical opposition to law-abiding society but something more like an apologetic failure, often more sinned against than sinning in his own eyes. We call these justifications of deviant behavior techniques of neutralization; and we believe these techniques make up a crucial component of Sutherland's "definitions favorable to the violation of law." It is by learning these techniques that the juvenile becomes delinquent, rather than by learning moral imperatives, values or attitudes standing in direct contradiction to those of the dominant society. In analyzing these techniques, we have found it convenient to divide them into five major types.

## The Denial of Responsibility

Insofar as the delinquent can define himself as lacking responsibility for his deviant actions, the disapproval of self or others is sharply reduced in effectiveness as a restraining influence. As Justice Holmes has said, even a dog distinguishes between being stumbled over and being kicked, and modern society is no less careful to draw a line between injuries that are unintentional, i.e., where responsibility is lacking, and those that are intentional. As a technique of neutralization, however, the denial of responsibility extends much further than the claim that deviant acts are an "accident" or some similar negation of personal accountability. It may also be asserted that delinquent acts are due to forces outside of the individual and beyond his control such as unloving parents, bad companions, or a slum neighborhood. In effect, the delinquent approaches a "billiard ball" conception of himself in which he sees himself as helplessly propelled into new situations. From a psychodynamic viewpoint, this orientation toward one's own actions may represent a profound alienation from self, but it is important to stress the fact that interpretations of responsibility are cultural constructs and not merely idiosyncratic beliefs. The similarity between this mode of justifying illegal behavior assumed by the delinquent and the implications of a "sociological" frame of reference or a "humane" jurisprudence is readily apparent. It is not the validity of this orientation that concerns us here, but its function of deflecting blame attached to violations of social norms and its relative independence of a particular personality structure. By learning to view himself as more acted upon than acting, the delinquent prepares the way for deviance from the dominant normative system without the necessity of a frontal assault on the norms themselves.

## The Denial of Injury

A second major technique of neutralization centers on the injury or harm involved in the delinquent act. The criminal law has long made a distinction between crimes which are *mala in se* and *mala prohibita*—that is between acts that are wrong in themselves and acts that are illegal but not immoral—and the delinquent can make the same kind of distinction in evaluating the wrongfulness of his behavior. For the delinquent, however, wrongfulness may turn on the question of whether or not anyone has clearly been hurt by his deviance, and this matter is open to a variety of interpretations. Vandalism, for example, may be defined by the delinquent simply as "mischief"—after all, it may be claimed, the persons whose property has been destroyed can well afford it. Similarly, auto theft may be viewed as "borrowing," and gang fighting may be seen as a private quarrel, an agreed upon duel between two willing parties, and thus of no concern to the community at large. We are not suggesting that this technique of neutralization, labelled the denial of injury, involves an explicit dialectic. Rather, we are arguing that the delinquent frequently, and in a hazy fashion, feels that his behavior does not really cause any great harm despite the fact that it runs counter to law. Just as the link between the individual and his acts may be broken by the denial of responsibility, so may the link between acts and their consequences be broken by the denial of injury. Since society sometimes agrees with the delinquent, e.g., in matters such as truancy, "pranks," and so on, it merely reaffirms the idea that the delinquent's neutralization of social controls by means of qualifying the norms is an extension of common practice rather than a gesture of complete opposition.

## The Denial of the Victim

Even if the delinquent accepts the responsibility for his deviant actions and is willing to admit that his deviant actions involve an injury or hurt, the moral indignation of self and others may be neutralized by an insistence that the injury is not wrong in light of the circumstances. The injury, it may be claimed, is not really an injury; rather, it is a form of rightful retaliation or punishment. By a subtle alchemy the delinquent moves himself into the position of an avenger and the victim is transformed into a wrong-doer. Assaults on homosexuals or suspected homosexuals, attacks on members of minority groups who are said to have gotten "out of place," vandalism as revenge on an unfair teacher or school official, thefts from a "crooked" store owner—all may be hurts inflicted on a transgressor, in the eyes of the delinquent. As Orwell has pointed out, the type of criminal admired by the general public has probably changed over the course of years and Raffles no longer serves as a hero; but Robin Hood, and his latter day derivatives such as the tough detective seeking justice outside the law, still capture the popular imagination, and the delinquent may view his acts as part of a similar role.

To deny the existence of the victim, then, by transforming him into a person deserving injury is an extreme form of a phenomenon we have mentioned before, namely, the delinquent's recognition of appropriate and inappropriate targets for his delinquent acts. In addition, however, the existence of the victim may be denied for the delinquent, in a somewhat different sense, by the circumstances of the delinquent act itself. Insofar as the victim is physically absent, unknown, or a vague abstraction (as is often the case in delinquent acts committed against property), the awareness of the victim's existence is weakened. Internalized norms and anticipations of the reactions of others must somehow be activated, if they are to serve as guides for behavior; and it is possible that a diminished awarenes of the victim plays an important part in determining whether or not this process is set in motion.

## The Condemnation of the Condemners

A fourth technique of neutralization would appear to involve a condemnation of the condemners or, as McCorkle and Korn have phrased it, a rejection of the rejectors. The delinquent shifts the focus of attention from his own deviant acts to the motives and behavior of those who disapprove of his violations. His condemners, he may claim, are hypocrites, deviants in disguise, or impelled by personal spite. This orientation toward the conforming world may be of particular importance when it hardens into a bitter cynicism directed against those assigned the task of enforcing or expressing the norms of the dominant society. Police, it may be said, are corrupt, stupid, and brutal. Teachers always show favoritism and parents always "take it out" on their children. By a slight extension, the rewards of conformity—such as material success—become a matter of pull or luck, thus decreasing still further the stature of those who stand on the side of the law-abiding. The validity of this jaundiced viewpoint is not so important as its function in turning back or deflecting the negative sanctions attached to violations of the norms. The delinquent, in effect, has changed the subject of the conversation in the dialogue between his own deviant impulses and the reactions of others; and by attacking others, the wrongfulness of his own behavior is more easily repressed or lost to view.

## The Appeal to Higher Loyalties

Fifth, and last, internal and external social controls may be neutralized by sacrificing the demands of the larger society for the demands of the smaller social groups to which the delinquent belongs such as the sibling pair, the gang, or the friendship clique. It is important to note that the delinquent does not necessarily repudiate the imperatives of the dominant normative system, despite his failure to follow them. Rather, the delinquent may see himself as caught up in a dilemma that must be resolved, unfortunately, at the cost of violating the law. One aspect of this situation has been studied by Stouffer and Toby in their research on the conflict between particularistic and universalistic demands, between the claims of friendship and general social obligations, and their results suggest that "it is possible to classify people according to a predisposition to select one or the other horn of a dilemma in role conflict." For our purposes, however, the most important point is that deviation from certain norms may occur not because the norms are rejected but because other norms, held to be more pressing or involving a higher loyalty, are accorded precedence. Indeed, it is the fact that both sets of norms are believed in that gives meaning to our concepts of dilemma and role conflict.

The conflict between the claims of friendship and the claims of law, or a similar dilemma, has of course long been recognized by the social scientist (and the novelist) as a common human problem. If the juvenile delinquent frequently resolves his dilemma by insisting that he must "always help a buddy" or "never squeal on a friend," even when it throws him into serious difficulties with the dominant social order, his choice remains familiar to the supposedly law-abiding. The delinquent is unusual, perhaps, in the extent to which he is able to see the fact that he acts in behalf of the smaller social groups to which he belongs as a justification for violations of society's norms, but it is a matter of degree rather than of kind.

"I didn't mean it." "I didn't really hurt anybody." "They had it coming to them." "Everybody's picking on me." "I didn't do it for myself." These slogans or their variants, we hypothesize, prepare the juvenile for delinquent acts. These "definitions of the situation" represent tangential or glancing blows at the dominant normative system rather than the creation of an opposing ideology; and they are extensions of patterns of thought prevalent in society rather than something created *de novo*.

Techniques of neutralization may not be powerful enough to fully shield the individual from the force of his own internalized values and the reactions of conforming others, for as we have pointed out, juvenile delinquents often appear to suffer from feelings of guilt and shame when called into account for their deviant behavior. And some delinquents may be so isolated from the world of conformity that techniques of neutralization need not be called into play. Nonetheless, we would argue that techniques of neutralization are critical in lessening the effectiveness of social controls and that they lie behind a large share of delinquent behavior. Empirical research in this area is scattered and fragmentary at the present time, but the work of Redl, Cressy, and others has supplied a body of significant data that has done much to clarify the theoretical issues and enlarge the fund of supporting evidence. Two lines of investigation seem to be critical at this stage. First, there is need for more knowledge concerning the differential distribution of techniques of neutralization, as operative patterns of thought, by age, sex, social class, ethnic group, etc. On *a priori* grounds it might be assumed that these justifications for deviance will be more readily seized by segments of society for whom a discrepancy between common social ideals and social practice is most apparent. It is also possible however, that the habit of "bending" the dominant normative system—if not "breaking" it—cuts across our cruder social categories and is to be traced primarily to patterns of social interaction within the familial circle. Second, there is need for a greater understanding of the internal structure of techniques of neutralization, as a system of beliefs and attitudes, and its relationship to various types of delinquent behavior. Certain techniques of neutralization would appear to be better adapted to particular deviant acts than to others, as we have suggested, for example, in the case of offenses against property and the denial of the victim. But the issue remains far from clear and stands in need of more information.

In any case, techniques of neutralization appear to offer a promising line of research in enlarging and systematizing the theoretical grasp of juvenile delinquency. As more information is uncovered concerning techniques of neutralization, their origins, and their consequences, both juvenile delinquency in particular, and deviation from normative systems in general may be illuminated.

# CONTEMPORARY RETROSPECTIVE ON DIFFERENTIAL ASSOCIATION AND SOCIAL LEARNING THEORIES

## LEARNING THEORY: FROM SEMINAL STATEMENTS TO HYBRIDIZATION

*J. Mitchell Miller, University of Texas at San Antonio;*
*J. Eagle Shutt, University of Louisville; and*
*J. C. Barnes, Florida State University*

A longstanding argument in criminology concerns whether crime is more a function of biological or sociological determinants. In presenting differential association theory, Edwin Sutherland (1939, 1947) outlined classical learning theory as an extreme form of nurture in the nature versus nurture debate. Criminal behavior, like all behavior, was considered to be heavily influenced by the environment. That is, behavior was viewed as the result of social factors rather than inherited genetic and biological traits (both physical and psychological). Criminal behavior, more specifically, was not attributable to rational choice and biosocial determinants such as genes or hormones, mental defects and neuroses, or lack of inner or external controls. Rather, crime was thought to result from influences external to individuals.

From the learning theory perspective, then, crime is culturally defined, normative in some environments, and transmitted to others through observation and interaction. Human nature is not innate but analogous to an empty vessel that becomes filled through social interactions with others. Sutherland's learning theory perspective has garnered numerous adherents and is now considered a dominant strand of criminological thought.

Classic learning theory's precursors, however, were noncriminological—a somewhat obvious statement in that Sutherland is widely recognized as the founder of, at least American, criminology. Earlier philosophers such as Descartes assumed that human nature is, at its essence, *tabula rasa*—a blank slate. Twentieth-century anthropologists such as Boas, Kroeber, and Mead assumed that human behavior was infinitely malleable and denied the existence of cultural universals. Contemporaneously, several social scientists underscored the primacy of imitation (see Trotter, 1919, for herd behaviors; Veblen, 1899, for emulation of high-status individuals) and the social construction of meaning (Mead, 1934). Building on Aristotle's claim that humans are social animals, Simmel and Wolff (1950) noted that humans prefer imitation, due, in part, to impulses to sociability and belonging. Perhaps most importantly, Gabriel Tarde (1912) influenced learning theory through his laws of imitation. Tarde noted a universal tendency to imitation in four related stages: (1) close contact, (2) imitation of superiors, (3) understanding of concepts, and (4) role model behavior.

Pre-Sutherland, crime was typically explained via biology or psychology rather than social environments. Individuals were considered criminals because of their body types (Lombroso, 1876/2006) or neuroses (Freud, 1901). Sutherland, though, had prompted the beginning of a shift in criminology toward environmental or sociological explanations of crime. Drawing on Park, Burgess, and McKenzie (1925) and other members of the Chicago School, Sutherland noted that particular locations exhibited consistently higher crime rates than others, giving rise to the still ongoing analysis of how environments are criminogenic. He also argued (1939, 1942, 1947) that such environments caused crime via socialization, a diachronic process of individual learning from immediate surroundings. Like any other form of behavior, criminal behavior was learned via interaction with other individuals and groups primarily through observation and communication. Over time, individuals acquire specific ideas and values, including (1) favorable or unfavorable definitions of criminal codes, (2) specific motives, drives, rationalizations, and attitudes supporting or opposing crime, and (3) specific techniques of crime.

The foremost determinant of individual criminality is considered *differential association* with delinquent peers, which denotes individual differences in exposure to specific information and definitions:

> A person becomes a delinquent because of an excess of definitions favorable to violation of law over definitions unfavorable to violation of law. . . . [T]he principle of differential association . . . refers to both criminal and anticriminal associations and has to do with counteracting forces. When persons become criminal, they do so because of contacts with criminal patterns and also because of isolation from anticriminal patterns. Any person inevitably assimilates the surrounding culture unless other patterns are in conflict. Negatively, this proposition also means that associations which are neutral so far as crime is concerned have little or no effect on the genesis of criminal behavior. (Sutherland & Cressey, 1970, pp. 75–76)

Through association with others, then, people are exposed to information via socialization agents who example favorable and/or unfavorable values (definitions) toward the criminal code. These definitions determine the direction of motivation or drive to commit crime and, ultimately, constitute a cause of crime.

The effect of an individual's exposure to specific agents of socialization (differential association) varies by (1) frequency, (2) duration, (3) priority, and (4) intensity. In other words, individuals tended to adopt information from agents of socialization involving frequent, persistent, early, and close contacts, such as family and close friends. Individuals exhibiting high criminality are exposed to more procrime definitions than anticrime definitions and thereby internalize unfavorable definitions of the criminal code. Particular incidents of crime occur when individuals define situations as appropriate occasions for violating the law.

Over the past 70 years, Sutherland's theory has gradually evolved from its pure sociological roots to a hybrid of sociology, psychology, and, arguably, even biology. By the 1960s, learning research had exposed a possible weakness in differential association theory. While criminal behavior may in fact be learned, there was no clear mechanism to explain how the process exactly transpired. Post-Sutherland learning research (Akers, 1973; Bandura, 1977; Rotter, 1954; Skinner, 1953) identified specific mechanisms for human learning. Humans were structured to learn via operant conditioning, a process wherein individuals acquired rewarded behaviors and discarded punished behaviors as reinforced by both positive and negative stimuli. This conditioning process has its maximal effect at early ages, suggesting that early experiences are disproportionately important in the development of criminal behavior.

Ronald Akers, in collaboration with Robert Burgess, perceived the utility of these newly discovered learning mechanisms for differential association theory. Their reformulation of differential association theory as *social learning theory* (Burgess & Akers, 1966) was innovative in that operant conditioning and observational learning were integrated into a distinct original theory featuring more precise definitions of learning process elements. In the following sections we will briefly critique these two leading learning theories: Sutherland (1939, 1947) and Burgess and Akers (1966). Discussion then turns to consideration of the level of empirical support for learning theory as evident in the existent literature, followed by a brief presentation of the recent expansions/refinements that have been put forth by leading theorists. Finally, we will briefly consider policy implications germane to the learning theory perspective.

## Critiques of Learning Theories

This section presents critiques of Sutherland's differential association theory as well as its major reformulation, social learning theory. Specific critiques emphasize fundamental limitations surrounding both theories as well as the potential advantages that might be realized by addressing the concerns identified.

### Sutherland's differential association theory

As originally formulated, differential association theory contained several possible deficiencies. First, in assuming that crime resulted from the social environment, rather than the physical environment, Sutherland eliminated nonsocial explanations of behavior in favor of pure symbolic interactionism. Socially constructed meanings were a reality in themselves, and the significance and ontology of biological perceptions of pain or pleasure was discounted. Following this reasoning to its logical conclusion, sugar's sweetness and fire's pain were purely social constructions and existed only due to socialization. As Burgess and Akers (1966) argued, however, nonsocial explanations for crime must exist. For example, stealing a loaf of bread effects pleasure from the food itself without the necessity of any social explanation; the pleasure received could encourage further stealing.

Second, Sutherland relied on an oversimplified model of human learning. In the context of the nature–nurture debate, Sutherland represented an extreme form of nurture. Human nature was represented as *tabula rasa,* or a blank slate, the content of which was entirely a product of the social environment. More recent psychological research (Bandura, 1977) has suggested that human nature is not so malleable in motives or drives as Sutherland first assumed. Humans as well as other animals are structured to seek pleasure and avoid pain centered in the brain. Skinner (1953, 1976), for example, suggested that behaviors across all species could be promoted by positive stimuli and eliminated by negative stimuli.

Finally, by Sutherland's own admission, the theory failed to account for differences in opportunities to commit crime, as well as personality differences. Even within criminal subcultures, individuals differed in the situations that they encountered. Likewise, due to personality differences, some individuals would be introverted and retiring, whereas others would be extroverted and gregarious. Thus, it appeared logical to expect considerable intragroup individual variation in crime, even among individuals with similar definitions.

### Burgess and Akers's social learning theory

While learning theory variables have been conclusively correlated to a broad variety of delinquent behaviors, social learning theory is not general enough to account for all crime variation—a fact that Akers freely admits:

> Neither social learning theory nor any other theory of crime and deviance has been able to explain all instances or variation in such behavior and none can withstand an absolute standard of necessary and sufficient causation with 100 percent of the variance explained. By that standard all current and past theories fail. (Akers & Jensen, 2006, p. 43)

Today, virtually all criminologists would agree that crime has more than one cause. If we are seeking a complete explanation of crime, the ideal multivariate equation would include other variables along with social learning theory predictors. In the post-Merton age of middle-range theories, general theories are typically greeted with skepticism. Any truly general theory must be able to account for the fact that other general theories of crime, such as Gottfredson and Hirschi's (1990) self-control theory, have been consistently correlated with a range of delinquent behaviors—thus, suggesting that more than one theoretical approach latches onto empirical realities of crime causation.[1]

A recent expansion of social learning theory increasing its explanative potential includes social structure as part of the theoretical construct. Akers (2005) has also moved

---

[1]Interestingly, scientists commonly accept that many pathologies, such as cancer, have multiple causes. Criminology has produced many correlates of crime as well, such as social disorganization variables, personality traits, and even biological traits. Nevertheless, general theories continue to garner numerous adherents and significant scholarly resources.

to unify social learning theory and Gottfredson and Hirschi's self-control theory (1990), though not Hirschi's 2004 reformulation of self-control.[2] Gottfredson and Hirschi (1990) argued that stable personality differences in self-control are formed in humans by ages 10–12 and, once formed, are relatively stable. Like learning theory, Gottfredson and Hirschi presumed that socialization processes, such as parental discipline and peer influence, were entirely responsible for the development of self-control. Akers reasoned that self-control has received considerable empirical support, is not incompatible with social learning theory, and is based on a consistent fundamental process (socialization).

Recent self-control research (Beaver & Wright, 2005) suggests that personality traits are at least partially inheritable. Evidence regarding the relationship between biology and personality traits is compelling and increasingly interdisciplinary. Personality traits have been linked to genetic variation (Blasi et al., 2005; Meyer-Lindenberg et al., 2006; for a thorough discussion of the literature, see Beaver, Wright, & Delisi, 2007), fetal development (Beaver & Wright, 2005), and damage to specific brain regions (Cardinal, Pennicott, Sugathapala, Robbins, & Everitt, 2001). Impulsiveness has been associated with dopamine production and frontal lobe activity, both of which have genetic underpinnings (Congdon & Canli, 2005). Impulsivity, a key component of Gottfredson and Hirschi's self-control, has been found more consequential with animals (Isles, Humby, Walters, & Wilkinson, 2004; James et al., 2007) than in humans. As a consequence, some self-control theorists have called for a revision of self-control to include biological factors, such as genetics, hormones, brain structures, and developmental processes.

If self-control is partially biological, and if self-control and social learning theory are to be integrated, a key issue becomes, what, if any, aspects of social learning processes are affected, though maybe not completely determined, by biology? Recall that even Sutherland questioned learning theory's ability to account for individual personality differences, which he felt might be relevant to learning. It is possible that reinforcement itself may display variation across individuals, leading to operationalization and measurement issues. In other words, a person's reinforcement perception, or his or her susceptibility to peer influence, may be experienced more strongly than another's, at least in some cases. More troublesome, however, is that learning theory may oversimplify the relationship between learning and personality.

Complicating the issue is social learning theory's aging behaviorist learning foundation, which, like both self-control and differential association theories, may profit from recent learning research. First, Skinner's operant conditioning approach has been generally discredited as an oversimplification of learning processes. Though Skinner (1976) argued for the general plasticity of brain function, the emerging picture of the brain suggests that it is structured to learn certain things easily and in set fashions (see Condon & Sander, 1974, for the synchronization of neonate movement with adult speech; see Piaget, 1963, for critical learning stages, language, and intelligence) even without being taught (e.g., geometry; see Duchaine, Yovel, Butterworth, & Nakayama, 2006). Social behaviors once thought abiological, such as reciprocal altruism (Rilling, Gutman, Thorsten, & Pagnoni, 2002), cooperation, self-regulation (Beaver, Wright, & DeLisi, 2007), and moral

---

[2]Hirschi, however, has resisted a unification approach, instead subscribing to what Akers termed an "oppositional strategy."

judgments (Greene, Nystrom, Engell, Darley, & Cohen, 2004; Koenigs et al., 2007), have since been partially related to biological factors such as genes, hormones, prenatal development, and functional brain regions. Research has shown that the brain has numerous unconscious modules (Duchaine, Cosmides, & Tooby, 2001; for a general discussion, see Cohen & Tong, 2001), characterized by rapid operation, automaticity, domain-specificity, information encapsulation, neural specificity, and innateness (Fodor, 1983, 2001). For example, the ability to recognize faces is located within a particular area of the brain; individuals with damage to or dysfunction in this site have prosopagnosia or faceblindness (Duchaine, 2006) and are unable to recognize others (Duchaine et al., 2006).

There is a growing body of research suggesting that the human sensitivity and susceptibility to social learning and imitation is related to a social information module (Gallese, 2005; Ramachandran, 2000, 2006), a type of primary value that orients humans toward others. Imitation itself appears to be hardwired into humans, which have a system of mirror neurons that fire when observing the behavior of others (Rizzolatti, Fadiga, Gallese, & Fogassi, 1996). When observing social behavior, even infants (Falck-Ytter, Gredeback, & von Hofsten, 2006) exhibit increased activity in mirror neurons (Iacoboni et al., 1999; Rizzolatti et al., 1996) and covert mimicry (Markovsky & Berger, 1983). Observing others in pain, for example, results in the activation of brain regions associated with pain (Singer et al., 2004). Individuals with autistic spectrum disorders, such as Asperger's syndrome, have dysfunctional mirror-neuronal systems (Dapretto et al., 2005; Oberman et al., 2005) and exhibit a range of deficits in processing social information. They pay less attention to social stimuli, have difficulty processing social information, and have difficulty modeling and predicting human perceptions and behavior (Baron-Cohen, Jolliffe, Mortimore, & Robertson, 1997). Thus, the learning process itself is inherently biological (Boeringer, 1992).

If learning theory is to be updated, and if social learning and self-control theories are to be integrated, the new learning model must account for biosocial factors. Unfortunately, however, most criminologists are both ill equipped for, and disposed to, biological research. Following Akers's lead (1991), we suggest a theoretical research program to explore an integrated model of social learning, social structure, and self-control, which accounts for, or at least does not exclude, personality traits and biology.

A theoretical research program (TRP) is an anatomic "set of related theories" (Wagner, 1984, p. 90) that is collectively engaged in by scientists. The TRP's orienting strategy (the unresolvable quasi-theory, such as the adaptationist working strategy) controls the types of issues and strategies employed by researchers. A TRP is composed of core and auxiliary formal theory sets, both of which may be falsifiable. Program growth occurs either through "composition of the sets or . . . in the organization, clarity, or refinement of elements already in the set" (p. 91). Thus, a TRP leads to theory growth in five possible ways: elaboration, variation, proliferation, integration, and competition.

Elaboration occurs when a new theory assumes a structure similar to an old theory but is "more comprehensive, more precise, more rigorous, or has greater empirical support" (Wagner, 1984, p. 39). Variation occurs when a new theory is a slight modification of a prior theory, typically conflicting over a small part of a domain. Proliferation occurs when a new theory adopts a structure similar to an old theory but the predictions apply to different explanatory domains. Integration occurs when a new theory consolidates two other theories and subsumes many (though typically not all) of the predictions of the old theories. Competition, perhaps the least successful method of theory growth, occurs when two contradictory theories struggle for dominance in the marketplace of ideas.

Learning theory has already benefited from a concerted research program with contributions from numerous researchers on a wide variety of behaviors (Akers, La Greca, Cochran, & Sellers, 1989). The proposed theoretical research program would build on the existent knowledge base by examining the relationship between personality traits, biology, and learning. Social learning theory itself exemplified elaboration, integration, and proliferation. Akers has elaborated on Sutherland's principles to create more precise predictions, integrated new theoretical concepts into differential association theory, and expanded the old theory's general structure to different explanatory domains—especially nonsocial reinforcement.

Subsequent research in social learning theory, as discussed, has found empirical support for social learning theory across a wide variety of criminal, delinquent, and/or deviant acts. The new task is to engage cross-disciplinary researchers to elaborate on Akers's revised social learning theory, while retaining its core theoretical structure, which clearly latches onto empirical realities. Such cross-disciplinary research would draw on knowledge of biological, criminological, and learning theories and likely would require a team of researchers with complementary skill sets. A key problem facing such research is a dearth of biologically informed criminological datasets. The few such sets available, such as the AddHealth dataset, include only limited genetic markers and potentially inadequate social learning theory variables. New, likely capital-intensive, studies informed by the latest neuroscientific, genetic, and learning research are needed to investigate the respective roles of learning, personality traits, and biosocial factors. Additionally, relevant learning genes and social learning information modules (if any) remain mysterious.

## Empirical Evaluations of Learning Theories

Learning theory has been arguably the most tested criminological theory, garnering consistently strong qualitative (Cressey, 1953; Sutherland, 1937) and quantitative empirical support across distinct subgroups (such as juveniles and the elderly) and cultures (see, e.g., Wang & Jensen, 2003) and for a wide range of behaviors such as smoking, substance abuse, violence, and sexual coercion (Akers & Lee, 1999; Ardelt & Day, 2002; Batton & Ogle, 2003; Brezina & Piquero, 2003; Chappell & Piquero, 2004; Gordon et al., 2004; Haynie, 2002; Kim & Goto, 2000; McGloin, Pratt, & Maahs, 2004; Rebellon, 2002; Rogers, 2001; Sellers, Cochran, & Winfree, 2003; Warr, 2002). For a comprehensive listing of empirical treatments of learning theory, see Akers and Jensen (2006).

Most learning theory research has relied on self-report data. Differential association measures have typically involved either the proportion of friends engaged in delinquency or Sutherland's differential association modalities (frequency, duration, intensity, and priority). Definitions have generally been measured by endorsements of positive or negative attitudes, beliefs, or neutralizing attitudes. Differential reinforcement has been measured by peer reactions, parental or legal sanctions, or actual or unanticipated rewards or punishments. Imitation has rarely been tested.

Learning theory has proven difficult to test, principally because the reinforcement process occurs over time, involving a complex series of feedbacks and inputs. As a consequence, the entire process of learning cannot be tested directly. Most criminological research has tended to use synchronic rather than diachronic approaches (i.e., cross-sectional, survey, or single-time-period data sources rather than the nonrecursive relationships of social learning theory), which could best be approximated using longitudinal methods. This problem has been exemplified by recent peer delinquency research. If learning theory is accurate, individuals would tend to adopt the attitudes of their peers, using the differential association measures outlined earlier. In this logic, we should expect individuals with high rates of contact to exhibit similar behaviors. But the temporal sequence of learning delinquency from delinquent peers has been questioned (Akers, 1989; Sampson & Laub, 1993). It could be that if "birds of a feather flock together," then delinquency (the "feathering") was established prior to peer association and delinquent peers have sought each other out (the "flocking," or assortive pairing).

Akers (1991) countered that assertive pairing does not contradict differential association, stating that "[s]ocial learning admits that birds of a feather do flock together; but it also admits that if the birds are humans, they also will influence one another's behavior, in both conforming and deviant directions" (pp. 83–84). Longitudinal research, moreover, has supported Akers's contention that peer associations are significantly associated with the initiation of deviance (Warr, 1993). For example, while assortive pairing occurred in drug contexts, peer drug use was a significant factor in an individual's initiation of drug use (Kandel & Davies, 1991).

Compared to other general theories of crime, social learning theory has been shown to be as, or more, predictive of criminal behavior. In a series of tests of integrated theory models, a range of behaviors (substance abuse, smoking, drinking, and sexual coercion) have shown explanatory power:

> The social learning variables of association, reinforcement, definitions, and imitation explain the self-perceived likelihood of using force to gain sexual contact or committing rape by college men (55 percent explained variance). They also account for the actual use of drugs or alcohol, non-physical coercion, and physical force by males to obtain sex (20 percent explained variance). Social bonding, self-control, and relative deprivation (strain) models account for less than 10 percent of the variance in these variables. (Akers, 2000, p. 89)

Thus, when controlling for other standard criminological predictors, social learning theory variables retain their significance, and, within the integrated model's context, are more robust. Despite the robustness of these findings, some researchers contend that social learning theories of delinquency disproportionately explain minor forms of deviance, and as a result, neglect more serious forms of deviant behavior (Warr, 2002).

Some social learning theory research may overestimate the effect of social learning variables. Since many learning theory studies have relied on self-report data for both individual and peer delinquency in synchronic studies, there is a danger of skewed measurement in favor of learning theory predictions. Self-report data are fraught with problems: lying on the self-report, assertive pairing, reiterating the same delinquency (i.e., the self-reported delinquency was the same act that the juvenile and the friend engaged in together), and projecting one's own delinquency as his or her peers' behavior. As a result, Kandel (1996) concluded that learning theory estimates of peer socialization effects on delinquency may overestimate up to fivefold in self-report measures.

A recent study by Haynie and Osgood (2005), however, provide at least partial answers to these critiques via a longitudinal design that (1) accounted for differences in situational opportunities; (2) controlled for assortive pairing; and (3) avoided self-report bias by obtaining independent assessments from the original respondent, as well as individual assessments from the respondent's peers. Using National Longitudinal Study of Adolescent Health longitudinal data of social networks, Haynie and Osgood found that as Akers's (1998) new model predicts, social structure was related to delinquency in that unstructured socializing with friends was correlated with increased delinquency. However, the normative influence of peers on delinquency was not as strong as expected and did not increase with closeness or duration.

Irrespective of methodological differences, the best available research suggests that social learning variables, while not accounting for all of the variation, remain robust predictors of delinquency. Accordingly and justifiably so, social learning theory remains at the forefront of criminological thinking.

## Theoretical Refinements

Although there have been several revisions (see, e.g., Cressey, 1960; Glaser, 1956, 1960) of Sutherland's differential association theory, none have had the impact of Burgess and Akers's (1966). A social-psychology hybrid that merged differential association with Rotter's (1954) noncriminological social learning theory and Skinner's operant conditioning, social learning theory has now long been a leading crime theory. While Rotter (1954) formulated the original, noncriminological social learning theory that allowed for both social and nonsocial effects on behavior, Akers predicted that an individual's deviant behavior results from the same processes that produce conformist behaviors as shaped by prior reinforcement experiences. Unlike differential association theory, reinforcement could be either social (such as reactions from family and friends) or nonsocial (such as physical rewards). Like differential association theory, an individual's primary source of reinforcement came from particular groups.

In place of Sutherland's differential association propositions, Akers (1973) argues that (1) deviant behavior is learned according to the principles of operant conditioning; (2) deviant behavior is learned in both nonsocial and social situations that are reinforcing or discriminating; (3) learning of deviant behavior occurs in groups that are an individual's major source of reinforcements; (4) learning of deviant attitudes and techniques to engage in deviance and avoidance procedures are a function of the reinforcements that an individual receives from reference groups; (5) the types of behavior learned and their frequency of occurrence are based on the types of reinforcements received and the deviant or nondeviant direction of norms, rules, and definitions that accompany reinforcement; (6) the probability that a person would engage in deviant behavior increases when the reinforcement includes normative statements, definitions, and verbalizations that value deviant behavior over conformist behavior; and (7) deviants receive greater amounts of reinforcements, more frequent reinforcements, and higher probability of reinforcements from valued groups whose opinions are deviant in the first place.

Akers (2000) focused on four major concepts: (1) differential association, or the process during which an individual was exposed to favorable or unfavorable definitions of law-abiding behavior; (2) differential reinforcement, or the balance of anticipated or actual rewards resulting from an action; (3) imitation, or the copying of others' behaviors, whether direct (in person) or indirect (via media), which is dependent on the models themselves, the behaviors themselves, and the observed consequences; and (4) an individual's definitions, or the attitudes or beliefs attached to a particular behavior and may include orientations or rationalizations that define a particular behavior as right or wrong, good or bad, or justifiable or unjustifiable. Individuals differ in their associations with others and as in opportunities to imitate the behaviors, attitudes, and definitions of others, as well as reinforcers of their individual behaviors, ideas, and attitudes. While imitation is important in acquiring new behaviors, only imitated behaviors, attitudes, and definitions reinforced ostensibly continue. Akers retained Sutherland's prediction that peer groups had a greater effect when association was done with greater duration, frequency, and intensity. Once an individual had adopted definitions favorable to deviance, he or she was more likely to engage in deviance. Thus, the stronger an individual's definitions for an act, the more likely he or she was to engage in it (Akers, 2000, p. 77). On this point, Akers (1998) notes:

> The probability that persons will engage in criminal and deviant behavior is increased and the probability of their conforming to the norm is decreased when they differentially associate with others who commit criminal behavior and espouse definitions favorable to it, are relatively more exposed in-person or symbolically to salient criminal/deviant models, define it as desirable or justified in a situation discriminative of the behavior, and have received in the past and anticipate in the current or future situation relatively greater reward than punishment for the behavior. (p. 50)

Social learning theory, like differential association theory, has been unfairly criticized as a cultural deviance theory that could explain deviant groups but not deviant individuals (Gottfredson & Hirschi, 1990; Hirschi, 1969). Akers's approach, however, allowed for individual differences via both differential exposure and individual experiences and expectations.

Since an individual will tend to acquire behaviors of those with whom he or she comes into contact, deviant individuals should come from deviant peers and, it is argued, from places where deviant norms and opportunities exist. Recognizing these patterns, over the past decade Akers has moved learning theory toward a more integrated model. Akers (1998) addressed learning theory's inability to account for individual differences in opportunities to commit crime by integrating social structure into social learning theory. In the revised model, social structure–social learning (SSSL) theory, social learning theory variables were still the immediate microlevel causes of crime; however, Akers recognized that different types of social structures created patterns of crime opportunities, as well as patterns of criminal-behavior reinforcement, that served as primary distal macrolevel and mesolevel causes of crimes (Akers, 1998). Social structure created the context for microlevel reinforcement and was relevant to crime in four ways: (1) differential social organization, or structural correlates of crime in a social setting, such as age composition; (2) differential location in the social structure, or social demographic characteristics of individuals and social groups, such as class, race, and marital status; (3) theoretically defined structural variables, such as variables from criminogenic conditions including anomie, oppression, or social disorganization theories; and (4) differential social location, or an individual's relationship to primary, secondary, and reference groups.

Despite Akers's aversion, his revised SSSL approach has untapped utility to explain cultural deviance (Akers, 1996). Two key problems in criminology are explaining (1) the relationship between culture and crime and (2) cultural change over time. Whereas it is foundational to learning theory that an individual's values and norms are related to crime, we may infer that a group's values and norms are likewise related to rates of intra-group crime (see, e.g., cultural transmission theory, Shaw & McKay, 1942). In broadening social learning theory via integrating mesolevel and macrolevel perspectives, Akers provides a potential tool to predict cultural change over time because, at least theoretically, meso- and macrolevel structures should partially shape the direction of microlevel processes. For example, areas characterized by high social disorganization (macrolevel) or high percentages of single-parent households (mesolevel, although the categories are not mutually exclusive) should create recurring, systematic patterns of reinforcement for deviant behavior. Over time, this handedness, or bias from randomness, in favor of deviant behavior should produce both subcultural values and norms favoring deviance within a particular community and between-group variation. Eventually, two specific areas could be characterized by the differences, or deviations, in common behaviors and norms exhib-ited by residents.

Unfortunately, however, an SSSL cultural deviance approach by itself cannot account adequately for value and norm formation and is plagued by the same ontological prob-lems that have faced classical and modern subcultural theories (Cohen, 1955; Nisbett & Cohen, 1996; Wolfgang & Ferracuti, 1967), as well as epidemiological theories of violence (Fagan, Wilkinson, & Davies, 2007). While different cultures will develop dif-ferent values and norms under specific conditions, it is unclear what these cultural ele-ments are, how they are acquired, and how they spread to others. Typically, subcultural theory has viewed subcultural formation as a group adaptation to individual-level needs. For example, applying Cohen (1955), a street youth internalizes middle-class goals but feels status frustration at not being able to attain them; as an adaptation to reduce status frustration, the youth may engage in delinquency and join with others to form gangs, which themselves create opportunities for subcultures. Problematically, however, it is unclear how the new group responds to create new values, particularly since (1) the group does not exist outside the individual (i.e., most sociologists now reject Durkheim's [1895/1982] metaphysical argument that social facts have an independent ontological reality); and (2) any group responses are, in fact, individual-level responses occurring on larger scales. There is no clear mechanism, therefore, for why certain cultural elements come to predominate. Even modern subcultural theory formulations fail to provide clear mechanisms for differential value and norm formation over time. For example, Nisbett and Cohen (1996) provide a plausible argument for the rise of honor-related values in a specific context, namely, Scotch-Irish herding societies; however, they fail to account for any intervening causal influences over the subsequent two centuries. Culture is treated as a monolithic, relatively unchanging mass of values and norms imparted generation to generation.

The key problems, then, involve the definition of values and norms and their differen-tial dissemination across groups over time. Fortunately, since subcultural theory's incep-tion, noncriminological theory and research development has developed two new lenses for viewing cultural change and norm formation, which may provide fruitful vehicles for integration with SSSL: (1) the memetics quasi-theoretical perspective, best exemplified by

Boyd and Richerson's (1985, 2005; Richerson & Boyd, 2005) dual inheritance theory; and (2) norm formation literature (see, e.g., Horne, 2001).

Boyd and Richerson (2005) conceptualized culture as being composed of information elements defined as ideas, values, beliefs, attitudes, and norms. Analogous to genes, these information elements are subject to selection in that (1) the persistence and prevalence of these information elements depend on their transmission host to host, generation to generation; and (2) some information elements will exhibit a bias, or nonrandom deviation, in their favor in the transmission process and thereby become more prevalent. Like social learning theory, dual inheritance theory is biologically grounded. Dual inheritance itself refers to human genetic and cultural evolution, and Boyd and Richerson stress that human behavior and cultural evolution are not random, but biased by human nature itself. Analogous to social learning theory, behaviors, values, and attitudes that individuals perceive as pleasurable, desirable, or profitable are more likely to be acquired.

Cultural deviance itself depends on differential norm formation; however, norms themselves are an oft-discussed but little studied topic within criminology. Typically, criminologists discuss norms without defining them, presuming that readers know what they are. This ignorance is unfortunate, even shocking, in a discipline oriented to a study of deviant behavior that definitionally and demarcationally involves norms. Social norms were featured in functionalist theories (see, e.g., Durkheim, 1903/1953; Parsons, 1952/1954; Shaw & McKay, 1942) as regulators of social behavior. Societies that failed to establish effective social norms were viewed as "sick" or dysfunctional, whereas effective normative regulation promoted consensus, harmony, and health. From the 1950s to the present, subcultural theorists have viewed norms as collective responses to individual needs (see, e.g., Cohen, 1955; Nisbett & Cohen, 1996). Learning theorists (see, e.g., Sutherland) viewed norms, or their absence, within individuals as predictive of behavior. More recently, rational choice theorists have attempted to explain the evolution of norms using rational choice assumptions. Norms have thus been posited as solutions to rational choice difficulties in explaining group coordination, such as queuing, cooperation, and crime (see Hechter & Opp, 2001, p. xii; see also Axelrod, 1984; MacCormick, 1998; Sampson et al., 1997). The modern view of norms, typically subtypified as either regulatory or oughtness, is that they are self-regulating, can form and dissolve, and demonstrate rational choice and information cascade effects (Horne, 2001). At minimum, a social norm is a socially enforced rule. In rational choice terms, Voss (2001) defines a norm as a regularity R in a population P of actors such that (1) R arises in recurrent interactions among the agents of population P; (2) almost every member of P prefers to conform to R on the condition that almost every other member of P also conforms to R; (3) almost every member of P believes that almost every other member of P conforms to R; (4) almost every member of P expects that nonconformity to R is likely to be punished with negative sanctions, and this expectation is the reason for conditions 2 and 3; and (5) R is a Nash equilibrium of the recurrent interaction (pp. 108–109). As the definition illustrates, norm formation and continuance involve a complex series of processes that, at a minimum, must be studied to understand cultural deviance.

In conjunction with memetics and norm formation approaches, SSSL may provide a viable mechanism, albeit incomplete, to explain the differential dissemination of information elements across groups, allowing for predictions of cultural change based on mesolevel, microlevel, and macrolevel factors. Potentially, theoretical predictions could be used to guide policy to favor selection of socially desirable information elements over time. Additionally, the new approach may help explain diverse cultural phenomena, such as social contagion of violence (Fagan et al., 2007) and diffusion of innovations (Rogers, 1983).

## Policy Implications

Regardless of social learning theory's future directions, its past has yielded clear implications for criminal justice policy. Social learning theory's central propositions have been used as the basis for an extensive range of rehabilitative, prevention, and behavior modification programs in correctional and therapeutic contexts (Akers & Jensen, 2006). In a very real sense, social learning theory has given academic credence and, if not true implementation intensity, a sense of evidence-based practice to a wide range of prosocial skills enhancement, role modeling, peer norming, and various other related rehabilitative programs at both the juvenile and adult levels throughout the justice system. Perhaps social learning theory's key policy lesson, then, has been that incarceration and probation are unlikely to succeed *sans* real rehabilitation components. Since character is formed by peer associations over time, criminal justice interventions that cluster delinquent offenders with similar others are likely to have a criminogenic, as opposed to a deterrent, effect. Social learning theory's central propositions provide a ready explanation for the common recidivism failures of juvenile justice incarceration interventions. Likewise, adult incarceration alone, particularly without further intervention to provide positive reinforcement, is likely doomed to current success levels that too often represent expensive failure. Successfully rehabilitating offenders is, in effect, a conditioning process that will involve patterns of reinforcement over time—a literal reworking of offenders' psyche.

In sum, findings culled from tests of learning theory indicate that the current criminal justice responses to crime (predominantly incarceration) have both direct and indirect negative impacts on juveniles. On the other hand, some alternatives to incarceration, such as juvenile deferment programs, may have more positive effects when prosocial definitions are emphasized. From a learning theory perspective, the best way to alter an adolescent's behavior is to alter his or her "definitions" of law-abiding behavior through environmental factors such as positive social networks.

# PART VII

# CONTROL THEORIES

# SOCIAL CONTROL THEORIES

## SELF CONCEPT AS AN INSULATOR AGAINST DELINQUENCY

*Walter C. Reckless, Simon Dinitz, and Ellen Murray*

This study is concerned with sixth-grade boys in the highest delinquency areas in Columbus, Ohio, who have not become delinquent and who are not expected to become delinquent. What insulates an early teen-age boy against delinquency? Is it possible to identify certain components that enable young adolescent boys to develop or maintain non-delinquent habits and patterns of behavior in the growing up process.

### Methodology

In order to study the non-delinquent boy, all 30 sixth-grade teachers in schools located in the highest white delinquency areas in Columbus were asked to nominate those white boys in their school rooms who would not, in their opinion, ever experience police or juvenile court contact. Treating each nominee separately, the teachers were then requested to indicate their reasons for the selection of a particular boy. Of the eligible students, 192, or just over half, were selected and evaluated by their teachers as being "insulated" against delinquency. A check of police and juvenile court records revealed that 16 (8.3 per cent) of those nominated had some type of law enforcement record, and these boys were eliminated from further consideration. Repeated neighborhood visits failed to locate 51 others. In the remaining cases both the boy and his mother were interviewed.

The 125 "good" boys comprising the final sample were given a series of four self-administered scales to complete. These included, in somewhat modified form, (1) the delinquency proneness and (2) social responsibility scales of the Gough California Personality Inventory, (3) an occupational preference instrument, (4) and one measuring the boy's conception of self, his family and other interpersonal relations. At the same time, though not in the presence of the nominee, the mother or mother-surrogate was interviewed with an open-ended schedule to determine the boy's developmental history, his patterns of association, and the family situation. (Now nearing completion is a comparable study of sixth-grade boys in the same classrooms who were nominated by the same teachers as being likely to come into contact with the police and juvenile court.)

### Findings

An analysis of the scores made by these 125 nominees on the delinquency vulnerability (De) and social responsibility (Re) scales seemed to justify their selection as "good" boys. Out of a possible total (De) score of 54, scores ranged from a low of 4 to a high of 34 with a mean of 14.57 and a standard deviation of 6.4. This mean score was significantly lower than that of school behavior problem boys, young delinquents or reformatory inmates investigated in other studies. In fact, the average De score of the sample subjects was below that obtained in all but one previous study using the same scale.

For a twelve year old group, the nominees scored remarkably high on the social responsibility scale. The mean Re score for the group was 28.86 with a standard deviation of 3.60 and a range of 12 to 40 out of a possible 42 points. This mean score was appreciably higher than that achieved by school disciplinary cases, delinquents, and prisoners tested in other studies. The correlation between the two sets of scores was $-.605$, indicating a significant and negative relationship between delinquency vulnerability and social responsibility as measured by these instruments.

In response to self-evaluation items, the 125 boys portrayed themselves as law-abiding and obedient. Specifically, the vast majority defined themselves as being stricter about right and wrong than most people, indicated that they attempted to keep out of trouble at all costs and further indicated that they tried to conform to the expectations of their parents, teachers and others. The nominees did not conceive of themselves as prospects for juvenile court action or detention, and they stated that their participation in such activities as stealing had been minimal and that their friends were either entirely or almost completely free of police and juvenile court contact. As part of their conformity pattern, the respondents rarely played "hookey" from school and almost without exception indicated a liking for school. Finally, the "good" boys visualized themselves as being about average in ability, activity level, and aggressiveness. When asked "What do you think keeps boys out of trouble?" the respondents listed parental direction (a good home), non-deviant companions, and work, as well as other conventional answers. It would therefore appear that the internalization of these non-deviant attitudes played a significant role in the "insulation" of these boys.

Nominee perceptions of family interaction also appeared to be highly favorable. As noted in a previous paper, the 125 families were stable maritally, residentially, and economically. There appeared to be close parental supervision of the boys' activities and associates, an intense parental interest in the welfare of the children, and a desire to indoctrinate them with non-deviant attitudes and patterns. This parental supervision and interest seemed to be the outstanding characteristic of the family profiles. It extended over the entire range of their sons' activities—from friendship patterns, leisure activities, and after school employment to movie attendance and the performance of well-defined duties at home. Thus, as regards companions for example, the mothers almost without exception stated that they knew the boys' friends, that these friends were good boys and that, in fact, the boys couldn't have chosen better companions. The mothers also knew the whereabouts of their sons at almost all times and many insisted on this knowledge.

Despite this intensive supervision, the boys did not feel themselves to be unduly restricted. In general, the nominees appeared satisfied with the amount of parental affection and attention and with the quality of discipline and punishment given them. They viewed their home life as pleasant and their parents as understanding.

Low and high scorers on the delinquency proneness scale and their respective mothers did not differ significantly in their evaluations of these various aspects of family interaction. Of the 22 home background variables tested—ranging from the percentage of boys from broken homes to parental favoritism—none was found to be significantly related to the delinquency proneness scores. This finding was hardly surprising in view of the non-representative character of the sample group and the relatively small amount of variation in the family settings. It may also well be that in defining his interpersonal and family relationships favorably, the "good" boy, regardless of the degree of his "goodness" as measured by various scales, is in fact expressing the positive attitudes and perceptions that are important components in his "goodness."

While there was no appreciable variation in aspects of family interaction between the low and high scorers, the boys as a group and their mothers as a group did differ significantly in some of their evaluations. These differences were largely centered around the activity level of the boys, the definitions of the fairness and severity of parental punishment, and the amount of bickering in the home. Mothers thought theirs sons to be more active, punishment to be less frequent and severe, and parental tranquility to be more pervasive than did the nominees. Most significantly, perhaps, the mothers expressed less satisfaction with the role played by the boys' fathers than did the boys. Briefly, the mothers pictured their husbands as being relatively aloof and rigid in their affectional relationships with their sons. The nominees, however, could not differentiate between their parents in this regard.

These divergences in perceptions may largely reflect age, sex, and role differences in expectations of what constitutes satisfactory family relationships. Consequently, predictive tables based on the parents' conceptions of the boy and his relationships would necessarily be different in many particulars from those based on the boys' conceptions.

## Conclusion

"Insulation" against delinquency on the part of these boys may be viewed as an ongoing process reflecting an internalization of non-delinquent values and conformity to the expectations of significant others. Whether the subjects, now largely unreceptive to delinquent norms of conduct, will continue to remain "good" in the future remains problematic. The answer to this question, it is felt, will depend on their ability to maintain their present self-images in the face of mounting situational pressures.

While this pilot study points to the presence of a socially acceptable concept of self as the insulator against delinquency, the research does not indicate how the boy in the high delinquency area acquired his self image. It may have been acquired by social definition of role from significant figures in his milieu, such as a mother, a relative, a priest, a settlement house worker, a teacher, etc. It might have been a by-product of effective socialization of the child, which had the good fortune of not misfiring. On the other hand, it may have been an outgrowth of discovery in social experience that playing the part of the good boy and remaining a good boy bring maximum satisfactions (of acceptance) to the boy himself. Finally, there is a strong suspicion that a well-developed concept of self as a "good boy" is the component which keeps middle- and upper-class boys, who live in the better neighborhoods, out of delinquency. The point is that this component seems to be strong enough to "insulate" the adolescent against delinquency in the unfavorable neighborhoods.

# A CONTROL THEORY OF DELINQUENCY

*Travis Hirschi*

Control theories assume that delinquent acts result when an individual's bond to society is weak or broken. Since these theories embrace two highly complex concepts, the bond of the individual to society, it is not surprising that they have at one time or another formed the basis of explanations of most forms of aberrant or unusual behavior. It is also not surprising that control theories have described the elements of the bond to society in many ways, and that they have focused on a variety of units as the point of control.

I begin with a classification and description of the elements of the bond to conventional society. I try to show how each of these elements is related to delinquent behavior and how they are related to each other. I then turn to the question of specifying the unit to which the person is presumably more or less tied, and to the question of the adequacy of the motivational force built into the explanation of delinquent behavior.

## Elements of the Bond

### Attachment

In explaining conforming behavior, sociologists justly emphasize sensitivity to the opinion of others. Unfortunately, . . . they tend to suggest that man is sensitive to the opinion of others and thus exclude sensitivity from their explanations of deviant behavior. In explaining deviant behavior, psychologists, in contrast, emphasize insensitivity to the opinion of others. Unfortunately, they too tend to ignore variation, and, in addition, they tend to tie sensitivity inextricably to other variables, to make it part of a syndrome or "type," and thus seriously to reduce its value as an explanatory concept. The psychopath is characterized only in part by "deficient attachment to or affection for others, a failure to respond to the ordinary motivations founded in respect or regard for one's fellows"; he is also characterized by such things as "excessive aggressiveness," "lack of superego control," and "an infantile level of response." Unfortunately, too, the behavior that psychopathy is used to explain often becomes part of the *definition* of psychopathy. As a result, in Barbara Wootton's words: "[The psychopath] is . . . *par excellence,* and without shame or qualification, the model of the circular process by which mental abnormality is inferred from anti-social behavior while anti-social behavior is explained by mental abnormality."

The problems of diagnosis, tautology, and name-calling are avoided if the dimensions of psychopathy are treated as causally and therefore problematically interrelated, rather than as logically and therefore necessarily bound to each other. In fact, it can be argued that all of the characteristics attributed to the psychopath follow from, are effects of, his lack of attachment to others. To say that to lack attachment to others is to be free from moral restraints is to use lack of attachment to explain the guiltlessness of the psychopath, the fact that he apparently has no conscience or superego. In this view, lack of attachment to others is not merely a symptom of psychopathy, it is psychopathy; lack of conscience is just another way of saying the same thing; and the violation of norms is (or may be) a consequence.

For that matter, given that man is an animal, "impulsivity" and "aggressiveness" can also be seen as natural consequences of freedom from moral restraints. However, since the view of man as endowed with natural propensities and capacities like other animals is peculiarly unpalatable to sociologists, we need not fall back on such a view to explain the amoral man's aggressiveness. The process of becoming alienated from others often involves or is based on active interpersonal conflict. Such conflict could easily supply a reservoir of *socially derived* hostility sufficient to account for the aggressiveness of those whose attachments to others have been weakened.

Durkheim said it many years ago: "We are moral beings to the extent that we are social beings." This may be interpreted to mean that we are moral beings to the extent that we have "internalized the norms" of society. But what does it mean to say that a person has internalized the norms of society? The norms of society are by definition shared by the members of society. To violate a norm is, therefore, to act contrary to the wishes and expectations of other people. If a person does not care about the wishes and expectations of other people—that is, if he is insensitive to the opinion of others—then he is to that extent not bound by the norms. He is free to deviate.

The essence of internalization of norms, conscience, or superego thus lies in the attachment to others. This view has several advantages over the concept of internalization. For one, explanations of deviant behavior based on attachment do not beg the question, since the extent to which a person is attached to others can be measured independently of his deviant behavior. Furthermore, change or variation in behavior is explainable in a way that it is not when notions of internalization or superego are used. For example, the divorced man is more likely after divorce to commit a number of deviant acts, such as suicide or forgery. If we explain these acts by reference to the superego (or internal control), we are forced to say that the man "lost his conscience" when he got a divorce; and, of course, if he remarries, we have to conclude that he gets his conscience back.

This dimension of the bond to conventional society is encountered in most social control-oriented research and theory. F. Ivan Nye's "internal control" and "indirect control" refer to the same element, although we avoid the problem of explaining changes over time by locating the "conscience" in the bond to others rather than making it part of the personality. Attachment to others is just one aspect of Albert J. Reiss's "personal controls"; we avoid his problems of tautological empirical observations by making the relationship between attachment and delinquency problematic rather than definitional. Finally, Scott Briar and Irving Piliavin's "commitment" or "stake in conformity" subsumes attachment, as their discussion illustrates, although the terms they use are more closely associated with the next element to be discussed.

## Commitment

"Of all passions, that which inclineth men least to break the laws, is fear. Nay, excepting some generous natures, it is the only thing, when there is the appearance of profit or pleasure by breaking the laws, that makes men keep them." Few would deny that men on occasion obey the rules simply from fear of the consequences. This rational component in conformity we label commitment. What does it mean to say that a person is committed to conformity? In Howard S. Becker's formulation it means the following:

> First, the individual is in a position in which his decision with regard to some particular line of action has consequences for other interests and activities not necessarily (directly) related to it. Second, he has placed himself in that position by his own prior actions. A third element is present though so obvious as not to be apparent: the committed person must be aware [of these other interests] and must recognize that his decision in this case will have ramifications beyond it.

The idea, then, is that the person invests time, energy, himself, in a certain line of activity—say, getting an education, building up a business, acquiring a reputation for virtue. When or whenever he considers deviant behavior, he must consider the costs of this deviant behavior, the risk he runs of losing the investment he has made in conventional behavior.

If attachment to others is the sociological counterpart of the superego or conscience, commitment is the counterpart of the ego or common sense. To the person committed to conventional lines of action, risking one to ten years in prison for a ten-dollar holdup is stupidity, because to the committed person the costs and risks obviously exceed ten dollars in value. (To the psychoanalyst, such an act exhibits failure to be governed by the "reality-principle.") In the sociological control theory, it can be and is generally assumed that the decision to commit a criminal act may well be rationally determined—that the actor's decision was not irrational given the risks and costs he faces. Of course, as Becker points out, if the actor is capable of in some sense calculating the costs of a line of action, he is also capable of calculational errors: ignorance and error return, in the control theory, as possible explanations of deviant behavior.

The concept of commitment assumes that the organization of society is such that the interests of most persons would be endangered if they were to engage in criminal acts. Most people, simply by the process of living in an organized society, acquire goods, reputations, prospects that they do not want to risk losing. These accumulations are society's insurance that they will abide by the rules. Many hypotheses about the antecedents of delinquent behavior are based on this premise. For example, Arthur L. Stinchcombe's hypothesis that "high school rebellion . . . occurs when future status is not clearly related to present performance" suggests that one is committed to conformity not only by what one has but also by what one hopes to obtain. Thus "ambition" and/or "aspiration" play an important role in producing conformity. The person becomes committed to a conventional line of action, and he is therefore committed to conformity.

Most lines of action in a society are of course conventional. The clearest examples are educational and occupational careers. Actions thought to jeopardize one's chances in these areas are presumably avoided. Interestingly enough, even nonconventional commitments may operate to produce conventional conformity. We are told, at least, that boys aspiring to careers in the rackets or professional thievery are judged by their "honesty" and "reliability"—traits traditionally in demand among seekers of office boys.

### Involvement

Many persons undoubtedly owe a life of virtue to a lack of opportunity to do otherwise. Time and energy are inherently limited: "Not that I would not, if I could, be both handsome and fat and well dressed, and a great athlete, and make a million a year, be a wit, a bon vivant, and a lady killer, as well as a philosopher, a philanthropist, a statesman, warrior, and African explorer, as well as a 'tone-poet' and saint. But the thing is simply impossible." The things that William James here says he would like to be or do are all, I suppose, within the realm of conventionality, but if he were to include illicit actions he would still have to eliminate some of them as simply impossible.

Involvement or engrossment in conventional activities is thus often part of a control theory. The assumption, widely shared, is that a person may be simply too busy doing conventional things to find time to engage in deviant behavior. The person involved in conventional activities is tied to appointments, deadlines, working hours, plans, and the like, so the opportunity to commit deviant acts rarely arises. To the extent that he is engrossed in conventional activities, he cannot even think about deviant acts, let alone act out his inclinations.

This line of reasoning is responsible for the stress placed on recreational facilities in many programs to reduce delinquency, for much of the concern with the high school drop-out, and for the idea that boys should be drafted into the Army to keep them out of trouble. So obvious and persuasive is the idea that involvement in conventional activities is a major deterrent to delinquency that it was accepted even by Sutherland: "In the general area of juvenile delinquency it is probable that the most significant difference between juveniles who engage in delinquency and those who do not is that the latter are provided abundant opportunities of a conventional type for satisfying their recreational interests, while the former lack those opportunities or facilities."

The view that "idle hands are the devil's workshop" has received more sophisticated treatment in recent sociological writings on delinquency. David Matza and Gresham M. Sykes, for example, suggest that delinquents have the values of a leisure class, the same values ascribed by Veblen to *the* leisure class: a search for kicks, disdain of work, a desire for the big score, and acceptance of aggressive toughness as proof of masculinity. Matza and Sykes explain delinquency by reference to this system of values, but they note that adolescents at all class levels are "to some extent" members of a leisure class, that they "move in a limbo between earlier parental domination and future integration with the social structure through the bonds of work and marriage." In the end, then, the leisure of the adolescent produces a set of values, which, in turn, leads to delinquency.

### Belief

Unlike the cultural deviance theory, the control theory assumes the existence of a common value system within the society or group whose norms are being violated. If the deviant is committed to a value system different from that of conventional society, there is, within the context of the theory, nothing to explain. The question is, "Why does a man violate the rules in which he believes?" It is not, "Why do men differ in their beliefs about what constitutes good and desirable conduct?" The person is assumed to have been social-ized (perhaps imperfectly) into the group whose rules he is violating; deviance is not a question of one group imposing its rules on the members of another group. In other words, we not only assume the deviant *has* believed the rules, we assume he believes the rules even as he violates them.

How can a person believe it is wrong to steal at the same time he is stealing? In the strain theory, this is not a difficult problem. . . . The motivation to deviance adduced by the strain theorist is so strong that we can well understand the deviant act even assuming the deviator believes strongly that it is wrong. However, given the control theory's assumptions about motivation, if both the deviant and the nondeviant believe the deviant act is wrong, how do we account for the fact that one commits it and the other does not?

Control theories have taken two approaches to this problem. In one approach, beliefs are treated as mere words that mean little or nothing if the other forms of control are missing. "Semantic dementia," the dissociation between rational faculties and emotional control which is said to be characteristic of the psychopath, illustrates this way of handling the problem. In short, beliefs, at least insofar as they are expressed in words, drop out of the picture; since they do not differentiate between deviants and nondeviants, they are in the same class as "language" or any other characteristic common to all members of the group.

Since they represent no real obstacle to the commission of delinquent acts, nothing need be said about how they are handled by those committing such acts. The control theories that do not mention beliefs (or values), and many do not, may be assumed to take this approach to the problem.

The second approach argues that the deviant rationalizes his behavior so that he can at once violate the rule and maintain his belief in it. Donald R. Cressey has advanced this argument with respect to embezzlement and Sykes and Matza have advanced it with respect to delinquency. In both Cressey's and Sykes and Matza's treatments, these rationalizations (Cressey calls them "verbalizations," Sykes and Matza term them "techniques of neutralization") occur prior to the commission of the deviant act. If the neutralization is successful, the person is free to commit the acts in question. Both in Cressey and in Sykes and Matza, the strain that prompts the effort at neutralization also provides the motive force that results in the subsequent deviant act. Their theories are thus, in this sense, strain theories. Neutralization is difficult to handle within the context of a theory that adheres closely to control theory assumptions, because in the control theory there is no special motivational force to account for the neutralization. This difficulty is especially noticeable in Matza's later treatment of this topic, where the motivational component, the "will to delinquency" appears after the moral vacuum has been created by the techniques of neutralization. The question thus becomes: Why neutralize?

In attempting to solve a strain theory problem with control theory tools, the control theorist is thus led into a trap. He cannot answer the crucial question. The concept of neutralization assumes the existence of moral obstacles to the commission of deviant acts. In order plausibly to account for a deviant act, it is necessary to generate motivation to deviance that is at least equivalent in force to the resistance provided by these moral obstacles. However, if the moral obstacles are removed, neutralization and special motivation are no longer required. We therefore follow the implicit logic of control theory and remove these moral obstacles by hypothesis. Many persons do not have an attitude of respect toward the rules of society; many persons feel no moral obligation to conform regardless of personal advantage. Insofar as the values and beliefs of these persons are consistent with their feelings, and there should be a tendency toward consistency, neutralization is unnecessary; it has already occurred.

Does this merely push the question back a step and at the same time produce conflict with the assumption of a common value system? I think not. In the first place, we do not assume, as does Cressey, that neutralization occurs in order to make a specific criminal act possible. We do not assume, as do Sykes and Matza, that neutralization occurs to make many delinquent acts possible. We do not assume, in other words, that the person constructs a system of rationalizations in order to justify commission of acts he *wants* to commit. We assume, in contrast, that the beliefs that free a man to commit deviant acts are *unmotivated* in the sense that he does not construct or adopt them in order to facilitate the attainment of illicit ends. In the second place, we do not assume, as does Matza, that "delinquents concur in the conventional assessment of delinquency." We assume, in contrast, that there is *variation* in the extent to which people believe they should obey the rules of society, and, furthermore, that the less a person believes he should obey the rules, the more likely he is to violate them.

In chronological order, then, a person's beliefs in the moral validity of norms are, for no teleological reason, weakened. The probability that he will commit delinquent acts is therefore increased. When and if he commits a delinquent act, we may justifiably use the weakness of his beliefs in explaining it, but no special motivation is required to explain either the weakness of his beliefs or, perhaps, his delinquent act.

The keystone of this argument is of course the assumption that there is variation in belief in the moral validity of social rules. This assumption is amenable to direct empirical test and can thus survive at least until its first confrontation with data. For the present, we must return to the idea of a common value system with which this section was begun.

The idea of a common (or, perhaps better, a single) value system is consistent with the fact, or presumption, of variation in the strength of moral beliefs. We have not suggested that delinquency is based on beliefs counter to conventional morality; we have not suggested that delinquents do not believe delinquent acts are wrong. They may well believe these acts are wrong, but the meaning and efficacy of such beliefs are contingent upon other beliefs and, indeed, on the strength of other ties to the conventional order.

## Relations among the Elements

In general, the more closely a person is tied to conventional society in any of these ways, the more closely he is likely to be tied in the other ways. The person who is attached to conventional people is, for example, more likely to be involved in conventional activities and to accept conventional notions of desirable conduct. Of the six possible combinations of elements, three seem particularly important and will therefore be discussed in some detail.

### Attachment and commitment

It is frequently suggested that attachment and commitment (as the terms are used here) tend to vary inversely. Thus, according to delinquency research, one of the lower-class adolescent's "problems" is that he is unable to sever ties to parents and peers, ties that prevent him from devoting sufficient time and energy to educational and occupational aspirations. His attachments are thus seen as getting in the way of conventional commitments. According to stratification research, the lower-class boy who breaks free from these attachments is more likely to be upwardly mobile. Both research traditions thus suggest that those bound to *conformity* for instrumental reasons are less likely to be bound to conformity by emotional ties to conventional others. If the unattached compensate for lack of attachment by commitment to achievement, and if the uncommitted make up for their lack of commitment by becoming more attached to persons, we could conclude that neither attachment nor commitment will be related to delinquency.

Actually, despite the evidence apparently to the contrary, I think it is safe to assume that attachment to conventional others and commitment to achievement tend to vary together. The common finding that middle-class boys are likely to choose instrumental values over those of family and friendship while the reverse is true of lower-class boys cannot, I think, be properly interpreted as meaning that middle-class boys are less attached than lower-class boys to their parents and peers. The zero-sum methodological model that produces such findings is highly likely to be misleading. Also, although many of the characteristics of the upwardly mobile alluded to by Seymour M. Lipset and Reinhard Bendix could be accounted for as consequences rather than causes of mobility, a methodological critique of these studies is not necessary to conclude that we may expect to find a positive relation between attachment and commitment in the data to be presented here. The present study and the one study Lipset and Bendix cite as disagreeing with their general conclusion that the upwardly mobile come from homes in which interpersonal relations were unsatisfactory are both based on high school samples. As Lipset and Bendix note, such studies necessarily focus on aspirations rather than actual mobility. For the present, it seems, we must choose between studies based on hopes for the occupational future and those based on construction or reconstruction of the familial past. Interestingly enough, the former are at least as likely to be valid as the latter.

## Commitment and involvement

Delinquent acts are events. They occur at specific points in space and time. For a delinquent act to occur, it is necessary, as is true of all events, for a series of causal chains to converge at a given moment in time. Events are difficult to predict, and specification of some of the conditions necessary for them to occur often leaves a large residue of indeterminacy. For example, to say that a boy is free of bonds to conventional society is not to say that he will necessarily commit delinquent acts; he may and he may not. All we can say with certainty is that he is *more likely* to commit delinquent acts than the boy strongly tied to conventional society.

It is tempting to make a virtue of this defect and espouse "probabilistic theory," since it, and it alone, is consistent with "the facts." Nevertheless, this temptation should be resisted. The primary virtue of control theory is not that it relies on conditions that make delinquency possible while other theories rely on conditions that make delinquency necessary. On the contrary, with respect to their logical framework, these theories are superior to control theory, and, if they were as adequate empirically as control theory, we should not hesitate to advocate their adoption in preference to control theory.

But they are not as adequate, and we must therefore seek to reduce the indeterminacy within control theory. One area of possible development is with respect to the link between elements of the bond affecting the probability that one will be exposed to temptation.

The most obvious link in this connection is between educational and occupational aspirations (commitment) and involvement in conventional activities. We can attempt to show how commitment limits one's opportunities to commit delinquent acts and thus get away from the assumption implicit in many control theories that such opportunities are simply randomly distributed through the population in question.

## Attachment and belief

That there is a more or less straightforward connection between attachment to others and belief in the moral validity of rules appears evident. The link we accept here and which we shall attempt to document is described by Jean Piaget:

> It is not the obligatory character of the rule laid down by an individual that makes us respect this individual, it is the respect we feel for the individual that makes us regard as obligatory the rule he lays down. The appearance of the sense of duty in a child thus admits of the simplest explanation, namely that he receives commands from older children (in play) and from adults (in life), and that he respects older children and parents.

In short, "respect is the source of law." Insofar as the child respects (loves and fears) his parents, and adults in general, he will accept their rules. Conversely, insofar as this respect is undermined, the rules will tend to lose their obligatory character. It is assumed that belief in the obligatory character of rules will to some extent maintain its efficacy in producing conformity even if the respect which brought it into being no longer exists. It is also assumed that attachment may produce conformity even in the face of beliefs favorable to nonconformity. In short, these two sources of moral behavior, although highly and complexly related, are assumed to have an independent effect that justifies their separation.

## The Bond to What?

Control theorists sometimes suggest that attachment to any object outside one's self, whether it be the home town, the starry heavens, or the family dog, promotes moral behavior. Although it seems obvious that some objects are more important than others and that the important objects must be identified if the elements of the bond are to produce the consequences suggested by the theory, a priori rankings of the objects of attachment have proved peculiarly unsatisfactory. Durkheim, for example, concludes that the three groups to whom attachment is most important in producing morality are the family, the nation, and humanity. He further concludes that, of these, the nation is most important. All of which, given much contemporary thinking on the virtues of patriotism, illustrates rather well the difficulty posed by such questions as: Which is more important in the control of delinquency, the father or the mother, the family or the school?

Although delinquency theory in general has taken a stand on many questions about the relative importance of institutions (for example, that the school is more important than the family), control theory has remained decidedly eclectic, partly because each element of the bond directs attention to different institutions. For these reasons, I shall treat specification of the units of attachment as a problem in the empirical interpretation of control theory, and not attempt at this point to say which should be more or less important.

## Where Is the Motivation?

The most disconcerting question the control theorist faces goes something like this: "Yes, but why do they do it?" In the good old days, the control theorist could simply strip away the "veneer of civilization" and expose man's "animal impulses" for all to see. These impulses appeared to him (and apparently to his audience) to provide a plausible account of the motivation to crime and delinquency. His argument was *not* that delinquents and criminals alone are animals, but that we are all animals, and thus all naturally capable of committing criminal acts. It took no great study to reveal that children, chickens, and dogs occasionally assault and steal from their fellow creatures; that children, chickens, and dogs also behave for relatively long periods in a perfectly moral manner. Of course the acts of chickens and dogs are not "assault" or "theft," and such behavior is not "moral"; it is simply the behavior of a chicken or a dog. The chicken stealing corn from his neighbor knows nothing of the moral law; he does not *want* to violate rules; he wants merely to eat corn. The dog maliciously destroying a pillow or feloniously assaulting another dog is the moral equal of the chicken. No motivation to deviance is required to explain his acts. So, too, no special motivation to crime within the human animal was required to explain his criminal acts.

Times changed. It was no longer fashionable (within sociology, at least) to refer to animal impulses. The control theorist tended more and more to deemphasize the motivational component of his theory. He might refer in the beginning to "universal human needs," or some such, but the driving force behind crime and delinquency was rarely alluded to. At the same time, his explanations of crime and delinquency increasingly left the reader uneasy. What, the reader asked, is the control theorist assuming? Albert K. Cohen and James F. Short answer the question this way:

> ... it is important to point out one important limitation of both types of theory. They [culture conflict and social disorganization theories] are both *control* theories in the sense that they explain delinquency in terms of the *absence* of effective controls. They appear, therefore, to imply a model of motivation that assumes that the impulse to delinquency is an inherent characteristic of young people and does not itself need to be explained; it is something that erupts when the lid—i.e., internalized cultural restraints or external authority—is off.

There are several possible and I think reasonable reactions to this criticism. One reaction is simply to acknowledge the assumption, to grant that one is assuming what control theorists have always assumed about the motivation to crime—that it is constant across persons (at least within the system in question): "There is no reason to assume that only those who finally commit a deviant act usually have the impulse to do so. It is much more likely that most people experience deviant impulses frequently. At least in fantasy; people are much more deviant than they appear." There is certainly nothing wrong with *making* such an assumption. We are free to assume anything we wish to assume; the truth of our theory is presumably subject to empirical test.

A second reaction, involving perhaps something of a quibble, is to defend the logic of control theory and to deny the alleged assumption. We can say the fact that control theory suggests the absence of something causes delinquency is not a proper criticism, since negative relations have as much claim to scientific acceptability as do positive relations. We can also say that the present theory does not impute an inherent impulse to *delinquency* to anyone. That, on the contrary, it denies the necessity of such an imputation: "The desires, and other passions of man, are in themselves no sin. No more are the actions, that proceed from those passions, till they know a law that forbids them."

A third reaction is to accept the criticism as valid, to grant that a complete explanation of delinquency would provide the necessary impetus, and proceed to construct an explanation of motivation consistent with control theory. Briar and Piliavin provide situational motivation: "We assume these acts are prompted by short-term situationally induced desires experienced by all boys to obtain valued goods, to portray courage in the presence of, or be loyal to peers, to strike out at someone who is disliked, or simply to 'get kicks.'" Matza, too, agrees that delinquency cannot be explained simply by removal of controls:

> Delinquency is only epiphenomenally action. ... [It] is essentially infraction. It is rule-breaking behavior performed by juveniles aware that they are violating the law and of the nature of their deed, and made permissible by the neutralization of infractious [!] elements. Thus, Cohen and Short are fundamentally right when they insist that social control theory is incomplete unless it provides an impetus by which the potential for delinquency may be realized.

The impetus Matza provides is a "feeling of desperation," brought on by the "mood of fatalism," "the experience of seeing one's self as effect" rather than cause. In a situation in which manliness is stressed, being pushed around leads to the mood of fatalism, which in turn produces a sense of desperation. In order to relieve his desperation, in order to cast off the mood of fatalism, the boy "makes things happen"—he commits delinquent acts.

There are several additional accounts of "why they do it" that are to my mind persuasive and at the same time generally compatible with control theory. But while all of these accounts may be compatible with control theory, they are by no means deducible from it. Furthermore, they rarely impute built-in, unusual motivation to the delinquent: he is attempting to satisfy the same desires, he is reacting to the same pressures as other boys (as is clear, for example, in the previous quotation from Briar and Piliavin). In other words, if included, these accounts of motivation would serve the same function in the theory that "animal impulses" traditionally served: they might add to its persuasiveness and plausibility, but they would add little else, since they do not differentiate delinquents from nondelinquents.

In the end, then, control theory remains what it has always been: a theory in which deviation is not problematic. The question "Why do they do it?" is simply not the question the theory is designed to answer. The question is, "Why don't we do it?" There is much evidence that we would if we dared.

# CRIME IN THE MAKING: PATHWAYS AND TURNING POINTS THROUGH LIFE

*Robert J. Sampson and John H. Laub*

Our theory emphasizes the importance of informal social ties and bonds to society at all ages across the life course. Hence the effects of informal social control in childhood, adolescence, and adulthood are central to our theoretical model. Virtually all previous studies of social control in criminology have focused either on adolescents or on official (that is, formal) social control mechanisms such as arrest and imprisonment. As a result, most criminological studies have failed to examine the processes of informal social control from childhood through adulthood.

We differentiate the life course of individuals on the basis of age and argue that the important institutions of informal and formal social control vary across the life span. For example, the dominant institutions of social control in childhood and adolescence are the family, school, peer groups, and the juvenile justice system. In the phase of young adulthood, the institutions of higher education or vocational training, work, and marriage become salient. The juvenile justice system is also replaced by the adult criminal justice system. Finally, in middle adulthood, the dominant institutions of social control are work, marriage, parenthood, investment in the community, and the criminal justice system.

Within this framework, our organizing principle derives from the central idea of social control theory: crime and deviance result when an individual's bond to society is weak or broken. Many sociologists mistakenly think of social control solely in terms of social repression and State sanctions (for example, surveillance, enforced conformity, incarceration). By contrast, we adopt a more general conceptualization of social control as the capacity of a social group to regulate itself according to desired principles and values, and hence to make norms and rules effective. We further emphasize the role of *informal* social controls that emerge from the role reciprocities and structure of interpersonal bonds linking members of society to one another and to wider social institutions such as work, family, and school.

In applying these concepts to the longitudinal study of crime, we examine the extent to which social bonds inhibit crime and deviance early in the life course, and the consequences this has for later development. Moreover, we examine social ties to both institutions and other individuals in the adult life course, and identify the transitions within individual trajectories that relate to changes in informal social control. In this context we contend that pathways to crime *and* conformity are mediated by social bonds to key institutions of social control. Our theoretical model focuses on the transition to adulthood and, in turn, the new role demands from higher education, full-time employment, military service, and marriage. Hence, we explore the interrelationships among crime and informal social control at all ages, with particular attention devoted to the assessment of within-individual change.

We also examine social relations between individuals (for example, parent-child, teacher-student, and employer-employee) at each stage of the life course as a form of social investment or social capital. Specifically, we posit that the social capital derived from strong social relations (or strong social bonds), whether as a child in a family, as an adolescent in school, or as an adult in a job, dictates the salience of these relations at the individual level. If these relations are characterized by interdependence, they represent social and psychological resources that individuals can draw on as they move through life transitions that traverse larger trajectories. Thus, we see both social capital and informal social control as linked to social structure, and we distinguish both concepts as important in understanding changes in behavior over time.

Recognizing the importance of both stability and change in the life course, we develop three sets of thematic ideas regarding age-graded social control. The first concerns the structural and intervening sources of juvenile delinquency; the second centers on the consequences of delinquency and antisocial behavior for adult life chances; and the third focuses on the explanation of adult crime and deviance in relation to adult informal social control and social capital. Although this model was developed in the ongoing context of our analysis of the Gluecks' data and represents the best fit between our conceptual framework and available measures, we believe that our theoretical notions have wider appeal and are not solely bound by these data.

## Structure and Process in Adolescent Delinquency

In explaining the origins of delinquency, criminologists have embraced either structural factors (such as poverty, broken homes) or process variables (such as attachment to parents or teachers). We believe such a separation is a mistake. We join structural and process variables together into a single theoretical model. In brief, we argue that informal social controls derived from the family (for example, consistent use of discipline, monitoring, and attachment) and school (for instance, attachment to school) mediate the effects of both individual and structural background variables. For instance, previous research on families and delinquency often fails to account for social structural disadvantage and how it influences family life. Socioeconomic disadvantage has potentially adverse effects on parents, such that parental difficulties are more likely to develop and good parenting is impeded. If this is true, we would then expect poverty and disadvantage to have their effects on delinquency transmitted through parenting.

The effects of family process are hypothesized to mediate structural context in other domains as well. Our model and data enable us to ascertain the direct and indirect effects of other key factors such as family disruption, parental criminality, household crowding, large family size, residential mobility, and mother's employment. All of these structural background factors have traditionally been associated with delinquency. It is our major contention, however, that these structural factors will strongly affect family and school social control mechanisms, thereby playing a largely indirect (but not unimportant) role in the explanation of early delinquency. The intervening processes of primary interest are family socialization (discipline, supervision, and attachment), school attachment, and the influence of delinquent siblings and friends.

### The Importance of Continuity between Childhood and Adulthood

Our second theme concerns childhood antisocial behavior (such as juvenile delinquency, conduct disorder, or violent temper tantrums) and its link to troublesome adult behaviors. As noted earlier, the theoretical importance of homotypic continuity has been largely ignored among sociological criminologists. Criminologists still focus primarily on the teenage years in their studies of offending, apparently disregarding the connections between childhood delinquency and adult crime. Reversing this tide, our main contention is that antisocial and delinquent behavior in childhood—measured by both official and unofficial sources—is linked to later adult deviance and criminality in a variety of settings (for example, family violence, military offenses, "street crime," and alcohol abuse). Moreover, we argue that these outcomes occur independent of traditional sociological and psychological variables such as class background, ethnicity, and IQ.

Although some criminologists have explored the connections among conduct disorder, juvenile delinquency, and adult crime, we argue that the negative consequences of childhood misbehavior extend to a much broader spectrum of adult life, including economic dependence, educational failure, employment instability, and marital discord. We explore the adult worlds of work, educational attainment, and marriage as well as involvement in deviant behavior generally. Delinquent and criminal events "are linked into life trajectories of broader significance, whether those trajectories are criminal or noncriminal in form." Because most research by criminologists has focused either on the teenage years or on adult behavior limited to crime, this basic idea has not been well integrated into the criminological literature.

### The Significance of Change in the Life Course

Our third focus, drawing on a developmental perspective and stepping-stone approach, is concerned with changes in deviance and offending as individuals age. Our thesis concerns adult behavior and how it is influenced not just by early life experiences, but also by social ties to the adult institutions of informal social control (such as family, school, and work). We argue that trajectories of both crime and conformity are significantly influenced over the life course by these adult social bonds, regardless of prior individual differences in self-control or criminal propensity.

The third major theme of our research, then, is that changes that strengthen social bonds to society in adulthood will lead to less crime and deviance. Conversely, changes in adulthood that weaken social bonds will lead to more crime and deviance. This premise allows us to explain desistance from crime as well as late onset. In addition, unlike most researchers, we emphasize the quality, strength, and interdependence of social ties more than the occurrence or timing of discrete life events. In our view, interdependent social bonds increase social capital and investment in social relations and institutions. Our theoretical model rests on social ties to jobs and family as the key inhibitors to adult crime and deviance. . . .

Unlike most researchers in the life-course mold, we emphasize the quality or strength of social ties more than the occurrence or timing of discrete life events. For example, we agree that the structural institution of marriage per se does not increase social control. However, strong attachment to a spouse (or cohabitant) combined with close emotional ties creates a social bond or interdependence between two individuals that, all else being equal, should lead to a reduction in deviant behavior. Similarly, employment alone does not increase social control. It is employment coupled with job stability, job commitment and mutual ties to work (that is, employee-employer interdependence) that should increase social control and, all else being equal, lead to a reduction in criminal and deviant behavior.

The logic of our argument suggests that it is the social investment or *social capital* in the institutional relationship, whether it involves a family, work, or community setting, that dictates the salience of informal social control at the individual level. The distinguishing feature of social capital lies in the structure of interpersonal relations and institutional linkages. Social capital is created when these relations change in ways that facilitate action. In other words, "social capital is productive, making possible the achievements of certain ends that in its absence would not be possible." By contrast, physical capital is wholly tangible, being embodied in observable material form, and human capital is embodied in the skills and knowledge acquired by an individual. Social capital is even less tangible, for it is embodied in the *relations among persons*. A core idea, then, is that independent of the forms of physical and human capital available to individuals (for example, income, occupational skill), social capital is a central factor in facilitating effective ties that bind a person to societal institutions.

Coleman's notion of social capital can be linked with social control theory in a straightforward manner—lack of social capital is one of the primary features of weak social bonds as defined earlier. The theoretical task is to identify the characteristics of social relations that facilitate the social capital available to individuals, employers, and other social actors. According to Coleman, one of the most important factors is the closure (that is, connectedness) of networks among actors in a social system. In a system involving employers and employees, for example, relations characterized by an extensive set of obligations, expectations, and interdependent social networks are better able to facilitate social control than are jobs characterized by purely utilitarian objectives and nonoverlapping social networks. Similarly, the mere presence of a relationship (such as marriage) between adults is not sufficient to produce social capital, and hence the idea of social capital goes beyond simple structural notions of marital status.

According to this theoretical conception, adult social controls are not as direct or external as for juveniles (for example, monitoring, supervision of activities). Rather, adult social ties are important insofar as they create interdependent systems of obligation and restraint that impose significant costs for translating criminal propensities into action. It is unrealistic to expect that adults with a criminal background (or low self-control) can be wholly transformed by institutions (marriage or work), or that such institutions are even capable of imposing direct controls like surveillance. Nevertheless, we believe that adults, regardless of delinquent background, will be inhibited from committing crime to the extent that they have social capital invested in their work and family lives. By contrast, those subject to weak systems of interdependence and informal social control as an adult (for example, weak attachment to the labor force or noncohesive marriages) are freer to engage in deviant behavior—even if nondelinquent as a youth. This dual premise allows us to explain desistance from crime as well as late onset.

We also emphasize the reciprocal nature of social capital invested by employers and spouses. For example, employers often take chances in hiring workers, hoping that their investment will pay off. Similarly, prospective marriage partners may be aware of a potential spouse's delinquent background but may nonetheless invest their future in that person. This investment by the employer or spouse may in turn trigger a return investment in social capital by the employee or husband. The key theoretical point is that social capital and interdependence are reciprocal and are embedded in the social ties that exist between individuals and social institutions. This conception may help explain how change in delinquent behavior is initiated. . . .

At first blush, our focus on change may seem at odds with the findings that (1) criminal behavior is stable over time and (2) the formation of adult social bonds is negatively related to juvenile delinquency. We reconcile these facts in two ways. First, not only is continuity far from perfect, it refers to the aggregate of interindividual differences and does not capture within-individual change. In this regard, our theoretical framework implies that adult social ties can modify childhood trajectories of crime despite the general stability of between-individual differences.

Second, weak adult social bonds may also serve as a mediating and hence sequential link between early delinquency and adult criminal behavior. The idea of cumulative continuity suggests that delinquency tends to "mortgage" one's future by generating negative consequences for life chances (for example, arrest, official labeling, and incarceration, which in turn spark failure in school, unemployment, weak community bonds). Serious delinquency in particular may lead to the "knifing off" of opportunities such that participants have fewer options for a conventional life. The concept of "knifing off" appears to be especially applicable to the structurally constrained life chances of the disadvantaged urban poor.

On the other hand, the absence or infrequency of delinquency—especially encounters with the police and/or institutionalization—provides opportunities for prosocial attachments to take firm hold in adulthood. Thus, nondelinquents are not just more motivated (presumably), but also better able structurally to establish strong social ties to conventional lines of adult activity. If nothing else, incumbency in prosocial roles provides advantages in maintaining the status quo and counteracting negative life events (for example, last hired, first fired). In this sense we emphasize the state-dependence notion that history matters—where one has been and how long one has been in that state are crucial in understanding adult developmental patterns.

Our theoretical perspective is also consistent with the argument that the incidence of criminal acts is problematic and varies when self-control is held constant. That is, variations in criminal propensity reflected by early delinquency provide an incomplete explanation of adult crime because the latter's realization is dependent, among other things, on opportunity (for instance, lack of guardianship or surveillance). Ties to work and family in adulthood influence opportunities and hence the probability that criminal propensities will be translated into action. For example, all else being equal, those in stable employment and marital relations are subject to more continuity in guardianship than those in unstable employment or marital roles.

In brief, ours is a dynamic theory of social capital and informal social control that at once incorporates stability and change in criminal behavior. Change is central to our model because we propose that variations in adult crime cannot be explained by childhood behavior alone. We specifically hypothesize that the strength of adult social bonds has a direct negative effect on adult criminal behavior, controlling for childhood delinquency. At the same time our model incorporates the link between childhood delinquency and adult outcomes, implying a cumulative, developmental process whereby delinquent behavior attenuates the social and institutional bonds linking adults to society. As such, adult social bonds not only have important effects on adult crime in and of themselves, but also help to explain the probabilistic links in the chain connecting early childhood differences and later adult crime. . . .

## Summary of Theoretical Model

Our theoretical framework has three major themes. The first is that structural context is mediated by informal family and school social controls, which in turn explain delinquency in childhood and adolescence. The second theme is that there is strong continuity in antisocial behavior running from childhood through adulthood across a variety of life domains. The third theme is that informal social capital in adulthood explains changes in criminal behavior over the life span, regardless of prior individual differences in criminal propensity. In our view, childhood pathways to crime and conformity over the life course are significantly influenced by adult social bonds.

Although we reject the "ontogenetic" approach dominant in developmental psychology, our theoretical framework nonetheless follows a developmental strategy. Loeber and LeBlanc define "developmental criminology" as strategies that examine within-individual changes in offending over time. Moreover, the developmental approach that we take views causality as "best represented by a developmental network of causal factors" in which dependent variables become independent variables over time. Developmental criminology recognizes continuity and change over time and focuses on life transitions as a way of understanding patterns of offending. This strategy has also been referred to as a "stepping stone approach," where factors are time ordered by age and assessed with respect to outcome variables.

A similar perspective can be found in interactional theory. In our theoretical framework, we draw on the key idea of interactional theory that causal influences are bidirectional or reciprocal over the life course. Interactional theory embraces a developmental approach and argues convincingly that delinquency may contribute to the weakening of social bonds and informal social control over time. In particular, Thornberry maintains that interactional theory offers an explanation for continuity in criminal trajectories over time: "The initially

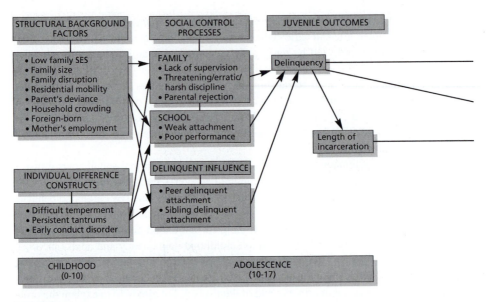

**FIGURE 1**
Dynamic theoretical model of crime, deviance, and informal social control over the life course
of 1,000 Glueck men, circa 1925–1975. (In the *UJD* design, delinquent and nondelinquent males
were matched on age, race/ethnicity, neighborhood SES, and IQ.)

weak bonds lead to high delinquency involvement, the high delinquency involvement further weakens the conventional bonds, and in combination both of these effects make it
extremely difficult to reestablish bonds to conventional society at later ages. As a result, all
of the factors tend to reinforce one another over time to produce an extremely high probability of continued deviance."

Thornberry's perspective is also consistent with a person-centered approach to development. In our analysis of the Gluecks' qualitative data we focused explicitly on "persons" rather than "variables" by examining individual life histories over time. This focus
complemented our quantitative analyses and offered insight into the social processes of intra-
individual developmental change in criminal behavior over the life course.

A summary representation of our sociogenic developmental theory as applied to the
Gluecks' data is presented in Figure 1. In essence this model explains probabilistic links
in the chain of events from childhood to adult criminal behavior. It is our view that family
and school processes of informal social control provide the key causal explanation of delinquency in childhood and adolescence. Structural background characteristics are important in
terms of their effects on informal family and school processes, but these same characteristics
have little direct influence on delinquency. Individual characteristics like temperament and
early conduct disorder are also linked to both family and school social control processes as
well as delinquency itself, but these same factors do not significantly diminish the effects of
social bonding in family and school on delinquency.

The theory embodied in Figure 1 explicitly links delinquency and adult crime to
childhood and adolescent characteristics as well as socializing influences in adulthood.
Early delinquency predicts weak adult social bonds, and weak adult social bonds predict

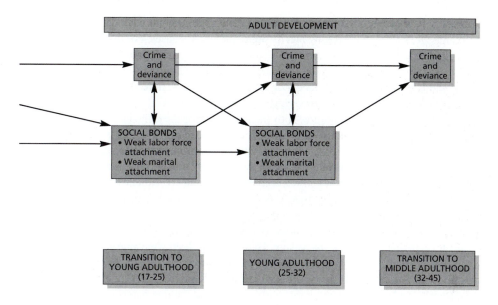

concurrent and later adult crime and deviance. The process is one in which childhood antisocial behavior and adolescent delinquency are linked to adult crime and deviance in part through weak social bonds. We also believe that salient life events and socialization experiences in adulthood can counteract, at least to some extent, the influence of early life experiences. For instance, late onset of criminal behavior can be accounted for by weak social bonds in adulthood, despite a background of nondelinquent behavior. Conversely, desistance from criminal behavior in adulthood can be explained by strong social bonds in adulthood, despite a background of delinquent behavior. In contrast to many life-course models, our theory emphasizes the quality or strength of social ties more than the occurrence or timing of life events. Thus, our theory provides a sociological explanation of stability and change in crime and deviance over the life course with an explicit focus on within-individual changes in offending and deviance. . . .

# CONTEMPORARY RETROSPECTIVE ON SOCIAL CONTROL THEORIES

## INTRODUCTION TO SOCIAL CONTROL THEORIES OF CRIME

*Christopher J. Schreck, Rochester Institute of Technology*

Shortly before noon on April 20, 1999, at Columbine High School in Littleton, Colorado, two students began opening fire on their teachers and classmates. The ensuing massacre, long planned by the gunmen, killed 12 people and injured 23 more. What took place during the shooting is not as much of interest to this chapter as the two teenaged shooters: Eric Harris and Dylan Klebold. Why did they do it?

After the shooting, there was considerable debate about the reasons the two boys went on a rampage. The media certainly had its share of favorite causes. For instance, Columbine High School was notorious for cliques of students, in particular the athletes who tormented and bullied other students and suffered few sanctions when they violated school rules. Harris and Klebold were not members of the popular cliques. Indeed, like many unpopular kids they resented the students who seemed to have it made. And they hung out with other unpopular kids, having in common with them a hatred of the athletes. And so, where the elites often wore white athletic caps, Harris and Klebold's group were sometimes distinguished by their black trench coats, thus earning them the moniker of "Trenchcoat Mafia." The two boys also got into trouble with school authorities and police, such as for breaking into a van to steal tools. Harris and Klebold were even fans of violent video games.

One of the reasons we have theory is to help us make sense of the facts we encounter, especially in an otherwise confusing event. Many facts appear in this story, enough at least to where we are forced to figure out which ones matter and which only represent plausible-sounding false trails. To be sure, Harris and Klebold were angry. They also played shoot-'em-up games like Doom. But other facts are also evident from this brief account that may be even more important to what allowed the crime to take place. Social control theories, for instance, are less impressed by the evident anger and gaming habits of the two gunmen than the fact of their relative isolation from others. Harris and Klebold had no close friends. Or maybe they did: Although the news reported some individuals who knew the boys alleging that the two gunmen were members of a tight circle of friends, it is noteworthy that—to our best knowledge—not one person in this "tight" group inspired in Harris or Klebold enough trust or confidence to ever learn of their plans. We can thus probably discount the hearsay claims of especially strong ties between members of the Trenchcoat Mafia. The gunmen lived with their parents, but they might as well have been boarders rather than sons in view of how little the parents really knew anything about them. Thus freed from caring what anyone thought, the two boys were answerable only to themselves insofar as the moral consequences of their actions were concerned. The video game playing and the hanging out with peers in no way differed from how many kids, popular or unpopular, might occupy their time.

The readings on social control theory included in this text focus on some of the leading social control theories, and outline the conditions that leave a person free to commit delinquency. This introduction will present some of the background on social control theories and describe why the theorists focus on *restraints* or barriers against crime rather than motives for crime (like anger). In addition, we will examine some of the research that has taken place testing these theories. And we shall see what various commentators or critics have had to say over the years about social control theory and its policy implications.

## History of Social Control Theory

Up until the late 1960s, the theories most criminologists thought were probably correct were two approaches that had originated in sociology and that had emphasized motive: strain/anomie and differential association. (Because sociology was then the dominant discipline in the study of crime, psychological and biological theories had long been ignored.) Since about 1970, social control theories became the third major sociological tradition within criminological theory and are arguably the leading explanation of crime today.

Social control theories developed slowly before the late 1960s. From the beginning, however, these theories focused on factors that inhibited or caged human action. One of the claims of social disorganization theory, which had emerged in the 1940s, was that high-crime areas in the inner city were due to the inability of residents to collectively control the behavior of one another (see Kornhauser, 1978). Social disorganization theory had little effect on the direction of criminology at that time. Several criminologists did occasionally expound the ideas of social control theory. Albert Reiss (1951), Ivan Nye (1958), and Walter Reckless (1961) wrote about a variety of "controls" on human behavior that could shape the amount of crime a person committed: personal and social controls, direct and indirect controls, and internal and external "containments." Yet these various descriptions of social control theory were not broadly influential either, and their ultimate destiny was to be overshadowed by later work.

Travis Hirschi's (1969) book *Causes of Delinquency* would take the laurels as the dominant statement on social control theory. A very good question is why Hirschi's social control theory succeeded where the others were ignored. Perhaps one reason is that most of Hirschi's book reported the results of a test of social control theory as well as an assessment of how well the claims of competing theories stood up to empirical fact. This powerful aspect of Hirschi's work—the use of data analysis to support or refute theoretical predictions—was somewhat unique at the time. Theorists were largely content to do no more than outline their theories and, perhaps, cite other research in support. But theories, if they are to be any good, have to conform to reality, and Hirschi's evidence largely confirmed the predictions of social control theory and revealed the weakness of other leading theories. Ruth Kornhauser (1978), a sociologist whose career began in the 1960s, provided a striking personal account of the impact of Hirschi's work. Kornhauser described herself as a supporter of Merton's anomie theory until she read Hirschi's book. After that, she became a control theorist. Social control theory was now not only a socially acceptable theoretical perspective for scientific study, but also had become a power in its own right. For a 25-year period, Hirschi's social control theory would enjoy the status of being the most frequently tested theory of crime, appearing in many dozens of journal articles and PhD dissertations (Stitt & Giacopassi, 1992).

The years did not pass by with social control theory unchanged. By 1993, Robert Sampson and John Laub published a variation of Hirschi's theory that would, in its turn, become the leading statement of social control theory thus far into the twenty-first century. Interested in why crime seemed to occur disproportionately often during adolescence and then start declining in frequency beginning in the early adult years, Sampson and Laub proposed an "age-graded theory of informal social control." If one is to judge the worth of a theory on its impact in shaping the direction of research, then this recent modification to Hirschi's theory has been very successful. Sampson and Laub, in various studies outlining and testing their theory of informal social control, are among the most-cited contemporary criminologists. Social control theory thus remains a leading force in criminological research.

## Theoretical Foundations

If Isaac Newton indeed saw further by standing on the shoulders of giants, then so too did social control theorists. Scientists draw inspiration from the work of others, learn from them, and then use their understanding in an original way to push the limits of knowledge still further. Some ideas that are fundamental to social control theory date back almost to Newton. The oldest ideas speak to basic assumptions about human nature, which all social control theories share. In fact, social control theories have a close link with the work of Enlightenment social philosophers like Jeremy Bentham and Cesare Beccaria.

Bentham and Beccaria tell us that action arises through a calculation of the advantages and costs. A simple example illustrates how calculation translates into action. For instance, why do people get out of bed and go to work when their alarm clock goes off and they are still sleepy? They get up because they weigh the costs and benefits of going to work and figure that working produces greater net benefits than not going to work. The same sort of calculation holds for any action, whether good or bad, legal or illegal. This does not mean that people are bad or evil, but rather their underlying reason for whatever they do is self-interest (of course they may not ever admit that to others, but that sort of protestation is simply for appearance's sake). When we do harm to others, it is because the act resulting in the harm brings pleasure or advantage. Stealing brings obvious rewards: money or a desirable object. Hitting someone brings status, a feeling of justice, or is a way for us to control the actions of another (Felson, 1998). When we do good—such as by helping someone at a soup kitchen—it is because we benefit in some way. We earn approval and trust from others, which we can use to our advantage. Thus, we have the basis for the saying "virtue is its own reward." If we didn't benefit from virtue in some respect, then no one would be virtuous. From this point of view, there is no meaningful distinction between criminals and noncriminals. Any one of us would commit crime if the temptation was great enough.

So the basic question is not why do people commit crime, but rather why do we choose not to break the law even when we have an opportunity to do so. The desire for crime is natural to us, insofar as it is natural for a person to gravitate toward doing things that are rewarding. Turning to Harris and Klebold, their anger is not unique. All of us get angry, often to the point of wishing to retaliate against those we view as responsible. And it is fair to say that frustration with some aspect of our lives is ubiquitous (if it wasn't, we would have no reason to do much of anything). Yet violence very seldom happens, even in the presence of a seemingly powerful motive. Here is another way of phrasing the control theorists' question: how do people resist criminal temptation? And why do most people resist temptation even when they think they can get away with it? In short, the control theorists' answer to crime is to simply make the costs such that the apparent advantages of the crime, whatever they may be, no longer have any appeal.

If all this so far sounds like deterrence theory, then you would be correct. Control theories, deterrence theories, and rational choice theories share the same basic principles. Their differences lie in emphasis. Deterrence theory makes the claim that to get people to behave themselves we need to make the legal system administer punishments that are certain, swift, and severe. Control theories, in contrast, would question whether the legal system is the most effective means of control. Hirschi's (1969) social control theory, for instance, highlighted how the fear of other people's opinions dissuades us from crime. Here is how opinion works more effectively than the courts: Unlike the criminal court, my opinion of others requires no due process or evidentiary procedure. It is not a docket that must wait until a hearing. My opinion is judge, jury, and executioner. I am not obliged to clemency or even to listen to appeals. Punishment is as swift as a thought, inflicted upon the offender the instant I withdraw my approval or trust. There are tangible outcomes as well that are not very pleasant. If a boss no longer trusts you, your continued employment is in jeopardy. If friends lose their respect for you, be prepared for lonely times. And so, compared to public opinion, the legal system is at best a crude, clumsy, and slow deterrent. Many people are fond of saying "I do not care what anyone else thinks of me." If they are being sincere (and most, fortunately, aren't), then you would do well to hold your wallet or pocketbook as close as you can.

Social control theories also see the law as generally a reflection of societal consensus. From this point of view, people essentially agree on the broad features of criminal action. There may be gray areas, like the criminality of marijuana or alcohol use, but there will be ubiquitous opposition to such actions as robbery, rape, and homicide. Crime is a quick and easy way for an individual to gain some personal advantage, but its *harm* to society is self-evident to everyone else. Thus, one's delinquency is likely to impact all manner of relationships, whether family, friends, work, or school. Bosses would oppose theft among their workers because presumably they can foresee themselves as future victims should they condone it. Friends often resent any assaults committed by their peers because the next time it could be them or their loved ones. While some people may be permissive toward the offending of others, most people will disapprove. Commit crime, according to social control theory, and you will find that people will change their opinion of you for the worse (with all of the attendant consequences that would follow).

## Empirical Evaluations

So, does the theory work? One complaint about learning criminological theory is that theory classes spend so much time presenting theories that sound good and then turn out to be wrong. The purpose of theory instructors doing this is not to dash students' hopes. All theories that have inspired scientists—even the wrong ones—appeal to common sense on some level. They have plausibility, and that is the trap for the unwary. To prevent ourselves from falling back into explanations of crime that have the fatal defect of not depicting reality, we have to know something about the empirical tests. Social control theories, it turns out, fare better than many other theories in this regard.

Much of the work on Hirschi's social control theory has focused on bonds between the individual and such institutions as the family, the school, and religion. Theorists have long attributed social problems to the breakdown of the family (e.g., Emile Durkheim); however, the family has not always been deemed important to the understanding of crime. Wilkinson (1974), for instance, noted that theorists' attention to the family was relatively intense during the early twentieth century, but had fallen from favor during the mid-twentieth century. Not surprisingly, the theories developed at this time, particularly differential association and strain theories, had almost nothing to say about the family. School, if it was mentioned at all in criminological theory during the mid-twentieth century, was linked with negative behaviors. Albert Cohen (1955) in particular targeted the school as the source of strain and subsequent malicious delinquency among lower-class boys, who invariably failed to meet the middle-class measuring rod established by their middle-class schoolmates and teachers.

Sheldon and Eleanor Glueck (1950) were responsible for much of the pioneering work on understanding how family factors—especially the quality of the relationships between children and parents—affected offending. Their own research had examined the level of supervision, the type of discipline parents used, as well as the level of affection between children and parents. The Gluecks examined the role of religious factors as well, finding that even while many delinquents attended church regularly, a higher proportion of nondelinquents did so. Ivan Nye (1958) reported similar patterns of results to that of the Gluecks. Nye found that families that had strained relationships among the members tended to have children who were more delinquent. Religious activity was also correlated somewhat with delinquency, with those who were more active religiously tending to be less delinquent. Nye's results, however, implicated the family as being the main force behind the religion–delinquency connection. Or, put another way, the reason why kids attended church and were less delinquent seemed to have more to do with the fact that they came from a closer and more cohesive family. The growing acceptance of the family among criminologists as a central determinant of problem behavior, and the newly created empirical literature supporting such a link, helped set the stage for Hirschi's landmark book.

Building from the work of the Gluecks and Nye, Travis Hirschi's (1969) *Causes of Delinquency* was important not only for its statement of social control theory, but also because it presented compelling evidence in support of that theory. Hirschi had collected data from over 4,000 adolescents attending schools in the San Francisco–Oakland area during the mid-1960s (the Richmond Youth Project). The data showed that children who had warm and close relationships with their parents—as measured by intimacy of communication, level of affection, and identification with parents—on average tended to be less delinquent than those children whose relationships with parents were not so close. It did not even matter if the parents were in poverty, as social bonds appeared to insulate children from delinquency. Or, put another way, it was in no way preordained that parents of lower socioeconomic status would produce delinquent children; strong bonds of attachment between parents and children remained effective barriers against offending whether one was rich or poor. Bonds of attachment and commitment with the school operated similarly, Hirschi found. Those kids who were most delinquent generally lacked educational accomplishments, disliked their school and teachers, and had less ambition to continue their education into college than their less-delinquent peers. The element of involvement, however, was not consistently connected with delinquency. That is, spending time doing conventional things did not seem to successfully inhibit offending.

In another paper, Hirschi and his colleague Rodney Stark (1969) examined the religiosity–delinquency connection using the Richmond Youth data. They considered many different dimensions of religiosity beyond attendance, such as moral values and belief in the supernatural. Their results were quite interesting. Attendance did not predict how strongly individuals held moral values or believed in the supernatural. Believing that one's moral lapses would be punished in the afterlife, or even whether one attended church or not, also had no connection with whether one offended. That is, the correlation between religion and delinquency was probably due to other factors.

Part of the scientific process involves other researchers independently replicating and verifying results. Empey and Lubeck (1971) compared family and school factors, finding that both contributed in a noteworthy way to delinquency. Michael Hindelang (1973) replicated Hirschi's results with respect to parental attachment corresponding with less delinquency, this time with a sample of youth living in upstate New York. Tests comparing the effect of the elements of the social bond on crime with other concepts, like differential association, however, seem to indicate that social bonds have a modest influence on crime while the measures of differential association have stronger effects (e.g., Conger, 1976). (I will have more on this finding, and its impact on social control theory, in the next section.) Kimberly Kempf-Leonard (1993) provides a detailed account of the research on Hirschi's theory over a period of two decades, most of which confirms Hirschi's original findings.

## Critiques

Theorists cannot foresee every contingency. Sometimes research results not anticipated by the theory—or indeed, results contrary to the theory—turn out to be true. Aspects of the theory might not survive scientific scrutiny, or do not seem to. Although criticism is seldom pleasant, skepticism and scrutiny are an essential part of the scientific process. You should not take the theorist at his or her word, especially when available credible facts seem to contradict some of the theory's predictions. Effective responses to criticism help maintain the vitality of a theory and enable it to grow. Note the qualifier "effective": Not all suggestions for revising theories are necessarily good suggestions. The theorist should (and often does) treat criticism and "constructive advice" with equal skepticism and scrutiny.

There are many criticisms of social control theory, far more than I can easily summarize here, but one issue would suffice to illustrate the process outlined just now. One question that Hirschi's social control theory has faced since its inception relates to the role of delinquent peers. Does having friends who commit crime have any causal impact on one's own crime? Hirschi dismissed the importance of criminal peers in delinquency causation. Indeed, his theory was clear that even delinquents would react negatively to their friends' acts of delinquency, so stronger attachment to criminal others should result in less rather than more delinquency. That did not turn out to be the case; apparently, strong attachment to delinquents was associated with more delinquency (Conger, 1976; Elliott et al., 1985). The peer effect still independently predicted crime, and moreover had a larger statistical influence on offending than measures of elements of the social bond. Proponents of social learning theory then argued that this was evidence against social control theory and in favor of their theory (see Akers & Sellers, 2004). Over a number of years, there were many efforts among criminologists to integrate social control and social learning theories, with the idea that peers teach their friends to commit crime (e.g., Elliott et al., 1985; Johnson, 1979; Thornberry, 1987).

Hirschi (1989) resisted these, observing that the two theories, if combined, would contain fatal internal contradictions (social control theories assume that crime is natural while social learning theories assume crime can only be learned; both assumptions cannot peacefully coexist). Yet the delinquent peer effect would not go away. Its presence forced social control theory to confront a fact seemingly in contradiction to its internal logic. Some commentators attempted to explain the role of delinquent peers without violating the assumptions of control theory. Marcus Felson (1998), for instance, argued that delinquent peers make delinquency easier, thus increasing the temptation of a crime by lowering its costs. Put another way, criminal friends do not teach criminality, but rather they create the situation allowing one's latent criminality greater scope of expression. After all, it is often easier to assault someone when one has several friends in support.

Others responding to the critics questioned whether studies demonstrating the importance of the peer effect even rested on sound data collection methods. If the data collection procedures are faulty, then the seemingly strong evidence supporting the delinquent peers–delinquency correlation is also faulty. Hirschi (1987) argued that the delinquent peers–delinquency connection is misleading for just this reason. Most studies of delinquent peers ask subjects to describe their friends. Hirschi claimed that what is likely happening is projection: That people, when describing their friends, in fact describe themselves. Haynie and Osgood (2005) reported results verifying that this seemed to be the case. Using data collected from the peers themselves, Haynie and Osgood found that the delinquent peer effect—which was once arguably the largest predictor of crime known—was modest. As you can see, criticism helped develop the ability of social control theory to account for new facts and even resulted in new questioning of well-established facts. Note that the end results of criticisms of criminological theory do not necessarily take the form the original critics had purposed.

## Theoretical Refinements

The deductive scientific process, as outlined in undergraduate research methods textbooks, begins with theory. Scientists then derive research questions from that theory, examine the data to see whether the theory successfully answers them, and then (if necessary) recommend refinements so that—in the next round of research—the theory might do better. In light of many years of research, researchers have looked upon Hirschi's social control theory and offered modifications. A number have proposed integrating social control theory with the other leading sociological theories of crime: differential association and strain theories being the foremost among these (e.g., Elliott et al., 1985; Thornberry, 1987). Whereas some of these integrated theories have generated research attention, almost none have resulted in particularly broad-based acceptance and interest among researchers. Perhaps Hirschi (1989) was correct: these theories sounded reasonable, but could offer no especially new risk factors for crime or research questions. Without the ability to support a sustained original research agenda, calls for theoretical integration as a means of developing social control theory have so far proved a dead end.

One refinement, however, has effectively supplanted Hirschi's theory as the leading model of social control. Hirschi's theory had left open the possibility that the strength of social bonds changed over a person's life span; however, by 1983 Hirschi and his colleague Michael Gottfredson explicitly rejected the value of life-course theories and ultimately held that criminality, once established in late childhood, stabilized and did not change (see Gottfredson & Hirschi, 1990). Put another way, if you were to rank three kids (Timmy, Joey, and Bob) based on their criminality at age 8, that same rank order would essentially hold at age 15 and any other age thereafter. One of the central debates of the 1980s and 1990s in criminology concerned the ability of criminological theory to explain the relationship between age and crime (Greenberg, 1985; Hirschi & Gottfredson, 1985, 1995; Sampson & Laub, 1995).

Sampson and Laub, using the data originally collected by the Gluecks (and that had been gathering dust in a filing cabinet at Harvard University for several decades), in 1993 published a book—*Crime in the Making*—that examined the connection of social bonds with crime over the life course. The underlying premise was that people can change with respect to their level of criminality over their lifetimes, and that social bonds were the primary agent for this happening. This section on social control theory includes a reading of Sampson and Laub's work and so I will not detail their theory here, but the essential features of Hirschi's social control theory exist in Sampson and Laub's framework. Their lasting contributions to social control theory consisted of the introduction of life-course concepts and methodology to research on the effects of social bonds.

Citations in many dozens of journal articles and PhD dissertations attest to the importance of Sampson and Laub's work (see Piquero & Mazerolle, 2001). Several studies are representative of this literature. Sampson and Laub's (1993) research of the Glueck data, like Hirschi's (1969), was supportive of their theory and highly influential. A few years later, Julie Horney and her colleagues (1995) examined a sample of ex-offenders to see whether turning points (e.g., living with a girlfriend or wife, finding work) influenced the former stability of their offending patterns. Their results indicated that the emergence and termination of social bonds in many cases resulted in short-term fluctuation in individual crime patterns. More recently, Sampson, Laub, and Wimer (2006) reported that marriage had a substantial causal influence on crime. Presently, one of the central debates regarding the future direction of life-course theories of crime concerns the existence of multiple "types" of offenders, each with unique points of origin and patterns of crime over the life span (e.g., Nagin & Tremblay, 2005a, 2005b; Sampson & Laub, 2003, 2005). Suffice to say that the presence of distinct classes of offenders would have a profound effect on the evolution of social control theory, and, as noted earlier, Sampson and Laub (like Hirschi) are tough in responding to their critics. The next stage of development for social control theory is not yet clear, but something new may well emerge in response to this debate or—more likely—something new will come from a completely unexpected direction or set of research findings.

## Policy Implications

Ultimately, the object of understanding how crime happens is to guide society's response. If we know the reasons crime flourishes, then by removing those reasons we can lessen the amount of crime.

Hirschi (1969), in outlining his theory, actually had little to say about policy. He later would publish or coauthor policy papers where he clearly indicated his sentiments on what needed to be done about the crime problem as well as how the currently favored policies create difficulties. Most criminal justice responses to crime follow what Gottfredson and Hirschi (1995) described as the "administrative criminology" model. That is, our policy initiatives designed to deal with crime focus primarily on strengthening the criminal justice system by increasing funding for law enforcement, eliminating problematic civil liberties (so police can "do their jobs"), and toughening sanctions against offenders. These approaches to crime control reflect not so much an objective analysis of the crime problem but rather the vested interests of policy decision makers within the criminal justice system. The approach is rather like: "We—and only we—can solve the crime problem and protect you from the evil-doers who wish to harm you."

Social control theories are very much critical of this approach. As noted earlier, social control theories are skeptical of the value of the legal system as a barrier against crime.

Moreover, if the weakness of social bonds is the root of the crime problem, then it follows that strengthening the ties between the individual and society would produce a person with an interest in conformity. Does sending people to prison—removing them from their jobs, family, or children—strengthen their bonds with society? Or does it leave them, upon release, with nothing to lose?

Thus, the most straightforward way to reduce the crime problem, according to the theory, is to help individuals intensify their relationships with society. This is trickier than it sounds. One cannot simply give an offender a spouse and children and a job. Consider the following two situations and answer the question: Who is more likely to value a relationship?

1. A person who worked hard to develop the relationship.
2. A person who had the relationship given, and was not obliged to stake much time or effort in developing the relationship.

This perhaps helps explain such otherwise baffling crimes as that of Jamar Hornsby. Hornsby was a full-scholarship football player at the University of Florida and was potentially a starter. One of his teammates and the teammate's girlfriend had been killed in an accident, and Hornsby offered to help the dead player's parents box up their son's belongings. Hornsby helped himself as well, and stole the girlfriend's credit card. He then proceeded to run up over $3,000 in charges, which earned him a criminal charge and got him booted from the team. The point here is to show that people can be offered opportunities to develop stakes in conformity, but they are more apt to squander them. This situation is not unlike that of lottery winners who blow through all their money. This problem of how to get people to respect social bonds is one of the policy challenges of social control theory.

Life-course theories add that offenders require age-appropriate intervention. Family interventions, for instance, would make the most sense at shaping young children. Interventions might include training parents on how to observe their child's behavior and punish inappropriate conduct. Indeed, the work of some scholars indicates that such programs reduce harsh and inconsistent parenting, resulting in children who appear better adjusted in school (e.g., Tremblay et al., 1992). We do not know much about how Eric Harris's and Dylan Klebold's parents did their jobs, but we can surmise that for whatever reason they did not supervise their children or inspire in them love and trust. Consequently, they were free to do as they pleased, with tragic consequences in this case. The readings in this section may help us better understand such happenings and be more sensitive to what it takes to prevent them.

# SELF-CONTROL THEORY

## A GENERAL THEORY OF CRIME

*Michael R. Gottfredson and Travis Hirschi*

### The Nature of Criminality: Low Self-Control

Theories of crime lead naturally to interest in the propensities of individuals committing criminal acts. These propensities are often labeled "criminality." In pure classical theory, people committing criminal acts had no special propensities. They merely followed the universal tendency to enhance their own pleasure. If they differed from noncriminals, it was with respect to their location in or comprehension of relevant sanction systems. For example, the individual cut off from the community will suffer less than others from the ostracism that follows crime; the individual unaware of the natural or legal consequences of criminal behavior cannot be controlled by these consequences to the degree that people aware of them are controlled; the atheist will not be as concerned as the believer about penalties to be exacted in a life beyond death. Classical theories on the whole, then, are today called *control* theories, theories emphasizing the prevention of crime through consequences painful to the individual.

Although, for policy purposes, classical theorists emphasized legal consequences, the importance to them of moral sanctions is so obvious that their theories might well be called underdeveloped *social control* theories. In fact, Bentham's list of the major restraining motives—motives acting to prevent mischievous acts—begins with goodwill, love of reputation, and the desire for amity. He goes on to say that fear of detection prevents crime in large part because of detection's consequences for "reputation, and the desire for amity." Put another way, in Bentham's view, the restraining power of legal sanctions in large part stems from their connection to social sanctions.

If crime is evidence of the weakness of social motives, it follows that criminals are less social than noncriminals and that the extent of their asociality may be determined by the nature and number of their crimes. Calculation of the extent of an individual's mischievousness is a complex affair, but in general the more mischievous or depraved the offenses, and the greater their number, the more mischievous or depraved the offender. (Classical theorists thus had reason to be interested in the seriousness of the offense. The relevance of seriousness to current theories of crime is not so clear.)

Because classical or control theories infer that offenders are not restrained by social motives, it is common to think of them as emphasizing an asocial human nature. Actually, such theories make people only as asocial as their acts require. Pure or consistent control theories do not add criminality (i.e., personality concepts or attributes such as "aggressiveness" or "extraversion") to individuals beyond that found in their criminal acts. As a result, control theories are suspicious of images of an antisocial, psychopathic, or career offender, or of an offender whose motives to crime are somehow larger than those given in the crimes themselves. Indeed, control theories are compatible with the view that the balance of the total control structure favors conformity, even among offenders. . . .

Positivism brought with it the idea that criminals differ from noncriminals in ways more radical than this, the idea that criminals carry within themselves properties peculiarly and positively conducive to crime. Being friendly to both the classical and positivist traditions, we expected to end up with a list of individual properties reliably identified by competent research as useful in the description of "criminality"—such properties as aggressiveness, body build, activity level, and intelligence. We further expected that we would be able to connect these individual-level correlates of criminality directly to the classical idea of crime. As our review progressed, however, we were forced to conclude that we had overestimated the success of positivism in establishing important differences between "criminals" and "noncriminals" beyond their tendency to commit criminal acts. Stable individual differences in the tendency to commit criminal acts were clearly evident, but many or even most of the other differences between offenders and nonoffenders were not as clear or pronounced as our reading of the literature had led us to expect.

If individual differences in the tendency to commit criminal acts (within an overall tendency for crime to decline with age) are at least potentially explicable within classical theory by reference to the social location of individuals and their comprehension of how the world works, the fact remains that classical theory cannot shed much light on the positivistic finding (denied by most positivistic theories) that these differences *remain reasonably stable with change in the social location of individuals and change in their knowledge of the operation of sanction systems.* This is the problem of self-control, the differential tendency of people to avoid criminal acts whatever the circumstances in which they find themselves. Since this difference among people has attracted a variety of names, we begin by arguing the merits of the concept of self-control.

### Self-control and alternative concepts

Our decision to ascribe stable individual differences in criminal behavior to self-control was made only after considering several alternatives, one of which (criminality) we had used before. A major consideration was consistency between the classical conception of crime and our conception of the criminal. It seemed unwise to try to integrate a choice theory of crime with a deterministic image of the offender, especially when such integration was unnecessary. In fact, the compatibility of the classical view of crime and the idea that people differ in self-control is, in our view, remarkable. As we have seen, classical theory is a theory of social or external control, a theory based on the idea that the costs of crime depend on the individual's current location in or bond to society. What classical theory lacks is an explicit idea of self-control, the idea that people also differ in the extent to which they are vulnerable to the temptations of the moment. Combining the two ideas thus merely recognizes the simultaneous existence of social and individual restraints on behavior. . . .

We are now in position to describe the nature of self-control, the individual characteristic relevant to the commission of criminal acts. We assume that the nature of this characteristic can be derived directly from the nature of criminal acts. We thus infer from the nature of crime what people who refrain from criminal acts are like before they reach the age at which crime becomes a logical possibility. We then work back further to the factors producing their restraint, back to the causes of self-control. In our view, lack of self-control does not require crime and can be counteracted by situational conditions or other properties of the individual. At the same time, we suggest that high self-control effectively reduces the possibility of crime—that is, those possessing it will be substantially less likely at all periods of life to engage in criminal acts.

### The elements of self-control

Criminal acts provide *immediate* gratification of desires. A major characteristic of people with low self-control is therefore a tendency to respond to tangible stimuli in the immediate environment, to have a concrete "here and now" orientation. People with high self-control, in contrast, tend to defer gratification.

Criminal acts provide *easy or simple* gratification of desires. They provide money without work, sex without courtship, revenge without court delays. People lacking self-control also tend to lack diligence, tenacity, or persistence in a course of action.

Criminal acts are *exciting, risky, or thrilling.* They involve stealth, danger, speed, agility, deception, or power. People lacking self-control therefore tend to be adventuresome, active, and physical. Those with high levels of self-control tend to be cautious, cognitive, and verbal.

Crimes provide *few or meager long-term benefits.* They are not equivalent to a job or a career. On the contrary, crimes interfere with long-term commitments to jobs, marriages, family, or friends. People with low self-control thus tend to have unstable marriages, friendships, and job profiles. They tend to be little interested in and unprepared for long-term occupational pursuits.

Crimes require *little skill or planning.* The cognitive requirements for most crimes are minimal. It follows that people lacking self-control need not possess or value cognitive or academic skills. The manual skills required for most crimes are minimal. It follows that people lacking self-control need not possess manual skills that require training or apprenticeship.

Crimes often result in *pain or discomfort for the victim.* Property is lost, bodies are injured, privacy is violated, trust is broken. It follows that people with low self-control tend to be self-centered, indifferent, or insensitive to the suffering and needs of others. It does not follow, however, that people with low self-control are routinely unkind or antisocial. On the contrary, they may discover the immediate and easy rewards of charm and generosity.

Recall that crime involves the pursuit of immediate pleasure. It follows that people lacking self-control will also tend to pursue immediate pleasures that are *not* criminal: they will tend to smoke, drink, use drugs, gamble, have children out of wedlock, and engage in illicit sex.

Crimes require the interaction of an offender with people or their property. It does not follow that people lacking self-control will tend to be gregarious or social. However, it does follow that, other things being equal, gregarious or social people are more likely to be involved in criminal acts.

The major benefit of many crimes is not pleasure but relief from momentary irritation. The irritation caused by a crying child is often the stimulus for physical abuse. That caused by a taunting stranger in a bar is often the stimulus for aggravated assault. It follows that people with low self-control tend to have minimal tolerance for frustration and little ability to respond to conflict through verbal rather than physical means.

Crimes involve the risk of violence and physical injury, of pain and suffering on the part of the offender. It does not follow that people with low self-control will tend to be tolerant of physical pain or to be indifferent to physical discomfort. It does follow that people tolerant of physical pain or indifferent to physical discomfort will be more likely to engage in criminal acts whatever their level of self-control.

The risk of criminal penalty for any given criminal act is small, but this depends in part on the circumstances of the offense. Thus, for example, not all joyrides by teenagers are equally likely to result in arrest. A car stolen from a neighbor and returned unharmed before he notices its absence is less likely to result in official notice than is a car stolen from a shopping center parking lot and abandoned at the convenience of the offender. Drinking alcohol stolen from parents and consumed in the family garage is less likely to receive official notice than drinking in the parking lot outside a concert hall. It follows that offenses differ in their validity as measures of self-control: those offenses with large risk of public awareness are better measures than those with little risk.

In sum, people who lack self-control will tend to be impulsive, insensitive, physical (as opposed to mental), risk-taking, short-sighted, and nonverbal, and they will tend therefore to engage in criminal and analogous acts. Since these traits can be identified prior to the age of responsibility for crime, since there is considerable tendency for these traits to come together in the same people, and since the traits tend to persist through life, it seems reasonable to consider them as comprising a stable construct useful in the explanation of crime.

### The many manifestations of low self-control

Our image of the "offender" suggests that crime is not an automatic or necessary consequence of low self-control. It suggests that many noncriminal acts analogous to crime (such as accidents, smoking, and alcohol use) are also manifestations of low self-control. Our image therefore implies that no specific act, type of crime, or form of deviance is uniquely required by the absence of self-control.

Because both crime and analogous behaviors stem from low self-control (that is, both are manifestations of low self-control), they will all be engaged in at a relatively high rate by people with low self-control. Within the domain of crime, then, there will be much versatility among offenders in the criminal acts in which they engage.

Research on the versatility of deviant acts supports these predictions in the strongest possible way. The variety of manifestations of low self-control is immense. In spite of years of tireless research motivated by a belief in specialization, no credible evidence of specialization has been reported. In fact, the evidence of offender versatility is overwhelming.

By versatility we mean that offenders commit a wide variety of criminal acts, with no strong inclination to pursue a specific criminal act or a pattern of criminal acts to the exclusion of others. Most theories suggest that offenders tend to specialize, whereby such terms as robber, burglar, drug dealer, rapist, and murderer have predictive or descriptive import. In fact, some theories create offender specialization as part of their explanation of crime. For example, Cloward and Ohlin create distinctive subcultures of delinquency around particular forms of criminal behavior, identifying subcultures specializing in theft, violence, or drugs. In a related way, books are written about white-collar crime as though it were a clearly distinct specialty requiring a unique explanation. Research projects are undertaken for the study of drug use, or vandalism, or teen pregnancy (as though every study of delinquency were not a study of drug use and vandalism and teenage sexual behavior). Entire schools of criminology emerge to pursue patterning, sequencing, progression, escalation, onset, persistence, and desistance in the career of offenses or offenders. These efforts survive largely because their proponents fail to consider or acknowledge the clear evidence to the contrary. Other reasons for survival of such ideas may be found in the interest of politicians and members of the law enforcement community who see policy potential in criminal careers or "career criminals."

Occasional reports of specialization seem to contradict this point, as do everyday observations of repetitive misbehavior by particular offenders. Some offenders rob the same store repeatedly over a period of years, or an offender commits several rapes over a (brief) period of time. Such offenders may be called "robbers" or "rapists." However, it should be noted that such labels are retrospective rather than predictive and that they typically ignore a large amount of delinquent or criminal behavior by the same offenders that is inconsistent with their alleged specialty. Thus, for example, the "rapist" will tend also to use drugs, to commit robberies and burglaries (often in concert with the rape), and to have a record for violent offenses other than rape. There is a perhaps natural tendency on the part of observers (and in official accounts) to focus on the most serious crimes in a series of events, but this tendency should not be confused with a tendency on the part of the offender to specialize in one kind of crime.

Recall that one of the defining features of crime is that it is simple and easy. Some apparent specialization will therefore occur because obvious opportunities for an easy score will tend to repeat themselves. An offender who lives next to a shopping area that is approached by pedestrians will have repeat opportunities for purse snatching, and this may show in his arrest record. But even here the specific "criminal career" will tend to quickly run its course and to be followed by offenses whose content and character is likewise determined by convenience and opportunity (which is the reason why some form of theft is always the best bet about what a person is likely to do next).

The evidence that offenders are likely to engage in noncriminal acts psychologically or theoretically equivalent to crime is, because of the relatively high rates of these "noncriminal" acts, even easier to document. Thieves are likely to smoke, drink, and skip school at considerably higher rates than nonthieves. Offenders are considerably more likely than nonoffenders to be involved in most types of accidents, including household fires, auto crashes, and unwanted pregnancies. They are also considerably more likely to die at an early age.

Good research on drug use and abuse routinely reveals that the correlates of delinquency and drug use are the same. As Akers has noted, "compared to the abstaining teenager, the drinking, smoking, and drug-taking teen is much more likely to be getting into fights, stealing, hurting other people, and committing other delinquencies." Akers goes on to say, "but the variation in the order in which they take up these things leaves little basis for proposing the causation of one by the other." In our view, the relation between drug use and delinquency is not a causal question. The correlates are the same because drug use and delinquency are both manifestations of an underlying tendency to pursue short-term, immediate pleasure. This underlying tendency (i.e., lack of self-control) has many manifestations, as listed by Harrison Gough:

> unconcern over the rights and privileges of others when recognizing them would interfere with personal satisfaction in any way; impulsive behavior, or apparent incongruity between the strength of the stimulus and the magnitude of the behavioral response; inability to form deep or persistent attachments to other persons or to identify in interpersonal relationships; poor judgment and planning in attaining defined goals; apparent lack of anxiety and distress

over social maladjustment and unwillingness or inability to consider maladjustment qua maladjustment; a tendency to project blame onto others and to take no responsibility for failures; meaningless prevarication, often about trivial matters in situations where detection is inevitable; almost complete lack of dependability . . . and willingness to assume responsibility; and, finally, emotional poverty.

. . .

Note that these outcomes are consistent with four general elements of our notion of low self-control: basic stability of individual differences over a long period of time; great variability in the kinds of criminal acts engaged in; conceptual or causal equivalence of criminal and noncriminal acts; and inability to predict the specific forms of deviance engaged in, whether criminal or noncriminal. In our view, the idea of an antisocial personality defined by certain behavioral consequences is too positivistic or deterministic, suggesting that the offender must do certain things given his antisocial personality. Thus we would say only that the subjects in question are *more likely* to commit criminal acts (as the data indicate they are). We do not make commission of criminal acts part of the definition of the individual with low self-control.

Be this as it may, retrospective research shows that predictions derived from a concept of antisocial personality are highly consistent with the results of prospective longitudinal and cross-sectional research: offenders do not specialize; they tend to be involved in accidents, illness, and death at higher rates than the general population; they tend to have difficulty persisting in a job regardless of the particular characteristics of the job (no job will turn out to be a good job); they have difficulty acquiring and retaining friends; and they have difficulty meeting the demands of long-term financial commitments (such as mortgages or car payments) and the demands of parenting.

Seen in this light, the "costs" of low self-control for the individual may far exceed the costs of his criminal acts. In fact, it appears that crime is often among the least serious consequences of a lack of self-control in terms of the quality of life of those lacking it.

### The causes of self-control

We know better what deficiencies in self-control lead to than where they come from. One thing is, however, clear: low self-control is not produced by training, tutelage, or socialization. As a matter of fact, all of the characteristics associated with low self-control tend to show themselves in the absence of nurturance, discipline, or training. Given the classical appreciation of the causes of human behavior, the implications of this fact are straightforward: the causes of low self-control are negative rather than positive; self-control is unlikely in the absence of effort, intended or unintended, to create it. (This assumption separates the present theory from most modern theories of crime, where the offender is automatically seen as a product of positive forces, a creature of learning, particular pressures, or specific defect.

At this point it would be easy to construct a theory of crime causation, according to which characteristics of potential offenders lead them ineluctably to the commission of criminal acts. Our task at this point would simply be to identify the likely sources of impulsiveness, intelligence, risk-taking, and the like. But to do so would be to follow the path that has proven so unproductive in the past, the path according to which criminals commit crimes irrespective of the characteristics of the setting or situation.

We can avoid this pitfall by recalling the elements inherent in the decision to commit a criminal act. The object of the offense is clearly pleasurable, and universally so. Engaging in the act, however, entails some risk of social, legal, and/or natural sanctions. Whereas the pleasure attained by the act is direct, obvious, and immediate, the pains risked by it are not obvious, or direct, and are in any event at greater remove from it. It follows that, though there will be little variability among people in their ability to see the pleasures of crime, there will be considerable variability in their ability to calculate potential pains. But the problem goes further than this: whereas the pleasures of crime are reasonably equally distributed over the population, this is not true for the pains. Everyone appreciates money; not everyone dreads parental anger or disappointment upon learning that the money was stolen.

So, the dimensions of self-control are, in our view, factors affecting calculation of the consequences of one's acts. The impulsive or short-sighted person fails to consider the negative or painful consequences of his acts; the insensitive person has fewer negative consequences to consider; the less intelligent person also has fewer negative consequences to consider (has less to lose).

No known social group, whether criminal or noncriminal, actively or purposefully attempts to reduce the self-control of its members. Social life is not enhanced by low self-control and its consequences. On the contrary, the exhibition of these tendencies undermines harmonious group relations and the ability to achieve collective ends. These facts explicitly deny that a tendency to crime is a product of socialization, culture, or positive learning of any sort.

The traits composing low self-control are also not conducive to the achievement of long-term individual goals. On the contrary, they impede educational and occupational achievement, destroy interpersonal relations, and undermine physical health and economic well-being. Such facts explicitly deny the notion that criminality is an alternative route to the goals otherwise obtainable through legitimate avenues. It follows that people who care about the interpersonal skill, educational and occupational achievement, and physical and economic well-being of those in their care will seek to rid them of these traits.

Two general sources of variation are immediately apparent in this scheme. The first is the variation among children in the degree to which they manifest such traits to begin with. The second is the variation among caretakers in the degree to which they recognize low self-control and its consequences and the degree to which they are willing and able to correct it. Obviously, therefore, even at this threshold level the sources of low self-control are complex.

There is good evidence that some of the traits predicting subsequent involvement in crime appear as early as they can be reliably measured, including low intelligence, high activity level, physical strength, and adventuresomeness. The evidence suggests that the connection between these traits and commission of criminal acts ranges from weak to moderate. Obviously, we do not suggest that people are born criminals, inherit a gene for criminality, or anything of the sort. In fact, we explicitly deny such notions. What we do suggest is that individual differences may have an impact on the prospects for effective socialization (or adequate control). Effective socialization is, however, always possible whatever the configuration of individual traits.

Other traits affecting crime appear later and seem to be largely products of ineffective or incomplete socialization. For example, differences in impulsivity and insensitivity become noticeable later in childhood when they are no longer common to all children. The ability and willingness to delay immediate gratification for some larger purpose may therefore be assumed to be a consequence of training. Much parental action is in fact geared toward suppression of impulsive behavior, toward making the child consider the long-range consequences of acts. Consistent sensitivity to the needs and feelings of others may also be assumed to be a consequence of training. Indeed, much parental behavior is directed toward teaching the child about the rights and feelings of others, and of how these rights and feelings ought to constrain the child's behavior. All of these points focus our attention on child-rearing.

### Child-rearing and self-control: The family

The major "cause" of low self-control thus appears to be ineffective child-rearing. Put in positive terms, several conditions appear necessary to produce a socialized child. Perhaps the place to begin looking for these conditions is the research literature on the relation between family conditions and delinquency. This research has examined the connection between many family factors and delinquency. It reports that discipline, supervision, and affection tend to be missing in the homes of delinquents, that the behavior of the parents is often "poor"; and that the parents of delinquents are unusually likely to have criminal records themselves. Indeed, according to Michael Ruter and Henri Giller, "of the parental characteristics associated with delinquency, criminality is the most striking and most consistent."

Such information undermines the many explanations of crime that ignore the family, but in this form it does not represent much of an advance over the belief of the general public (and those who deal with offenders in the criminal justice system) that "defective upbringing" or "neglect" in the home is the primary cause of crime.

To put these standard research findings in perspective, we think it necessary to define the conditions necessary for adequate child-rearing to occur. The minimum conditions seem to be these: in order to teach the child self-control, someone must (1) monitor the child's behavior; (2) recognize deviant behavior when it occurs; and (3) punish such behavior. This seems simple and obvious enough. All that is required to activate the system is affection for *or* investment in the child. The person who cares for the child will watch his behavior, see him doing things he should not do, and correct him. The result may be a child more capable of delaying gratification, more sensitive to the interests and desires of others, more independent, more willing to accept restraints on his activity, and more unlikely to use force or violence to attain his ends.

When we seek the causes of low self-control, we ask where this system can go wrong. Obviously, parents do not prefer their children to be unsocialized in the terms described. We can therefore rule out in advance the possibility of positive socialization to unsocialized behavior (as cultural or subcultural deviance theories suggest). Still, the system can go wrong at any one of four places. First, the parents may not care for the child (in which case none of the other conditions would be met); second, the parents, even if they care, may not have the time or energy to monitor the child's behavior; third, the parents, even if they care *and* monitor, may not see anything wrong with the child's behavior; finally, even if everything else is in place, the parents may not have the inclination or the means to punish the child. So, what may appear at first glance to be nonproblematic turns out to be problematic indeed. Many things can go wrong. According to much research in crime and delinquency, in the homes of problem children many things have gone wrong: "Parents of stealers do not track ([they] do not interpret stealing . . . as 'deviant'); they do not punish; and they do not care."

Let us apply this scheme to some of the facts about the connection between child socialization and crime, beginning with the elements of the child-rearing model.

**The attachment of the parent to the child.** Our model states that parental concern for the welfare or behavior of the child is a necessary condition for successful child-rearing. Because it is too often assumed that all parents are alike in their love for their children, the evidence directly on this point is not as good or extensive as it could be. However, what exists is clearly consistent with the model. Glueck and Glueck report that, compared to the fathers of delinquents, fathers of nondelinquents were twice as likely to be warmly disposed toward their sons and one-fifth as likely to be hostile toward them. In the same sample, 28 percent of the mothers of delinquents were characterized as "indifferent or hostile" toward the child as compared to 4 percent of the mothers of nondelinquents. The evidence suggests that stepparents are especially unlikely to have feelings of affection toward their stepchildren, adding in contemporary society to the likelihood that children will be "reared" by people who do not especially care for them.

**Parental supervision.** The connection between social control and self-control could not be more direct than in the case of parental supervision of the child. Such supervision presumably prevents criminal or analogous acts and at the same time trains the child to avoid them on his own. Consistent with this assumption, supervision tends to be a major predictor of delinquency, however supervision or delinquency is measured.

Our general theory in principle provides a method of separating supervision as external control from supervision as internal control. For one thing, offenses differ in the degree to which they can be prevented through monitoring; children at one age are monitored much more closely than children at other ages; girls are supervised more closely than boys. In some situations, monitoring is universal or nearly constant; in other situations monitoring for some offenses is virtually absent. In the present context, however, the concern is with the connection between supervision and self-control, a connection established by the stronger tendency of those poorly supervised when young to commit crimes as adults.

**Recognition of deviant behavior.** In order for supervision to have an impact on self-control, the supervisor must perceive deviant behavior when it occurs. Remarkably, not all parents are adept at recognizing lack of self-control. Some parents allow the child to do pretty much as he pleases without interference. Extensive television-viewing is one modern example, as is the failure to require completion of homework, to prohibit smoking, to curtail the use of physical force, or to see to it that the child actually attends school. (As noted, truancy among second-graders presumably reflects on the adequacy of parental awareness of the child's misbehavior.) Again, the research is not as good as it should be, but evidence of "poor conduct standards" in the homes of delinquents is common.

**Punishment of deviant acts.** Control theories explicitly acknowledge the necessity of sanctions in preventing criminal behavior. They do not suggest that the major sanctions are legal or corporal. On the contrary, as we have seen, they suggest that disapproval by people one cares about is the most powerful of sanctions. Effective punishment by the parent or major caretaker therefore usually entails nothing more than explicit disapproval of unwanted behavior. The criticism of control theories that dwells on their alleged cruelty is therefore simply misguided or ill informed.

Not all caretakers punish effectively. In fact, some are too harsh and some are too lenient. Given our model, however, rewarding good behavior cannot compensate for failure to correct deviant behavior.

Given the consistency of the child-rearing model with our general theory and with the research literature, it should be possible to use it to explain other family correlates of criminal and otherwise deviant behavior.

*Parental criminality.* Our theory focuses on the connection between the self-control of the parent and the subsequent self-control of the child. There is good reason to expect, and the data confirm, that people lacking self-control do not socialize their children well. According to Donald West and David Farrington, "the fact that delinquency is transmitted from one generation to the next is indisputable." Of course our theory does not allow transmission of criminality, genetic or otherwise. However, it does allow us to predict that some people are more likely than others to fail to socialize their children and that this will be a consequence of their own inadequate socialization. The extent of this connection between parent and child socialization is revealed by the fact that in the West and Farrington study fewer than 5 percent of the families accounted for almost half of the criminal convictions in the entire sample. (In our view, this finding is more important for the theory of crime, and for public policy, than the much better-known finding of Wolfgang and his colleagues that something like 6 percent of *individual* offenders account for about half of all criminal acts.) In order to achieve such concentration of crime in a small number of families, it is necessary that the parents and the brothers and sisters of offenders also be unusually likely to commit criminal acts.

Why should the children of offenders be unusually vulnerable to crime? Recall that our theory assumes that criminality is not something the parents have to work to produce; on the contrary, it assumes that criminality is something they have to work to avoid. Consistent with this view, parents with criminal records do *not* encourage crime in their children and are in fact as disapproving of it as parents with no record of criminal involvement. Of course, not wanting criminal behavior in one's children and being upset when it occurs do not necessarily imply that great effort has been expended to prevent it. If criminal behavior is oriented toward short-term rewards, and if child-rearing is oriented toward long-term rewards, there is little reason to expect parents themselves lacking self-control to be particularly adept at instilling self-control in their children.

Consistent with this expectation, research consistently indicates that the supervision of delinquents in families where parents have criminal records tends to be "lax," "inadequate," or "poor." Punishment in these families also tends to be easy, short-term, and insensitive— that is, yelling and screaming, slapping and hitting, with threats that are not carried out.

Such facts do not, however, completely account for the concentration of criminality among some families. A major reason for this failure is probably that the most subtle element of child-rearing is not included in the analysis. This is the element of *recognition* of deviant behavior. Many parents do not even recognize *criminal* behavior in their children, let alone the minor forms of deviance whose punishment is necessary for effective child-rearing. For example, when children steal outside the home, some parents discount reports that they have done so on the grounds that the charges are unproved and cannot therefore be used to justify punishment. By the same token, when children are suspended for misbehavior at school, some parents side with the child and blame the episode on prejudicial mistreatment by teachers. Obviously, parents who cannot see the misbehavior of their children are in no position to correct it, even if they are inclined to do so.

Given that recognition of deviant acts is a necessary component of the child-rearing model, research is needed on the question of what parents should and should not recognize as deviant behavior if they are to prevent criminality. To the extent our theory is correct, parents need to know behaviors that reflect low self-control. That many parents are not now attentive to such behaviors should come as no surprise. The idea that criminal behavior is the product of deprivation or positive learning dominates modern theory. As a consequence, most influential social scientific theories of crime and delinquency ignore or deny the connection between crime and talking back, yelling, pushing and shoving, insisting on getting one's way, trouble in school, and poor school performance. Little wonder, then, that some parents do not see the significance of such acts. Research now makes it clear that parents differ in their reaction to these behaviors, with some parents attempting to correct behaviors that others ignore or even defend. Because social science in general sees little connection between these acts and crime, there has been little systematic integration of the child development and criminological literatures. Furthermore, because the conventional wisdom disputes the connection between child training and crime, public policy has not focused on it. We do not argue that crime is caused by these early misbehaviors. Instead, we argue that such behaviors indicate the presence of the major individual-level cause of crime, a cause that in principle may be attacked by punishing these early manifestations. Nor do we argue that criminal acts automatically follow early evidence of low self-control. Because crime requires more than low self-control, some parents are lucky and have children with low self-control who still manage to avoid acts that would bring them to the attention of the criminal justice system. It is less likely (in fact unlikely), however, that such children will avoid altogether behavior indicative of low self-control. Put another way, low self-control predicts low self-control better than it predicts any of its specific manifestations, such as crime.

# CONTEMPORARY RETROSPECTIVE ON SELF-CONTROL THEORY

## OVERVIEW OF SELF-CONTROL THEORY

*Nicole Leeper Piquero, Virginia Comonwealth University; and*
*Alex R. Piquero, University of Maryland*

Building off of a frustration with criminological theory's inability to account for the enduring relationship between age and crime, Gottfredson and Hirschi's (1990) *A General Theory of Crime* outlined a theory of crime that set out to distinguish crime from criminality. In doing so, they focused on answering one important question: what do all crimes have in common? After defining crime as an event involving force or fraud that satisfies self-interest, the authors (p. 15) contended that all crimes have several character-istics in common. That is, crimes are easy to commit, require little skill or systematic plan-ning, and, perhaps most importantly, bring the offender immediate excitement and pleasure (p. 20). In other words, the motivation for crime is the pursuit of self-interest.

Given this nature of crime, the authors hypothesized that the principal cause of crime and other risk-taking behaviors over the life course is an enduring and stable individual characteristic they termed low self-control. It is comprised of six elements: impulsivity, preference for simple tasks, risk-seeking, a preference for physical as opposed to men-tal tasks, self-centeredness, and a quick temper. Further, the six elements are believed to coalesce in the same person. As defined by Gottfredson and Hirschi (1990), low self-control is the inability to defer immediate gratification. As such, when those with lower levels of self-control (i.e., offenders) are confronted with opportunities to engage in crimi-nal behavior, they tend to cast aside considerations of long-term costs associated with acts of force and fraud and instead focus on and seize the momentary benefits that they believe the criminal acts produce.

Low self-control is believed to be crystallized by early adolescence (generally by age eight) as a result of poor parental practices; that is, when parents fail to monitor their child's behavior, recognize the child's deviant behavior, and appropriately punish the delin-quent behavior. Differences in levels of self-control between persons are believed to be relatively stable over the life course. Thus, while individuals can gain or lose self-control, the relative ranking differences between individuals remains similar. In short, individuals with lower amounts of self-control in adolescence will tend to also have and display lower amounts of self-control in adulthood. Furthermore, as deficiencies in self-control are dif-ficult to overcome once set into motion, external life events such as marriage and employ-ment will do little to alter or repair the shortcomings associated with low self-control.

Persons low in self-control will also manifest these self-control deficiencies across an array of crime and noncrime domains, including health, education, employment, alco-hol and drug use, and relationship problems. The reach of these self-control problems is such that individuals low in self-control will tend not to concentrate their involvement in problematic behaviors in any one particular domain but will experience similar problems across many if not all domains of life. Thus, Gottfredson and Hirschi (1990) suggest a versatility thesis that views offenders as being adaptable and able to engage in a full array of negative behaviors as the various opportunities present themselves. The prospects for changing individuals with already established levels of low self-control are virtually zero, and there does not appear to be much that can be done with respect to deterring the behavior of these individuals via the criminal justice system. Therefore, the best policy responses seem to lie in (1) the development of self-control early in the life course, gear-ing parenting efforts to instill adequate self-control in children, and ensuring, as best as possible, that parents themselves do not have self-control problems that they will transmit to their offspring; and (2) in altering criminal opportunities.

## Critiques

Since its original formulation and statement, the general theory of crime has been subject to a number of theoretical and empirical critiques. Seven specific critiques are outlined here. The first and perhaps most challenging critique emerged from social learning theorist

Ronald Akers (1991), and concerned the linkage between the independent and dependent variables in the general theory. Akers contends that the use of self-control as an organizing construct to explain the many alternative manifestations of deficiencies in self-control amounts to a tautological argument that renders the theory untestable. Akers (2000) argues that since Gottfredson and Hirschi hypothesize that low self-control is the cause of the propensity toward criminal behavior and do not define self-control separately from this propensity, that the propensity toward crime and low self-control appear to be one in the same. In other words, low self-control causes low self-control (p. 112).

Second, many commentators believed that Gottfredson and Hirschi provided the criminological community with very little guidance on how best to operationalize and empirically measure self-control. Therefore, early research conducted by Grasmick, Tittle, Bursik, and Arneklev (1993) utilized a 24-item self-report scale that measures self-control as a unidimensional construct comprised of the six attitudinal measures laid out in the theory. Other researchers prefer to rely on behavioral indicators of self-control (Evans, Cullen, Burton, Dunaway, & Benson, 1997; Keane, Maxim, & Teevan, 1993; Paternoster & Brame, 1998), which allowed for the tautology critique to reemerge. The issue of tautology once again emerges as part of the methodological critique when low self-control is viewed as the cause of both crime and analogous behaviors, especially when the analogous behaviors are used as measures of low self-control in predicting crime (Pratt & Cullen, 2000; Stylianou, 2002). In further examining the methodological issues some research suggests that it does not matter whether an attitudinal or behavioral measure of self-control is used, since each taps into a different aspect of self-control and the results appear to be in the expected directions (Tittle, Ward, & Grasmick, 2003; Turner & Piquero, 2002).

Third, Gottfredson and Hirschi have been faulted for failing to pay homage and attention to the historical placement of the term *self-control* in other disciplines that have used the term, primarily in psychology. In that discipline, self-control has a long-established theoretical and operational set of definitions and constructs that the theorists did not recognize, or if they did recognize it, they did not devote much substantive attention to it in their writings.

A fourth critique concerned Gottfredson and Hirschi's insistence that there are no reliable differences between offenders and/or crime types. In other words, for these theorists typologies of offenders (i.e., high-rate, low-rate, adolescence-limited, life-course-persistent) were not worth the added complexity associated with them, largely because deficits in self-control were common to all of them. Further, Gottfredson and Hirschi believed that adjudication between crime types was also not worth the added complexity because the characteristics of all crimes, at all times and at all places were the same. For example, whereas Gottfredson and Hirschi (1990, see also Hirschi & Gottfredson, 1987, 1989) argue that their theory can account for white-collar crimes, they also contend that there is no theoretical value in distinguishing white-collar crime from other crime types since all crime is motivated by the pursuit of self-interest. For those crime types that did not readily fall under the purview of their theory (i.e., corporate crimes), the authors summarily dismissed them as being too small in number or significance to warrant a sustained, or original, theoretic formulation.

Fifth, although Gottfredson and Hirschi did discuss biology with respect to the original formulation of the theory, they have been criticized for not devoting much attention to the importance of biology, especially with respect to individual differences in self-control as well as (the potential) biological transmission of parts of self-control that have been studied in great detail by psychologists and medical doctors alike (e.g., Cauffman, Steinberg, & Piquero, 2005).

Sixth, as a general theory of crime, the theorists made the bold and sometimes simplistic statement that self-control accounts for all demographic and cultural differences observed in crime rates, including race, gender, culture, and nation-level differences. Thus, for Gottfredson and Hirschi, the only reason that males commit more crime is simply because they tend to have (exhibit) more low self-control than their female counterparts. The same can be said for race differences and differences across cultures and nations. Yet, these statements have been criticized by many scholars as not being nuanced to the important differences that exist across situations, structural positions, cultures, and nation states, which are believed to also exert—in addition to personal, individual differences—some level of effect on crime (Miller & Burack, 1993; Vazsonyi, Pickering, Junger, & Hessing, 2001).

Finally, Gottfredson and Hirschi's theory has been criticized for not being a general theory in that the level of variation explained by self-control among and across crime types has not been very strong. Although the theorists are clear in explicating that, as a general theory self-control should only be held up against its ability to relate to a great number of outcomes and not necessarily that it accounts for all of the variation in those outcomes, the theory has still come under question about its ability to explain much of the variation in crimes, especially when compared to several extant criminological theories, especially those that purport to explain a much greater share of the lion's variation in crime (i.e., social learning theory).

## Empirical Evaluation

Since its original publication, the theory has been subject to a great many empirical tests ranging from assessments of its hypotheses regarding (1) that all six characteristics of self-control come together in the same person; (2) that self-control differences remain relatively stable between persons over the life course; (3) that offenders are versatile and not specialized and that self-control relates to a wide range of negative outcomes in both crime and noncrime domains; (4) that self-control accounts for differences in crime across demographic characteristics; (5) that self-control is impervious to change by external agents of social control; (6) that self-control is the only enduring personal characteristic implicated in deviant, delinquent, and criminal behavior over the life course; and (7) that self-control is the most important correlate of crime, above and beyond all other sources of crime that are believed by other theorists to relate to criminal activity (i.e., peers, marriage, etc.).

Although a detailed overview of all empirical tests is beyond the scope of this essay, it is useful to briefly note here, with respect to each of these seven hypotheses, what the current research indicates. First, studies appear to indicate that the six characteristics of self-control tend to coalesce in the same person. That is, persons with a quick temper are also the same persons who are impulsive and enjoy taking risks. Although the available evidence does point to some nuanced differences with respect to sample types (high school students, college students, drug offenders, U.S.- and non-U.S.-based samples, etc.), the general trend noted is fairly consistent across studies. Second, with respect to the hypothesis of rank stability in self-control, the small number of studies shows that while self-control does appear to change within persons, with persons almost always gaining as opposed to losing self-control, the rank stability between them tends to be stable. Aside from there being a handful of studies on this question, the main limitation of these efforts is that they are based on a small number of observation periods and for short swaths of individuals' lives. Third, the self-control–versatility hypothesis has held up well against the empirical research. Individuals low in self-control tend to engage in a wide array of criminal and negative, noncriminal acts; however, research examining white-collar and corporate crimes has been less supportive (Benson & Moore, 1992; Simpson & Piquero, 2002). Fourth, the linkage between self-control and crimes of force and fraud appear to hold reasonably well across almost all demographic correlates, the majority of research being conducted with respect to the gender and cross-national correlate investigations. There have been few investigations of the link of self-control to crime across race, and surprisingly only a handful of studies on the relationship of self-control to crime or deviance across age (Tittle & Grasmick, 1997). Fifth, there have been few policy investigations of how self-control changes within persons in response to changes in social controls, but in those studies that do examine this issue (albeit more indirectly because of little attention being paid to measures of self-control before and after social control changes) there do appear to be changes in outward expressions of self-control (i.e., less crime in response to changes in social controls; see Horney et al., 1995; Laub, Nagin, & Sampson, 1998; Piquero, Brame, Mazerolle, & Haapanen, 2002). At the same time, there does exist some evidence from a handful of studies that measures of self-control in children do change in response to changes in parenting practices (Tremblay et al., 1992). Sixth, Gottfredson and Hirschi's argument that self-control is the sole personal characteristic implicated across crime types has not been subject to intense empirical scrutiny. However, in the handful of investigations that exist with respect to this hypothesis, the data do not appear to be in the theorists' favor. At least two empirical investigations (Cauffman et al., 2005; Piquero, Schoepfer, & Langton, in press) show that while self-control is an important correlate, so too are other personal(ity) factors, and consideration of differences in self-control does not eliminate the influence of these other personal(ity) characteristics. Seventh, the effect of self-control across a wide range of studies is impressive, but it does not eliminate all other sources of crime. Most, if not all empirical investigations fail to confirm the theorists' hypothesis that self-control eliminates all other correlates of crime, including both demographic and social correlates.

Pratt and Cullen's (2000) summary statement provides a nice overview of the empirical status of Gottfredson and Hirschi's theory. First, self-control is related to a wide swath of negative outcomes in both crime and noncrime domains. Second, the amount of variation explained across these behaviors can be characterized as moderate. Third, self-control appears to be an equally viable correlate of crime across a wide array of demographic groups. Fourth, the effect of self-control on crime was virtually the same, regardless if it was measured using attitudinal or cognitive schemes or behavioral measurement strategies. And fifth, self-control is not the sole correlate of crime; that is, even after self-control as a correlate is taken into consideration in empirical models, it does not eliminate other sources of crime, most notably the effect of delinquent peers. Adjudication of other empirical issues such as the role of self-selection and ones circulating around the operationalization and measurement of self-control remain underresearched and unanswered.

## Theoretical Refinement

Gottfredson and Hirschi have remained steadfast with respect to the original theoretical formulation of the general theory of crime, and have themselves made very few changes. In fact, they have made only two alterations to the original statement of the theory on two fronts. First, they have come to dismiss the role of opportunities as being an important part of the genesis of crime. Recall that in the original theory, self-control met with opportunities to produce crime. Most recently, however, Gottfredson and Hirschi (2003) contend that because opportunities for (at least some type of) crime are available to most persons at all times, it can be largely treated as a constant; thus, the theorists now view self-control as being the sole correlate of criminal activity. The second change is much more subtle, but has significant implications for the theory and ensuing research.

Recently, Hirschi (2004) has presented a restatement of self-control. Specifically, he now suggests that self-control be conceived as "the tendency to consider the full range of potential costs of a particular act [that] moves the focus from the *long-term* implications of the act to its *broader* and often contemporaneous implications" (p. 543, emphasis in original). For Hirschi these costs or inhibitions "vary in number and salience" (p. 545), may be far reaching, are not latent or hidden to the offender, nor do they refer to previous criminal or delinquent acts. Hirschi offers that this new definition is consistent with how self-control affects would-be offenders' calculation of the consequences of their acts at the point of decision making, and he believes it clarifies some of the conceptual ambiguities that have caused misinterpretations of the theory and as a consequence, ensuing empirical research. To do so, and paying homage to the friendliness between social control and rational choice theories of crime, Hirschi argued that the reformulated self-control definition should contain elements of both cognizance and rational choice. This exercise led him to consider and define self-control as the "set of inhibitions one carries with one wherever one happens to go" (p. 543).

One empirical study of Hirschi's redefined self-control has emerged. Piquero and Bouffard (2007) collected data from a sample of young adults, measured Hirschi's redefined and reconceptualized self-control concept, and compared its predictive ability to the most commonly used attitudinal measure of self-control, the Grasmick et al. (1993) self-report self-control measure. Their analysis indicated that Hirschi's redefined self-control was significantly associated with two types of crime, and that it reduced to insignificance the effect of the Grasmick et al. self-control measure. Their study ended with the suggestion that self-control be considered as a situational characteristic, one that may not necessarily be stable within persons, over time, and across opportunities.

Before proceeding, it is important to note two recently developed theoretical refinements to the general theory. In the first, Tittle, Ward, and Grasmick (2004) have provided what may turn out to be a very useful theoretical modification to the general theory of crime, one that was not anticipated by Gottfredson and Hirschi. These authors identified an important theoretical distinction between one's desire to exercise self-control relative to one's ability to do so, and their analysis indicated strong support for this bifurcation. Recent work by Muraven, Pogarsky, and others also reconsiders self-control, both theoretically and empirically, and provides consideration of self-control acting as a muscle, being exerted in different ways and formats throughout the course of an offender's life, and the toll it (i.e., exertion) takes on the offender.

The second theoretical extension was put forth by Pratt et al. (2004) and Turner, Pratt, and Piquero (2005), both of whom attempted to further explicate and develop the hypothesis surrounding the development of self-control. Integrating insights from the social disorganization literature, Pratt and his colleagues found that neighborhood socialization factors, in addition to the parenting sources, are also an important source of variation in self-control. Meanwhile Turner and his colleagues found that even into adolescence, external efforts aimed at self-control changes (in their study by the school) can serve as an important source of the development of self-control in addition to what is gained from parenting. Importantly, neither effort denies the import of parenting being a (or the) principal source of self-control; instead, both believe that the development of self-control, in its original and ongoing formats, is a process comprised of myriad sources that include parents, but also other important sources unrecognized by Gottfredson and Hirschi.

Gottfredson and Hirschi's (1990) theory was developed originally to explain participation in criminal and analogous behaviors. Nevertheless, they note that "victims and offenders tend to share all or nearly all social and personal characteristics. Indeed the correlation between self-reported offending and self-reported victimization is, by social science standards, very high" (p. 17). Even before the publication of *A General Theory of Crime*, Gottfredson (1981) argued that "the factors most closely associated with victimization are factors which have also been found to be associated with offending. That is, by and large, combinations of characteristics predictive of offending are also predictive of victimization" (pp. 725–726). With this as a launching pad, several scholars have examined whether self-control can be used to explain criminal victimization (Piquero, MacDonald, et al., 2005; Schreck, 1999; Schreck, Stewart, & Fisher, 2006; Stewart, Elifson, & Sterk, 2004). The central argument is that if self-control is a significant predictor of criminal offending and victims and offenders share common characteristics, it is reasonable to anticipate that self-control is a significant predictor of criminal victimization (Piquero, MacDonald, et al., 2005). Although small in number, recent empirical studies have confirmed this link between self-control and criminal victimization.

It is not that individuals with low self-control consciously or intentionally place themselves in vulnerable situations, but that the lack of self-control precludes an awareness of the potential deleterious outcomes of their own risky behaviors and includes a particularly strong taste for action and danger. Several elements of self-control can be reformulated to account for victimization. First, individuals with low self-control are impulsive and have difficulty in delaying gratification. They tend to adopt a "here and now" approach to life and seek immediate gratification in most circumstances. Because of their impulsivity, they typically fail to see the long-term consequences of their decisions and interactions with others. Stewart et al. (2004) suggest that "individuals with low self-control tend to have difficulty succeeding in social institutions, conventional activities, and personal relationships that require delayed gratification or planning" (p. 176).

Second, individuals with low self-control typically find themselves in risky situations and behaviors. They often gravitate toward risky activities without much thought of taking appropriate precautions (Schreck et al., 2006). For example, persons with low self-control would be more likely to provoke and antagonize others without considering fully the potential for others to retaliate against them. Similarly, assuming there is an opportunity to avoid a confrontation, those with lower levels of self-control may be less likely to "walk away" from verbal or physical provocation.

Third, individuals with low self-control tend to prefer physical activities over mental activities. They look for physical stimulation and action. Sitting quietly, being still, and thinking are perceived to be unpleasant. They often fail to assess cognitively the risky contexts that they find themselves in. In situations where conflict appears likely, they may become defensive or antagonistic, rather than contemplative or conciliatory.

Fourth, individuals with low self-control tend to have low frustration tolerance and quick tempers. They tend to become angry or upset with only minimal provocation and may engage in a verbal or physical attack or counterattack against others. Given the substantial overlap between offending and victimization in many crimes, individuals with quick tempers may become both offenders and victims within the same context. As Schreck (1999) observes, "the difference between offending and being victimized depends on who wins the fight" (p. 636).

## Policy Application

From the description provided earlier, it can readily be seen that Gottfredson and Hirschi offer a very short window for significant alterations to the principal cause of crime, self-control. Recall that once established, by early adolescence self-control is believed to be impervious to change, such that there is little rehabilitation that can be effectively garnered for offenders, and that offenders themselves, because of the ready stock of opportunities for some type of crime at all times, are not deterred by social control and/or criminal justice agents. On the policy front then, there are only a few significant places for reductions in crime, and these stem largely from what can be undertaken in the first decade of life.

The first and perhaps most important policy proscription emanating from the general theory of crime deals with paying specific attention to parenting efforts. Recall that for Gottfredson and Hirschi, parenting provides the key processual mechanism for the development of self-control. Thus, policy efforts at helping parents better monitor their child's behavior, recognize deviant behavior when it occurs, and effectively and appropriately punish such behavior when it is recognized can go a long way toward improving their child's self-control, and in turn, reducing the probability and frequency of negative behaviors in crime and noncrime domains. There are several such programmatic efforts that have been carried out for improving children's self-control. Several have shown improvements of self-control in children as well as reductions in delinquency and crime (see Greenwood, 2006; Tremblay et al., 1992).

The second policy proscription, admittedly more controversial, also stems directly from the theory, and deals with an external change in behavior. At one point, Gottfredson and Hirschi (1995) argued that the disbursement of condoms would serve as a cheap, but effective approach to better gains in self-control (and hence less crime in the long run) because it would prevent certain individuals (would-be parents who demonstrate deficiencies in self-control because of their involvement in unprotected sexual behavior) from conceiving children at an early age, an age at which they themselves have not developed sufficient self-control and who also do not have the resources (educational and economic) to help children overcome any early-life self-control deficits. This policy proscription has not been effectively studied, especially within the context of the general theory of crime.

One part of the theory that remains underdeveloped, the distribution of opportunities, is perhaps the only other place where policy interventions such as situational crime prevention efforts may come into play. Given that the theory says very little about criminal opportunities other than the fact that they are assumed to be more or less constant for everyone, this is one area in which there may be a possibility for crime reduction, especially given the number of existing individuals with low self-control. At first glance situational crime prevention strategies and Gottfredson and Hirschi's theory may seem like an odd pairing, but as suggested by Benson and Madensen (2007), the two theoretical perspectives make a similar distinction—that is, the starting point designating a difference between crime and criminality. However, some purists of the general theory would suggest that situational crime prevention strategies do not fall under the purview of changes within offenders (i.e., changes to their self-control) and thus should not be part and parcel of the policy implications or efforts that emerge from and are attributed to the general theory of crime.

## Where the Theory Is Now and Where It Needs to Go

It is clear that Gottfredson and Hirschi's general theory of crime has become virtually the null hypothesis in criminological theory. By explication of a (virtually) sole-source hypothesis of crime and criminals, it stands on a Chinese proverb: there is beauty in simplicity. Of course, any time a theorist makes the claim that crimes and criminals are easy to understand, he or she is surely to come under critique, and the general theory is not exempt from this role. But at the same time, the theory's reach and impact is immeasureable. All theories of crime must confront the need for complexity; all theories of crime must consider whether there is a need to adjudicate within offenders and within types of crime; and all theories of crime must consider whether their accounts apply equally well across demographic factors. On these fronts, Gottfredson and Hirschi have done the field of criminology a service.

But more work remains to be done on their theory. Heeding the call of Tittle, Moffitt, Agnew, and other prominent criminologists, Gottfredson and Hirschi do not own their theory. Much like contributors to Wikipedia, the theory is out in public view for all to consume, consider, and modify as they see fit and useful. On this front, the theory is broad and general enough, and the field's knowledge of crime and criminals small and specific enough that much can be gleaned both theoretically and methodologically from tackling their original hypotheses and developing new hypotheses, as Tittle, Pogarsky, Pratt, and others have done, that seek to further unpack the scope of statements associated with the general theory. Here, it is likely that the most gains will be garnered with further attention to the role of self-control, within persons, as it relates to its stability (or lack thereof), its response to efforts to change it, as well as to whether it remains the sole or at the very least most important personal correlate of all crimes, at all times. Does the field need developmental or group-based theories of crime? Does the field need a theory for understanding complicated corporate crimes? These are age-old questions in criminology, but sometimes the age-old questions are the most fundamental ones for a discipline that seeks to understand why people do what they do.

# PURE SOCIOLOGY

## CRIME AS SOCIAL CONTROL

*Donald Black*

There is a sense in which conduct regarded as criminal is often quite the opposite. Far from being an intentional violation of a prohibition, much crime is moralistic and involves the pursuit of justice. It is a mode of conflict management, possibly a form of punishment, even capital punishment. Viewed in relation to law, it is self-help. To the degree that it defines or responds to the conduct of someone else—the victim—as deviant, crime is social control. And to this degree it is possible to predict and explain crime with aspects of the sociological theory of social control, in particular, the theory of self-help. . . .

### Modern Self-Help

A great deal of the conduct labelled and processed as crime in modern societies . . . is intended as a punishment or other expression of disapproval, whether applied reflectively or impulsively, with coolness or in the heat of passion. Some is an effort to achieve compensation, or restitution, for a harm that has been done. The response may occur long after the offense, perhaps weeks, months, or even years later; after a series of offenses, each viewed singly as only a minor aggravation but together viewed as intolerable; or as an immediate response to the offense, perhaps during a fight or other conflict, or after an assault, theft, insult, or injury.

Most intentional homicide in modern life is a response to conduct that the killer regards as deviant. In Houston during 1969, for instance, over one-half of the homicides occurred in the course of a "quarrel," and another one-fourth occurred in alleged "self-defense" or were "provoked," whereas only a little over one-tenth occurred in the course of predatory behavior such as burglary or robbery. Homicide is often a response to adultery or other matters relating to sex, love, or loyalty, to disputes about domestic matters (financial affairs, drinking, housekeeping) or affronts to honor, to conflicts relating to debts, property, and child custody, and to other questions of right and wrong. . . .

Many crimes involving the confiscation or destruction of property also prove to have a normative character when the facts come fully to light. There are, for example, moralistic burglaries, thefts, and robberies. Over one-third of the burglaries in New York City resulting in arrest involve people with a prior relationship, and these not infrequently express a grievance the burglar has against his victim. . . . In a case in New York City, one resulting in two arrests for burglary, two black women barged into the home of an elderly white woman at midnight to confront her because earlier in the day she had remonstrated with their children for throwing rocks at her window. . . .

Another possible mode of self-help is robbery, or theft involving violence. Thus, in New York City, where over one-third of the people arrested for robbery are acquainted with their victims, the crime often arises from a quarrel over money. In one case, for example, a woman reported that her sister and her sister's boyfriend had taken her purse and $40 after assaulting her and threatening to kill her baby, but she later explained that this had arisen from a misunderstanding: The boyfriend wanted reimbursement for a baby carriage that he had bought for her, whereas she thought it had been a gift. . . .

Conduct known as vandalism, or malicious destruction of property, proves to be a form of social control in many cases as well. . . . Thus, in one American neighborhood where parking spaces on the street are scarce, the residents have evolved their own distribution system, with its own customary rules and enforcement procedures. In the winter, one such rule is that whoever shovels the snow from a parking space is its "owner," and persistent violators may find that their automobile has been spraypainted or otherwise abused. . . .

Finally, it might be noted that the practice of collective liability—whereby all of the people in a social category are held accountable for the conduct of each of their fellows—occurs in modern as well as traditional societies. . . .

Crime by young people against adult strangers may also have this logic in some cases: All adults might be held liable for the conduct of those known personally, such as police, teachers, and parents. Among young people themselves, particularly in large American cities, rival "gangs" may engage in episodic violence resembling the feud in traditional settings, where each member of a feuding group is liable—to injury or even death—for the conduct of the other members. . . .

## Theoretical Considerations

When a moralistic crime is handled by the police or prosecuted in court, the official definition of the event is drastically different from that of the people involved, particularly from that of the alleged offender. . . . The victim thus becomes the offender, and vice versa. . . . The offense lies in how the grievance was pursued. The crime is self-help.

It should be apparent from much of the foregoing that in modern society the state has only theoretically achieved a monopoly over the legitimate use of violence. . . . Many people still "take the law into their own hands." They seem to view their grievances as their own business, not that of the police or other officials, and resent the intrusion of law. They seem determined to have justice done, even if this means that they will be defined as criminals. . . . [T]hey do what they think is right, and willingly suffer the consequences.

### Deterrence and self-help

To the degree that people feel morally obligated to commit crimes, it would seem that the capacity of the criminal law to discourage them—its so-called deterrent effect—must be weakened. For example, homicides committed as a form of capital punishment would seem to be more difficult to deter than those committed entirely in pursuit of personal gain. . . . That the desirability of killing another person is entertained at all is remarkable, however, particularly when the death penalty is believed to be a possible result. . . . [A] theory of deterrence surely should recognize that the power of punishment to deter crime partly depends upon whether a given crime is itself a form of social control.

A related question is the extent to which victimizations are deterred by self-help rather than—or in addition to—law. Although many citizens are entirely dependent upon legal officials such as the police to handle criminal offenders, others are prepared to protect themselves and their associates by any means at their disposal, including violence. . . .

Thus, a burglar or robber might be executed by his intended victim, though burglary and robbery are generally not capital crimes in modern codes of law. Accordingly, to the degree that self-help is effectively repressed by the state, crime of other kinds might correspondingly increase. . . . Perhaps some of the predatory crime in modern society is similarly a result of a decline in self-help. . . .

### The theory of self-help

Several centuries ago, Thomas Hobbes argued that without a sovereign state—without law—a "war of every one against every one" would prevail, and life would be "solitary, poor, nasty, brutish, and short.". . .

Hobbesian theory would lead us to expect more violence and other crimes of self-help in those contemporary settings where law—governmental social control—is least developed, and, indeed, this appears to fit the facts: Crimes of self-help are more likely where law is less available. This is most apparent where legal protection is withheld as a matter of public policy, such as where a contract violates the law. A gambling debt is not legally enforceable, for example, and the same applies to transactions in illicit narcotics, prostitution, stolen goods, and the like. Perhaps for this reason many underworld businesses find it necessary to maintain, in effect, their own police, such as the "strong-arms" of illegal loan operations and the "pimps" who oversee the work of prostitutes. Furthermore, it appears that social control within settings of this kind is relatively violent. . . .

In all of these settings neglected by law, crimes of self-help are comparatively common. There are, so to speak, stateless locations in a society such as modern America, and in them the Hobbesian theory appears to have some validity.

Before closing, it is possible to specify the relationship between law and self-help more precisely. The likelihood of self-help is not merely a function of the availability of law, and, moreover, crimes of self-help are not always handled leniently by legal officials. Different locations and directions in social space have different patterns. In other words, the relationship between law and self-help depends upon who has a grievance against whom.

Four patterns can be identified: First, law may be relatively unavailable both to those with grievances and to those who are the objects of self-help, as when people of low status and people who are intimate have conflicts with each other. Secondly, law may be relatively unavailable to those with grievances in comparison to those who have offended them. Should the former employ self-help, they may therefore be vulnerable to harsh treatment by legal officials. This is the situation of people with a grievance against a social superior, such as a teenager with a grievance against an adult, and may help to explain why they tend to develop their own techniques of social control, including, for instance, covert retaliation, self-destruction, and flight. Those with grievances against a social inferior illustrate a third pattern: Law is readily available to them, but not to those against whom they might employ self-help. In this situation, the aggrieved party seemingly has a choice of law or self-help. A man might easily obtain legal help against his teenaged son, for example, but if he simply beats the boy instead—a kind of self-help—he is unlikely to be handled with severity by the police or other officials. The fourth possibility, where law is readily available both to those with grievances and to those who have offended them, is seen where people of high status, and also people who are strangers, have conflicts with each other. Here self-help seems to be relatively infrequent. In sum, law and self-help are unevenly distributed across social space, and each is relevant to the behavior of the other.

## Conclusion

The approach taken in this paper departs radically from traditional criminology. Indeed, the approach taken here is, strictly speaking, not criminological at all, since it ignores whatever might be distinctive to crime as such (including, for example, how criminals differ from other people or how their behavior differs from that which is not prohibited). Instead it draws attention to a dimension of many crimes that is usually viewed as a totally different—even opposite—phenomenon, namely, social control. Crime often expresses a grievance. This implies that many crimes belong to the same family as gossip, ridicule, vengeance, punishment, and law itself. It also implies that to a significant degree we may predict and explain crime with a sociological theory of social control, specifically a theory of self-help. Beyond this, it might be worthwhile to contemplate what else crime has in common with conduct of other kinds. For instance, some crime may be understood as economic behavior, and some as recreation. In other words, for certain theoretical purposes we might usefully ignore the fact that crime is criminal at all.

# CONTEMPORARY RETROSPECTIVE ON PURE SOCIOLOGY

## TWENTY-FIVE YEARS OF "CRIME AS SOCIAL CONTROL"

*Scott Jacques, University of Missouri–St. Louis*[1]

Black's (1983a) classic article "Crime as Social Control" provides students of crime with three important insights: (1) some criminal actions are punishment for wrongdoing, or "self-help"; (2) self-help can deter crime, such as predatory robbery or burglary; and (3) self-help is most likely to occur among persons and groups who receive little assistance from the government in righting wrong.

This essay begins by differentiating the theoretical foundation for Black's theory of self-help from other criminological perspectives. It reviews quantitative and qualitative studies of the drug world that serve as empirical evaluations of the theory. The essay then examines the relevance of the theory for drug policy and reducing criminal retaliation, and concludes by considering a troubling critique.

## Theoretical Foundation

Black's theory of self-help is nested within the paradigm of pure sociology (Black 1976, 1995, 1998). "As a novel theoretical paradigm pure sociology diverges sharply from traditional criminological thinking as exemplified in . . . the dominant explanations of crime, such as social learning, strain, control, rational choice, and phenomenological theory" (Cooney, 2006, p. 52). Pure sociology is valuable to criminology because it provides a system of

---

[1] I thank Richard Wright for comments on an earlier draft.

conceptualizations that allow for the construction of general, testable, simple, and, perhaps, valid theories. The paradigm is useful and unique because it avoids one-dimensionality, microcosms and macrocosms, anthropocentrism, and teleology (Black, 1995, p. 847).

Pure sociology avoids one-dimensionality by synthesizing the major themes of sociological theory (Black, 1995, pp. 851–852). The task for pure sociologists is to find patterns among a multitude of social characteristics—such as income, family, intimacy, employment, memberships, knowledge, conventionality, and deviant past—and variation in the form, style, and magnitude of social behaviors, such as getting a job, joining a gang, going to college, or being arrested.[2]

Most theories in criminology are microoriented and focused on explaining the behavior of individuals (e.g., Hirschi, 1969) or macrooriented and concerned with explaining the behavior of groups (e.g., Sampson et al., 1997). Microcosms and macrocosms are inherently limited because no person or group behaves the same way all of the time. Social behaviors, rather than people or groups, should be the focus of *social* theory. Pure sociology's approach is to

> explain human behavior with the shape of social space. . . . Social space is neither . . . a microcosm [nor a] macrocosm, neither a person nor a [group]. Its size is variable. . . . The shape of social space is defined and measured by the social characteristics of everyone involved in every instance of human behavior. . . . Each instance of human behavior, large or small, has its own multidimensional location and direction in social space. Each has a social structure. . . . A case [of behavior] might . . . be high and upward, high and lateral, low and downward, low and lateral, downward and distant . . . , upward and distant . . . , and so on. The same case has a radial location and direction—outward (from the center), inward (from the margin), or lateral—measured by the social participation of everyone involved. . . . The social characteristics of the all the third parties—partisan or nonpartisan—similarly define the social location and direction of a [behavior]: Each third party may be higher, lower, or equal to each [other actor] in various ways, relationally and culturally close or distant from each, and so on. All these locations and directions together comprise the multidimensional shape of social space of each [behavior]—its social structure. And the social structure of a [behavior] . . . predicts and explains its fate. (Black, 1995, pp. 853–854)

Another attribute of pure sociology that sets it apart from other theoretical frameworks is the absence of anthropocentrism. Theories are anthropomorphic to the degree that they attempt to explain the behavior of people rather than the behavior of social life, a subtle but important distinction. Again, rather than try to explain variation between people or groups of people, pure sociology explains variation in social behavior from one case to the next.

Finally, pure sociology is unique in criminology because it intentionally avoids teleology. There are no assumptions about the motives, goals, objectives, or wants of individuals or groups. The problem with such teleological assumptions is that they are forever beyond

---

[2]Since Black's "Crime as Social Control" was first published, the theory of self-help has been refined as pure sociologists specify the various links between self-help and social structure, and has been applied to crimes such as domestic violence, dueling, feuding, genocide, lynching, and terrorism. Although space limitations preclude a detailed discussion of each refinement and application of the theory of self-help, interested readers should consult the works of Baumgartner (1988, 1992, 1993); Black (1983a, 1983b, 1998, 2000, 2004a, 2004b); Campbell (2005, 2006); Cooney (1997a, 1997b, 1998, 2003); Horwitz (1990); Michalski (2004); Phillips (2003); Phillips and Cooney (2005); Senechal de la Roche (1996, 2001, 2004); and Tucker and Ross (2004).

observation, and so they have more to do with philosophy than science. Pure sociology "predicts and explains what happens, how social life actually behaves, without regard to whether it contributes to anything—whether it has particular consequences, whether it is supposed to happen, or whether it works" (Black, 1995, p. 862).

## Crime as Social Control

As noted in the conclusion to "Crime as Social Control," Black's (1983a) theory of self-help "is, strictly speaking, not criminological at all, since it ignores whatever might be distinctive to crime as such. . . . Instead it draws attention to a dimension of many crimes that is usually viewed as a totally different phenomenon, namely, social control" (p. 42). Social control is defined as "how people define and respond to deviant behavior" (Black, 1998, p. 4), and "is found wherever and whenever people hold each other to standards, explicitly or implicitly, consciously or not: on the street, in prison, at home, at a party" (Black, 1976, p. 105). Social control includes a number of behaviors (Black, 1983b, 1983c, 1998; Horwitz, 1990; Jacques & Wright, 2008), such as calling the police (Black, 1976, 1980, 1989, 1998), avoidance (Baumgartner, 1988), gossip (Merry, 1984), and negotiation (Black, 1998, pp. 83–85). "Self-help is the handling of a grievance by unilateral aggression" (Black, 1998, p. 74). When self-help is illegal, crime is social control.

However, "[n]ot all criminal behavior is a form of social control. Some crime is exploitative or predatory, some is lifestyle related or expressive, and some is capitalistic or entrepreneurial" (Cooney, 2006, p. 58). Black's theory of self-help *does not* attempt to explain all crimes, but only crimes of self-help. For instance, the theory of self-help does not explain predatory robberies, frauds, or burglaries (but see Cooney, 2006; Cooney & Phillips, 2002), nor does it predict variation in illicit drug dealing—an entrepreneurial crime (but see Jacques & Wright, 2006). Black's (1983a) theory is restricted to criminal acts that are, at the same time, social control accomplished through self-help.[3]

## Empirical Evaluations

Although Black's theory of self-help is applicable across time and place, this essay restricts its attention to empirical evaluations of self-help related to the drug world in the United States. Simply put, compared to a social context where drugs are legal, *illicit* drug traders and users have less access to law when victimized (Black, 1976, 1983a) and, for that reason, are more often involved with self-help (Black, 1983a; also see Cooney, 1998; Horwitz, 1990; Jacques and Wright, in press). A number of studies demonstrate the empirical connection between illegality, drugs, and retaliation predicted by Black's theory of self-help.

America's prohibition of alcohol during the 1920s exemplifies how illegality can influence criminal violence. Before prohibition, persons in drug market conflicts were afforded

---

[3]This does not mean, however, that pure sociology is inherently restricted to social control. "As a general theoretical paradigm, applicable to all social behavior, pure sociology should predict and explain forms of criminal behavior that are not acts of social control" (Cooney, 2006, p. 58).

more protection and assistance by the police, but outlawing alcohol diminishes access to law and can thereby increase the odds of criminal retaliation. Miron's (2004) study of the Prohibition era and violence demonstrates this relationship. Miron finds that "the homicide rate was high in [the] 1920–1933 period, when constitutional prohibition of alcohol was in effect. . . . After repeal of alcohol prohibition, the homicide rate dropped quickly and remained low" (p. 48; also see Jensen, 2000).

More recently, the illegality of the crack and cocaine trades has contributed to high rates of violence in those markets. Goldstein and others, for example, collected data on about 400 homicides in New York City in 1988. The analysis shows that many of the homicides were cases of self-help related to illicit drugs.

> The most striking finding in [the] study was that about two-fifths of all the homicide events we studied (162 or 39%) and nearly three-fourths of all the drug-related homicides (162 or 74.3%) had to do with the exigencies of the illicit market system . . . *the vast bulk of crack-related homicides occurred between dealers or dealers and users.* They did not involve the murder of strangers outside the crack world. (Goldstein, Brownstein, Ryan, & Bellucci, 1997, p. 118, emphasis in original)

The study shows that at least 79% of 106 crack-related homicides, 55% of 45 cocaine-related homicides, and 63% of 11 other drug-homicides are instances of self-help related to either territorial disputes, the collection of debts, punishment of workers, disputes over drug theft, or bad merchandise being sold (percentages calculated from Table 6-3 in Goldstein et al., 1997, p. 119).

The city of St. Louis, Missouri, has been called the most violent place in America (but see Rosenfeld & Lauritsen, 2008). Qualitative data from interviews with active drug dealers in St. Louis illustrate how persons without access to law are more likely to engage in self-help. Topalli, Wright, and Fornango (2002) tell the story of Stub, "a heroin dealer who was robbed and shot on the street corner by one of his regular customers" (p. 342). Stub was taken to the hospital and required a four-day stay before being sent home to recuperate. Shortly thereafter Stub enacted the ultimate revenge:

> *Interviewer:* So what did you do?
>
> *Stub:* After [being shot], I got out [of the hospital] for about two weeks, recuperated, and got back to doing the same thing [dealing heroin].
>
> *Interviewer:* What about this guy though?
>
> *Stub:* He got his.
>
> *Interviewer:* If you don't mind, we'd like you to tell us about it. You don't have to, you know.
>
> *Stub:* In so many details . . . he got his, he's no longer.
>
> *Interviewer:* He's no longer?
>
> *Stub:* In existence.

Stub was asked "why such drastic measures were necessary," and the dealer's response reflects Black's thoughts on the deterrent effect of self-help on predatory crime:

> *Stub:* See, you have to realize if I didn't get back at him, you and him could say [Stub's] a punk. Everybody can go take [Stub's] shit. So if he [gets] hurt, everybody

knew who hurt him. . . . [S]ee the thing is, if somebody robbed you and you in the dope game, you don't want to be robbed first off cause then . . . I got the fucking city saying you can rob him. So if you handle your business you ain't got to even worry about it cause they gonna say that [so-and-so] robbed [Stub], and shit he came up missing. So that gonna give them the fear right there not to fuck with you.

In other words, drug dealers, in their own minds, see self-help as a method of retribution but also as a necessary measure in deterring victimization from occurring in the first place.

## Policy Relevance

To my knowledge, Black's (1983a) theory of self-help has never been used to guide public policy; nevertheless, the theory has important policy implications, especially for the drug world. To the degree that drug traders do not have access to law when victimized, self-help will emerge as a method of retribution. As discussed, illicit drug dealers and users have relatively little access to law when victimized, and, for this reason, they are more likely to engage in retaliatory violence, fraud, or theft. What that suggests is that criminal retaliation in a municipality increases as the amount of law applied to drugs increases. It naturally flows from this that criminal retaliation (self-help) can be reduced by decriminalizing drugs or reducing the amount of law directed against drugs.

The decriminalization or legalization of many drugs, it would seem, is unlikely to occur in the immediate future, and so alternative strategies for reducing criminal retaliation should be considered. Although drug traders have relatively little access to *formal* settlement, such as police and courts, disputes can also be managed with *informal* settlement. For instance, a parent may decide the fate of a dispute between children, or a coach may decide which of two players instigated a fight and deserves punishment. Similarly, a community member may mediate a dispute with illicit drug traders who do business or live in the neighborhood. Consider, for example, a drug-related dispute in Chicago between gang members, who were led by Big Cat, and neighborhood residents, who were led by Marlene, that was informally settled by a person of relatively high social status, Pastor Wilkins:

Big Cat's thrust outward, from the sphere of drug distribution into other hidden economic arenas, took on greater force in 2000, when the gang began taking over Homans Park. . . . Marlene Matteson, president of the 1700 South Maryland Avenue Block Club, and her neighbors saw in Big Cat's advances several threats to their welfare. Their children could lose a place to play in relative safety because the gang wanted to turn Homans Park into a bazaar filled with . . . illicit traders whom they would tax. Parents feared that the gang's presence would threaten the safety of children and their guardians who had to walk by on their way to school and work. . . . Marlene and her neighbor were stuck, unsure how to respond. *Historically, they had little success enlisting the police, so while they thought of calling on law enforcement, they almost by instinct sought other opportunities.* . . . Believing they could never entirely eradicate underground economies outside their homes, they had to find a rapprochement with the shady traders arriving in Homans Park. . . . Marlene's neighbors permitted her to explore deals with the gang . . . [and] they decided to enlist the services of Pastor Wilkins. (Venkatesh, 2006, pp. 291–293; emphasis added)

Pastor Wilkins agreed to mediate the conflict and invited Marlene and Big Cat to his church so that they could solve the problem with a nonviolent, informal solution:

> In a damp basement . . . they sat at a large table and discussed their respective concerns. *Even Big Cat's presence was remarkable, but such was the clergy's power [or status] in Maquis Park.* . . . The following interchange occurred at the . . . meeting that Wilkins mediated: "What worries me," said Marlene, "is that there's about seventy children on my block who use that park—and that's not counting the ones who live on the other side. Can't have them around your boys. . . . If you're in our park, we can't be. It's as simple as that. . . . I'll give you the nighttime, but that's going to be tough. But, bottom line, baby, is we can't have you all there during the day." "Okay," interjected Wilkins. "Now, you have to stop for the summer Big Cat. We're not asking for a two-year thing, or nothing like that. Just when the kids are outside." [Big Cat replied:] "I guess I could work it on 59th, but that Arab keeps telling us he don't want us around, keeps calling the cops." [Wilkins replied:] "If I get him to leave you alone during the day, and you can hang out in that parking lot on the other side of the store, you'll leave the park for the summer." "Yeah," Big Cat replied, dejected at the compromise. "Okay, we'll be gone." (Venkatesh, 2006, pp. 293–295; emphasis added)

Cooney (1998, pp. 140–149; also see Jacobs & Wright, 2006, pp. 129–134) suggests that one strategy for reducing criminal retaliation in communities is to increase access to informal settlement agents. According to Cooney (1998), "[i]f third parties are to promote the peaceful settlement of conflict, they should neither be too low nor too high in status relative to the principals" (pp. 140–141). It is possible to imagine an established system of popular justice built around two kinds of third parties: "elders" and "peacemakers" (p. 142). Elders need not be representatives of religion, such as Pastor Wilkins; any person—given a status that is neither too high nor too low—could serve as an elder who would "establish and staff tribunals dedicated to settling disputes in a consultative manner" (p. 142). Distinct from elders are peacemakers, who "would be members of the local community trained to intervene quickly in disputes in order to prevent them from escalating into" retaliation (pp. 144–145). In short, Cooney suggests a system of informal social control that relies on community members—not police, prosecutors, or judges—to intervene in disputes, which, in theory, will reduce criminal retaliation. If informal settlement can solve disputes, then criminal retaliation is less likely to occur.

### Critique and Conclusion

Theory nested in the paradigm of pure sociology, such as Black's (1983a) theory of self-help, has been critiqued on a number of grounds (see Frankford, 1995; Gottfredson & Hindelang, 1979; Greenberg, 1983; Hagan, 1985; Rosenfeld, 2001; Sciulli, 1995). This essay addresses the critique that, at least for me, is most troubling.

As noted earlier, pure sociology is free from "teleology—the understanding of anything as a means to an end" (Black, 1998, p. xix), and social control is defined as "how people define and respond to deviant behavior" (Black, 1998, p. 4). What is "deviant"? According to pure sociology, any behavior is deviant to the degree that it is socially controlled, through self-help, law, avoidance, negotiation, or toleration (Black, 1998). The question becomes: Is it possible to observe deviance separately from social control and without teleological assumptions?

Without teleological assumptions "about needs, functions, values, interests, and goals" (Black, 1998, p. xix), how can we know whether any given criminal act—such as a robbery or burglary—is self-help or predation? For instance, imagine that we witness two robberies, one retaliatory and the other predatory. How can we *empirically* tell which robbery is predatory and which is retaliatory without teleology? One method would be to ask each robber whether the act was more about money or revenge. But asking a person why he or she does something seems to invoke teleology. We could restrict our attention to the events that led up to each robbery, but how do we know which preceding behaviors are deviant and which are not? It could be argued that if someone was assaulted and then robbed the assaulter, that could be reasonably classified as a case of self-help, but it nevertheless seems teleological—an assumption, imputation, or inference about behavior.

It is difficult to "get your head around" how self-help is a nonteleological concept, and "solving" this conundrum is beyond the scope of this essay. However, even if the theory of self-help does rely on teleology, it is worth pointing out that it is no more teleological than any other psychological, sociological, or social-psychological theory of crime. At best, the theory of self-help is free from teleology and, for that reason, superior to other theories of crime.[4] At worst, the theory of self-help is teleological, but—because almost all other theories of crime are admittedly teleological—it is the "best worst" choice for explaining crime currently available to students.

---

[4]Holding constant other factors, such as generality, simplicity, originality, and validity of theories (Black, 1995).

# PART VIII

# INTERACTIONIST THEORIES

# LABELING THEORIES

## CRIME AND THE COMMUNITY

*Frank Tannenbaum*

### A Matter of Definition

In the conflict between the young delinquent and the community there develop two opposing definitions of the situation. In the beginning the definition of the situation by the young delinquent may be in the form of play, adventure, excitement, interest, mischief, fun. Breaking windows, annoying people, running around porches, climbing over roofs, stealing from pushcarts, playing truant—all are items of play, adventure, excitement. To the community, however, these activities may and often do take on the form of a nuisance, evil, delinquency, with the demand for control, admonition, chastisement, punishment, police court, truant school. This conflict over the situation is one that arises out of a divergence of values. As the problem develops, the situation gradually becomes redefined. The attitude of the community hardens definitely into a demand for suppression. There is a gradual shift from the definition of the specific acts as evil to a definition of the individual as evil, so that all his acts come to be looked upon with suspicion. In the process of identification his companions, hang-outs, play, speech, income, all his conduct, the personality itself, become subject to scrutiny and question. From the community's point of view, the individual who used to do bad and mischievous things has now become a bad and unredeemable human being. From the individual's point of view there has taken place a similar change. He has gone slowly from a sense of grievance and injustice, of being unduly mistreated and punished, to a recognition that the definition of him as a human being is different from that of other boys in his neighborhood, his school, street, community. This recognition on his part becomes a process of self-identification and integration with the group which shares his activities. It becomes, in part, a process of rationalization; in part, a simple response to a specialized type of stimulus. The young delinquent becomes bad because he is defined as bad and because he is not believed if he is good. There is a persistent demand for consistency in character. The community cannot deal with people whom it cannot define. Reputation is this sort of public definition. Once it is established, then unconsciously all agencies combine to maintain this definition even when they apparently and consciously attempt to deny their own implicit judgment.

Early in his career, then, the incipient professional criminal develops an attitude of antagonism to the regulated orderly life that he is required to lead. This attitude is hardened and crystallized by opposition. The conflict becomes a clash of wills. And experience too often has proved that threats, punishments, beatings, commitments to institutions, abuse and defamation of one sort or another, are of no avail. Punishment breaks down against the child's stubbornness. What has happened is that the child has been defined as an "incorrigible" both by his contacts and by himself, and an attempt at a direct breaking down of will generally fails.

The child meets the situation in the only way he can, by defiance and escape—physical escape if possible, or emotional escape by derision, anger, contempt, hatred, disgust, tantrums, destructiveness, and physical violence. The response of the child is just as intelligent and intelligible as that of the schools, of the authorities. They have taken a simple problem, the lack of fitness of an institution to a particular child's needs, and have made a moral issue out of it with values outside the child's ken. It takes on the form of war between two wills, and the longer the war lasts, the more certainly does the child become incorrigible. The child will not yield because he cannot yield—his nature requires other channels for pleasant growth; the school system or society will not yield because it does not see the issues involved as between the incompatibility of an institution and a child's needs, sometimes physical needs, and will instead attempt to twist the child's nature to the institution with that consequent distortion of the child which makes an unsocial career inevitable. The verbalization of the conflict in terms of evil, delinquency, incorrigibility, badness, arrest, force, punishment, stupidity, lack of intelligence, truancy, criminality, gives the innocent divergence of the child from the straight road a meaning that it did not have in the beginning and makes its continuance in these same terms by so much the more inevitable.

The only important fact, when the issue arises of the boy's inability to acquire the specific habits which organized institutions attempt to impose upon him, is that this conflict becomes the occasion for him to acquire another series of habits, interests, and attitudes as a substitute. These habits become as effective in motivating and guiding conduct as would have been those which the orderly routine social institutions attempted to impose had they been acquired.

This conflict gives the gang its hold, because the gang provides escape, security, pleasure, and peace. The gang also gives room for the motor activity which plays a large role in a child's life. The attempt to break up the gang by force merely strengthens it. The arrest of the children has consequences undreamed-of, for several reasons.

First, only some of the children are caught though all may be equally guilty. There is a great deal more delinquency practiced and committed by the young groups than comes to the attention of the police. The boy arrested, therefore, is singled out in specialized treatment. This boy, no more guilty than the other members of his group, discovers a world of which he knew little. His arrest suddenly precipitates a series of institutions, attitudes, and experiences which the other children do not share. For this boy there suddenly appear the police, the patrol wagon, the police station, the other delinquents and criminals found in the police lock-ups, the court with all its agencies such as bailiffs, clerks, bondsmen, lawyers, probation officers. There are bars, cells, handcuffs, criminals. He is questioned, examined, tested, investigated. His history is gone into, his family is brought into court. Witnesses make their appearance. The boy, no different from the rest of his gang, suddenly becomes the center of a major drama in which all sorts of unexpected characters play important roles. And what is it all about? about the accustomed things his gang has done and has been doing for a long time. In this entirely new world he is made conscious of himself as a different human being than he was before his arrest. He becomes classified as a thief, perhaps, and the entire world about him has suddenly become a different place for him and will remain different for the rest of his life.

## The Dramatization of Evil

The first dramatization of the "evil" which separates the child out of his group for specialized treatment plays a greater role in making the criminal than perhaps any other experience. It cannot be too often emphasized that for the child the whole situation has become different. He now lives in a different world. He has been tagged. A new and hitherto non-existent environment has been precipitated out for him.

The process of making the criminal, therefore, is a process of tagging, defining, identifying, segregating, describing, emphasizing, making conscious and self-conscious; it becomes a way of stimulating, suggesting, emphasizing, and evoking the very-traits that are complained of. If the theory of relation of response to stimulus has any meaning, the entire process of dealing with the young delinquent is mischievous in so far as it identifies him to himself or to the environment as a delinquent person.

The person becomes the thing he is described as being. Nor does it seem to matter whether the valuation is made by those who would punish or by those who would reform. In either case the emphasis is upon the conduct that is disapproved of. The parents or the policeman, the older brother or the court, the probation officer or the juvenile institution, in so far as they rest upon the thing complained of, rest upon a false ground. Their very enthusiasm defeats their aim. The harder they work to reform the evil, the greater the evil grows under their hands. The persistent suggestion, with whatever good intentions, works mischief, because it leads to bringing out the bad behavior that it would suppress. The way out is through a refusal to dramatize the evil. The less said about it the better. The more said about something else, still better. . . .

The dramatization of the evil therefore tends to precipitate the conflict situation which was first created through some innocent maladjustment. The child's isolation forces him into companionship with other children similarly defined, and the gang becomes his means of escape, his security. The life of the gang gives it special mores, and the attack by the community upon these mores merely overemphasizes the conflict already in existence, and makes it the source of a new series of experiences that lead directly to a criminal career.

In dealing with the delinquent, the criminal, therefore, the important thing to remember is that we are dealing with a human being who is responding normally to the demands, stimuli, approval, expectancy, of the group with whom he is associated. We are dealing not with an individual but with a group.

> In a study of 6,000 instances of stealing, with reference to the number of boys involved, it was found that in 90.4 per cent of the cases two or more boys were known to have been involved in the act and were consequently brought to court. Only 9.6 per cent of all the cases were acts of single individuals. Since this study was based upon the number of boys brought to court, and since in many cases not all of the boys involved were caught and brought to court, it is certain that the percentage of group stealing is therefore even greater than 90.4 per cent. It cannot be doubted that delinquency, particularly stealing, almost invariably involves two or more persons.

That group may be a small gang, a gang of children just growing up, a gang of young "toughs" of nineteen or twenty, or a gang of older criminals of thirty. If we are not dealing with a gang we may be dealing with a family. And if we are not dealing with either of these especially we may be dealing with a community. In practice all these factors—the family, the gang, and the community—may be important in the development and the maintenance of that attitude towards the world which makes a criminal career a normal, an accepted and approved way of life.

Direct attack upon the individual in these circumstances is a dubious undertaking. By the time the individual has become a criminal his habits have been so shaped that we have a fairly integrated character whose whole career is in tune with the peculiar bit of the environment for which he has developed the behavior and habits that cause him to be apprehended. In theory isolation from that group ought to provide occasion for change in the individual's habit structure. It might, if the individual were transplanted to a group whose values and activities had the approval of the wider community, and in which the newcomer might hope to gain full acceptance eventually. But until now isolation has meant the grouping in close confinement of persons whose strongest common bond has been their socially disapproved delinquent conduct. Thus the attack cannot be made without reference to group life.

The attack must be on the whole group; for only by changing its attitudes and ideals, interests and habits, can the stimuli which it exerts upon the individual be changed. Punishment as retribution has failed in reform, that is, to change character. If the individual can be made aware of a different set of values for which he may receive approval, then we may be on the road to a change in his character. But such a change of values involves a change in stimuli, which means that the criminal's social world must be changed before he can be changed.

### The Scapegoat Is a Snare and a Delusion

The point of view here developed rejects all assumptions that would impute crime to the individual in the sense that a personal shortcoming of the offender is the cause of the unsocial behavior. The assumption that crime is caused by any sort of inferiority, physiological or psychological, is here completely and unequivocally repudiated.

This of course does not mean that morphological or psychological techniques do not have value in dealing with the individual. It merely means that they have no greater value in the study of criminology than they would have in the study of any profession. If a poor IQ is a bad beginning for a career in medicine, it is also a poor beginning for a career in crime. If the psychiatrist can testify that a psychopath will make an irritable doctor he can prove the same for the criminal. But he can prove no more. The criminal differs from the rest of his fellows only in the sense that he has learned to respond to the stimuli of a very small and specialized group; but that group must exist or the criminal could not exist. In that he is like the mass of men, living a certain kind of life with the kind of companions that make that life possible.

This explanation of criminal behavior is meant to apply to those who more or less consistently pursue the criminal career. It does not necessarily presume to describe the accidental criminal or the man who commits a crime of passion. Here perhaps the theories that would seek the cause of crime in the individual may have greater application than in attempting to deal with those who follow a life of crime. But even in the accidental criminal there is a strong presumption that the accident is the outcome of a habit situation. Any habit tends to have a background of social conditioning.

> A man with the habit of giving way to anger may show his habit by a murderous attack upon some one who has offended. His act is nonetheless due to habit because it occurs only once in his life. The essence of habit is an acquired predisposition to *ways* or modes of response, not to particular acts except as, under special conditions, these express a way of behaving. Habit means special sensitiveness or accessibility to certain classes of stimuli, standing predilections and aversions, rather than bare recurrence of specific acts. It means will.

In other words, perhaps the accidental criminal also is to be explained in terms such as we used in discussing the professional criminal.

# SOCIAL PATHOLOGY

*Edwin Lemert*

## A Sociological Approach to the Study of Sociopathic Behavior

The early tendency to regard sociology as a synthetic discipline which combines items of biological, psychological, psychiatric, geographic, and demographic knowledge in order to explain human behavior has pretty well disappeared. Sociologists now hold to the notion that theirs is a separate field of study requiring concepts and generalizations which are unique to this field. Sociologists now generalize at "their own level" rather than trying to reduce their generalizations to the level of other fields. The only remnants of the synthetic tradition, if it can be called that, lie in a certain amount of confusion over how to reckon theoretically with nonsociological factors which have a marginal or indirect bearing upon human behavior.

Our own position on this matter is that the direct or significant factors of sociopathic behavior are sociological or sociopsychological in nature, expressible by such concepts as social structure, group, role, status, and symbolic interaction. To the extent that factors falling outside of those which are strictly sociological must be taken into consideration in analyzing pathological human behavior they must be related in a verifiable way to the sociological variables. Such factors as physical size and strength, biological anomalies, aggressiveness, hallucinations, monetary income, age, sex, and position in space can be applied in only a limited way to explain variation in social and cultural factors, which in turn are the chief interacting determiners of human behavior. Where variables such as the former must be taken into account, it must be shown how they affect social organization, role, status, social participation, self-definitions, and the other variables which we define as "sociological." The actual details of effective causation can be given at this last, a sociological or sociopsychological level. Starting with these assumptions as to the nature of the sociological approach and guided by the criteria of a systematic theory, we can now proceed to the series of propositions or postulates which are the elements of our theory of sociopathic behavior.

## A General Statement of Our Theory

Stated in the most general way, our theory is one of social differentiation, deviation, and individuation. For a summary description we may turn to an excerpt from a paper by the present writer:

> We may pertinently ask at this juncture whether the time has not come to break abruptly with the traditions of older social pathologists and abandon once and for all the archaic and medicinal idea that human beings can be divided into normal and pathological, or, at least, if such a division must be made, to divest the term "pathological" of its moralistic unscientific overtones. As a step in this direction, the writer suggests that the concepts of social differentiation and individuation be rescued from the limbo of older textbooks on sociology, dusted off, and given scientific airing, perhaps being supplemented and given statistical meaning with the perfectly usable concept of deviation. There seems to be no cogent reason why the bulk of the data discussed in textbooks and courses on social pathology cannot be treated as a special phase of

social and cultural differentiation and thus conveniently integrated with general sociological theory as taught in courses in introductory sociology. . . .

Because some method must be found to distinguish that portion of differentiation which can be designated as appropriately falling within the field of social pathology, the second necessary postulate is that there is a space-time limited societal awareness and reaction to deviation, ranging from strong approval through indifference to strong disapproval. Thus, by further definition, sociopathic phenomena simply become differentiated behavior which at a given time and place is socially disapproved even though the same behavior may be socially approved at other times and in other places.

To recapitulate, then, we start with the idea that persons and groups are differentiated in various ways, some of which result in social penalties, rejection, and segregation. These penalties and segregative reactions of society or the community are dynamic factors which increase, decrease, and condition the form which the initial differentiation or deviation takes. This process of deviation and societal reaction, together with its structural or substantive products, can be studied both from its collective and its distributive aspects. In the first instance, we are concerned with sociopathic differentiation; and, in the second, our concern is with sociopathic individuation.

## Breaking Down the Theory into Its Postulates

In order to give further precision to the above statement, it can be resolved into a series of postulates. These postulates are simple statements of fact for which the writer feels no obligation to supply proof. They differ from axioms, upon which mathematical and symbolic systems are constructed, in that they contain empirical elements. They are the building blocks for the theory of this treatise and *ipso facto* they must be accepted as points of departure for the analysis which follows. The question as to whether these postulates are the relevant ones or whether they are too few must await answer until after the theory has been tested. The postulates are as follows:

1. There are modalities in human behavior and clusters of deviations from these modalities which can be identified and described for situations specified in time and space.
2. Behavioral deviations are a function of culture conflict which is expressed through social organization.
3. There are societal reactions to deviations ranging from strong approval through indifference to strong disapproval.
4. Sociopathic behavior is deviation which is *effectively* disapproved.
5. The deviant person is one whose role, status, function, and self-definition are importantly shaped by how much deviation he engages in, by the degree of its social visibility, by the *particular* exposure he has to the societal reaction, and by the nature and strength of the societal reaction.
6. There are patterns of restriction and freedom in the social participation of deviants which are related directly to their status, role, and self-definitions. The biological strictures upon social participation of deviants are directly significant in comparatively few cases.
7. Deviants are individuated with respect to their vulnerability to the societal reaction because: (*a*) the person is a dynamic agent, (*b*) there is a structuring to each personality which acts as a set of limits within which the societal reaction operates.

## The Place of This Theory in General Sociological Theory

In keeping with our high scientific resolve the various terms employed in stating our postulates are intended to be amoral and nonevaluational, having obvious statistical implications and derivations. There is no intimation that concepts like "restricted participation," "sociopathic behavior," or "deviation" connote either goodness or badness. The objective of this work is to study a limited part of deviation in human behavior and a certain range of societal reactions, together with their interactional products, and by the methods of science to arrive at generalizations about the uniformities in these events. The aim is to study sociopathic behavior in the same light as normal behavior and, by implication, with extensions or derivations of general sociological theory. By the same token, we hold that, with certain modifications in our frame of reference, variations from social norms in desirable and enviable directions should be explored as profitably as the more frequently studied sociopathic variations. The behavior of the genius, the motion-picture star, the exceptionally beautiful woman, and the renowned athlete should lend itself to the same systematic analysis as that which is applied to the criminal, the pauper, or the sex delinquent.

A question for parenthetical consideration is whether or not it is possible to apply our theory with logical extensions to the analysis of behavior systems and persons which are differentiated but which do not excite polarized reactions of social approbation or disapproval. In data like these the chief conditioning factors appear to be the special qualities of the societal reaction. Thus, for example, the primary influences in forming the occupational personality of a locomotive engineer are such things as time, mobility, and income. The small amount of dislike for the railroad man sometimes found in small towns has little to do with the formation of his role and self-conception. Whatever may be the answer to our question, we can readily recognize the gains to be made by integrating the growing body of research on behavior systems of occupational and functional groups and the sort of trend in sociological analysis this book represents. Such an integration would broaden the possible scope of this kind of research and generalization to encompass such monographic studies as those of the railroader, the waitress, and the musician, as well as those of the professional thief, the hobo, or the beggar. . . .

## The Relationship of Deviation and the Societal Reaction

The degree of deviation shown by an individual or a group can be taken as a partial gauge of the probable societal reaction. Other things being equal or ignored, a particularly heinous crime will arouse more public action than a mild one, or an increase in the number of traffic offenses will cause more vigorous policing of the community. In order to predict societal reactions, techniques for estimating deviation are necessary. However, few efforts have been made to measure deviational behavior. Hypothetically, the sum total of deviation in a given situation will consist of the variance of the actions from prescribed social norms multiplied by the number of persons who engage in such actions. Measured or informally estimated in this way, the deviation in disapproved categories should be reciprocated by a comparatively intense reaction from the aggregates and groups whose sanctions have been violated. However, there are at least two other factors which interact with the gross deviation to condition the extent and nature of the societal reaction. One of these is the social visibility of the deviation.

## Social Visibility

In order for deviation to provoke a community reaction, it must have a minimum degree of visibility, that is, it must be apparent to others and be identified as deviation, A vast amount of sexual deviation in our society is clandestine and consequently escapes the public eye, which is to say that it has a low visibility, a fact probably related to the puritanical background of our culture. This is not to say that no social influence is present, since the deviant in such cases may still, through the action of covert symbolic processes, imagine the reaction of "others" to his behavior and acquire feelings of guilt or anxiety. However, he or she does avoid the traumatic impact of public identification as an immoral person and also evades the sequence of differential reactions and penalty which follow such an identification.

Criminal statistics are generally held to be unreliable for the very reason that such a vast amount of crime escapes the notice and records of the law-enforcement agencies. Low-visibility crimes include hundreds of thousands of abortions, many sexual crimes, passing of counterfeit money, shortchanging of business patrons, confidence games, pocket picking, shoplifting, gambling, and many others.

While many forms of criminal deviation remain concealed in our society, in other forms of deviation a high degree of visibility is present because of the intrinsic qualities of the behavior involved, because of the nature of the situation, or because of the physical and social characteristics of the persons involved. It is ordinarily believed that the misconduct of members of racial minorities receives more publicity than similar violations by majority-group persons. It has been the habit of many newspapers to call attention to the fact that a person committing a crime is a Negro or a Mexican, or an Indian, or an alien. This operates strongly to build up a stereotype of the group in question as being a criminally inclined "race" and thus heightens the societal reaction to their future violations. The low economic and unpropertied status of minority-group members means that they seldom appear as plaintiffs in civil and criminal proceedings and nearly always as defendants. This, too, heightens their visibility as deviants.

The member of an immigrant group living in an area not predominantly inhabited by persons of his own nationality is also likely to be more conspicuous when he transgresses the rules of society. The member of an upper social class is apt to have his behavior more carefully scrutinized for shortcomings when he is interacting with persons of low status than when he is with his compeers, although this probably varies a good deal.

A factor which has considerable effect in magnifying the visibility of any given deviation emerges from the adjustment which the deviants make to such a deviation. The adjustment consists of secondary, often habitual or unverbalized, responses which may be either compensatory in nature, or an integral part of a formalized deviant role. Reference intended here is to such things as the grimaces the stutterer makes in trying to speak, the bizarre posturings of crippled or blind persons, the mannerisms which the professional criminal elects to symbolize his difference from other members of society or from other criminals, or, finally, the flamboyant dress of the traditional prostitute. . . .

## The Societal Reaction

The socially visible deviations within a group, community, or society stir its members to a wide variety of expressive reactions and attitudes, depending upon the nature of the deviations and the expectancies of the conforming majority. Admiration, awe, envy, sympathy, fear, repulsion, disgust, hate, and anger are felt and manifested by those confronted by departures from their sanctioned ways of behaving. These are the elemental stuff from which the societal reaction is compounded.

### The pristine form of the societal reaction

In informally organized groups and communities there is a direct and spontaneous quality in the societal reaction which tends to be immediately relevant to the deviation. This continues to be the case, even in more formally organized groups and communities, so long as there is a close correspondence between the informal and formal organizations. Under these conditions the societal reaction tends to be a pure function of the interaction of deviation and the norms of the group which are transgressed. Other things being equal, the societal reaction will reciprocate in intensity the degree, amount, and visibility of the deviation. Beyond these, the compulsiveness of the norms violated or deviated from interacts to limit the severity of the societal reaction. Given constants and similarity of deviation, the public reaction in two different communities will vary with the respective importance attached to norms covering the deviations.

To illustrate what has been said in the preceding paragraph, we may take drunkenness for our example. Ordinarily, when a man is brought into court on a charge of "drunk and disorderly," he is warned or lectured and his case is dismissed. However, subsequent offenses are apt to result in fines and jail sentences. Ultimately, if his alcoholic disturbances persist over a long period of time, he may be placed in an institution.

This is a common pattern of reaction to drunken misdemeanants in many American communities. But from one community to another there may be variations in the policy for dealing with drunken persons. Drunkenness is handled with differing amounts of leniency because of the varying conceptions of the importance of sobriety. Some communities do not arrest drunks at all, but hold them in protective custody until they are sober again. In communities with heavy contingents of foreign-born in the population, the public reactions to drunkenness may be mitigated by the receptive attitudes of these groups toward this behavior. On the other hand in many Methodist communities in Kansas and Mormon communities in Utah, we see much greater public disapproval of drunkenness than in most other American communities.

In pursuing the more complex aspects of the societal reaction, some distinction must be observed between "innovating" and "recurrent" deviations. A sociopathic deviation which is entirely new and for which there is no historical antecedent often leaves a group or society at a loss for effective means of coping with it. This has often been the case where alcoholic liquors have been introduced by white men into primitive societies, leading to drunkenness which heretofore had been outside the experience of the group. Under conditions such as these the members of the group must rely or fall back upon informal expressions of their disapproval. These reactions may make the deviants uncomfortable and distressed but they do not necessarily impair their formal status.

Recurrent deviations and the growth of a deviant population bring alterations in the culture and social organization of the community within which they occur. Mythologies, stigma, stereotypes, patterns of exploitation, accommodation, segregation, and methods of control spring up and crystallize in the interaction between the deviants and the rest of society. The informal societal reaction is extended and formalized in the routinized procedures of agents and agencies delegated with direct responsibility for penalizing and restraining or reforming the deviants. The status of the deviants is redefined, and special pariah roles may be assigned to them.

### Spurious qualities of the societal reaction

The simple factoring of the societal reaction which we have done thus far is not sufficient to explain its complexities in groups or societies where the close organic relation between the deviation and attitudinal responses to it is mediated by a chain of formal relationships. Out of these a greatly attenuated societal reaction may appear, even in cases where there has been extensive, visible deviation from highly compulsive norms. It is fairly easy to think of situations in which serious offenses against laws commanding public respect have brought only a mild penalty or have gone entirely unpunished. Conversely, cases are easily discovered in which a somewhat minor violation of legal rules has provoked surprisingly stringent penalties. The societal reaction, especially under the second condition, has a spurious quality out of proportion to the deviation which engendered it. This spurious surplus of the societal reaction results in an exaggeration and distortion of the facts of deviation, so that a large measure of the deviation becomes "putative." The putative deviation is that portion of the societal definition of the deviant which has no foundation in his objective behavior. Frequently these fallacious imputations are incorporated into myth and stereotype and mediate much of the formal treatment of the deviant. We shall find many examples of this in the folklore about various specific forms of deviation which are to be treated in later chapters. One quick illustration is the common belief in our culture that the taking of narcotic drugs disposes people to sexual depravity and criminality—beliefs for which there is little or no proof.

To take into our reckoning all the factors which produce disproportions in the reciprocal relationship between deviation and the societal reaction would carry us too far afield into the subjects of public opinion and social control. Let it suffice to mention a few of the factors involved and then dwell upon one of the more important of these. Such things as purely technical demands of formal procedure, lack of resources and personnel of control agencies, personal idiosyncrasies of the persons in power, the nature and jurisdiction of the authority held by formal community agencies and the bureaucratic encystment of such agencies, isolating them from public opinion, should all be counted as significant variables in the formal societal reaction. . . .

### Sequence in the societal reaction

Despite the fact that when it first appears deviation can theoretically provoke approval, indifference, or disapproval, there is reason to believe that all innovations in behavior arouse some initial disapproval. The reason for this lies in the difficulty of immediately demonstrating the utility of the new behavior. Utility, is a function of understanding the deviation and is not always at once apparent to the great majority of people. Thus in the past many inventions, such as anesthesia and vaccination, were resisted by the public and even by members of the medical profession itself. Another reason why early departures from customary ways of behaving are unfavorably received by society or groups is that they upset a system of reciprocity between groups, extending to groups and persons who receive no direct value from the innovation. Moreover, the normative or value-systems of individuals may be so strongly reified that variations from expected behavior automatically awaken hostile reactions.

Once an innovation in behavior occurs and takes hold of a sizable number of persons, a dynamic interplay is observable between it and the social situation in which it takes place. Presumably there is a patterning in the sequence of events associated with the societal reaction. At least in such things as reform movements in urban politics there seems to be a similarity sufficiently recognizable to justify the terms "sequence" or "cycle." One attempt at analysis of the sequential aspects of communal reactions to disapproved behavior has been undertaken under the heading of "the natural history of a social problem." The deviation under consideration in this study was the appearance in Detroit, Michigan, of the pattern of family living in trailers and the growth of trailer camps in places where these families congregated and set up subcommunity organizations among themselves. The societal reaction to this new development was found to fall into three phases: (1) awareness, (2) policy determination, and (3) reform.

The time span between the first trailer-camp establishments and the peak of the community agitation and reaction to the "problem" was from ten to fifteen years. Visibility of the behavior was very low at first, then it tended to spread through geographic and social space until newspapers began to reflect the strong concern of many community groups at different social levels. As the hostility toward the inhabitants of these camps mounted, other groups were drawn into the situation, on the side of the trailer people as well as among their opponents. The chief advocates of the new behavior and defenders of the trailer dwellers were the companies manufacturing trailers and trailer equipment. Conflicts over policy gave rise to alignments of groups for and against various proposals to control the situation or to do away with the behavior. Finally, after a period of public controversy, the reaction to the "problem" tended to shift to an administrative level, with new ordinances and regulations put into effect by city and county officials. We are left to believe that the behavior which in its original form was disapproved of was finally integrated into the community culture.

### No one sequence or pattern in the societal reaction

While the analysis has much to commend it, there is some doubt as to whether it is a sufficient one. It is questionable whether the community reaction to variant behavior always follows the course and eventuates in the manner indicated by this research. The sequence described seems entirely too unilinear and mechanical. At least three possible end products of the community reaction are indicated: (1) ultimate acceptance of the variant behavior and its integration into the general, local, or special culture; (2) an unstable equilibrium or symbiotic relationship between the aberrant social organization and the normal; and (3) complete and unqualified rejection of the sociocultural novelty. The first alternative, which impressed the students of the Detroit situation, simply means that the deviation and societal reaction become a phase of social and cultural change. History records many similar instances of this sort. Trailer housing is not only well established in given localities but is pretty well accepted throughout our entire society. The use of lipstick, rouge, silk stockings, and smoking and drinking were all once confined to women with low social status or to prostitutes, yet today they are universally sanctioned as normal behavior for women of all classes. The Republican and Democratic parties in the United States have promoted and passed legislation in recent years which was once condemned as being socialistic and communistic. The proposals for graduated income taxes and the income tax generally were held to be radical and subversive in principle when first proposed; nevertheless, today these taxes are regarded as necessary parts of our whole financial structure.

### Unstable equilibrium in the societal reaction

The second large alternative, societal reaction, seems to be present in conjunction with many of our historically old "social problems," such as pauperism and many kinds of crime and prostitution, the forms of which have their roots in our European cultural antecedents. The societal reaction to these sociopathic behaviors in many areas is a compound of acceptance and rejection, frequently manifesting itself as the tacit tolerance of variant social patterns coupled with a nominal or formal disapproval and rejection. In this case the waxing deviation seems to have been halted at a certain point, giving rise to a tenuous integration between it and the older, accepted social organization. A situation obtains in which community tolerance is precariously stabilized just short of a critical point in the tolerance quotient at which collective action is taken.

The impasse which is reached in the societal reaction is partly explained by generalized culture conflict which affects such a large majority of the population that little consistent action is possible. This can be seen in ambivalent attitudes toward such things as begging and gambling. In the latter case most people realize that it is a costly and meaningless form of behavior, but the attitude is complicated by the fact that most people have gambled at some time or another. Even our churches have utilized gambling to raise money. In other words, gambling is both situational and systematic deviation. Consequently, fears are easily awakened that controls set up to eliminate the systematic gambling will be applied to gambling in other contexts. Drawing up legislation which will penalize the unwanted deviation without jeopardizing the status of the numerous casual participants is exceedingly difficult.

Other forms of sociopathic behavior are strictly systematic, and a sharp distinction can be made between the minority of persons who participate in it and the majority who do not. Here the explanation of the truncated societal reaction must be sought in the structuring of group relationships and the distribution of power within the community. The socially disapproved behavior in question may stir up a fairly strong and constant desire in the community for change and reform, but its importance in a reciprocal economy of group relations makes it impossible to root it out and destroy it. . . .

## Sociopathic Individuation

The deviant person is a product of differentiating and isolating processes. Some persons are individually differentiated from others from the time of birth onward, as in the case of a child born with a congenital physical defect or repulsive appearance, and as in the case of a child born into a minority racial or cultural group. Other persons grow to maturity in a family or in a social class where pauperism, begging, or crime are more or less institutionalized ways of life for the entire group. In these latter instances the person's sociopsychological growth may be normal in every way, his status as a deviant being entirely caused by his maturation within the framework of social organization and culture designated as "pathological" by the larger society. This is true of many delinquent children in our society.

The same sort of gradual, unconscious process which operates in the socialization of the deviant child may also be recognized in the acquisition of socially unacceptable behavior by persons after having reached adulthood. However, with more verbal and sophisticated adults, step-by-step violations of societal norms tend to be progressively rationalized in the light of what is socially acceptable. Changes of this nature can take place at the level of either overt or covert behavior, but with a greater likelihood that adults will preface overt behavior changes with projective symbolic departures from society's norms. When the latter occur, the subsequent overt changes may appear to be "sudden" personality modifications. However, whether these changes are completely radical ones is to some extent a moot point. One writer holds strongly to the opinion that sudden and dramatic shifts in behavior from normal to abnormal are seldom the case, that a sequence of small preparatory transformations must be the prelude to such apparently sudden behavior changes. This writer is impressed by the day-by-day growth of "reserve potentialities" within personalities of all individuals, and he contends that many normal persons carry potentialities for abnormal behavior, which, given proper conditions, can easily be called into play.

### Personality changes not always gradual

This argument is admittedly sound for most cases, but it must be taken into consideration that traumatic experiences often speed up changes in personality. Nor can the "trauma" in these experiences universally be attributed to the unique way in which the person conceives of the experience subjectively. Cases exist to show that personality modifications can be telescoped or that there can be an acceleration of such changes caused largely by the intensity and variety of the social stimulation. Most soldiers undoubtedly have entirely different conceptions of their roles after intensive combat experience. Many admit to having "lived a lifetime" in a relatively short period of time after they have been under heavy fire in battle for the first time. Many generals have remarked that their men have to be a little "shooted" or "blooded" in order to become good soldiers. In the process of group formation, crises and interactional amplification are vital requisites to forging true, role-oriented group behavior out of individuated behavior.

The importance of the person's conscious symbolic reactions to his or her own behavior cannot be overstressed in explaining the shift from normal to abnormal behavior or from one type of pathological behavior to another, particularly where behavior variations become systematized or structured into pathological roles. This is not to say that conscious choice is a determining factor in the differentiating process. Nor does it mean that the awareness of the self is a purely conscious perception. Much of the process of self-perception is doubtless marginal from the point of view of consciousness. But however it may be perceived, the individual's self-definition is closely connected with such things as self-acceptance, the subordination of minor to major roles, and with the motivation involved in learning the skills, techniques, and values of a new role. *Self-definitions or self-realizations are likely to be the result of sudden perceptions and they are especially significant when they are followed immediately by overt demonstrations of the new role they symbolize.* The self-defining junctures are critical points of personality genesis and in the special case of the atypical person they mark a division between two different types of deviation.

### Primary and secondary deviation

There has been an embarrassingly large number of theories, often without any relationship to a general theory, advanced to account for various specific pathologies in human behavior. For certain types of pathology, such as alcoholism, crime, or stuttering, there are almost as many theories as there are writers on these subjects. This has been occasioned in no small way by the preoccupation with the origins of pathological behavior and by the fallacy of confusing *original* causes with *effective* causes. All such theories have elements of truth, and the divergent viewpoints they contain can be reconciled with the general theory here if it is granted that original causes or antecedents of deviant behaviors are many and diversified. This holds especially for the psychological processes leading to similar pathological behavior, but it also holds for the situational concomitants of the initial aberrant conduct. A person may come to use excessive alcohol not only for a wide variety of subjective reasons but also because of diversified situational influences, such as the death of a loved one, business failure, or participating in some sort of organized group activity calling for heavy drinking of liquor. Whatever the original reasons for violating the norms of the community, they are important only for certain research purposes, such as assessing the extent of the "social problem" at a given time or determining the requirements for a rational program of social control. From a narrower sociological viewpoint the deviations are not significant until they are organized subjectively and transformed into active roles and become the social criteria for assigning status. The deviant individuals must react symbolically to their own behavior aberrations and fix them in their sociopsychological patterns. The deviations remain primary deviations or symptomatic and situational as long as they are rationalized or otherwise dealt with as functions of a socially acceptable role. Under such conditions normal and pathological behaviors remain strange and somewhat tensional bedfellows in the same person. Undeniably a vast amount of such segmental and partially integrated pathological behavior exists in our society and has impressed many writers in the field of social pathology.

Just how far and for how long a person may go in dissociating his sociopathic tendencies so that they are merely troublesome adjuncts of normally conceived roles is not known. Perhaps it depends upon the number of alternative definitions of the same overt behavior that he can develop; perhaps certain physiological factors (limits) are also involved. However, if the deviant acts are repetitive and have a high visibility, and if there is a severe societal reaction, which, through a process of identification is incorporated as part of the "me" of the individual, the probability is greatly increased that the integration of existing roles will be disrupted and that reorganization based upon a new role or roles will occur. (The "me" in this context is simply the subjective aspect of the societal reaction.) Reorganization may be the adoption of another normal role in which the tendencies previously defined as "pathological" are given a more acceptable social expression. The other general possibility is the assumption of a deviant role, if such exists; or, more rarely, the person may organize an aberrant sect or group in which he creates a special role of his own. *When a person begins to employ his deviant behavior or a role based upon it as a means of defense, attack, or adjustment to the overt and covert problems created by the consequent societal reaction to him, his deviation is secondary.* Objective evidences of this change will be found in the symbolic appurtenances of the new role, in clothes, speech, posture, and mannerisms, which in some cases heighten social visibility, and which in some cases serve as symbolic cues to professionalization.

### Role conceptions of the individual must be reinforced by reactions of others

It is seldom that one deviant act will provoke a sufficiently strong societal reaction to bring about secondary deviation, unless in the process of introjection the individual imputes or projects meanings into the social situation which are not present. In this case anticipatory fears are involved. For example, in a culture where a child is taught sharp distinctions between "good" women and "bad" women, a single act of questionable morality might conceivably have a profound meaning for the girl so indulging. However, in the absence of reactions by the person's family, neighbors, or the larger community, rein-forcing the tentative "bad-girl" self-definition, it is questionable whether a transition to secondary deviation would take place. It is also doubtful whether a temporary exposure to a severe punitive reaction by the community will lead a person to identify himself with a pathological role, unless, as we have said, the experience is highly traumatic. Most fre-quently there is a progressive reciprocal relationship between the deviation of the indi-vidual and the societal reaction, with a compounding of the societal reaction out of the minute accretions in the deviant behavior, until a point is reached where ingrouping and outgrouping between society and the deviant is manifest. At this point a stigmatizing of the deviant occurs in the form of name calling, labeling, or stereotyping.

The sequence of interaction leading to secondary deviation is roughly as follows: (1) primary deviation; (2) social penalties; (3) further primary deviation; (4) stronger penalties and rejections; (5) further deviation, perhaps with hostilities and resentment beginning to focus upon those doing the penalizing; (6) crisis reached in the tolerance quotient, expressed in formal action by the community stigmatizing of the deviant; (7) strengthening of the deviant conduct as a reaction to the stigmatizing and penalties; (8) ultimate acceptance of deviant social status and efforts at adjustment on the basis of the associated role.

As an illustration of this sequence the behavior of an errant schoolboy can be cited. For one reason or another, let us say excessive energy, the schoolboy engages in a classroom prank. He is penalized for it by the teacher. Later, due to clumsiness, he creates another disturbance and again he is reprimanded. Then, as sometimes happens, the boy is blamed for something he did not do. When the teacher uses the tag "bad boy" or "mischief maker" or other invidious terms, hostility and resentment are excited in the boy, and he may feel that he is blocked in playing the role expected of him. Thereafter, there may be a strong temptation to assume his role in the class as defined by the teacher, particularly when he discovers that there are rewards as well as penalties deriving from such a role. There is, of course, no implication here that such boys go on to become delinquents or criminals, for the mischief-maker role may later become integrated with or retrospectively rationalized as part of a role more acceptable to school authorities. If such a boy continues this unac-ceptable role and becomes delinquent, the process must be accounted for in the light of the general theory of this volume. There must be a spreading corroboration of a sociopathic self-conception and societal reinforcement at each step in the process.

The most significant personality changes are manifest when societal definitions and their subjective counterpart become generalized. When this happens, the range of major role choices becomes narrowed to one general class. This was very obvious in the case of a young girl who was the daughter of a paroled convict and who was attending a small Middle Western college. She continually argued with herself and with the author, in whom she had confided, that in reality she belonged on the "other side of the railroad tracks" and that her life could be enormously simplified by acquiescing in this verdict and living accordingly. While in her case there was a tendency to dramatize her conflicts, nevertheless there was enough societal reinforcement of her self-conception by the treatment she received in her relationship with her father and on dates with college boys to lend it a painful reality. Once these boys took her home to the shoddy dwelling in a slum area where she lived with her father, who was often in a drunken condition, they abruptly stopped seeing her again or else became sexually presumptive.

# CRIME, SHAME AND REINTEGRATION

## *John Braithwaite*

The theory in this [chapter] suggests that the key to crime control is cultural commitments to shaming in ways that I call reintegrative. Societies with low crime rates are those that shame potently and judiciously; individuals who resort to crime are those insulated from shame over their wrongdoing. However, shame can be applied injudiciously and counterproductively; the theory seeks to specify the types of shaming which cause rather than prevent crime. . . .

Figure 1 provides a schematic summary of the theory. In the first part of this chapter clear definitions are attempted for the key concepts in Figure 1. The cluster of six variables around interdependency at the top left of Figure 1 are characteristics of individuals; the three at the top right are characteristics of societies; while high levels of crime and shaming are variables which apply to both individuals and societies. The theory as summarized in Figure 1 thus gives an account both of why some kinds of individuals and some kinds of societies exhibit more crime.

We could get a more parsimonious theory by collapsing the similar constructs of interdependency (an individual-level variable) and communitarianism (a societal variable) into a single construct, but then we would no longer have a framework to predict both which individuals and which societies will have more crime. On the desirability of being able to do this I can only agree with Cressey:

> A theory explaining social behavior in general, or any specific kind of social behavior, should have two distinct but consistent aspects. First, there must be a statement that explains the statistical distribution of the behavior in time and space (epidemiology), and from which predictive statements about unknown statistical distributions can be derived. Second, there must be a statement that identifies, at least by implication, the process by which individuals come to

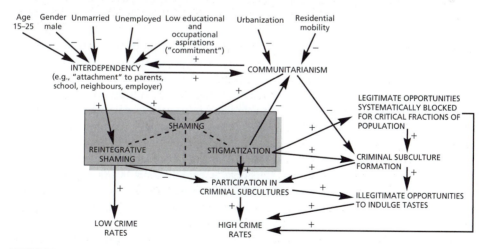

**FIGURE 1**
Summary of the theory of reintegrative shaming.

exhibit the behavior in question, and from which can be derived predictive statements about the behavior of individuals.

## Key Concepts

*Interdependency* is a condition of individuals. It means the extent to which individuals participate in networks wherein they are dependent on others to achieve valued ends and others are dependent on them. We could describe an individual as in a state of interdependency even if the individuals who are dependent on him are different from the individuals on whom he is dependent. Interdependency is approximately equivalent to the social bonding, attachment and commitment of control theory.

*Communitarianism* is a condition of societies. In communitarian societies individuals are densely enmeshed in interdependencies which have the special qualities of mutual help and trust. The interdependencies have symbolic significance in the culture of group loyalties which take precedence over individual interests. The interdependencies also have symbolic significance as attachments which invoke personal obligation to others in a community of concern, rather than simply interdependencies of convenience as between a bank and a small depositor. A communitarian culture rejects any pejorative connotation of dependency as threatening individual autonomy. Communitarian cultures resist interpretations of dependency as weakness and emphasize the need for mutuality of obligation in interdependency (to be both dependent and dependable). The Japanese are said to be socialized not only to *amaeru* (to be succored by others) but also to *amayakasu* (to be nurturing to others).

*Shaming* means all social processes of expressing disapproval which have the intention or effect of invoking remorse in the person being shamed and/or condemnation by others who become aware of the shaming. When associated with appropriate symbols, formal punishment often shames. But societies vary enormously in the extent to which formal punishment is associated with shaming or in the extent to which the social meaning of punishment is no more than to inflict pain to tip reward–cost calculations in favor of certain outcomes. Shaming, unlike purely deterrent punishment, sets out to moralize with the offender to communicate reasons for the evil of her actions. Most shaming is neither associated with formal punishment nor perpetrated by the state, though both shaming by the state and shaming with punishment are important types of shaming. Most shaming is by individuals within interdependent communities of concern.

*Reintegrative shaming* is shaming which is followed by efforts to reintegrate the offender back into the community of law-abiding or respectable citizens through words or gestures of forgiveness or ceremonies to decertify the offender as deviant. Shaming and reintegration do not occur simultaneously but sequentially, with reintegration occurring before deviance becomes a master status. It is shaming which labels the act as evil while striving to preserve the identity of the offender as essentially good. It is directed at signifying evil deeds rather than evil persons in the Christian tradition of "hate the sin and love the sinner." Specific disapproval is expressed within relationships characterized by general social approval; shaming criminal behavior is complemented by ongoing social rewarding of alternative behavior patterns. Reintegrative shaming is not necessarily weak; it can be cruel, even vicious. It is not distinguished from stigmatization by its potency, but by (a) a finite rather than open-ended duration which is terminated by forgiveness; and by (b) efforts to maintain bonds of love or respect throughout the finite period of suffering shame.

*Stigmatization* is disintegrative shaming in which no effort is made to reconcile the offender with the community. The offender is outcast, her deviance is allowed to become a master status, degradation ceremonies are not followed by ceremonies to decertify deviance.

*Criminal subcultures* are sets of rationalizations and conduct norms which cluster together to support criminal behavior. The clustering is usually facilitated by subcultural groups which provide systematic social support for crime in any of a number of ways—supplying members with criminal opportunities, criminal values, attitudes which weaken conventional values of law-abidingness, or techniques of neutralizing conventional values.

## Short Summary of the Theory

The following might serve as the briefest possible summary of the theory. A variety of life circumstances increase the chances that individuals will be in situations of greater interdependency, the most important being age (under 15 and over 25), being married, female, employed, and having high employment and educational aspirations. Interdependent persons are more susceptible to shaming. More importantly, societies in which individuals are subject to extensive interdependencies are more likely to be communitarian, and shaming is much more widespread and potent in communitarian societies. Urbanization and high residential mobility are societal characteristics which undermine communitarianism.

The shaming produced by interdependency and communitarianism can be either of two types—shaming that becomes stigmatization or shaming that is followed by reintegration. The shaming engendered is more likely to become reintegrative in societies that are communitarian. In societies where shaming does become reintegrative, low crime rates are the result because disapproval is dispensed without eliciting a rejection of the disapprovers, so that the potentialities for future disapproval are not dismantled. Moreover, reintegrative shaming is superior even to stigmatization for conscience-building.

Shaming that is stigmatizing, in contrast, makes criminal subcultures more attractive because these are in some sense subcultures which reject the rejectors. Thus, when shaming is allowed to become stigmatization for want of reintegrative gestures or ceremonies which decertify deviance, the deviant is both attracted to criminal subcultures and cut off from other interdependencies (with family, neighbors, church, etc.). Participation in subcultural groups supplies criminal role models, training in techniques of crime and techniques of neutralizing crime (or other forms of social support) that make choices to engage in crime more attractive. Thus, to the extent that shaming is of the stigmatizing rather than the reintegrative sort, and that criminal subcultures are widespread and accessible in the society, higher crime rates will be the result. While societies characterized by high levels of stigmatization will have higher crime rates than societies characterized by reintegrative shaming, the former will have higher or lower crime rates than societies with little shaming at all depending largely on the availability of criminal subcultures.

Yet a high level of stigmatization in the society is one of the very factors that encourages criminal subculture formation by creating populations of outcasts with no stake in conformity, no chance of self-esteem within the terms of conventional society—individuals in search of an alternative culture that allows them self-esteem. A communitarian culture, on the other hand, nurtures deviants within a network of attachments to conventional society, thus inhibiting the widespread outcasting that is the stuff of subculture formation.

For clarity of exposition the two types of shaming have been presented as a stark dichotomy. In reality, for any society some deviants are dealt with in ways that are more stigmatic while others receive more reintegrative shaming. Indeed, a single deviant will be responded to more stigmatically by some, more reintegratively by others. To the extent that the greater weight of shaming tends to stigmatization, the crime-producing processes on the right of Figure 1 are more likely to be triggered; to the extent that the balance of shaming tips toward reintegration, informal processes of crime control are more likely to prevail over these crime-producing processes.

The other major societal variable which fosters criminal subculture formation is systematic blockage of legitimate opportunities for critical fractions of the population. If black slum dwellers are systematically denied economic opportunities because of the stigma of their race and neighborhood, then criminal subcultures will form in those outcast neighborhoods. It can be seen that stigmatization (as opposed to social integration) as a cultural disposition may contribute to the systematic blockage of these economic opportunities; but cultural variables like stigmatization will be of rather minor importance compared with structural economic variables in determining opportunities. I have argued that the blockages in this part of the theory are not restricted to closed opportunities to climb out of poverty; systematically blocked opportunities for ever greater wealth accumulation by the most affluent of corporations often lead to corporate criminal subculture formation.

Criminal subcultures are the main mechanism for constituting illegitimate opportunity structures—knowledge on how to offend, social support for offending or communication of rationalizations for offending, criminal role models, subcultural groups which assist with the avoidance of detection and which organize collective criminal enterprises. However, illegitimate opportunities are greater in some societies than others for a variety of further reasons which are not incorporated within the theory. While the effects of legitimate and illegitimate opportunities on crime are mostly mediated by participation in criminal subcultures, the blockage of legitimate opportunities combined with the availability of illegitimate opportunities can independently increase crime. Whether illegitimate opportunities to engage in crime are supplied by participation in criminal subcultures or otherwise, they must be opportunities that appeal to the tastes of tempted individuals for them to result in crime.

This summary is crudely simple because it ignores what goes on within the shaming box in Figure 1. That is, it ignores the treatment of the social processes that combine individual acts of shaming into cultural processes of shaming which are more or less integrative: gossip, media coverage of shaming incidents, children's stories, etc. In turn, the summary has neglected how these macro processes of shaming feed back to ensure that micro practices of shaming cover the curriculum of crimes. . . .

### Capacity of the Theory to Explain What We Know about Crime

. . . What is the capacity of the theory to explain [the correlates of crime]? Some indeterminacy arises over the different effects of reintegrative shaming versus stigmatization. For example, what does the theory predict should be the association between gender and crime? Figure 1 shows that being female increases interdependency, which in turn fosters shaming. If the extra shaming produced is reintegrative, being female is associated with low crime rates. However, if the extra shaming amounts to stigmatization, higher crime rates become possible where subcultural support is found for the outcast status.

To solve this problem we make a rather modest assumption. This assumption, as argued earlier, is that in most societies criminal subcultures are minority phenomena—narrowly diffused—so that stigmatization will in only a minority of cases be followed by an opportunity to participate in a subculture which is attractive to the individual. It follows that the level of shaming should be unambiguously negatively related to the crime rate because most shaming will be either reintegrative shaming, or stigmatic shaming which does not lead to subcultural attachments, and both of these options will reduce crime. In any case, as is clear from Figure 1, variables (like gender) which increase interdependency have their effect on shaming partly through increasing communitarianism, and shaming which is a product of communitarianism is most likely to be reintegrative. Interdependency both increases the prospects of shaming and decreases the chances that such shaming as occurs will be stigmatic.

Thus the characteristics associated with low interdependency—being male, 15–25 years of age, unmarried, unemployed, and with low educational and vocational aspirations—should all be associated with high involvement in crime. Urbanization and high residential mobility are also predicted by the theory as correlates of crime. It is concluded that all of these characteristics are strong and consistent correlates of crime.

In establishing the relationship between communitarianism and crime, we rely far too heavily on qualitative evidence from Japan and more doubtful qualitative evidence from a handful of other societies. The association between interdependency as a characteristic of individuals and crime, on the other hand, is well established. Control theory has spawned impressive evidence that young people who are "attached" to their parents and to the school are less likely to engage in delinquency.

There is not such an impressive and unambiguous literature on "attachment" to neighbors and crime. The recent review of sixty-five studies of religiosity and deviance by Tittle and Welch suggests the possibility, contrary to some conventional wisdom in criminology, that interdependency via church affiliation may reduce crime. Tittle and Welch concluded that "the evidence seems remarkably consistent in suggesting that religion is related to deviant behavior. Indeed, only a few variables in social science (possibly gender and age) have proven to be better predictors of rule breaking." . . .

. . . The theory of reintegrative shaming provides an explanation for why unemployed people should engage in less crime in terms of their loss of interdependency. Beyond unemployment, being at the bottom of the class structure means blocked legitimate opportunities and an increased likelihood of access to certain kinds of subcultures which supply illegitimate opportunities.

The theory offers a convincing explanation of why crime rates have been increasing in most Western societies since World War II. The recent development of Western societies has been associated with a decline of interdependency and communitarianism and a progressive uncoupling of punishment and shaming. This has been a period when urbanization, residential mobility, delayed marriage and marriage breakdown, and an explosion of the 15–25 age group have occurred in most countries.

Finally, that young people who associate with criminals are more likely to engage in crime themselves, approximates one of the propositions of the theory—that participating in a criminal subculture leads to crime. Sharing a criminal subculture was argued to be a route to crime partly because the subculture transmits qualifications or neutralizations to belief in the importance of complying with the law.

In summary, the theory accounts for the best established findings of criminology as corollaries of the theory and one as a postulate of the theory.

# CONTEMPORARY RETROSPECTIVE ON LABELING THEORIES

## LABELING AND SECONDARY DEVIANCE

*Jón Gunnar Bernburg, University of Iceland*

Labeling theory focuses on the consequences of societal reactions to deviance, emphasizing the ways in which society labels and stigmatizes social deviants (criminals, persons who are mentally ill, gays and lesbians, and so on), and on the consequences of such processes for labeled individuals. Key statements on the labeling approach are found in the early works of Tannenbaum (1938) and Lemert (1951), and in a series of works that came out during the 1960s, including the works of Becker (1963), Goffman (1963), Scheff (1966), and others.

An important proposition that surfaces in these writings is that societal reactions to deviance can trigger processes that tend to reinforce or amplify subsequent deviance. The criminological version of this proposition, presented in the writings of Tannenbaum, Lemert, and Becker, focuses on the effect of criminal labeling on subsequent criminal behavior. Thus, once significant aspects of the social environment have defined or labeled the individual as a criminal or a delinquent, the labeled individual is associated with widespread, negative stereotypes, and is often seen by others as fundamentally different from other people. The individual is labeled and cast into a stigmatized social status, which therefore may trigger several criminogenic processes, including (1) changes in the individual's definition of self, (2) reduced integration into the conventional social structure, and (3) increased association with deviant groups.

An emphasis on the effect of labeling on the individual's definition of self is found in the works of Edwin Lemert. Lemert (1951) argues that deviations are "primary" as long as individuals rationalize or otherwise deal with the deviations "as functions of a socially acceptable role" (p. 75). However, repeated deviations that have high visibility and that lead to severe societal reaction can lead to a definition of "me" as a deviant—that is, the individual may develop a conception of self as a deviant, which therefore may lead to more stable involvement in deviance. "Objective evidences of this change will be found in the symbolic appurtenances of the new role, in clothes, speech, posture, and mannerisms, which in some cases heighten social visibility" (p. 76). At this point, deviant behavior is "secondary" as it is no longer merely a function of the conditions or problems that initially triggered the deviant behavior. Deviant behavior now reflects a changed definition of self.

Labeling and stigmatization may have negative consequences for ties to conventional groups and for access to mainstream opportunities, hence increasing the likelihood of future involvement in crime and deviance. Moreover, reduced integration into conventional social structure can lead to increased associations with deviant groups, which also increases the likelihood of stable deviant and criminal behavior. According to theorists (Becker, 1963; Tannenbaum, 1938), criminal labeling can trigger rejection and other negative responses by conventional others, including peers, community members, and gatekeepers in the opportunity structure (e.g., employers). Becker tackles this notion by using the concept of *master status*, underscoring that the deviant status can override other statuses a person has. Thus, conventional others often define labeled individuals on the basis of stereotypes, which therefore can trigger fear, mistrust, and other negative perceptions of labeled individuals. Therefore, conventional agents tend to reject individuals that have been labeled deviant. Also, people may reject labeled individuals to avoid being associated with stigma themselves. Finally, as Tannenbaum (1938, p. 17) points out, labeling may also trigger reduced ties to the conventional order due to defiance. Once key actors in the community have defined the individual as bad, "he is not believed if he is good," which therefore can lead to "defiance" and "escape" from the institutional order.

Thus, we can see that although labeling research has often focused on the exclusionary effects of formal labeling such as arrest or conviction (e.g., Schwartz & Skolnick, 1962), labeling theory emphasizes informal as well as formal labeling. In fact, given the theory's focus on social interaction and social status, informal labeling is a central factor in the labeling process (Matsueda, 1992; Paternoster & Iovanni, 1989). Significant others and gatekeepers in the institutional order—local community, school, family, workplace, and so on—play key roles in defining the individual's social status and self-concept.

But, formal labeling plays a crucial role in the labeling process as well, because formal reactions and sanctions may trigger or escalate informal labeling. Lemert (1951) points out, "Deviation is criminal only if effectively reacted to and symbolized as such" (p. 284). To be formally processed as a deviant lends special and enhanced significance to the status of the person as a "criminal." Tannenbaum's (1938) notion of the dramatization of evil underscores the same point; that is, criminal justice reactions, such as arrest, trial, and imprisonment, signify the individual as a delinquent or criminal, and thus constitute public designations of the individual's immorality and inability to follow rules and social norms. Moreover, experiencing formal reactions may have a direct impact on self-definitions. This point is emphasized by Lemert (1951), who argues that social sanctions convey powerful messages to offenders about what others now think of them. For example, "The symbolic environment of the prison converts the more general societal definition of the criminal into variations on a common theme . . . 'once a crook always a crook'" (p. 315).

Labeling theory has gone through periods of controversy and debate, not surprisingly given that the theory entails a proposition that directly contradicts traditional ideas about the role of punishment in crime deterrence. The labeling approach was widely popular in the field of deviance and crime during the 1960s and early 1970s, but it became discredited within criminology after a series of critical papers that came out during the 1970s and 1980s. The critics argued that labeling theory was vague and trivial, and, to the extent that it could be regarded as a theory, its claims were not supported by empirical research (Hirschi, 1980; Mankoff, 1971; Tittle, 1980; Wellford, 1975). When reading the original texts by Tannenbaum, Lemert, and Becker, it is hard to deny that elaboration is needed on the processes involved, and that the theorists provided little research evidence that could verify their claims. However, as Paternoster and Iovanni (1989) have pointed out, much of the early critique was overly stringent, even antagonistic toward the labeling approach. Moreover, much of the critique aimed at the theory's supposed failure to receive empirical support was in fact not justified given that there was almost no valid research evidence at the time for or against labeling theory (Paternoster & Iovanni, 1989). This may have led to a premature demise of labeling theory within criminology.

Despite the tendency to ignore labeling effects in criminological research (Hagan & Palloni, 1990), recent decades have seen some buildup of constructive work on the labeling approach. First, while the classic statements on labeling theory were indeed vague and fragmented, and provided only blueprints for theoretical processes, more recent work has provided elaboration and refinement of the labeling approach. Second, there have been improvements in the empirical research, which is significant given that research on labeling effects has often been plagued by methodological problems (Paternoster & Iovanni, 1989). In what follows, I discuss the current literature on labeling theory, turning my attention first to refinement and elaborations of labeling theory.

## Refinement and Elaboration

Attempts to clarify and elaborate on the mechanisms through which labeling may influence the development of deviance and crime have provided much needed theoretical clarity to the labeling literature. Matsueda (1992) has provided a refinement of the argument that labeling influences deviance through its effect on the self-concept. Building on the social psychology of George H. Mead (1934), Matsueda assumes that the self arises in problematic situations when individuals perform *role-taking;* that is, when individuals take the role of a significant other and see themselves from their standpoint. In Matsueda's terms, the self-concept is shaped in the process of *reflected appraisals,* in which individuals give meaning to themselves based on how they perceive themselves from the standpoint of others. Accordingly, when individuals perceive themselves as delinquent from the standpoint of others, they tend to form perceptions of themselves as delinquents, which therefore can lead to commitment to delinquent roles.

The work of Link, Cullen, Struening, Shrout, and Dohrenwend (1989) on mental illness labeling provides another significant theoretical elaboration that seems relevant for criminal labeling. Link et al. argue that labeling may lead to reduced social ties and life chances due to not only actual rejection or discrimination by others but also anticipated rejection and social withdrawal. Thus, labeled individuals, having exposure to the same stereotypes as others, often anticipate that others will devalue or reject them. Situations that entail such reactions by others are perceived to trigger feelings of shame and embarrassment (see Goffman, 1963, p. 13), and hence labeled individuals may often avoid social situations that, in their minds, could entail uncomfortable interaction dynamics, including rejection and devaluation by others. In turn, "withdrawal may lead to constricted social networks and fewer attempts at seeking more satisfying, higher paying jobs" (Link et al., 1989, p. 403).

Labeling theory can be integrated with other sociological theories, and such integration is emphasized in some of the early works on labeling theory, including the works of Becker and Tannenbaum. The current labeling literature emphasizes that labeling theory complements other sociological theories of crime and deviance. Sampson and Laub (1997) have argued that labeling theory can be integrated into the life-course approach to crime, which focuses on the development of social bonds in the life course. According to

Sampson and Laub, labeling and stigmatization (among other factors) can have a negative impact on the individual's social bonds and life chances. Insofar as labeling undermines social bonding in areas of family, school, peer ties, or employment, labeling indirectly increases the likelihood of subsequent deviance. For example, formal labeling of children and adolescents may lead to parental stress and rejection of the child, which may increase the likelihood of poor parenting practices, and hence increase the likelihood of subsequent adolescent delinquent behavior (Stewart, Simons, Conger, & Scaramella, 2002). Moreover, Sampson and Laub emphasize that labeling may have long-term as well as short-term effects. Labeling that occurs during childhood or adolescence can have long-term effects on life changes and adult criminal behavior because it can lead to reduced educational attainment and restricted employment opportunities, thus weakening "social and institutional bonds linking adults to society" (Sampson & Laub, 1997, p. 144).

Labeling theorists have long implied the integration of labeling theory and social learning–differential association theory (Becker, 1963; Heimer & Matsueda, 1994; Kaplan & Johnson, 1991; Sampson & Laub, 1997; Tannenbaum, 1938). Social learning–differential association theory (see Akers, 1985) implies that deviant groups provide attitudes, rationalizations, role models, and opportunities that increase the likelihood of deviance and crime. Accordingly, insofar as labeling increases the likelihood of association with deviant groups, it indirectly influences subsequent delinquency.

In this vein, Bernburg, Krohn, and Rivera (2006) have pointed out that given the importance of peer influence in delinquent behavior, the effects of labeling on deviant peer association should be of major interest to criminologists. Bernburg et al. suggest several processes by which formal criminal labeling of juveniles may increase deviant peer associations. First, conventional peers in the local community may avoid or reject labeled peers because of their own negative perceptions (e.g., due to fear and mistrust), but also because their parents may expect them to avoid known delinquents. Second, anticipating stigmatization and embarrassment, labeled youths may withdraw from conventional social situations, which therefore reduces their involvement in conventional peer networks. For example, a youth who is known as a delinquent in the community may avoid going to a friend's house because meeting the friend's parents may entail shame or embarrassment. Both rejection and withdrawal in turn increase association with deviant peer groups, which represent a source of social support in which deviant labels are accepted. Finally, the formation of a deviant self-concept may increase association with deviant groups because individuals tend to become friends with those whom they perceive as similar to themselves.

Braithwaite's (1989) *shaming theory* offers an ambitious attempt to integrate several sociological theories, including labeling theory, into a broad, multilevel theory of criminal behavior. A key notion in Braithwaite's work is the distinction between *reintegrative* and *disintegrative* shaming (shaming generally refers to societal responses that express disapproval and aim to invoke remorse in the offender). Reintegrative shaming is when shaming is followed by efforts to bring the person back into the community by gestures of acceptance and forgiveness. Thus, the person is not labeled and stigmatized but seen as a normal person who has done wrong. By contrast, disintegrative shaming refers to the type of processes described by labeling theory, namely, shaming that entails labeling, stigmatization, social exclusion, and defiance. Thus, this approach argues that social sanctions do not necessarily entail labeling and stigmatization. Such harmful processes tend to occur only when societal reactions fail to convey the message to the offender that he or she is still considered a full member of the social group.

According to Braithwaite's theory, social context specifies the tendency for shaming to be either reintegrative or disintegrative. Shaming tends to be reintegrative when there is a high level of interdependency in the social group as a whole and between the offender and the group. Preexisting bonds between the offender and the group provide means to communicate not only moral condemnation but also gestures of forgiveness and acceptance. Preexisting bonds also create the perception that the offender is a real person, and hence he or she is less likely to be defined on the basis of stereotypes. Also, members of groups that are characterized by high levels of social cohesion, trust, and group loyalty presumably are more concerned and more willing to participate in reintegrative shaming. Accordingly, reintegrative shaming is most likely to be found in social contexts that are characterized by interdependence and communitarianism. By contrast, individualistic groups and societies have fewer procedures to reintegrate offenders; in such contexts shaming is more likely to result in labeling, stigmatization, and social exclusion.

Aside from Braithwaite's theory, scholars have pointed out that other situational and structural factors may specify labeling effects. The emphasis of labeling theory on social status and identity has prompted scholars to consider whether initial social status may specify the effects of labeling. Such considerations, however, have led to opposite hypotheses regarding the role of social status in specifying labeling effects (Sherman & Smith, 1992). On the one hand, labeling may have a larger, detrimental effect on disadvantaged individuals, including minorities and the impoverished, because these groups tend to lack economic and social resources to resist labeling and stigmatization. For example, in comparison with poor, nonwhite parents, white, middle- or upper-class parents should be more likely to be able to convince the school authorities that their child is not destined to be a criminal and should get a second change (see Bodwhich, 1993). Bernburg and Krohn (2003) have suggested that formal labeling may be more likely to trigger informal labeling and stigmatization of disadvantaged individuals, because such individuals are associated with stigma to begin with.

On the other hand, since disadvantaged individuals are already associated with stigma, they may have reduced stakes in maintaining a respectable identity, thus they may be less likely to be affected by labeling (Ageton & Elliott, 1974; Hirschfield, 2008). Hirschfield has suggested that in severely disadvantaged inner-city communities arrests are common and perceived as a normal aspect of male adolescence, and hence carry little stigma in such contexts.

Finally, scholars have pointed out that there may be an interaction effect between formal and informal labeling. Paternoster and Iovanni (1989) have pointed out that formal labeling may not influence individual development much if it does not lead to labeling in informal social settings. Again, significant others and gatekeepers in the institutional order play key roles in defining the individual's social status and self-concept. Thus, formal labeling, such as an arrest or a conviction, may have little or no impact on a person's social status as long as it is kept secret from community members, employers, teachers, and so on. But, if the formal labeling becomes widely known, the individual may find himself or herself cast into a stigmatized social status. This argument has important implications for research on labeling effects, as the effect of formal labeling on negative outcomes should be more pronounced if the formal label becomes known to actors that play a key role in defining the individual's social status and self-concept (see Hjalmarsson, 2008).

## Empirical Evaluation

In an important review article written about two decades ago, Paternoster and Iovanni (1989) argued that the bulk of the research on labeling effects on delinquency and crime was plagued by methodological problems, and hence there were few conclusions that could be drawn about the general validity of labeling theory. Specifically, Paternoster and Iovanni discussed four problems in their review. First, studies on the effect of formal labeling on delinquency had often used samples that comprised formally labeled offenders only (e.g., offenders on record, or ex-convicts). Such data often do not entail the necessary comparison between individuals who have been labeled and individuals who have not been labeled. Second, the bulk of the research had failed to examine directly the processes that, according to labeling theory, should mediate the effects of labeling on subsequent delinquency and crime. Third, labeling research had often failed to specify and examine potential contingent effects of labeling. Finally, most of the research had studied only formal labeling, while informal labeling effects were rarely examined.

During the past two decades, there have been attempts to improve the research with respect to some of these methodological issues. Researchers have used longitudinal survey studies based on samples from general populations (as opposed to populations of offenders on record) to examine the effect of labeling on subsequent delinquency. Such studies tend to find a positive effect of formal labeling on subsequent delinquency, net of initial delinquency and other controls (Bernburg & Krohn, 2003; Hagan & Palloni, 1990; Johnson, Simons, & Conger, 2004; Palarma, Cullen, & Gersten, 1986; Ray & Downs, 1986; Stewart et al., 2002). For example, in a study on British working-class boys, Hagan and Palloni (1990) found a positive effect of formal juvenile labeling (conviction) on subsequent delinquency, while controlling for initial delinquent behavior, as well as for "characterological processes" (parenting practices, family income, IQ score at ages eight to nine, conduct problems at ages eight to nine, etc.). Hagan and Palloni also found evidence for contingent effects of labeling. The effect of formal labeling on subsequent delinquency turned out to be significantly larger among boys whose parents had a criminal conviction. Hagan and Palloni argued that formal labeling of youths may be more likely to trigger informal labeling and stigma in the context of a stigmatized family.

The study by Hagan and Palloni (1990) underscores a general point discussed earlier, namely, that the informal social environment may be more likely to stigmatize individuals that are associated with stigma to begin with (Bernburg & Krohn, 2003). Another study that supports this notion is a study by Palarma et al. (1986) who found that arrest had a larger effect on subsequent delinquency among youths who also had a mental illness label. The findings by Hagan and Palloni are also consistent with Lemert's (1951) suggestion that when youths are exposed to stigmatized role models (especially parents), "chances are greater that societal definitions of 'criminal' applied to the young deviant will be incorporated as the fulcrum of self" (p. 318).

Labeling theory has received support in experimental research that randomizes formal reaction to apprehended offenders. Klein (1986) conducted a field experiment that randomized the formal action taken against a sample of apprehended youths. The youths were at random (1) counseled and released or (2) referred to the social service system, referred with purchase of service, or petitioned toward juvenile court. The study found that youths who were counseled and released had a lower probability of recidivism after

27 months than youths who experienced further reaction. In fact, the highest recidivism rate was found in the group that was petitioned toward juvenile court. Sherman and Smith (1992) conducted field experiments to examine the effect of arrest for domestic violence on subsequent domestic violence (see also Berk, Campbell, Klap, & Western, 1992). The study found that arrest for domestic violence was associated with an increased likelihood of subsequent violence, but these effects were observed among unemployed individuals only. These field experiments underscore that properly designed studies on samples comprised only of offenders on record can provide meaningful tests of labeling theory.

Chiricos, Barrick, Bales, and Bontrager (2007) examined the effect of formal adjudication on recidivism in a sample of adults found guilty of a felony and sentenced to probation in Florida between 2000 and 2002. Although the study was not an experiment, the study's setting provided a meaningful comparison between formally labeled individuals and individuals who have "escaped" formal labeling, because judges in Florida have the option to withhold formal adjudication of guilt for convicted felons who are sentenced to probation. Offenders who have adjudication withheld can say on employment applications and elsewhere that they have not been convicted for a felony, and thus they lose no civil rights. The study found that formal adjudication increased the likelihood of recidivism, net of prior record, type and seriousness of the offense, and social demographic factors. Chiricos et al. also examined whether the effect of formal adjudication on recidivism was contingent on social background characteristics as well as neighborhood context. The findings showed that formal adjudication had a significantly larger effect on recidivism among white offenders, but the effect did not interact with neighborhood disadvantage. Finally, Chiricos et al. found that the effect of adjudication on recidivism was stronger among individuals who did not have a prior criminal record before the age of 30. This finding is consistent with research that has shown that novice offenders are affected more by formal labeling than individuals who have developed a pattern of delinquent behavior prior to labeling (Horowitz & Wasserman, 1979).

Elaborations of theoretical processes have guided researchers in examining intervening processes in the effect of labeling on subsequent deviance. Matsueda (1992) has used longitudinal survey data on male youths to examine the effect of reflected appraisals on delinquent behavior (see the prior discussion). As discussed, Matsueda's approach implies that in order to evaluate the effect of labeling on the self-concept, two key factors need to be examined, namely, the appraisals of others (perceptions of others toward an individual) and reflected appraisals (perceived perceptions of others toward self). Matsueda used interviews with parents as well as their children and was able to measure key variables in his argument, such as parental appraisal of the child as a rule-violator (parental perception of the child as a rule-violator); youth's appraisal of self as a rule-violator (youth's own perception of whether friends, parents, and teachers see him or her as a rule-violator), and self-reported delinquent behavior. The findings supported Matsueda's key hypotheses. Thus, both parental appraisals of their child as a rule-violator as well as the youth's reflected appraisal as a rule-violator had positive effects on subsequent delinquent behavior (net of social background and initial delinquency). In a subsequent analysis of the same data, Heimer and Matsueda (1994) found that association with delinquent peers mediated a part of the effect of parental and self-appraisals on subsequent delinquency.

Few studies have examined the intermediate role of ties to conventional others, although some research lends support for this process. Stewart et al. (2002) found that formal labeling (an index for police contacts and involvement with the juvenile justice system) had a positive effect on subsequent delinquent behavior, in part through a positive effect of formal labeling on poor parenting practices. Other studies have confirmed that formal labeling negatively influences conventional social ties (Zhang, 1994; Zhang & Messner, 1994).

There is evidence for the negative effect of formal labeling on life chances, especially on employment (e.g., Pager, 2003; Schwartz & Scolnick, 1962; Western & Beckett, 1999), but few studies have directly examined whether reduced life chances mediate the effect of labeling on subsequent delinquency and crime. There is some research, though, that supports this process (Bernburg & Krohn, 2003; De Li, 1999; Sampson & Laub, 1993). Bernburg and Krohn (2003) used longitudinal data on urban males to examine the effect of formal labeling during adolescence on criminal behavior during early adulthood. Bernburg and Krohn used alternative indicators of formal labeling. Thus, police records were used to examine whether the youths had been arrested or had experienced police contact, and self-report data were used to examine whether the subject had experienced juvenile justice intervention (put on probation, placed in a correctional center, community service, or detention, brought to court, placed in a treatment program). The findings showed, first, that formal labeling during adolescence had a positive effect on crime in late adolescence and early adulthood, net of initial delinquency and other controls. Second, the study found that educational attainment and employment stability mediated a part of the effect of formal labeling on early adulthood crime. Finally, Bernburg and Krohn found that formal labeling during adolescence had a larger effect on young adulthood crime among African Americans and among individuals who had impoverished family backgrounds. These findings were thus contrary to the findings of Chiricos et al. (2007) on adult offenders that, again, found larger labeling effects among whites.

Some research supports the intermediate role of deviant peer associations. Bernburg et al. (2006) examined whether the effect of formal labeling on subsequent delinquency was mediated by association with delinquent peers, using three successive time-points (six-month intervals) from longitudinal data on urban adolescents. The study found that juvenile justice intervention influenced subsequent delinquency, net of initial delinquency and other controls. Moreover, gang membership and association with delinquent peers mediated a part of this effect. A few other studies indicate that formal labeling has a positive effect on association with delinquent peers (Johnson et al., 2004; Kaplan & Johnson, 1991; but see Farrington, 1977). And, again, there is some research that supports the effect of informal labeling on delinquent peer associations (Heimer & Matsueda, 1994).

With the exception of Matsueda's (1992) study of reflected appraisals, and subsequent analyses of these same data (e.g., Heimer & Matsueda, 1994; Tripplett & Jarjoura, 1994), labeling research has paid limited attention to informal labeling. I have pointed out elsewhere (Bernburg, in press) that the lack of direct research of informal labeling constitutes a serious limitation of the research literature. Thus, for example, there is research that indicates that formal labeling is associated with reduced ties to conventional people and mainstream opportunity structures, but there has not been much research on the processes that may be involved. Some research exists though. Experimental research has shown that employers often reject applicants that have a formal criminal label (Pager, 2003; Schwartz & Skolnick, 1962).

As discussed, Link et al. (1989) imply that in order to tackle the processes triggered by labeling, research needs to go beyond examining only objective (formal and informal) labeling; it also needs to focus on perceived and anticipated labeling and stigma, as well as efforts by labeled individuals to withdraw from social situations. Such research has been rare, although a recent study by Winnick and Bodkin (2008) provides an example of how withdrawal processes can be examined. Winnick and Bodkin conducted a survey among convicts, asking the convicts about how they intended to manage their status as ex-convicts upon release from prison. The study found that many convicts believe that most people distrust and reject ex-convicts, a belief that was positively associated with an intention to withdraw from social participation upon release from prison.

As discussed, the effects of societal reactions on individual development, including subsequent involvement in delinquency and crime, may be contingent on social context. As we have seen, research has revealed a few significant contingencies, including preexisting stigma (Hagan & Palloni, 1990; Palarma et al., 1986), minority status and disadvantage (Berk et al., 1992; Bernburg & Krohn, 2003; Chiricos et al., 2007; Sherman & Smith, 1992), and prior involvement in delinquency and crime (Chiricos et al., 2007; Horowitz & Wasserman, 1979). Furthermore, Braithwaite's shaming theory provides a comprehensive theory of contingent effects, implying that social sanctions are more likely to trigger labeling and stigmatization in social contexts that are characterized by low levels of interdependency and cohesion. Although comprehensive tests have been rare, there is some research that has examined isolated aspects of this proposition (see Tittle, Bratton, & Gertz, 2003, for a critical review of this work). Using survey data from China, Lu, Zhang, and Miethe (2002) examined whether social interdependency influenced people's willingness to practice reintegrative shaming toward offenders. Lu et al. measured both family interdependency (respondents' attachments to their family) and neighborhood interdependency (frequency of respondents' interaction with neighbors). Reintegrative shaming was measured with questions about respondents' willingness to disprove of others' wrongdoing, and about their willingness to welcome the offender back into the community after the offender had served the punishment. Consistent with Braithwaite's theory, the study found interdependency to be positively related to a willingness to practice reintegrative shaming. But, we should keep in mind that this study did not examine the effects of such practices on the offenders themselves.

Braithwaite's theory has implications for societal-level analysis, implying that societal reactions to crime should be less likely to result in labeling and stigma in communitarian societies, which are characterized by high aggregate levels of interdependency. Baumer, Wright, Kristinsdottir, and Gunnlaugsson (2002) compared recidivism rates across several industrialized nations to test Braithwaite's proposition. Baumer et al. focused on Iceland as a test case for Braithwaite's theory, arguing that this small island nation in the North Atlantic provided an example of a highly communitarian society that practices reintegrative shaming, and hence should exhibit lower recidivism rates than many other industrialized nations. However, the study found no support for this prediction, as recidivism rates in Iceland turned out to be comparable to recidivism rates in other industrialized nations. We should keep in mind that the researchers did not provide any direct data to demonstrate their presumption that reintegrative shaming is in fact more prevalent in Iceland than elsewhere (see the review by Tittle, Bratton, et al., 2003).

In conclusion, the current research has provided support for the effect of labeling on subsequent crime and delinquency, and it has provided some support for the intermediate processes specified by labeling theory, including reflected appraisals, reduced ties to conventional groups, blocked opportunities, and association with deviant groups. Moreover, the research has revealed some of the conditions that we would expect to enhance the impact of labeling on subsequent deviance. However, the research is still limited in important respects (see the review by Bernburg, in press). The volume of research is limited, and hence key findings need to be replicated. Second, the intermediate processes are usually studied separately, so we have no way of telling whether there is an overlap among the mediating factors. Finally, despite the central role of informal labeling and stigmatization in labeling theory, there have been few attempts to examine these concepts directly. These limitations need to be addressed in future research.

## A Final Word: Implications for Social Policy

If the labeling approach adds a distinct dimension to the study of crime and deviance, it also has distinct implications for social policy. Labeling theory challenges the classical notion of specific deterrence that argues that the pain of punishment deters the individual from engaging in crime in the future. Labeling theory argues that formal reactions to deviance often transcend their manifested goals, producing more and not less deviance and crime. In this context, it may be noted that comprehensive reviews of the individual-level research on the effects of formal sanctions on subsequent delinquent behavior lend more support for labeling theory than for the theory of specific deterrence (Huizinga & Henry, 2008).

As Braithwaite (1989) has argued, when seen in this light, heavy-handed criminal justice is a misguided social policy. The state has been all too ready to transfer massive social and economic resources to the traditional instruments of criminal justice—namely, law enforcement and prisons—but little has been done by way of counteracting the harmful effects of formal sanctions. A general implication of labeling research is that formal reactions and sanctions should be used with caution, and in a way that minimizes labeling and stigmatization; for example, by allowing most offenders to conceal their experiences with criminal justice (see Chiricos et al., 2007; Hjalmarsson, 2008). Furthermore, Braithwaite's (1999) discussion of *restorative justice* as a means to make punishment reintegrative is particularly interesting in this context.

But, we should note that the macrolevel implications of labeling theory are not as straightforward as one might expect. Labeling theory would expect a heavy-handed criminal justice policy to create a large pool of stigmatized individuals, which therefore may lead to higher crime rates (see Western & Beckett, 1999). However, there is a general principle in social science research that tells us that individual-level processes cannot be inferred directly to the societal level (Lieberson, 1985). For example, labeling theory does not contradict the notion of general deterrence, namely, the notion that punishment deters the general public from committing criminal offenses. It could even be argued that the general deterrence effects of punishment stem in part from people's fear of being stigmatized. But, we should also note that general deterrence is only one of many macrolevel processes that need to be considered. As Rose and Clear (1998) have discussed, the macrolevel effects of criminal justice policy on crime rates are likely to entail a complex of processes that go beyond the notion of general deterrence. The point here is that although formal sanctions may make offenders more, rather than less, likely to violate the law in the future, such microlevel findings may not be directly inferred to aggregate-level or macrolevel effects of punishment on crime rates. Only aggregate-level research can provide answers to aggregate-level questions.

Aside from the question of secondary deviance, which has been the main focus of this essay, research indicates that criminal labeling disproportionally influences the lives of people in the lower social strata. Racial minorities are more likely than others to come into contact with the criminal justice system and research suggests that when they do, they are treated more harshly (Donziger 1999). There is research that suggests that when accused of a crime, nonwhites are significantly more likely to be incarcerated than are whites, net of the seriousness of the offense and prior offending record (Steffensmeier, Ulmer, & Kramer 1998). And, during police–citizen encounters, the police are more likely to arrest nonwhite suspects, net of the seriousness of the offense, suspect demeanor, and other factors (Worden & Shepard, 1996). Labeling theory highlights the consequences of labeling not only for criminal behavior but also for identity, social integration, and life chances, and thus underscores the importance of reforming criminal justice to ensure equal opportunity as well as fairness and due process.

# SYMBOLIC INTERACTIONIST AND PHENOMENOLOGICAL THEORIES

## SEDUCTIONS OF CRIME: MORAL AND SENSUAL ATTRACTIONS IN DOING EVIL

*Jack Katz*

The study of crime has been preoccupied with a search for background forces, usually defects in the offenders' psychological backgrounds or social environments, to the neglect of the positive, often wonderful attractions within the lived experience of criminality. The novelty of this [chapter] is its focus on the seductive qualities of crimes: those aspects in the foreground of criminality that make its various forms sensible, even sensually compelling, ways of being.

   The social science literature contains only scattered evidence of what it means, feels, sounds, tastes, or looks like to commit a particular crime. Readers of research on homicide and assault do not hear the slaps and curses, see the pushes and shoves, or feel the humiliation and rage that may build toward the attack, sometimes persisting after the victim's death. How adolescents manage to make the shoplifting or vandalism of cheap and commonplace things a thrilling experience has not been intriguing to many students of delinquency. Researchers of adolescent gangs have never grasped why their subjects so often stubbornly refuse to accept the outsider's insistence that they wear the "gang" label. The description of "cold-blooded, senseless murders" has been left to writers outside the social sciences. Neither academic methods nor academic theories seem to be able to grasp why such killers may have been courteous to their victims just moments before the killing, why they often wait until they have dominated victims in sealed-off environments before coldly executing them, or how it makes sense to them to kill when only petty cash is at stake. Sociological and psychological studies of robbery rarely focus on the *distinctive* attractions of robbery, even though research has now clearly documented that alternative forms of criminality are available and familiar to many career robbers. In sum, only rarely have sociologists taken up the challenge of explaining the qualities of deviant experience.

   The statistical and correlational findings of positivist criminology provide the following irritations to inquiry: (1) whatever the validity of the hereditary, psychological, and social-ecological conditions of crime, many of those in the supposedly causal categories do not commit the crime at issue, (2) many who do commit the crime do not fit the causal categories, and (3) and what is most provocative, many who do fit the background categories and later commit the predicted crime go for long stretches without committing the crimes to which theory directs them. Why are people who were not determined to commit a crime one moment determined to do so the next?

   I propose that empirical research turn the direction of inquiry around to focus initially on the foreground, rather than the background of crime. Let us for once make it our first priority to understand the qualities of experience that distinguish different forms of criminality. What concerns can guide such an inquiry? How can the explanation of the qualities of criminality be pursued without starting an undisciplined pursuit of experiential evidence?

## The Magic in Motivation

Whatever the relevance of antecedent events and contemporaneous social conditions, something causally essential happens in the very moments in which a crime is committed. The assailant must sense, then and there, a distinctive constraint or seductive appeal that he did not sense a little while before in a substantially similar place. Although his economic status, peer group relations, Oedipal conflicts, genetic makeup, internalized machismo, history of child abuse, and the like remain the same, he must suddenly become propelled to commit the crime. Thus, the central problem is to understand the emergence of distinctive sensual dynamics.

To believe that a person can suddenly feel propelled to crime without any independently verifiable change in his background, it seems that we must almost believe in magic. And, indeed, this is precisely what we must do. When they are committing crimes, people feel drawn and propelled to their criminality, but in feeling determined by outside forces, they do nothing morally special. The particular seductions and compulsions they experience may be unique to crime, but the sense of being seduced and compelled is not. To grasp the magic in the criminal's sensuality, we must acknowledge our own.

A sense of being determined by the environment, of being pushed away from one line of action and pulled toward another, is natural to everyday, routine human experience. We are always moving away from and toward different objects of consciousness, taking account of this and ignoring that, and moving in one direction or the other between the extremes of involvement and boredom. In this constant movement of consciousness, we do not perceive that we are controlling the movement. Instead, to one degree or another, we are always being seduced and repelled by the world. "This *is* fascinating (interesting, beautiful, sexy, dull, ugly, disgusting)," we know (without having to say), as if the thing itself possessed the designated quality independent of us and somehow controlled our understanding of it. Indeed, the very nature of mundane being is emotional; attention is feeling, and consciousness is sensual.

Only rarely do we actually experience ourselves as subjects directing our conduct. How often, when you speak, do you actually sense that you are choosing the words you utter? As the words come out, they reveal the thought behind them even to the speaker whose lips gave them shape. Similarly, we talk, walk, and write in a sense of natural competence governed by moods of determinism. We rest our subjectivity on rhythmic sensibilities, feelings for directions, and visions of unfolding patterns, allowing esthetics to guide us. Self-reflexive postures in which one creates a distance between the self and the world and pointedly directs the self into the world, occur typically in an exceptional mood of recognizing a malapropism, after a misstep, or at the slip of the pen. With a slight shock, we recognize that it was not the things in themselves but our perspective that temporarily gave things outside of us the power to seduce or repel.

Among the forms of crime, the range of sensual dynamics runs from enticements that may draw a person into shoplifting to furies that can compel him to murder. If, as social researchers, we are to be able to explain more variation in criminality than background correlations allow, it appears that we must respect these sensual dynamics and honor them as authentic. But now we seem caught in a new dilemma. How can we simultaneously discredit the determinism of psychological and social background factors while crediting the determinism of sensually dynamic attractions and compulsions? Put another way, how can we find, through studying how people construct their experience as an artifact, the emergence of new forces that shape the actors themselves? Can we really see any novel causal forces in the black box between background factors and subsequent acts? After we have refined correlations between problematic acts and explanatory background factors, is there anything more to say other than that those whose actions do and those whose actions do not line up with predictions just "choose" to act that way?

For clues to the resolution of the dilemma, we may consider the dynamics of inter-action between interrogator and interrogee, drawing specifically on the American mili-tary experience in Vietnam. The interrogation of Vietnamese peasants routinely included physical assaults—at a minimal level, slapping. Intelligence officers often began a session in the spirit of many routine, civilian work assignments, as an obligation, without marked enthusiasm, only to discover overriding sensual dimensions in the process.

These were not extraordinary happenings. Unless one sets out to do so, it is actu-ally difficult to avoid the development of an involving esthetic in the sounds and rhythms of repeatedly slapping another person. To maintain the controlled assault of an interro-gating slapping and pushing, the officer must repeatedly adjust his body in relation to the responding movement of the interrogee. If a resonant slap was used to articulate the imposition of pressure and if the pressure is not to dissipate, the audible universe must be further managed, perhaps through making the subsequent slap louder or through the cun-ning use of silence. Attention to the esthetics of sound and interrelated body movements is not perverse but practically essential if the significance and spirit of "pressure" is to be maintained.

In the interrogator's attentiveness to rhythm and intensity as essential concerns for sustaining the metaphysics of "pressure," there is a move into the spirit of determinism. The interrogator has created themes that, through their evolving apparent requirements, he must acknowledge. Although he began the line of action, now it constrains his further creativity. He may walk away at any moment, but if he is to keep the pressure on, there are certain things he must now do.

From here, the interrogator may spin off along one of the many alternative paths of determinism. Patterns of slapping freely suggest various metaphors, and authority may be shaped to play out any of the symbolic possibilities that have sprung up. For example, despite repeated slaps that audibly ring in his head, the interrogee will not pick up on requests for information. What does the "ringing" and the refusal to "pick up" suggest? A metaphor, the dictates of which the interrogator may now enact under the rubric, the "Bell Telephone Hour": "You take a field telephone, wire it up around the man's testicles, you ring him up and he always answers."

Another path of escalating determinism became known as the "Americal Rule": "if he wasn't a Vietcong then, he sure as hell is one now." At the start, interrogators were often unsure of the political sympathies of the interrogee, but, in the end, it did not matter. Either the interrogee was a Vietcong sympathizer or, if not, the eminently dispassionate reason-ing went, he was likely to turn hostile after being slapped unjustly. In either case, it was reasonable after a while to consider his failure to cooperate as being motivated by malevo-lence. At that point, the interrogee's hostility is blocking the progress of the interrogation and thus is provocative: the *interrogee* is giving the *interrogator* a hard time!

The moral responsibility, and in a strictly empirical perspective, the causal respon-sibility has been shifted to the victim. Now the interrogator, just by insistently repeating questions, establishes the interrogee's region of freedom not to respond, emphasizing in turn the constraints of the process on the interrogator's freedom. But if the peasant will not answer the questions, if the peasant's information is beyond the control of Authority, the peasant's suffering is not. The peasant's suffering is conveniently in front of Authority; it offers itself as an object that can be juxtaposed against the interrogator's frustrations and constructed to fit the military will. The dialectic of freedom and restraint has reversed. Just as Authority was beginning to become disciplined to the requirements of the process— doing what is necessary to sustain pressure and responding to the interrogee's hostility—it discovers a new region of freedom.

Occasionally, this process would turn into frenzied slaughter; more commonly, it would cause a modest increase in brutalization. In either case, Authority set into motion a process that it could go with. But this process is always vulnerable to an interruption of its implicit sensual logic. The interrogator, no matter how carried away he may feel, can always stop.

In one instance, a peasant woman "shit in her pants . . . [and became] very embarrassed." In odor and in moral sensibility, the interrogee violated the esthetics and the moral stance underlying the ongoing dynamic. Suddenly her spontaneous bowel movement perfectly if unwittingly reversed the esthetic preconditions and moral thrust of the process. The soldier stopped. "I'm beating up this girl, for what? What the fuck am I doing? I just felt like a shit."

In another incident, a Marine was showing the peasants that the Marines were in charge by recklessly driving a truck. His dominance was spatially and audibly established; up in the noisy truck, he did not bother to count how many he hit. Somehow a 15-year-old boy on a bicycle got caught in the wheels. The driver came down to look and found "this kid who just stared back at him with an absolutely level stare." Silence and spatial equality broke the momentum. The Marine, previously above and behind a wall of noise, was suddenly on the same plane with his victim, with nothingness audibly around. This time, he walked off.

The challenge for explanation is to specify the steps of the dialectic process through which a person empowers the world to seduce him to criminality. On the one hand, we must explain how the individual himself *conjures up* the spirit. On the other hand, we must accept the attraction or compulsion as *authentic*.

It is not a simple matter to raise these spirits. One cannot be blindly enraged, cooly sadistic, or secretly thrilled at will, simply by the conscious choice to be evil, no more than one can transport himself to erotic heights simply and instantly by opting for pleasure. For a person to experience being influenced or determined, he must lose a reflective awareness of the abiding, constructive workings of his subjectivity. Thus, part of the challenge is to recognize steps in raising a spirit of determinism that are sufficiently subtle that their contingencies go unnoticed.

Typically, the person will not be able to help us with the analysis because he is taken in by his efforts to construct the dynamic. If we ask, "Why did you do it?" he is likely to respond with self-justifying rhetoric. But he can help us with a detailed account of the processual development of his experience. If we ask, "How did you do that? And then what did you do?" we are likely to discover some poignant moments. And, because the person constructs his definition of the situation through bodily comprehension, we may catch the conditions of his involvement in exceptional circumstances when it is undermined by an incongruent sensuality. Thus, the interrogator's victim may defecate, triggering a life-saving perception by her torturer that *he* is the shit. Or, to offer an erotic example, the lovers' child may suddenly walk in and prove that what they had sensed as an abandoned involvement was not.

That emotions are contingent on definitions of the situation is a commonplace both in existentialist writing and in the sociological tradition of symbolic interaction. What has been more difficult to appreciate is the ontological validity of passion—the authentic efficacy of sensual magic. In sex, as well as in mock fighting on street corners, initially lighthearted thrusts and parries may turn into the real thing without warning. Such preliminaries to passion are playful in an existentially specific sense: the participants are playing with the line between the sense of themselves as subject and object, between being in and out of control, between directing and being directed by the dynamics of the situation. To complete successfully the transition from subject to object and achieve the emotional extremes of eros or thanatos, a person may have to arrange the environment to "pacify" his subjectivity. He may then submit to forces that transcend his subjectivity even while he tacitly controls the transition.

What phenomenology uniquely has appreciated is not simply that a person's lived world is his artifact but that by experiencing himself as an object controlled by transcendent forces, an individual can genuinely experience a new or different world. By pacifying his subjectivity, a person can conjure up a magic so powerful that it can change his ontology. What begins as idle slapping or fondling may lead to the discovery of rare truths or the acquisition of a new incompetence.

It is necessary to indulge a fiction or invoke a ritual to begin the process, but if one does not hedge on the commitment of faith, otherwise inaccessible phenomena may come into reach, bringing revelations or shutting off part of one's freedom and confirming that the initial commitment was authentic. In religious practice, we may find the results of this dialectical process inspiring; in sex, delightful. As unattractive morally as crime may be, we must appreciate that there is *genuine experiential creativity* in it as well. We should then be able to see what are, for the subject, the authentic attractions of crime and we should then be able to explain variations in criminality beyond what can be accounted for by background factors.

## Criminal Projects

Approaching criminality from the inside, social research takes as its subject the morally exceptional conduct that the persons themselves regard as criminally sanctionable in official eyes. Since there is an enormous variety of criminal phenomena, how can one demarcate and set up for explanation a limited number of subjectively homogeneous offenses? I suggest that a seemingly simple question be asked persistently in detailed application to the facts of criminal experience: what are people trying to do when they commit a crime?

The resulting topics will not necessarily follow official crime categories. Crimes, as defined in statutes, surveys of citizens, and police records, take definitional shape from the interests of victims and from practical problems of detection and punishment, not necessarily from the experience of those committing the crimes. But if one begins with rough conventional or folk categories, such as hot-blooded murder, gang violence, adolescent property crime, commercial robbery, and "senseless" and "cold-blooded" murder, and refines the concepts to fit homogeneous forms of experience, one can arrive at a significant range of criminal projects: committing righteous slaughter, mobilizing the spirit of a street elite, constructing sneaky thrills, persisting in the practice of stickup as a hardman, and embodying primordial evil.

By way of explanation, I will propose for each type of crime a different set of individually necessary and jointly sufficient conditions, each set containing (1) a path of action—distinctive practical requirements for successfully committing the crime, (2) a line of interpretation—unique ways of understanding how one is and will be seen by others, and (3) an emotional process—seductions and compulsions that have special dynamics. Raising the spirit of criminality requires practical attention to a mode of executing action, symbolic creativity in defining the situation, and esthetic finesse in recognizing and elaborating on the sensual possibilities.

Central to all these experiences in deviance is a member of the family of moral emotions: humiliation, righteousness, arrogance, ridicule, cynicism, defilement, and vengeance. In each, the attraction that proves to be most fundamentally compelling is that of overcoming a personal challenge to moral—not to material—existence. For the impassioned killer, the challenge is to escape a situation that has come to seem otherwise inexorably humiliating. Unable to sense how he or she can move with self-respect from the current situation, now, to any mundane-time relationship that might be reengaged, then, the would-be killer leaps at the possibility of embodying, through the practice of "righteous" slaughter, some eternal, universal form of the Good.

For many adolescents, shoplifting and vandalism offer the attractions of a thrilling melodrama about the self as seen from within and from without. Quite apart from what is taken, they may regard "getting away with it" as a thrilling demonstration of personal competence, especially if it is accomplished under the eyes of adults.

Specifically "bad" forms of criminality are essentially addressed to a moral challenge experienced in a spatial metaphor. Whether by intimidating others' efforts to take him into their worlds ("Who you look-in' at?") or by treating artificial geographic boundaries as sacred and defending local "turf" with relentless "heart," "badasses" and *barrio* warriors celebrate an indifference to modern society's expectation that a person should demonstrate a sensibility to reshape himself as he moves from here to there.

To make a habit of doing stickups, I will argue, one must become a "hardman." It is only smart to avoid injuring victims unnecessarily, but if one becomes too calculating about the application of violence, the inherent uncertainties of face-to-face interaction in robberies will be emotionally forbidding. Beneath the surface, there may be, to paraphrase Nietzsche, a ball of snakes in chaotic struggle. But the stickup man denies any uncertainty and any possibility of change with a personal style that ubiquitously negates social pressures toward a malleable self.

Perhaps the ultimate criminal project is mounted by men who culminate a social life organized around the symbolism of deviance with a cold-blooded, "senseless" murder. Mimicking the ways of primordial gods as they kill, they proudly appear to the world as astonishingly evil. Through a killing only superficially justified by the context of robbery, they emerge from a dizzying alternation between affiliation with the great symbolic powers of deviant identity and a nagging dis-ease that conformity means cowardice.

Overall, my objective is to demonstrate that a theory of moral self-transcendence can make comprehensible the minutia of experiential details in the phenomenal foreground, as well as explain the general conditions that are most commonly found in the social backgrounds of these forms of criminality. This inquiry will best serve those who wish to address evil—not as judged by moral philosophy or imputed by political ideology but as lived in the everyday realities of contemporary society. In the end, I suggest that the dominant political and sociological understanding that crime is motivated by materialism is poorly grounded empirically—indeed, that it is more a sentimentality than a creditable causal theory. Because of its insistence on attributing causation to material conditions in personal and social backgrounds, modern social thought has been unable either to acknowledge the embrace of evil by common or street criminals, or, and for the same reason, develop empirical bite and intellectual depth in the study of criminality by the wealthy and powerful. By opening up systematic, theoretical, and empirical inquiry into the experience of criminality, this study points toward a comparative sociology that is capable of examining the seductions of crime as they are experienced up and down the social and political order. Those who follow the argument to its end may not find encouragement for broad-based social welfare policies, but readers should discover that the domestic deceits and foreign atrocities of our elites are no longer tangential to social research on crime. . . .

If the preceding contributes to the study of crime, it is only because the readily available, detailed meaning of common criminality has been systematically ruled out as ineligible for serious discussion in the conventions of modern sociological and political thought. Something important happened when it became obscenely sensational or damnably insensitive to track the lived experience of criminality in favor of imputing factors to the background of crime that are invisible in its situational manifestation. Somehow in the psychological and sociological disciplines, the lived mysticism and magic in the foreground of criminal experience became unseeable, while the abstractions hypothesized by "empirical theory" as the determining background causes, especially those conveniently quantified by state agencies, became the stuff of "scientific" thought and "rigorous" method.

Whatever the historical causes for treating background factors as the theoretical core for the empirical study of crime, the point of this volume is to demonstrate that it is not necessary to constitute the field back to front. We may begin with the foreground, attempting to discover common or homogeneous criminal projects and to test explanations of the necessary and sufficient steps through which people construct given forms of crime. If we take as our primary research commitment an exploration of the distinctive phenomena of crime, we may produce not just ad hoc bits of description or a collection of provocative anecdotes but a systematic empirical theory of crime—one that explains at the individual level the causal process of committing a crime and that accounts at the aggregate level for recurrently documented correlations with biographical and ecological background factors.

## VIOLENT CRIMINAL ACTS AND ACTORS REVISITED

*Lonnie Athens*

### Self as Process: Interpretation of the Situation

In the entire intellectual arsenal of the interpretive approach, there is no more potent notion than that of the "interpretation of the situation." Consequently I gathered data on the interpretations of the situations that the fifty-eight violent offenders formed when they committed their violent crimes. The information needed on these interpretive or self processes was gleaned by having these offenders describe to me in as much detail as possible what happened during the situations in which they committed their violent crimes and what, if anything, they thought and felt as these situations unfolded.

My study of these data reveals two things. First, it reveals that violent people always *do* interpret the situations in which they commit violent criminal acts. Further, the interpretations that they form of these situations account for their violent actions. In all the cases I found that the individuals committing the violent acts did at least two things. (1) By assuming the attitudes of their victims, they implicitly or explicitly indicated to themselves the meaning or character of the victim's gestures. (2) By assuming an attitude of their generalized others, they implicitly or explicitly indicated to themselves that they *ought* to take violent action. Thus the data reveal that violent people *consciously construct* violent plans of action before they commit violent criminal acts.

This conclusion almost completely contradicts the previous literature on this issue. With only one exception, psychiatrists, psychologists, and sociologists have argued that most violent criminal acts are committed as a result of *unconscious* motivations, *deep* emotional needs, *inner* psychic conflicts, or sudden *unconscious* emotional bursts. For example, Banay, a psychiatrist, asserts that "the true nature of the psychological phenomena of violence which causes one human being to inflict death upon another will remain shrouded in mystery unless a detailed psychiatric study traces down the inner motivations." Similarly Abrahamsen states that "it is safe to say that unconscious elements play an overwhelming part in homicide, and if uncovered, they will provide us with material enabling us to establish the dynamic connection between the killer's mind and his homicide." Tanay, another psychiatrist, asserts that "ego-dystonic homicide describes a killing that occurs against the conscious wishes of the perpetrator," and he later adds that "the majority of homicides are ego-dystonic." Further, on the bases of their review of the literature on "murderers and murders," the Lesters, two psychologists, state: "Real murderers are not usually motivated by any long-range plans or conscious desires. Most commonly, they kill during some trivial quarrel, or their acts are triggered by some apparently unimportant incident, while deep and unconscious emotional needs are their basic motivation. Most murders occur on sudden impulse and in the heat of passion, in situations where the killer's emotions overcome his ability to reason."

Finally, in their joint works, Wolfgang, a sociologist, and Ferracuti, a psychologist, contend that 90 percent of criminal homicides are "passion crimes," acts that "are unplanned, explosive, determined by sudden motivational bursts." Wolfgang and Ferracuti add that in such aggressive crimes the offender acts "quickly," so that "neither reasoning nor time for it are at his disposal."

The data from my study also reveal that the interpretations of situations in which violent criminal acts are committed are not homogeneous but fall into four distinct types. The following discussion of each of these types of interpretation should clarify how individuals construct interpretations of the situations in which they commit violent criminal acts.

### Physically defensive interpretations

The first type of interpretation is "physically defensive." There are two essential steps in forming physically defensive interpretations of a situation. First, by assuming the attitude of the victim, the perpetrator implicitly or explicitly indicates to himself that the victim's gestures mean either (1) that the victim will soon physically attack him or an intimate, such as a spouse or child, or (2) that the victim is already physically attacking him or an intimate. Second, by assuming an attitude of his generalized other, the perpetrator then implicitly or explicitly indicates to himself that he ought to respond violently toward the victim and calls out within himself a violent plan of action. The perpetrator forms his violent plan of action because he sees violence as the only means of preventing another person from inflicting physical injury on him or an intimate. The key feature of all physically defensive interpretations is that the victim makes a gesture that the perpetrator designates to himself as foreshadowing or constituting a physical attack, generating a grave sense of fear in him for his own or an intimate's physical safety. . . .

Further, when a perpetrator injures or kills another person as a result of forming a physically defensive interpretation, his violent criminal act is *victim precipitated*. My definition of victim precipitation is not reducible to the positivistic one that Marvin Wolfgang popularized, however. According to Wolfgang, victim precipitation is where "the role of the victim is characterized by his having been the first in the homicide drama to use physical force directed against his subsequent slayer. The victim precipitated cases are those in which the victim was the first to show and use a deadly weapon, to strike a blow in an altercation—in short, the first to commence the interplay or resort to physical violence." In a later paper he explicitly states that the criteria that he used "to classify . . . victims as precipitators of their own deaths were based on overt physical behavior" and that "words alone were not enough."

Using Wolfgang's positivistic definition and my interpretive one to determine whether to classify violent criminal acts as victim precipitated readily shows the differences between our respective definitions. First, a violent criminal act can be victim precipitated according to Wolfgang's definition and also follow from a physically defensive interpretation. The individual takes violent action in such a case, but only after indicating to himself that his antagonists have already physically attacked him or an intimate and through further self-indication judges that physical retaliation is the best means of preventing his antagonists from inflicting further injuries on him or an intimate. Second, a violent criminal act can be non–victim precipitated according to Wolfgang's definition but follow from a physically defensive interpretation. Here the individual resorts to physical violence first but does so only after indicating to himself that his antagonists' gestures indicate that a physical attack on him or an intimate is imminent and through further self-indication judges that a preemptive strike is the best means of protecting his or an intimate's physical safety. Third, a violent criminal act can be non–victim precipitated according to Wolfgang's definition and also not follow from a physically defensive interpretation. In this case the perpetrator resorts to physical violence first, but without forming a physically defensive interpretation of the situation. Before taking his violent action, the individual neither indicates to himself that his protagonists are either physically attacking him or an intimate or threatening to do so nor through further self-indication judges that a retaliatory or preemptive strike is the best means of stopping their present or soon anticipated physical attack on him or an intimate.

Finally, a violent criminal act can be victim precipitated according to Wolfgang's definition but not follow from a physically defensive interpretation. Here the victim strikes first, but the blow struck is so slight that the perpetrator does not define it as imperiling either him or an intimate, as in the case of a bumping. If physical gestures that are not physically threatening are considered to satisfy the requirement for victim precipitation, however, then it becomes necessary for the sake of consistency to consider as well physical gestures where no physical contact is made with the perpetrator, as in the case of obscene gestures. Consequently, if the victim made any physical gesture toward the perpetrator before being attacked, then the violent criminal act would have to be considered as victim precipitated.

The relationship between these two ways of defining victim precipitation not only makes it clear that the two definitions are not synonymous. It also exposes the fundamental weakness in Wolfgang's positivistic definition of victim precipitation. The positivistic conception ignores the meaning of precipitation to the victim and offender. Moreover Wolfgang's deprecation of the importance of "words" in precipitating physical altercations is at odds not only with the interpretive approach taken here but also now with criminal law. Thus the positivistic conception leaves out far too many cases in which the victim *is* a genuine contributing factor in the offense and includes far too many cases in which the victim is not a genuinely contributing factor in the offense.

### Frustrative interpretations

The second type of interpretation of situations in which violent criminal acts are committed is "frustrative." Frustrative interpretations are formed in two basic steps. First, by assuming the attitude of the victim, the perpetrator implicitly or explicitly indicates to himself that the victim's gestures mean either (1) that the victim is resisting or will resist the *specific* course of action that the perpetrator seeks to carry out or (2) that the perpetrator should cooperate in a *specific* course of action that he does not want carried out. Second, by assuming an attitude of his generalized other, the perpetrator then implicitly or explicitly indicates to himself that he ought to respond violently toward the victim and calls out within himself a violent plan of action. The perpetrator forms this violent plan of action because he sees violence as the most appropriate way to handle another person's potential or attempted blockage of the larger act that the perpetrator wants to carry out—for example, robbery, sexual intercourse, car theft—or to block the larger act that the other person wants to carry out—for example, calling the police or arresting the perpetrator. The mark of all frustrative interpretations is that the perpetrator becomes angry after designating to himself the direction along which the larger act is heading and his desire for the act not to follow that course. . . .

### Malefic interpretations

The third type of interpretation of situations in which violent criminal acts are committed is "malefic." Malefic interpretations are formed in a three-step process. First, by assuming the attitude of the victim, the perpetrator implicitly or explicitly indicates to himself that the victim's gestures mean that the victim is deriding or badly belittling the perpetrator. Second, by assuming an attitude of his generalized other, the perpetrator implicitly or explicitly indicates to himself that the victim is an extremely evil or malicious person. Finally, by making further self-indications from the same attitude of his generalized other, the perpetrator implicitly or explicitly indicates to himself that he ought to respond violently toward the victim and calls out within himself a violent plan of action. The perpetrator forms his violent plan of action because he sees violence as the most fitting way of handling evil or malicious people who make derogatory gestures. The key feature of all malefic interpretations is that the perpetrator judges the victim to be extremely evil or malicious, which in turn ignites his hatred for the victim. . . .

### Frustrative-malefic interpretations

The final type of interpretation of situations in which violent criminal acts are committed is "frustrative-malefic," which combines features of the prior two types. Frustrative-malefic interpretations are formed in a three-step process. First, by assuming the attitude of the victim, the perpetrator implicitly or explicitly indicates to himself that the victim's gestures mean either that the victim is resisting some *specific* line of action that the perpetrator wants to carry out or that he wants the perpetrator to cooperate in some *specific* line of action that the perpetrator does not want carried out. Second, by assuming an attitude of his generalized other, the perpetrator implicitly or explicitly indicates to himself that the victim's gestures are irksome or malicious and consequently that the victim is evil or malicious. Finally, by making further self-indications from the same attitude of his generalized other, the perpetrator implicitly or explicitly indicates to himself that he ought to respond violently toward the victim and calls out within himself a violent plan of action. The perpetrator forms this violent plan of action because he sees violence as the most appropriate way to deal with an evil or malicious person's potential or attempted blockage of the larger act that he seeks to carry out or as the most appropriate way to block the larger act that an evil or malicious person wants to carry out. The perpetrator views the victim not only as an adversary but as a particularly loathsome one as well. The mark of all frustrative-malefic interpretations is that they start out as frustrative interpretations. Before the perpetrator mounts his violent attack, however, the interpretations become malefic, with pure hatred always displacing the anger that the perpetrator earlier felt toward his victim. . . .

## The Larger Theoretical Implications

. . . The basic assumption behind my theory is that crime is a product of *social retardation*. Social retardation exists when people guide their actions toward themselves and others from the standpoint of an underdeveloped, primitive phantom community, an "us" that hinders them from cooperating in the ongoing social activities of their corporal community or the larger society in which it is embedded.

More than thirty years ago Marshall B. Clinard stated a still much overlooked point that has profound implications for criminology: "The act as well as the actor must be considered." I had failed to realize fully not only that I had developed a theory but also that my theory conforms with five brute facts about violent criminal acts and actors.

The first brute fact to which my theory conforms is that more than one type of violent criminal act exists. Since my theory portrays violent criminal acts as resulting from any one of four interpretations of conflictive situations, it implies that there are four distinct types of violent criminal acts: physically defensive, pure frustrative, pure malefic, and frustrative-malefic. It should be noted that the first type, the physically defensive violent criminal act, comprises violent acts that fail, for one reason or another, to meet the legal requirements for self-defense, so that as perfect instances of "imperfect self-defenses," they qualify as bona fide acts of criminal violence. Thus the brute fact that there are multiple types of violent criminal acts contradicts any theory in which all or most criminal violent acts are crammed into a single form, as is done in the case of the "character contest" model.

It should be also noted that there are two subtypes of my frustrative type of violent criminal act. Frustrative violent criminal acts are products of "frustrative interpretations" of conflictive situations, which can be formed in either of two distinct ways. First, by assuming the attitudes of his soon-to-be victims, the perpetrator of violence tells himself that the victims intend to resist the specific line of action that he wants to execute. Next, by assuming the attitude of his phantom community, he tells himself that he should respond violently toward the victims and calls out a violent plan of action from within himself. The other distinct way in which an individual can form a frustrative interpretation is as follows. First, by assuming his soon-to-be victims' attitudes, he tells himself that they want him to cooperate in a specific line of action that he does not want to carry out. Next, by assuming the attitude of his phantom community, he tells himself that he should respond violently, once again calling out a violent plan of action from within himself. The two ways that an individual can form a frustrative interpretation thus have the same second steps, but the initial steps differ, giving these acts a slightly different meaning for the actor and thereby creating two subtypes of the pure frustrative violent criminal acts. In the first, "coercive" subtype, the individual considers his violent plan of action to be the best means of overpowering other people's resistance to the larger act that he wants to carry out, such as sexual intercourse or robbery. In the second, "resistive" subtype, the individual sees his violent plan of action as the most effective way to block the larger act that other people want carried out but that he does not, such as divorce or arrest.

That there is more than one type of violent criminal is the second brute fact to which my theory conforms. According to my theory, three types of violent criminals can be distinguished on the basis of their phantom communities (formerly generalized others) and self-conceptions: (1) "marginally violent," (2) "violent," and (3) "ultraviolent." Ultraviolent criminals inhabit unmitigated violent phantom communities and paint violent portraits of themselves. Violent criminals inhabit mitigated violent phantom communities and paint incipiently violent self-portraits, whereas the marginally violent criminals inhabit nonviolent phantom communities and, naturally, paint only nonviolent portraits of themselves. Finally, each of these types of violent individuals stands on clearly different steps on a violence progression ladder. The marginally violent individual stands on the first rung, the violent individual stands on the middle rung, and the ultraviolent individual stands on the top rung.

The third brute fact to which my theory conforms is that different types of violent criminals are capable of engaging in quite different types of violent criminal acts. If violent criminals are not equally violent, then common sense dictates that they should not commit the same kinds of violent criminal acts. According to my theory, ultraviolent criminals will commit physically defensive, pure frustrative, pure malefic, or frustrative-malefic violent criminal acts. Violent criminals will commit both physically defensive and frustrative-malefic violent criminal acts, whereas marginally violent ones will commit only physically defensive violent criminal acts. Thus a comprehensive theory of violent criminals must explain the violence capability of each different type of violent criminal, not just the most violent type—the ultraviolent criminal—as Katz, for example, does.

More than seven decades ago the famous sociological tandem of Robert Park and Ernest Burgess originally drew the distinction between "expressive" and "positive," or instrumental, behavior: "A very much larger part of human behavior than we ordinarily imagine is merely expressive . . . activity carried out for its own sake. Only work, action which has some ulterior motive or is performed from a conscious sense of duty, falls wholly and without reservation into the second class." Four decades later the positivistic psychologist Arnold Buss distinguished "instrumental" from "angry," or expressive, aggression, a distinction that has subsequently become a standard part of psychologists', sociologists', and criminologists' vernacular. Instrumental aggression is only a means to another end, whereas angry aggression is the end in itself. Although using an obvious means/end scheme, Buss sought to avoid any reference to the aggressor's intention so as to cast his distinction as strictly as possible in positivistic terms:

> There are two reasons for excluding the concept of intent. . . . First, it implies teleology, a purposive act directed toward a future goal, and this view is inconsistent with the behavioral approach adopted in this book. Secondly, and more important, is the difficulty of applying this term to behavioral events. . . .
>   In summary, *intent* is both awkward and unnecessary in the analysis of aggressive behavior.

In disavowing intention Buss becomes guilty of reductionism. He mistakenly reduces a social act to a purely physical act. About twenty years earlier Park humorously illustrated the nature of this mistake:

> If innocently . . . I am walking along the street and a brick falls on my head or close enough at least to interrupt my meditations, that in itself is a mere physical fact. If, however, looking up I see a face grinning down on me maliciously from the wall from which the brick came, the fall of the brick ceases to be a mere physical phenomenon and becomes a social fact. It changes its character as soon as I interpret it as an expression of an attitude or intent rather than an act of God . . . that is wholly without intention of any sort, and one therefore, for which no one can be made responsible.

In a much later and more enlightened discussion, Buss distinguishes instrumental aggression from angry aggression on the basis of "the stimuli that elicit them, the accompanying emotion, and the consequences" but still not on the basis of actors' varying interpretations of the conflictive situations that confront them:

> The first class, angry aggression, is commonly incited by insult, attack, or annoyances. The usual emotional reaction is anger. . . . The usual consequence of angry aggression is pain and discomfort of the victim; the intent of the aggressor is to harm the victim. . . . The second class, instrumental aggression, is caused by competition or by any of the usual incentives that motivate behavior (dominance, food, mate, . . . ). There may be an emotional reaction (anger), but it is not a necessary part of the sequence. The usual consequence is success in competition or attainment of the incentive; any harm to the victim is incidental.

If the interpretive process is included rather than excluded from Buss's classificatory scheme, then it can subsume the four types of violent criminal acts that I found my three different types of violent criminals to commit. More specifically, physically defensive and frustrative violent criminal acts are purely instrumental. Malefic violent criminal acts are purely expressive, and frustrative-malefic violent criminal acts are combined instrumental-expressive violent criminal acts. Because marginally violent criminals commit only physically defensive violent criminal acts, they engage in only purely instrumental extreme acts of aggression. Because violent criminals commit physically defensive and frustrative-malefic violent criminal acts, they engage in both purely instrumental and combined instrumental/expressive extreme acts of aggression. Finally, because ultraviolent criminals commit physically defensive, pure frustrative, pure malefic, and frustrative-malefic violent criminal acts, they engage in purely instrumental, purely expressive, and combined instrumental/expressive extreme acts of aggression. Classifying the violent criminal actors and acts distinguished in my theory on the basis of whether they engage in expressive or instrumental extreme acts of aggression demonstrates that only the most dangerous violent criminals will engage in purely expressive acts of extreme aggression. Thus, when revised, Buss's classification system adds a bit of insight to my findings.

The fourth brute fact to which my theory conforms is that violent criminal actors and acts are not evenly spread across the social landscape but pop up more frequently in some places than they do in others. According to Park, every corporal community is "a mosaic of minor communities, many of them strikingly different from one another, but all more or less typical." He considers minor communities to be synonymous with "natural areas." In every natural area, or minor community, there are certain types of individuals whose impact on the flavor and tempo of their community's daily life far exceeds their absolute numbers. Since conflict is indigenous to human group life, conflict inevitably breaks out between the members of any minor community. To varying degrees a community's members will inform one another about how conflicts are handled in their communities. Thus, on the basis of the nature of a community's predominant individual types and the prevailing wisdom for handling interpersonal conflicts, three kinds of communities can be demarcated: *civil, malignant*, and *turbulent*. In civil minor communities the predominant individual type is the marginally violent person, whose nonviolent phantom community is congruent with that of his minor community and the larger corporal community that encompasses it. Among the members of civil minor communities, the prevailing wisdom is that interpersonal conflicts should be handled by nonviolent means, such as gossiping about one another and ostracizing, snubbing, and avoiding each other. They will use physical violence only as a last resort when they are physically attacked and must do for themselves what the police cannot do at that moment. Violent criminal acts of any type thus occur rarely in such a community. Nevertheless, because the boundaries between different natural areas are permeable, individuals prone to greater violence may always wander into and occasionally try to settle in civil communities, making the threat of violent criminal acts a remote but ever-present possibility.

In malignant minor communities the predominant individual type is the ultraviolent person, whose unmitigated phantom community is congruent with that of his minor corporal community but in conflict with that of the larger corporal community of which it is part. Members of malignant communities know that the prevailing wisdom is that physical violence is the most effective means for handling serious conflicts. Any time a serious conflict arises, it is taken for granted that one must be prepared to use deadly force, as well as to be the recipient of it. The members of these communities live with the bleak realization that at any time they could become embroiled in a conflict in which they could either kill or be killed. The marginally violent individuals who become trapped in these communities must endure the harsh reality that they or one of their loved ones could at any time be added to their violent and ultraviolent neighbors' lists of victims, whereas violent individuals brace themselves for the inevitable day when they will clash with each other or one of their ultraviolent neighbors. As Elijah Anderson perceptively observes: "They must be on guard even against people they have known over many years." Thus malignant communities constitute virtual combat zones where violent criminal acts of all types—pure frustrative, pure malefic, frustrative-malefic, and physically defensive—occur with such depressing frequency that they become commonplace.

A young man laments the extraordinary safety precautions that his mother must take to survive in the malignant community in which she lives:

> My mother goes through a lot of changes, just to live from day to day. . . . I remember when she
> got a new fridge one time, she just cut the box up and put out a little each week. . . . She didn't

want her neighbors to know she'd gotten something, because that meant either she had money or there was something in there to steal. . . .

And whenever she'd go to church, she would put her pocketbook over her shoulder, and then put her coat on over the pocket book. . . . And no jewelry. Even if she was gonna get a ride. . . . She'd wait till she got in the car, and then on the way to where she was going put it on. On the way back, she'd take it off. It's a hell of a way to live, but that's how she avoided problems.

In contrast to the situation in both civil and malignant communities, in turbulent minor communities no individual type has gained the upper hand, so that there is no predominant individual type but instead an admixture of types. Thus ultraviolent people with their unmitigated violent phantom communities, violent people with their mitigated violent phantom communities, and marginally violent people with their nonviolent phantom communities all come to live, work, and play in close physical proximity with one another. The odd mixture of uncongenial individual types that characterizes turbulent communities creates a social environment where, as Park says, "everything is loose and free, but everything is problematic." There exists, therefore, no prevailing wisdom for handling interpersonal conflicts among members of these communities. Conflict arises not only over this or that particular issue but also over the appropriate means for their resolution. Since community members are not sure what to expect when conflicts erupt, life in the community is chaotic. This creates the potentially dangerous situation that Park describes in his foreword to *The Gold Coast and the Slum* as being one "in which the physical distances and the social distances do not coincide; a situation in which people who live side by side are not, and—because of the divergence of their interests and their heritages—cannot, even with the best of good will, become neighbors." Thus, as expected, sundry violent criminal acts occur more frequently in turbulent communities than in civil communities, although much less frequently than in malignant communities.

In *Street Wise* Anderson succinctly but sublimely describes a turbulent community that he dubs the "Village":

A perfunctory look at the Village streets in daytime would lead one to believe that this is indeed a pleasant neighborhood whose residents get along well, and that there is genuine comity among the various kinds of people who live there. And to a large extent this is true. As residents stroll up and down the tree-lined streets, there is often a pleasant show of civility, if not intimacy, between neighbors. . . .

Yet many residents are concerned about the strangers with whom they must share the public space, including wandering homeless people, aggressive beggars, muggers, anonymous black youths, and drug addicts. . . .

Increasingly, people see the streets as a jungle, especially at night. . . . They are then on special alert, carefully monitoring everyone who passes and giving few people the benefit of the doubt. . . . Although there is a general need to view the Village as an island of civility. . . . the underlying sense is that the local streets and public spaces are uncertain at best and hostile at worst.

Social segregation is the common social process through which all three of these different minor communities, or natural areas, are created. According to Park, "The natural areas into which the urban—and every other type of community, in fact—resolves itself are, at least, in the first instance, the products of a sifting and sorting process which we may call segregation." Blumer points out that "segregation is a primary means by which a human society develops an inner organization." "One can say," he adds, "that the process of segregation in one form or another is accepted, employed, and condoned by all human societies."

Although operating on a large-scale basis and producing long-lasting consequences, social segregation is ultimately a product of people's interpretations of a recurrent problem. Because people must always live somewhere, the problem becomes where to lay their hats and rest their heads. They must separately or jointly decide where it is best for people to reside given their life circumstances. In deciding on a minor community or neighborhood in which to settle, they may take into account a whole array of factors, including the cost of housing, the reputation of the schools, the proximity to public transportation, and the physical distance to their present or anticipated places of employment, as well as the social distance between them and their likely neighbors. Although all these factors will be important in this decision, none will be any more important than the fear of violent crime. Rich, poor, or in-between, few people would wish to move into or long remain in a community where they would likely brush shoulders with violent and ultraviolent criminals.

Nevertheless the communities created from this social segregation process are not static entities that, once formed, never change. On the contrary they are always evolving by moving back and forth from a state of relative stability to one of transition. As ultraviolent criminals invade civil communities and marginally violent people flee from them, these communities slowly degenerate into malignant ones. Likewise, as ultraviolent criminals are driven from malignant communities and marginally violent people move into them, the community progressively becomes more civil. Turbulent communities are those that are caught in the middle of this larger process of community change. They represent communities in which, in Park's apt words, "the old order is passing, but the new order has not yet arrived." Thus turbulent communities are either in transition from civil into malignant communities or from malignant into civil communities.

Park views social segregation and the community change that it brings about as occurring inside the larger social process of "succession":

> Although the term succession, as originally employed by sociologists, would seem to be more appropriately applied to movements of population and to such incidental social and cultural changes as these movements involve, there seems to be no sound reason why the same term should not be used to describe any orderly and *irreversible series of events*, provided they are to such an extent correlated with other less obvious and more fundamental social changes that they may be used as indices of these changes.

Later he formally defines succession as follows: "Changes, when they are recurrent, so that they fall into a temporal or spatial series—particularly if the series is of such a sort that the effect of each succeeding increment of change reinforces or carries forward the effects of the proceeding—constitute what is described in this paper as succession."

Contrary to Park's notion of succession, community change is a precarious process capable of reversing direction. Unforeseen contingencies can always arise that affect the course of a community's life no less than the lives of the individuals who inhabit it. A civil community that changes into a turbulent one may always revert to a civil one without becoming a malignant one. The invasion of ultraviolent criminals into a civil community may always be halted before they become the predominant individual type. Likewise a malignant community that becomes a turbulent one may always revert to a malignant one without becoming a civil one. Marginally violent people may always be frightened away before they can establish a beachhead and later become the predominant individual type in a malignant community. In both instances the succession process is rudely interrupted before it reaches the expected destination. Moreover, before the ultimate direction of a turbulent community's further evolution becomes apparent, the community may stay in its present state for a long period.

In all fairness, I must admit that Park recognized the problems with his use of succession to explain community change. In an attempt to salvage the idea, he broadened his earlier definition to include the forms of community change that happen in civil, turbulent, and malignant communities: "In view, however, of the complexity of social change . . . it seems desirable to include within the perspective and purview of the concept, and of studies of succession, every possible form of orderly change so far as it affects the interrelations of individuals in a community or the structure of the society of which these individuals are part."

Unfortunately there are limits to which the meaning of any concept can be stretched before its meaning is lost. The idea of succession clearly implies that communities change over an endless cycle or series of irreversible stages. It does not merely imply, as Park belatedly suggests, any change that follows an orderly process. To the contrary, it definitely implies a particular kind of orderly process of change, where one stage inevitably comes after another in an irreversible sequence. Consequently the notion should be discarded.

The fifth and final brute fact about violent criminal acts and actors to which my theory conforms is that both may change over time by becoming either more or less violent. The latter, salutary development takes place in the case of de-escalating violent careers, and the former, unfortunate one takes place in the case of escalating violent ones. In retrospect I also discovered that the stable "violent" career, a subtype of the more general stable career, is merely a methodological artifact. My second study included many middle-aged offenders who, because of the sheer amount of elapsed time, were simply unable to recall much about the earlier periods of their lives when they held nonviolent self-conceptions and had not performed any substantially violent acts. I had created this erroneous subtype on the basis of my study of their cases. Thus I mistakenly classified these violent criminals as undergoing stable violent careers when, undoubtedly, they had undergone escalating ones.

Although slow to recognize that I had developed a new theory congruent with the five brute facts about violent criminal acts and actors just described, I recognized immediately that female violent criminals did not constitute an anomaly as far as this theory is concerned. Because I had strategically used female violent offenders in constructing the theory, my explanation could account for women's violent crimes. In fact including women in my second study was responsible for my discovery that violent criminal actors can have mitigated violent phantom communities (formerly generalized others) and incipiently violent self-conceptions. Their inclusion also helped me to discover that these phantom communities, and to a lesser extent self-images, play a pivotal part in a normal progression through an escalating and de-escalating violent criminal career.

# CONTEMPORARY RETROSPECTIVE ON SYMBOLIC INTERACTIONIST AND PHENOMENOLOGICAL THEORIES

## THE EMBEDDEDNESS OF SYMBOLIC INTERACTIONISM IN CRIMINOLOGY

*Jeffrey T. Ulmer, Pennsylvania State University*

To study sociological criminology is to be conversant with a variety of symbolic inter-actionist ideas and concepts (whether one knows it or not). Many theories at the core of criminology are imbued with symbolic interactionism. This is no accident, since symbolic interactionism and the sociological study of crime have common roots in the distinctive Chicago School approach to sociology (see the reviews by Maines, 2001; Strauss, 1993).

### What Is Symbolic Interactionism?

It is surprisingly difficult to state precisely what symbolic interactionism is and isn't in con-temporary sociology, for two reasons. First, as Maines (2001) and Fine (1993) have argued, sociology has increasingly adopted into its mainstream concepts and propositions—such as self, identity, definitions of the situation, agency, meaning—that are at the heart of sym-bolic interactionism (see the reviews by Hall, 2007; Maines, 2001). Second, researchers in the symbolic interactionist tradition have increasingly broadened their empirical focus to a wide range of topics, and have engaged with a broad range of theoretical traditions and even disciplines (cognitive psychology, cultural studies, communication studies, feminist theory, and postmodernist perspectives, to name a few). Fortunately, several excellent sum-maries and discussions of symbolic interactionism exist, such as Shalin (1986), Fine (1993), Strauss (1993), Maines (2001), and Hall (2007). Readers interested in a fuller treatment of symbolic interactionism's history, key concepts and propositions, and place in sociology should consult these resources. In addition, symbolic interactionism has its own profes-sional association (the Society for the Study of Symbolic Interaction, founded in 1977) with its own academic journal (*Symbolic Interaction*) and website, and a research annual devoted to interactionist work (*Studies in Symbolic Interaction*, published by Elsevier Sciences).

The most narrow answer to the question "what is symbolic interactionism" is that it is the social psychology of the self and identity, stemming from the pioneering theories of George Herbert Mead, Charles Horton Cooley, William James, and John Dewey (see Charmaz's 2007 comprehensive treatment of interactionist conceptions of the self and iden-tity). Many introductory sociology and social psychology textbooks define symbolic inter-actionism in this way. Symbolic interactionism emphasizes that humans have the capacity to regard their own minds and behavior as objects through a process known as "reflexivity." This reflexive experience of one's own existence and self-awareness is the *self*. Mead, following William James, famously conceived of the impulsive, creative, energetic phase of the self as the "I," and the reflexive, socialized phase of the self as the "me." The "me" phase of the self assesses the "I" through an ongoing internal conversation, in light of the views and norms of larger groups that the individual has internalized. Lonnie Athens (1994) later usefully conceptualized this internalized collection of social norms and directives as one's "phantom community." Following the lead of Herbert Blumer (1937), Mead's most authoritative early interpreter for sociology, interactionists have made the reflexive self central to any understandings of human behavior, and have emphasized the multifaceted and dynamic nature of the self (see especially Blumer's 2004 posthumously published and comprehensive explanation of Mead's thoughts on the self and social interaction).

Starting in the 1950s, interactionists such as Anselm Strauss, Howard Becker, Gregory Stone, and Erving Goffman extended this focus on the self to the notion of *identity*. In the works of these authors, identities are social locations that are transacted in social interaction. In other words, identities are social identifications that enable individuals to place one another in social space. Identities are also the social interactional face of the self—that is, identities are dimensions of self that we present in interaction, and that other parties to the interaction know us by. We also define ourselves in terms of our identities, and how others react to them and treat us as we enact them (these are known as "reflected appraisals"). In an important implication for labeling theory in criminology, deviant *stigma* is, in the words of Erving Goffman, "spoiled identity." A stigma is a devalued identity that is imposed upon a person. Stigma strongly tends to mobilize negative behavioral expectations and attributions of character among others who meet the stigmatized person.

In the 1970s and 1980s, Sheldon Stryker (1980; Stryker & Burke, 2000) and others articulated a formal identity theory, which, like earlier treatments, emphasized role identities (such as father, professor, sister, etc.) and categorical identities (such as gender, race, ethnicity, socioeconomic status, religion, etc.) as a key link between the self and social structure. Stryker and his disciples also described how different identities have different subjective salience for the self (for example, one's identity of "spouse" or "daughter" is likely much more salient, or important, to one's self-concept and self-esteem than the identity of "golfer" or "soccer fan"). Thus, we each interact on the basis of many identities, which all are arranged in a *hierarchy of salience* for defining the self.

Many symbolic interactionist scholars would argue for a much broader definition of their perspective, however (see Fine, 1993; Hall, 2007; Maines, 2001; Shalin, 1986; Strauss, 1993, as just a few presentations of this broader position). This broader definition certainly includes, but goes considerably beyond, the social psychology of self and identity described earlier. From this broader perspective, interactionism is a generic sociological perspective that is based on the philosophy of American pragmatism (Mead, Dewey, James, and Cooley, mentioned previously, were noted pragmatist philosophers as well as psychologists and sociologists). Indeed, Herbert Blumer, who was seen as the authoritative spokesperson of the perspective until his death in 1987, coined the term *symbolic interactionism* in 1937 to simply identify a broad and somewhat amorphous approach to sociology that incorporated the insights of Mead and other pragmatists as well as early Chicago School sociologists W. I. Thomas and Robert Park. As such, symbolic interactionism is not so much a formalistic theory, with predictive propositions and hypotheses (though one could perhaps derive such hypotheses), as it is a paradigm or overarching conceptual framework that shapes one's approach to theorizing about and researching any sociological topic. On this view, symbolic interactionism has at least four defining features (see Hall, 2007; Maines, 2001).

**1. *An emphasis on interpretation and meaning:*** Symbolic interactionism rests on three simple propositions distilled from the thought of Mead, Dewey, James, Cooley, and other early pragmatists: (1) people act on the basis of meanings that they have for them; (2) meanings emerge, or are created from, interactions between social actors (which importantly can include not just individuals but groups such as organizations, communities, and the like—Blumer often used the terms "acting units," "group actors," and "collective actors"); and (3) meanings are maintained and/or changed through a dynamic process in which people keep or adjust their definitions based on responses and consequences.

According to Blumer, these three propositions are the absolute bedrock of symbolic interactionism. This means that interactionism is at its heart an interpretive perspective—that is, it emphasizes the way people and groups interpret the world around them, and act on the basis of those interpretations. Thus, W. I. Thomas and D. S. Thomas's concept of the *definition of the situation* is central to symbolic interactionism (and, an interactionist would argue, all of sociology). The famous "Thomas theorem" says that what people define as real becomes real in its consequences. People act in social situations toward objects and other people on the basis of their interpretations and definitions. Note also that social actors' definitions can vary a great deal in accuracy and effectiveness (at least as perceived by others), but the crucial point is that it is those definitions, and not some "objective" reality or stimuli, that drive behavior. As will be shown later, this interactionist principle is at the heart of Sutherland's differential association theory and Akers's social learning theory in criminology.

**2. *An emphasis on process:*** Process, change, evolution, and emergence were central concerns of the early pragmatist philosophers and their early sociological interpreters, such as Park, Thomas, and Blumer. Interactionists focus on how individuals and their social worlds are always active, in process, ongoing, becoming, and changing. In other words, all of society, social organization, and social structure rest on, are made up of, and are transformed by myriad and complex ongoing processes of social interaction, in much the same way that a solid object such as a table or steel bar is made up of atomic and subatomic particles in interactive motion (Perinbanayagam, 1986). Nothing is seen as static: even stability takes action to maintain. In fact, symbolic interactionist conceptions of social organization and structure rest on these views of structure and organization as ongoing interaction process, or what Blumer called "joint action" (see Blumer, 2004; Hall, 1987, 2003; Maines, 2001; Strauss, 1993). According to Blumer (2004):

> Organization must be seen as arising in the process of fitting components, individual acts, to each other—a process in which the participating individuals are forging their individual adjustive acts in terms of the definitions and expectations imposed on them, their own interests, the constraints the situation places on them, and the opportunities afforded for distinctive lines of individual action. (p. 99)

**3. *An emphasis on human agency:*** Humans do not just automatically or passively respond to stimuli (as older behaviorist psychological imagery would have it), nor is human behavior predetermined by instinct. People define the objects, events, and others around them, and act with intention. People create, innovate, formulate goals, make choices, and attempt to achieve those goals (with varying degrees of success). People can also flexibly adapt and adjust their lines of action to the changing demands and opportunities of the situations around them. This emphasis on agency therefore explains the centrality of the self and identity in interactionist thought. The self is the *agent* who acts and interacts, and in doing so, constitutes society.

To emphasize agency is not to say, however, that interactionism ignores constraint, including constraint from social structures. Instead, interactionists see agency as being in a *dialectical relationship* with biological and social constraints of various kinds.

**4. *Dialectical thinking, and a rejection of dualisms or false dichotomies:*** Interactionism emphasizes relationships of mutual interdependence and mutual determinism. Dialectical thinking of this sort was a key feature of American pragmatist thought, and it fundamentally shapes symbolic interactionist sociology. For interactionists, to say that two phenomena form a dialectic is to say that they mutually interrelate in a manner that is practically inseparable. In fact, two dialectical phenomena can be said to mutually create one another, in the sense that one cannot exist without the other, and one has no meaning without reference to the other. Thus, interactionists generally do not believe in many dualisms (that is, opposed dichotomies) commonly discussed in social science, such as "body vs. mind," "nature vs. nurture," "individual vs. society," "micro- vs. macro-" social phenomena, "stability vs. change," "consensus vs. conflict." Instead, most interactionists would argue that no single part of these dichotomies can be studied without reference to its counterpart. For example, individual social behavior makes sense only in the context of some larger community of organization and culture, so studying individual behavior (even individual self and identity) is rather pointless without reference to his or her surrounding social world. At the same time, interactionists have difficulty with the notion that macrolevel social structures (nations, states, corporations, etc.) can be meaningfully studied without reference to the individuals, interactions, and joint acts that constitute them.

In sum, the broadest definition of symbolic interaction is that it is a sociology that is founded in pragmatist philosophical assumptions, especially the ones listed previously. Whether one uses a broad or narrow definition, however, symbolic interaction has profoundly shaped criminology.

## Empirical Applications: Symbolic Interactionism and Core Criminological Theories

In discussing the place of symbolic interactionism in sociology, David Maines (2001) identifies three categories of influence and use of interactionist work: interactionist promoters, interactionist utilizers, and unaware interactionists. Basically, any scholar of criminal activity who draws on, applies, or tests the core criminological theories discussed earlier is arguably an interactionist utilizer (if the scholar acknowledges the theoretical connections to interactionism), or an unaware interactionist (if he or she does not acknowledge such connections). Obviously, then, there is a great deal of both interactionist utilization and unaware interactionism in criminology.

Five of the major criminological theories are either directly influenced by symbolic interactionism, or share common roots and key pragmatist assumptions: social disorganization, differential association/social learning, social control, and labeling theories (for a more thorough discussion, see Ulmer, 2000; Ulmer & Spencer, 1999).

Social disorganization theory, of course, developed more or less simultaneously with symbolic interactionism proper at the University of Chicago. The term *social disorganization* was coined by W. I. Thomas and Florian Znaniecki (1918), and was applied to the study of crime by Chicago scholars like Shaw and McKay (1931). Social disorganization theory in criminology, which thrives in empirical research to this day (see Bursik & Grasmick, 1993b; Kubrin & Weitzer, 2003a; Rose & Clear, 1998), grew out of the early Chicago School's life history and social ecological approaches, which were themselves steeped in a pragmatist approach to sociological inquiry (see Maines, Bridger, & Ulmer, 1996).

Opportunity theory (Cloward & Ohlin, 1960) represents the marriage of Robert Merton's notion of structural strain with differential association theory (Cullen, 1988; Merton, 1997). As explained in the following text, differential association theory itself was influenced by and based in the same pragmatist approach to sociology as social disorganization theory. Furthermore, later extensions of opportunity theory clearly link it with interactionist themes such as situational-level interaction, definitions of situations, socialization, culture, and decision making (see Cullen, 1988; Steffensmeier, 1983; Ulmer, 2000).

Social control theory (Hirschi, 1969) and its recent extensions (Laub & Sampson, 2003; Sampson & Laub, 1993) argue that people refrain from committing crime and deviance because of social bonds to conventional others, institutions, and norms. The four elements of these social bonds are known as stakes in conformity: attachment to conventional others, commitment to conventional lines of action, involvement in conventional activities, and belief in conventional norms. Hirschi's conceptualization of attachment and commitment was influenced by Erving Goffman (1961), and his treatment of them as stakes in conformity derives many ideas from both Goffman's (1961, 1963) and Becker's (1960) notion of commitments as "side bets."

The two criminological theories that are most identified with symbolic interactionism, however, are differential association/social learning theory and labeling theory. I therefore discuss these in greater detail.

### Differential association/social learning, and neutralizations

The name "symbolic interactionism" had not yet been coined by Herbert Blumer when Edwin Sutherland, arguably the founder of sociological criminology in the United States as we know it, first formulated differential association theory in 1924. Sutherland and Blumer were, in fact, products of the sociology department at University of Chicago, and both of them absorbed pragmatist assumptions and perspectives through the work of Robert Park, G. H. Mead, Louis Wirth, John Dewey, and others. Sutherland was especially influenced by the work of W. I. Thomas and his notion (with Dorothy Swain Thomas) of the definition of the situation. This concept—fundamental to symbolic interactionism—would become the bedrock upon which he constructed his generic theory of crime and deviance, differential association.

Sutherland's theory is one of *differences in association with messages and opportunities favorable to crime*. It posits that deviant/criminal behavior, like most social behavior, is learned and that it is learned through processes of social interaction. In Sutherland's definitive statement of the theory (1947), criminal or delinquent behavior involves the learning of (a) techniques of committing crimes and (b) orientations (vocabularies of motives, drives, rationalizations) and attitudes favorable to crime. Differential association/social learning theory is supported by an impressive array of quantitative, qualitative, historical, and cross-cultural evidence (for a definitive treatment of differential association/social learning theory, see Akers, 1998).

The concept of normative conflict frames the theory. This is simply the notion that various groups and subgroups in society differ in terms of definitions of right and wrong, and in their definitions of whether individuals are obligated to follow laws (either particular ones or laws in general). These groups can include subcultures, professional and occupational groups, ethnic groups, voluntary associations, religious groups, neighborhoods, and other collectivities. This normative conflict, in turn, is played out at both the individual and group levels.

The structural, group-level manifestation of normative conflict is *differential social organization*. The norms, values, meanings, skills, and definitions found within these groups can be favorable to particular kinds of crime, or crime in general. In addition, cultural, subcultural, or group messages or definitions can be *supportive, neutral, hostile,* or *mixed* toward crime. Groups' organization (the social and cultural organization of various groups or settings) can potentially be favorable for crime in general, and/or for specific kinds of crimes, or for specific kinds of crimes in specific circumstances. Sutherland (1940) describes the effect of differential social organization this way: "The law is pressing in one direction, and other forces are pressing in the opposite direction" (p. 12).

Later, Daniel Glaser (1956) linked "association" more closely with the symbolic interactionist perspective Glaser acquired from Herbert Blumer at Chicago. Focusing on the subjective role-taking process that occurs in both social interaction and private thought, Glaser suggested that Sutherland's theory be reconceptualized as "differential identification." Defining "identification" as "the choice of another from whose perspective we view our own behavior," he expressed the essence of his revision as "[a] person pursues criminal behavior to the extent that he identifies himself with real or imaginary persons from whose perspective his criminal behavior seems acceptable" (p. 440).

Neutralization theory, formulated by Sykes and Matza (1957), noted that delinquents and criminals usually have both criminal and noncriminal values, expressing the former in their lawbreaking while at the same time maintaining at least some allegiance to conventional norms. Sykes and Matza drew upon C. Wright Mills's (1940) concept of "vocabularies of motive," and identified a process by which would-be deviants or criminals suspend or rationalize conduct that violates norms in which the actor otherwise believes. These vocabularies of motive allow the actor to then engage in the chosen form of deviant activity. They called this prebehavior rationalization process "neutralization," and identified five common and nonmutually exclusive techniques of neutralization: "denials of responsibility" (e.g., blaming their crimes on their circumstances), "denials of the victim" (e.g., claiming that their victim "had it coming"), "denials of injury" (e.g., saying that their victims have plenty and won't miss it), "condemning their condemners" (e.g., accusing their prosecutors of prejudice), and "appeals to higher loyalties" (e.g., saying that they did it for their friends or family). Accounts are similar to neutralizations, but are articulated after deviant behavior to retrospectively excuse or rationalize the violation of norms to self and others (Scott & Lyman, 1968). In general, accounts and neutralizations are examples of a broader concept that interactionists call "aligning actions" (Stokes & Hewitt 1976), or rhetoric and actions aimed at repairing disrupted social situations and damaged identity.

Bruce Jacobs (1992) and Volkan Topalli (2005) have further extended neutralization theory in ways that broaden it, and ground it on even more solid interactionist footing. These two scholars found that neutralizations and accounts do not just apply to deviance/crime. Rather, they can be used by people embedded in deviant subcultures to excuse conventional actions that would call into question their identity and standing in the deviant group. Jacobs found that undercover police had to provide accounts and neutralizations for *not* using drugs in front of drug dealers and other users so as to not blow their own cover. Topalli found that "hardcore" gang members often had to provide accounts and neutralizations for otherwise conventional behavior. For example, they often had to account to their gangster peers for situations where they chose *not* to violently retaliate against someone who wronged them.

Akers (1998) combines Sutherland's ideas with Glaser's (1956) notion of differential identification, Sykes and Matza's (1957) theory of vocabularies of motive and deviance, and developments in social psychology that postdated Sutherland to articulate a social learning theory of crime that specifies the process of differential association in more detail and specificity. According to Akers, crime is learned through three conceptually distinct— but usually interrelated—social processes: differential association, differential reinforcement (receiving positive reinforcement for deviant behavior), and differential identification or deviant role modeling.

In sum, socialization favorable to crime involves learning definitions, attitudes, behaviors, skills, and vocabularies of motive favorable to given forms of deviance, as well as forming of relationships with deviant others and self-definitions in terms of deviant identities. Differential association/social learning theory incorporates several symbolic interactionist themes: an emphasis on interpretive meanings and definitions of situations as the proximal causes of behavior, an emphasis on the importance of interaction processes and how they are shaped by larger social contexts, and the importance of self-definitions and identities (see Akers, 1998).

### Labeling theory

Labeling theory has long been closely identified with symbolic interactionism (Steffensmeier & Terry, 1975). Its early proponents, such as G. H. Mead, Frank Tannenbaum, Edwin Lemert, Howard Becker, Alfred Lindesmith, Erving Goffman, and Edwin Schur, were either proponents of interactionism or were substantially influenced by pragmatist or interactionist work. Key interactionist elements that suffuse labeling theory are (1) an emphasis on social process; (2) an emphasis on the importance of the construction of meaning and the interpretive definition of social objects; (3) the importance of the dialectic between selves, identities, and situations; and (4) the dialectic between agency and constraint.

Contemporary labeling theory's themes include (1) the situational and larger scale definition of deviance; (2) the role of social statuses and identities in affecting whether one gets negatively labeled; (3) the consequences of deviant labels for the careers and selves of individuals labeled deviant; and (4) the consequences of the creation and labeling of deviance for society. Labeling theory also predicts that negative labeling of behavior in question (either informally for deviance or formally for crime) depends on the following situational contingencies: (1) the meaning and consequences of the act; (2) the identity and statuses of the actor; (3) the audience of the act; and (4) the context of the act (for a systematic treatment of the role of status, demeanor, appearance, audience, and context in social reaction to deviance, see Steffensmeier & Terry, 1975). Readers interested in a definitive review of the history, central ideas, and criticisms of labeling theory should see Joel Best's *Deviance: Career of a Concept* (2004).

One of labeling theory's main themes is the effect of being labeled unfavorably (e.g., as delinquent or criminal) on a person's subsequent life history. More recently, Laub and Sampson (2003; Sampson & Laub, 1993), among others, have demonstrated that arrests and convictions among young offenders tend to reverberate throughout the life course, producing negative consequences and cumulative disadvantages in education, employment, family life, substance abuse, and further criminal behavior (see also Pager, 2003).

Differential association and labeling theory also have a symbiotic relationship (Ulmer, 1994). One basic contention of labeling theory is that sanctions against crime/deviance can inadvertently contribute to continuity in deviant activity and careers. This occurs because punitive sanctions can potentially (1) restrict opportunities for conventional employment and relationships, (2) open up illegitimate opportunities and access to deviant networks or subcultures, and (3) lead to the development of deviant self-identities and a sense of estrangement from conventional society. In other words, labeling can open up criminal/ deviant learning and performance opportunities, and produce further differential association processes that entrench an individual into crime or deviance (Ulmer, 1994, 2000).

Another interactionist feature shared by labeling theory and differential association theory is an emphasis on careers and process (see Ulmer & Spencer, 1999). In particular, labeling theory argues that the original causes of criminal behavior may not be the same as the eventual causes that reproduce or sustain criminal behavior (or, as Howard Becker [1963] put it, the deviant behavior in time produces its own set of deviant motivations). In general, differential association and labeling and have been influential in the current focus on the life course and crime/deviance (see Benson, 2002; Laub & Sampson, 2003; Sampson & Laub, 1997).

Another important extension of labeling theory is the theory of reintegrative shaming and restorative justice. Notable symbolic interactionist themes that the theory of reintegrative shaming draws on include labeling and stigmatization, self and identity, symbolic representations of social order, and recent interactionist research in the sociology of emotions. John Braithwaite (1989) first articulated the theory of reintegrative shaming and helped lay the foundation for the contemporary restorative justice movement in Australia and New Zealand, Europe, and (to a lesser extent) the United States. In a nutshell, Braithwaite argued that sanctions against rule breaking can either be stigmatizing or reintegrative. Stigmatizing sanctions are well described by labeling theory: an offender is ritually stigmatized, placed in a spoiled identity, and punished. Spoiled identities (e.g., "ex-con," "felon") then mobilize exclusionary reactions from conventional relationships and institutions even after formal punishment has ended and may sometimes foster entrenched commitment to deviant groups. Thus stigmatizing sanctions alienate the offender from the community. Reintegrative styles of justice, however, are built around shaming, respecting, and giving voice to victims; atonement or restitution; and then restoration of the offender as a valued member of the community. Different societies and cultures vary in the extent to which their systems of justice are stigmatizing or reintegrative. Japan, aboriginal tribes of Australia and New Zealand, and some Native American tribes, for example, exhibit more reintegrative styles of justice, while the United States and similar nations are presented as examples of systems of stigmatizing sanctioning.

Braithwaite and colleagues' *Shame Management through Reintegration* (Ahmed, Harris, Braithwaite, & Braithwaite, 2001) is a valuable extension of the theory of reintegrative shaming and restorative justice. The authors review the growing body of research from sociology, psychology, criminology, and anthropology (including much cross-cultural research) on the topics of shaming, stigmatization, and restorative sanctions, and they also empirically apply their theoretical framework to data on drunk driving and school bullying. Though the literature is still limited, the research and policy experiments in restorative justice that do exist have met with noticeable success (as measured by likelihood of reoffending, as well as victim and offender satisfaction with the perceived justice of sanctions) in Australia, New Zealand, Europe, Japan, and (to a much lesser extent) the United States, at least when they have been properly implemented.

## Theoretical Refinements: Contemporary Criminology

There are too many examples of interesting research and theorizing done by contemporary interactionist utilizers to discuss in this chapter, but I will select a few who I think are particularly interesting exemplars. First, Bruce Jacobs, Richard Wright, Jody Miller, and Lisa Maher have produced compelling street ethnographies of the social worlds of crack dealing, robbery, drug robbery, and other street crime (Jacobs, 1996; Jacobs, Topalli, & Wright, 2000; Jacobs & Wright, 1999, 2006; Maher & Daly, 1996; Miller, 1998). With ethnographic meticulousness that would make a cultural anthropologist proud, their work provides a wealth of data on the structural situations, networks of relationships, and interpretive strategies of the lives of a variety of male and female street criminals. Their analyses of these data draw explicitly and implicitly on many interactionist themes. In particular, these scholars focus on the interpretive processes of the people involved, as well as the dialectic of situational agency and constraint.

### Interactionist utilizers

Ross Matsueda and his colleagues have been extending, testing, and refining interactionist-based ideas from differential association and labeling theory for two decades (Matsueda, 1982, 1988, 1992; Matsueda & Heimer, 1997). In particular, Matsueda and his colleagues focus on the nature and role of peer relationships and interaction in producing crime and delinquency, as well as the role of negative reflected appraisals from parents and other authority figures in solidifying deviant identities among juveniles. The influence of Sheldon Stryker's (1980) work is especially strong in Matsueda's work.

Richard Felson's instrumental theory of aggression and violence (1992, 1993) draws from rational choice theory, but elements of it are quite interactionist-friendly. Felson's theory is influenced by the work of Sheldon Stryker, Peter Burke, Erving Goffman, and others (Richard Felson studied under Sheldon Stryker at Indiana University). Felson argues that violence is usually instrumental, used to gain compliance, settle disputes, or otherwise exercise coercive power. His account depicts violence as arising from interpretive decision processes in which actors assess rewards and costs, the likelihood of success of violence or aggression, the audience, and the context.

Robert Agnew's "general strain theory" (1992) expands traditional Mertonian notions of strain and brings the concept to bear on individual actors and their decisions about engaging in crime and deviance. Agnew identifies different types of structural and situational strain in everyday life, and explains how different modes of adaptation and coping with such strain are criminogenic or not. Agnew (1995) has also extended David Matza's (1964) well-known notion of "drift" into deviance and crime, and explores the implications for determinacy and indeterminacy in criminal and deviance careers.

Another symbolic interactionist utilization in criminology is Jack Katz's *Seductions of Crime* (1988), which focuses on the self-conceptions that offenders gain from lawbreaking.

The immediate thrill of risk-taking and getting away with it pervades the autobiographical accounts of successful prior crimes that he collected. These tales range from essays that college students wrote for him on their juvenile shoplifting, a type of delinquency that anonymous questionnaires indicate is committed by most youths of all socioeconomic classes, to reports of unprosecuted murders and rapes that are included in life histories from prison inmates who were interviewed while serving long terms for other crimes.

The work of Neal Shover (1983, 1996) studies the criminal careers of property offenders and follows them through the life course. In doing so, he focuses on their interpretive definitions of themselves and their situations, their exercise of agency within structural constraints, and the role of emergence and contingency in their criminal careers.

Beyond these few among many possible examples of the use of interactionism, what are some examples of, to use Maines's (2001) term, "promotion" of symbolic interactionism per se in the field? We discuss two (out of several possible) examples of "interactionist promoters" in criminology. A more comprehensive review of interactionist contributions to criminology can be found in Ulmer and Spencer (1999).

### Interactionist promoters: Three examples

First, thanks to journalist Richard Rhodes's (1999) book *Why They Kill: Discoveries of a Maverick Criminologist*, a vast academic and public audience has been introduced to Lonnie Athens's theory and research on violence, and core tenets of symbolic interactionism as well. Athens's theorizing and research on violent crime reflect his study under Herbert Blumer at Berkeley, and it is steeped in the thought of Blumer and Mead (whose theory of the self Athens [1994, 1995] has also refined). He analyzed the careers of serious violent offenders and offenders' decisions to commit homicide, rape, robbery, and/or aggravated assault (Athens, 1989, 1997, 2003). As Blumer points out in the foreword to *Violent Criminal Acts and Actors Revisited* (1997), Athens was able to "have his informants describe their violent acts in a way that would allow him to identify their situations as seen by them . . . and to trace their interpretations of these . . . situations," because he gained good rapport with them and developed familiarity with their worlds (p. 5).

The prime movers driving Athens's theory of violent acts are situational definitions conducive to violence, self-images consistent with violent behavior, self-conversations with phantom communities that provide moral justification for violence, and corporal (physical) communities whose norms favor the use of violence in dominance disputes (see Athens, 1997, 2003). Athens's *The Creation of Dangerous Violent Criminals* (1989) delineates a theory of "violentization" (or violent socialization) in which serious violent offenders are distinguished by their having passed through six career phases: violent subjugation, personal horrification, violent coaching, belligerency, violent performance, and virulency.

Second, Steffensmeier and Ulmer (2005) integrate several core theories of criminal and deviant behavior into an interactionist-based learning/opportunity/commitment framework (see also Ulmer, 2000). For example, they argue that criminal/deviant socialization (differential association) and conventional social control both consist of a generic sociological process—the development and experience of structural, personal, and moral commitments (for the original statement of the interactionist theory of structural, personal, and moral commitment, see Johnson, 1991).

Commitment processes can produce continuity in criminal behavior both by fostering a *desire* for criminal activities and choices, and/or by *constraining* individuals from pursuing alternatives. For example, personal commitment to criminal activities develops through learning positive attitudes toward criminal activities and criminal others, and adopting criminal self-definitions. Moral commitment constrains individuals from terminating criminal lines of action once one has become involved in them through internalized cultural and subcultural norms of exchange and obligation. Structural commitment constrains the termination of criminal careers, and is produced by the relative availability and attractiveness of conventional and criminal *opportunities*, irretrievable investments in criminal activity, and social reactions from criminal associates. Both differential association into crime/deviance and conventional social control entail developing all of these kinds of commitments (to either deviance or conformity, or both), and the concept of structural commitment also embeds the individual in structural contexts, large and small. Steffensmeier and Ulmer (2005) introduce the term "commitment portfolio" to refer to an individual's "accumulated and valued interests and allegiances, as represented by his or her structural, moral, and personal commitments" (p. 174). They argue that stability and change in criminal careers can be explained with reference to individuals' commitment portfolios. For example, building a portfolio of conventional commitments as one gets older explains the typical desistence from crime with aging. On the other hand, some offenders do not develop such conventional commitments, and/or continue to develop strong criminal commitment portfolios as they get older. These kinds of offenders would persist in crime throughout the life course (or until such time as their commitment portfolios changed to favor conventional commitments).

Furthermore, the negative consequences of labeling work through commitment processes (Steffensmeier & Ulmer, 2005; Ulmer, 1994). Commitment processes are the "intervening variables" between negative social reaction and what Lemert (1951) calls secondary deviance, when one becomes entrenched in a deviant or criminal identity and career. That is, punitive or exclusionary social reactions to crime or deviance can rearrange structural, personal, or moral commitments to deviance versus conventional activity, and entrench individuals in criminal identities and careers.

Third, Giordano and her colleagues (Giordano, Cernkovich, & Rudolph, 2002; Giordano, Cernkovich, & Holland, 2003; Giordano, Schroeder & Cernkovich, 2007) present what they call "a symbolic interactionist theory of desistance" from criminal activity and test it with longitudinal quantitative (self-report questionnaires) and qualitative (narrative life history interviews) data from a broadly varying sample of men and women. They find substantial support for their theory, and claim that it outperforms alternatives. Among the benefits Giordano et al. (2002) claim for their interactionist theory of desistance are (1) offering a balanced emphasis on the importance of both agency and constraint in the life course, (2) explaining why some individuals do not desist from crime even when opportunity structures are favorable for them to do so, and (3) offering better explanations for why men's and women's criminal careers and desistance processes differ considerably. In addition, Giordano et al. (2007) expand this interactionist theory of desistence to include a focus on emotions and how emotional selves influence long-term continuity and change in crime.

## Policy Applications

Although there has been little explicit symbolic interactionist discussion of policy with regard to crime and justice, one can think of several policy directions that would be compatible with interactionism. In general, symbolic interactionism would emphasize policies that took seriously the main themes of interactionist and interactionist-inspired research in criminology: socialization and social learning, self and identity, commitments, and labeling processes.

Symbolic interactionist compatible efforts at preventing crime and rehabilitating offenders would be similar to those suggested by differential association/social learning theory (for fuller development of these policy prescriptions, see Akers, 1998). That is, policies to prevent crime would most effectively focus on fostering communities and other social contexts that provide young people with learning opportunities for conventional norms, skills, definitions, and behaviors. Interactionist-compatible policies to prevent crime would provide people of all ages the opportunities to build commitment portfolios that favored conventional activity over crime. These commitment portfolios would particularly include an emphasis on building conventional identities and definitions of self rather than differential identification with criminal role models.

Giordano et al.'s (2002, 2003, 2007) interactionist theory of desistence from crime coined the term *hooks for change*. These hooks for change are said to be vitally necessary for individuals to choose to leave behind criminal behavior and lifestyles and embrace conventional ones. Hooks for change are opportunities, relationships, and experiences that offer those entrenched in criminal careers the incentive to adopt new, noncriminal identities and new conventional self-definitions (Giordano et al., 2002), as well as fostering decreased negative emotions that motivate crime, and increased skill in managing one's emotions (Giordano et al., 2007). It follows that interactionist-inspired rehabilitation policies would foster such hooks for change. Giordano and her colleagues make several specific recommendations for such policies in their work (2002, 2003, 2007). In sum, symbolic interactionism would favor rehabilitative policies that fostered conventional social learning; the development of portfolios of conventional structural, personal, and moral commitments; and hooks for change that foster the development of conventional identities and selves.

The theory of reintegrative shaming has particularly well-developed policy implications. Ahmed and colleagues (2001) present nine social justice policy prescriptions from a reintegrative shaming perspective, and these are very compatible with symbolic interactionism, since reintegrative shaming theory incorporates labeling theory and recent interactionist work on the sociology of emotions. Among the latter are (1) reducing stigmatization and its alienating effects; (2) seeking reintegrative ways to communicate disapproval of crime and other harmful acts; (3) helping victims and offenders acknowledge and discharge shame; (4) reducing procedural injustice (e.g., inequalities in the enforcement of laws and in punishments) and distributive injustice (e.g., status or economic inequalities); (5) supporting social movements and institutions with agendas that disapprove of crimes of domination and that confront distributive and procedural injustice; (6) strengthening the justice and care of familial, economic, and political institutions and thus increasing public trust in them; and (7) regulating crime responsively—that is, trying restorative justice first and falling back on deterrence and incapacitation only when restorative justice fails. This last prescription bears some elaboration because it demonstrates that the theory's authors are not just naive utopians. They fully realize that restorative justice and reintegrative shaming will not work for all disapproved behaviors or rule breakers and that the effectiveness of these sanctions depends on the "ethical identities" and rationality of offenders. They argue that restorative procedures are the preferred sanctions for rational and ethical offenders, deterrence is appropriate for rational offenders who lack conventional ethical commitments, and incapacitation is appropriate for the irrational offender. Ultimately, its proponents argue that reintegrative shaming/restorative justice is relevant not only to crime but to social justice of all kinds (e.g., environmental justice, economic justice) and to social order itself.

Finally, a good deal of symbolic interactionist research has examined the policy-making process itself, and this research sounds a caution regarding the implementation of crime prevention or rehabilitation efforts. The research refers to policy formation and implementation as "the transformation of intentions" (Estes & Edmonds, 1981; Hall, 1997; Hall & McGinty, 1997; Ulmer, 2005). This means that policies are at the mercy of those who implement them, and formal policy goals can be transformed or even subverted by local officials. According to Hall (1997), on one hand, "policy actors, dependent upon those who follow them to complete their intentions, set the terms that both limit and facilitate later actions" (p. 401). On the other hand, "later actors may reinforce, clarify, subvert, or amend initial intentions and content" (p. 401). Thus, symbolic interactionism would draw attention to the implementation process and the ways well-intentioned crime policies could get sidetracked. Since, for interactionists, social order exists in and through processes of social interaction, it follows that crime policies depend on the quality of their implementation by local individuals and participants.

Symbolic interactionism is a vital part of sociology today, and many of its key ideas and concepts are taken for granted by nearly all sociologists. This perspective has shaped sociological criminology since its inception. As long as the links between interactionism and criminology remain viable, interactionism will direct criminologists' attention to the importance of interpretive meaning, interaction processes, human agency, self, and identity, and the dialectical interrelationships between individuals, situations, and larger social contexts.

# PART IX

# CRITICAL THEORIES

# CONFLICT AND RADICAL THEORIES

## CRIMINALITY AND ECONOMIC CONDITIONS

*William Adrian Bonger*

. . . [I]t is certain that man is born with social instincts, which, when influenced by a favorable environment can exert a force great enough to prevent egoistic thoughts from leading to egoistic acts. And since crime constitutes a part of the egoistic acts, it is of importance, for the etiology of *crime in general*, to inquire whether the present method of production and its social consequences are an obstacle to the development of the social instincts, and in what measure. We shall try in the following pages to show the influence of the economic system and of these consequences upon the social instincts of man.

After what we have just said it is almost superfluous to remark that the egotisic tendency does not *by itself* make a man criminal. For this something else is necessary. It is possible for the environment to create a great egoist, but this does not imply that the egoist will necessarily become criminal. For example, a man who is enriched by the exploitation of children may nevertheless remain all his life an honest man from the legal point of view. He does not think of stealing, because he has a surer and more lucrative means of getting wealth, although he lacks the moral sense which would prevent him from committing a crime if the thought of it occurred to him. We shall show that, as a consequence of the present environment, man has become very egoistic and hence more *capable of crime*, than if the environment had developed the germs of altruism.

*The present economic system* is based upon exchange. As we saw at the end of the preceding section such a mode of production cannot fail to have an egoistic character. A society based upon exchange isolates the individuals by weakening the bond that unites them. When it is a question of exchange the two parties interested think only of their own advantage even to the detriment of the other party. In the second place the possibility of exchange arouses in a man the thought of the possibility of converting the surplus of his labor into things which increase his well-being in place of giving the benefit of it to those who are deprived of the necessaries of life. Hence the possibility of exchange gives birth to cupidity.

The exchange called simple circulation of commodities is practiced by all men as consumers, and by the workers besides as vendors of their labor power. However, the influence of this simple circulation of commodities is weak compared with that exercised by capitalistic exchange. It is only the exchange of the surplus of labor, by the producer, for other commodities, and hence is for him a secondary matter. As a result he does not exchange with a view to profit, (though he tries to make as advantageous a trade as possible) but to get things which he cannot produce himself.

Capitalistic exchange, on the other hand, has another aim—that of making a profit. A merchant, for example, does not buy goods for his own use, but to sell them to advantage. He will, then, always try, on the one hand, to buy the best commodities as cheaply as possible, by depreciating them as much as he can; on the other hand, to make the purchaser pay as high a price as possible, by exaggerating the value of his wares. *By the nature of the mode of production itself* the merchant is therefore forced to make war upon two sides, must maintain his own interests against the interests of those with whom he does business. If he does not injure too greatly the interests of those from whom he buys, and those to whom he sells, it is for the simple reason that these would otherwise do business with those of his competitors who do not find their interest in fleecing their customers. Wherever competition is eliminated for whatever cause the tactics of the merchant are shown in their true light; he thinks only of his own advantage even to the detriment of those with whom he does business. "No commerce without trickery" is a proverbial expression (among consumers), and with the ancients Mercury, the god of commerce, was also the god of thieves. This is true, that the merchant and the thief are alike in taking account *exclusively* of their own interest to the detriment of those with whom they have to do.

The fact that in our present society production does not take place generally to provide for the needs of men, but for many other reasons, has important effects upon the character of those who possess the means of production. Production is carried on for profit exclusively; if greater profits can be made by stopping production it will be stopped—this is the point of view of the capitalists. The consumers, on the other hand, see in production the means of creating what man has need of. The world likes to be deceived, and does not care to recognize the fact that the producer has only his own profit in view. The latter encourages this notion and poses as a disinterested person. If he reduces the price of his wares, he claims to do it in the interest of the public, and takes care not to admit that it is for the purpose of increasing his own profits. This is the falsity that belongs inevitably to capitalism.

In general this characteristic of capitalism has no importance for the morality of the consumer, who is merely duped, but it is far otherwise with the press, which is almost entirely in the power of the capitalists. The press, which ought to be a guide for the masses, and is so in some few cases, in the main is in the hands of capitalists who use it only as a means of making money. In place of being edited by men who, by their ability and firmness, are capable of enlightening the public, newspapers are carried on by persons who see in their calling only a livelihood, and consider only the proprietor of the sheet. In great part the press is the opposite of what it ought to be; it represents the interests of those who pay for advertisements or for articles; it increases the ignorance and the prejudices of the crowd; in a word, it poisons public opinion.

Besides this general influence upon the public the press has further a special place in the etiology of crime, from the fact that most newspapers, in order to satisfy the morbid curiosity of the public, relate all great crimes in extenso, give portraits of the victims, etc., and are often one of the causes of new crimes, by arousing the imitative instinct to be found in man.

As we have seen above the merchant capitalist makes war in two directions; his interests are against those of the man who sells to him, and of the man who buys from him. This is also true of the industrial capitalist. He buys raw materials and sells what he produces. But to arrive at his product he must buy labor, and this purchase is "sui generis."

Deprived as he is of the means of production the working-man sells his labor only in order not to die of hunger. The capitalist takes advantage of this necessitous condition of the worker and exploits him. We have already indicated that capitalism has this trait in common with the earlier methods of production. Little by little one class of men has become accustomed to think that the others are destined to amass wealth for them and to be subservient to them in every way. Slavery, like the wage system, demoralizes the servant as well as the master. With the master it develops cupidity and the imperious character which sees in a fellow man only a being fit to satisfy his desires. It is true that the capitalist has not the power over the proletarian that the master has over his slave; he has neither the right of service nor the power of life and death, yet it is none the less true that he has another weapon against the proletarian, a weapon whose effect is no less terrible, namely enforced idleness. The fact that the supply of manual labor always greatly exceeds the demand puts this weapon into the hands of every capitalist. It is not only the capitalists who carry on any business that are subjected to this influence, but also all who are salaried in their service.

Capitalism exercises in still a third manner an egoistic influence upon the capitalistic "entrepreneur." Each branch has more producers than are necessary. The interests of the capitalists are, then, opposed not only to those of the men from whom they buy or to whom they sell, but also to those of their fellow producers. It is indeed claimed that competition has the effect simply of making the product better and cheaper, but this is looking at the question from only one point of view. The fact which alone affects criminality is that competition forces the participants, under penalty of succumbing, to be as egoistic as possible. Even the producers who have the means of applying all the technical improvements to perfect their product and make it cheaper, are obliged to have recourse to gross deceits in advertising, etc., in order to injure their competitors. Rejoicing at the evil which befalls another, envy at his good fortune, these forms of egoism are the inevitable consequence of competition. . . .

What are the conclusions to be drawn from what has gone before? When we sum up the results that we have obtained it becomes plain that economic conditions occupy a much more important place in the etiology of crime than most authors have given them.

First we have seen that the present economic system and its consequences weaken the social feelings. The basis of the economic system of our day being exchange, the economic interests of men are necessarily found to be in opposition. This is a trait that capitalism has in common with other modes of production. But its principal characteristic is that the means of production are in the hands of a few, and most men are altogether deprived of them. Consequently, persons who do not possess the means of production are forced to sell their labor to those who do, and these, in consequence of their economic preponderance, force them to make the exchange for the mere necessaries of life, and to work as much as their strength permits.

This state of things especially stifles men's social instincts; it develops, on the part of those with power, the spirit of domination, and of insensibility to the ills of others, while it awakens jealousy and servility on the part of those who depend upon them. Further the contrary interests of those who have property, and the idle and luxurious life of some of them, also contribute to the weakening of the social instincts.

The material condition, and consequently the intellectual condition, of the proletariat are also a reason why the moral plane of that class is not high. The work of children brings them into contact with persons to associate with whom is fatal to their morals. Long working hours and monotonous labor brutalize those who are forced into them; bad housing conditions contribute also to debase the moral sense, as do the uncertainty of existence, and finally absolute poverty, the frequent consequence of sickness and unemployment. Ignorance and lack of training of any kind also contribute their quota. Most demoralizing of all is the status of the lower proletariat.

The economic position of woman contributes also to the weakening of the social instincts.

The present organization of the family has great importance as regards criminality. It charges the legitimate parents with the care of the education of the child; the community concerns itself with the matter very little. It follows that a great number of children are brought up by persons who are totally incapable of doing it properly. As regards the children of the proletariat, there can be no question of the education properly so-called, on account of the lack of means and the forced absence of one or both of the parents. The school tends to remedy this state of things, but the results do not go far enough. The harmful consequences of the present organization of the family make themselves felt especially in the case of the children of the lower proletariat, orphans, and illegitimate children. For these the community does but little, though their need of adequate help is the greatest.

Prostitution, alcoholism, and militarism, which result, in the last analysis, from the present social order, are phenomena that have demoralizing consequences.

As to the different kinds of crime, we have shown that the very important group of economic criminality finds its origin on the one side in the absolute poverty and the cupidity brought about by the present economic environment, and on the other in the moral abandonment and bad education of the children of the poorer classes. Then, professional criminals are principally recruited from the class of occasional criminals, who, finding themselves rejected everywhere after their liberation, fall lower and lower. The last group of economic crimes (fraudulent bankruptcy, etc.) is so intimately connected with our present mode of production, that it would not be possible to commit it under another.

The relation between sexual crimes and economic conditions is less direct; nevertheless these also give evidence of the decisive influence of these conditions. We have called attention to the four following points.

First, there is a direct connection between the crime of adultery and the present organization of society, which requires that the legal dissolution of a marriage should be impossible or very difficult.

Second, sexual crimes upon adults are committed especially by unmarried men; and since the number of marriages depends in its turn upon the economic situation, the connection is clear; and those who commit these crimes are further almost exclusively illiterate, coarse, raised in an environment almost without sexual morality, and regard the sexual life from the wholly animal side.

Third, the causes of sexual crime upon children are partly the same as those of which we have been speaking, with the addition of prostitution.

Fourth, alcoholism greatly encourages sexual assaults.

As to the relation between crimes of vengeance and the present constitution of society, we have noted that it produces conflicts without number; statistics have shown that those who commit them are almost without exception poor and uncivilized, and that alcoholism is among the most important causes of these crimes.

Infanticide is caused in part by poverty, and in part by the opprobrium incurred by the unmarried mother (an opprobrium resulting from the social utility of marriage).

Political criminality comes solely from the economic system and its consequences.

Finally, economic and social conditions are also important factors in the etiology of degeneracy, which is in its turn a cause of crime.

Upon the basis of what has gone before, we have a right to say that the part played by economic conditions in criminality is preponderant, even decisive.

This conclusion is of the highest importance for the prevention of crime. If it were principally the consequence of innate human qualities (atavism, for example), the pessimistic conclusion that crime is a phenomenon inseparably bound up with the social life would be well founded. But the facts show that it is rather the optimistic conclusion that we must draw, that where crime is the consequence of economic and social conditions, we can combat it by changing those conditions. . . .

"It is society that prepares the crime", says the true adage of Quetelet. For all those who have reached this conclusion, and are not insensible to the sufferings of humanity, this statement is sad, but contains a ground of hope. It is sad, because society punishes severely those who commit the crime which she has herself prepared. It contains a ground of hope, since it promises to humanity the possibility of some day delivering itself from one of its most terrible scourges.

# CULTURE CONFLICT AND CRIME

*Thorsten Sellin*

## Culture Conflicts as Conflicts of Cultural Codes

There are social groups on the surface of the earth which possess complexes of conduct norms which, due to differences in the mode of life and the social values evolved by these groups, appear to set them apart from other groups in many or most respects. We may expect conflicts of norms when the rural dweller moves to the city, but we assume that he has absorbed the basic norms of the culture which comprises both town and country. How much greater is not the conflict likely to be when Orient and Occident meet, or when the Corsican mountaineer is transplanted to the lower East Side of New York. Conflicts of cultures are inevitable when the norms of one cultural or subcultural area migrate to or come in contact with those of another, and it is interesting to note that most of the specific researches on culture conflict and delinquency have been concerned with this aspect of conflict rather than the one mentioned earlier.

Conflicts between the norms of divergent cultural codes may arise

1. when these codes clash on the border of contiguous culture areas;
2. when, as may be the case with legal norms, the law of one cultural group is extended to cover the territory of another; or
3. when members of one cultural group migrate to another.

Speck, for instance, notes that "where the bands popularly known as Montagnais have come more and more into contact with Whites, their reputation has fallen lower among the traders who have known them through commercial relationships within that period. The accusation is made that they have become less honest in connection with their debts, less trustworthy with property, less truthful, and more inclined to alcoholism and sexual freedom as contacts with the frontier towns have become easier for them. Richard White reports in 1933 unusual instances of Naskapi breaking into traders' store houses."

Similar illustrations abound in the works of the cultural anthropologists. We need only to recall the effect on the American Indian of the culture conflicts induced by our policy of acculturation by guile and force. In this instance, it was not merely contact with the white man's culture, his religion, his business methods, and his liquor, which weakened the tribal mores. In addition, the Indian became subject to the white man's law and this brought conflicts as well, as has always been the case when legal norms have been imposed upon a group previously ignorant of them. Maunier, in discussing the diffusion of French law in Algeria, recently stated: "In introducing the *Code Pénal* in our colonies, as we do, we transform into offenses the ancient usages of the inhabitants which their customs permitted or imposed. Thus, among the Khabyles of Algeria, the killing of adulterous wives is ritual murder committed by the father or brother of the wife and not by her husband, as elsewhere. The woman having been sold by her family to her husband's family, the honor of her relatives is soiled by her infidelity. Her father or brother has the right and the duty to kill her in order to cleanse by her blood the honor of her relatives. Murder in revenge is also a duty, from family to family, in case of murder of or even in case of insults to a relative: the vendetta, called the *rekba* in Khabylian, is imposed by the law of honor. But these are crimes in French law! Murder for revenge, being premeditated and planned, is assassination, punishable by death! . . . What happens, then, often when our authorities pursue the criminal, guilty of an offense against public safety as well as against morality: public enemy of the French order, but who has acted in accord with a respected custom? The witnesses of the assassination, who are his relatives, or neighbors, fail to lay charges against the assassin: when they are questioned, they pretend to know nothing; and the pursuit is therefore useless. A French magistrate has been able to speak of 'the conspiracy of silence among the Algerians'; a conspiracy aiming to preserve traditions, always followed and obeyed, against their violation by our power. This is the tragic aspect of the conflict of laws. A recent decree forbids the husband among the Khabyles to profit arbitrarily by the power given him according to this law to repudiate his wife, demanding that her new husband pay an exorbitant price for her—this is the custom of the *lefdi*. Earlier, one who married a repudiated wife paid nothing to the former husband. It appears that the first who tried to avail himself of the new law was killed for violating the old custom. The abolition of the ancient law does not always occur without protest or opposition. That which is a crime was a duty; and the order which we cause to reign is sometimes established to the detriment of 'superstition'; it is the gods and the spirits, it is believed, that would punish any one who fails to revenge his honor."

When Soviet law was extended to Siberia, similar effects were observed. Anossow and Wirschubski both relate that women among the Siberian tribes, who in obedience to the law, laid aside their veils were killed by their relatives for violating one of the most sacred norms of their tribes.

The relations between delinquency and the migration of the members of one cultural group to the area of another will be discussed later in this chapter.

We have noted that culture conflicts are the natural outgrowth of processes of social differentiation, which produce an infinity of social groupings, each with its own definitions of life situations, its own interpretations of social relationships, its own ignorance or misunderstanding of the social values of other groups. The transformation of a culture from a homogeneous and well-integrated type to a heterogeneous and disintegrated type is therefore accompanied by an increase of conflict situations. Conversely, the operation of integrating processes will reduce the number of conflict situations. Such conflicts within a changing culture may be distinguished from those created when different cultural systems come in contact with one another, regardless of the character or stage of development of these systems. In either case, the conduct of members of a group involved in the conflict of codes will in some respects be judged abnormal by the other group.

## The Study of Culture Conflicts

In the study of culture conflicts, some scholars have been concerned with the effect of such conflicts on the conduct of specific persons, an approach which is naturally preferred by psychologists and psychiatrists and by sociologists who have used the life history technique. These scholars view the conflict as internal. Wirth states categorically that a culture "conflict can be said to be a factor in delinquency only if the individual feels it or acts as if it were present." Culture conflict is mental conflict, but the character of this conflict is viewed differently by the various disciplines which use this term. Freudian psychiatrists regard it as a struggle between deeply rooted biological urges which demand expression and the culturally created rules which give rise to inhibitive mechanisms which thwart this expression and drive them below the conscious level of the mind, hence they rise either by ruse in some socially acceptable disguise, as abnormal conduct when the inhibiting mechanism breaks down, or as neuroses when it works too well. The sociologist, on the other hand, thinks of mental conflict as being primarily the clash between antagonistic conduct norms incorporated in personality. "Mental conflict in the person," says Burgess in discussing the case presented by Shaw in *The Jack-Roller*, "may always be explained in terms of the conflict of divergent cultures."

If this view is accepted, sociological research on culture conflict and its relationships to abnormal conduct would have to be strictly limited to a study of the personality of cultural hybrids. Significant studies could be conducted only by the life-history case technique applied to persons in whom the conflict is internalized, appropriate control groups being utilized, of course. Only studies of persons falling within the "reduced group resistance" category would produce etiological generalizations of any relevancy to the problem of causation.

The absence of mental conflict, in the sociological sense, may, however, be well studied in terms of culture conflict. An example may make this clear. A few years ago a Sicilian father in New Jersey killed the sixteen-year-old seducer of his daughter, expressing surprise at his arrest since he had merely defended his family honor in a traditional way. In this case a mental conflict in the sociological sense did not exist. The conflict was external and occurred between cultural codes or norms. We may assume that where such conflicts occur violations of norms will arise merely because persons who have absorbed the norms of one cultural group or area migrate to another and that such conflict will continue so long as the acculturation process has not been completed. Only then may the violations be regarded in terms of mental conflict.

If culture conflict may be regarded as sometimes personalized, or mental, and sometimes as occurring entirely in an impersonal way solely as a conflict of group codes, it is obvious that research should not be confined to the investigation of mental conflicts and that contrary to Wirth's categorical statement that it is impossible to demonstrate the existence of a culture conflict "objectively . . . by a comparison between two cultural codes" this procedure has not only a definite function, but may be carried out by researches employing techniques which are familiar to the sociologist.

The emphasis on the life history technique has grown out of the assumption that "the experiences of one person at the same time reveals the life activities of his group" and that "habit in the individual is an expression of custom in society." This is undoubtedly one valid approach. Through it we may hope to discover generalizations of a scientific nature by studying persons who (1) have drawn their norms of conduct from a variety of groups with conflicting norms, or (2) who possess norms drawn from a group whose code is in conflict with that of the group which judges the conduct. In the former case alone can we speak of mental or internal culture conflict; in the latter, the conflict is external.

If the conduct norms of a group are, with reference to a given life situation, inconsistent, or if two groups possess inconsistent norms, we may assume that the members of these various groups will individually reflect such group attitudes. Paraphrasing Burgess, the experiences of a group will reveal the life activities of its members. While these norms can, no doubt, be best established by a study of a sufficient number of representative group members, they may for some groups at least be fixed with sufficient certainty to serve research purposes by a study of the social institutions, the administration of justice, the novel, the drama, the press, and other expressions of group attitudes. The identification of the groups in question having been made, it might be possible to determine to what extent such conflicts are reflected in the conduct of their members. Comparative studies based on the violation rates of the members of such groups, the trends of such rates, etc., would dominate this approach to the problem.

In conclusion, then, culture conflict may be studied either as mental conflict or as a conflict of cultural codes. The criminologist will naturally tend to concentrate on such conflicts between legal and nonlegal conduct norms. The concept of conflict fails to give him more than a general framework of reference for research. In practice, it has, however, become nearly synonymous with conflicts between the norms of cultural systems or areas. Most researches which have employed it have been done on immigrant or race groups in the United States, perhaps due to the ease with which such groups may be identified, the existence of more statistical data recognizing such groupings, and the conspicuous differences between some immigrant norms and our norms.

## CLASS, STATE, AND CRIME: ON THE THEORY AND PRACTICE OF CRIMINAL JUSTICE

*Richard Quinney*

A Marxist analysis of crime begins with the recognition that crime is basically a material problem. In fact, the crucial phenomenon to be considered is not crime per se, but the historical development and operation of the capitalist economy. Any study of crime involves an investigation of such natural products and contradictions of capitalism as poverty, inequality, unemployment, and the economic crisis of the capitalist state. Ultimately, however, to understand crime we must understand the development of the political economy of capitalist society.

The necessary condition for any society, according to the materialist method and conception of reality, is that its members produce their material means of subsistence. Social production is therefore the primary process of all social life. Moreover, in the social production of our existence we enter into relations that are appropriate to the existing forces of production. It is this "economic" structure that provides the foundation for all social and political institutions, for everyday life, and for social consciousness. Our analysis thus begins with the *material conditions* of social life.

The *dialectical method* allows us to comprehend the world as a complex of processes, in which all things go through a continuous process of coming into being and passing away. All things are studied in the context of their historical development. Dialectical materialism allows us to learn about things as they are in their actual interconnection, contradiction, and movement. In dialectical analysis we critically understand our past, informing our analysis with the possibilities for our future.

A Marxist analysis shares in the larger *socialist struggle*. There is the commitment to eliminating exploitation and oppression. Being on the side of the oppressed, only those ideas are advanced that will aid in transforming the capitalist system. The objective of the Marxist analysis is change—revolutionary change. The purpose of our intellectual labors is to assist in providing knowledge and consciousness for building a socialist society. Theories and strategies are developed to increase conscious class struggle; ideas for an alternative to capitalist society are formulated; and strategies for achieving the socialist alternative are proposed. In the course of intellectual-political work we engage in the activities and actions that will advance the socialist struggle.

With these notions of a Marxist analysis—encompassing a dialectical-historical analysis of the material conditions of capitalist society in relation to socialist revolution—we begin to formulate the significant substantive questions about crime. In recent years, as socialists have turned their attention to the study of crime, the outline for these questions has become evident. At this stage in our intellectual development the important questions revolve around *the meaning of crime in capitalist society*. Furthermore, there is the realization that the meaning of crime changes in the course of the development of capitalism.

The basic problem in any study of the meaning of crime is that of integrating the two sides of the crime phenomenon: placing into a single framework (1) the defining of behavior as criminal (i.e., *crime control*) and (2) the behavior of those who are defined as criminal (i.e., *criminality*). Thus far, the analysis of crime has focused on one side or the other, failing to integrate the two interrelated processes into one scheme. In pursuing a Marxist analysis, however, the problem of the dual nature of the concept of crime is solved by *giving primacy to the underlying political economy*.

The basic question in the Marxist analysis of crime is thus formulated: What is the meaning of crime in the development of capitalism? In approaching this question, we must give attention to several interrelated processes: (1) the development of capitalist political economy, including the nature of the forces and relations of production, the formulation of the capitalist state, and the class struggle between those who do and those who do not own and control the means of production; (2) the systems of domination and repression that are established in the development of capitalism, operating for the benefit of the capitalist class and secured by the capitalist state; (3) the forms of accommodation and resistance to the conditions of capitalism, by all people oppressed by capitalism, especially the working class; and (4) the relation of the dialectics of domination and accommodation to patterns of crime in capitalist society, producing the crimes of domination and the crimes of accommodation. As indicated in Figure 1, all these processes are dialectically related to the developing political economy. Crime is to be understood in terms of the development of capitalism.

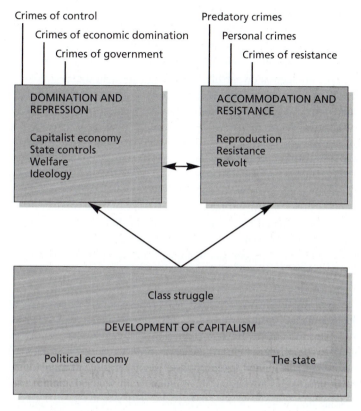

**FIGURE 1**
Crime and the development of capitalism.

## Development of Capitalist Economy

Crime, as noted, is a manifestation of the material conditions of society. The failure of conventional criminology is to ignore, by design, the material conditions of capitalism. Since the phenomena of crime are products of the substructure—are themselves part of the superstructure—any explanation of crime in terms of other elements of the superstructure is no explanation at all. Our need is to develop a general materialist framework for understanding crime, beginning with the underlying historical processes of social existence.

Production, as the necessary requirement of existence, produces its own forces and relations of social and economic life. The material factors (such as resources and technology) and personal factors (most importantly the workers) present at any given time form the productive *forces* of society. In the process of production, people form definite relations with one another. These *relations* of production, in reference to the forces of production, constitute the particular *mode* of production of any society at any given time. The economic mode of production furnishes society with its substructure, on which the social and political institutions (including crime control) and supporting ideologies are built.

Once the outlines of *political economy* (the productive forces, the relations of production, and the superstructure) have been indicated, the *class structure* and its dynamics can be recognized. A class society arises when the system of production is owned by one segment of the society to the exclusion of another. All production requires ownership of some kind; but in some systems of production ownership is private rather than social or collective. In these economies social relations are dependent on relations of domination and subjection. Marxist economists thus observe: "Relations of domination and subjection are based on private ownership of the means of production and express the exploitation of man by man under the slave-owning, feudal and capitalist systems. Relations of friendly co-operation and mutual assistance between working people free of exploitation are typical of socialist society. They are based on the public ownership of the means of production, which cut out exploitation."

All social life in capitalist society, including everything associated with crime, therefore, must be understood in terms of the economic conditions of production and the struggle between classes produced by these conditions. In other words, in capitalist society the life and behavior of any group in the society, or any individual group member, can be understood only in terms of the conflict that characterizes class relations, which in turn is produced by the capitalist system of production. The life and behavior of one class are seen in relation to that of the other. . . .

Hence, class in capitalist society is analyzed in reference to the relationship to the process of production and according to the relationship to other classes in the society.

Moreover, the problematics of *labor* (as the foremost human activity) characterize the nature and specific relationship of the classes. For the capitalist system to operate and survive, the capitalist class must exploit the labor (appropriate the *surplus labor*) of the working class. As Maurice Dobb notes,

> the relationship from which in one case a common interest in preserving and extending a particular economic system and in the other case an antagonism of interest on this issue can alone derive must be a relationship with a particular mode of extracting and distributing the fruits of surplus labour, over and above the labour which goes to supply the consumption of the actual producer. Since this surplus labor constitutes its life-blood, any ruling class will of necessity treat its particular relationship to the labour-process as crucial to its own survival; and any rising class that aspires to live without labour is bound to regard its own future career, prosperity and influence as dependent on the acquisition of some claim upon the surplus labour of others.

The capitalist class survives by appropriating the surplus labor of the working class, and the working class as an exploited class exists as long as surplus labor is required in the productive process: each class depends on the other for its character and existence.

The amount of labor appropriated, the techniques of labor exploitation, the conditions of working-class life, and the level of working-class consciousness have all been an integral part of the historical development of capitalism. In like manner, the degree of antagonism and conflict between classes has varied at different stages in the development. Nevertheless, it is the basic contradiction between classes, generalized as class conflict, that typifies the development of capitalism. Class conflict permeates the whole of capitalist development, represented in the contradiction between those who own property and those who do not, and by those who oppress and those who are oppressed. All past history, that involving the development of capitalism, is the history of class struggle.

Capitalism as a system of production based on the exploitation by the ruling capitalist class that owns and controls the means of production is thus a dynamic system that goes through its own stages of development. In fact, capitalism is constantly transforming its own forces and relations of production. As a result, the whole of capitalist society is constantly being altered—within the basic framework of capitalist political economy.

The Marxian view stresses the qualitative changes in social organization and social relations as well as (or in relation to) the quantitative changes in the economic system. Capitalism transforms itself, affecting the social existence of all who live under it. This is the basic dynamic of capitalist development, an interdependence between production, the relations of production, and the social superstructure of institutions and ideas. "For it is a requirement of all social production that the relations which people enter into in carrying on production must be suitable to the type of production they are carrying on. Hence, it is a general law of economic development that the relations of production must necessarily be adapted to the character of the forces of production."

As the preceding discussion indicates, analysis of the meaning of crime in the development of capitalism necessarily involves an investigation of the relation between the concrete stage of capitalist development and of the social relations that correspond to that stage of development. This is not to argue that the superstructure of social relations and culture is an automatic (directly determined) product of the economic substructure. After all, people may enter into relations of production in various ways in order to employ the given forces of production; and it is on the basis of these relations that they create further institutions and ideas. Since human social existence is in part a product of conscious activity and struggle, conscious life must be part of any analysis. Maurice Cornforth, in a discussion of historical materialism, puts it well:

> But ideas and institutions are not the automatic products of a given economic and class structure, but products of people's conscious activities and struggles. To explain the superstructure, these activities and struggles must be studied concretely, in their actual complex development. Therefore it is certainly not Marxism, just as it is certainly not science, to attempt to conclude from the specification of certain economic conditions what the form of the superstructure arising on that basis is going to be, or to deduce every detailed characteristic of the superstructure from some corresponding feature of the basis. On the contrary, we need to study how the superstructure actually develops in each society and in each epoch, by investigating the facts about that society and that epoch.

Such is the basic task in our study of the meaning of crime in the development of capitalism.

In addition, the more developed the productive forces under capitalism, the greater the discrepancy between the productive forces and the capitalist relations of production. Capitalist development, with economic expansion being fundamental to capitalist economic development, exacerbates rather than mitigates the contradictions of capitalism. Workers are further exploited, conditions of existence worsen, while the contradictions of capitalism increase. Capitalist development, in other words, and from another vantage point, creates the conditions for the transformation and abolition of capitalism, brought about in actuality by class struggle.

The history of capitalism can thus be traced according to the nature of capitalist development. The main contradictions of capitalism are concretely formed and manifested in each stage of development. The forms and intensity of exploitation are documented and understood in respect to the particular character of capitalism at each development stage. How crime—control of crime and criminality—plays its part in each stage of capitalist development is our concern in any investigation of the meaning of crime.

The periods of capitalist development, for our purposes, differ according to the ways in which surplus labor is appropriated. Capitalism, as distinct from other modes of production, has gone through periods that utilize various methods of production and create social relations in association with these productive forms. Each new development in capitalism, conditioned by the preceding historical processes, brings about its own particular forms of capitalist economy and social reality—and related problems of human existence.

Any investigation of the meaning (and changing meanings) of crime in America, therefore, requires a delineation of the periods of economic development in the United States. A few attempts at such delineation already exist, but for other than the study of crime. For example, Douglas Dowd in his book *The Twisted Dream* notes briefly three different periods of American development, with particular reference to the role of the state in American economic life: (1) American mercantilism, up to Jackson's Presidency; (2) laissez-faire capitalism, coming to a climax in the decades after the Civil War; and (3) maturing industrial capitalism, up to the present. Similarly, in another treatment, William A. Williams in his book *The Contours of American History* arranges American history according to the following periods: (1) the age of mercantilism, 1740–1828; (2) the age of laissez nous faire, 1819–96; and (3) the age of corporate capitalism, 1882 to the present. To this scheme, others add that American capitalism is now in the stage of either "monopoly capital" or "finance capital."

It is debatable, nevertheless, in our study of crime in the United States, whether America was capitalist from the beginning, with capitalism merely imported from the Old to the New World. Or whether, as James O'Connor has recently argued, capitalist development has occurred in only fairly recent times. For the first hundred years of nationhood the United States resisted large-scale capitalist production. Independent commodity production predominated; farmers, artisans, small manufacturers and other petty producers were the mainstay of the economy. Only as northern capitalists acquired land from the farmers (thus appropriating their labor power) and as immigrant labor power was imported from Europe did capitalism finally emerge in the United States. American capitalism emerged when capitalists won the battle as to who was to control labor power. Surplus labor was now in the hands of a capitalist ruling class. Workers could be exploited.

For certain, we are today in a stage of late, advanced capitalism in the United States. The current meaning of crime in America can be understood only in relation to the character of capitalism in the present era. Similarly, the meanings of crime at various times in the past have to be understood according to the particular stage of development. Only in the investigation of crime in the development of capitalism do we truly understand the meaning of crime. Concrete research will provide us with knowledge about the role of crime in the development of capitalism.

## Domination and Repression

The capitalist system must be continuously reproduced. This is accomplished in a variety of ways, ranging from the establishment of ideological hegemony to the further exploitation of labor, from the creation of public policy to the coercive repression of the population. Most explicitly, the *state* secures the capitalist order. Through various schemes and mechanisms, then, the capitalist class is able to dominate. And in the course of this domination, crimes are carried out. These crimes, committed by the capitalist class, the state, and the agents of the capitalist class and state, are the crimes of domination.

Historically the capitalist state is a product of a political economy that depends on a division of classes. With the development of an economy based on the exploitation of one class by another, there was the need for a political form that would perpetuate that kind of order. With the development of capitalism, with class divisions and class struggle, the state became necessary. A new stage of development, Frederick Engels observes, called for the creation of the state:

> Only one thing was wanting: an institution which not only secured the newly acquired riches of individuals against the communistic traditions of the gentile order, which not only sanctified the private property formerly so little valued, and declared this sanctification to be the highest purpose of all human society; but an institution which set the seal of general social recognition on each new method of acquiring property and thus amassing wealth at continually increased speed; an institution which perpetuated, not only this growing cleavage of society into classes, but also the right of the possessing class to exploit the non-possessing, and the rule of the former over the latter.
>
> And this institution came. The state was invented.

The state thus arose to protect and promote the interests of the dominant class, the class that owns and controls the means of production. The state exists as a device for controlling the exploited class, the class that labors, for the benefit of the ruling class. Modern civilization, as epitomized in capitalist societies, is founded on the exploitation of one class by another. Moreover, the capitalist state is oppressive not only because it supports the interests of the dominant class but also because it is responsible for the design of the whole system within which the capitalist ruling class dominates and the working class is dominated. The capitalist system of production and exploitation is secured and reproduced by the capitalist state.

The coercive force of the state, embodied in law and legal repression, is the traditional means of maintaining the social and economic order. Contrary to conventional wisdom, law instead of representing community custom is an instrument of the state that serves the interests of the developing capitalist ruling class. Law emerged with the rise of capitalism, as Stanley Diamond writes: "Law arises in the breach of a prior customary order and increases in force with the conflicts that divide political societies internally and among themselves. Law *and* order is the historical illusion; law versus order is the historical reality." Law and legal repression are, and continue to serve as, the means of enforcing the interests of the dominant class in the capitalist state.

Through the legal system, then, the state forcefully protects its interests and those of the capitalist ruling class. Crime control becomes the coercive means of checking threats to the existing social and economic order, threats that result from a system of oppression and exploitation. As a means of controlling the behavior of the exploited population, crime control is accomplished by a variety of methods, strategies, and institutions. The state, especially through its legislative bodies, establishes official policies of crime control. The administrative branch of the state establishes and enforces crime-control policies, usually setting the design for the whole nation. Specific agencies of law enforcement, such as the Federal Bureau of Investigation and the recent Law Enforcement Assistance Administration, determine the nature of crime control. And the state is able through its Department of Justice officially to repress the "dangerous" and "subversive" elements of the population.

Altogether, these state institutions attempt to rationalize the legal system by employing the advanced methods of science and technology. And whenever any changes are to be attempted to reduce the incidence of crime, rehabilitation of the individual or reform within the existing institutions is suggested. Drastically to alter the society and the crime-control establishment would be to alter beyond recognition the capitalist system.

Yet the coercive force of the state is but one means of maintaining the social and economic order. A more subtle reproductive mechanism of capitalist society is the perpetuation of the capitalist conception of reality, a nonviolent but equally repressive means of domination. As Alan Wolfe has shown, in the manipulation of consciousness the existing order is legitimated and secured:

> The most important reproductive mechanism which does not involve the use of state violence is consciousness-manipulation. The liberal state has an enormous amount of violence at its disposal, but it is often reluctant to use it. Violence may breed counter-violence, leading to instability. It may be far better to manipulate consciousness to such an extent that most people would never think of engaging in the kinds of action which could be repressed. The most perfectly repressive (though not violently so) capitalist system, in other words, would not be a police state, but the complete opposite, one in which there were no police because there was nothing to police, everyone having accepted the legitimacy of that society and all its daily consequences.

Those who rule in capitalist society—with the assistance of the state—not only accumulate capital at the expense of those who work but impose their ideology as well. Oppression and exploitation are legitimized by the expropriation of consciousness; since labor is expropriated, consciousness must also be expropriated. In fact, *legitimacy* of the capitalist order is maintained by controlling the consciousness of the population. A capitalist hegemony is established.

Thus, through its various reproductive mechanisms capitalism is able to maximize the possibility of control over the citizens of the state. Ranging from control of production and distribution to manipulation of the mind, capitalism operates according to its own form of dictatorship. André Gorz writes:

> The dictatorship of capital is exercised not only on the production and distribution of wealth, but with equal force on the manner of producing, on the model of consumption, and on the manner of consuming, the manner of working, thinking, living. As much as over the workers, the factories, and the state, this dictatorship rules over the society's vision of the future, its ideology, its priorities and goals, over the way in which people experience and learn about themselves, their potentials, their relations with other people and with the rest of the world. This dictatorship is economic, political, cultural and pyschological at the same time: it is total.

Moreover, a society that depends on surplus labor for its existence must not only control that situation but also must cope with the problems that economic system naturally creates. The capitalist state must therefore provide "social services" in the form of education, health, welfare, and rehabilitation programs of various kinds, to deal with the problems that could otherwise be dealt with only by changing the capitalist system. These state services function as a repressive means of securing the capitalist order.

Capitalism systematically generates a *surplus population*, an unemployed sector of the working class either dependent on fluctuations in the economy or made obsolete by new technology. With the growth of the surplus population, pressures build up for the growth of the welfare system. The function of expanding welfare, with its host of services, is to control the surplus population politically. Moreover, O'Connor observes, "Unable to gain employ-ment in the monopoly industries by offering their laborpower at lower than going wage rates (and victimized by sexism and racism), and unemployed, underemployed, or employed at low wages in competitive industries, the surplus population increasingly becomes depen-dent on the state." An unsteady alliance is thus formed between the casualties it naturally produces. Only a new economic order could replace the need for a welfare state.

Repression through welfare is in part the history of capitalism. The kinds of services have varied with the development of economic conditions. In the same way, relief policies have varied according to specific tensions produced by unemployment and subsequent threats of disorder. As Frances Fox Piven and Richard A. Cloward write in their study of the modern welfare system:

> Relief arrangements are ancillary to economic arrangements. Their chief function is to regulate labor, and they do that in two general ways. First, when mass unemployment leads to outbreaks of turmoil, relief programs are ordinarily initiated or expanded to absorb and control enough of the unemployed to restore order; then, as turbulence subsides, the relief system contracts, expel-ling those who are needed to populate the labor market. Relief also performs a labor-regulating function in this shrunken state, however. Some of the aged, the disabled, the insane, and others who are of no use as workers are left on the relief rolls, and their treatment is so degrading and punitive as to instill in the laboring masses a fear of the fate that awaits them should they relax into beggary and pauperism. To demean and punish those who do not work is to exalt by con-trast even the meanest labor at the meanest wages. These regulative functions of relief, and their periodic expansion and contraction, are made necessary by several strains toward instability inherent in capitalist economies.

Control through welfare can never be a permanent solution for a system based on appropri-ation of labor. As with all the forms of control and manipulation in capitalist society, wel-fare cannot completely counter the basic contradictions of a capitalist political economy.

Although the capitalist state creates and manages the institutions of control (employing physical force *and* manipulation of consciousness), the basic contradictions of the capital-ist order are such that this control is not absolute and, in the long run, is subject to defeat. Because of the contradictions of capitalism, the capitalist state is more weak than strong. Eventually the capitalist state loses its legitimacy, no longer being able to perpetuate the ideology that capital accumulation for capitalists (at the expense of workers) is good for the nation or for human interests. The ability of the capitalist economic order to exist according to its own interests is eventually weakened. The problem becomes especially acute in periods of economic crisis, periods that are unavoidable under capitalism.

In the course of reproducing the capitalist system crimes are committed. It is a contra-diction of capitalism that some of its laws must be violated in order to secure the existing system. The contradictions of capitalism produce their own sources of crime. Not only are these contradictions heightened during times of crisis, making for increased crimes of dom-ination, but the nature of these crimes changes with the further development of capitalism.

The crimes of domination most characteristic of capitalist domination are those that occur in the course of state control. These are the *crimes of control*. They include the felonies and misdemeanors that law-enforcement agents, especially the police, carry out in the name of the law, usually against persons accused of other violations. Violence and brutality have become a recognized part of police work. In addition to these crimes of con-trol, there are the crimes of more subtle nature in which agents of the law violate the civil liberties of citizens, as in the various forms of surveillance, the use of provocateurs, and the illegal denial of due process.

Then there are the *crimes of government*, committed by the elected and appointed officials of the capitalist state. The Watergate crimes, carried out to perpetuate a particular governmental administration, are the most publicized instances of these crimes. There are also those offenses committed by the government against persons and groups who would seemingly threaten national security. Included here are the crimes of warfare and the political assassination of foreign and domestic leaders.

Crimes of domination also consist of those crimes that occur in the capitalist class for the purpose of securing the existing economic order. These *crimes of economic domination* include the crimes committed by corporations, ranging from price fixing to pollution of the environment in order to protect and further capital accumulation. Also included are the economic crimes of individual businessmen and professionals. In addition, the crimes of the capitalist class and the capitalist state are joined in organized crime. The more conventional criminal operations of organized crime are linked to the state in the present stage of capitalist development. The operations of organized crime and the criminal operations of the state are united in the attempt to assure the survival of the capitalist system.

Finally, many *social injuries* are committed by the capitalist class and the capitalist state that are not usually defined as criminal in the legal codes of the state. These systematic actions, involving the denial of basic human rights (resulting in sexism, racism, and economic exploitation) are an integral part of capitalism and are important to its survival.

Underlying all the capitalist crimes is the appropriation of the surplus value created by labor. The working class has the right to possess the whole of this value. The worker creates a value several times greater than the labor power purchased by the capitalist. The excess value created by the worker over and above the value of labor power is the surplus value which is appropriated by the capitalist. Surplus value, as exploitation, is essential to capitalism, being the source of accumulation of capital and expansion of production.

Domination and repression are a basic part of class struggle in the development of capitalism. The capitalist class and state protect and promote the capitalist order by controlling those who do not own the means of production. The labor supply and the conditions for labor must be secured. Crime control and the crimes of domination are thus necessary features and the natural products of capitalist political economy.

## The Political Economy of Criminal Justice

The capitalist state promotes the further development of the capitalist mode of production. The state, under late capitalism, must establish the general framework for capital accumulation and foster the conditions for maintaining the capitalist system. In assuring capital accumulation, exploitative social relations are reproduced and even heightened. The social problems generated by the capitalist system are increased with the further development of capitalism.

The class struggle under late capitalism must be regulated by the state. The repressive apparatus of the state becomes ever more important in the development of capitalism. Policies of control—especially crime control—are instituted in the attempt to regulate problems and conflicts that otherwise can be solved only by social and economic changes that go beyond capitalist reforms. Criminal justice, as the euphemism for controlling class struggle and administering legal repression, becomes a major type of social policy in the advanced stages of capitalism.

Emerging within the political economy of late capitalism is a political economy of criminal justice. The political economy of criminal justice is one of the fundamental characteristics of advanced capitalism. To understand its various features is to understand a crucial part of the capitalist system. Criminal justice will likely increase as a capitalist response to the contradictions of late capitalism.

### State expenditure on criminal justice

The capitalist state must increasingly expend its resources on programs that secure the capitalist order. These *social expenses* of the state, as defined by James O'Connor, consist of "projects and services which are required to maintain social harmony—to fulfill the state's 'legitimization' function". While *social capital* is expended in the promotion of profitable private accumulation, the social expenses of the state are not directly productive, producing no surplus value. They are designed to keep "social peace" among unemployed workers, or among the surplus population in general. Welfare and law enforcement are the primary forms of the state's social expenses, regulating class struggle, repressing action against the existing order, and giving legitimacy to the capitalist system. The creation and administration of the criminal justice system as a whole has become a principal social expense of the capitalist state.

The state in promoting capital accumulation in the monopoly sector stimulates overproduction and thereby creates a surplus population and the resulting need for state expenses to cope with the surplus population. Such social services as education, family support, health services, and housing benefits give legitimacy to the capitalist system and satisfy some of the needs of the working class. These services compensate in part for the oppression and suffering caused by capitalism.

The criminal justice system, on the other hand, serves more explicitly to control that which cannot be remedied by available employment within the economy or by social services for the surplus population. The police, the courts, and the penal agencies—the entire criminal justice system—expands to cope as a last resort with the problems of surplus population. As the contradictions of capitalism increase, the criminal justice system becomes a preventive institution as well as a control and corrective agency. State expenditures on criminal justice occupy a larger share of the state's budgetary expenses. Criminal justice as a social expense of the state necessarily expands with the further development of capitalism. . . .

As the crisis of the state and the capitalist economy accelerates, forms of control will be devised that attempt to be more pervasive and more certain and, at the same time, less of an expense for the state. The state and monopoly capital will try to create crime control programs that do not require a major outlay of capital, capital that does not promote further capital accumulation. For example, halfway-house programs may in some cases be substituted for large and costly institutions. Surveillance may replace some other forms of confinement and control. Yet the contradiction is only furthered: criminal justice is inevitably a losing battle under late capitalism.

In other words, criminal justice spending is only a partial, temporary, and self-defeating resolution to capitalist economic contradictions. The situation is similar to military spending. While expenditures on warfare and the military may have some immediate functions for the state and the economy, an economy based on such expenditure is subject to more contradictions than ultimate resolutions. A substantial criminal justice budget, similar to a military budget, cannot successfully solve the economic and political problems of the capitalist system. And in the long run, criminal justice as a social expenditure can only further the contradictions of capitalism. . . .

### Control of surplus population

Social expenditures on criminal justice necessarily increase with the development of advanced capitalism. In the late stages of capitalism the mode of production and the forms of capital accumulation accelerate the growth of the relative surplus population. The state must then provide social expense programs, including criminal justice, both to legitimate advanced capitalism and to control the surplus population. Rather than being capable of absorbing the surplus population into the political economy, advanced capitalism can only supervise and control a population that is now superfluous to the capitalist system. The problem is especially acute when the surplus population threatens to disturb the system, either by overburdening the system or by political action. Criminal justice is the modern means of controlling this surplus population produced by late capitalist development.

The state attempts to offset the social expense of criminal justice by supporting the growth of the criminal justice—industrial complex. The fiscal crisis of the capitalist state is temporarily alleviated by forming an alliance between monopoly capital and state-financed social programs. The social programs of the state are thereby transformed into social capital, providing subsidized investment opportunities for monopoly capital and ameliorating some of the material impoverishment of the surplus population. The new complex thus ties the surplus population to the state and to the political economy of advanced capitalism. While a growing segment of the population is absorbed into the system as *indirectly productive workers*—the army of government and office workers, paraprofessionals, and those who work in one way or another in the social expense programs—there is also a large surplus population that is controlled by these programs. These unemployed, underemployed, reserve army workers now find themselves dependent on the state. They are linked to the state (and to monopoly capital) for much of their economic welfare, and they are linked in being the object of the social control programs of the state. The criminal justice system is the most explicit of these programs in controlling the surplus population. Criminal justice and the surplus population are thus symbiotically interdependent.

As the surplus population grows with the development of capitalism, the criminal justice system or some equivalent must also grow. An expanding criminal justice system is the only way late capitalism can "integrate" the surplus population into the overall economic and political system. The notion that the social problems generated by capitalism can be solved becomes obsolete. Instead, problems such as crime are dealt with in terms of a *control* model. When the underlying conditions of capitalism cannot be changed—without changing the capitalist system itself—controlling the population oppressed by the existing conditions is the only "solution." . . .

On all levels of the criminal justice system new techniques of control are being developed and instituted. Not only has there been increased implementation of a military-hardware approach to criminal justice, but developing more recently alongside are more subtle approaches. A dual system is developing whereby some actions of the surplus population that are defined as criminal are dealt with harshly by strong-arm techniques and by punitive measures. Other actions by other portions of the surplus population are handled by such software techniques as diversion from the courts and community-based corrections. In general, however, whatever the current techniques, the new model is one of *pacification*. The surplus population is not only to be controlled, but it is to accept this control. The capitalist state, in alliance with monopoly capital, must continually innovate in expanding the criminal justice system.

Whatever the techniques of control, the fact remains that it is the surplus population that is in need of control, that is being controlled by the criminal justice system. Control is especially acute in those periods when the economic crisis is most obvious—during periods of depression and recession. It is during these times that the surplus population is affected most; and it is during these times that the surplus population grows through unemployment.

As usual during these periods, the hardest-hit groups are women, blacks, the young, and unskilled workers. . . .

A way of controlling this unemployed surplus population is simply and directly by confinement in prisons. The rhetoric of criminal justice—and that of conventional criminology—is that prisons are for incarcerating criminals. In spite of this mystification, the fact is that prisons are used to control that part of the surplus population that is subject to the discretion of criminal law and the criminal justice system. What is not usually presented are the figures and the conclusion that prisons are differentially utilized according to the extent of economic crisis. The finding is clear: the prison population increases as the rate of unemployment increases. Using admissions to federal prisons, the number of prison admissions varies directly with the rate of unemployment. Unemployment simultaneously makes actions of survival and frustration necessary on the part of the unemployed surplus population and makes some form of controlling that population necessary by the state. Containment of the unemployed in prison is a certain way of controlling a threatening surplus population. Until other solutions of control are found, the capitalist state will need the certainty of the prison for controlling portions of the surplus population.

# CONTEMPORARY RETROSPECTIVE ON CONFLICT AND RADICAL THEORIES

## CONFLICT CRIMINOLOGY: DEVELOPMENTS, DIRECTIONS, AND DESTINATIONS PAST AND PRESENT

*Bruce A. Arrigo, University of North Carolina–Charlotte; and
Christopher R. Williams, University of West Georgia*

Though its intellectual roots lie with Hegel, Marx, Weber, and other classical theorists (Bernard, 1983), conflict theory did not fully emerge as a potent theoretical force within the criminological community until the late 1960s and early 1970s (e.g., Quinney, 1970)—a time at which broader social turmoil highlighted the centrality of conflict within American culture. The civil rights and women's movements, the Vietnam War, Watergate, and an emerging counterculture inspired academics and laypersons alike to critically assess existing power structures and the ways in which powerful interests shaped nearly every aspect of social life. Scholars of crime, law, and justice began to ask questions about the role of power in the construction of crime and in an effort to control persons whose behavior corresponded to those constructions. Thereafter, "power," "inequality," "social class," and related concepts would become points of theoretical convergence within a new brand of criminology (Arrigo, 1999, p. 6).

Thorstein Sellin (1938) and George Vold (1958) had laid the early foundations of conflict criminology with their articulations of culture conflict and group conflict, respectively. Central to both was a critique of the consensus tradition within crime and justice studies—a tradition within which norms, values, and interests are regarded as shared, agreed-upon, and a potential source of order rather than disorder. The United States, each argued, is better characterized as grounds for continual struggle, on which diverse peoples with manifold values and interests compete to further the welfare of their own culture or social standing. From its beginnings, the conflict tradition explicitly identified law as a principle force in such struggles. Law is an outcome of conflict, its content a reflection of the values and interests of those groups who have emerged victorious from economic, political, and social contestation. As well, once particular groups or segments attain some advantage, their access to law provides a means by or through which they can maintain or further their progress. Rather than being value-neutral, representing the common good, and augmenting equally the needs and interests of all (as is often claimed to be their function), laws are codifications of the interests and legitimations of the behavior of those groups with sufficient power and resources to influence them (Williams & Arrigo, 2007).

This theme became more prominent beginning in the late 1960s, as Austin Turk (1969), Richard Quinney (1970), and others further detailed the ways in which social, economic, and political power impacted lawmaking and, by extension, definitions of lawbreaking. In his classic work *The Social Reality of Crime,* Richard Quinney (1970) echoed the contentions of earlier conflict theorists in noting that law represents the interests of "specific persons and groups . . . who have the power to translate their interests into public policy" (p. 35). One consequence of this power differential is that those with authority to influence the construction of law, the definition of crime, and the enforcement of justice are less likely to have their own actions ("behavioral patterns") labeled criminal and subjected to legal consequence (Chambliss & Seidman, 1971; Quinney, 1970, 1980). By logical extension, groups lacking sufficient power and resources to shape lawmaking find their voices silenced and, in some cases, their behavior criminalized. Even where law violations occur by members of more powerful groups, their greater resources allow them to better conceal their actions and defend themselves from accusations (e.g., Bernard, 1981). Overall, then, the higher one's economic and political position, the less likely it is that one's routine behavior will be defined as criminal, and the less likely it will be for that individual to be subjected to enforcement efforts when his or her behavior is classified as criminal. Unsurprisingly, then, persons belonging to groups with less power and influence will be disproportionately represented in official crime rates (e.g., Williams & Arrigo, 2007).

Though the logic that linked power, lawmaking, and crime attracted many criminologists to the conflict camp, none of the aforementioned theorists had specifically identified the root source of power. Consequently, conflict theory was primed for a new wave of theorists who would more openly and unambiguously describe the dynamics of power.

The works of Sellin, Vold, Turk, and the early work of Quinney are often categorized as belonging to the "pluralist" tradition within conflict theory, as each understood society to be "comprised of numerous interest groups in a constant competitive struggle for the power to define events or control issues they consider[ed] important" (Einstadter & Henry, 1995, p. 238). Beginning in the 1970s, however, a number of criminologists began to explicitly incorporate elements of Marxist social theory (which was not widely available or known in the United States before the 1960s) into their critical works on law, crime, and justice (e.g., Balbus, 1977a, 1977b; Beirne & Sharlet, 1980; Milovanovic, 1981). The Marxist, or *radical*, conflict tradition surfaced with a more direct focus on the relationship between crime, conflict, and *capitalism* (Taylor et al., 1973; Taylor, Walton, & Young, 1975; see also Bohm, 1982, for an overview). Rather than numerous interest groups competing for representation in law and policy, there were only two groups of any real significance: the ruling class and the working class.

In the context of criminological theory, the turn toward a Marxist-inspired conflict theory was a crucial juncture. As Bernard (1981) asserted, most radical criminologists of the 1980s would have considered themselves conflict criminologists only a decade earlier (p. 362). Thus, many working within the conflict tradition adopted and began to work within the tenets of radical criminology—to such an extent that very few criminologists today would regard themselves as traditional (i.e., pluralist) conflict criminologists. From the 1980s onward, the radical variant of conflict theory would be its most forceful and influential manifestation (Arrigo, 1999). In light of this, it may be valuable to further review the basic principles of radical criminology, distinguishing it from earlier pluralist versions of conflict theory.

Radical criminologists argue that power and conflict are direct outcomes of the political economy of capitalism, and that the former is expressly rooted in the ownership of the *means of production* (e.g., Arrigo & Bernard, 1997; Bernard, 1981; Lynch & Groves, 1989). In other words, those who own fields, mines, factories and, in postindustrial societies, corporations possess a disproportionate degree of wealth, resources, and influence on government processes such as the making of law and policy (e.g., Michalowski, 1985). Class-based or economic inequalities are the most potent source of power, and the most fundamental source of conflict, crime, and other social problems. On the one hand, class-based inequalities create social conditions conducive to criminal motivation and subsequent illicit behavior; and, on the other hand, the privileged standing the ruling class enjoys—especially with making and administering law—means that the "normal" behavior of those occupying a lower socioeconomic status is more likely to be identified as criminal. Indeed, as Sheldon (2001) explained, social class is a fundamental determinant of *what* behaviors are defined as crimes and subjected to enforcement, *who* is identified as a criminal, to what extent the criminal justice system becomes involved in a particular case, and the ultimate disposition of any given criminal matter (pp. 3–4).

Because of its focus on the influence of economic power on law and justice, radical conflict criminology is sometimes classified as a theory of *lawmaking* rather than one of *lawbreaking* (Williams & Arrigo, 2007). In other words, the tradition of radical criminology is one within which the majority of attention has been directed toward critiquing criminal justice and offering a framework for the pursuit of social justice rather than on explaining criminal behavior (Arrigo, 1999). Our system of justice, radical theorists have argued, exists and operates within a society marked by class- (as well as race- and gender-)

based inequalities. And, as Sheldon (2001) noted, "*equal justice cannot be achieved in an unequal society*" (p. 3). In its current form, the criminal justice system serves simply to perpetuate and reproduce existing inequalities and injustices. Some radical criminologists more specifically regard the criminal justice system as an instrument of the ruling class and a means by which the ruling class is able to assert and maintain control over the lower classes (Michalowski, 1985).

Economic power provides influence not only on the making of law and policy, but also over the enforcement of law and the processing and punishment of lawbreakers. Reiman (1995), for instance, argued that it is largely the lower class that is controlled by the criminal justice system, with prisons and jails being warehouses for the economically marginalized segment of our society (pp. 133–134). Radical criminologists have been quick to point out that even where the ruling classes are subjected to control (e.g., administrative laws), the rules themselves and the consequences for deviation from that control are typically less severe and less stigmatizing. As Box (1983) maintained:

> Rather than being a fair reflection of those behaviours objectively causing us the most avoidable suffering, criminal law . . . criminalize[s] only some victimizing behaviours, usually those more frequently committed by the relatively powerless, and . . . exclude[s] others, usually those frequently committed by the powerful. (p. 7)

While it could be argued that the deviations of the ruling class are less harmful than those considered typical for the lower class, radical criminologists suggest that the former (e.g., fraud, corporate tax evasion, environmental hazards; price fixing and gouging) devastate far more people and carry a far more significant price tag (Lynch & Groves, 1989). By focusing on crimes of the powerless, however, the criminal justice system deflects attention away from more serious harms that result from the behavior of the ruling classes. Sheldon (2001) summarized this position amply when he wrote, "*the criminal justice system focuses primarily on those crimes that have the highest probabilities of being committed by the poorest segments of our society and almost virtually ignores those crimes committed by the richest segments of our society, crimes that actually harm us the most*" (p. 6, italics in original).

While this critique of lawmaking and law enforcement has been more central to the radical conflict tradition, criminologists have utilized, to a lesser extent, its tenets as tools for explaining lawbreaking (Arrigo & Bernard, 1997). Although Marx himself did not have much to say on the subject of crime, several theses concerning crime causation and criminal behavior can be extrapolated or inferred from what little he did offer. Most generally, inequalities and subsequent differentials in the distribution of power that are inevitable results within capitalist economic structures are *criminogenic* (i.e., crime-generating or producing). Some of Marx's work, for instance, suggests that routine forms of crime result from the demoralization of the chronically un- and underemployed (i.e., the *lumpenproletariat*) (Lynch, Michalowski, & Groves, 2000). For some such persons, the absence of meaningful prospects for labor leaves them prone to street crime (e.g., theft, robbery) as a "last resort" vehicle for survival. In other cases, the least well-off are forced to turn to demoralizing forms of employment such as prostitution to subsist (Bernard, 1981, p. 365).

Others working within the Marxist tradition focused on the impact of capitalism on individual and social character. Bonger (1916/1969), for instance, argued that capitalism gives rise to a certain form of moral character—namely, one driven by egoism, greed, and competitiveness—which, in turn, generates antisocial behavioral patterns within the population. Because capitalism encourages competition for scarce resources, conflict in the course of pursuing those resources is to be expected. Where people are fighting with one another for power and wealth, we should not expect cooperative, harmonious social relations. Importantly, Bonger's thesis accounts for both crimes of the powerless, as well as crimes of the powerful. As the ruling classes are no less egoistic and greedy, they become just as likely to engage in behaviors that harm others. The key difference, as previously discussed, is that the harmful behaviors of the ruling class are less likely to be defined as criminal, making it appear as though crime is a lower-class problem.

## Critiques

Conflict criminology in all of its variations has not been without abundant criticism from a number of sources (including conflict theorists themselves). First, because they focus on structural or macrolevel factors, conflict criminologists rarely give due attention to explanations of and research on human behavior that link its deviant manifestations to individualistic concerns such as biological and/or psychological functioning. Conflict criminologists, in turn, assert that their neglect of microlevel variables is intentional. By focusing on arrest, prosecution, and punishment of individual criminal offenders as a solution to the social problem of crime, the criminal justice system deflects attention away from the root causes of crime (e.g., Reiman, 2007). Similarly, by focusing on individual or small-group characteristics as causes of crime, criminological theorists mostly overlook the deeper social forces that give rise to individual and small-group behavioral patterns that generally create conditions within which crime is likely to flourish (e.g., Arrigo, 1999; Quinney, 1970). The "rational choices" of individuals, for instance, always take place within social, cultural, and historical circumstances that have a formative influence on those choices.

   While the claim that mainstream criminology has tended to ignore the impact of economic, political, and social inequality on lawmaking and lawbreaking holds merit, conflict criminologists can be equally criticized for discounting much useful theory and research that suggests or demonstrates links between crime and biological, psychological, and immediate social environments. Indeed, most criminologists would agree that a comprehensive theory of crime applicable in a wide range of contexts would need to account for different levels of influence on human behavior, including the effects of evolution, genetics, and neurochemistry on our biological disposition; the impact of early childhood experiences on the shaping of our values, beliefs, and psychological tendencies; the ways in which our social interactions inform our psychosocial development; and macrolevel concerns such as the influence of neighborhood environment, culture, and the political economy on the construction of identity. The consensus tradition tends to ignore the latter, but the conflict tradition has largely neglected the former.

   Another prominent criticism of radical criminology is that it lacks a solid scientific foundation. In other words, it is a "dogmatic ideology rather than . . . a testable theory" (Akers & Sellers, 2004, p. 220; see also Akers, 1979, 1980). Not all radical criminologists would take issue with this criticism. Indeed, some have argued that attempting to reduce radical theory to a set of scientific foundations contradicts its very aim (see the "Empirical Evaluations" section that follows). Those who have endeavored to provide testable hypotheses have, by most accounts, met with only modest success. The very nature of conflict criminology as a macrolevel theory of crime founded upon a critique of social and economic structures makes its reduction to empirically testable propositions quite difficult. It is likely that conflict theory generally, and radical conflict criminology specifically, will never accumulate the quantity of empirical support enjoyed by many mainstream, consensus theories of crime (e.g., Arrigo & Williams, 2006).

A third criticism comes from within conflict criminology itself. Some have argued that radical criminologists have placed too much emphasis on class. Bernard (1981), for instance, observed that "[a]lthough some form of loose class system exists in America today, class arguably is no longer the clearly defined phenomenon it was in the time of Karl Marx" (p. 372). While at some historical point it may have been useful to divide persons and assess behavioral patterns on the basis of class position (defined in terms of their relationship to the means of production), the contemporary United States cannot so easily be divided into a working class and a ruling class. Rather, whatever class system is in place today it is far more complex, requiring criminologists to "go to considerable lengths to relate this confusing picture of class structure, ownership, and control of the means of production to the contemporary crime problem" (Bernard, 1981, p. 372). A related criticism has been launched by radical criminologists who believe that the privileging of class is misguided, not strictly because of the complex nature of the concept of "class," but because other variables such as race and gender are equally—if not more—important for understanding crime, law, and justice (e.g., Chesney-Lind, 1997; Lynch & Patterson, 1996; Martin & Jurik, 2006; Schwartz & Milovanovic, 1999).

Finally, radical criminologists have been criticized for the assumption that law and policy always represent the interests and work to the benefit of the ruling class. Even a cursory examination of existing law and policy, as well as their effects and functions, reveal that some of these so-called benefits are direct contradictions of ruling-class values and interests. Radical criminologists have responded to this criticism by noting that the ruling class does not always seek to further its material well-being in the short term. In fact, the long-term interests of the ruling class may be better served by foregoing short-term political-economic needs, thereby providing the appearance that current law and policy favor the values of the working class (Arrigo & Bernard, 1997; Bernard, 1981). This strategy pacifies the masses and ensures that the majority will be less likely to demand significant change that would otherwise threaten the power and control of the ruling elite (Arrigo, 1999; Lynch et al., 2000).

## Empirical Evaluations

As noted earlier, a perceived lack of empirical support for radical criminological claims has been one of the most salient criticisms of the theory. Indeed, empirical knowledge amassed by radical criminologists has been minimal in comparison with that produced by mainstream criminological theorists. In response, some radical criminologists have argued that their criminology is not meant to have such groundings. As Bernard (1981) explained, their "primary purpose is political and action-oriented, rather than empirical and scientific"

(p. 376). As much as some criminologists claim to engage in research that is "value-free" and "objective," radical criminologists argue that no criminology—or research, for that matter—can be value-neutral and objective. Instead, all theory and research are informed by and privilege certain values and represent certain interests (Arrigo, 1999). Conventional or mainstream theory and research on crime and justice is thus inherently political, but presented under the guise of being apolitical. By conforming to the expectations of the status quo, mainstream liberal and conservative criminologists are merely accepting and reinforcing the dominant ideologies that maintain existing power structures and perpetuate inequalities. In short, examinations of crime, law, and justice that conform to the positivist paradigm ultimately serve the interests of powerful social groups or classes (Arrigo & Bernard, 1997).

Notwithstanding the conscious objections of some radical criminologists to empirically driven research, others have endeavored to substantiate their claims. Whereas mainstream theories of crime look to individual-level factors in their explanatory efforts, radical criminologists contend that crime must be understood in relation to the larger social structures and contexts within which individuals function in society. As Lynch, Schwendinger, and Schwendinger (2004) offered:

> For radicals, these structures—which include economic forces and conditions; class, gender, and race relationships, structures, hierarchies, and identities; and political and other elements of social structure—not only affect the individual's actions and *motivations*, but an individual's *opportunities* for conformity and crime, the individual's *life-course*, the range of actions that are defined and sanctioned as crime within a society, and the probability that a sanction *will be applied.* (p. 192)

Research efforts undertaken by radical criminologists consequently look beyond individuals and small groups. In recent decades, radical criminologists have examined the impact of various economic forces and variables on crime, including recession (Box, 1983), surplus value (Lynch, 1988), and economic or business cycles (e.g., Carlson & Michalowski, 1997). One of the more widely studied variables is that of unemployment (e.g., Chiricos & DeLone, 1992; Reiman, 2007). Research has consistently demonstrated a link between crime and unemployment (e.g., Currie, 1993, 1997; Young, 1997). While mainstream criminologists have not neglected this relationship, rarely do their analyses incorporate consideration for the causes of unemployment itself. Unemployment is only modestly related to the personal troubles of jobless individuals (e.g., lack of motivation). More commonly, it is a function of corporate practices endemic to late-stage capitalistic economies. To illustrate, unemployment is meaningfully linked to corporate downsizing, outsourcing of jobs, and the increased mechanization of labor (Lynch & Stretesky, 1999, p. 14). In turn, these business practices are motivated by the desire on the part of wealthy capitalists (i.e., owners) to accumulate even more capital, often by cutting costs or improving the efficiency of production. Although these profit-minded strategies may make sense from the perspective of those who stand to gain from increases in corporate earnings, they can have significant and obvious deleterious costs to employees, families, and communities. Outsourcing of jobs to other countries, for instance, can result in factory closings within communities which, in turn, can lead to fewer employment opportunities, a loss of tax revenue, and depleted funds for education, health care, and community development, increasing levels of disorganization within those communities (e.g., Sampson & Groves,

1989; Sampson et al., 1997), and a corresponding increase in social problems such as poverty, homelessness, and crime within those environs (e.g., Wilson, 1996).

Consistent with their ongoing critique of the criminal justice system, radical criminologists have offered empirical investigations not only of crime and victimization, but also of policing, court processes, and patterns and trends in punishment. Specifically, radical criminologists have been interested in the ways in which some persons, by virtue of class position, race, gender, and so on, are disadvantaged by or subject to injustices as a function of criminal justice processes. To illustrate, consider that in the contemporary United States social class is crucially linked to criminal behavior, but also to such issues as availability and quality of legal counsel and likelihood of pretrial release (i.e., bail) following arrest. If set at $20,000, 70% of felony defendants will be unable to make bail. Poorer defendants are therefore considerably more likely to be held in jail awaiting trial than wealthier defendants accused of the same offense. Moreover, being detained in jail while awaiting trial potentially has a number of adverse effects, including job loss, housing/mortgage difficulties, family stress, and so forth. Not least importantly, research has demonstrated that defendants who make bail are less likely to be found guilty—perhaps because they are better able to assist in the preparation of their defense when not confined to a jail cell (e.g., Reaves, 1992). Consequently, poorer defendants are more likely to be found guilty than wealthier defendants accused of the same crimes. While this logic may not provide convincing evidence for the notion that the criminal justice system serves the purpose of controlling the lower classes, it does support the more general claim by conflict criminologists that persons of lower social class and status are regularly disadvantaged through the routine functioning of that system.

## Theoretical Refinements

Subsequent to the emergence and continued development of radical conflict criminology, the remaining decades of the twentieth century (carrying over into the twenty-first century) saw an array of additional theoretical perspectives materialize, each broadly rooted in the tradition of conflict but unique in its particular source and focus of concern. Our focus in this section will thus be contemporary theoretical offshoots of the conflict tradition more so than refinements of its original principles. What can generally be referred to as *critical criminology* is typically regarded as including Marxist or radical conflict criminology, as well as alternative perspectives such as anarchist criminology, feminist criminology, critical race theory, postmodern criminology, cultural criminology, left realism, and peacemaking criminology (e.g., Arrigo, 1999; DeKeseredy & Perry, 2006; Schwartz & Hatty, 2003). Because an entire chapter could easily be dedicated to each of these theories, this section will focus only on a few key arguments and developments proposed by representative critical criminological perspectives.

### Anarchist criminology

Like Marxism, anarchism as a social theory and political movement has a rich and storied history, typified by the works of pioneering theorists such as Peter Kropotkin, Michael Bakunin, and William Godwin. Anarchist criminology can be regarded as a variation of conflict theory that incorporates a critique of existing power structures and inequalities as sources of social problems, and promotes the displacement of coercive authority in the interest of realizing a more natural form of justice (e.g., Ferrell, 1999; Tifft, 1979). The word *anarchism* stems from the Greek *anarchos*, meaning "no rule" and, indeed, anarchists argue that social justice demands that all forms of authority be eliminated and replaced by a classless society, egalitarian social relations, and shared commitment to communal or collective good. Regulations that come in the form of laws and formal rules would be replaced, in Kropotkin's (1912) words, by "mutual agreement between the members of that society" (p. 68). In other words, rather than rules being imposed upon citizens by authoritarian institutions and their representatives, they would be created (and continually adjusted) by citizens themselves in the process of working toward productive human relationships and flourishing communities (e.g., Williams & Arrigo, 2001).

Indeed, law is theorized by anarchist criminologists to be counterproductive, causing more problems than it solves. Kropotkin (1885/1992) summarized this notion well in his classic essay on law and authority:

> When there is ignorance in the heart of a society and disorder in people's minds, laws become numerous. [People] expect everything from legislation and, each new law being a further miscalculation of reality, they are led to demand incessantly when should emerge from themselves . . . a new law is considered a remedy for all ills. (p. 145)

When laws—or, for that matter, law enforcement, courts, prisons, etc.—are seen as the solution to our problems, we encourage the strengthening of government and the consequent weakening of community-based problem solving. Under ideal circumstances, authoritarian institutions (such as law) and their representatives are to be replaced by voluntary forms of social order wherein the natural inclinations of human beings allow for cooperative solutions to crime and other social problems. Unlike forms of social and criminological theory that hold human beings to be naturally antisocial and prone to violence, anarchists see people as inclined by nature toward compassionate and cooperative relations with one another. Antisocial and criminal behavior patterns evident in industrial and postindustrial societies are an outgrowth of forms of social organization (e.g., capitalism) that discourage these natural inclinations from manifesting and simultaneously encourage—even necessitate—negative emotions and interpersonal tendencies (e.g., competitiveness, selfishness, greed, envy).

### Left realism

Since its emergence in the 1980s, left realism has endeavored to chart significant inroads for theory, research, and policy in criminology that share in the assumptions of, but differ notably from, Marxist-inspired radical criminology (e.g., Lea & Young, 1984; MacLean & Milovanovic, 1991). The latter has been sharply criticized for its idealism and corresponding failure to offer viable proposals for the prevention and reduction of crime and victimization. As Lea and Young (1984) put it, the radical tradition of criminology had "tended to be idealistic in nature and . . . failed to provide any solutions for crime and policing in a realistic way" (p. 358). Partly in response to such criticism, one of the guiding principles of left realism is that radical criminology should refocus its energies toward finding "realistic" policy alternatives that would meaningfully impact crime and injustice (see the section "Policy Applications" for several examples).

Left realists take a more practical interest in the everyday realities of crime and victimization—particularly as those realities disproportionately impact the working class.

A second criticism of the radical tradition that left realists have sought to challenge is that it has been too heavily "focused on crimes of the powerful at the expense of a realistic analysis of predatory crimes directed towards the working class" (Lea & Young, 1984, p. 358). Left realists have argued that radical criminologists have tended to place too little emphasis on inner-city crime (that committed by the working class against the working class) in part out of fear that such a focus would energize conservative crime control policies (e.g., Currie, 1992). While advocating for renewed attention to working-class crime and victimization, left realists have also been careful not to "trivialize the degree of public harm done by affluent offenders" (DeKeseredy, MacLean, & Schwartz, 1997, p. 19).

Left realist criminologists also deviate from traditional radical criminology in their utilization of "both quantitative and qualitative research methods to elicit rich data about crime, victims, and criminal justice processing" (DeKeseredy et al., 1997, p. 21). In part, the exercise of empirical methodologies in researching crime is a response to those who have discounted Marxist criminology as lacking in scientific foundations. As well, the empirical efforts of left realists have provided data with which to "challenge right-wing discourses" concerning crime and the "ineffective conservative agenda aimed at curbing such problems" (DeKeseredy et al., 1997, p. 21).

### Postmodern criminology

Postmodernism is a broad philosophical movement that gained force within the humanities and social sciences beginning in the 1980s. It has since received increasing attention within criminological scholarship (Arrigo, 1995). Postmodernism can best be described as a theory of *knowledge* production and, more specifically, the ways in which knowledge is linked to power (e.g., Arrigo, 1996). It is in this respect that postmodernism can be regarded as a theory of social conflict (Arrigo & Bernard, 1997). Postmodern criminology does not, however, offer anything resembling a theory of crime causation.

The element of postmodernism that has most often been subject of criminological focus is that of *language*. Although postmodern criminologists do not explicitly address concerns of political economy, they argue that knowledge and language themselves operate as a form of political economy. As an "instrument of political and economic power" (Arrigo & Bernard, 1997, p. 40), language—like class, race, and gender—represents an important source of conflict. Language, postmodernists argue, "shapes, modifies, and defines all social relationships, all institutional practices, and all methods of knowing" (p. 39). Because the language we use structures the ways in which we think—especially if our language supports certain power arrangements—then we will tend to think about the world in terms of those arrangements and, consequently, act to maintain and further them (Arrigo, 2002).

The problem with these "arrangements" is that they exclude or discount alternative ways of knowing, replacement ways of experiencing, and novel ways of being/becoming (Arrigo & Milovanovic, 2009). Stated differently, if language structures the thoughts that we think in ways that are not neutral, in ways that endorse circumscribed views of crime, law, and justice (e.g., of "offenders," "victims," "punishment," "restoration," "reasonableness," "harm"), then these privileged standpoints reduce difference to sameness, homogenize identity, and territorialize knowledge. This is the manifestation of oppression assuming a discursive linguistic form. Lost in this process of reality construction are the possibilities for more completely embodying and legitimizing lived experience in all of its conformities and contradictions, consistencies and anomalies, predictabilities and irregularities, sensibilities and absurdities. Lost in this process of reality construction is the possibility for more fully celebrating our evolving kaleidoscopic humanity.


## Policy Applications

The policy implications of conflict theory—particularly its radical variation—have been on the receiving end of much criticism. Because they locate the root causes of crime within social arrangements, most strains of conflict theory have historically conceded that the only effective means of preventing or reducing crime is to make significant changes to those arrangements. Within the Marxist tradition, the only meaningful course of action to reduce social problems is to replace the capitalist system—ultimately, the root of inequality, poverty, and so on—with one conforming to the tenets of socialism. This implication is one for which radical criminologists have been heavily criticized. This is particularly the case given that socialist societies past and present have not been able to eliminate crime, and this fact alone seems to refute the premise that the implementation of a socialist state will have their desired effect.

Other conflict traditions have offered policy recommendations less radical than a replacement of the capitalist state. It is important to note, however, that just as different theories of social conflict focus on different forms of conflict (e.g., interest group, economic, race-, gender-, or language-based), the policy implications of specific variants of conflict theory will vary modestly from one another. For instance, critical theorists focusing on the criminogenic quality of racial inequality are likely to recommend courses of action that will reduce economic, political, and social disparities between races. All conflict theories, however, recommend law and policy changes directed toward altering the fundamental inequalities upon which social arrangements are formed.

Conflict criminologists share the assertion that crime, as well as unemployment, homelessness, and other maladies, are not the result of antisocial motivations traceable to select individuals within a society. Rather, they are social problems and, consequently, are a function of the way in which society is politically and economically organized—specifically, that form of social organization which follows from late-stage capitalism and the practices common to it. If we wish to understand the development and continued existence of crime and other social problems, we must consider the ways in which the routine operation of capitalism produces great inequalities in the distribution of wealth and resources, disparities in life circumstances and prospects, and a host of other societal concerns that are either directly or indirectly associated with crime and criminality. We cannot expect to curb criminal behavior by punishing, deterring, incapacitating, or even rehabilitating individual criminals. As crime is a *social problem* correlated with social factors, its prevention or reduction requires *social change*. Specifically, social change requires social reorganization; that is, taking steps toward remedying the rampant economic inequalities that plague extant social relations.

Although conflict theorists are quick to point to the ways in which the criminal justice system sustains and even perpetuates inequalities, this status quo maintaining apparatus "cannot be a meaningful avenue of social change" (Lynch & Groves, 1989, p. 108). Unlike theories of crime and justice that advocate reform at the level of individuals, families, or neighborhoods, conflict theorists argue that such reforms do little to remedy the inequalities that represent the ultimate source of crime and other social problems. Reform is merely "patching up the problems" (Einstadter & Henry, 1995, p. 250) while doing little to alter the variables that give rise to those problems. Changes to the system of justice are not separable from changes to the political economy. Meaningful and lasting reductions in antisocial behavior can be attained only by "restructuring the distribution of wealth and ownership, thereby narrowing the vast chasms of inequality that now exist and that produce the propensity toward crime" (p. 250).

Indeed, conflict theorists have argued that structural changes that minimize disparities in wealth will produce *less need* for a system of criminal justice, as motivations for criminal behavior will dissipate. Where differences in wealth are minimized, persons are equally capable of pursuing the satisfaction of their needs and interests. Thus, not only are inequities in the distribution of wealth and other social conditions that give rise to crime reduced, the psychological motives for criminal behavior (e.g., egoism, competitiveness) that are inevitable products of capitalism are diminished as well. Where the motivation for crime is limited, crime is prevented and thus it need not be controlled or monitored through the means typically associated with criminal justice (e.g., law enforcement, formal courts of law, prison).

Where undesirable behavior does occur, some conflict theorists have envisioned an informal, collective approach to managing it. Anarchist criminologists in particular point out that informal social control has always been a more effective means of controlling behavior than formal, state-sponsored interventions. In fact, as labeling theorists have demonstrated, formal procedures often make matters worse. Processing offenders through a formal system of justice and subjecting them to punishment can have a detrimental impact on self-image, generate hostility and resentment, and, perhaps most importantly, does little to reconnect the offender to the community of which she or he is a part. What is needed in these situations is a collective, community-based effort whereby the offender's conduct (not the person) is met with disapproval, the individual is encouraged to authentically accept responsibility for her or his actions, is empowered to understand the harm these actions caused to others, and, ultimately, is reconnected to the broader community and social fabric, always and already in positional, relational, and provisional ways (Arrigo, 1995).

More recently, some criminologists have begun to advocate less radical avenues of change. This is particularly true of left realists, for whom social change should be "practical" and "progressive" (DeKeseredy et al., 1997, p. 21). DeKeseredy (2003), for instance, suggests job creation and training programs, higher minimum wages, government-sponsored day care, housing assistance, universal health care, and other attainable initiatives that would help lower unemployment, poverty, and other criminogenic conditions (p. 37).

# FEMINIST THEORIES

## SISTERS IN CRIME: THE RISE OF THE
## NEW FEMALE OFFENDER

*Freda Adler*

Women are no longer indentured to the kitchens, baby carriages, or bedrooms of America. The skein of myths about women is unraveling, the chains have been pried loose, and there will be no turning back to the days when women found it necessary to justify their existence by producing babies or cleaning houses. Allowed their freedom for the first time, women—by the tens of thousands—have chosen to desert those kitchens, and plunge exuberantly into the formerly all-male quarters of the working world. . . .

In the same way that women are demanding equal opportunity in fields of legitimate endeavor, a similar number of determined women are forcing their way into the world of major crimes. . . .

It is this segment of women who are pushing into—and succeeding at—crimes which were formerly committed by males only. Females . . . are now being found not only robbing banks single-handedly, but also committing assorted armed robberies, muggings, loan-sharking operations, extortion, murders, and a wide variety of other aggressive, violence-oriented crimes which previously involved only men. . . .

By every indicator available, female criminals appear to be surpassing males in the rate of increase for almost every major crime. Although males continue to commit the greater absolute number of offenses, it is the women who are committing those same crimes at yearly rates of increase now running as high as six and seven times greater than those for males. . . .

In summary, what we have described is a gradual but accelerating social revolution in which women are closing many of the gaps, social and criminal, that have separated them from men. The closer they get, the more alike they look and act. This is not to suggest that there are no inherent differences. Differences do exist and will be elaborated later in this book, but it seems clear that those differences are not of prime importance in understanding female criminality. The simplest and most accurate way to grasp the essence of women's changing patterns is to discard dated notions of femininity. That is a role that fewer and fewer women are willing to play. In the final analysis, women criminals are human beings who have basic needs and abilities and opportunities. Over the years these needs have not changed, nor will they. But women's abilities and opportunities have multiplied, resulting in a kaleidoscope of changing patterns whose final configuration will be fateful for all of us. . . .

## Social Differences

Whatever equality may have existed between Adam and Eve before the Fall, there was a clear distinction in their social roles afterward. Adam was thenceforth required to till the soil and earn his bread by the sweat of his brow; Eve was condemned to painful childbirth and total submission to her husband. In one august decree, her reproductive role and social role were established and fixed. To be a woman, then as now, meant not just to be a distinctive blend of physiological and psychological characteristics. It meant and means that one is perceived differently, treated differently, responded to differently, and the subject of different expectations. Given the varying social forces that weigh unequally on the sexes in creatures as culture-dependent as humans, it seems clear that the resulting differences in behavior owe more to wide disparities in social-role than to the narrow differences in physical and psychological makeup.

The answer to the nursery-rhyme question, "what are little girls made of?" is revealing at several different levels. The list of ingredients—"sugar and spice and everything nice"—contains both a biological theory and a social demand. We are told, first of all, that little girls are good because of their inherent structure, and secondly, that they had better be good if they hope to enjoy the status of femininity and avoid the social disapproval which accompanies deviancy. Little boys, too, are under social pressure, but of a different kind. They are made of "snakes and snails and puppy-dog tails"—a combination designed to contrast mischievously and dynamically with the inert and saccharine constitution of their female counterparts. They, too, are saddled with social and presumed biological imperatives which compress the wide-ranging human potential for variation into the narrow confines of social-role expectation. There is hardly any important individual or social area—play, personal hygiene, manners, discipline, dependency, dress, activity, career, sexual activity, aggressiveness, etc.—which has not been polarized and institutionalized as a sex-role difference. While it is true that men have tended to stigmatize women as a group, deviation from social standards is even worse—e.g., the "effeminate" man and the "masculine" woman.

Traditionally, the little girl and later the woman are confined to a low-level of noise, dirt, disorder, and physical aggression. They must be obedient, dependent, modest about their bodies, and avoid sex play as well as rough and tumble competition. But life is not all no-no's: for her pains she is allowed to turn more readily to others for gratification, to cry when hurt, to be spontaneously affectionate, and to achieve less in school and work. Whatever the natural inclination of the sexes may be, society does not depend on spontaneous acquisition of the profile it considers desirable: besides identification with the parent of the same sex, which is probably the single most important determinant of behavior, it selects out from the random range of childhood activities those certain ones which will be accentuated or discarded. The shaping process includes toys—mechanical and problem-solving for boys, and soft and nonchallenging for girls—social structuring, individual rewards and punishments, and the satisfactions apparently inherent in conforming to role expectations. The development of aggressive and dependent traits, both of which are considered to be sex-related, is a case in point. One research study found that while aggressive boys become aggressive men and dependent girls become dependent women, the reverse was true for dependent boys and aggressive girls: as they approach maturity, they reverse themselves and also become aggressive men and dependent women, respectively. Similarly, there is a greater overlap of sex-role personality traits when the sibling in a two-child family is of the opposite sex, and this effect is greater with the younger siblings than with the older ones. Clearly, learning and social pressure are influential in effecting sex-role expectations. Extending the argument that social roles are related to biological processes only indirectly, presumably a technology which permitted father to nurture the child could result in a complete social-role reversal. In a pithy and accurate observation, Simone de Beauvoir summed up the consensus of current thinking when she said, "One is not born, but rather becomes, a woman."

In the interests of clarity, I have spoken separately of the major physical, psychological, and social characteristics which distinguish women from men, although obviously each molds the final form of the other, both clinically and theoretically. Investigations of animal behavior demonstrate, for example, that rat pups who are psychologically stimulated develop larger and presumably smarter brains than those exposed to sensory isolations; a litter born to a low-status African wild dog is less likely to survive than one born to a high-status female because the pups are less well fed and less protected by the pack; the male offspring of low-status baboon females, regardless of their innate characteristics, are less likely to become dominant than those born to high-status females because the latter spend more time in physical proximity to the inner circle of dominant males and learn dominance behavior; and the ovulatory cycle of a dove is retarded when a glass partition is placed between her and the rest of the flock, and it is stopped altogether if she is isolated in a room, unless there is a mirror. The interdependency between biological drive and learning is described in Konrad Lorenz's formulation of the concept of "instinct-training interlocking behavior": he describes this as a blend of instinctive and learned components, with instinct guaranteeing the readiness for certain kinds of learning and behavior to occur but experience shaping its final form.

In summary, females are smaller and meeker than men, they are less stable physiologically, they produce fewer androgenic hormones, and they have been socially shaped toward passivity, dependency, and conformity. Men are bigger, stronger, more aggressive, achievement-oriented, and more willing to break rules and take risks. This profile of the "normal" male and the "normal" female is consistent with the traditional differences which, until the last few decades, have prevailed for their criminal counterparts. However, the increasing "masculinization" of female social and criminal behavior forces us to reexamine the basis for her previous feminine limitations. A common-sense approach, and one followed by even such uncommon men as Freud and Adler, would suggest that what is natural to the female could be inferred from a factual description of the way the majority of females think and feel and act. Understandably, this is what has been done, and just as understandably it has been wrong. . . .

## Female Passivity: Genetic Fact or Cultural Myth?

In the past, aggression was thought to be chiefly a biologically controlled trait. As a matter of their birth and ongoing internal chemistry, males were assumed to be "naturally aggressive"—hence the explanation of their historic roles as soldiers, hard-boiled businessmen, and merciless criminals. Women, on the other hand, were thought to be innately timid, passive, and conforming. Their general failure to be anything but mothers and housewives was offered as proof of their inability to be aggressive.

Of all the differences between the sexes, only four—size, strength, aggression, and dominance—have been implicated in any way with the overrepresentation of males in the criminal system.

The first two are biological givens; the other two are largely, if not entirely, socially learned. Let us examine them separately. In non-technological societies and in earlier periods in industrial societies, physical strength was often the final arbiter of social interaction, but even so, it was not the only one. In man as well as in the apes, psychological factors including social manipulation, ruses, and group alliances were often decisive for leadership and effective action. In animals as well as men, the battle did not always go to the strong nor the race to the swift. But even if it did, this edge has been diminished by the technology of modern weapons. The deadliness of a gun is not necessarily less dangerous in the hands of a woman—although some have claimed that her lack of aggressiveness makes her a very unlikely and ineffective gunslinger. This is an interesting assumption because it is a common stereotype and is grounded in studies of male hormonal influences on lower animals, which gives it a ring of biological authenticity. There is much truth in this, but it is only a partial truth which, when stretched beyond its limits, conveys a falsehood. The truth is that in lower animals males are characteristically more aggressive, and this aggression is so directly linked to male hormones that if the male is castrated or injected with estrogen (the female hormone) he will stop fighting. Likewise, the prenatal administration of testosterone to pregnant monkeys results in pseudohermaphroditic female offspring who even three years after birth are more aggressive than normal females. However, it would be misleading to formulate the equation androgen = aggression or estrogen = nonaggression for all but the simplest and least socially developed species. Furthermore, it cannot be claimed that aggression is the exclusive prerogative of males. Mature female chimpanzees regularly drive off lower status males and any female mammal's defense of her cubs is as fierce as it is legendary.

But relevant as this is in establishing that aggression can co-exist with estrogen and can be unrelated to male hormones in mammals, the evidence for hormonal-behavioral detachment is even more compelling in subhuman primates and men. It is not possible to understand the behavior of social animals outside the context of a social situation. For example, an electric shock applied to an animal in a dominant position vis-à-vis another will result in an attack; the same stimulus applied to the same animal who is in a subdominant position vis-à-vis another will result in cringing, submissive behavior. Likewise, the response of anger vs. fear or fight vs. flight depends less on the release of specific chemicals than on whether we perceive the threatening stimulus, in relation to ourselves, to be smaller or larger. The human capacity for abstraction and symbol formulation extends the range of "size" to include factors only remotely related to actual mass, so that characteristics such as wealth, lineage, social connections, skill, and intelligence may be perceived as "big" and accorded dominance. In the evolutionary progression toward higher mammals, there is a decreasing dependency between hormones and behavior, and in humans we find an almost complete cultural "override" of innate drives and tendencies. Thus, while status and dominance appear to be constants throughout the order of social primates, culture defines which characteristics will be labeled as dominant. Likewise, the distinctive sex-appropriate behaviors so rigidly controlled by hormones in lower animals have yielded to a rich variety of gender roles in human societies.

In *Sex and Temperament in Three Primitive Societies*, Margaret Mead described three revealing cultural variations. In one tribe, both sexes acted in the mild, parental, responsive manner we expect of women; in a second, both sexes acted in the fierce initiating fashion we expect of men; in a third, the men were chatty, wore curls, and went shopping in the manner of our stereotype of women, while the women were their unadorned, managerial, energetic partners. She concluded that sex roles were

> mere variations of human temperament, to which the members of either or both sexes may, with more or less success in the case of different individuals, be educated to approximate.

She also concluded that regardless of what social role the male plays, it is always the lead.

Regardless of what his characteristic behavior may be and even when it is imitative of "feminine behavior," it is considered high status when he adopts it. While historically and universally it is indeed a man's world, it does not follow that modern industrial man is innately more dominant than modern woman. It could be argued that the equalizing effects of a technological civilization like ours is without historical parallel and that the universal dominance of men may have resulted more from the institutionalization of man's superior strength than from any innate feminine submissiveness.

Western history is replete with examples of women who have risen above their cultural stereotype to become leaders of vigor and acclaim. Nor has their reign or tenure in office been particularly noteworthy for its tranquillity, peacefulness, or lack of aggressive adventures, all characteristics of their countrywomen in the social role of housewife. These women have, in fact, displayed a remarkable talent for ruthless and highly aggressive leadership. For instance, few world leaders have ever been so renowned for their tyrannical, belligerent rule as the English queens. One can still be stirred by the picture of Elizabeth I attired with her gold crown and shining breast-plate, mounted on a white stallion, and moving like an avenging angel through her army of twenty thousand men at Tilbury . . .; Cleopatra of ancient Egypt, a biological woman's woman by any standards, was known for her shrewd political manipulations and insatiable appetite for military conquests; Maria Theresa was the founder of the modern Austrian state; the Russian Empress Catherine, who mothered a dozen children during her reign, still found time to annex ever-widening territories and seek new armies to defeat. In the present day, it is noteworthy that the two major countries with female rulers have both been at war within the last few years: Indira Gandhi of India and Golda Meir of Israel have shown no timidity—each, in wars across her border, has wielded political and military might as effectively as any man. Of course, such women as these who have risen to national leadership possess extraordinary characteristics which distinguish them from the mass of women—and the mass of men, for that matter. The very capacity and drive for ascension through a male world involved a selection process which would have discouraged weaker women. Notwithstanding their small numbers, the resoluteness, and fortitude of such women challenge the myth of innate female passivity. On a broader scope, and one which encompassed more ordinary women, was the female incursion into criminal areas, previously considered male, during World War II. In law-enforcing as well as law-breaking, it would appear that social position and social-role expectations are more important than sex in determining behavior.

During the early 1940s, the mobilization of males from the civil to the military sector resulted in the necessity for a large number of women to fill positions previously held by men. And fill them they did, in a way not altogether anticipated. It had been known and expected that lesser men often rise to the stature of a role thrust on them by circumstance. It should not have been surprising, therefore, that "lesser men" who happen to be women would do the same thing. What was most portentous, however, about this vocational shift was not that women could assume men's jobs, but that in doing so they could also presume

to men's social roles. One need not look to psychological theories to explain the enthusiasm with which women embraced men's esteemed positions. Their own, as housewife and
playmate, had been eroding for years and a desperately labor-short male establishment had
further devalued it in the interests of national defense, as something akin to indolence, if
not disloyalty. "Rosie the Riveter," symbol of the women working for the war, was proclaimed a heroine in song and style by a grateful country. As the residence of female status
shifted from the home to the office or factory, a trip that men had made long before, the
American woman accommodated so congenially to the change that few people at the time
challenged her credentials to perform. However, many were concerned that she was not
just commuting to her new-found roles but might settle down to stay. In unprecedented
numbers women crossed the sex-role line in their jobs and in their crimes during the war
years, 1940 to 1945. In that period, the crimes committed by women almost doubled in
number and even began to assume the same patterns as male crime. The trend peaked in
1945 and declined rapidly after the war with the return of men to their jobs, but it could
never be the same. Women were now urged to act more like women by a male establishment which wanted to return to the position it had temporarily (it hoped) vacated. But in
social evolution as in biological evolution, there is no easy road back, especially since in a
very profound sense the women could not go home again. Labor-saving household appli-
ances and the denigration of the domestic work ethic they conveyed rendered her old position untenable. In addition, there was a shift in the male attitude. Men were seeing women
as worthy rivals and feeling considerably less charitable and more competitive toward
them. Furthermore, in a world grown too full of people, even the once sacrosanct status
of motherhood was beginning to bear unhappy resemblances to overproductive pollution.
With zero population as a national goal and household drudgery an accepted epithet, where
was the woman to go? The road back was blocked, and while the road forward was not
completely open it was now more accessible than ever before.

The pressure was all for discarding the separate-but-equal provisions of the old social
contract and opting for a chance to compete in the same field and under the same conditions as men. Unfortunately, the men were not as ready for this change as the women. Psy-
choanalysts, long accustomed to the futile penis envy of women, were now talking about
breast envy and womb envy, an example of male jealousy toward women almost unheard
of in Freud's day.

While women proceeded to widen their social and criminal roles, many men, especially middle- and lower-class men, who had the least ground to yield in the status hierarchy, resisted in every way they could. . . .

## Gender Equality and Crime

The old ways do indeed die hard, not only because we need our stereotypes and our sub-
dominants, but also because cognitive systems tend to become security blankets to which
we cling most tenaciously just when we are most threatened. It is perhaps for these reasons
that the coming of age of the Western woman was not forecast by the behavioral scientists
who should have known, but instead it caught us unaware and overtook our comfortable
prejudices with a *fait accompli*. While most were predicting that it was impossible and
many were arguing that it wasn't happening, it had already occurred. It is tempting to think

no deeper than an apparent fact, and it must be admitted that the "facts" of female inferiority were apparent to all who could read the figures that supported them. It did not seem productive to search out the reasons behind the figures. They were self-evident because they confirmed what we already knew about the natural superiority of men. If it were otherwise, we surely would have been told by this time. But, indeed, we were being told new "facts" in compelling ways by new figures which were challenging old theories.

In the countless indices which measure female output of degrees and income and factory production, and in the Uniform Crime Reports which tabulate her legal transgressions, these rising figures were intruding not only on our beliefs but on the mores which supported them. At first, the rising crime rates were greeted as an apparition, a mirage; at first, they were dismissed as an aberration which would correct itself by statistical adjustments; at last, they were recognized as ancient female strengths which had always been latent and were just now, at this sociotechnological juncture of history, realizing their potential. Everything we know about the history of woman and everything we see about her current behavior tells us that her past limitations as a worker and law-breaker have been largely, if not entirely, the result of her physical weakness and the cultural institutions which derived from that fact. Save only her inferiority in size and strength, her differences from men are just *that*, differences. Some confer an advantage, others a disadvantage, depending on the particular culture. In our own, given her education, aspirations (these, too, have been liberated), freedom from unwanted pregnancies, healthy assertiveness, and access to labor-saving devices, including guns, she shares the same fortunate or unfortunate criminogenic qualities as men.

I have not contended here that women are equal *to* men, simply that they are potentially the equal of men. There are many differences which we have described and no doubt more will be discovered, but all evidence points to two complementary conclusions: First, the small natural differences between the sexes have been polarized and institutionalized in special ways by different cultures to produce a gender disparity which reveals more about emotional needs of the society than about the innate possibilities of the individual. And second, when size and strength between the sexes are discounted by technology, as they have been within the ranks of men, social expectations and social roles, including the criminal roles, tend increasingly to merge.

There was a time early in the history of the physical sciences, before the concepts of mass and gravity were formulated, when the weight of an object was thought to reside within the physical boundaries of the object. Because weight is palpable and measurable, it was a conclusion which met the requirements of common sense and common experience. But the limitation of common sense is that it owes too much allegiance to the past to permit conceptual breakthroughs to the future. It is a better follower than leader. As physicists later discovered, the weight of an object is not inherent within it but rather the measure of an outside gravitational pull acting upon it. In an analogous manner, scientific thinking about human behavior has evolved in the same centrifugal direction. From the predecessors of Lombroso to the followers of Freud and into modern times, the search for the causes of female criminality have focused on her biology with scant heed to her sociology. We have only recently recognized that the clothes of social-role expectations not only make the man, they also form the woman.

Even if it is established that humans have innate biological drives, and even if it were confirmed that females have a different biogrammar (i.e., a behavioral repertoire of signals) from males, the social forces which impinge on her from without would still be decisive for her conformist as well as her deviant behavior. In the profoundest evolutionary sense, the social factors which sustain and suspend us also create our destiny, and biology must follow where society leads.

## DOING FEMINIST CRIMINOLOGY

*Meda Chesney-Lind*

I can still vividly recall hearing a male researcher who, reporting on fertility rates at a population meeting in Seattle, referred to his subjects using male pronouns throughout his presentation. Since it was clear from the content of his talk that his subjects were female (we are after all the only ones who can give birth), I was puzzled. A graduate student attending my first national meeting and rather daunted by the setting. I waited until the break to ask him about his word choice. Without any embarrassment, he informed me that "I say he or him because to say she or her would trivialize my research."

For many years, criminology was not haunted by this problem. Unlike demography, it was seen as an incontrovertibly male, even "macho" field. Crime has, in fact, sometimes been described as an ultimate form of masculinity. In Albert Cohen's words, "the delinquent is a rogue male" whose behavior no matter how it is condemned on moral grounds "has at least one virtue: it incontestably confirms, in the eyes of all concerned, his essential masculinity."

The criminological fascination with male deviance and crime—which I have flippantly dubbed the "Westside Story Syndrome"—is not, as some might contend, simply a reflection of the American crime problem. I suspect that it is also explained by Margaret Mead's observation that whatever men do, even if it is dressing dolls for religious ceremonies, has higher status and is more highly rewarded than whatever women do. For this reason, fields focus on male activities and attributes wherever possible: to study them is to convey higher status to the researcher.

The question now is whether theories of delinquency and crime, which were admittedly developed to explain male behavior, can be used to understand female crime, delinquency, and victimization. Clearly these theories have been much affected by notions that class and protest masculinity were at the core of criminal behavior. Will the "add women and stir" approach to criminological theory be sufficient? Are these really, despite their origins, general theories, as some have argued?

My research experience convinces me that they are not. About fifteen years ago, when I was reading files compiled on youth referred to Honolulu's family court during the first half of this century, I ran across what I considered to be a bizarre pattern. Over half of all the girls had been referred to court for "immorality" and another third were charged with being "wayward." In reading the files, I discovered that this meant that the young women were suspected of being sexually active. Evidence of this "exposure" was vigorously pursued in all cases—and this was not subtle. Virtually all girl's files contained gynecological examinations (sometimes there were stacks of these forms). Doctors, who understood the purpose of such examinations, would routinely note the condition of the hymen on the form: "admits intercourse, hymen ruptured," "hymen ruptured," "no laceration" as well as comments about whether the "laceration" looks new or old were typical notations.

Later analysis of the data would also reveal the harsh sanctions imposed on those girls found guilty of these offenses. Thus, despite widespread repetitions about the chivalrous treatment of female offenders, I was finding in the then skimpy literature on women's crime that large numbers of these girls were being incarcerated for non-criminal offenses. For example, in Honolulu, girls' referred to court in the 1930s were twice as likely as boys to be detained; they spent, on the average five times as long as males in detention facilities; and they were three times as likely to be sent to training schools. Later research would confirm that this pattern was also found in other parts of the country and that similar though less extreme bias against girls existed well into the 1960s.

Reflecting on this pattern recently, it occurred to me that girls were being treated in this fashion as the field of criminology was developing—these were, after all the halcyon years of theory building. So while criminologists—mostly male—were paying a lot of attention to the male delinquent, large numbers of girls were being processed, punished and incarcerated. Indeed, one of the classic excuses for neglecting female offenders—their relatively small numbers—did not hold during these years. I found, for example, that girls made up half of those committed to Hawaii training schools well into the 1950s.

One reason for this neglect of girls may have been the inability of researchers to identify with their problems or situations. By contrast, I was not able to distance myself from their lives. At that time, the women's movement was a major part of my life. For the first time, I was seeing the connections between my life and the lives of other women. In small groups, in Honolulu as elsewhere, we were discovering that the personal was political, that sisterhood was a source of power, and that women's experiences, though academically invisible, were important. I knew, first hand, about physical examinations and knew that even under the best of circumstances they were stressful. I imagined what it would have been like to be a 13 or 14 year-old, to be arrested on my family's orders, taken to a detention center and forcibly examined by a doctor I didn't know. Later, I would also read of legal cases where girls, in other states, were held in solitary confinement for refusing such examinations, and I would talk to women who had had this experience as girls. Their comments and experiences confirmed the degradation and personal horror of this experience.

I bring up this particular point simply to demonstrate that the administration of a medical examination, the larger meaning of that medical examination in the girl's delinquent "career" as an "immoral" or wayward or incorrigible offender, and the harsh response to the girl so identified had no place in the delinquency theories I had studied.

Certainly, one can patch together, as I did, notions of stigma, degradation rituals, and labelling, but the job was not complete and the picture imperfect. I have come increasingly to the conclusion that my own research results plus the work of other feminist researchers argue for a feminist revision of delinquency, crime and criminal victimization—a feminist criminology.

Though I see the need for this, I am keenly aware that professional rewards for such an undertaking may be slow in coming. The work I just described on female delinquency was completed for my Master's thesis. The sociology department where I did this research failed to perceive its import. In order to complete my work for the Ph.D., I was forced to abandon the topic of women and crime and venture into population research—that's how I got to Seattle to hear that even women's ability to give birth can be obfuscated.

Despite the professional liabilities, I would argue that an overhaul of criminological theory is essential. The extensive focus on disadvantaged males in public settings has meant that girls' victimization, the relationship between that experience and girls' crime, and the relationship between girl's problems and women's crime have been systematically ignored. Feminist research has established that many of the young women who ran away from home, for example, were running from homes that were sexually and physically abusive. These backgrounds often lead to a street life, also rigidly stratified by gender, that pushes girls further into the criminal world and, for some, into adult crime.

Also missed has been the central role played by the juvenile justice system in the sexualization of female delinquency and the criminalization of girl's survival strategies. In a very direct way, the family court's traditional insistence that girls "obey" their parents has forced young women, on the run from brutal or negligent families, into the lives of escaped convicts. It could be suggested that the official actions of the juvenile justice system should be understood as major forces in girls' oppression as they have historically served to reinforce the obedience of all young women to the demands of patriarchal authority no matter how abusive and arbitrary.

But the evidence supporting the undertaking of such a thorough rethinking and revision of criminological theory comes from many directions—of which my own work is only a small part. Consider the pioneering work of feminist researchers on the significance of the victimization of women—particularly the importance of sexual assault and wife battering—and the generation of women's fear of victimization at the hands of males. Their work has gone a long way to identify and rectify problems within standard criminological paradigms all of which ignored or minimized the significance of women's abuse.

Examples of these problems abound. Consider, for example, the many years during which the lethality of wife battering was unmentioned, or worse, the women blamed for having "precipitated" the assault. Consider the overwhelming gender differences between the characteristics of the victims and the assailants that were routinely obscured by language which implied mutuality of victimization ("spouse abuse," "domestic violence," "family-related sexual abuse" and "sexual harassment"). Consider the tacit approval found in many studies of police and court minimization of women's victimization. Consider the methodologies that obscure that same victimization by, for example, soliciting information on assault in the presence of other family members. And finally, consider the studies which continued to puzzle over women's fear of crime in the face of the enormous official efforts to ignore, disbelieve and trivialize women's victimization.

Feminist criminology, by contrast, argues that the criminal justice system plays a major role in maintaining the place of women in male society. Feminist criminologists are not, by this approach, simply discussing the power of gender roles (though this power is undeniable) in the production of conformity and crime. Instead, feminist research is making it increasingly clear that gender stratification in partriarchal society is as powerful a system as class. Efforts must be undertaken to understand female and male deviance and conformity in the context of a ubiquitous system of male control of and power over women's labor and sexuality.

This work will not be easy. Efforts to construct a feminist model of delinquency and crime must first and foremost be sensitive to the situations of girls and women—including the special impact of poverty, racism and sexism on women's choices. And because it is vital to an understanding of offender's definitions of their own situations, choices, and behavior, time must be spent listening to girls and women. Finally, current qualitative research on the reaction of official agencies to female delinquency and crime must be conducted. Only in this way, can a full understanding of women's crime and official constructions and reactions to that behavior be achieved.

Failure to consider the existing empirical evidence about women's lives, or to seek information where none is available, can quickly lead to stereotyped thinking and theoretical dead ends. An example of this sort of flawed theory building was the early fascination with the notion that the women's movement was causing an increase in women's crime; a notion that is now more or less discredited. More recent notions, such as the idea that mothers' employment might somehow increase their daughter's crimes must also consult the actual life situations of women and girls.

But what does this have to do with "real" criminology, the study of the male offender and official reactions to him? What's in this for the criminologist who is not specifically interested in research on gender and crime? In my view, a lot. The early insights into male crime were largely gleaned by intensive field observation. This work needs to be re-thought with an eye toward the meaning of these behaviors within patriarchy. New work on male crime and official responses to this behavior must continually ask what the impact of this particular behavior is on the patriarchal order. Does it empower men at the expense of women? Does it replicate (in the underclass) the gender divisions of the dominant society or not? Does it encourage female reliance on male protection (dubious though it may be)? There are many new questions to ask about old data, many new avenues of inquiry opened once these issues are considered. And the work will be important.

And finally, a plea. Let's not see any more studies of "delinquency" and "crime" that either exclude female subjects or suggest that they will be considered in a future paper (which is often never written). If female behavior does not fit into the conceptual framework or the data on women "foul up" the results, then its time to rethink the theory.

# GENDER AND CRIME: TOWARD A
# GENDERED THEORY OF FEMALE OFFENDING

*Darrell Steffensmeier and Emilie Allan*

The principal goal of this article is to advance theory and research by advancing a gendered paradigm of female offending which builds on existing theory and on the growing body of work on gender; and by proposing a series of recommendations for further research. . . .

No satisfactorily unified theoretical framework has yet been developed for explaining female criminality and gender differences in crime. Criminologists disagree as to whether gender-neutral (i.e. traditional theories derived from male samples) or gender-specific theories (i.e. recent approaches derived from female samples and positing unique causal paths for female as compared to male criminality) are better suited to these tasks. We take the position that the traditional gender-neutral theories provide reasonable explanations of less serious forms of female and male criminality, and for gender differences in such crime categories. Their principal shortcoming is that they are not very informative about the specific ways in which differences in the lives of men and women contribute to gender differences in type, frequency, and context of criminal behavior. Gender-specific theories are likely to be even less adequate if they require separate explanations for female crime and male crime.

Here we build on a framework for a "gendered" approach begun elsewhere. This approach is compatible with the traditional, gender-neutral theories. The broad social forces suggested by traditional theories exert general causal influences on both male and female crime. But it is gender that mediates the manner in which those forces play out into sex differences in types, frequency, and contexts of crime involvements.

## Key Elements of a Gendered Approach

A gendered approach should include at least four key elements. First, the perspective should help explain not only female criminality but male criminality as well, by revealing how the organization of gender deters or shapes delinquency by females but encourages it by males. We use the term "organization of gender" to refer broadly to things gendered—norms, identities, arrangements, institutions, and relations by which human sexual dichotomy is transformed into something physically and socially different.

Second, a gendered perspective should account not only for gender differences in type and frequency of crime, but also for differences in the context of offending. Even when men and women commit the same statutory offense, the "gestalt" of their offending is frequently quite different. Because the gender differences in context are small for trivial or mild forms of lawbreaking, but large for violent and other serious forms of crime, contextual analysis can shed light on the gender differences for serious offenses—hitherto the most difficult to explain.

Third, compared to theories based on male crime, we need to consider several key ways in which women's routes to crime (especially serious crime) may differ from those of men. Building on the work of Daly and Steffensmeier, such differences include: (a) the more blurred boundaries between victim and victimization in women's than men's case histories; (b) women's exclusion from most lucrative crime opportunities; (c) women's ability to exploit sex as an illegal money-making service; (d) consequences (real or anticipated) of motherhood and child care; (e) the centrality of greater relational concerns among women, and the manner in which these both shape and allow women to be pulled into criminal involvements by men in their lives; (f) the greater need of street women for protection from predatory or exploitative males.

Fourth, the perspective should explore the extent to which gender differences in crime derive not only from complex social, historical, and cultural factors, but from biological and reproductive differences as well.

Figure 1 summarizes a gendered paradigm of offending that takes into account the four criteria enunciated above. We sketch here key features of this paradigm that affect men and women differently in terms of willingness and ability to commit crime.

## The Organization of Gender

The organization of gender together with sex differences in physical/sexual characteristics contributes to male and female differences in several types of relatively enduring characteristics that increase the probability of prosocial and altruistic response on the part of females but antisocial and predatory response on the part of males.

In the discussion that follows we elaborate briefly on five areas of life that inhibit female crime but encourage male crime: gender norms, moral development and affiliative

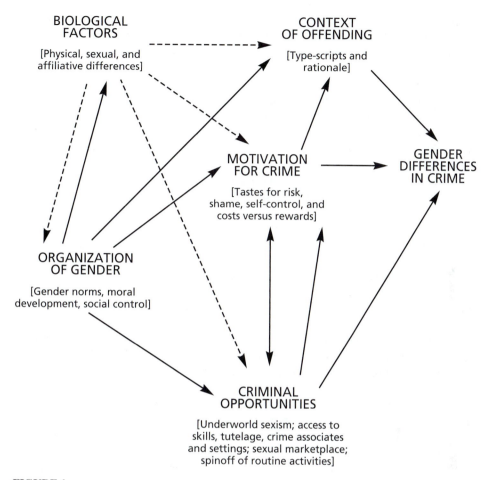

**FIGURE 1**

Gendered model of female offending and gender diiferences in crime. *Broken line* indicates weak effect; *solid line* signifies strong effect.

concerns, social control, physical strength and aggression, and sexuality. Gender differences in these areas condition gender differences in patterns of motivation and access to criminal opportunities, as well as gender differences in the type, frequency, and context of offending. These areas are not discrete, but rather they overlap and mutually reinforce one another.

### Gender norms

The greater taboos against female crime stem largely from two powerful focal concerns ascribed to women: (i) nurturant role obligations and (ii) female beauty and sexual virtue. In varied settings or situations, these concerns shape the constraints and opportunities of girls' and women's illicit activities.

Women are rewarded for their ability to establish and maintain relationships and to accept family obligations, and their identity tends to be derived from key males in their lives (e.g. father, husband). Derivative identity constrains deviance on the part of women involved with conventional males but encourages the criminal involvements of those who become accomplices of husbands or boyfriends. Greater child-rearing responsibilities further constrain female criminality.

Femininity stereotypes (e.g. weakness, submission, domestication, nurturance, and "ladylike" behavior) are basically incompatible with qualities valued in the criminal underworld. The cleavage between what is considered feminine and what is criminal is sharp, while the dividing line between what is considered masculine and what is criminal is often thin. Crime is almost always stigmatizing for females, and its potential cost to life chances is much greater than for males.

Expectations regarding sexuality and physical appearance reinforce greater female dependency as well as greater surveillance by parents and husbands. These expectations also shape the deviant roles available to women (e.g. sexual media or service roles). Moreover, fear of sexual victimization diverts women from crime-likely locations (bars, night-time streets) and reduces their opportunities to commit crimes.

### Moral development and amenability to affiliation

Gender differences in moral development and an apparent greater inherent readiness of women to learn parenting and nurturing predispose women toward an "ethic of care" that restrains women from violence and other criminal behavior injurious to others. Women are socialized not only to be more responsive to the needs of others but also to fear the threat of separation from loved ones. Such complex concerns inhibit women from undertaking criminal activities that might cause hurt to others and shape the "gestalt" of their criminality when they do offend.

In contrast, men who are conditioned toward status-seeking, yet marginalized from the world of work, may develop an amoral world view in which the "takers" gain superior status at the expense of the "givers." Such a moral stance obviously increases the likelihood of aggressive criminal behavior on the part of those who become "convinced that people are at each other's throats increasingly in a game of life that has no moral rules."

### Social control

Social control powerfully shapes women's relative willingness and ability to commit crime. Female misbehavior is more stringently monitored and corrected through negative stereotypes and sanctions. The greater supervision and control reduces female risk-taking and increases attachment to parents, teachers, and conventional friends, which in turn reduces influence by delinquent peers. Encapsulation with in the family and the production of "moral culture" restricts the freedom even of adult women to explore the temptations of the world.

### Physical strength and aggression

The demands of the crime environment for physical power and violence help account for the less serious nature and less frequent incidence of crimes by women compared to those by men. Women may lack the power, or may be perceived by themselves or by others as lacking the violent potential, for successful completion of certain types of crime or for protection of a major "score." Hustling small amounts of money or property protects female criminals against predators who might be attracted by larger amounts. Real or perceived vulnerability can also help account for female restriction to solo roles, or to roles as subordinate partners or accomplices in crime groups. This can be seen in a variety of female offense patterns, including the exigencies of the dependent prostitute-pimp relationship. Together, physical prowess and muscle are useful for committing crimes, for protection, for enforcing contracts, and for recruiting and managing reliable associates.

### Sexuality

Reproductive-sexual differences (especially when combined with sexual taboos and titillations of the society as a whole) contribute to the far greater sexual deviance and infidelity among males. Women, on the other hand, have expanded opportunities for financial gain through prostitution and related illicit sexual roles. The possibilities in this arena reduce the need to commit the serious property crimes that so disproportionately involve males.

Although female offenders may use their sexuality to gain entry into male criminal organizations, such exploitation of male stereotypes is likely to limit their criminal opportunities within the group to roles organized around female attributes. The sexual dimension may also heighten the potential for sexual tension which can be resolved only if the female aligns herself with one man sexually, becoming "his woman."

Even prostitution—often considered a female crime—is essentially a male-dominated or -controlled criminal enterprise. Police, pimps, businessmen who employ prostitutes, and clients—virtually all of whom are male—control, in various ways, the conditions under which the prostitute works.

## Access to Criminal Opportunity

The factors above—gender norms, social control, and the like—restrict female access to criminal opportunity, which in turn both limits and shapes female participation in crime. Women are also less likely than men to have access to crime opportunities as a spin-off of legitimate roles and routine activities. Women are less likely to hold jobs as truck driver, dockworker, or carpenter that would provide opportunities for theft, drug dealing, fencing, and other illegitimate activities. In contrast, women have considerable opportunity for commission, and thus for surveillance and arrest for petty forms of fraud and embezzlement.

Females are most restricted in terms of access to underworld crimes that are organized and lucrative. Institutional sexism in the underworld severely limits female involvement in crime groups, ranging from syndicates to loosely structured groups. As in the upperworld, females in the underworld are disadvantaged in terms of selection and recruitment, in the range of career paths and access to them, and in opportunities for tutelage, skill development, and rewards.

## Motivation

Gender norms, social control, lack of physical strength, and moral and relational concerns also limit female willingness to participate in crime at the subjective level—by contributing to gender differences in tastes for risk, likelihood of shame or embarrassment, self-control, and assessment of costs versus rewards of crime. Motivation is distinct from opportunity, but the two often intertwine, as when opportunity enhances temptation. As in legitimate enterprise, being able tends to make one more willing, just as being willing increases the prospects for being able. Like male offenders, female offenders gravitate to those activities that are easily available, are within their skills, provide a satisfactory return, and carry the fewest risks.

Criminal motivations and involvements are also shaped by gender differences in risk preferences and in styles of risk-taking. For example, women take greater risks to sustain valued relationships, whereas males take greater risks for reasons of status or competitive advantage. Criminal motivation is suppressed by the female ability to foresee threats to life chances and by the relative unavailability of type scripts that could channel females in unapproved behaviors.

## Context of Offending

Many of the most profound differences between the offenses committed by men and women involve the context of offending, a point neglected by quantitative studies based on aggregate and survey data. "Context" refers to the characteristics of a particular offense, including both the circumstances and the nature of the act. Contextual characteristics include, for example, the setting, whether the offense was committed with others, the offender's role in initiating and committing the offense, the type of victim, the victim-offender relationship, whether a weapon was used, the extent of injury, the value or type of property destroyed or stolen, and the purpose of the offense. Even when males and females participate in the same types of crimes, the "gestalt" of their actions may differ markedly. Moreover, the more serious the offense, the greater the contextual differences by gender.

A powerful example of the importance of contextual considerations is found in the case of spousal murders, for which the female share of offending is quite high—at least one third, and perhaps as much as one half. Starting with Wolfgang's classic study of homicide, a number of writers propose that husbands and wives have equal potential for violence. However, Dobash et al. point out that the context of spousal violence is dramatically different for men and women. Compared to men, women are far more likely to kill only after a prolonged period of abuse, when they are in fear for their lives and have exhausted all alternatives. A number of patterns of wife-killing by husbands are rarely if ever found when wives kill husbands: murder-suicides, family massacres, stalking, and murder in response to spouse infidelity.

In common delinquency, female prevalence approaches that of males in simple forms of delinquency like hitting others or stealing from stores or schools, but girls are far less likely to use a weapon or to intend serious injury to their victims, to steal things they cannot use, and to steal from building sites or break into buildings.

Similarly, when females commit traditional male crimes like burglary, they are less likely to be solitary, more likely to serve as an accomplice (e.g. drop-off driver), and less likely to receive an equal share of proceeds. Also, female burglaries involve less planning and are more spontaneous, and they are more likely to occur in daytime in residences where no one is at home and with which they have prior familiarity as an acquaintance, maid, or the like.

## Application of Gendered Perspective to Patterns of Female Crime

The utility of a gendered perspective can be seen in its ability to explain both female and male patterns of criminal involvement as well as gender differences in crime. The perspective predicts, and finds, that female participation is highest for those crimes most consistent with traditional norms and for which females have the most opportunity, and lowest for those crimes that diverge the most from traditional gender norms and for which females have little opportunity. Let us briefly review some examples of property, violent, and public order offending patterns that can be better understood from a gendered perspective.

In the area of property crimes we have already noted that the percentage of female arrests is highest for the minor offenses like small thefts, shoplifting and passing bad checks—offenses compatible with traditional female roles in making family purchases. The high share of arrests for embezzlement reflects female employment segregation: women constitute about 90% of lower level bookkeepers and bank tellers (those most likely to be arrested for embezzlement), but slightly less than half of all accountants or auditors. Further, women tend to embezzle to protect their families or valued relationships, while men tend to embezzle to protect their status.

Despite Simon's claim that female involvement in white collar crime was on the increase, in fact it is almost nonexistent in more serious occupational and/or business crimes, like insider trading, price-fixing, restraint of trade, toxic waste dumping, fraudulent product commerce, bribery, and official corruption, as well as large-scale governmental crimes (for example, the Iran-Contra affair and the Greylord scandal). Even when similar on-the-job opportunities for theft exist, women are still less likely to commit crime.

The lowest percentage of female involvement is found for serious property crimes whether committed on the "street" such as burglary and robbery or in the "suite" such as insider trading or price-fixing. These sorts of offenses are very much at odds with traditional feminine stereotypes, and ones to which women have very limited access. When women act as solo perpetrators, the typical robbery is a "wallet-sized" theft by a prostitute or addict. However, females frequently become involved in such crimes as accomplices to males, particularly in roles that at once exploit women's sexuality and reinforce their traditional subordination to men.

Female violence, although apparently at odds with female gender norms of gentleness and passivity, is also closely tied to the organization of gender. Unlike males, females rarely kill or assault strangers or acquaintances; instead, the female's victim tends to be a male intimate or a child, the offense generally takes place within the home, the victim is frequently drunk, and self-defense or extreme depression is often a motive. For women to kill, they generally must see their situation as life-threatening, as affecting the physical or emotional well-being of themselves or their children.

The linkage between female crime and the gendered paradigm of Figure 1 is perhaps most evident in the case of certain public order offenses with a high percentage of female involvement, particularly the sex-related categories of prostitution and juvenile runaways—the only offense categories where female arrest rates exceed those of males. The high percentage of female arrests in these two categories reflects both gender differences in marketability of sexual services and the continuing patriarchal sexual double standard. Although customers must obviously outnumber prostitutes, they are less likely to be sanctioned. Similarly, although self-report studies show male rates of runaways to be as high as female rates, suspicion of sexual involvement makes female runaways more likely to be arrested.

Female substance abuse (as with other patterns of female crime) often stems from relational concerns or involvements, beginning in the context of teenage dating or following introduction to drugs by husbands or boyfriends. Women tend to be less involved in heavy drinking or hard drug use—those drugs most intimately tied to drug subcultures and the underworld more generally. Female addicts are less likely to have other criminal involvements prior to addiction, so the amplification of income-oriented crime is greater for female drug users. Female addict crimes are mainly prostitution, reselling narcotics or assisting male drug dealers, and property crimes such as shoplifting, forgery, and burglary.

## Advantages of Paradigm

A gendered approach helps to clarify the gendered nature of both female and male offending patterns. For women, "doing gender" preempts criminal involvement or directs it into scripted paths. For example, prostitution draws on and affirms femininity, while violence draws on and affirms masculinity.

At present it is unclear whether nontraditional roles for women will contribute to higher or lower rates of female offending. Traditional roles constrain most women from crime but may expose others to greater risks for criminal involvement. Wives playing traditional roles in patriarchal relationships appear to be at greatest risk both for victimization and for committing spousal homicide. Similarly, women emotionally dependent on criminal men are more easily persuaded to "do it all for love." (Note, nevertheless, that men are also more easily persuaded by other men.) Cross-cultural differences complicate the issue further. For example, among gypsies, traditional gender roles prevail and male dominance is absolute. Yet, because gypsy women do practically all the work and earn most of the money, their culture dictates a large female-to-male involvement in thievery.

A gendered approach can also help explain both stability and variability in the gender effect. A growing body of historical research indicates that the gender differences in quality and quantity of crime described here closely parallel those that have prevailed since at least the thirteenth century. Even where variability does exist across time, the evidence suggests that changes in the female percentage of offending (i) are limited mainly to minor property crimes or mild forms of delinquency and (ii) are due to structural changes other than more equalitarian gender roles such as shifts in economic marginality of women, expanded availability of female-type crime opportunities, and greater formalization of social control. The considerable stability in the gender gap for offending can be explained in part by historical durability of the organization of gender. Certainly for recent decades, research suggests that the core elements of gender roles and relationships have changed little, if at all. Underlying physical/sexual differences (whether actual or perceived) may also play a part. Human groups, for all their cultural variation, follow basic human forms. . . .

Our knowledge about fundamental issues in the study of gender and crime has expanded greatly with the proliferation of studies over the past several decades, although significant gaps still exist. Given the relatively low frequency and less serious nature of female crime, expanding research on female offending may seem hard to justify. But research on the gendered nature of crime contributes to the understanding of male as well as female crime. Furthermore, the study of gender and crime is a productive arena for exploring the nature of gender stratification and the organization of gender more generally.

# CONTEMPORARY RETROSPECTIVE ON FEMINIST THEORIES

## LOOKING BACK, LOOKING AHEAD: ASSESSING CONTEMPORARY FEMINIST CRIMINOLOGY[1]

*Amanda Burgess-Proctor, Oakland University*

Given the ubiquitous nature of the sex differential in crime and in deviance in general, any generalizing theory must point to factors which operate with very different effects upon men and women or, alternatively, that their like deviance is dealt with in very different manners by facets of the social system. Indeed whether a particular theory explains feminine delinquency as well as masculine and offers within its framework an explanation for the apparent difference in rats is often a useful touchstone of its validity. (Heidensohn, 1968, pp. 164–165)

From its inception until as recently as the early 1970s, modern criminology existed almost entirely free from the influence of feminist thought. As a result, theories developed to explain criminal behavior also were largely uninformed by feminism, until 1968 when Frances Heidensohn "launched the first missile" of feminist criticism at mainstream criminology (Simpson & Gibbs, 2006, p. 269). Pioneering feminist criminologists like Heidensohn, Dorie Klein (1973), Freda Adler (1975), Rita Simon (1975), and Carol Smart (1976) strongly criticized existing criminological theories, lamenting the near total absence of gender from explanations of offending behavior. Although many of these early criticisms were advanced by liberal feminists whose ideas about sex role socialization and criminality have been dismissed by radical and socialist feminist criminologists more recently (Daly & Chesney-Lind, 1988; Kruttschnitt, 1996; see also Miller, 1986), concerns about the absence of gender from criminological scholarship still resonate today.

The purpose of this essay is to assess the state of contemporary feminist criminological theory. I begin by providing a brief overview of the theoretical foundation of feminist criminology in order to answer the question, "What is feminist criminology?" In this section I outline three important feminist criticisms of traditional criminological theories as well as solutions offered by feminist scholarship. Next, I outline some of the criticisms that, in turn, have been directed at feminist criminology. I then provide examples of contemporary empirical investigations that aim to develop, refine, and test feminist criminological theories. Finally, I offer suggestions for theoretical advancement in contemporary feminist criminology and discuss the relevance of this advancement for criminal justice policy.

### Theoretical Foundation: What Is Feminist Criminology?

It is inaccurate to think of "feminist criminology" as a single theory, like differential association or general strain theory, for example. Instead, feminist criminology is better understood as a collection of theories, perspectives, and methodologies that consider how gendered social relations influence the commission of crime, the processing of offenders in

---

[1]Many thanks to Hillary Potter for her insightful comments on an earlier draft of this manuscript.

the criminal justice system, the behavior and application of criminal laws, and other social processes related to issues of crime and justice. Indeed, feminist theories have been offered to explain a wide variety of criminological phenomena, from offending behaviors like rape and intimate partner violence to processing decisions including arrest and sentencing. Moreover, feminist criminology—like feminism itself—consists of multiple perspectives, each having distinct assumptions about the source (or sources) of women's oppression (Barak, Flavin, & Leighton, 2001; Daly & Chesney-Lind, 1988; Price & Sokoloff, 2004). For example, liberal feminists attribute women's oppression primarily to gender role socialization, whereas radical feminists fault patriarchy and male-dominated social relations (Burgess-Proctor, 2006, for a review). Although the diverse perspectives found in feminist criminology share commonalities in that they "focus on women's interests, are overtly political, and strive to present a new vision of equality and social justice" (Flavin, 2001, p. 272; see also Rafter & Heidensohn, 1995), the multiplicity of perspectives nonetheless make feminist criminology somewhat challenging to succinctly define.

Instead, it may be more useful to consider that a primary goal of feminist criminology is to address and correct the historical exclusion of gender (and other sources of inequality such as race/ethnicity, class, and sexuality) from mainstream criminological scholarship. To that end, feminist criminology offers three important criticisms of traditional criminological theories. These criticisms, along with the theoretical solutions offered by feminist criminological scholarship, provide insight into the theoretical foundation of feminist criminology.

### Feminist criticism #1: The generalizability issue

*What is the problem?*   The first important feminist criticism of traditional criminological theories is that they are presumed to explain both men's and women's offending. Daly and Chesney-Lind (1988) call this approach to theory building the "generalizability problem" (p. 508). It is well established that, almost without exception, most criminological theories were developed by male scholars to explain crimes committed by men and boys, and were tested using male-only samples (Belknap, 2001; Chesney-Lind & Pasko, 2004a; Daly & Chesney-Lind, 1988; Flavin, 2001; Miller, 2004; Morash, 1999; Simpson, 1989). Thus, the question for feminists is whether and/or to what extent these theories can explain women's offending. In other words, the problem is that male-centered theories are generalized to the entire population of offenders and are uncritically presented by their proponents as being applicable to all types of offending behavior by both men and women (see, for example, Akers, 1997; Gottfredson & Hirschi, 1990). Absent from these theories, though, is consideration of whether the etiology of women's offending is better explained by alternative, gender-specific theories. Regarding the issue of generalizability, the question for feminist criminologists can be put simply: "Do theories of men's crime apply to women? Can the logic of such theories be modified to include women?" (Daly & Chesney-Lind, 1988, p. 514).

Notwithstanding the fundamental external validity problems inherent in making claims about groups that one has not directly sampled or studied, mainstream criminological theories have been criticized by feminist scholars for failing to consider how gender inequality shapes opportunities and motivations for committing crime. For example, Daly and Chesney-Lind (1988) question what it means "to develop a gender-neutral theory of crime . . . when neither the social order nor the social structure of crime is gender-neutral" (p. 516). In other words, given that traditional criminological theories are posited to be gender-neutral (and universal) yet have been developed without consideration of how gender structures human behavior, what are the implications of theories that ignore gender in the face of real-life gender inequality and discrimination? Clearly, such theories lack relevance in explaining the behavior of individuals—both male and female—whose opportunities and motivations for engaging in crime are structured by gender.

In a different vein, feminist criminologists also have criticized mainstream criminological scholarship for failing to capitalize on the contributions gender-based explanations can offer the field. For example, Morash (1999) notes that "gender-focused theories are particularly relevant to explaining crime . . . [because] they stimulate a reconceptualization of crime, and related new approaches to measuring it. . . . An important result of revised concepts and increased understanding of the effect of gender on crime is implications for the choice of interventions to prevent and control crime" (p. 454). Thus, theories that fail to account for the influence of gender may not be able to adequately inform crime prevention and control strategies.

Specific criminological theories have been criticized by feminist scholars for ignoring gender differences in the etiology of offending. For example, Belknap (2001) observes that strain theory, as developed by Merton (1938), Cohen (1955), and Cloward and Ohlin (1960), considers strain only in the context of economic inequality, and that class-based explanations lose relevance for explaining female offending once it is considered that women are the most impoverished group in nearly every Western society, yet commit far fewer crimes than men. In other words, economic strains likely do not motivate female offenders to commit crime in the same way that they motivate male offenders, and therefore are not generalizable to women's experiences. Criticizing perhaps the most famous "general" theory of crime, Belknap (2001) points out that Gottfredson and Hirschi's (1990) self-control theory ignores gender dynamics within the family setting, where, according to Gottfredson and Hirschi, "proper" discipline is thought to ensure the development of self-control in children (see also Flavin, 2001). Finally, Morash (1999) faults Akers's (1997) theory of social learning and social structure for failing to recognize that "social structure not only produces differential learning, but also produces differences in power, opportunities, and resources" for men and women (p. 457). That is, though Akers's "general theory" (like Gottfredson and Hirschi's "general theory") purports to explain all types of deviant behavior, it fails to consider the influence of gender on men's and women's criminal offending.

***What theoretical solutions does feminist criminology offer?***   According to Daly and Chesney-Lind (1988), the absence of women's experiences from mainstream criminological theories cannot be rectified by a simple "add women and stir" approach (see also Barak et al., 2001), but rather "a reconceptualization of analytic categories is necessary" (p. 504). Put differently, simply appending women's experiences onto the experiences of men does not constitute theoretical advancement. Rather, criminological theoretical advancement occurs through the reconceptualization of key concepts and ideas (Morash, 1999). Thus, criminologists must not engage in the uncritical application of existing theories to women's experiences, but instead should identify new theoretical concepts and propositions that are informed by feminist insights (Daly & Chesney-Lind, 1988).

An example of the type of reconceptualization advocated by feminist criminologists is "blurred boundaries" (Daly & Maher, 1998), a term that refers to the confluence of women's victimization and criminalization experiences. Recent feminist explanations of female offending propose that women's previous experiences with victimization are inextricably linked with their later offending behaviors (e.g., Gaarder & Belknap, 2002; Miller, 2004). This proposition states that "criminalization is connected to women's subordinate position in society where victimization by violence coupled with economic marginality related to race, class, and gender all too often blur the boundaries between victims and offenders" (Gilfus, 1992, p. 86). A related example is "feminist pathways" research (Belknap, 2001). Feminist pathways studies reconceptualize ideas used in traditional life-course theories (for example, as advanced by Sampson & Laub, 1992) by using women's and girls' voices to identify life-course events that may particularly influence female offending (Belknap, 2001). For instance, Richie (1996) used feminist pathways analysis to develop her theory of gender entrapment, which she uses to explain criminal offending among black battered women. These theoretical advancements respond to the first feminist criticism of main-stream criminological theory (the issue of generalizability) by reconceptualizing existing mainstream theoretical perspectives to reflect feminist insights.

### Feminist criticism # 2: The gender gap issue

***What is the problem?***  The second important feminist criticism of traditional crimi-nological theories is that they fail to adequately explain the gender disparity in offending, or what Daly and Chesney-Lind (1988) call the "gender-ratio problem" (p. 508). Perhaps the most robust of all criminological findings is that men are more likely to commit crimes than women, yet traditional criminological theories have been unable to adequately explain why this gender gap exists (Britton, 2000; Daly & Chesney-Lind, 1988; Liu & Kaplan, 1999; Miller, 2004). Extending the issue of generalizability, then, feminist criminolo-gists assert that even if it can be shown that the same processes explain male and female offending, a void remains when it comes to explaining why men offend in greater num-bers than women. The questions for feminist criminologists, then, are: "Why are women less likely than men to be involved in crime? Conversely, why are men more crime prone than women? What explains [these] gender differences?" (Daly & Chesney-Lind, 1988, p. 515). Feminist criminologists have observed that the exclusion of gender from mainstream theories of crime is particularly regrettable given that gender is such an impor-tant predictor of crime (Belknap, 2001; Daly & Chesney-Lind, 1988). That is, attempts to identify processes that explain men's and women's offending still leave unanswered the question of why there exists a gender gap in offending.

Further, feminists also recognize that although women as a group are less likely to offend than men, black women have higher levels of involvement in offending than white women (e.g., Belknap, 2001; Daly, 1997). Thus, the gender-ratio problem becomes more complicated when considered within the context of race/ethnicity (and class), further underscoring the failure of mainstream criminological theories to explain race- and class-based variations in gendered patterns of offending. As a result, gender—both alone and in conjunction with race/ethnicity—remains undertheorized in mainstream criminology.

***What theoretical solutions does feminist criminology offer?***  The absence of suffi-cient explanations for the gender gap in offending has prompted feminist criminologists to develop new theories that can account for variation in men's and women's offending rates. One such theory is power-control theory, as developed by John Hagan and his col-leagues (Hagan, 1989; Hagan, Gillis, & Simpson, 1985; Hagan, Simpson, & Gillis, 1987).

Power-control theory combines insights from Marxist and feminist approaches to offer a structural explanation for the gender gap in offending. Specifically, power-control theory suggests that girls are less deviant than boys because they are subjected to greater parental (specifically, *maternal*) social control that emphasizes and reinforces their risk-avoidant behavior (Hagan et al., 1985, 1987). Specifically, Hagan and his colleagues argue that daughters in "patriarchal" families, in which the father is the authority figure and the mother is not employed outside the home, are subjected to greater parental control than daughters in "egalitarian" families, in which both parents share authority and work outside of the home, and consequently engage in less deviant behavior (Hagan et al., 1987). Though power-control theory is an example of feminist-oriented theoretical reconceptualization, it has also been criticized by feminists for suggesting that girls' criminality is rooted in their mothers' liberation and workforce participation (e.g., Chesney-Lind & Pasko, 2004a).

A second feminist theory that addresses the gender-gap issue is Messerchmidt's structured action theory (Messerschmidt, 1993, 1997; see also Miller, 2002). Structured action theory, simply put, states that crime is associated with power. One key proposition of this theory is that because women are excluded from gaining broad-based social power, and because crime and power are linked, men will be more likely than women to engage in criminal behavior (Messerschmidt, 1997). Moreover, men's tendencies to engage in criminality can be explained in terms of their efforts to "do gender." Thus, a second proposition of structured action theory is that crime is one means for men to express their masculinity (Messerschmidt, 1997). According to a structured action approach, then, "Women and men 'do gender' or behave in gendered ways, in response to normative beliefs about femininity and masculinity. . . . [T]his approach has been incorporated into feminist accounts of crime as a means of explaining differences in men's and women's offending . . . and can help account for men's greater involvement in particular types of crimes (e.g., violence)" (Miller, 2004, p. 54; see also Miller, 2002). These theoretical advancements respond to the second feminist criticism of mainstream criminological theory (the issue of the gender gap in offending) by offering explanations for the criticism.

### Feminist criticism #3: The appropriate methodology issue

*What is the problem?* The third important feminist criticism of mainstream criminological theories is that they have been developed and tested using quantitative methodologies, which arguably are not well suited to generating detailed descriptions about the ways in which gender structures criminal behavior. Although quantitative analyses formed the foundation of early efforts at answering the gender-ratio problem (Kruttschnitt, 1996) and may have a measure of success in attempting to answer the "generalizability problem" (e.g., see Liu & Kaplan, 1999), they are not designed to provide detailed, descriptive information about the gender–crime relationship. However, these quantitative methodologies are given priority in mainstream criminology, thereby stunting opportunities for theory building using qualitative methods (Daly & Chesney-Lind, 1988). Unfortunately, "quantitative advances have outrun theoretical developments pertaining to the gender-crime relationship. Accordingly, it is time to start focusing on the question of what observed gender differences *mean* in terms of the life course experiences that ultimately result in patterned differences in offending" (Kruttschnitt, 1996, p. 154, emphasis added).

The problem, as feminists have pointed out, is that quantitative analyses often fail to capture important contextual information that can shed light on the impact of gender on offending (Daly & Chesney-Lind, 1988; Morash, 1999). Although feminist criminologists interested in placing offending in a gendered context may wish to do so using qualitative methodologies that make use of in-depth interviews and observations, these methods often are ignored, trivialized, or dismissed within mainstream criminology in favor of more highly valued quantitative approaches (Daly & Chesney-Lind, 1988). Still, feminists argue, criminological theoretical development sometimes necessitates the use of qualitative techniques:

> The problem of measures that fail to validly reflect crime can sometimes be solved by using qualitative data as the basis for the development of multidimensional, quantitative measures; however, in some case only qualitative data adequately reflect the phenomenon being studied. (Morash, 1999, pp. 454–455)

An example of the failure of quantitative methodologies to "adequately reflect the phenomenon being studied" is the proposition that perpetration of intimate partner violence (IPV) is gender-symmetric. Using a survey instrument called the Conflict Tactics Scale (CTS), Straus and Gelles (1990) and their colleagues (Stets & Straus, 1990) have conducted several broad-based national surveys that measure incidents of violence between intimate partners. Comparing the number of violent incidents reported by men and women, these and other researchers who use the CTS have concluded that women are as violent as men, leading to the formulation of gender-symmetric theories of IPV (e.g., see Dutton, 2006). However, as feminist critics have repeatedly countered (DeKeseredy & Dragiewicz, 2007; DeKeseredy & MacLean, 1990; Dobash & Dobash, 1992; Dobash, Dobash, Wilson, & Daly, 1992; Johnson, 1998; Morash, 1999), the CTS merely "counts blows" and fails to place women's use of IPV in its appropriate context (for example, by considering when women use violence against their partners in self-defense). By simply summing aggressive acts, the CTS "inadequately captures the seriousness of wife abuse, and exaggerates the seriousness of women's abuse of men" (Morash, 1999, p. 435). Thus, IPV theories that are based solely on quantitative data may miss important contextual and structural factors that shape men's and women's use of violence.

***What theoretical solutions does feminist criminology offer?*** All of this is *not* to say that quantitative methods have no place in feminist criminology or are inherently antifeminist (or, conversely, that qualitative methods are automatically feminist). Indeed, Kruttschnitt (1996) demonstrates the merits of quantitative methodologies for developing and testing gender-based theories of crime, while Johnson (1998) uses data from the Violence Against Women Survey (VAWS) to underscore that statistical data are indeed useful in understanding violence against women. Still, quantitative methodologies alone may fail to capture important contextual information necessary for the development of theory, feminist or otherwise. Thus, one solution is to develop theories using mixed-methods designs, for example, by developing quantitative variables derived from open-ended responses (Kruttschnitt, 1996; Morash, 1999). An alternative strategy is to supplement quantitative data with descriptive data obtained by qualitative methods (Kruttschnitt, 1996). In contrast, Daly and Chesney-Lind (1988) advocate the development of "gender-linked" theories using strictly qualitative methods that allow criminologists to "get our hands dirty" and "plunge more deeply into the social world of girls and women" (p. 519).

For example, Miller's (1986) ethnographic study of female street hustlers in Milwaukee led to important theoretical contributions. Among Miller's most critical discoveries was that women are recruited into offending behaviors by their integration into "deviant street networks" (p. 35). As suggested by Daly and Chesney-Lind (1988), Miller "gets her hands dirty" by investigating how women's social worlds shape their participation in illegal work, and how their social worlds are modeled by structural and cultural changes at the macro-social level. With respect to IPV research, feminist scholars express preference for theoretical frameworks that consider the context within which IPV occurs (e.g., Dobash & Dobash, 1979, 1992). For example, regarding the limited selection of "options" available to battered women in isolated rural areas, Websdale (1998) remarks, "Rural battered women's 'choices' often boil down to remaining with abusers and enduring/resisting violence, leaving the abuser and enduring poverty under the welfare system, or leaving the abuser and entering wage work in a hostile gendered capitalist economy" (p. 171). Such frameworks are often, but not always, developed using qualitative methods. Thus, these theoretical advancements respond to the third feminist criticism of mainstream criminological theory (the appropriate methodology issue) by relying upon methodological strategies that can offer a detailed, nuanced, and contextualized picture of the relationship between gender and crime.

## Empirical Evaluations

As described earlier, feminist criminology consists of an array of theories and perspectives that consider gender (as well as race/ethnicity, class, sexuality, and other systems of power) in the study of crime, law, and deviance. However, the multifaceted nature of feminist criminology does not mean that feminist theories are empirically untestable. In fact, the opposite is true: the last decade in particular has seen a proliferation of empirical work aimed at developing, advancing, and testing feminist criminological theories.

Some of these empirical evaluations address the first feminist criticism of traditional criminological theories: the generalizability issue. Recall that some feminist scholarship aimed at developing gender-specific theories of women's offending uses the concept of "blurred boundaries" to demonstrate how women's prior victimization experiences are inextricably linked with their later offending and use of violence (Daly & Maher, 1998). Recent feminist empirical investigations offer support for this idea. For example, Gaarder and Belknap (2002) conducted in-depth interviews with 22 girls incarcerated in an adult women's prison in order to identify their pathways to crime. Their analysis reveals that intersecting sources of oppression (e.g., race/ethnicity, class, gender, and sexuality) are salient in the lives of these young women, and that many of their lives are characterized by a confluence of victimization and offending (Gaarder & Belknap, 2002). Similarly, Makarios (2007) uses prospective cohort data to examine the relationship between race, abuse, and girls' use of violence, and observes that abuse is a stronger predictor of female violence than male violence (although this effect does not vary across race).

Other empirical evaluations address the second feminist criticism of traditional criminological theories: the gender gap issue. One particularly good example of this type of research is Bufkin's (1999) study of bias crimes, which uses the concepts found in Messerschmidt's structured action theory to account for men's greater participation in bias crimes. In her analysis of both quantitative and qualitative data, Bufkin concludes that bias crime is one means by which men "do gender." In other words, men attempt to express their masculinity by assaulting and victimizing people who contradict the hegemonic masculine ideal (e.g., women, gays and lesbians, and racial and ethnic minorities). She also uses this theoretical framework to address female bias crime, suggesting that such offenses are used by women as a means of gaining power that routinely is denied to them in a patriarchal society. Bufkin therefore theorizes that bias crimes are an attempt to reproduce hegemonic masculine ideals, and thus are more likely to be committed by men than women.

Additionally, Heimer and DeCoster (1999) combine elements of differential association and feminist theories to advance a gendered theory of violent delinquency. An empirical test of their theoretical model using data from the National Youth Survey suggests that violent delinquency is a gendered phenomenon. In particular, the authors conclude that

> girls are less violent than boys because they are influenced more strongly by bonds to family, learn fewer violent definitions, and are taught that violence is inconsistent with the meaning of being female. These mechanisms appear to be so effective among girls that direct, overt controls like supervision and coercive discipline contribute little to the explanation of variation in female violence, while they are important for explaining variation in male violence. (p. 303)

Still other empirical evaluations address the third important feminist criticism of traditional criminological theories: the appropriate methodology issue. Contemporary feminist scholars have heeded the call to utilize qualitative (and mixed-methods) designs to develop and test a variety of feminist criminological theories. As previously mentioned, Richie's (1996) life-history analysis of incarcerated battered women and the resulting gender entrapment theory she develops to explain criminality among black battered women is an excellent example of this type of research. Another is Maher's (1997) ethnography of women drug users, an exemplary feminist study in which the author develops a theoretical framework that situates women's participation in the street-level drug economy within intersecting systems of race/ethnicity, class, and gender.

Finally, some empirical evaluations of feminist theories concern issues related to gender and crime more broadly, such as the relationship between gender equality and intimate partner violence, rape, and other forms of violence against women. For example, Yodanis's (2004) cross-national study of violence against women makes an important theoretical contribution. Feminists assert that violence against women is higher in societies in which gender inequality is high, and in which women occupy low social status relative to men. Noting the importance of conducting international and comparative analyses, Yodanis uses data from the International Crime Victims Survey and from the United Nations to examine the relationship between gender inequality, fear, and violence against women. She finds that, in accordance with feminist theory, sexual violence against women in a particular country is negatively correlated with women's status in that country. "The results show that social structural characteristics, particularly women's access to and position in social institutions, are related to rates of sexual violence, and that rates of sexual violence, in turn, are related to women's fear" (p. 672). Similarly, Martin et al. (2006) test feminist models of rape using data from U.S. cities and discover that rape rates are lower in cities where women enjoy higher absolute status (e.g., have higher incomes, percentage of college degrees, labor force participation, and occupational status). Paradoxically, the authors also find rape rates to be *higher* in cities having higher gender equality, which they suggest is indicative of a "backlash effect" (p. 333). Martin and colleagues conclude that, taken together, results of their analysis offer support for a socialist feminist model of rape that integrates class- and gender-based explanations of women's oppression.

## Critiques

Previously I outlined three important feminist criticisms of traditional criminological theories. Feminist criminology has, in turn, received its own fair share of criticism, though the most intense criticism of feminist criminology has come not from mainstream criminologists but from other feminists. Of course, some mainstream criminologists have been critical of feminist scholarship, often on the grounds that it is unscientific, lacks objectivity, has political underpinnings, or is otherwise a threat to "authentic" social science (e.g., see Dutton, 2006). However, more pointed (and legitimate) criticisms have been leveled against feminist criminology from within feminist circles.

For example, writing at the beginning of feminism's third wave in the 1980s and 1990s,[2] feminist scholars lamented advancement of the "liberation hypothesis" a decade before to explain women's offending (e.g., Belknap, 2001; Daly & Chesney-Lind, 1988; Miller, 1986). In the mid-1970s, liberal feminists including Freda Adler (1975) and Rita Simon (1975) hypothesized that the gender gap in offending could be explained by the fact that women's traditional societal roles limit their opportunities for committing crime. Accordingly, an important proposition of this hypothesis is that women's offending rates eventually will converge with those of men due to women's "liberation" through employment outside the home and/or entrance into the managerial and professional ranks—in other words, as women become more like men. However, women's offending rates have remained relatively stable over the last three decades, thereby discrediting this explanation (Belknap, 2001; Kruttschnitt, 1996). For example, after analyzing FBI arrest statistics for men and women at three points in time—1960, 1975, and 1990—Steffensmeier and Allan (1996) conclude:

> Although some authors profess to see major changes over time in the female percentage of arrests (e.g. Adler 1975, Simon 1975), the numbers for 1960, 1975, and 1990 are perhaps more remarkable for their similarity than for their differences. For all three periods, the female share of arrests for most categories was 15% or less and was typically smallest for the most serious offenses." (p. 463)

Steffensmeier and Allan further note that the FBI arrest data are corroborated by official victimization data and self-report survey data, both of which suggest that women's participation in serious offending has remained consistently lower than men's over time.

Similarly, Messerschmidt (2002) recognized that, as in the case of the female gang members he studied, women and girls who commit violent crime do not necessarily exhibit masculine characteristics. Critics argued that the liberation hypothesis was especially damaging because it created a moral panic over a new "female offender" that was "more myth than

---

[2]Historically, the feminist movement is divided into three eras or "waves." The first wave of feminism began in the United States with the birth of the abolitionist and women's suffrage movements in the mid-to-late 1800s. The women's liberation and civil rights movements of the 1960s and 1970s marked the onset of feminism's second wave. Currently, feminism is in the midst of its third wave, which began during the 1980s and 1990s.

reality," and shifted attention away from more radical feminist criminological approaches focused on men's control of women (Simpson, 1989, p. 610). As noted, these same criticisms also have been directed at more contemporary theories deemed to be mere variations of the liberation hypothesis, including power-control theory (Chesney-Lind & Pasko, 2004a).

More recently, feminists of color, lesbian feminists, and other feminists who felt marginalized within the mainstream feminist movement have condemned the hegemony of white women's experiences both in the broader feminist movement and in feminist criminology specifically (Collins, 2000; Daly & Stephens, 1995; Zinn & Dill, 1996). These scholars, also writing during the genesis of third-wave feminism, recognized that mainstream feminism essentialized women by allowing the experiences of privileged, white women to represent those of all women (Burgess-Proctor, 2006). Just as pioneering feminists protested the absence of gender from mainstream criminology, contemporary feminists have protested the absence of race/ethnicity, class, sexuality, nationality, and other locations of inequality from feminist criminology (Britton, 2000; Daly & Stephens, 1995; Potter, 2006). Consequently, contemporary feminist criminologists have advocated for integrated, intersectional theoretical frameworks that attend to other systems of power besides simply gender (Barak, et al., 2001; Britton, 2000; Burgess-Proctor, 2006; Daly & Stephens, 1995; Flavin, 2001; Potter, 2006; Simpson & Gibbs, 2006), as described in the following section.

## Theoretical Refinements

In the roughly 40 years since feminists first made inroads into criminology, there have been tremendous theoretical advancements, as demonstrated by the examples outlined in this essay. In fact, today entire journals are devoted to publishing feminist criminological scholarship, a scenario that was unimaginable during the formative years of feminist criminology. These are remarkable achievements, to be sure, but there is always room for improvement. I have argued elsewhere that theoretical advancement in contemporary feminist criminology requires development of frameworks that simultaneously consider multiple sources of oppression to understand criminological phenomena (Burgess-Proctor, 2006). Here I refine this argument even further, and suggest two specific feminist perspectives that are essential for achieving this type of theoretical advancement.

The first essential feminist perspective is *multiracial feminist criminology (MFC)*. MFC is rooted in multiracial feminism, a perspective developed by women of color who recognized the need to construct approaches to studying gender that included considerations of race/ethnicity, class, and other systems of power (Zinn & Dill, 1996). The term *multiracial feminism* emphasizes "race as a power system that interacts with other structured inequalities to shape genders" (Zinn & Dill, 1996, p. 324), and the main focus of this perspective is on interlocking and multiple inequalities (Thompson, 2002; Zinn & Dill, 1996). According to this perspective, gendered relations occur within a complex power hierarchy involving race/ethnicity, class, sexuality, nationality, and other systems of power, and in which people are situated in relation to one another (Zinn & Dill, 1996). Feminists who operate from this perspective advocate for an intersectional approach to studying gender that attends to multiple sources of inequality that simultaneously operate at both the macrolevel and microlevel (Andersen & Collins, 2004; Weber, 2001).

Multiracial feminist criminology, and the intersectional race–class–gender framework through which it operates, is essential to the advancement of feminist criminology because it enables the development of theories that attend to the influence of social location—that is, where one is situated in the societal power hierarchy—on motivations and opportunities for committing crime, as well as on the processing of offenders in the criminal justice system. Additionally, the focus of multiracial feminism on advancing social justice (Zinn & Dill, 1996) allows criminologists to parlay theoretical discoveries into real-world strategies that benefit women, as well as men (Burgess-Proctor, 2006). For example, recent feminist scholarship aimed at theorizing about marginalized women's experiences with intimate partner violence offers guidance for developing culturally sensitive, competent, relevant, and, hopefully, more effective services for battered women, especially those from marginalized social groups (Burgess-Proctor, 2008; see also Sokoloff & Dupont, 2005).

The second essential feminist perspective is *black feminist criminology (BFC)*. Developed by Potter (2006), BFC draws upon feminist criminology, black feminist theory, and critical race feminist theory to illuminate structural, cultural, and familial forces that shape black women's experiences with intimate partner abuse. Echoing the intersectional principles of MFC, Potter proposes a BFC model that "incorporates the tenets of interconnected identities, interconnected social forces, and distinct circumstances to better theorize, conduct research, and inform policy regarding criminal behavior and victimization among African Americans" (p. 109). Potter notes that traditional feminist criminology is rooted in mainstream feminism, which historically has ignored issues of race/ethnicity in favor of a focus on gender discrimination, as discussed previously. As a corrective, then, BFC "extends beyond traditional feminist criminology to view African American women (and conceivably, other women of color) from their multiple marginalized and dominated positions in society, culture, communities, and families" (p. 107).

Specifically, four themes are considered within Potter's (2006) BFC framework: social structural oppression, black community and culture, intimate and familial relations, and the black woman as an individual. To demonstrate the utility of BFC for feminist criminology, Potter uses these four themes to illuminate black women's experiences with IPV. For example, with respect to the third theme—intimate and familial relations—Potter explains that consideration of generational characteristics of black families, such as embeddedness in "othermothers" and extended family members, can help explain the preference of many black battered women to avoid formal help resources in favor of familial sources of support.

Potter's (2006) black feminist criminology framework is an extremely important—and urgently needed—refinement of feminist criminological theory. In addition, multiracial feminist criminology offers a similarly integrated theoretical framework for understanding the complex linkages between race/ethnicity, class, gender, and crime. However, these are nascent perspectives that have yet to be fully developed by feminist criminologists; indeed, this essay constitutes a first attempt to articulate a specific "multiracial feminist criminology" framework. It is the task of contemporary feminist criminologists, then, to pursue the development of these and other theoretical frameworks that move feminist criminology toward a more inclusive understanding of the complex power hierarchy within which the relationship between gender and crime operates.

## Policy Applications

Feminist criminological research has informed, and will continue to inform, crime and justice policies because feminist scholars prioritize the translation of research into action

(Flavin, 2001). Indeed, feminism is defined in part by a commitment to developing strategies for change (Daly & Chesney-Lind, 1988), and support for public policies that enhance equality and social justice is a similarly integral feature of feminism, particularly multiracial feminism (Thompson, 2002). To date, feminist scholarship and activism has shaped a wide variety of public policies, including the development of shelters, hotlines, and other resources for battered women (e.g., see Yllö & Bograd, 1988), the reformation of state rape laws (Berger, Searles, & Neuman, 1988), and the adoption (and subsequent questioning) of mandatory- and pro-arrest laws for IPV (Chesney-Lind, 2002). Contemporary feminist criminologists continue to produce research aimed at influencing and improving any number of criminal justice policies both in the United States and abroad.

For example, feminist criminologists in the United States are conducting policy-relevant research about the American juvenile justice and capital punishment systems. First, Belknap and Holsinger (2006) analyzed data from over 400 incarcerated Ohio youth to explore how risk factors for delinquency are gendered. Though girls in their sample reported higher levels of abuse and victimization than boys, boys self-reported abuse at an "alarmingly high" rate, leading the authors to conclude that intervention strategies for abused children are essential for deterring delinquency (p. 65). Conversely, the authors also recommend that treatment programs in detention facilities be properly equipped to address youths' abuse histories, in order to facilitate desistance upon their release.

Meanwhile, Westervelt and Cook (2007) are conducting truly groundbreaking feminist research with U.S. death-row exonerees. Clearly, improved understanding of how innocent people came to (wrongfully) serve time on death row offers tremendous opportunities for policy refinement, especially with respect to U.S. capital punishment laws. As of this writing the authors remain in the data analysis phase of their project so published results of their study are as yet forthcoming. Of their efforts to approach their research from a solidly feminist perspective, however, the authors write:

> We have been explicit in our attempts to maintain our feminist integrity in the research process while studying a group of people whose lived experiences have not been central to most feminist concerns. Thus, we ask: how do we accomplish feminist methodology in the process of interviewing innocent individuals who have been exonerated of capital crimes? Given that our interview participants are predominately men, how do we keep feminist concerns and techniques central to our method? (p. 21)

Feminists outside the United States are engaging in similar policy-rich research, particularly in the area of IPV. One prominent example is efforts of Canadian scholars to counter the developing antifeminist domestic violence and men's/fathers' rights movements both in Canada and across North America (Dragiewicz, 2008; Mann, 2008). Drawing upon the body of research, described previously, that suggests gender parity in perpetration of IPV, men's rights advocates "argue that women are equally or indeed more violent in domestic contexts than men, and that abused women shelters, restraining orders, anti-stalking laws, risk assessment tools, and other feminist-supported anti–domestic violence interventions promote hatred of and bias against men" (Mann, 2008, pp. 44–45). Anti-feminist activism in Canada often manifests in requests for the Canadian government to stop funding the women's research agency Status of Women Canada (Mann, 2008), while in the United States such activism often manifests in intense challenges to the federal Violence Against Women Act (Dragiewicz, 2008). Noting that these movements have had a measurable, negative impact on services and programs for battered women, Dragiewicz asserts that IPV scholars and practitioners "need to understand the tactics of backlash and how they work in order to advance efforts to protect victims of abuse and decrease the occurrence of violence" (p. 138).

In Asia, Haarr's (2007) investigation of Tajik women's attitudes about wife abuse also reveals important insights for the development of antiviolence strategies, this time in nations adhering to strict, patriarchal value systems. For example, the 400 Tajik women Haarr surveyed indicated widespread approval of and tolerance for abuse of women by their husbands and/or mothers-in-law, even going so far as to suggest various circumstances under which wife abuse would be justified. Not surprisingly, justifiable transgressions typically included violations of women's gender-role expectations in traditional Tajik-Islamic culture, such as leaving the house without a husband's permission or being suspected of having extramarital relations. Thus, Haarr concludes that "the challenge facing international organizations and local nongovernmental organizations in Tajikistan is to confront cultural norms and conceptualizations of gender identities, women's roles, wife abuse, and women's rights in awareness-raising events and educational programs" (p. 267).

As these examples reveal, contemporary feminist criminologists frequently engage in research that is aimed at *in*forming and *re*forming criminal justice policy. Both inside and outside the United States, feminist scholarship has wide-ranging implications for criminal justice policy. Of course, these policy implications often have a particular goal of improving the lives of women and girls—especially those who come into contact with the criminal justice system.


## Conclusion

The goal of this essay is to provide readers with a clearer idea of where feminist criminology is today, and also of where it is heading. Despite the major inroads made by feminist scholars in the field of criminology, opportunities for growth remain:

> Compared to thirty years ago, more research and policymaking efforts consider feminist theoretical contributions. By and large, however, feminist theories have not been fully integrated into the study and practice of criminal justice and consequently have not received the same attention as varieties of strain theories, social control theories, or individualist theories. As a result, the richness and insight of feminist perspectives have yet to be widely appreciated. (Flavin, 2001, p. 277)

Hopefully, this essay underscores the benefit of feminist theoretical developments in criminology, and in turn encourages new scholars to appreciate the insights feminist theories can offer the discipline. With continued appreciation of the many benefits of feminist scholarship, the goal many feminists share of witnessing complete integration of feminist theories alongside strain, control, and other canonical criminological frameworks may soon be realized.

# REFERENCES

Abercombie, N., Hill, S., & Turner, B. S. (1988). *The Penguin dictionary of sociology.* Harmondsworth, England: Penguin.

Adler, F. (1975). *Sisters in crime: The rise of the new female offender.* New York: McGraw-Hill.

Ageton, S., & Elliott, D. (1974). The effect of legal processing on delinquent orientations. *Social Problems, 22,* 87–100.

Agnew, R. (1983). Social class and success goals: An examination of relative and absolute aspirations. *The Sociological Quarterly, 24,* 435–452.

Agnew, R. (1984). Goal achievement and delinquency. *Sociology and Social Research, 68,* 435–451.

Agnew, R. (1985). A revised strain theory of delinquency. *Social Forces, 64,* 151–167.

Agnew, R. (1989). A longitudinal test of revised strain theory. *Journal of Quantitative Criminology, 5,* 373–387.

Agnew, R. (1992). Foundation for a general strain theory of crime and delinquency. *Criminology, 30,* 47–87.

Agnew, R. (1995). Determinism, indeterminism, and crime: An empirical exploration. *Criminology, 33,* 83–110.

Agnew, R. (1999). A general strain theory of community differences in crime rates. *Journal of Research in Crime and Delinquency, 36,* 123–155.

Agnew, R. (2001a). Building on the foundation of general strain theory: Specifying the types of strain most likely to lead to crime and delinquency. *Journal of Research in Crime and Delinquency, 38,* 319–361.

Agnew, R. (2001b). *Juvenile delinquency: Causes and control.* Los Angeles: Roxbury.

Agnew, R. (2006a). General strain theory. In S. Henry & M. Lanier (Eds.), *The essential criminology reader* (pp. 154–163). Boulder, CO: Westview Press.

Agnew, R. (2006b). *Pressured into crime: An overview of general strain theory.* New York: Oxford University Press.

Agnew, R., & White, H. R. (1992). An empirical test of general strain theory. *Criminology, 30,* 475–500.

Agnew, R., Brezina, T., Wright, J. P., & Cullen, F. T. (2002). Strain, personality traits, and delinquency: Extending general strain theory. *Criminology, 40*, 43–72.

Ahmed, E., Harris, N., Braithwaite, J., & Braithwaite, V. (2001). *Shame management through reintegration.* New York: Cambridge University Press.

Aichorn, A. (1979). Wayward youth. In J. E. Jacoby (Ed.), *Classics of criminology* (2nd ed., pp. 167–171). Prospect Heights, IL: Waveland. (Original work published 1925)

Akers, R., & Sellers, C. (2009). *Criminological theories: Introduction, evaluation, and application* (5th ed.). Cary, NC: Oxford University Press.

Akers, R. L. (1973). *Deviant behavior: A social learning approach.* Belmont, CA: Wadsworth.

Akers, R. L. (1979). Theory and ideology in Marxist criminology. *Criminology, 16*, 527–544.

Akers, R. L. (1980). Further critical thoughts on Marxist criminology: Comment on Turk, Toby, and Klockars. In J. Inciardi (Ed.), *Radical criminology: The coming crises.* Beverly Hills, CA: Sage.

Akers, R. L. (1985). *Deviant behavior: A social learning approach* (3rd ed.). Belmont, CA: Wadsworth.

Akers, R. L. (1989). Social learning and alcohol behavior among the elderly. *The Sociological Quarterly, 30*, 625–663.

Akers, R. L. (1991). Self-control as a general theory of crime. *Journal of Quantitative Criminology, 7*, 201–211.

Akers, R. L. (1996). Is differential association/social learning cultural deviance theory? *Criminology, 34*, 229–247.

Akers, R. L. (1997). *Criminological theories.* Los Angeles: Roxbury.

Akers, R. L. (1998). *Social learning and social structure: A general theory of crime and deviance.* Boston: Northeastern University Press.

Akers, R. L. (2000). *Criminological theories: Introduction, evaluation, and application* (3rd ed.). Los Angeles: Roxbury.

Akers, R. L. (2005). Self-control, social learning, and positivistic theories of crime. In E. Goode (Ed.), *Evaluating the general theory of crime.* New York: Cambridge University Press.

Akers, R. L., & Jensen, G. F. (2006). Empirical status of social learning theory: Past, present, and future. In F. T. Cullen, J. P. Wright, & K. R. Blevins (Eds.), *Taking stock: The status of criminological theory: Vol. 15. Advances in criminological theory* (pp. 37–76). New Brunswick, NJ: Transaction.

Akers, R. L., & Lee, G. (1999). A longitudinal test of social learning theory: Adolescent smoking. *Journal of Drug Issues, 26*, 317–343.

Akers, R. L., & Sellers, C. S. (2004). *Criminological theories: Introduction, evaluation, and application* (4th ed.). Los Angeles: Roxbury.

Amendola, A. M., & Scozzle, S. (2004). Promising strategies for reducing violence. *Reclaiming Children and Youth, 13*, 51–53.

Andersen, M., & Collins, P. H. (2004). *Race, class, and gender* (5th ed.). Belmont, CA: Wadsworth.

Anderson, E. (1994). The code of the streets. *The Atlantic Monthly, 273*, 82–94.

Anderson, E. (1999). *Code of the street: Decency, violence, and moral life of the inner city.* New York: Norton.

Ardelt, M., & Day, L. (2002). Parents, siblings, and peers: Close social relationships and adolescent deviance. *Journal of Early Adolescence, 22*, 310–349.

Arnold, R., Keane, C., & Baron, S. (2005). Assessing risk of victimization through epidemiological concepts: An alternative analytic strategy applied to routine activities theory. *Canadian Review of Sociology & Anthropology, 42*, 345–364.

Arnold, W. R., & Brungardt, T. M. (1983). *Juvenile misconduct and delinquency.* Boston: Houghton Mifflin.

Arrigo, B. A. (1995). The peripheral core of law and criminology: On postmodern social theory and conceptual integration. *Justice Quarterly, 12*, 447–472.

Arrigo, B. A. (1996). *The contours of psychiatric justice: A postmodern critique of mental, criminal insanity, and the law*. New York/London: Garland.

Arrigo, B. A. (Ed.). (1999). *Social justice/criminal justice: The maturation of critical theory in law, crime, and deviance*. Belmont, CA: Wadsworth.

Arrigo, B. A. (2002). *Punishing the mentally ill: A critical analysis of law and psychiatry*. New York: State University of New York Press.

Arrigo, B. A., & Bernard, T. (1997). Postmodern criminology in relation to radical and conflict criminology. *Critical Criminology, 8*(2), 39–60.

Arrigo, B. A., & Milovanovic, D. (2009). *Revolution in penology: Rethinking the society of captives*. New York: Rowman and Littlefield.

Arrigo, B. A., & Williams, C. R. (Eds.). (2006). *Philosophy, crime, and criminology*. Urbana/Chicago: University of Illinois Press.

Arseneault, L., Moffitt, T. E., Caspi, A., Taylor, A., Rijsdijk, F. V., Jaffee, S. R., et al. (2003). Strong genetic effects on cross-situational antisocial behavior among 5-year-old children according to mothers, teachers, examiner-observers, and twins' self-reports. *Journal of Child Psychology and Psychiatry, 44*, 832–848.

Aseltine, R. H., Jr., Gore, S., & Gordon, J. (2000). Life stress, anger and anxiety, and delinquency: An empirical test of general strain theory. *Journal of Health and Social Behavior, 41*, 256–275.

Athens, L. (1989). *The creation of dangerous violent criminals*. Urbana: University of Illinois Press.

Athens, L. (1994). The self as a soliloquy. *The Sociological Quarterly, 35*, 521–532.

Athens, L. (1995). Dramatic self change. *The Sociological Quarterly, 36*, 571–586.

Athens, L. (1997). *Violent criminal acts and actors revisited*. Chicago: University of Illinois Press.

Athens, L. (2003). Violentization in larger context. In L. Athens & J. Ulmer (Eds.), *Violent acts and violentization: Assessing, applying, and developing Lonnie Athens' theories*. Oxford, England: Elsevier Sciences.

Austin, R. L. (1980). Adolescent subcultures of violence. *The Sociological Quarterly, 21*, 545–561.

Axelrod, R. (1984). *The evolution of cooperation*. New York: Basic Books.

Balbus, I. D. (1977a). Commodity form and legal form: An essay on the relative autonomy of the law. *Law & Society Review, 11*, 571–587.

Balbus, I. D. (1977b). *The dialectics of legal repression: Black rebels before the American criminal courts*. New Brunswick, NJ: Transaction.

Ball, R. A. (1966). An empirical exploration of neutralization theory. *Criminology, 4*, 22–32.

Ball-Rokeach, S. J. (1973). Values and violence: A test of the subculture of violence thesis. *American Sociological Review, 38*, 736–749.

Bandura, A. (1973). *Aggression: A social learning analysis*. Englewood Cliffs, NJ: Prentice Hall.

Bandura, A. (1977). *Social learning theory*. Englewood Cliffs, NJ: Prentice Hall.

Banfield, E. C. (1970). *The unheavenly city*. Boston: Little, Brown.

Barak, G., Flavin, J. M., & Leighton, P. S. (2001). *Class, race, gender, and crime: Social realities of justice in America*. Los Angeles: Roxbury.

Barclay, P., Buckley, J., Brantingham, P., Brantingham, P., & Whin-Yates, T. (1996). Preventing auto-theft in suburban Vancouver commuter lots: Effects of a bike patrol. *Crime Prevention Studies, 6*, 133–161.

Baron, S. W. (2004). General strain, street youth, and crime: A test of Agnew's revised theory. *Criminology, 42*, 457–484.

Baron-Cohen, S., Jolliffe, T., Mortimore, C., & Robertson, M. (1997) Another advanced test of theory of mind: Evidence from very high functioning adults with autism or Asperger syndrome. *Journal of Child Psychology and Psychiatry, 38*, 813–822.

Basinger, S. (2001). *A bounded rationality model of "crime & punishment": Integrating formal theory and experimental research*. Panel 8-4, annual meetings of the American Political Science Association.

Batton, C., & Jensen, G. (2002). Decommodification and homicide rates in the 20th-century United States. *Homicide Studies, 6*, 6–38.

Batton, C., & Ogle, R. S. (2003). "Who's it gonna be—you or me?": The potential of social learning for integrated homicide-suicide theory. In R. L. Akers & G. F. Jensen (Eds.), *Social learning theory and the explanation of crime: A guide for the new century: Vol. 11. Advances in criminological theory* (pp. 85–108). New Brunswick, NJ: Transaction.

Baumer, E. P. (2007). Untangling research puzzles in Merton's multilevel anomie theory. *Theoretical Criminology, 11*, 63–93.

Baumer, E. P., & Gustafson, R. (2007). Social organization and instrumental crime: Assessing the empirical validity of classic and contemporary anomie theories. *Criminology, 45*, 617–663.

Baumer, E. P., Horney, J., Felson, R., & Lauritsen, J. (2003). Neighborhood disadvantage and the nature of violence. *Criminology, 40*, 579–616.

Baumer, E. P., & South, S. J. (2001). Community effects on youth sexual activity. *Journal of Family Issues, 22*, 1025–1043.

Baumer, E. P., Wright, R., Kristinsdottir, K., & Gunnlaugsson, H. (2002). Crime, shame, and recidivism: The case of Iceland. *British Journal of Criminology, 42*, 40–59.

Baumgartner, M. P. (1988). *The moral order of a suburb*. New York: Academic Press.

Baumgartner, M. P. (1992). War and peace in early childhood. In J. Tucker (Ed.), *Virginia review of sociology: Law and conflict management*. Greenwich, CT: JAI Press.

Baumgartner, M. P. (1993). Violent networks: The origins and management of domestic conflict. In R. B. Felson & J. T. Tedeschi (Eds.), *Aggression and violence: Social interactionist perspectives*. Washington, DC: American Psychological Association.

Beaver, K. M. (2008). Nonshared environmental influences on adolescent delinquent involvement and adult criminal behavior. *Criminology, 46*(2), 341–370.

Beaver, K. M., & Wright, J. P. (2005). Evaluating the effects of birth complications on low self-control in a sample of twins. *International Journal of Offender Therapy and Comparative Criminology, 49*, 450–471.

Beaver, K. M., Wright, J. P., & Delisi, M. (2007). Self-control as an executive function: Reformulating Gottfredson and Hirschi's parental socialization thesis. *Criminal Justice and Behavior, 34*, 1345–1361.

Beaver, K. M., Wright, J. P., DeLisi, M., Daigle, L. E., Swatt, M. L., & Gibson, C. L. (2007). Evidence of a gene x environment interaction in the creation of victimization: Results from a longitudinal sample of adolescents. *International Journal of Offender Therapy and Comparative Criminology, 51*, 620–645.

Beaver, K. M., Wright, J. P., DeLisi, M., Walsh, A., Vaughn, M. G., Boisvert, D., et al. (2007). A gene x gene interaction between DRD2 and DRD4 is associated with conduct disorder and antisocial behavior in males. *Behavioral and Brain Functions, 3*, 30.

Beccaria, C. (1986). *On crimes and punishments*. Hackett. (Original work published 1764)

Becker, G. S. (1968). Crime and punishment: An economic approach. *Journal of Political Economy, 76*, 169–217.

Becker, H. (1960). Notes on the concept of commitment. *American Journal of Sociology, 66*, 32–40.

Becker, H. (1963). *Outsiders*. New York: Macmillan.

Beirne, P., & Sharlet, R. (Eds.). (1980). *Pashukanis: Selected writings on Marxism and law.* New York: Academic Press.

Belknap, J. (2001). *The invisible woman: Gender, crime, and justice* (2nd ed.). Belmont, CA: Wadsworth/Thomson Learning.

Belknap, J., & Holsinger, K. (2006). The gendered nature of risk factors for delinquency. *Feminist Criminology, 1*(1), 48–71.

Bennett, D. S., & Gibbons, T. A. (2000). Efficacy of child cognitive-behavioral interventions for antisocial behavior: A meta-analysis. *Child and Family Behavior Therapy, 22,* 1–15.

Bennett, R. (1991). Routine activities: A cross-national assessment of a criminological perspective. *Social Forces, 70,* 143–163.

Benson, M. L. (2002). *Crime and the life course.* Los Angeles: Roxbury.

Benson, M. L., & Madsensen, T. D. (2007). Situational crime prevention and white-collar crime. In H. N. Pontell & G. Geis (Eds.), *International handbook of white-collar and corporate crime* (pp. 609–626). New York: Springer.

Benson, M. L., & Moore, E. (1992). Are white-collar and common offenders the same? An empirical and theoretical critique of a recently proposed general theory of crime. *Journal of Research in Crime and Delinquency, 29,* 251–272.

Berger, R. J., Searles, P., & Neuman, W. L. (1988). The dimensions of rape reform legislation. *Law & Society Review, 22*(2), 329.

Berk, R. A., Campbell, A., Klap, R., & Western, B. (1992). The deterrent effect of arrest in incidents of domestic violence: A Bayesian analysis of four field experiments. *American Sociological Review, 57,* 698–708.

Berkowitz, L. (1989). Frustration-aggression hypothesis: Examination and reformulation. *Psychological Bulletin, 106,* 59–73.

Bernard, T. J. (1981). The distinction between conflict and radical criminology. *The Journal of Criminal Law and Criminology, 72,* 362–379.

Bernard, T. J. (1983). *The consensus-conflict debate: Form and content in social theories.* New York: Columbia University Press.

Bernard, T. J. (1984). Control criticisms of strain theories: An assessment of theoretical and empirical adequacy. *Journal of Research in Crime and Delinquency, 21,* 353–372.

Bernard, T. J. (1990). Angry aggression among the "truly disadvantaged." *Criminology, 28,* 73–96.

Bernburg, J. G. (in press). Labeling theory. In M. D. Krohn, A. Lizotte, & G. P. Hall (Eds.), *The handbook of crime and deviance.* Springer Science.

Bernburg, J. G., & Krohn, M. D. (2003). Labeling, life chances, and adult crime: The direct and indirect effects of official intervention in adolescence on crime in early adulthood. *Criminology, 41,* 1287–1318.

Bernburg, J. G., Krohn, M. D., & Rivera, C. (2006). Official labeling, criminal embeddedness, and subsequent delinquency: A longitudinal test of labeling theory. *Journal of Research in Crime and Delinquency, 43,* 67–88.

Bernburg, J. G. & Thorlindsson, T. (2001). Routine activities in social context: A closer look at the role of opportunity in deviant behavior. *Justice Quarterly, 18,* 543–567.

Best, J. (2004). *Deviance: Career of a concept.* Belmont, CA: Wadsworth.

Black, D. (1976). *The behavior of law.* New York: Academic Press.

Black, D. (1980). *The manners and customs of the police.* New York: Academic Press.

Black, D. (1983a). Crime as social control. *American Sociological Review, 48,* 34–45.

Black, D. (Ed.). (1983b). *Toward a general theory of social control: Vol. 1. Fundamentals.* Orlando, FL: Academic Press.

Black, D. (Ed.). (1983c). *Toward a general theory of social control: Vol. 2. Selected problems.* Orlando, FL: Academic Press.

Black, D. (1989). *Sociological justice.* New York: Oxford University Press.

Black, D. (1995). The epistemology of pure sociology. *Law & Social Inquiry, 20,* 829–870.

Black, D. (1998). *The social structure of right and wrong* (Rev. ed.). San Diego, CA: Academic Press.

Black, D. (2000). On the origin of morality. *Journal of Consciousness Studies, 7,* 107–119.

Black, D. (2004a). The geometry of terrorism. *Sociological Theory, 22,* 14–25.

Black, D. (2004b). Violent structures. In M. A. Zahn, H. H. Brownstein, & S. L. Jackson (Eds.), *Violence: From theory to research.* Cincinnati, OH: Anderson.

Blair, J., Mitchell, D., & Blair, K. (2005). *The psychopath: Emotion and the brain.* Malden, MA: Blackwell.

Blalock, H. (1969). *Theory construction.* Englewood Cliffs, NJ: Prentice Hall.

Blasi, G., Mattay, V. S., Bertolino, A., Elvevag, B., Callicott, J. H., & Das, S. (2005). Effect of catechol-O-methyltransferase val158met genotype on attentional control. *Journal of Neuroscience, 25,* 5038–5045.

Blonigen, D. M., Hicks, B. M., Krueger, R. F., Patrick, C. J., & Iacono, W. G. (2005). Psychopathic personality traits: Heritability and genetic overlap with internalizing and externalizing psychopathology. *Psychological Medicine, 35,* 637–648.

Blumer, H. (1937). Social psychology. In E. P. Schmidt (Ed.), *Man and society.* New York: Prentice Hall.

Blumer, H. (2004). *George Herbert Mead and human conduct.* Walnut Creek, CA: AltaMira.

Bobb, A. J., Castellanos, F. X., Addington, A. M., & Rapoport, J. L. (2006). Molecular genetic studies of ADHD: 1991 to 2004. *American Journal of Medical Genetics Part B (Neuropsychiatric Genetics), 141B,* 551–565.

Bodwitch, C. (1993). Getting rid of troublemakers: High school disciplinary procedures and the production of dropouts. *Social Problems, 40,* 493–509.

Boeringer, S. (1992). *Sexual coercion among college males: Assessing three theoretical models of coercive sexual behavior.* Unpublished doctoral dissertation, University of Florida.

Bohle, H. H. (1975). *Soziale abweichung und erfolgschancen. Die anomietheorie in der diskussion* [Social deviance and chances of success. The anomie theory in discussion]. Neuwied und Darmstadt: Luchterland Verlag.

Bohm, R. M. (1982). Radical criminology: An explication. *Criminology, 19,* 565–589.

Bonger, W. A. (1969). *Crime and economic conditions.* Boston: Little, Brown. (Original work published 1969)

Bouffard, J. A. (2002). Methodological and theoretical implications of using subject generated consequences in testing rational choice theory. *Justice Quarterly, 19,* 747–771.

Bouffard, J. A. (2007). Predicting differences in the perceived relevance of crime's costs and benefits in a test of rational choice theory. *International Journal of Offender Therapy and Comparative Criminology, 51,* 461–485.

Bowers, K. J., Johnson, S. D., & Hirschfield, A.F.G. (2004). Closing off opportunities for crime: An evaluation of alleygating. *European Journal on Criminal Policy and Research, 10,* 283–308.

Box, S. (1983). *Power, crime, and mystification.* London: Tavistock.

Boyd, R., & Richerson, P. J. (1985). *Culture and the evolutionary process.* Chicago: University of Chicago Press.

Boyd, R., & Richerson, P. J. (2005). *The origin and evolution of cultures.* Oxford, England: Oxford University Press.

Braga, A. A., Weisburd, D. L., Waring, E. J., Mazerolle, L. G., Spelman, W., & Gajewski, F. (1999). Problem-oriented policing in violent crime places: A randomized controlled experiment. *Criminology, 37*, 541–580.

Braithwaite, J. (1989). *Crime, shame, and reintegration*. Cambridge, MA: Cambridge University Press.

Braithwaite, J. (1999). Restorative justice: Assessing optimistic and pessimistic accounts. *Crime and Justice: A Review of Research, 25*, 1–127.

Brantingham, P., & Brantingham, P. (1981). *Environmental criminology*. Beverly Hills, CA: Sage.

Brantingham, P., & Brantingham, P. (1995). Criminality of place: Crime generators and crime attractors. *European Journal on Criminal Policy and Research, 3*, 5–26.

Bratton, W. J., & Knobler, P. (1998). *Turnaround: How America's top cop reversed the crime epidemic*. New York: Random House.

Brezina, T. (1996). Adapting to strain: An examination of delinquent coping responses. *Criminology, 34*, 39–60.

Brezina, T., & Piquero, A. R. (2003). Exploring the relationship between social and non-social reinforcement in the context of social learning theory. In R. L. Akers & G. F. Jensen (Eds.), *Social learning theory and the explanation of crime: A guide for the new century: Vol. 11. Advances in criminological theory* (pp. 265–288). New Brunswick, NJ: Transaction.

Brezina, T., Piquero, A. R., & Mazerolle, P. (2001). Student anger and aggressive behavior in school: An initial test of Agnew's macro-level strain theory. *Journal of Research in Crime and Delinquency, 38*, 362–386.

Britton, D. M. (2000). Feminism in criminology: Engendering the outlaw. *The ANNALS of the American Academy of Political and Social Science, 571*, 57–76.

Broidy, L. (2001). A test of general strain theory. *Criminology, 39*, 9–35.

Broidy, L., & Agnew, R. (1997). Gender and crime: A general strain theory perspective. *Journal of Research in Crime and Delinquency, 34*, 275–306.

Brownfield, D. (1986). Social class and violent behavior. *Criminology, 24*, 421–438.

Brownfield, D. (1996). Subcultural theories of crime and delinquency. In J. Hagan, A. R. Gillis, & D. Brownfield (Eds.), *Criminological controversies* (pp. 99–123). Boulder, CO: Westview Press.

Brunson, R. K. (2007). Police don't like black people: African-American young men's accumulated police experiences. *Criminology & Public Policy, 6*, 71–102.

*Buck v. Bell*, 274 U.S. 200 (1927).

Bufkin, J. L. (1999). Bias crime as gendered behavior. *Social Justice, 26*(1), 155–176.

Burgess, E. W. (1967). The growth of the city: An introduction to a research project. In R. E. Park, E. W. Burgess, & R. D. McKenzie (Eds.), *The city* (pp. 47–62). Chicago: University of Chicago Press.

Burgess, R. L., & Akers, R. L. (1966). A differential association-reinforcement theory of criminal behavior. *Social Problems, 14*, 128–147.

Burgess-Proctor, A. (2006). Intersections of race, class, gender, and crime: Future directions for feminist criminology. *Feminist Criminology, 1*(1), 27–47.

Burgess-Proctor, A. (2008). *Understanding the help-seeking of marginalized battered women*. Unpublished doctoral dissertation, Michigan State University.

Bursik, R. J. (1986). Ecological stability and the dynamics of delinquency. In A. J. Reiss & M. Tonry (Eds.), *Communities and crime* (pp. 35–66). Chicago: University of Chicago Press.

Bursik, R. J. (1988). Social disorganization and theories of crime and delinquency: Problems and prospects. *Criminology, 26*, 519–551.

Bursik, R. J., & Grasmick, H. G. (1993a). Economic deprivation and neighborhood crime rates. *Law & Society Review, 27,* 263–283.

Bursik, R. J., & Grasmick, H. (1993b). *Neighborhoods and crime: The dimensions of effective community control.* New York: Lexington Books.

Bursik, R. J., & Webb, J. (1982). Community change and patterns of delinquency. *American Journal of Sociology, 88,* 24–42.

Burton, V. S., & Cullen, F. T. (1992). The empirical status of strain theory. *Journal of Crime and Justice, 15,* 1–30.

Byrne, J. M., & Sampson, R. J. (1986). *The social ecology of crime.* New York: Springer-Verlag.

Campbell, B. (2005). *Genocide as social control.* Paper presented at the annual meeting of the Southern Sociological Association, Charlotte, NC.

Campbell, B. (2006). *The collectivization of genocide.* Paper presented at the annual meeting of the American Society of Criminology, Los Angeles, CA.

Cao, L. (2004). Is American society more anomic? A test of Merton's theory with cross-national data. *International Journal of Comparative and Applied Criminal Justice, 28,* 17–31.

Cao, L., Adams, A., & Jensen, V. (1997). A test of the black subculture of violence thesis. A research note. *Criminology, 35,* 367–379.

Cao, L., & Maume, D. (1993). Urbanization, inequality, lifestyles and robbery: A comprehensive model. *Sociological Focus, 26,* 11–26.

Cardinal, R. N., Pennicott, D. R., Sugathapala, C. L., Robbins, T. W., & Everitt, B. J. (2001). Impulsive choice induced in rats by lesions of the nucleus accumbens core. *Science, 292,* 2499–2501.

Carlson, S., & Michalowski, R. (1997). Crime, unemployment, and social structures of accumulation: An inquiry into historical contingency. *Justice Quarterly, 14,* 209–241.

Caspi, A., Henry, B., McGee, R. O., Moffitt, T. E., & Silva, P. A. (1995). Temperamental origins of child and adolescent behavior problems: From age three to age fifteen. *Child Development, 66,* 55–68.

Caspi, A., McClay, J., Moffitt, T. E., Mill, J., Martin, J., Craig, I. W., et al. (2002). Role of the genotype in the cycle of violence in maltreated children. *Science, 297,* 851–854.

Cauffman, E., Steinberg, L., & Piquero, A. R. (2005). Psychological, neuropsychological, and physiological correlates of serious antisocial behavior. *Criminology, 43,* 133–176.

Chambliss, W., & Seidman, R. (1971). *Law, order, and power.* Reading, MA: Addison-Wesley.

Chamlin, M. B., & Cochran, J. K. (1995). Assesssing Messner and Rosenfeld's institutional anomie theory: A partial test. *Criminology, 33,* 411–429.

Chamlin, M. B., & Cochran, J. K. (1997). Social altruism and crime. *Criminology, 35,* 203–228.

Chappell, A. T., & Piquero, A. R. (2004). Applying social learning theory to police misconduct. *Deviant Behavior, 25,* 89–108.

Charmaz, K. (2007). Self. In G. Ritzer (Ed.), *Blackwell encyclopedia of sociology.* Boston: Blackwell.

Chesney-Lind, M. (1997). *The female offender: Girls, women, and crime.* Thousand Oaks, CA: Sage.

Chesney-Lind, M. (2002). Criminalizing victimization: The unintended consequences of pro-arrest policies for girls and women. *Criminology & Public Policy, 2*(1), 81–90.

Chesney-Lind, M., & Pasko, L. (2004a). *The female offender: Girls, women, and crime* (2nd ed.). Thousand Oaks, CA: Sage.

Chesney-Lind, M., & Pasko, L. (Eds.). (2004b). *Girls, women, and crime: Selected readings.* Thousand Oaks, CA: Sage.

Chiricos, T. G., Barrick, K., Bales, W., & Bontrager, S. (2007). The labeling of convicted felons and its consequences for recidivism. *Criminology, 45*, 547–581.

Chiricos, T. G., & DeLone, M. (1992). Labor surplus and punishment: A review and assessment of theory and evidence. *Social Problems, 39*, 421–446.

Clark, K. (1965). *Dark ghetto, dilemmas of social power*. New York: Harper and Row.

Clinard, M. B. (1964). *Anomie and deviant behavior*. New York: Free Press.

Cloward, R. A., & Ohlin, L. E. (1960). *Delinquency and opportunity: A theory of delinquent gangs*. New York: Free Press.

Cohen, A. K. (1955). *Delinquent boys: The culture of the gang*. New York: Free Press.

Cohen, A. K. (1997). An elaboration of anomie theory. In R. Agnew & N. Passas (Eds.), *The future of anomie theory* (pp. 52–61). Boston: Northeastern University Press.

Cohen, J. D., & Tong, F. (2001). Neuroscience: The face of controversy. *Science, 293*, 2405–2407.

Cohen, L., & Cantor, D. (1980). The determinants of larceny: An empirical and theoretical study. *Journal of Research in Crime and Delinquency, 17*, 140–159.

Cohen, L., Cantor, D., & Klueger, J. (1981). Robbery victimization in the U.S.: Social and economic determinants of potentially violent event. *Social Science Quarterly, 63*, 644–657.

Cohen, L., & Felson, M. (1979). Social change and crime rate trends: A routine activity approach. *American Sociological Review, 44*, 588–608.

Cohen, L., & Felson, M. (1981). Modeling crime trends: A criminal opportunity perspective. *Journal of Research in Crime and Delinquency, 18*, 138–164.

Cole, S. (1975). The growth of scientific knowledge: Theories of deviance as a case study. In L. A. Coser (Ed.), *The idea of social structure: Papers in honor of Robert K. Merton* (pp. 175–220). New York: Harcourt Brace Jovanovich.

Coleman, J. S. (1988). Social capital in the creation of human capital. *American Journal of Sociology, 94*, 95–120.

Coleman, J. S. (1990). *Foundations of social theory*. Cambridge, MA: Harvard University Press.

Collins, J., Cox, B., & Langan, P. (1987). Job activities and personal crime victimization: Implications for theory. *Social Science Research, 16*, 345–360.

Collins, P. H. (2000). *Black feminist thought: Knowledge, consciousness, and the politics of empowerment* (2nd ed.). New York: Routledge.

Comings, D. E., Gade-Andavolu, R., Gonzalez, N., Wu, S., Muhleman, D., Blake, H., et al. (2000a). Comparison of the role of dopamine, serotonin, and noradrenaline genes in ADHD, ODD, and CD: Multivariate regression analysis of 20 genes. *Clinical Genetics, 57*, 178–196.

Comings, D. E., Gade-Andavolu, R., Gonzalez, N., Wu, S., Muhleman, D., Blake, H., et al. (2000b). Multivariate analysis of associations of 42 genes in ADHD, ODD, and CD. *Clinical Genetics, 58*, 31–40.

Condon, W. S., & Sander, L. W. (1974). Neonate movement is synchronized with adult speech: Interactional participation and language acquisition. *Science, 183*, 99–101.

Congdon, E., & Canli, T. (2005). The endophenotype of impulsivity: Reaching consilience through behavioral, genetic, and neuroimaging approaches. *Behavioral and Cognitive Neuroscience Reviews, 4*, 262–281.

Conger, R. (1976). Social control and social learning models of delinquency: A synthesis. *Criminology, 14*, 17–40.

Cook, P. (1987). Robbery violence. *Journal of Criminal Law and Criminology, 78*, 357–376.

Cooney, M. (1997a). The decline of elite homicide. *Criminology, 35*, 381–407.

Cooney, M. (1997b). From Warre to tyranny: Lethal conflict and the state. *American Sociological Review, 62*, 316–338.

Cooney, M. (1998). *Warriors and peacemakers: How third parties shape violence.* New York: New York University Press.

Cooney, M. (2003). The privatization of violence. *Criminology, 41,* 1377–1406.

Cooney, M. (2006). The criminological potential of pure sociology. *Crime, Law, & Social Change, 46,* 51–63.

Cooney, M., & Phillips, S. (2002). Typologizing violence: A Blackian perspective. *International Journal of Sociology and Social Policy, 22,* 75–108.

Cooter, R., and Ulen, T. (1997). *Law and economics.* New York: Addison-Wesley.

Cooter, R. D. (2000a). Do good laws make good citizens? An economic analysis of internalized norms. *Virginia Law Review, 86,* 1577–1601.

Cooter, R. D. (2000b). Three effects of social norms on law: Expression, deterrence,and internalization. *Oregon Law Review, 79,* 1–22.

Copes, H. (1999). Routine activities and motor vehicle theft: A crime-specific approach. *Journal of Crime and Justice, 22,* 125–146.

Cornish, D. B., & Clark, R. (Eds.). (1986). *The reasoning criminal: Rational choice perspectives on offending.* New York: Springer-Verlag.

Cressey, D. R. (1953). *Other people's money: A study in the social psychology of embezzlement.* Glencoe, IL: Free Press.

Cressey, D. R. (1960). Epidemiology and individual conduct: A case from criminology. *Pacific Sociological Review, 3,* 47–58.

Cressey, D. R. (1968). Culture conflict, differential association, and normative conflict. In M. Wolfgang (Ed.), *Crime and culture* (pp. 43–55). New York: Wiley.

Cullen, F. (1984). *Rethinking crime and deviance theory: The emergence of a structuring condition.* Totowa, NJ: Rowman and Allanheld.

Cullen, F. T. (1988). Were Cloward and Ohlin strain theorists? Delinquency and opportunity revisited. *Journal of Research in Crime and Delinquency, 25,* 214–241.

Cullen, F. T., & Gilbert, K. E. (1982). *Reaffirming rehabilitation.* Cincinnati, OH: Anderson.

Cullen, F. T., & Wright, J. P. (1997). Liberating the anomie-strain paradigm: Implications from social-support theory. In N. Passas & R. Agnew (Eds.), *The future of anomie theory* (pp. 187–206). Boston: Northeastern University Press.

Cullen, F. T., Wright, J. P., & Blevins, K. R. (Eds.). (2006). *Taking stock: The status of criminological theory: Vol. 15. Advances in criminological theory.* New Brunswick, NJ: Transaction.

Cullen, J. B., Parboteeach, K. P., & Hoegle, M. (2004). Cross-national differences in managers' willingness to justify ethically suspect behaviors: A test of institutional anomie theory. *Academy of Management Journal, 47,* 411–421.

Currie, E. (1992). Retreatism, minimalism, realism: Three styles of reasoning on crime and drugs in the United States. In J. Lowman & B. MacLean (Eds.), *Realist criminology: Crime control and policing in the 1990's.* Toronto, Ontario, Canada: University of Toronto Press.

Currie, E. (1993). *Reckoning: Drugs, the cities, and the American future.* New York: Hill and Wang.

Currie, E. (1997). Market society and social disorder. In B. MacLean & D. Milovanovic (Eds.), *Thinking critically about crime.* Vancouver, British Columbia, Canada: Collective Press.

Daly, K. (1997). Different ways of conceptualizing sex/gender in feminist theory and their implications for criminology. *Theoretical Criminology, 1*(1), 25–51.

Daly, K., & Chesney-Lind, M. (1988). Feminism and criminology. *Justice Quarterly, 5*(4), 497–538.

Daly, K., & Maher, L. (Eds.). (1998). *Criminology at the crossroads: Feminist readings in crime and justice.* New York: Oxford University Press.

Daly, K., & Stephens, D. (1995). The "dark figure" of criminology: Towards a black and multi-ethnic feminist agenda for theory and research. In N. Rafter & F. Heidensohn (Eds.), *International feminist perspectives in criminology: Engendering a discipline* (pp. 189–215). Philadelphia: Open University Press.

Damasio, A. R. (1994). *Descarte's error: Emotion, reason and the human brain.* New York: G. P. Putnam.

Dapretto, M., Davies, A., Pfeifer, J., Scott, A., Sigman, M., Bookheimer, S., et al. (2005). Understanding emotions in others: Mirror neuron dysfunction in children with autism spectrum disorders. *Nature Neuroscience, 9,* 28–30.

Dau-Schmidt, K. G. (1990). An economic analysis of the criminal law as a preference shaping policy. *Duke Law Journal, 1,* 1–18.

Davidson, R. N. (1981). *Crime and environment.* New York: St. Martin's Press.

DeKeseredy, W., & Dragiewicz, M. (2007). Understanding the complexities of feminist perspectives on woman abuse: A commentary on Dutton's *Rethinking Domestic Violence. Violence Against Women, 13*(8), 874–884.

DeKeseredy, W., & MacLean, B. (1990). Research on women abuse in Canada: A realist critique of the Conflict Tactics Scale. *Canadian Review of Social Policy, 25,* 19–27.

DeKeseredy, W., MacLean, B., & Schwartz, M. (1997). Thinking critically about left realism. In B. MacLean & D. Milovanovic (Eds.), *Thinking critically about crime.* Vancouver, British Columbia, Canada: Collective Press.

DeKeseredy, W. S. (2003). Left realism on inner-city crime. In M. Schwartz & S. Hatty (Eds.), *Controversies in critical criminology.* Cincinnati, OH: Anderson.

DeKeseredy, W. S., & Perry, B. (Eds.). (2006). *Advances in critical criminology: Theory and application.* Lanham, MD: Lexington Books.

De Li, S. (1999). Legal sanctions and youths' status achievements: A longitudinal study. *Justice Quarterly, 16,* 377–401.

DeLisi, M. (2005). *Career criminals in society.* Thousand Oaks, CA: Sage.

DeLisi, M. (2008). Neuroscience and the Holy Grail: Genetics and career criminality. In A. Walsh & K. M. Beaver, *Introduction to biosocial criminology.* New York: Routledge.

Dobash, R. E., & Dobash, R. P. (1979). *Violence against wives.* New York: Free Press.

Dobash, R. E., & Dobash, R. P. (1992). *Women, violence, and social change.* London: Routledge.

Dobash, R. P., Dobash, R. E., Wilson, M., & Daly, K. (1992). The myth of sexual symmetry in marital violence. *Social Problems, 39,* 71–91.

Donziger, S. R. (1999). Prisons. In F. R. Scarpitti & A. L. Nielsen (Eds.), *Crime and criminals* (pp. 494–512). Los Angeles: Roxbury.

Dragiewicz, M. (2008). Patriarchy reasserted: Father's rights and anti-VAWA activism. *Feminist Criminology, 3,* 121–144.

Drapela, L. A. (2006). The effect of negative emotion on licit and illicit drug use among high school dropouts: An empirical test of general strain theory. *Journal of Youth and Adolescence, 35,* 755–770.

Dubin, R. (1959). Deviant behavior and social structure: Continuities in social theory. *American Sociological Review, 24,* 147–164.

Dubois, W.E.B. (1996). *The Philadelphia Negro, a social study.* Philadelphia: University of Pennsylvania Press. (Original work published 1899)

Duchaine, B. (2006). Selective deficits in developmental cognitive neuropsychology: An introduction. *Cognitive Neuropsychology, 23,* 675–679.

Duchaine, B., Cosmides, L., & Tooby, J. (2001). Evolutionary psychology and the brain. *Current Opinion in Neurobiology, 11,* 225–230.

Duchaine, B., Yovel, G., Butterworth, E., & Nakayama, K. (2006). Prosopagnosia as an impairment to face-specific mechanisms: Elimination of the alternative hypotheses in a developmental case. *Cognitive Neuropsychology, 23*(5), 714–747.

Dugdale, R. (1877). *The Jukes: A study in crime, pauperism, and heredity.* New York: G. P. Putman.

Durkheim, E. (1953). The determination of moral facts. In *Sociology and philosophy* (pp. 35–62). Glencoe, IL: Free Press. (Original work published 1903)

Durkheim, E. (1966). *Suicide: A study in sociology.* New York: Free Press. (Original work published 1897)

Durkheim, E. (1982). *The rules of the sociological method.* New York: Free Press. (Original work published 1895)

Dutton, D. G. (2006). *Rethinking domestic violence.* Vancouver, British Columbia, Canada: UBC Press.

Eck, J. E. (2002). Preventing crime at places. In L. W. Sherman, D. Farrington, B. Welsh, & D. L. MacKenzie (Eds.), *Evidence-based crime prevention.* New York: Routledge.

Ehrhardt-Mustaine, E., & Tewksbury, R. (1997). The risk of victimization in the workplace for men and women: An analysis using routine activities/lifestyle theory. *Humanity & Society, 21*, 17–38.

Ehrlich, I. (1996). Crime, punishment and the market for offenses. *Journal of Economic Perspectives, 10*, 43–67.

Einstadter, W., & Henry, S. (1995). *Criminological theory: An analysis of its underlying assumptions.* Orlando, FL: Harcourt Brace.

Ellickson, R. C. (1989). Bringing culture and human frailty to rational actors: A critique of classical law and economics. *Chicago-Kent Law Review, 65*, 23–55.

Elliott, D., Ageton, S., & Canter, R. (1979). An integrated theoretical perspective on delinquent behavior. *Journal of Research in Crime and Delinquency, 16*, 3–27.

Elliott, D., & Voss, H. (1974). *Delinquency and dropout.* Lexington, MA: Lexington Books.

Elliott, D. S., Huizinga, D., & Ageton, S. (1985). *Explaining delinquency and drug use.* Beverly Hills, CA: Sage.

Empey, L. (1956). Social class and occupational aspiration: A comparison of absolute and relative measurement. *American Sociological Review, 21*, 703–709.

Empey, L. T., & Lubeck, S. G. (1971). *The Silverlake experiment: Testing delinquency theory and community intervention.* Chicago: Aldine.

Erlanger, H. S. (1974). The empirical status of the subculture of violence thesis. *Social Problems, 74*, 280–292.

Estes, C., & Edmonds, B. (1981). Symbolic interaction and social policy analysis. *Symbolic Interaction, 4*, 75–86.

Evans, T., Cullen, F. T., Burton, V., Jr., Dunaway, R., & Benson, M. (1997). The social consequences of self-control: Testing the general theory of crime. *Criminology, 35*, 475–504.

Fagan, J., Wilkinson, D. L., & Davise, G. (2007). Social contagion of violence. In D. Flannery, A. Vazsonyi, & I. Waldman (Eds.), *The Cambridge handbook of violent behavior.* Cambridge, England: Cambridge University Press.

Falck-Ytter, T., Gredebäck, G., & von Hofsten, C. (2006). Infants predict other people's action goals. *Nature Neuroscience, 9*, 878–879.

Farrington, D. P. (1977). The effects of public labelling. *British Journal of Criminology, 17*, 112–125.

Farrington, D. P., & Welsh, B. C. (2007). *Saving children from a life of crime: Early risk factors and effective interventions.* New York: Oxford University Press.

Felson, M. (1986). Linking criminal choices, routine activities, informal social control, and criminal outcomes. In D. Cornish & R. Clarke (Eds.), *The reasoning criminal* (pp. 119–128). New York: Springer-Verlag.

Felson, M. (1987). Routine activities and crime prevention in the developing metropolis. *Criminology, 25,* 911–932.

Felson, M. (1994). *Crime and everyday life: Insight and implications for society.* Thousand Oaks, CA: Pine Forge Press.

Felson, M. (1998). *Crime and everyday life.* Thousand Oaks, CA: Pine Forge Press.

Felson, R. B. (1992). "Kick 'em when they're down": Explanations of the relationship between stress and interpersonal aggression and violence. *The Sociological Quarterly, 33,* 1–16.

Felson, R. B. (1993). Predatory and dispute-related violence: A social interactionist approach. In R. Clarke & M. Felson (Eds.), *Advances in criminological theory* (Vol. 5, pp. 189–235). New Brunswick, NJ: Transaction.

Felson, R. B., Liska, A., McNulty, T., & South, S. (1994). The subculture of violence and delinquency, individual vs. school context effects. *Social Forces, 73,* 155–173.

Fender, J. (1999). A general equilibrium model of crime and punishment. *Journal of Economic Behavior and Organization, 39,* 437–453.

Ferrell, J. (1999). Anarchist criminology and social justice. In B. Arrigo (Ed.), *Social justice/ criminal justice: The maturation of critical theory in law, crime, and deviance.* Belmont, CA: Wadsworth.

Fine, G. A. (1993). The sad demise, mysterious disappearance, and glorious triumph of symbolic interactionism. *Annual Review of Sociology, 19,* 61–87.

Fine, G. A., & Kleinman, S. (1979). Rethinking subculture: An interactionist analysis. *American Journal of Sociology, 85,* 1–20.

Fischer, C. (1995). The subcultural theory of urbanism, a twentieth year assessment. *American Journal of Sociology, 101,* 543–577.

Flavin, J. (2001). Feminism for the mainstream criminologist: An invitation. *Journal of Criminal Justice, 29,* 271–285.

Fodor, J. A. (1983). *The modularity of mind.* Cambridge, MA: MIT Press.

Fodor, J. A. (2001). *The mind doesn't work that way.* Cambridge, MA: MIT Press.

Forde, D., & Kennedy, L. (1997). Risky lifestyles, routine activities, and the general theory of crime. *Justice Quarterly, 14,* 265–289.

Frankford, D. M. (1995). Review: Social structure and right and wrong: Normativity without agents. *Law & Social Inquiry, 20,* 787–803.

Freud, S. (1901). *The psychopathology of everyday life.* Amazon Digital Services.

Froggio, G., & Agnew, R. (2007). The relationship between crime and "objective" versus "subjective" strains. *Journal of Contemporary Criminal Justice, 35,* 81–87.

Gaarder, E., & Belknap, J. (2002). Tenuous borders: Girls transferred to adult court. *Criminology, 40,* 481–517.

Gaetz, S. (2004). Safe streets for whom? Homeless youth, social exclusion, and criminal victimization. *Canadian Journal of Criminology and Criminal Justice, 46,* 423–455.

Gallese, V. (2005). "Being like me": Self-other identity, mirror neurons and empathy, In S. Hurley & N. Chater (Eds.), *Perspectives on imitation: From cognitive neuroscience to social science* (Vol. 1, pp. 101–118). Boston: MIT Press.

Garofalo, J., & Clark, D. (1992). Guardianship and residential burglary. *Justice Quarterly, 9,* 443–463.

Garofalo, J., Siegel, L., & Laub, J. (1987). School-related victimizations among adolescents: An analysis of National Crime Survey narratives. *Journal of Quantitative Criminology, 3,* 321–338.

Gastil, R. D. (1971). Homicide and a regional culture of violence. *American Sociological Review, 36,* 412–427.

Gau, J. M., & Pratt, T. C. (2008). Broken windows or window dressing? Citizens (in)ability to tell the difference between disorder and crime. *Criminology & Public Policy, 7,* 163–194.

Geertz, C. (1973). *The interpretations of cultures.* New York: Basic Books.

Geis, G. (2007). *White-collar and corporate crime.* Upper Saddle River, NJ: Pearson Prentice Hall.

Gibbs, J. P. (1985). The methodology of theory construction in criminology. In R. Meier (Ed.), *Theoretical methods in criminology* (pp. 23–50). Beverly Hills, CA: Sage.

Gibson, C. L., & Tibbetts, S. G. (2000). A biosocial interaction in predicting early onset of offending. *Psychological Reports, 86,* 509–518.

Gilfus, M. E. (1992). From victims to survivors to offenders: Women's routes of entry and immersion into street crime. *Women & Criminal Justice, 4,* 63–88.

Giordano, P., Cernkovich, S., & Holland, D. (2003). Changes in friendship relations over the life course: Implications for desistence from crime. *Criminology, 41,* 293–328.

Giordano, P., Cernkovich, S., & Rudolph, J. (2002). Gender, crime, and desistance: Toward a theory of cognitive transformation. *American Journal of Sociology, 107,* 990–1064.

Giordano, P., Schroeder, R., & Cernkovich, S. (2007). Emotions and crime over the life course: A neo-Meadian perspective on criminal continuity and change. *American Journal of Sociology, 112,* 1603–1661.

Glaser, D. (1956). Criminality theories and behavioral images. *American Journal of Sociology, 61,* 433–444.

Glaser, D. (1960). Differential association and criminological prediction. *Social Problems, 8,* 6–14.

Glueck S., & Glueck, E. (1950). *Unraveling juvenile delinquency.* Cambridge, MA: Harvard University Press.

Goddard, H. H. (1912). *The Kallikak family.* New York: Macmillan.

Goddard, H. H. (1914). *Feeble-mindedness.* New York: Macmillan.

Goffman, E. (1961). *Encounters.* Indianapolis, IN: Bobbs-Merrill.

Goffman, E. (1963). *Stigma: Notes on the management of a spoiled identity.* Englewood Cliffs, NJ: Prentice Hall.

Goldstein, P. J., Brownstein, H. H., Ryan, P. J., & Bellucci, P. A. (1997). Crack and homicide in New York City: A case study in the epidemiology of violence. In C. Reinarman & H. G. Levine (Eds.), *Crack in America: Demon drugs and social justice.* Los Angeles: University of California Press.

Gordon, R. A., Lahey, B. B., Kawai, E., Loeber, R., Stouthamer-Loeber, M., & Farrington, D. P. (2004). Anti-social behavior and youth gang membership: Selection and socialization. *Criminology, 42,* 55–87.

Gottfredson, M. R. (1981). On the etiology of criminal victimization. *Journal of Criminal Law and Criminology, 72,* 714–726.

Gottfredson, M. R., & Hindelang M. J. (1979). Theory and research in the sociology of law. *American Sociological Review, 44,* 27–37.

Gottfredson, M. R., & Hirschi, T. (1990). *A general theory of crime.* Stanford, CA: Stanford University Press.

Gottfredson, M. R., & Hirschi, T. (1995). National crime policy. *Society, 32,* 30–36.

Gottfredson, M. R., & Hirschi, T. (2003). Self-control and opportunity. In C. L. Britt & M. R. Gottfredson (Eds.), *Advances in criminological theory: Vol. 12. Control theories of crime and delinquency* (pp. 5–20). New Brunswick, NJ: Transaction.

Gould, S. J. (1996). *The mismeasure of man* (Rev. ed.). New York: Norton.

Grasmick, H. G., & Bursik, R. J. (1990). Conscience, significant others, and rational choice: Extending the deterrence model. *Law & Society Review, 24*, 837–861.

Grasmick, H. G., Bursik, R. J., & Kinsey, K. A. (1991). Shame and embarrassment as deterrents to noncompliance with the law: The case of an antilittering campaign. *Environment and Behavior, 23*, 233–251.

Grasmick, H. G., Tittle, C. R., Bursik, R. J., Jr., & Arneklev, B. K. (1993). Testing the core empirical implications of Gottfredson and Hirschi's general theory of crime. *Journal of Research in Crime and Delinquency, 30*, 5–29.

Greenberg, D. F. (1983). Donald Black's sociology of law: A critique. *Law & Society Review, 17*, 337–368.

Greenberg, D. F. (1985). Age, crime, and social explanation. *American Journal of Sociology, 91*, 1–21.

Greene, J. D., Nystrom, L. E., Engell, A. D., Darley, J. M., & Cohen, J. D. (2004). The neural bases of cognitive conflict and control in moral judgment. *Neuron, 44*, 389–400.

Greenwood, P. (2006). *Changing lives: Delinquency prevention as crime control policy.* Chicago: University of Chicago Press.

Haarr, R. (2007). Wife abuse in Tajikistan. *Feminist Criminology, 2*, 245–270.

Hagan, J. (1985). The science of social control. *Contemporary Sociology, 14*, 667–670.

Hagan, J. (1989). *Structural criminology.* New Brunswick, NJ: Rutgers University Press.

Hagan, J., Gillis, A. R., & Simpson, J. (1985). The class structure of gender and delinquency: Toward a power-control theory of common delinquent behavior. *American Journal of Sociology, 90*, 1151–1178.

Hagan, J., & McCarthy, B. (1997). Anomie, social capital, and street criminology. In N. Passas & R. Agnew (Eds.), *The future of anomie theory* (pp. 124–141). Boston: Northeastern University Press.

Hagan, J., & Palloni, A. (1990). The social reproduction of a criminal class in working-class London, 1950–1980. *American Journal of Sociology, 96*, 265–299.

Hagan, J., Simpson, J., & Gillis, A.R. (1987). Class in the household: A power-control theory of gender and delinquency. *American Journal of Sociology, 92*, 788–816.

Hall, P. (1987). Interactionism and the study of social organization. *The Sociological Quarterly, 28*, 1–22.

Hall, P. (1997). Meta-power, social organization, and the shaping of social action. *Symbolic Interaction, 20*, 397–418.

Hall, P. (2003). Interactionism, social organization, and social processes: Looking back and moving ahead. *Symbolic Interaction, 26*, 33–55.

Hall, P. (2007). Symbolic interaction. In G. Ritzer (Ed.), *Blackwell encyclopedia of sociology.* Boston: Blackwell.

Hall, P., & McGinty, P. (1997). Policy as the transformation of intentions: Producing program from statute. *The Sociological Quarterly, 38*, 439–467.

Hannerz, U. (1969). *Soulside: Inquiries into ghetto culture and community.* New York: Columbia University Press.

Hannon, L., & DeFronzo, J. (1998). The truly disadvantage, public assistance, and crime. *Social Problems, 45*, 383–392.

Harary, F. (1966). Merton revisited. A new classification for deviant behavior. *American Sociological Review, 31*, 693–697.

Harcourt, B. E. (2001). *Illusion of order: The false promise of broken windows policing.* Cambridge, MA: Harvard University Press.

Harcourt, B. E., & Ludwig, J. (2006). Broken windows: New evidence from New York City and a five-city social experiment. *The University of Chicago Law Review, 73*, 271–320.

Harer, M., & Steffensmeier, D. J. (1996). Race and prison violence. *Criminology, 34*, 323–355.

Harris, J. R. (1995). Where is the child's environment? A group socialization theory of development. *Psychological Review, 102*, 458–489.

Harris, J. R. (1998). *The nurture assumption: Why children turn out the way they do*. New York: Free Press.

Harris, J. R. (2007). *No two alike: Human nature and human individuality*. New York: Norton.

Hawdon, J. (1996). Deviant lifestyles: The social control of routine activities. *Youth and Society, 28*, 162–188.

Hawley, A. (1950). *Human ecology: A theory of community structure*. New York: Ronald Press.

Hay, C., & Evans, M. M. (2006). Violent victimization and involvement in delinquency: Examining predictions from general strain theory. *Journal of Criminal Justice, 34*, 261–274.

Haynie, D. L. (2002). Friendship networks and delinquency: The relative nature of peer delinquency. *Journal of Quantitative Criminology, 18*, 99–134.

Haynie, D. L., & Osgood, D. W. (2005). Reconsidering peers and delinquency: How do peers matter? *Social Forces, 84*(2), 1109–1130.

Hechter, M., & Kanazawa, S. (1997). Sociological rational choice theory. *Annual Review of Sociology, 23*, 191–214.

Hechter, M., & Opp, K. D. (2001). Introduction. In M. Hechter & K. D. Opp (Eds.), *Social norms* (pp. xi–xx). New York: Russell Sage.

Heidensohn, F. (1968). The deviance of women: A critique and an enquiry. *British Journal of Sociology, 19*, 160–175.

Heimer, K. (1997). Socioeconomic status, subcultural definitions, and violent delinquency. *Social Forces, 75*, 799–833.

Heimer, K., & DeCoster, S. (1999). The gendering of violent delinquency. *Criminology, 37*(2), 277–312.

Heimer, K., & Matsueda, R. L. (1994). Role-taking, role commitment, and delinquency: A theory of differential social control. *American Sociological Review, 59*, 365–390.

Heitgard, J. L., & Bursik, R. J. (1987). Extracommunity dynamics and the ecology of delinquency. *American Journal of Sociology, 92*, 775–787.

Hindelang, M. (1973). Causes of delinquency: A potential replication and extension. *Social Problems, 20*, 471–487.

Hindelang, M. J., Gottfredson, M. R., & Garofalo, J. (1978). *Victims of personal crime: An empirical foundation for a theory of personal victimization*. Cambridge, MA: Ballinger.

Hirschfield, P. J. (2008). The declining significance of delinquent labels in disadvantaged urban communities. *Sociological Forum, 23*, 575–601.

Hirschi, T. (1969). *Causes of delinquency*. Berkeley and Los Angeles: University of California Press.

Hirschi, T. (1980). Labelling theory and juvenile delinquency: An assessment of the evidence. In Walter Gove (Ed.), *The labelling of deviance: Evaluating a perspective* (2nd ed., pp. 271–302). New York: Wiley.

Hirschi, T. (1987). Review of *Explaining Delinquency and Drug Use*, by Delbert S. Elliott, David Huizinga, and Suzanne S. Ageton. *Criminology, 25*, 193–201.

Hirschi, T. (1989). Exploring alternatives to integrated theory. In S. F. Messner, M. D. Krohn, & A. E. Liska (Eds.), *Theoretical integration in the study of deviance and crime* (pp. 37–49). Albany: State University of New York Press.

Hirschi, T. (2004). Self-control and crime. In R. F. Baumeister & K. D. Vohls (Eds.), *Handbook of self-regulation: Research, theory and applications* (pp. 537–552). New York: Guilford Press.

Hirschi, T., & Gottfredson, M. (1983). Age and the explanation of crime. *American Journal of Sociology, 89*, 552–584.

Hirschi, T., & Gottfredson, M. (1985). Age and crime, logic and scholarship: Comment on Greenberg. *American Journal of Sociology, 91*, 22–27.

Hirschi, T., & Gottfredson, M. R. (1987). Causes of white-collar crime. *Criminology, 25*, 949–974.

Hirschi, T., & Gottfredson, M. R. (1989). The significance of white-collar crime for a general theory of crime. *Criminology, 27*, 359–371.

Hirschi, T., & Gottfredson, M. (1995). Control theory and the life-course perspective. *Studies on Crime and Crime Prevention, 4*, 131–142.

Hirschi, T., & Stark, R. (1969). Hellfire and delinquency. *Social Problems, 17*, 202–213.

Hjalmarsson, R. (2008). Criminal justice involvement and high school completion. *Journal of Urban Economics, 63*, 613–630.

Hoffmann, J. P. (2003). A contextual analysis of differential association, social control, and strain theories of delinquency. *Social Forces, 81*, 753–785.

Hoffmann, J. P., & Cerbone, F. G. (1999). Stressful life events and delinquency escalation in early adolescence. *Criminology, 37*, 343–374.

Hoffmann, J. P., & Ireland, T. (1995). Cloward and Ohlin's strain theory reexamined: An elaborated theoretical model. In F. Adler & W. S. Laufer (Eds.), *The legacy of anomie theory* (pp. 247–270). New Brunswick, NJ: Transaction.

Hoffmann, J. P., & Ireland, T. O. (2004). Strain and opportunity structures. *Journal of Quantitative Criminology, 20*, 263–292.

Hoffmann, J. P., & Miller, A. S. (1998). A latent variable analysis of general strain theory. *Journal of Quantitative Criminology, 14*, 83–110.

Hoffmann, J. P., & Su, S. S. (1997). The conditional effects of stress on delinquency and drug use: A strain theory assessment of sex differences. *Journal of Research in Crime and Delinquency, 34*, 46–78.

Hollenhorst, P. S. (1998). What do we know about anger management programs in corrections? *Federal Probation, 62*, 52–65.

Hollon, S. D., & Beck, A. T. (2003). Cognitive and cognitive behavioral therapies. In M. J. Lambert (Ed.), *Bergin and Garfield's handbook of psychotherapy and behavior change* (5th ed., pp. 447–492). New York: Wiley.

Horne, C. (2001). Sociological perspectives. In M. Hechter & K. D. Opp (Eds.), *Social norms* (pp. 3–34). New York: Russell Sage.

Horney, J. D., Osgood, D. W., & Marshall, I. H. (1995). Criminal careers in the short-term: Intra-individual variability in crime and its relation to local life circumstances. *American Sociological Review, 60*, 655–673.

Horowitz, A., & Wasserman, M. (1979). The effect of social control on delinquent behavior: A longitudinal test. *Sociological Focus, 12*, 53–70.

Horowitz, R., & Schwartz, G. (1974). Honor, normative ambiguity and gang violence. *American Sociological Review, 39*, 238–251.

Horwitz, A. V. (1990). *The logic of social control*. New York: Plenum Press.

Huizinga, D., & Henry, K. L. (2008). In A. M. Liberman (Ed.), *The long view of crime: A synthesis of longitudinal research* (pp. 220–254). New York: Springer.

Hyman, H. H. (1966). The value systems of different classes. A social psychological contribution to the analysis of stratification. In R. Bendix & S. M. Lipset (Eds.), *Class, status, and power* (pp. 488–499). New York: Free Press.

Iacoboni, M., Woods, R. P., Brass, M., Bekkering, H., Mazziotta, J. C., & Rizzolatti, G. (1999). Cortical mechanisms of human imitation. *Science, 286,* 2526–2528.

Ireland, T. O., Smith, C. A., & Thornberry, T. P. (2002). Developmental issues in the impact of child maltreatment on later delinquency and drug use. *Criminology, 40,* 359–400.

Isles, A. R., Humby, T., Walters, E., & Wilkinson, L. S. (2004). Common genetic effects on variation in impulsivity and activity in mice. *Journal of Neuroscience, 24,* 6733–6740.

Jackson, A., Gililand, K., & Veneziano, L. (2006). Routine activity theory and sexual deviance among male college students. *Journal of Family Violence, 21*(7), 449–460.

Jacobs, B. (1992). Undercover drug use evasion tactics: Excuses and neutralizations. *Symbolic Interaction, 15,* 435–454.

Jacobs, B. (1996). Crack dealers and restrictive deterrence: Identifying narcs. *Criminology, 34,* 409–432.

Jacobs, B., Topalli, V., & Wright, R. (2000). Managing retaliation: Drug robbery and informal sanction threat. *Criminology, 38,* 171–198.

Jacobs, B., & Wright, R. (1999). Stick-up, street culture, and offender motivation. *Criminology, 37,* 149–174.

Jacobs, B., & Wright, R. (2006). *Street justice: Retaliation in the criminal underworld.* New York: Cambridge University Press.

Jacques, S., & Wright R. (2006). *The costs and benefits of social distance and status in illicit drug sales.* Paper presented at the annual meeting of the American Sociological Association, Montreal, Canada.

Jacques, S., & Wright, R. (2008). The relevance of peace to studies of drug market violence. *Criminology, 46.*

Jacques, S., & Wright, R. (in press). Drug law and violent retaliation. In H. Barlow & S. Decker (Eds.), *Criminology and public policy: Putting theory to work* (2nd ed.). Philadelphia: Temple University Press.

Jaeger, G., & Selznick, P. (1964). A normative theory of culture. *American Sociological Review, 29,* 653–669.

Jaffee, S. R., Caspi, A., Moffitt, T. E., Dodge, K. A., Rutter, M., Taylor, A., et al. (2005). Nature x nurture: Genetic vulnerabilities interact with physical maltreatment to promote conduct problems. *Development and Psychopathology, 17,* 67–84.

James, A. S., Groman, S. M., Seu, E., Jorgensen, M., Fairbanks, L. A., & Jentschi, J. D. (2007). Dimensions of impulsivity are associated with poor spatial working memory performance in monkeys. *Journal of Neuroscience, 27,* 14358–14364.

Jang, S. J., & Johnson, B. R. (2003). Strain, negative emotions, and deviant coping among African-Americans: A test of general strain theory. *Journal of Quantitative Criminology, 19,* 79–105.

Jensen, G. F. (2000). Prohibition, alcohol, and murder: Untangling countervailing mechanisms. *Homicide Studies, 4,* 18–36.

Jensen, G. F. (2002). Institutional anomie and societal variations in crime: A critical appraisal. *International Journal of Sociology and Social Policy, 22,* 45–74.

Jensen, G. F. (2004). Prohibition, alcohol, and murder: Untangling countervailing mechanisms. *Homicide Studies, 4*(1), 18–36.

Johnson, H. (1998). Rethinking survey research on violence against women. In R. E. Dobash & R. P. Dobash (Eds.), *Rethinking violence against women* (pp. 23–51). Thousand Oaks, CA: Sage.

Johnson, L. M., Simons, R. L., & Conger, R. D. (2004). Criminal justice system involvement and continuity of youth crime. *Youth & Society, 36*, 3–29.

Johnson, M. (1991). Commitment to personal relationships. In W. Jones & D. Perlman (Eds.), *Advances in personal relationships* (Vol. 3, pp. 117–143). London: Jessica Kingsley.

Johnson, R. E. (1979). *Juvenile delinquency and its origins: An integrated theoretical approach.* New York: Cambridge University Press.

Jolls, C., Sunstein, C. R., & Thaler, R. (1998). A behavioral approach to law and economics. *Stanford Law Review, 50*, 1471–1550.

Kandel, D., & Davies, M. (1991). Friendship networks, intimacy, and illicit drug use in young adulthood: A comparison of two competing theories. *Criminology, 29*, 441–469.

Kandel, D. B. (1996). The parental and peer contexts of adolescent deviance: An algebra of interpersonal influences. *Journal of Drug Issues, 26*, 289–315.

Kaplan, H. B., & Johnson, R. J. (1991). Negative social sanctions and juvenile delinquency: Effects of labeling in a model of deviant behavior. *Social Science Quarterly, 72*, 98–122.

Katz, J. (1988). *Seductions of crime.* New York: Basic Books.

Keane, C., Maxim, P., & Teevan, J. (1993). Drinking and driving, self-control and gender: Testing a general theory of crime. *Journal of Research in Crime and Delinquency, 30*, 30–46.

Kelling, G. L., & Coles, C. M. (1996). *Fixing broken windows.* New York: Simon & Schuster.

Kelling, G. L., & Moore, M. H. (1988). The evolving strategy of policing. *Perspectives on Policing, 4*, 1–15. Washington, DC: National Institute of Justice.

Kelling, G. L., & Sousa, W. H., Jr. (2001). *Do police matter? An analysis of the impact of New York City's police reforms.* New York: The Manhattan Institute.

Kempf-Leonard, K. (1993). The empirical status of Hirschi's control theory. In F. Adler & W. S. Laufer (Eds.), *New directions in criminological theory: Advances in criminological theory* (pp. 145–187). New Brunswick, NJ: Transaction.

Kim, T. E., & Goto, S. G. (2000). Peer delinquency and parental social support as predictors of Asian American adolescent delinquency. *Deviant Behavior, 21*, 331–348.

Kitsuse, J. I., & Cicourel, A. V. (1963). A note on the uses of official statistics. *Social Problems, 11*, 131–139.

Klein, D. (1973). The etiology of female crime: A review of the literature. *Issues in Criminology, 8*, 3–29.

Klein, M. W. (1986). Labeling theory and delinquency policy: An experimental test. *Criminal Justice and Behavior, 13*, 47–79.

Koenigs, M., Young, L., Adolphs, R., Tranel, D., Cushman, F., Hauser, M., et al. (2007). Damage to the prefrontal cortex increases utilitarian moral judgements. *Nature, 446*, 901–911.

Kornhauser, R. R. (1978). *Social sources of delinquency: An appraisal of analytic models.* Chicago: University of Chicago Press.

Krahe, B. (2001). *The social psychology of aggression.* New York: Psychology Press.

Kropotkin, P. (1912). *Modern science and anarchism.* London: Unwin.

Kropotkin, P. (1992). *Words of a rebel* (G. Woodcock, Trans.). New York: Black Rose Books. (Original work published 1885)

Kruttschnitt, C. (1996). Contributions of quantitative methods to the study of gender and crime, or bootstrapping our way into the theoretical thicket. *Journal of Quantitative Criminology, 12*, 135–161.

Kubrin, C., & Weitzer, R. (2003a). New directions in social disorganization theory. *Journal of Research in Crime and Delinquency, 40*, 374–402.

Kubrin, C. E., & Weitzer, R. (2003b). Retaliatory homicide: Concentrated disadvantage and neighborhood culture. *Social Problems, 50*, 157–180.

LaGrange, T. (1999). The impact of neighborhoods, schools, and malls on the spatial distribution of property damage. *Journal of Research in Crime and Delinquency, 36*(4), 393–422.

Lasley, J. (1989). Drinking routines/lifestyles and predatory victimization: A causal analysis. *Justice Quarterly, 6*, 529–542.

Laub, J. H., Nagin, D. S., & Sampson, R. J. 1998. Trajectories of change in criminal offending: Good marriage and the desistance process. *American Sociological Review, 63*, 225–238.

Laub, J. H., & Sampson, R. (2003). *Shared beginnings, divergent lives: Delinquent boys to age 70*. Cambridge, MA: Harvard University Press.

Lea, J., & Young, J. (1984). *What is to be done about law and order?* Harmondsworth, England: Penguin.

LeBlanc, L. A., & Le, L. (1999). Behavioral treatment. In M. Hersen & R. T. Ammerman (Eds.), *Advanced abnormal child psychology* (pp. 197–218). Mahwah, NJ: Erlbaum.

Lemert, E. (1951). *Social pathology: A systematic approach to the theory of sociopathic behavior*. New York/Toronto/London: McGraw-Hill.

Levine, D. N. (1985). *The flight from ambiguity: Essays in social and cultural theory*. Chicago: University of Chicago Press.

Lewis, O. (1969). *A death in the Sanchez family*. New York: Random House.

Lieberson, S. (1985). *Making it count: The improvement of social research and theory*. Berkeley: University of California Press.

Liebow, E. (1967). *Tally's corner: A study of Negro street corner men*. Boston: Little, Brown.

Lilly, J. R., Cullen, F. T., & Ball, R. A. (1995). *Criminological theory: Context and consequences* (2nd ed.). Thousand Oaks, CA: Sage.

Lilly, J. R., Cullen, F. T., & Ball, R. A. (2007). *Criminological theory* (4th ed.). Thousand Oaks, CA: Sage.

Link, B. G., Cullen, F. T., Struening, E., Shrout, P. E., & Dohrenwend, B. P. (1989). A modified labeling theory approach to mental disorders: An empirical assessment. *American Sociological Review, 54*, 400–423.

Liska, A. E., & Messner, S. F. (1999). *Perspectives on crime and deviance* (3rd ed.). Upper Saddle River, NJ: Prentice Hall.

Listokin, Y. (2002). Efficient time bars: A new rationale for the existence of statutes of limitations in criminal law. *The Journal of Legal Studies, 31*, 99–118.

Listokin, Y. (2007). Crime and (with a lag) punishment: Equitable sentencing and implications of discounting. *American Criminal Law Review, 44*, 115–145.

Liu, X., & Kaplan, H. (1999). Explaining the gender difference in adolescent delinquent behavior: A longitudinal test of mediating mechanisms. *Criminology, 37*, 195–215.

Loeber, R., & Farrington, D. P. (2001). The significance of child delinquency. In R. Loeber & D. P. Farrington (Eds.), *Child delinquents: Development, intervention, and service needs* (pp. 1–24). Thousand Oaks, CA: Sage.

Lombroso, C. (2006). *Criminal man*. Durham, NC: Duke University Press. (Original work published 1876)

Lombroso-Ferrero, G. (1911). *Criminal man, according to the classification of Cesare Lombroso*. New York: G. P. Putnam.

Lowenkamp, C. T., Cullen, F. T., & Pratt, T. C. (2003). Replicating Sampson and Groves's test of social disorganization theory: Revisiting a criminological classic. *Journal of Research in Crime and Delinquency, 40*, 351–373.

Lu, H., Zhang, L., & Miethe, T. D. (2002). Interdependency, communitarianism and reintegrative shaming in China. *The Social Science Journal, 39*, 189–201.

Luckenbill, D., & Doyle, D. P. (1989). Structural position and violence. Developing a cultural explanation. *Criminology, 27*, 419–436.

Lynch, J. (1987). Routine activity and victimization at work. *Journal of Quantitative Criminology, 3*, 283–300.

Lynch, M. (1988). The extraction of surplus value, crime, and punishment: A preliminary empirical analysis for the U.S. *Contemporary Crises, 12*, 329–344.

Lynch, M., & Groves, B. (1989). *A primer in radical criminology* (2nd ed.). New York: Harrow and Heston.

Lynch, M., Michalowski, R., & Groves, B. (2000). *A primer in radical criminology: Critical perspectives on crime, power, and identity* (3rd ed.). New York: Criminal Justice Press.

Lynch, M., & Patterson, E. B. (Eds.). (1996). *Justice with prejudice: Race and criminal justice in America.* New York: Harrow & Heston.

Lynch, M., Schwendinger, H., & Schwendinger, J. (2004, November). *The status of empirical research in radical criminology.* Plenary Session paper delivered at the annual meeting of the American Society of Criminology, Nashville, TN.

Lynch, M., & Stretesky, P. (1999). Marxism and social justice: Thinking about social justice, eclipsing criminal justice. In B. Arrigo (Ed.), *Social justice/criminal justice: The maturation of critical theory in law, crime, and deviance.* Belmont, CA: Wadsworth.

MacCormick, N. (1998). Norms, institutions, and institutional facts. *Law and Philosophy, 17*, 301–345.

MacLean, B., & Milovanovic, D. (1991). *New directions in critical criminology.* Vancouver, British Columbia, Canada: Collective Press.

Madriz, E. (1996). The perception of risk in the workplace: A test of routine activity theory. *Journal of Criminal Justice, 24*, 407–412.

Maher, L. (1997). *Sexed work: Gender, race, and resistance in a Brooklyn drug market.* Oxford, England: Oxford University Press.

Maher, L., & Daly, K. (1996). Women in the street level drug economy: Continuity or change. *Criminology, 34*, 465–492.

Maines, D. R. (2001). *The faultline of consciousness: A view of interactionism in criminology.* New York: Aldine de Gruyter.

Maines, D. R., Bridger, J., & Ulmer, J. (1996). Mythic facts and Park's pragmatism: On predecessor selection and theorizing in human ecology. *The Sociological Quarterly, 37*, 521–549.

Makarios, M. D. (2007). Race, abuse, and female criminal violence. *Feminist Criminology, 2*, 100–116.

Makkai, T., & Braithwaite, J. (1994). The dialectics of corporate crime deterrence. *Journal of Research in Crime and Delinquency, 31*, 347–373.

Mankoff, M. (1971). Societal reaction and career deviance: A critical analysis. *The Sociological Quarterly, 12*, 204–217.

Mann, R. (2008). Men's rights and feminist advocacy in Canadian domestic violence policy arenas: Contexts, dynamics, and outcomes of antifeminist backlash. *Feminist Criminology, 3*, 44–75.

Markovsky, B., & Berger, S. M. (1983). Crowd noise and mimicry. *Personality and Social Psychology Bulletin, 9*, 90–96.

Markowitz, F., & Felson, R. B. (1998). Sociodemographic attitudes and violence. *Criminology, 36*, 117–138.

Martin, K., Vieraitis, L. M., & Britto, C. (2006). Gender equality and women's absolute status: A test of feminist models of rape. *Violence Against Women, 12*, 321–339.

Martin, S. E., & Jurik, N. S. (2006). *Doing justice, doing gender: Women in legal and criminal justice occupations.* Thousand Oaks, CA: Sage.

Mason, D. A., & Frick, P. J. (1994). The heritability of antisocial behavior: A meta-analysis of twin and adoption studies. *Journal of Psychopathology and Behavioral Assessment, 16*, 301–323.

Massey, D. S. (2002). A brief history of human society: The origin and role of emotion in social life. *American Sociological Review, 67*, 1–29.

Massey, D. S., & Denton, N. A. (1993). *American apartheid: Segregation and the making of the underclass*. Cambridge, MA: Harvard University Press.

Massey, J., Krohn, M., & Bonati, L. (1989). Property crime and routine activities of individuals. *Journal of Research in Crime and Delinquency, 26*, 378–400.

Matsueda, R. L. (1982). Testing control theory and differential association: A causal modeling approach. *American Sociological Review, 47*, 489–504.

Matsueda, R. L. (1988). The current state of differential association theory. *Crime and Delinquency, 34*, 277–306.

Matsueda, R. L. (1992). Reflected appraisals, parental labeling, and delinquency: Specifying a symbolic interactionist theory. *American Journal of Sociology, 97*, 1577–1611.

Matsueda, R. L, Drakulich, K., & Kubrin, C. E. (2006). Race and neighborhoods and violence. In R. Peterson, J. Krivo, & J. Hagan (Eds.), *The many colors of crime: Inequalities of race, ethnicity, and crime in America* (pp. 334–357). New York: New York University Press.

Matsueda, R. L., Gartner, R., Piliavin, I., & Polakowski, P. (1992). The prestige of criminal and conventional occupations. *American Sociological Review, 57*, 752–770.

Matsueda, R. L., & Heimer, K. (1987). Race, family structure, and delinquency: A test of differential association and social control theories. *American Sociological Review, 52*, 826–840.

Matsueda, R. L., & Heimer, K. (1997). Developmental theories of crime. In T. Thornberry (Ed.), *Advances in criminological theory* (pp. 174–186). New Brunswick, NJ: Transaction.

Matsueda, R. L., Kreager, D. A., & Huizinga, D. (2006). Deterring delinquents: A rational model of theft and vilence. *American Sociological Review, 71*, 95–122.

Matza, D. (1964). *Delinquency and drift*. Berkeley, CA: Wiley.

Matza, D. (1969). *Becoming deviant*. Englewood Cliffs, NJ: Prentice Hall.

Maume, M. O., & Lee, M. R. (2003). Social institutions and violence: A sub-national test of institutional anomie theory. *Criminology, 41*, 1137–1172.

Mazerolle, L. G., Roehl, J., & Kadleck, C. (1998). Controlling social disorder using civil remedies: Results from a randomized field experiment in Oakland, California. In L. G. Mazerolle & J. Roehl (Eds.), *Crime prevention studies* (pp. 141–159). Monsey, NY: Criminal Justice Press.

Mazerolle, P., Burton, V. S., Cullen, F. T., Evans, T. D., & Payne, G. L. (2000). Strain, anger, and delinquent adaptations specifying general strain theory. *Journal of Criminal Justice, 28*, 89–101.

Mazerolle, P., & Maahs, J. (2000). General strain and delinquency: An alternative examination of conditioning influences. *Justice Quarterly, 17*, 753–778.

Mazerolle, P., & Piquero, A. (1998). Linking exposure to strain with anger: An investigation of deviant adaptations. *Journal of Criminal Justice, 26*, 195–211.

McCart, M. R., Priester, P. E., Davies, W. H., & Azen, R. (2006). Differential effectiveness of behavioral parent-training and cognitive-behavioral therapy for antisocial youth: A meta-analysis. *Journal of Abnormal Child Psychology, 34*, 527–543.

McCarthy, B. (2002). The new economics of sociological criminology. *Annual Review of Sociology, 28*, 417–442.

McCarthy, B., & Hagan, J. (2001). When crime pays: Capital, competence, and criminal success. *Social Forces, 79*, 1035–1060.

McGloin, J. M., Pratt, T. C., & Maahs, J. (2004). Rethinking the IQ-delinquency relationship: A longitudinal analysis of multiple theoretical models. *Justice Quarterly, 21*, 603–631.

Mead, G. H. (1934). *Mind, self, and society*. Chicago: University of Chicago Press.

Meares, T. L., & Kahan, D. M. (1998). Law and (norms of) order in the inner city. *Law & Society Review, 32*, 805–837.

Meier, R. F., & Miethe, T. (1993). Understanding theories of criminal victimization. In M. Tonry (Ed.), *Crime and justice: An annual review of research* (pp. 459–499). Chicago: University of Chicago Press.

Menard, S. (1995). A developmental test of Mertonian anomie theory. *Journal of Research in Crime and Delinquency, 32*, 136–174.

Menard, S. (1997). A developmental test of Cloward's differential opportunity theory. In N. Passas & R. Agnew (Eds.), *The future of anomie theory* (pp. 142–186). Boston: Northeastern University Press.

Merry, S. E. (1984). Rethinking gossip and scandal. In D. Black (Ed.), *Toward a general theory of social control: Vol. 1. Fundamentals*. Orlando, FL: Academic Press.

Merton, R. K. (1938). Social structure and anomie. *American Sociological Review, 3*, 672–682.

Merton, R. K. (1964). Anomie, anomia and social interaction. In M. B. Clinard (Ed.), *Anomie and deviant behavior* (pp. 213–242). New York: Free Press.

Merton, R. K. (1968). *Social theory and social structure* (Rev. ed.). New York: Free Press.

Merton, R. K. (1997). On the evolving synthesis of differential association and anomie theory: A perspective from the sociology of science. *Criminology 35*, 517–525.

Messerschmidt, J. W. (1993). *Masculinities and crime*. Lanham, MD: Rowman and Littlefield.

Messerschmidt, J. W. (1997). *Crime as structured action: Gender, race, class, and crime in the making*. Thousand Oaks, CA: Sage.

Messerschmidt, J. W. (2002). Response to Miller. *Theoretical Criminology, 6*, 477–480.

Messner, S. F. (1983). Regional and racial effects on the urban homicide rate. The subculture of violence revisited. *American Journal of Sociology, 88*, 997–1007.

Messner, S. F. (1988). Merton's "social structure and anomie": The road not taken. *Deviant Behavior, 9*, 33–53.

Messner, S. F. (2003). An institutional-anomie theory of crime: Continuities and elaborations in the study of social structure and anomie. *Kölner Zeitschrift für Soziologie und Sozialpsychologie*, Sonderheft, 43, 93–109.

Messner, S. F. (in press). Robert K. Merton: Social structure and anomie. In F. T. Cullen & P. Wilcox (Eds.), *The encyclopedia of criminological theory*. Thousand Oaks, CA: Sage.

Messner, S. F., & Blau, J. (1987). Routine leisure activities and rates of crime: A macro-level analysis. *Social Forces, 65*, 1035–1052.

Messner, S. F., & Rosenfeld, R. (1997a) *Crime and the American dream* (2nd ed.). Belmont, CA: Thomson-Wadsworth.

Messner, S. F., & Rosenfeld, R. (1997b). Political restraint of the market and levels of criminal homicide: A cross-national application of institutional anomie theory. *Social Forces, 75*, 1393–1416.

Messner, S. F., & Rosenfeld, R. (2006). The present and future of institutional-anomie theory. In F. T. Cullen, J. P. Wright, & K. R. Blevins (Eds.), *Taking stock: The status of criminological theory* (pp. 127–148). New Brunswick, NJ: Transactions.

Messner, S. F., & Rosenfeld, R. (2007). *Crime and the American dream* (4th ed.). Belmont, CA: Thomson-Wadsworth.

Messner, S. F., Rosenfeld, R., & Baumer, E. (2004). Dimensions of social capital and rates of criminal homicide. *American Sociological Review, 69*, 882–903.

Messner, S. F., & Tardiff, K. (1985). The social ecology of urban homicide: An application of the routine activities approach. *Criminology, 23*, 241–267.

Meyer-Lindenberg, A., Buckholtz, J. W., Kolachana, B., Hariri, A. R., Pezawas, L., Blasi, G., et al. (2006). Neural mechanisms of genetic risk for impulsivity and violence in humans. *Proceedings of the National Academy of Sciences, 103*, 6269–6274.

Michalowski, R. (1985). *Order, law, and crime: An introduction to criminology*. New York: Random House.

Michalski, J. H. (2004). Making sociological sense out of trends in intimate partner violence: The social structure of violence against women. *Violence Against Women, 10*, 652–675.

Miethe, T., Stafford, M., & Long, J. (1987). Social differentiation in criminal victimization: A test of routine activities/lifestyles theories. *American Sociological Review, 52*, 184–194.

Miethe, T. D., & McDowall, D. (1993). Contextual effects in models of criminal victimization. *Social Forces, 71*, 741–759.

Miethe, T. D., & Meier, R. (1990). Opportunity, choice, and criminal victimization: A test of a theoretical model. *Journal of Research in Crime and Delinquency, 27*, 243–266.

Miles, D. R., & Carey, G. (1997). Genetic and environmental architecture of human aggression. *Journal of Personality and Social Psychology, 72*, 207–217.

Mill, J., Caspi, A., Williams, B. S., Craig, I., Taylor, A., Polo-Tomas, M., et al. (2006). Prediction of heterogeneity in intelligence and adult prognosis by genetic polymorphisms in the dopamine system among children with attention-deficit/hyperactivity disorder. *Archives of General Psychiatry, 63*, 462–469.

Miller, E. (1986). *Street woman*. Philadelphia: Temple University Press.

Miller, J. (1998). Up it up: Gender and the accomplishment of street robbery. *Criminology, 36*(1), 37–66.

Miller, J. (2002). The strengths and limits of "doing gender" for understanding street crime. *Theoretical Criminology, 6*, 433–460.

Miller, J. (2004). Feminist theories of women's crime: Robbery as a case study. In B. R. Price & N. Sokoloff (Eds.), *The criminal justice system and women* (pp. 51–67). Boston: McGraw-Hill.

Miller, S., & Burack, C. (1993). A critique of Gottfredson and Hirschi's general theory of crime: Selective (in)attention to gender and power positions. *Women and Criminal Justice, 4*, 115–134.

Miller, W. B. (1958). Lower-class culture as a generating milieu of gang delinquency. *Journal of Social Issues, 14*, 5–19.

Mills, C. W. (1940). Situated actions and vocabularies of motive. *American Sociological Review, 5*, 904–913.

Milovanovic, D. (1981). The commodity-exchange theory of law: In search of a perspective. *Crime and Social Justice, 16*, 41–49.

Miron, J. A. (2004). *Drug war crimes: The consequences of prohibition*. Oakland, CA: The Independent Institute.

Mizruchi, E. H. (1960). Social structure and anomia in a small city. *American Sociological Review, 25*, 645–654.

Mocan, H. N., & Rees, D. I. (2005). Economic conditions, deterrence and juvenile crime: Evidence from micro data. *American Law and Economic Review, 7*, 319–349.

Moffitt, T. E. (1990). The neuropsychology of juvenile delinquency: A critical review. In M. Tonry & N. Morris (Eds.), *Crime and justice: An annual review of Research* (Vol. 12, pp. 99–169). Chicago: University of Chicago Press.

Moffitt, T. E. (1993). Adolescence-limited and life-course-persistent antisocial behavior: A developmental taxonomy. *Psychological Review, 100*, 674–701.

Moffitt, T. E. (2005). The new look of behavioral genetics in developmental psychopathology: Gene-environment interplay in antisocial behaviors. *Psychological Bulletin, 131*, 533–554.

Moffitt, T. E., & Caspi, A. (2001). Childhood predictors differentiate life-course persistent and adolescence-limited pathways among males and females. *Development and Psychopathology, 13*, 355–375.

Morash, M. (1999). A consideration of gender in relation to social learning and social structure: A general theory of crime and deviance. *Theoretical Criminology, 3*, 451–462.

Morenoff, J. D., & Sampson, R. J. (1997). Violent crime and the spatial dynamics of neighborhood transition: Chicago, 1970–1990. *Social Forces, 76*, 31–64.

Moriarty, L., & Williams, J. (1996). Examining the relationship between routine activities theory and social disorganization: An analysis of property crime victimization. *American Journal of Criminal Justice, 21*, 43–59.

Moynihan, D. P. (1969). *Maximum feasible misunderstanding, community action in the war on poverty*. New York: Free Press.

Mustaine, E., & Tewksbury, R. (1999). A routine activities theory explanation for women's stalking victimization. *Violence Against Women, 5*, 43–62.

Mustaine, E., & Tewksbury, R. (2002). Sexual assault of college women: A feminist interpretation of a routine activities analysis. *Criminal Justice Review, 27*, 89–123.

Nagin, D. S., & Pogarsky, G. (2003). An experimental investigation of deterrence: Cheating, self-serving bias, and impulsivity. *Criminology, 41*, 501–527.

Nagin, D. S., & Tremblay, R. E. (2005a). Developmental trajectory groups: Fact or fiction? *Criminology, 43*, 873–904.

Nagin, D. S., & Tremblay, R. E. (2005b). From seduction to passion: A response to Sampson and Laub. *Criminology, 43*, 915–918.

Nisbett, R. E., & Cohen, D. (1996). *Culture of honor: The psychology of violence in the South*. Boulder, CO: Westview Press.

Novak, K. J., Harman, J. L., Holsinger, A. M., & Turner, M. G. (1999). The effects of aggressive policing of disorder on serious crime. *Policing: An International Journal of Police Strategies & Management, 22*, 171–190.

Nye, F. I. (1958). *Family relationships and delinquent behavior*. Westport, CT: Greenwood Press.

Oberman, L. M., Hubbard, E. M., McCleery, J. P., Altschuler, E. L., Ramachandran, V. S., & Pineda, J. A. (2005). EEG evidence for mirror neuron dysfunction in autism. *Cognitive Brain Research, 24*, 190–198.

Olds, D. (2002). Prenatal and infancy home visiting by nurses: From randomized trials to community replication. *Prevention Science, 3*, 153–172.

Olds, D., Henderson, C. R., Cole, R., Eckenrode, J., Kitzman, H., Luckey, D., et al. (1998a). Long-term effects of nurse home visitation on children's criminal and antisocial behavior. *Journal of the American Medical Association, 280*, 1238–1244.

Olds, D., Hill, P., Mihalic, S., & O'Brien, R. (1998b). *Blueprints for violence prevention: Book 7. Prenatal and infancy home visitation by nurses*. Boulder, CO: Center for the Study and Prevention of Violence.

Osgood, D., & Anderson, A. (2004). Unstructured socializing and rates of delinquency. *Criminology, 42*, 519–549.

Osgood, D., Wilson, J., O'Malley, P., Bachman, J., & Johnston, J. (1996). Routine activities and individual deviant behavior. *American Sociological Review, 61*, 636–655.

Pager, D. (2003). The mark of a criminal record. *American Journal of Sociology, 108*, 937–975.

Palarma, F., Cullen, F. T., & Gersten, J. C. (1986). The effect of police and mental health intervention on juvenile deviance: Specifying contingencies in the impact of formal reaction. *Journal of Health and Social Behavior, 27*, 90–105.

Park, R., Burgess, E. W., & McKenzie, R. D. (1925). *The city*. Chicago: University of Chicago Press.

Parsons, T. (1951). *The social system*. New York: Free Press.

Parsons, T. (1954). A sociologist looks at the legal profession. In *Essays in sociological theory*. New York: Free Press. (Original work published 1952)

Paternoster, R., & Brame, R. (1998) The structural similarity of processes generating criminal and analogous behavior. *Criminology, 36*, 633–670.

Paternoster, R., & Iovanni, L. (1989). The labeling perspective and delinquency: An elaboration of the theory and assessment of the evidence. *Justice Quarterly, 6*, 359–394.

Paternoster, R., & Mazerolle, P. (1994). General strain theory and delinquency: A replication and extension. *Journal of Research in Crime and Delinquency, 31*, 235–263.

Pease, K. (2002). Repeat victimization and the policing of communities. *International Review of Victimology, 9*, 137–148.

Perinbanayagam, R. (1986). The meaning of uncertainty and the uncertainty of meaning. *Symbolic Interaction, 9*, 105–126.

Pettigrew, T. F., & Spier, R. (1962). The ecological structure of Negro homicide. *American Journal of Sociology, 47*, 621–629.

Pezzin, L. E. (1995). Earnings prospects, matching effects, and the decision to terminate a criminal career. *Journal of Quantitative Criminology, 11*, 29–50.

Pfhol, S. (1985). *Images of deviance and social control. A sociological history*. New York: McGraw-Hill.

Phillips, S. (2003). The social structure of vengeance: A test of Black's model. *Criminology, 41*, 673–708.

Phillips, S., & Cooney, M. (2005). Aiding peace, abetting violence: Third parties and the management of conflict. *American Sociological Review, 70*, 334–354.

Piaget, J. (1963). *The origins of intelligence in children*. New York: Norton.

Piquero, A. R. (1999). The validity of incivility measures in public housing. *Justice Quarterly, 16*, 793–818.

Piquero, A. R., & Bouffard, J. (2007). Something old, something new: A preliminary investigation of Hirschi's redefined self-control. *Justice Quarterly, 24*, 1–27.

Piquero, A. R., Brame, R., Mazerolle, P., & Haapanen, R. (2002). Crime in emerging adulthood. *Criminology, 40*, 137–169.

Piquero, N. L., Exum, M. L., & Simpson, S. S. (2005). Integrating the desire-for-control and rational choice in a corporate crime context. *Justice Quarterly, 22*, 252–280.

Piquero, A. R., MacDonald, J., Dobrin, A., Daigle, L. E., & Cullen, F. T. (2005). Self-control, violent infractions, and homicide victimization: Assessing the general theory of crime. *Journal of Quantitative Criminology, 21*, 55–71.

Piquero, A. R., & Mazerolle, P. (Eds.). (2001). *Life course criminology: Contemporary and classic readings*. Belmont, CA: Wadsworth.

Piquero, A., & Piquero, N. L. (1998). On testing institutional anomie theory with varying specifications. *Studies on Crime and Crime Prevention, 7*, 61–84.

Piquero, N. L., Schoepfer, A., & Langton, L. (in press). Completely out of control or the desire to be in complete control? How low self-control and the desire-for-control relate to corporate offending. *Crime and Delinquency*.

Plomin, R., & Daniels, D. (1987). Why are children in the same family so different from one another? *Behavioral and Brain Sciences, 10*, 1–60.

Plomin, R., DeFries, J. C., Craig, I. W., & McGuffin, P. (2003). *Behavioral genetics in the post-genomic era*. Washington, DC: American Psychological Association.

Pogarsky, G. (2002). Identifying deterrable offenders: Implications for deterrence research. *Justice Quarterly, 19*, 431–452.

Pogarsky, G., Kim, K., & Paternoster, R. (2005). Perceptual change in the National Youth Survey: Lessons for deterrence theory and offender decision making. *Justice Quarterly, 22*, 1–29.

Poland, K. (1978). The subculture of violence. Youth offender value systems. *Criminal Justice and Behavior, 5*, 159–164.

Posner, R. A. (1992). *Economic analysis of the law* (4th ed.). Boston: Little, Brown.

Posner, R. A. (1998). Rational choice, behavioral economics, and the law. *Stanford Law Review, 50*, 1551–1575.

Potter, H. (2006). An argument for black feminist criminology: Understanding African American women's experiences with intimate partner abuse using an integrated approach. *Feminist Criminology, 1*, 106–124.

Pratt, T. C., & Cullen, F. T. (2000). The empirical status of Gottfredson and Hirschi's general theory of crime: A meta-analysis. *Criminology, 38*, 931–964.

Pratt, T. C., Cullen, F. T., Blevins K. R., Daigle, L. E., & Madensen, T. D. (2006). The empirical status of deterrence theory: A meta-analysis. In F. T. Cullen, J. P. Wright, & K. R. Blevins (Eds.), *Advances in criminological theory* (Vol. 15, pp. 367–396). Edison, NJ: Transaction.

Pratt, T. C., & Godsey, T. W. (2003). Social support, inequality, and homicide: A cross-national test of an integrated theoretical model. *Criminology, 41*, 611–643.

Pratt, T. C., Maahs, J., & Stehr, S. D. (1998). The symbolic ownership of the corrections "problem": A framework for understanding the development of corrections policy in the United States. *Prison Journal, 78*, 451–464.

Pratt, T. C., Turner, M. G., & Piquero, A. R. (2004). Parental socialization and community context: A longitudinal analysis of the structural sources of low self-control. *Journal of Research in Crime and Delinquency, 41*, 219–243.

Preston, C. (2007). Zoning the Internet: A new approach to protecting children online. *Brigham Young University Law Review*, 1417–1467.

Price, B., & Sokoloff, N. (2004). *The criminal justice system and women* (3rd ed.). New York: McGraw-Hill.

Quinney, R. (1970). *The social reality of crime*. Boston: Little, Brown.

Quinney, R. (1980). *Class, state, and crime* (2nd ed.). New York: Longman.

Rafter, N., & Heidensohn, F. (1995). *International feminist perspectives in criminology: Engendering a discipline*. Buckingham, England: Open University Press.

Raine, A. (1993). *The psychopathology of crime: Criminal behavior as a clinical disorder*. San Diego, CA: Academic Press.

Raine, A., Brennan, P., & Mednick, S. A. (1997). Interaction between birth complications and early maternal rejection in predisposing individuals to adult violence: Specificity to serious, early-onset violence. *American Journal of Psychiatry, 154*, 1265–1271.

Rainwater, L. (1970). *Behind ghetto walls: Black family life in a federal slum*. Chicago: Aldine de Gruyter.

Ramachandran, V. S. (2000, May 29). Mirror neurons and imitation learning as the driving force behind "the great leap forward" in human evolution. *Edge, 69*.

Ramachandran, V. S. (2006, January 12). Mirror neurons and the brain in the vat. *Edge, 176*.

Ray, M. C., & Downs, W. (1986). An empirical test of labeling theory using longitudinal data. *Journal of Research in Crime and Delinquency, 23*, 169–194.

Reaves, B. (1992). Pretrial release of felony defendants, 1990. *Bureau of Justice Statistics Bulletin*. Washington, DC: Office of Justice Programs, U.S. Department of Justice.

Rebellon, C. J. (2002). Reconsidering the broken homes/delinquency relationship and exploring its mediating mechanism(s). *Criminology, 40*, 103–136.

Reckless, W. C. (1961). A new theory of delinquency and crime. *Federal Probation, 25*, 42–46.

Reiman, J. (1995). *The rich get richer and the poor get prison* (2nd ed.). Boston: Allyn & Bacon.

Reiman, J. (2007). *The rich get richer and the poor get prison* (8th ed.). Boston: Allyn & Bacon.

Reiss, A. J. (1951). Delinquency as the failure of personal and social controls. *American Sociological Review, 16*, 196–207.

Retz, W., Retz-Junginger, P., Supprian, T., Thome, J., & Rosler, M. (2004). Association of serotonin transporter promoter gene polymorphism with violence: Relation with personality disorders, impulsivity, and childhood ADHD psychopathology. *Behavioral Sciences and the Law, 22*, 415–425.

Rhee, S. H., & Waldman, I. D. (2002). Genetic and environmental influences on antisocial behavior: A meta-analysis of twin and adoption studies. *Psychological Bulletin, 128*, 490–529.

Rhodes, R. (1999). *Why they kill: Discoveries of a maverick criminologist*. New York: Knopf.

Richerson, P. J., & Boyd, R. (2005). *Not by genes alone: How culture transformed human evolution*. Chicago: University of Chicago Press.

Richie, B. (1996). *Compelled to crime: The gender entrapment of black battered women*. New York: Routledge.

Rilling, J. K, Gutman, D. A., Thorsten, R. Z., & Pagnoni, G. (2002). A neural basis for social cooperation. *Neuron, 35*, 395–405.

Rizzolatti, G., Fadiga, L., Gallese, V., & Fogassi, L. (1996). Premotor cortex and the recognition of motor actions. *Cognitive Brain Research, 3*, 131–141.

Roberts, D. E. (1999). Race, vagueness, and the social meaning of order-maintenance policing. *Journal of Criminal Law & Criminology, 89*, 775–836.

Rodman, H. (1963/1964). The lower-class value stretch. *Social Forces, 42*, 203–215.

Rogers, E. (1983). *The diffusion of innovations*. New York: Free Press.

Rogers, M. (2001). *A social learning theory and moral disengagement analysis of criminal computer behavior: An exploratory study*. Doctoral dissertation, University of Manitoba, Winnipeg, Canada.

Roncek, D., & Bell, R. (1981). Bars, blocks, and crimes. *Journal of Environmental Systems, 11*, 35–47.

Roncek, D., & Maier, P. (1991). Bars, blocks, and crimes revisited: Linking the theory of routine activities to the empiricism of "hot spots." *Criminology, 29*, 725–753.

Rose, D., & Clear, T. (1998). Incarceration, social capital, and crime: Implications for social disorganization theory. *Criminology, 36*, 441–480.

Rosenfeld, R. (1994). Neighborhoods and crime: The dimensions of effective community control by R. J. Bursik, Jr. and H. G. Grasmick. *American Journal of Sociology*, 1387–1389.

Rosenfeld, R. (2001). The role of third parties in violent conflict: A comment on Cooney's theory of third parties. *Theoretical Criminology, 5*, 269–272.

Rosenfeld, R., Jacobs, B., & Wright, R. (2003). Snitching and the code of the street. *British Journal of Criminology, 43*, 291–309.

Rosenfeld, R., & Lauritsen, J. (2008). The most dangerous crime rankings. *Contexts, 7*, 66–67.

Rosenfeld, R., & Messner, S. F. (in press). The normal crime rate, the economy, and mass incarceration: An institutional-anomie perspective on crime-control policy. In S. Decker & H. Barlow (Eds.), *Criminology and public policy: Putting theory to work*. Philadelphia: Temple University Press.

Rothman, D. J. (1980). *Conscience and convenience: The asylum and its alternatives in progressive America*. Boston: Little, Brown.

Rotter, J. B. (1954). *Social learning and clinical psychology*. New York: Prentice Hall.

Rowe, D. C. (1987). Resolving the person-situation debate: Invitation to an interdisciplinary dialogue. *American Psychologist, 42*, 218–227.

Rowe, D. C. (1994). *The limits of family influence: Genes, experience, and behavior*. New York: Guilford Press.

Rowe, D. C. (2002). *Biology and crime*. Los Angeles: Roxbury.

Rowe, D. C., & Plomin, R. (1981). The importance of nonshared ($E_1$) environmental influences on behavioral development. *Developmental Psychology, 17*, 517–531.

Rushing, W. A. (1970). Class differences in goal orientations and aspirations: Rural patterns. *Rural Sociology, 35*, 377–395.

Rutter, M. (2005). Commentary: What is the meaning and utility of the psychopathy concept? *Journal of Abnormal Child Psychology, 33*, 499–503.

Ryan, J. P., & Testa, M. F. (2005). Child maltreatment and juvenile delinquency: Investigating the role of placement and placement instability. *Children and Youth Services Review, 27*, 227–249.

Sampson, R. J. (1986). Neighborhood family structure and the risk of personal victimization. In R. J. Sampson & J. M. Byrne (Eds.), *The social ecology of crime* (pp. 25–46). New York: Springer-Verlag.

Sampson, R. J. (1987a). Personal violence by strangers: An extension and test of the opportunity model of predatory victimization. *Journal of Criminal Law and Criminology, 78*, 327–356.

Sampson, R. J. (1987b). Urban black violence: The effect of male joblessness and family disruption. *American Journal of Sociology, 93*, 348–382.

Sampson, R. J. (2006). Collective efficacy theory: Lessons learned and directions for future inquiry. In F. T. Cullen, J. P. Wright, & K. R. Blevins (Eds.), *Taking stock: The status of criminological theory, advances in criminological theory* (Vol. 15, pp. 149–168). New Brunswick, NJ: Transaction.

Sampson, R. J., & Bartusch, D. J. (1998). Legal cynicism and (subculture?) tolerance of deviance: The neighborhood context of racial differences. *Law & Society Review, 32*, 777–804.

Sampson, R. J., & Bean, L. (2006). Cultural mechanisms and killing fields. A revised theory of community-level racial inequality. In R. Peterson, J. Krivo, & J. Hagan (Eds.), *The many colors of crime: Inequalities of race, ethnicity, and crime in America* (pp. 8–38). New York: New York University Press.

Sampson, R. J., & Groves, W. (1989). Community structure and crime: testing social disorganization theory. *American Journal of Sociology, 94*, 774–802.

Sampson, R. J., & Laub, J. (1992). Crime and deviance in the life course. *Annual Review of Sociology, 18*, 63–84.

Sampson, R. J., & Laub, J. (1993). *Crime in the making: Pathways and turning points through life*. Cambridge, MA: Harvard University Press.

Sampson, R. J., & Laub, J. H. (1995). Understanding variability in lives through time: Contributions of life-course criminology. *Studies on Crime and Crime Prevention, 4*, 143–158.

Sampson, R. J., & Laub, J. H. (1997). A life-course theory of cumulative disadvantage and the stability of delinquency. In T. P. Thornberry (Ed.), *Developmental theories of crime and delinquency* (pp. 133–161). New Brunswick, NJ: Transaction.

Sampson, R. J., & Laub, J. H. (2003). Life-course desisters? Trajectories of crime among delinquent boys followed to age 70. *Criminology, 41*, 555–592.

Sampson, R. J., & Laub, J. H. (2005). Seductions of method: Rejoinder to Nagin and Tremblay's "Developmental trajectory groups": Fact or useful fiction? *Criminology, 43*, 905–913.

Sampson, R. J., Laub, J. H., & Wimer, C. (2006). Does marriage reduce crime? A counterfactual approach to within-individual causal effects. *Criminology, 44*, 465–508.

Sampson, R. J., & Lauritsen, J. L. (1994). Violent victimization and offending: Individual-, situational-, and community-level risk factors. In A. J. Reiss & J. A. Roth (Eds.), *Understanding and preventing violence* (Vol. 3, pp. 1–114). Washington, DC: National Academy Press.

Sampson, R. J., Morenoff, J., & Raudenbush, S. (2005). Social anatomy of racial and ethnic disparities in violence. *American Journal of Public Health, 95*, 224–232.

Sampson, R. J., & Raudenbush, S. W. (1999). Systematic social observation of public spaces: A new look at disorder in urban neighborhoods. *The American Journal of Sociology, 105*, 603–651.

Sampson, R. J., & Raudenbush, S. W. (2004). Seeing disorder: Neighborhood stigma and the social construction of "broken windows." *Social Psychology Quarterly, 67*, 319–342.

Sampson, R. J., Raudenbusch, S., & Earls, F. (1997). Neighborhoods and violent crime: A multilevel study of collective efficacy. *Science, 227*, 918–924.

Sampson, R. J., & Wilson, W. J. (1995). Toward a theory of race, crime and urban inequality. In J. Hagan & R. D. Peterson (Eds.), *Crime and inequality* (pp. 37–54). Stanford, CA: Stanford University Press.

Sampson, R. J., & Wooldredge, J. (1987). Linking the micro- and macro-dimension of lifestyle-routine activity and opportunity models of predatory victimization. *Journal of Quantitative Criminology, 3*, 371–393.

Sasse, S. (2005). "Motivation" and routine activities theory. *Deviant Behavior, 26*, 547–570.

Savolainen, J. (2000). Inequality, welfare state, and homicide: Further support for the institutional anomie theory. *Criminology, 38*, 1021–1042.

Scarr, S. (1992). Developmental theories for the 1990s: Development and individual differences. *Child Development, 63*, 1–19.

Scarr, S., & Carter-Saltzman, L. (1979). Twin method: Defense of a critical assumption. *Behavior Genetics, 9*, 527–542.

Scarr, S., & McCartney, K. (1983). How people make their own environments: A theory of genotype → environment effects. *Child Development, 54*, 424–435.

Scarr, S., & Weinberg, R. A. (1978). The influence of "family background" on intellectual attainment. *American Sociological Review, 43*, 674–692.

Schafer, S. (1968). Anomie, culture conflict, and crime in disorganized and overorganized societies. In M. Wolfgang (Ed.), *Crime and culture* (pp. 83–93). New York: Wiley.

Scheff, T. H. (1966). *Becoming mentally ill*. Chicago: Aldine de Gruyter.

Schreck, C. J. (1999). Criminal victimization and low self-control: An extension and test of a general theory of crime. *Justice Quarterly, 16*, 633–654.

Schreck, C. J., & Fisher, B. (2004). Specifying the influence of the family and peers on violent and victimization. *Journal of Interpersonal Violence, 19*, 1021–1041.

Schreck, C. J., Stewart, E. A., & Fisher, B. S. (2006). Self-control, victimization, and their influence on risky lifestyles: A longitudinal analysis using panel data. *Journal of Quantitative Criminology, 22*, 319–340.

Schreck, C., Wright, R., & Miller, J. (2002). A study of individual and situational antecedents of violent victimization. *Justice Quarterly, 19*, 159–180.

Schwartz, M. D., DeKeseredy, W., Tait, D., & Alvi, S. (2001). Male peer support and a feminist routine activities theory: Understanding sexual assault on the college campus. *Justice Quarterly, 18*, 623–649.

Schwartz, M. D., & Hatty, S. (Eds.). (2003). *Controversies in crime and justice: Critical criminology*. Cincinnati, OH: Anderson.

Schwartz, M. D., & Milovanovic, D. (Eds.). (1999). *Race, gender, and class in criminology: The intersections*. New York: Garland.

Schwartz, M. D., & Pitts, V. (1995). Exploring a feminist routine activities approach to explaining sexual assault. *Justice Quarterly, 12*, 9–31.

Schwartz, R. D., & Skolnick, J. H. (1962). Two studies of legal stigma. *Social Problems, 10*, 133–143.

Sciulli, D. (1995). Donald Black's positivism in law and social control. *Law & Social Inquiry, 20*, 805–828.

Scott, M. B., & Lyman, S. M. (1968). Accounts. *American Sociological Review, 33*, 46–61.

Sellers, C. S., Cochran, J. K., & Winfree, L. T. (2003). Social learning theory and courtship violence: An empirical test. In R. L. Akers & G. F. Jensen (Eds.), *Social learning theory and the explanation of crime: A guide for the new century: Vol. 11. Advances in criminological theory* (pp. 109–128). New Brunswick, NJ: Transaction.

Sellin, T. (1938). *Culture conflict and crime*. New York: Social Science Research Council.

Senechal de la Roche, R. (1996). Collective violence as social control. *Sociological Forum, 11*, 97–128.

Senechal de la Roche, R. (2001). Why is collective violence collective? *Sociological Theory, 19*, 126–144.

Senechal de la Roche, R. (2004). Modern lynchings. In M. A. Zahn, H. H. Brownstein, & S. L. Jackson, (Eds.), *Violence: From theory to research*. Cincinnati, OH: Anderson.

Shalin, D. (1986). Pragmatism and social interactionism. *American Sociological Review, 51*, 9–29.

Shaw, C. R., & McKay, H. D. (1931). Social factors in juvenile delinquency. In National Commission on Law Observance and Enforcement (Report No. 13). *Report on the causes of crime* (Vol. 2). Washington, DC: U.S. Government Printing Office.

Shaw, C. R., & McKay, H. D. (1942). *Juvenile delinquency and urban areas*. Chicago: University of Chicago Press.

Shaw, C. R., & McKay, H. D. (1969). *Juvenile delinquency and urban areas* (Rev. ed.). Chicago: University of Chicago Press.

Sheldon, R. (2001). *Controlling the dangerous classes: A critical introduction to the history of criminal justice*. Boston: Allyn & Bacon.

Sherman, L., Gartin, P., & Buerger, M. (1989). Hot spots of predatory crime: Routine activities and the criminology of place. *Criminology, 27*, 27–55.

Sherman, L. W., & Smith, D. A. (1992). Crime, punishment, and stake in conformity: Legal and informal control of domestic violence. *American Sociological Review, 57*, 680–690.

Short, J. F., Jr., & Stodtbeck, F. I. (1965). *Groups process and gang delinquency*. Chicago: University of Chicago Press.

Shover, N. (1983). The later stages of ordinary property offender careers. *Social Problems, 31*, 208–218.

Shover, N. (1996). *Great pretenders: The pursuits and careers of persistent thieves*. Boulder, CO: Westview Press.

Shover, N., & Honaker, D. (1992). The socially bounded decision-making of persistent property offenders. *Howard Journal of Criminal Justice, 31*, 276–293.

Simmel, G., & Wolff, K. H. (1950). *The sociology of Georg Simmel*. Glencoe, IL: Free Press.

Simon, R. (1975). *Women and crime*. Lexington, MA: D.C. Health.

Simpson, S. S. (1989). Feminist theory, crime, and justice. *Criminology, 27*, 605–631.

Simpson, S. S. (2002). *Corporate crime, law and social control*. New York: Cambridge University Press.

Simpson, S. S., & Gibbs, C. (2006). Making sense of intersections. In C. Kruttschnitt & K. Heimer (Eds.), *New directions in the study of gender, offending, and victimization* (pp. 269–302). New York: New York University Press.

Simpson, S. S., & Piquero, N. L. (2002). Low self-control, organizational theory, and corporate crime. *Law & Society Review, 36*, 509–548.

Singer, T., Seymour, B., O'Doherty, J., Kaube, H., Dolan, R. J., & Frith, C. D. (2004). Empathy for pain involves the affective but not sensory components of pain. *Science, 303*, 1157–1162.

*Skinner v. Oklahoma*, 316 U.S. 535 (1942).

Skinner, B. F. (1953). *Science and human behavior.* New York: Macmillan.

Skinner, B. F. (1976). *About behaviorism.* New York: Vintage Press.

Sloan, J. J., III. (1994). The correlates of campus crime: An analysis of reported crimes on college and university campuses. *Journal of Criminal Justice, 22*, 51–61.

Small, M. L., & Newman, K. (2001). Urban poverty after the truly disadvantaged. The rediscovery of the family, neighborhood and culture. *Annual Review of Sociology, 27*, 23–45.

Smart, C. (1976). *Women, crime, and criminology: A feminist critique.* Boston: Routledge & Kegan Paul.

Smith, A. (1896). *Lectures on justice, police, revenue and arms, delivered in the University of Glasgow, reported by a student in 1763*, edited by Edwin Cannan. Oxford: Clarendon Press. (Original work published 1763)

Smith, C. A., & Thornberry, T. P. (1995). The relationship between child maltreatment and adolescent involvement in delinquency. *Criminology, 33*, 451–481.

Sokoloff, N., & Dupont, I. (2005). Domestic violence at the intersections of race, class, and gender. *Violence Against Women, 11*, 38–64.

Spano, R., & Nagy, S. (2005). Social guardianship and social isolation: An application and extension of lifestyle/routine activities theory to rural adolescents. *Rural Sociology, 70*, 414–437.

Spano, R., Rivera, C., & Bolland, J. (2006). The impact of timing of exposure to violence on violent behavior in a high poverty sample of inner city African-American youth. *Journal of Youth and Adolescence, 35*, 681–692.

Spelman, W. (2004). Optimal targeting of incivility-reduction strategies. *Journal of Quantitative Criminology, 20*, 63–88.

Steffensmeier, D. (1983). Organization properties and sex-segregation in the underworld: Building a sociological theory of sex differences in crime. *Social Forces, 6*, 1010–1032.

Steffensmeier, D., & Allan, E. (1996). Gender and crime: Toward a gendered theory of female offending. *Annual Review of Sociology, 22*, 459–487.

Steffensmeier, D., & Terry, R. (1975). *Examining deviance experimentally.* Washington, NY: Alfred.

Steffensmeier, D., & Ulmer, J. (2005). *Confessions of a dying thief: Understanding criminal careers and illegal enterprise.* New Brunswick, NJ: Aldine-Transaction.

Steffensmeier, D., Ulmer, J., & Kramer, J. (1998). The interaction of race, gender, and age in criminal sentencing: The punishment cost of being young, black, and male. *Criminology, 36*, 763–799.

Stets, J., & Strauss, M. A. (1990). Gender differences in reporting marital violence and its medical and psychological consequences. In M. A. Straus & R. J. Gelles (Eds.), *Physical violence in American families* (pp. 151–165). New Brunswick, NJ: Transaction.

Stewart, E., & Simons, R. (2006). Structure and culture in African-American adolescent violence. A partial test of the code of the street thesis. *Justice Quarterly, 23*, 1–33.

Stewart, E. A., Elifson, K. W., & Sterk, C. E. (2004). Integrating the general theory of crime into an explanation of violent victimization among female offenders. *Justice Quarterly, 21*(1), 159–181.

Stewart, E. A., Schreck, C. J., & Simons, R. L. (2006) "I ain't gonna let no one disrespect me": Does the code of the street reduce or increase violent victimization among African American adolescents? *Journal of Research in Crime and Delinquency, 43*, 427–458.

Stewart, E. A., Simons, R. L., Conger, R. D., & Scaramella, L. V. (2002). Beyond the interactional relationship between delinquency and parenting practices: The contribution of legal sanctions. *Journal of Research in Crime and Delinquency, 39*, 36–59.

Stitt, B. G., & Giacopassi, A. (1992). Trends in the connectivity of theory and research in criminology. *The Criminologist, 17*(1), 3–6.

Stokes, R., & Hewitt, J. (1976). Aligning actions. *American Sociological Review, 41*, 838–849.

Straus, M. A., & Gelles, R. J. (1990). Societal change and change in family violence from 1975–1985 as revealed by two national surveys. In M. A. Straus & R. J. Gelles (Eds.), *Physical violence in American families* (pp. 113–131). New Brunswick, NJ: Transaction.

Strauss, A. (1993). *Continual permutations of action.* New York: Aldine.

Stryker, S. (1980). *Symbolic interaction: A social structural version.* Menlo Park, CA: Benjamin/Cummings.

Stryker, S., & Burke, P. J. (2000). The past, present, and future of an identity theory. *Social Psychology Quarterly, 63*, 284–297.

Stucky, T. D. (2003). Local politics and violent crime in U.S. cities. *Criminology, 41*, 1101–1135.

Stults, B. J., & Baumer, E. P. (2008). Assessing the relevance of anomie theory for explaining spatial variation in lethal criminal violence: An aggregate-level analysis of homicide within the United States. *International Journal of Conflict and Violence, 2*, 215–247.

Stylianou, S. (2002). The relationship between elements and manifestations of low self-control in a general theory of crime: Two comments and a test. *Deviant Behavior, 23*, 531–557.

Sullivan, R. F. (1973). The economics of crime: An introduction to the literature. *Crime and Delinquency, 19*, 138–149.

Sutherland, E. H. (1937). *The professional thief.* Chicago: University of Chicago Press.

Sutherland, E. H. (1939). *Principles of criminology* (3rd ed.). Philadelphia: J. B. Lippincott.

Sutherland, E. H. (1940). White collar criminality. *American Sociological Review, 5*, 1–12.

Sutherland, E. H. (1942). Development of the theory. In K. Schuessler (Ed.), *Edwin Sutherland on analyzing crime* (pp. 13–29). Chicago: University of Chicago Press.

Sutherland, E. H. (1947). *Principles of criminology* (4th ed.). Philadephia: J. B. Lippincott.

Sutherland, E. H., & Cressey, D. R. (1970). *Criminology* (8th ed.). Philadelphia: J. B. Lippincott.

Suttles, G. D. (1968). *The social order of the slum.* Chicago: University of Chicago Press.

Swidler, A. (1986). Culture in action: Symbols and Strategies. *American Sociological Review, 51*, 273–286.

Sykes, G., & Matza, D. (1957). Techniques of neutralization: A theory of delinquency. *American Sociological Review, 22*, 664–670.

Sykes, G. M. (1978). *Criminology.* New York: Harcourt Press.

Tannenbaum, F. (1938). *Crime and the community.* Boston: Ginn and Company.

Tarde, G. (1912). *Penal philosophy.* Boston: Little, Brown.

Taylor, I., Walton, P., & Young, J. (1973). *The new criminology: For a social theory of deviance.* New York: Harper and Row.

Taylor, I., Walton, P., & Young, J. (1975). *Critical criminology.* London: Routledge & Kegan Paul.

Taylor, R. B. (2001). The ecology of crime, fear, and delinquency. In R. Paternoster & R. Bachman (Eds.), *Explaining criminals and crime: Essays in contemporary criminological theory* (pp. 124–139). Los Angeles: Roxbury.

Tewksbury, R., & Mustaine, E. (2000). Routine activities and vandalism: A theoretical and empirical study. *Journal of Crime & Justice, 23*, 81–110.

Thomas, W. I., & Znaniecki, F. (1918). *The Polish peasant in Europe and America* (Vol. 4). Chicago: University of Chicago Press.

Thompson, B. (2002). Multiracial feminism: Recasting the chronology of second wave feminism. *Feminist Studies, 28,* 337–360.

Thornberry, T. (1987). Towards an interactional theory of delinquency. *Criminology, 25,* 863–891.

Thrasher, F. M. (1927). *The gang.* Chicago: University of Chicago Press.

Tibbets, S. G., & Gibson, C. (2002). Individual propensities and rational decision making: Recent findings and promising approaches. In A. R. Piquero & S. Tibbetts (Eds.), *Rational choice and criminal behavior: Recent research and future challenges* (pp. 3–24). New York: Routledge.

Tibbetts, S. G., & Piquero, A. R. (1999). The influence of gender, low birth weight, and disadvantaged environment in predicting early onset of offending: A test of Moffitt's interactional hypothesis. *Criminology, 37,* 843–878.

Tifft, L. (1979). The coming redefinitions of crime: An anarchist perspective. *Social Problems, 26,* 392–402.

Tita, G., & Griffiths, E. (2005). Traveling to violence: The case for a mobility-based spatial typology of homicide. *Journal of Research in Crime and Delinquency, 42,* 275–308.

Tittle, C. H. (1980). Labeling and crime: An empirical evaluation. In W. Gove (Ed.), *The labelling of deviance: Evaluating a perspective* (2nd ed., pp. 241–263). New York: Wiley.

Tittle, C. H., Bratton, J., & Gertz, M. G. (2003). A test of micro-level application of shaming theory. *Social Problems, 50,* 593–618.

Tittle, C. R. (1983). Social class and criminal behavior: A critique of the theoretical foundation. *Social Forces, 62,* 334–358.

Tittle, C. R., Broidy, L. M., & Gertz, M. G. (2008). Strain, crime, and contingencies. *Justice Quarterly, 25,* 283–319.

Tittle, C. R., & Grasmick, H. G. (1997). Criminal behavior and age: A test of three provocative hypotheses. *Journal of Criminal Law & Criminology, 88,* 309–342.

Tittle, C. R., Ward, D. A., & Grasmick, H. G. (2003). Self-control and crime/deviance: Cognitive vs. behavioral measures. *Journal of Quantitative Criminology, 19,* 333–366.

Tittle, C. R., Ward, D. A., & Grasmick, H. G. (2004). Capacity for self-control and individuals' interest in exercising self-control. *Journal of Quantitative Criminology, 20,* 143–172.

Tittle, C., Wayne, R., & Villemez, J., & Smith, D. (1978). The myth of social class and criminality: An empirical assessment of the empirical evidence. *American Sociological Review, 43,* 643–656.

Topalli, V. (2005). When being good is bad: An expansion of neutralization theory. *Criminology, 43,* 797–835.

Topalli, V., Wright, R., & Fornango, R. (2002). Drug dealers, robbery and retaliation: Vulnerability, deterrence and the contagion of violence. *British Journal of Criminology, 42,* 337–351.

Tremblay, R. E., Vitaro, F., Bertrand, L., LeBlanc, M., Beauchesne, H., Bioleau, H., et al. (1992). Parent and child training to prevent early onset of delinquency: The Montreal longitudinal experimental study. In J. McCord & R. E. Tremblay (Eds.), *Preventing antisocial behavior: Interventions from birth through adolescence* (pp. 117–138). New York: Guilford Press.

Triplett, R. A., & Jarjoura, G. R. (1994). Theoretical and empirical specification of a model of informal labeling. *Journal of Quantitative Criminology, 10,* 241–276.

Trotter, W. (1919). *Instincts of the herd in peace and war.* New York: Macmillan.

Tseloni, A., Wittebrood, K., Farrell, G., & Pease, K. (2004). Burglary victimization in England and Wales, the United States and the Netherlands. *British Journal of Criminology, 44,* 66–91.

Tucker, J., & Ross, S. (2004). Corporal punishment and Black's theory of social control. In M. J. Donnelly & M. A. Strauss (Eds.), *Corporal punishment in theoretical perspective.* New Haven, CT: Yale University Press.

Turk, A. (1969). *Criminality and legal order.* Chicago: Rand.

Turner, M. G., & Piquero, A. R. (2002). The stability of self-control. *Journal of Criminal Justice, 30*, 457–471.

Turner, M. G., Pratt, T. C., & Piquero, A. R. (2005). The school context as a source of self-control. *Journal of Criminal Justice, 33*, 329–339.

Ulmer, J. T. (1994). Revisiting Stebbins: Labeling and commitment to deviance. *The Sociological Quarterly, 35*, 135–157.

Ulmer, J. T. (2000). Commitment, deviance, and social control. *The Sociological Quarterly, 41*, 315–336.

Ulmer, J. T. (2005). The localized uses of federal sentencing guidelines in four U.S. district courts: Evidence of processual order. *Symbolic Interaction, 28*, 255–279.

Ulmer, J. T., & Spencer, J. W. (1999). The contributions of an interactionist approach to research and theory on criminal careers. *Theoretical Criminology, 3*, 95–124.

Valentine, C. A. (1968). *Culture and poverty. Critique and counter proposals.* Chicago: University of Chicago Press.

Vazsonyi, A. T., Pickering, L. E., Junger, M., & Hessing, D. (2001). An empirical test of a general theory of crime: A four-nation comparative study of self-control and the prediction of deviance. *Journal of Research in Crime and Delinquency, 38*, 91–131.

Veblen, T. (1899). *The theory of the leisure class: An economic study of institutions.* New York: Macmillan.

Venkatesth, S. A. (2006). *Off the books: The underground economy of the urban poor.* Cambridge, MA: Harvard University Press.

Viding, E., Blair, R.J.R., Moffitt, T. E., & Plomin, R. (2005). Evidence for substantial genetic risk for psychopathy in 7-year-olds. *Journal of Child Psychology and Psychiatry, 46*, 592–597.

Viding, E., Frick, P. J., & Plomin, R. (2007). Aetiology of the relationship between callous-unemotional traits and conduct problems in children. *British Journal of Psychiatry, 190*, 33–38.

Vogel, R., & Himelein, M. (1995). Dating and sexual victimization: An analysis of risk factors among precollege women. *Journal of Criminal Justice, 23*, 153–162.

Vold, G. B. (1958). *Theoretical criminology.* New York: Oxford University Press.

Vold, G. B., Bernard, T. J., & Snipes, J. (2002). *Theoretical criminology.* New York: Oxford University Press.

Voss, T. (2001). Game-theoretical perspectives. In M. Hechter & K. D. Opp (Eds.), *Social norms* (pp. 105–136). New York: Russell Sage.

Wagner, D. G. (1984). *The growth of sociological theories.* Beverly Hills, CA: Sage.

Walker, S. (1984). "Broken windows" and fractured history: The use and misuse of history in recent police patrol analysis. *Justice Quarterly, 1*, 77–90.

Walsh, A. (2002). *Biosocial criminology: Introduction and integration.* Cincinnati, OH: Anderson.

Walsh, A., & Beaver, K. M. (2008). *Introduction to biosocial criminology.* New York: Routledge.

Walters, G. D., & Contri, D. (1998). Outcome expectancies for gambling: Empirical modeling of a memory network in federal prison inmates. *Journal of Gambling Studies, 14*, 173–191.

Wang, J. (2002). Bank robberies by an Asian gang: An assessment of the routine activities theory. *International Journal of Offender therapy and Comparative Criminology, 46*, 555–568.

Wang, S., & Jensen, G. F. 2003. Explaining delinquency in Taiwan: A test of social learning theory. In R. L. Akers & G. F. Jensen (Eds.), *Social learning theory and the explanation of crime: A guide for the new century: Vol. 11. Advances in criminological theory* (pp. 65–84). New Brunswick, NJ: Transaction.

Ward, D. A., Stafford, M. C., & Gray, L. N. (2006). Rational choice, deterrence, and theoretical integration. *Journal of Applied Social Psychology, 26,* 571–585.

Warner, B. D. (2003) The role of attenuated culture in social disorganization theory. *Criminology, 41,* 73–98.

Warner, B. D., & Rountree, P. (1997). Local social ties in a community and crime model: Questioning the systemic nature of informal social control. *Social Problems, 44,* 520–536.

Warr, M. (1993). Age, peers, and delinquency. *Criminology, 31,* 17–40.

Warr, M. (2002). *Companions in crime: The social aspects of criminal conduct.* Cambridge, England: Cambridge University Press.

Weber, L. (2001). *Understanding race, class, gender, and sexuality: A conceptual framework.* Boston: McGraw-Hill.

Websdale, N. (1998). *Rural woman battering and the justice system: An ethnography.* Thousand Oaks, CA: Sage.

Wellford, C. (1975). Labelling theory and criminology: An assessment. *Social Problems, 22,* 332–345.

Western, B., & Beckett, K. (1999). How unregulated is the U.S. labor market? The penal system as a labor market institution. *American Journal of Sociology, 104,* 1030–1060.

Westervelt, S. D., & Cook, K. J. (2007). Feminist research methods in theory and practice: Learning from death row exonerees. In S. Miller (Ed.), *Criminal justice research and practice: Diverse voices from the field* (pp. 21–38). Boston: University Press of New England.

Wilkinson, D. L. (2003). *Guns, violence, and identity among African American and Latino youth.* New York: LFB Scholarly Publishing.

Wilkinson, K. (1974). The broken home and juvenile delinquency: Scientific explanation or ideology? *Social Problems, 21,* 726–739.

Williams, C. R., & Arrigo, B. A. (2001). Anarchoas and order: On the emergence of social justice. *Theoretical Criminology, 5,* 223–252.

Williams, C. R., & Arrigo, B. A. (2007). Conflict theory and crime and delinquency. In G. Ritzer (Ed.), *The Blackwell encyclopedia of sociology* (pp. 665–668). New York: Blackwell.

Wilson, D. B., Bouffard, L. A., & Mackenzie, D. L. (2005). A quantitative review of structured, group-oriented, cognitive-behavioral program for offenders. *Criminal Justice and Behavior, 32,* 172–204.

Wilson, J. Q., & Herrnstein, R. (1985). *Crime and human nature.* New York: Simon & Schuster.

Wilson, J. Q., & Kelling, G. L. (1982, March). The police and neighborhood safety: Broken windows. *The Atlantic Monthly,* 29–38.

Wilson, W. J. (1987). *The truly disadvantaged: The inner-city, the underclass, and public policy.* Chicago: University of Chicago Press.

Wilson, W. J. (1996). *When work disappears: The world of the new urban poor.* New York: Knopf.

Winnick, T. A., & Bodkin, M. (2008). Anticipated stigma and stigma management among those to be labeled "ex-con." *Deviant Behavior, 29,* 295–333.

Wolfgang, M. E. (1958). *Patterns in criminal homicide.* Philadelphia: University of Pennsylvania Press.

Wolfgang, M. E., & Ferracuti, F. (1967). *The subculture of violence: Towards an integrated theory in criminology.* New York: Tavistock.

Wooldredge, J. (1998). Inmate lifestyles and opportunities for victimization. *Journal of Research in Crime and Delinquency, 35,* 480–502.

Wooldredge, J., Cullen, F., & Latessa, E. (1992). Victimization in the workplace: A test of routine activities theory. *Justice Quarterly, 9*, 325–335.

Worden, R., & Shepard, R. (1996). Demeanor, crime, and police behavior: A reexamination of the police services study data. *Criminology, 34*, 83–106.

Worrall, J. L. (2006). The discriminant validity of perceptual incivility measures. *Justice Quarterly, 23*, 360–383.

Wright, B.R.E., Caspi, A., Moffitt, T. E., & Paternoster, R. (2004). Does the perceived risk of punishment deter criminally-prone individuals? Rational choice, self-control, and crime. *Journal of Research in Crime and Delinquency, 41*, 180–213.

Wright, R., & Decker, S. (1994). *Burglars on the job.* Boston: Northeastern University Press.

Wright, R. A., & Miller, J. M. (1998). Taboo until today? The coverage of biological arguments in criminology textbooks, 1961 to 1970 and 1987 to 1996. *Journal of Criminal Justice, 26*, 1–19.

Yllö, K., & Bograd, M. (1988). *Feminist perspectives on wife abuse.* Thousand Oaks, CA: Sage.

Yodanis, C. L. (2004). Gender inequality, violence against women, and fear: A cross-national test of feminist theory of violence against women. *Journal of Interpersonal Violence, 19*, 655–675.

Young, J. (1997). Left realism: The basics. In B. MacLean & D. Milovanovic (Eds.), *Thinking critically about crime.* Vancouver, British Columbia, Canada: Collective Press.

Zhang, L. (1994). Peers rejection as a possible consequence of official reaction to delinquency in Chinese society. *Criminal Justice and Behavior, 21*, 387–402.

Zhang, L., & Messner, S. F. (1994). The severity of official punishment for delinquency and change in interpersonal relations in Chinese society. *Journal of Research in Crime and Delinquency, 31*, 416–433.

Zinn, M. B., & Dill, T. (1996). Theorizing difference from multiracial feminism. *Feminist Studies, 22*, 321–331.

# CREDITS

Page 308: From "Crime as Social Control" by Donald Black, *American Sociological Review,* Vol. 48. No.1 (Feb., 1983), pp.34–45. Reprinted with permission.

Page 320: From *Crime and the Community*, by F. Tannebaum. Copyright © 1938 Columbia University Press. Reprinted with permission of the publisher.

Page 324: Lemert, Edwin. *Social Pathology: A Systematic Approach to the Theory of Sociopathic Behavior.* McGraw-Hill Higher Education. 1951.

Page 335: From John Braithwaite, *Crime, Shame, and Reintegration*, 1989, © Cambridge University Press 1989, reproduced with permission.

Page 351: From *Seductions of Crime* by Jack Katz, copyright 1988. Reprinted by permission of Basic Books, a member of Perseus Books Group.

Page 357: Lonnie Athens. 1997. "Self as Process: Interpretation of the Situation." From *Violent Criminal Acts and Actors Revisited. pp.32–41*

Page 361: Lonnie Athens. 1997. "The Principal Phase, II: The Larger Theoretical Implications." From *Violent Criminal Acts and Actors Revisited. pp.144–154*

Page 382: Bonger, Willem. 1916. *Criminality and Economic Conditions.* [pp. 402–405, 667–669, 672]

Page 386: From *Culture, Conflict and Crime* by Thorsten Sellin, pp. 63–70, © 1938, New York: Social Science Research Council. Reprinted with permission.

Page 389: From *Class, State and Crime* by Richard Quinney, © 1980 New York: Longman. Reprinted with permission.

Page 413: Adler, Freda. 1975. Sisters in Crime: The Rise in the New Female Offender. New York: McGraw-Hill.

Page 420: Meda Chesney-Lind. 1988. "Doing Feminist Criminology." *The Criminologist. vol. 13 [1,3,16,17]* Reprinted, with permission, from the *American Society of Criminology.*

Page 423: Reprinted, with permission, from the *Annual Review of Sociology* Volume 22© 1996 by Annual Reviews.

# INDEX